Sherwood Anderson

Sherwood Anderson

A WRITER IN AMERICA

VOLUME 2

Walter B. Rideout

Introduction by Charles Modlin

The University of Wisconsin Press

The University of Wisconsin Press
1930 Monroe Street
Madison, Wisconsin 53711

www.wisc.edu/wisconsinpress/

3 Henrietta Street
London WC2E 8LU, England

1   3   5   4   2

Printed in the United States of America

Library of Congress Cataloging-in-Publication Data
Rideout, Walter B. (Walter Bates)
Sherwood Anderson : a writer in America / Walter B. Rideout ; introduction by Charles E. Modlin.
p. cm.
Includes bibliographical references and index.
ISBN 0-299-21530-X (cloth : alk. paper)
1. Anderson, Sherwood, 1876–1941. 2. Authors, American—20th century—Biography. I. Title.
PS3501.N4Z773   2005
813'.52—dc22   2005011164

ISBN 0-299-22020-6 (volume 2)

This book was published with the support of the Brittingham Fund and the Anonymous Fund for the
Humanities of the University of Wisconsin–Madison.

To Jean

Contents

Preface to Volume 2

IN ITS finished form Walter Rideout's long-anticipated biography of Sherwood Anderson turned out to be much more than a magisterial treatment of a single author and his work. It represents as well the story lines of author and editor and, in turn, the evolution of the text itself, all of which deserve comment because they are remarkable and inseparable.

Walter Rideout's graduate studies at Harvard had been interrupted by World War II, but he returned as a Navy veteran in 1946 to complete his doctorate in English with Howard Mumford Jones. In the early 1950s, as scholars were beginning to revisit and assess the life and work of Sherwood Anderson, who had died in 1941, Rideout collaborated with Jones in preparing the first collected edition of Anderson's letters (1953). By this time Rideout was deeply immersed in the study of Anderson. Although it is noted in the introduction that he began his research in 1959, there is abundant evidence that he had been interviewing individuals who had been close to Anderson in the early 1950s. About this time he signed a contract to write Anderson's biography, having received the blessing of Eleanor, the author's widow, who would support his work in innumerable ways until her death more than three decades later.

Rideout began his teaching career at Northwestern University in 1949 and in 1956 published his first major critical work, *The Radical Novel in the United States, 1900–1954*. In 1962 he accepted a visiting professorship at the University of Wisconsin–Madison, where he remained for the rest of his career, chairing the English Department from 1965 until 1968 and retiring in 1986 as Harry Hayden Clark Emeritus Professor of Twentieth-century American Literature. As one might expect, the demands of his academic career—such as chairing a large department, directing more than fifty dissertations, and accepting Fulbright and other lectureships—slowed his progress on the Anderson biography. Thus, a favorite question at conferences during the 1970s and '80s became "How far has Walter got on *the* biography?"

Although deterred, Rideout was never discouraged, and he made it known to fellow Andersonians that once he retired, he would devote his full time to a task that was now in its fourth decade. When completed, it was entering its fifth—surely one of the most protracted works of its kind in the history of American letters. But by now problems over which he had no control had emerged. His original editor had retired and was replaced by another who questioned the wisdom of publishing a manuscript of some 2,300 pages. Moreover, Rideout was experiencing early symptoms of dementia, which made the ultimate fate of the work even more doubtful. Then the University of Wisconsin Press emerged as the agent of salvation, by accepting the work for publication.

By the time the Press was ready to start preparing the biography for publication, however, Rideout was too ill to do anything himself about adding a still missing introduction or to participate in reading and correcting proofs. The editors thus turned to another accomplished Anderson scholar and good friend of Rideout's, Charles Modlin, to write an introduction and participate in preparing the material for final publication.

Modlin was an ideal choice, for he not only had a detailed grasp of Anderson's life and work, but his publications on the subject were distinguished in quality and in both breadth and depth. His editing was notable for accuracy, economy, and precision. The Jones-Rideout collection of Anderson's letters had drawn almost entirely from the extensive Newberry Collection, but Modlin's *Sherwood Anderson: Selected Letters* (1984) made available many other important letters not only from the Newberry, but from twenty-three additional libraries. With the blessing of Eleanor Anderson, his close friend, he next turned his attention to the extensive (some 1,400 letters), and long sealed, collection of letters that Anderson wrote to Eleanor from the time of their courtship until the end of his life. From this effort came his fascinating and informative *Sherwood Anderson's Love Letters to Eleanor Copenhaver Anderson* (1989).

Notable among Modlin's other projects is *Certain Things Last: The Selected Short Stories of Sherwood Anderson* (1992), a collection of thirty of Anderson's finest short stories, with judiciously edited or re-edited texts, including five fine stories that appear in print for the first time. He was, furthermore, a congenial, generous colleague, who coedited three collections of Anderson material in collaboration with other scholars.

Modlin completed an informative introduction to Rideout's biography—distinguished by his usual precision and economy of expression—and worked closely with the Press to provide whatever author's corrections were needed in volume 1. Before he completed these tasks, however, he was himself beset by a grave illness that would soon take his life. During periods of hospitalization, he would take the manuscript with him and continue proofreading. Only his death, on January 1, 2006, prevented him from assisting the press in preparing volume 2 for publication. Although Rideout could not comprehend the significance of the publication of volume 1, a copy was placed in his hands a few weeks before his death on April 8, 2006.

Walter Rideout and Charles Modlin: hail and farewell!

Hilbert H. Campbell and Welford D. Taylor
August 2006

Acknowledgments

PROFESSOR RIDEOUT had virtually finished his book before illness left him unable to complete the final touches, including a list of acknowledgments. It is impossible now to compile a complete one or to include the genial words of appreciation that he would certainly have written. But we have listed here the names, so far as we can determine them, of major informants, librarians, colleagues and friends, Anderson family members, and the University of Wisconsin Press staff who have contributed to the making of this biography. We apologize for the impersonality of the lists and for omissions:

Informants: Marc and Lucile Antony, Dorothy Bartlett, William Bird, Charles Bockler, George A. Bottger, Mrs. Lorenz Carstensen, Ralph Church, John Cournos, Mrs. John Craun, George M. Day, H. Kellogg Day, William R. Dennes, Burt L. Dickinson, Mrs. Jack Dillman, Margaret E. Edwards, Wharton Esherick, Ernestine Evans, Richard Faben, Richard Faxon, James K. Feibleman, Julius Friend, Mr. and Mrs. Clarence G. Fuller, Lewis Galantière, Albert Goldstein, Mildred Becker Fuller, Charles H. Funk, Glenn and Laura Gosling, Mrs. W. K. Graham, B. W. Huebsch, Herman Hurd, Thaddeus Hurd, Maria Jolas, Nellie Lewis, Dorothy Jones, Mr. and Mrs. W. Powell Jones, Mrs. Joel Harris Lawrence, Mrs. Alfred Newman, Anne Poor, Felix Russman, Adaline Katz Samuel, Alma Schiff, William Spratling, Mrs. James Stark, Joe Stephenson, Mrs. James Thomas, Margaret Bartlett Thornton, Raymond J. Toner, Harriet Walker Welling, Elizabeth Whaley, William L. White, Mrs. Frank Wilford, William Wright.

Librarians: Diana Haskell and Amy Wood Nyholm at the Newberry Library.

Andersonian colleagues: David D. Anderson, Hilbert H. Campbell, Charles E. Modlin, William A. Sutton, Welford D. Taylor, Kim Townsend, Ray Lewis White, Kenny Williams.

His colleagues and friends at the University of Wisconsin and elsewhere:

Jon S. Reilly, Phillip Harth, Sargent Bush, Susan Stanford Friedman, Thomas Schaub, Marton M. Sealtz Jr., Ron Wallace, and Phillip Certain.

Relatives of Anderson: Cornelia Anderson, Eleanor Copenhaver Anderson, Elizabeth Prall Anderson, John Anderson, Marion (Mimi) Anderson, Mary Chryst Anderson.

Those at the University of Wisconsin Press who have made it possible for this book to be published: Raphael Kadushin, Sheila Moermond, Sheila Leary, Mary Sutherland, and Adam Mehring.

The one person to whom he would have expressed his deepest indebtedness is his dear wife, Jean Rideout, to whom this book is dedicated.

Introduction
Charles E. Modlin

WALTER RIDEOUT'S *Sherwood Anderson: A Writer in America* is a seminal work that reintroduces us to an important American writer. All writers go in and out of fashion, but the best writers always weather the passing literary mode, and Anderson is due for the kind of rousing rediscovery that Rideout's book should help launch. In fact, no other existing Anderson biography is as thoroughly researched, as founded on primary sources and interviews with a range of Anderson friends and family members, or as complete in its vision of the man and the writer.

This biography is the result of exhaustive research begun in 1959. The results are impressive, not only adding a wealth of details to what was previously known but also uncovering much new information about events and people in Anderson's life. For example, Rideout reveals that Anderson suffered a breakdown in 1907 that prefigures his famous one in 1912. He also finds in Bertha Baynes, a young woman in Anderson's boyhood home of Clyde, Ohio, the prototype of Helen White and traces his companionship with Adaline Katz during his time in New Orleans that influenced his 1923 novel *Many Marriages*. With such a comprehensive perspective on Anderson the man, this book presents his many remarkable attributes more clearly than ever before. On the other hand, Rideout makes no attempt to overstate Anderson's virtues or to overlook his weaknesses and inconsistencies as they are occasionally displayed.

Rideout also provides perceptive analyses of many of Anderson's works, pointing out previously overlooked subtleties of structure, symbolism, and characterization. He also astutely places Anderson's life and writings in such broader movements of his times as the transition of American society from rural to industrial; the shaping of a midwestern literary tradition; and the political trends of socialism, communism, and Roosevelt's New Deal.

Of great assistance to Rideout in tracing these matters were the findings of other scholars whose publications led the renaissance of Anderson studies in the last four decades of the twentieth century. As the extensive documentation of this book acknowledges, they contributed mightily to its content. But time has taken its toll, and the production of Anderson studies has lagged in recent years. Nonetheless, signs of new interest are evident in a reprint of *A Story Teller's Story,* a critical study by Robert Dunne, and a collection of Anderson's poetry.

~

Anderson's life is an absorbing story in its own right, but in many ways it also provides the best possible background for an appreciation of his literary accomplishments, especially his fiction. As Anderson himself acknowledged, his fiction is often autobiographical and his memoirs are fictionalized. Professor Rideout ably sorts out the subtleties resulting from such crossovers. He shows on the one hand how Anderson's life does frequently enrich his fiction and, on the other, how the autobiographical works, even when they are embroidered by Anderson's fancy, still reveal an imaginative truth of their own.

The signature event in Sherwood Anderson's life was his dramatic departure from his Elyria, Ohio, business in 1912 and embarkation upon a career as an author. As Rideout explains, the circumstances at the time were not as simple as Anderson would have us believe in *A Story Teller's Story,* yet this important event, even as altered in Anderson's imagination, well demonstrates the cyclical course of his life. "I'm trying again . . . a man has to begin over and over . . . ," he wrote to Roger Sergel a year before his death, and indeed his life consisted of many stops and starts, which not only reveal an important part of his psychological makeup but also provide convenient demarcations of the major phases of his life.

Anderson's early years growing up in Clyde, Ohio, were a strong formative influence on him, and he drew freely from them in many of his writings. In fact his interest in the resonance of youthful experience became a major theme in his fiction. It is rendered masterfully in such short stories as "The Man Who Became a Woman" and "Death in the Woods," in which the narrators come to terms with events in their youth, though for quite different purposes. In "The Man Who Became a Woman," the narrator tells his story as a "kind of confession" that he hopes will put to rest his memories of nightmarish experiences from boyhood. The narrator of "Death in the Woods" combines his memories of an event in his childhood with adult experience and insights to piece together the full story. As he explains: "The whole thing, the story of the old woman's death, was to me as I grew older like music heard from far off. The notes had to be picked up slowly one at a time."

One of the most telling uses of Anderson's boyhood in both his fiction and autobiographies is his manner of depicting the influence of his mother and father, Emma and Irwin Anderson. Looking back upon his mother's death, which occurred in 1895 when he was eighteen, he identifies her as the main source of his artistic bent. In the dedication to her in *Winesburg, Ohio,* which remarkably anticipates his approach to the characters in the book, he credits her with having awakened in him "the hunger to see beneath the surface of lives. . . ." As he remembers her in his autobiographical works, she also becomes the victim of her husband's irresponsible conduct, having to take in laundry because of his inability to hold a job. In *Winesburg* George Willard's parents are similarly contrasted, with his mother representing the source of his capacity to dream, while his father, who is ineffectual as a provider, lectures George to "Keep your eyes on your money. Be awake." At the end of the book, when George Willard, much like Anderson himself, leaves town, he intends to follow his mother's dream of finding artistic fulfillment in his writing. But he is also aware, as he counts the money in his pocketbook, of his father's admonition to mind his finances. In 1932 when Anderson was planning a dramatic version of *Winesburg,* he identified this conflict between the mother and father as "the central theme of the play." Such opposing demands of artistic and material success would recur to the end in Anderson's life and works.

⁓

Anderson's business career, in a sense, actually began in Clyde, when he worked at such a variety of jobs that he acquired the nickname "Jobby." But it was in Chicago, following a period of manual labor, a stint in the army during the Spanish-American War, and a year at the Wittenberg Academy in Springfield, Ohio, that he began to write copy for an advertising agency. In 1904 he married Cornelia Lane, and they subsequently had three children. In the meantime he became the head of a mail-order firm in Cleveland and then another in Elyria, Ohio. Following his walking away from the Elyria business, his marriage also collapsed, and in 1913 he moved back to Chicago to resume his advertising job. He later came to despise such work, mainly because he felt that it interfered with his own writing and was a debased use of the language, manipulating words for financial profit.

Despite this apparent conflict between his business and writing careers, the fact is that Anderson did some of his finest writing, including

Winesburg, Ohio, the book generally considered to be his masterpiece, while working as an ad man. In some ways the job even provided unexpected opportunities to pursue his writing. He claimed for example to have written one of his finest short stories, "I'm a Fool," while appearing to be working on an advertisement. In *A Story Teller's Story* he recalls an occasion during a dull meeting about plows when he transformed one of the speakers into a character in a story that played out in his imagination while the meeting dragged on. In addition he enjoyed the stimulating contact with coworkers such as George Daugherty, who was gifted as an oral storyteller but unable to write up his stories and thus provided Anderson with material for his writing. The job also afforded him occasional opportunities to escape Chicago and to develop friendships with favorite clients, notably W. A. Steele and Dave Bohon in Owensboro and Harrodsburg, Kentucky, respectively, the latter even figuring in Anderson's story "I Want to Know Why." The same mix of good and bad impressions may be seen in his reactions a few years later to his lecture tours. He often complained about them, but he also enjoyed the stimulation of traveling to new places, speaking to particularly receptive audiences, and meeting interesting people.

∽

Anderson's career as a full-time writer could be said to have begun in 1922 when he left Chicago on a train, leaving behind his advertising work and his second wife, Tennessee Mitchell. On his way to New York, he stopped off in Elyria, where he revisited his old factory, found his name missing from the door of his old office, and realized anew that he was now a writer. By the time he and his third wife, Elizabeth Prall, settled in New Orleans, he had published *Many Marriages* and *Horses and Men,* and virtually completed *A Story Teller's Story.* He was a renowned author when he became a mentor of sorts for the young William Faulkner, not only helping him to publish his first novel, *Soldier's Pay,* but, more importantly, as Faulkner explained, encouraging him to write about the world he knew best, the "little patch up there in Mississippi" that he was to draw upon in shaping the fictional world of Yoknapatawpha County.

Another change followed in 1925. After a vacation in southwestern Virginia that summer, Anderson became so fond of the people and the countryside there that he bought farm property. The following year, using the royalties from his best-selling novel *Dark Laughter,* he built a fine country house near the village of Troutdale that he called Ripshin. Within a year he had tired of being the gentleman farmer and, being anxious to take on a new role for himself, he moved to Marion, about twenty-two miles from Ripshin, to become publisher and editor of the two local newspapers. Although the work amounted to a retreat from the literary world and a return to business, he enjoyed it for awhile, especially as it afforded frequent opportunities to talk with the citizenry of that area. He wrote a large number of editorials, features, and news stories for the papers, some of which were collected in *Hello Towns!* By the end of 1928, however, he was ready for a change. Turning over the papers to his son Robert and, separating from Elizabeth Prall, he struck out in yet another new direction.

In early January 1929, Anderson began a friendship and correspondence with Eleanor Copenhaver, a Marion native who frequently returned home from her job as an industrial secretary for the YWCA in New York. Much of her work involved travel throughout the South promoting better working and housing conditions for women. Anderson not only fell in love with her but also became interested, through her influence, in factory conditions in the South. Anderson's interest in the emerging world of American industry had previously been reflected in the agrarian-industrial conflict in *Winesburg, Ohio, Poor White,* and many of his short stories, including "The Egg" and "Ohio Pagan." Now, however, his concern with industrialism became much more politically focused. Within a few months of their meeting, he began a long courtship of Eleanor that included following her movements throughout the South and using the occasions to tour mills and factories and to become involved in the labor movement. The literary results of these experiences were *Perhaps Women, Beyond Desire,* and numerous essays.

After Anderson and Eleanor Copenhaver were married in 1933, he enjoyed his only thoroughly successful marriage, his interest in radical politics waned, and his writing career took new directions. He was once again beginning a new cycle—his final one. He continued to write some fine short stories, many of which he collected in *Death in the Woods,* and also became interested in the theater. His most notable play was an adaptation of *Winesburg,* which for various reasons, especially his difficulties in attempting to collaborate with New York playwright Arthur Barton, never succeeded. At about the same time, he became attracted to the Roosevelt administration and agreed to travel around the country, meeting people and assessing their recovery from the Depression in a series of articles for *Today,* a pro-New Deal magazine. In 1935 some of these were included in his book *Puzzled America.* A year later he published his last novel, *Kit Brandon,* about rum-running during the Prohibition era.

Given the cyclical pattern of Anderson's life, it is appropriate that his last published book was *Home Town,* a pleasant paean to small-town life that in a way brought him back full-circle to his own origins. Still, he remained the restless traveler to the end. He and Eleanor were on their way to South America to visit friends in Valparaiso and to settle into the life of a small town in Chile when he died on March 8, 1941.

One can only speculate on how the South American trip would have worked out for Anderson during the planned six-month visit. Being so fond of visiting new places and meeting people, he would undoubtedly have enjoyed the South American friends he had already made and the literary figures they would have put him in touch with. However, his dream of becoming close to the ordinary people there might have been difficult because of the language barrier. Despite his diligent efforts to learn Spanish, he probably would have had the same problems communicating with non-English-speaking people that had previously frustrated him in France and Mexico. In any case it seems likely that his restlessness and longing to return to his home in Virginia would have been strong by the time for his return trip.

After Anderson's death, Eleanor resumed her work with the YWCA, which included an assignment in post–World War II Italy. She also preserved Ripshin much as her husband had left it. Over the years until her own death in 1985, she was the faithful steward of Anderson's literary estate. In 1947 she gave most of the manuscripts and correspondence that were still in her possession to the Newberry Library in Chicago, stimulating a major outpouring of critical and editorial work on Anderson that culminates in this eagerly awaited biography.

∽

Sherwood Anderson's life and writings as expressions of his Americanism have long been of interest to Walter Rideout. He and Howard Mumford Jones gave as one basis for their selection of letters for *Letters of Sherwood Anderson* "the place (or lack of place) of the writer in America"; similarly the full title of the present biography is *Sherwood Anderson: A Writer in America*. In both books the theme is only suggestive, but the distinctly American patterns of Anderson's life, both as aspiring businessman and writer, are evident. As he leaves the small midwestern town of his youth to make his mark in the big world, he is squarely in the tradition of the American Dream made famous in Benjamin Franklin's autobiography, the life of Abraham Lincoln, and the novels of Horatio Alger. When Anderson picks up stakes and starts anew, he is also the characteristic American nomad, as he acknowledges in *A Story Teller's Story:* "Like all real American men of our day I wander constantly from place to place striving to put down roots into the American soil and not quite doing it." But he greatly enjoyed his many opportunities to discover and write about the places and people in all regions of the country.

Ultimately his pursuit of success, both material and artistic, became disappointing. In later years he lamented his diminished capacity to produce publishable work and the low income from work that was published. At the same time, he battled with various financial distractions such as his arrangement with publisher Horace Liveright in 1925 by which he would receive an advance of $100 a week for five years, the troublesome patronage of Mary Emmett, and his embarrassment at having to live on Eleanor's YWCA income. But eventually, as his literary reputation declined, he came to a fairly serene acceptance of his fate and adopted a kind of anti-American Dream—maintaining the importance of "thinking small" and shunning the corruptive search for success. Instead, the process, not the achievement, became the important thing. He wrote to Roger Sergel in 1927, soon after buying the Marion newspapers, that "work accomplished means so little. It is in the past. What we all want is the glorious and living present."

On the other hand, his interest in discovering America and its people never subsided. His many chances to travel, whether as businessman, writer, or tourist, helped to sustain his wandering ways. No pattern for living could be easier for Anderson because one of his remarkable gifts was his ability to be equally at home working on his farm, attending dinners with the literati in New York, visiting a men's club at a church in South Dakota, conversing with a brakeman on a train in California or coal miners in West Virginia; he made new friends wherever he traveled. He could never be an expatriate like his sometime friend Ernest Hemingway and insisted many times throughout his life that his writing was inextricably connected with his identity as an American. He was, he explained in a letter to Van Wyck Brooks on July 30, 1923, "because of the accident of my position as a man of letters, . . . a kind of composite essence of it all." In 1937 Thomas Wolfe wrote to him that "I think of you with Whitman and with Twain—that is, with men who have seen America with a poet's vision." Anderson could have wished for no finer compliment.

Sherwood Anderson

1

Break-Up

THROUGH MUCH of 1928, Anderson immersed himself in the small sea of Marion and Smyth County life, observing, probing, recording. In addition to his regular beat of town council and service club meetings and court trials, he attended boxing matches, occasional concerts, ball games, the Fourth of July celebration and the county fair in August, kept a close eye on the activities of the fire department and of Sheriff Dillard, watched the weather season by season, followed lambing time in February, spring planting, summer crop growing, autumn harvesting, and wrote them all up, often with Buck Fever's help. Among many other matters, he detailed the affectionate life and untimely death of Nellie the Printshop Cat, Dooney Hester's one-hundred-hour, nonstop drive around Marion's streets in a sealed Chevrolet from the Sprinkle Motor Company, and interviews with such local personalities as Tom Greer, a mountain boy who over the years had built up a nationally known dealership in roots, herbs, and barks. He collected Personals sent in to the newspaper office or picked up from his conversations with the habitués of the "Senate Chamber," the gathering place at the rear of Doc Thompson's City Drug Store; he wrote editorials and "What Say!" columns in his *Notebook* fashion on any subject that came into his head; he printed obituaries, stipulating only one to a person since, he announced using the editorial we, "To tell the truth we are a thousand times more interested in the living than in the dead."[1]

That more than six hundred subscriptions, mostly local ones, came in during the first three months of his editorship shows that people liked his efforts; but the papers were "a constant weekly problem," he admitted to John, and in the first two months of the year he had almost no time for other writing except for a brief article, "The Young Writer," which he contributed, apparently on request, to the first issue of a journal started by literary undergraduates at Washington and Lee University. "To really be a writer," he advised his college audience, "is a lifetime job," one demanding devotion, not to making money, but to being "essentially a lover . . . in love with some infinitely difficult notion of perfection in his art that is never quite achieved." Nevertheless, his editorials and columns often showed writerly qualities. In Washington early in February to interview Herbert Hoover, Secretary of Commerce and probable Republican candidate for the presidency, he reported his experience for his papers in "In Washington," an article using the apparently casual but actually careful voice and structuring along with the balance between interior consciousness and external event that appear in his better stories. Uninterested in politics, he goes first in the nation's capital to the recently opened Freer Gallery of Art, where he passes quickly by the paintings of the famous but to him "vastly overestimated" James Whistler and goes on to view closely the older Chinese and Japanese pieces. The subsequent meeting with Hoover is unlike that in the Chinese painting he admires of the Emperor Weu meeting the sage, Chiang-Tzu-ya, not because Anderson is no sage but because the painting with its setting of quiet nature gives a sense "of infinite time, space, distance." Hoover, on the other hand, like Anderson "a bit too fat," sits in his modern office and is all efficiency and immediate business. He refuses to be interviewed but agrees to talk. He is certain that the Mississippi River, which Anderson thinks of as uncontrollable Mother Mississippi, can be controlled by engineering to prevent a repetition of the terrible 1927 flood. He gives Anderson "long rows of figures showing how the industrialists have improved things for the common man" and approves industrialism's standardization; though once he seems momentarily uncomfortable when Anderson suggests that because of standardization individualism is dying out. Anderson leaves Hoover, feeling that they have "got nowhere." Walking the streets of Washington for hours afterwards, he decides that Hoover, engineer and businessman, "has developed the ideal brain for his time." He admires him but does not feel "warmed" by him. Passing the White House, he thinks of the very human Lincoln living there and then goes back to the Freer Gallery for one more look at the Chinese art "but it was closed for the night."[2]

At the beginning of January, the Andersons had given up their weekends at Ripshin and stayed on in their hotel room. On March 1, they moved from this confining space to one of the three small apartments on the second floor of the print shop building. Burt Dickinson, who lived in the apartment beside theirs, became companionable with them both, though he knew Sherwood better because of courthouse activity. To him they seemed quite different in temperament. Elizabeth once told him that she thought all problems could be solved by the use of intellect and reason; whereas he knew Sherwood's approach was quite the opposite: problems could be solved by feeling and intuition and, if these were unsuccessful, were simply to be escaped from physically. Only subsequently did

Dickinson realize through hindsight that the Andersons had been carefully keeping up a front about the "trouble" between them. By coincidence, two days before they moved into the apartment, Bab Finley had married Dr. E. Vernon Hahn of Indianapolis. Presumably she had written Anderson earlier about her intention, but of her side in the whole correspondence only two letters exist; if he replied, no such letter or letters survive. The correspondence would continue for several additional years, becoming more and more desultory, but now in March of 1928 Anderson might very well have felt that his different relationships with two women were drawing toward an end.[3]

The papers were always there, demanding his attention and time but also providing him an opportunity to be more the reformer he had claimed not to be. His first cause was a campaign, starting in the March 1 issue of the *News,* to beautify the community and his own view from the print shop window by getting the town's machinery out of the ugly lot at the rear of the courthouse and by planting grass and trees, at his own expense if necessary, to turn this "eyesore" into "a pleasant place, here in the very heart of town." After Buck Fever and his "boss" had pushed the campaign for "Henry Mencken Park" for three months, the town council voted to move its machinery to another lot. People from all over the county began to bring in shrubs and bulbs, and at the end of August the council officially and amusedly named the new park Sherwood Forest. Meanwhile, in mid-May Anderson began calling for contributions to help Beulah Bowman, a severely crippled mountain girl who had been successfully operated on at the expense of the Kiwanis Club and now needed funds for her education at an industrial school; by the end of the month $118 had been collected at the office for her.[4]

There was no better influence than "country papers," the new editor began to believe, "to get after better county government, check brutalities, give voice to the better influences already in the county"; but two other causes required more pushing against the status quo. Back in December when he was still feeling his way as editor and town citizen, Anderson had had Buck Fever praise the Christmas dinner served the inmates of the county jail, which also faced the town eyesore, and offer to be incarcerated the following Christmas. Since then, Anderson had begun to get beneath the surface of things. On April 12, grown more self-confident and also pleased by the *Roanoke Times*'s editorial comment that he was "getting out two of the most newsy weeklies in the State," he published, without Buck as a cover, a shocked attack on the jail conditions. In "The Black Hole of Marion" he described the one crowded room for women and the two crowded cages for men, where girls and boys were confined with "hardened" adult prisoners, where there was a single open toilet in each of these three spaces and no bathing facilities, and where some of the older prisoners were

"Syphilitics, tuberculars, dopes, etc." Of course it would take tax money to replace this "pest hole" with a larger, hygienic humane county jail, but, he concluded, "The county that permits such conditions to go on is as guilty as the men who commit the crimes and are thrown in there for committing them." It would take a year of much "pounding" by Anderson, friend of the despised and neglected, and by others; but then a bond issue was put through by the county, and "a decent sanitary jail" was built.[5]

The other cause was the need for a new "colored school," as he and his invented Mrs. Homing-Pigeon put it, the present one being "disreputable beyond words." This campaign began in early June when he applauded at length the town council's vote to move the machinery from "Henry Mencken Park" and applauded briefly its vote to furnish the building materials with which, as agreed, "the colored mechanics of the town would build the new [school] building free of labor cost"—a voluntary contribution of labor, neither council nor Anderson seems to have perceived, that would not be expected of white mechanics if a new white school were to be built. Careful not to exacerbate the white racial prejudice in a small Southern town by "scolding," as he later put it, he and Mrs. Homing-Pigeon linked the need for a new jail with that for a new segregated school on the grounds that both buildings were so unsanitary that disease threatened to spread at any time from either through the community as a whole. He continued his careful "fight" for the school for at least a year, and the project would have gone through, he later explained, "but a colored preacher—a rather self-assertive man—antagonized a lot of people and spoiled things." Possibly the preacher had asked why black mechanics should be expected to contribute their labor free to a county responsibility, and possibly Anderson had underestimated white resistance to the needs of the black population. He had his own lesser form of resistance too. In the papers he gave greater attention to the need for a new jail, arguing not just on the grounds of hygiene, as he mostly did with the school, but of personal decency as well; and even before either campaign began he had openly revealed how his primitivistic attitude toward blacks limited his views on their education. In "Negro Singing," a report in the March 15 News, he praised a concert given in Marion by the black Hampton Quartette but found these trained singers inferior both to trained white ones—"the white man will beat [the black] a thousand miles at all of the sophisticated arts"—and to the illiterate black workers, "real black boys," whose work song he had heard one night back in 1920 on a boat up the Mobile River and which "seemed a real part of the lonely forests, of the river, the night." Just as the white race has lost the "unconscious giving of [self] to the song," which is "inherent in the negro race," so will blacks lose it; for "Surely education is all right, but education, in the white man's sense, does something to the black and brown man." Unexpressed but obvious, then, would have been Anderson's racist reservations about the schooling of black children. Nevertheless, he wrote and lived in a Southern town in 1928, not now, and in 1928 he did begin and continue a campaign, however circumspect, to make people "feel" that the "present colored school [was] a disgrace to the county."[6]

He had other schemes for civic betterment as well. He had frequently printed his own and others' stories and articles in the papers, not simply to fill space but in this context to get people to read them and not be put off by the notion that they were "high brow stuff." His readers had approved. Since there were no bookstores in town, in early April he established in his print shop office the nonprofit Marion Publishing Company Library, largely of contemporary books, which one joined with a refundable deposit of $1.50 and from which one could borrow books for a week at fifteen cents a volume, any income to be used for the purchase of new books. This lending library helped to make the print shop "a small center of movement," as he wrote Bab, one of the town's gathering places where all sorts of people dropped in casually or on business and where he could talk, pick up news for the papers, and feel himself part of the flow of community life. Less successful than the lending library was his attempt to introduce the townspeople to modern art. They had liked the realistic prints that the Virginia artist J. J. Lankes had sent him and which he had framed and hung on the print shop walls; but the citizens tended to turn away in silent puzzlement from the dozen or more framed reproductions of paintings he began displaying months later, despite his warning that they required new kinds of responses in order to understand them. More to the townspeople's taste, apparently, was a spare, beautifully balanced line drawing of Buck Fever sent in by Wharton Esherick, Anderson's friend from Fairhope days. Made into a newspaper cut at the head of the "Buck Fever Says" column, it suggested in the lazily sprawled sitting posture of the mountain man one of Anderson's own favorite positions.[7]

With the approach of spring he began to feel more at ease with the papers and to find some time to write. Having been too busy to contribute a piece to the March issue of *Vanity Fair,* he sent in for the April one, "Just Walking," a purportedly personal experience interweaving three instances of long walks through the beauty of different nights, two of the instances being tales within the major tale set in a small midwestern town where during the day, contrastingly, a sensational murder trial is being observed by several bored newspaper reporters. The tales are not only interwoven but unobtrusively cumulative as well. In the first, Anderson recalls walking silently for hours with another guest after a party through the night streets of a New York made white with soft clinging snow; in the second, as he walks out in the countryside with a group of reporters on a warm, late fall evening, he and one reporter get ahead of the others, and the reporter tells him of walking on a different evening with a man who had "a fine baritone voice" and who kept singing out of sheer pleasure; in the third, the group has reached a hill overlooking a farmhouse and another reporter begins to sing with "a really lovely voice." From the house half a dozen farm people begin coming out to listen, and then as "a sort of finishing touch to our walk" a woman among the farm people sings a song in response, after which Anderson and the reporters simply walk back to their hotels. Although Anderson had come to think of his *Vanity Fair* pieces as done primarily for the money, he tried not to let them be hack work, and "Just Walking" culminates in one of his most lyrical moments of human communication.

For the same April number of *Vanity Fair* when the magazine sent him and nine other "famous people" a form, he returned it with his evaluations of 223 past and present persons and things on a scale of twenty-five as highest down to zero, evaluations that, with some surprises, sketch his admirations and dislikes. He awarded only eight 25s: six writers (Dostoyevsky, Fielding, Flaubert, Homer, Melville, Shakespeare), one painter (Cézanne), one thing (the Ten Commandments). He gave three 24s (Aristotle, Keats, George Moore), several 23s, including Whitman and, unexpectedly, Henry James, and a number of 22s, including Aeschylus, Bach, Degas, Hardy, and Ibsen. Lardner received a 22, Dreiser a 21, Gertrude Stein a 20, and Freud a 19, while Fitzgerald, Hemingway, Joyce, and Picasso got a middling 16. At the lower end he gave 6s to Sinclair Lewis, Longfellow, and the movies. (Although his books were said to have no "pictures possibilities," he wrote one Harry Dimand, "Someday, of course, someone will get at it and make some pictures showing more of the drama of the insides of people.") Among the many to whom he gave the lowest score of zero were Dante, Henry Ford, Greta Garbo, Edgar Guest, and Upton Sinclair. The names of Anderson favorites George Borrow, Lincoln, Turgenev, Twain, and Van Gogh did not appear on the list, but even so Anderson and Ferenc Molnar were noted as "the most generously minded" of the ten evaluators.[8]

With the change of season he suddenly plunged into a new novel, one built around his earlier Mary Cochran figure. "I write in the shop, in my room at night, even get up in the night to write," he told Bab. On Easter Sunday, April 8 that year, he and Elizabeth resumed their weekends at Ripshin, and he wrote that morning with his back to an open fire and in front of an open window through which came the low sound of the stream and the song of birds in the apple trees. As details about Mary Cochran's life slipped from his pen onto the paper, he began giving her quite different "surroundings and circumstances." Happy with the way the writing was going, he looked out on a hillside field a tall mountain man had plowed for him and reflected how the neighboring men had come to see him the day before to bring the latest bits of gossip, showing him that he "was accepted now as one of themselves, a man of the countryside." He knew that the men would cheat in a horse trade, steal his whiskey, and be dangerous when drunk, but otherwise were honest and dependable. They knew they could come to Ripshin any time of day or night and be sure of a welcome and, if needed, assistance, as when he took a sick boy to the doctor in his car in the middle of the night. Bill Wright had told him that Troutdale had been a vicious community before he arrived; people "planted evil weeds in other people's gardens—literally." Anderson could take satisfaction in changing this with what Wright later called the "spirit of kindliness" which he introduced into the whole Ripshin area.[9]

Easter Sunday was a good day, and others followed. For a brief while he was writing fairly steadily, sensing a "little music under the pen." As always he was experimenting, hunching out his own method and goal, he told Bab.

> What I have to say I have to say in my own way. If there is an art for me it must be my own art.
> Something indefinable—lets call it "it" toward which a man goes.
> Trying to go by some other man's road only leads to confusion.
> I have to get people as they are in nature, trees, skies, plowed fields.

A short story he wrote at this time, "The Lost Novel," shows him transposing personal experience more fully than usual into fiction. In March, Roger Sergel had written that he had given up his teaching job at the University of Pittsburgh and moved to Chicago to take over The Dramatic Publishing Company, which his uncle had founded. That his and Ruth's apartment address was now 6016 Stony Island Avenue sent Anderson into nostalgic memories of first meeting artists in the Fifty-seventh Street and Stony Island bohemia and of "wandering about . . . at night and dreaming" and having "All sorts of love adventures" in adjacent Jackson Park. "Did I ever tell you the story of my lost novel?" he asked. "That happened on what is called the Japanese Island in Jackson Park." Anderson's one disguise in his brief story is to assign his own experience to an English writer rather like his London friend John Cournos in appearance though not in background, reserving for himself the role of unnamed narrator. As the narrator begins his tale, and at other points throughout, Anderson provides him with remarks relevant to his own current life and thinking. Thus the narrator and the English writer agree that "no man ever quite got at—the thing," that is, the "indefinable . . . 'it'" of the letter to Bab; the two men spend "a half-hour going over names" of certain "old fellows" who have nearly "got at—the thing," coming up with Keats and Shakespeare, whom Anderson had picked out for a 24 and a 25 in his recently submitted evaluations for *Vanity Fair;* artists, the narrator declares, "may be the only lovers," as Anderson in "The Young Writer" had declared that "Your real writer, or your real artist in any art, is essentially a lover"; and the writer at one point tries "automatic writing," which the narrator later hears was taken up by "a group of young poets in Paris," such as those Anderson had learned about in 1927 from Jolas's *transition* group. In the personal history of the writer, the story itself, one repeatedly recognizes Anderson's own beneath the thin surface of applied Englishness. The writer marries a woman "above him in station" who like Cornelia "had been to a woman's college" and, the writer feels, probably thinks him "an ignorant man." After he has taken a job as a clerk in London and they have had two children, he suddenly begins to write, neglecting his job and family. He locks himself in an upstairs room and writes and writes, he loses his job, and his wife, as Anderson would write of Cornelia in the *Memoirs,* sits crying on the stairs outside the locked door, ruthlessly ignored by the writer since, as Anderson had repeatedly stated, the artist's devotion must be to his art. The writer finishes his book, "a real book"— as Anderson would tell Otto Liveright, with intended or unintended double meaning, "his completed tale was a very real story"—and gains "some fame." Then breaking with wife and children but feeing guilty for doing so, he is blocked in writing his second novel, as Anderson had only too recently been blocked in his own writing. One midafternoon the writer, hungry and weary, goes to Hyde Park and has the experience Anderson refers to as "my lost novel" in Chicago's Jackson Park and hence must be essentially replicating here. Suddenly he begins writing his second novel, writing intensely hour after hour, and feeling that "all the love he had in his being" had gone into it, finishes it in one sitting. He takes the manuscript to his room, lays it on his desk, satisfied that he has "done—the thing," goes out to eat and walk, returns at daylight, and sleeps through the day. Awakening, he goes to look at his novel, "really [knowing] all the time it wasn't there," and "of course" finds on the desk "nothing but blank empty sheets of paper." Thereupon the writer says to the narrator: "Anyway . . . this I know. I never will write such a beautiful novel as that one was." The narrator concludes the tale by saying:

> Of course when he said it he laughed.
> I do not believe there are too many people in the world who will know exactly what he was laughing about.[10]

Presumably the writer is not laughing at the inherent improbability of the event, personal experience of the author or not, and so at his own predetermined discovery of the blank pages, which comes close to being a trick ending, nor at the suggestion that "all the love he had in his being" was in fact none at all. What the narrator presumably understands from the laugh is that not even in the imagination and much less in the actuality can the artist reach that "indefinable 'it'" of art, that, as Anderson had written in "The Young Writer," the "real artist . . . is essentially . . . in love with some infinitely difficult notion of perfection in his art that is never quite achieved." Such is the absurdity and the glory of the artist's endeavor, which is why Anderson was so happy on that Easter morning and at the time he wrote "The Lost Novel," since this fiction was "of course" really true for himself.

Even so there were days in April when what he was after became "so elusive, hard to grasp" that his writing went dead. If at such times he was at Ripshin, he could still be helped by the "quiet stately thing in nature." Knowing that "A seed has to rot before it can grow," he would go outdoors, sit on a fallen apple tree, look at the plowed hillside field, now planted to oats, and in a healing act of empathy with natural process

try to go down into the ground, feel the harrow raking me, the rain falling on me, the spring sun creeping down to me.

If I am to grow green again and put forth fruit it must be a slow patient process.

Toward the end of April the patient process was interrupted by an unexpected visit from young Bob, who had been spending his first year at the University of Virginia. Lonely, unable or unwilling to fit in, unhappy that his father had been too busy to write him frequently or send more money, he arrived in Marion convinced that he would not return to the university and proceeded to get wildly drunk. Feeling guilty for neglecting him, understanding that the drunkenness was an act of desperation not a moral collapse, the father sobered the son up, bought him new shoes, gave him some money and had a long talk with him during which he persuaded him to return to the university for the year at least. Bob, he felt, was much like what he considered the "worse" part of his own nature, sometimes given to "talking sheer nonsense" and at those times unable "to take a great leap over it," and because of the likeness he often felt he was unfair to him. He could not love the older son as he did the younger one, but after Bob left, he felt that they were getting on better. Very probably it was at this time that he began to think seriously of having Bob help out with the newspapers if they got to be too much for him to handle.[11]

During the first six months of his editorship, he explained to Burton Emmett early in May, he and Elizabeth had handled the business side of the papers successfully, a point he knew his benefactor was interested in. Although they had put perhaps a thousand dollars into replenishing paper stock and making mechanical improvements, they had set enough money aside to "make the payments as per program," presumably to Cox and on the bank loan. To meet other costs he had agreed with Colston Leigh to lecture two weeks in the fall and two in the spring of 1929, and he had the additional income from the monthly pieces for *Vanity Fair*. Further, although in "the American scene now the artist has no place," the papers gave him "a definite place in the life of the community"; and best of all, when writing on his novel "does not come as I want it to I do not sit, twirl my thumbs and eat myself up with remorse that I cannot do more and better work."

Things were looking up financially in general. He sent "The Lost Novel" to Otto Liveright on May 1 and urged him to sell it to some magazine for five hundred dollars because he needed the money. Liveright obliged by placing the story for that sum at *Scribner's Magazine,* and he helped Anderson obtain a contract for further pieces for *Vanity Fair* which allowed him to continue choosing his own subjects to write about, a necessity for him, he insisted to Otto, since writing on assigned subjects would make him "a mere hack." He had already contributed more pieces to the magazine than his original contract had called for, and he now began a series, usually entitled "Small Town Notes," describing ordinary people who "Like people everywhere are essentially lonely" and like everyone else resort to "all sorts of little subterfuges to get through life." For each piece he received as before three hundred dollars. Temporarily feeling well to do in early June, he bought a new Star automobile from the local dealer, Quincy Calhoun.[12]

He also decided on a quick trip to New York in mid-June to ease the weekly pressure of the papers, to settle the contract with *Vanity Fair,* and to discuss with Horace Liveright the possibilities of a new project he had recently begun thinking about, a book made up of selections from a year's issue of the papers, a book which "should be as absorbing as a great novel." Liveright approved of the project, Anderson finished the rest of his business quickly, and he surrendered himself to the exultation, as he would call it, of being for three days and two nights in his favorite city with its crowds and boulevards, its smartly dressed women, its rivers of beautiful shiny cars, its energetic men who knew how to play and who did business casually in expensive restaurants. He dined with his New Orleans friend Lyle Saxon and avoided most of the literary parties; though at one he was told happily by a woman that he and Dreiser were both "dead," shortly to be supplanted by "a new giant emerging on the horizon," obviously Thomas Wolfe, an admirer of Anderson, whose huge manuscript of the novel which became *Look Homeward, Angel* had recently been turned down by Boni and Liveright and accepted by Scribner's. On the radios, which now seemed blaring everywhere, he heard that Amelia Earhart had just flown across the Atlantic—that was June 18, and she had been the passenger on the *Friendship* with two men as pilot and co-pilot but received most of the publicity—and he read "to-day" in the June 19 *Times*

her "poem of courage," which he would reprint in *Hello Towns!*, the
projected book he had discussed with Liveright. On the nineteenth he returned to Marion, writing "Exultation," an impressionistic account of his
glorious New York "spree," on the train.[13]

Refreshed, he began writing "almost constantly," he told Burton Emmett, and shortly he let two stories "flow out as they came into my head,"
a first draft of "Fred" and "Alice," the latter of which, after "tightening
up," he sent off to Otto Liveright on July 17. "Alice" describes three instances of beauty seen by men "in the most unexpected places"—in a young
girl walking toward a slovenly cabin in the Ozarks, in a barefoot woman
walking along a muddy country road with a rough band of horse traders,
and especially in Alice herself, a Tennessee mountain woman once a tall
"half-vulgar, half lovely" singer who took many lovers and, as one of them
said, walked unforgettably "like a queen" across a stage or a room. Now
aging, her voice gone, her figure stout and unkempt, she has not lost her
shrewd, sympathetic understanding of people or her enormous generosity
toward them. The last time the narrator sees her, however, she is for the
moment "spiritually flat," trying to get past one of "what she called the
'times between.'" Having climbed a mountain in the Adirondacks one
evening, the two are descending along a road, Alice in the lead. She has
shaken off some unhappy memory, and when she crosses a moonlit stretch
of road, the narrator, stopping behind her, suddenly perceives her tall and
young walking like a queen. For the moment he loves her so madly that he
drops the cane he has carried, dismanned as had been the man who had
seen the barefooted woman in a country road and had dropped the corn-
cutting knife he was working with. By such framing action Anderson suggests that a man's awareness of a woman's beauty flashing out of drab,
even ugly surroundings may be sexually-tinged but is essentially aesthetic,
as was the awareness of another narrator of a tired old-young woman
dead in a moonlit opening in snowy woods; indeed, it is beauty revealing
itself from within the ordinary that has the most immediate, powerful, and
memorable effect on the observer. "Alice" thus becomes a parable about
Anderson's view of his own art.[14]

The major pieces of news in June were that Breece Perkins's big store
in Troutdale, built only the previous year, had burned to the ground, leaving the half-deserted lumber town more abandoned than ever; that the
Marion town council had purchased the new place for storing the town's
machinery; and that on the twenty-eighth Al Smith had been nominated as
the Democratic candidate for the presidency. Anderson announced that he
would not state his own position in the election fight—in the November
number of *Vanity Fair* he would be listed as one of sixty-seven of the "One
Hundred Celebrated Artists" who would vote for Smith—and cautioned
his readers that Democrats and Republicans would have to live together

after the election. Don't insult your friends was his advice; just hit them with a brick since the wound would heal more quickly. He himself had spent the evening when Smith was nominated at the Democratic convention in the office of a Virginia city newspaper, waiting for the word of the nomination but especially admiring the big modern presses. If he were a city newspaperman, he afterward wrote in "The Newspaper Office," he would want to do his writing in the press room in their presence.

> I suggested this idea once to a New York newspaperman, but he said it was not practical. To me it seemed that, if men had to work in the presence of the great presses, presently there would be a new dignity creep into their work. Suppose a man could write prose as fine as these presses. Or something worthy of the linotype machine.
> Suppose a man could write prose that did its work as smoothly and as well as a modern automobile.

Anderson had written and lectured on the beauty of modern machines before, but this piece coming near the end of the twenties seems unusually prophetic of what would be a consuming interest for him beginning in 1930. No longer should writing try to match the grace and courage of the trotting horse or be worthy of being read aloud to a field of growing corn; rather, writing should try to attain "the worth and dignity of the presses themselves." Equally prophetic was the corollary he had warned his readers and listeners of before, including Secretary of Commerce Hoover.

> In spite of all their efforts to prevent it, the modern newspaper, like most modern things, has lost all track of life. Life has pretty nearly been syndicated out of it.
> In almost every factory the men look small beside the machines they operate.

His own grass roots approach to life through the small town weekly seemed to him the more human one.[15]

Now that it was full summer, the Andersons went every weekend to Ripshin. Cornelia had agreed that John and Mimi should spend the summer there with their father, and Sherwood found that he got much from having his two younger children with him. He and Bob continued not to "touch each other much," he confessed to Bab. "Alas, it may simply be that I do not love him much." Presumably it was a relief to both when Bob went off to Philadelphia to work on the *Bulletin*. Anderson was writing little except for the papers, but this kind of writing was giving him satisfaction.

I am often full of joy that I can write so that some heavy handed farmer will come down the street to the shop and take my hand. "It's good," he says. That pleases me more than most anything I have had happen in my life. Or the coal miner, over the line in West Virginia, who tells me that he and his wife read my column in the paper aloud to each other and talk about it after they go to bed.

Because of the pressure of the papers, the Andersons had almost no guests, although the photographer Doris Ulmann came for a few days in mid-July and took many photographs of Ripshin and the area, including at least one of Anderson that would be reproduced in a note on him as contributor in *Scribner's Magazine* accompanying the publication of "The Lost Novel." The photograph shows him sitting, body and face a quarter turned to the right. The face is still fairly firm, but the neck is thickening, and the tousled hair shows streaks of gray. He is wearing a light-colored suit with what appears in black and white to be a gaudy, diamond-patterned tie, but the tie is conventionally knotted as befits one with community status.[16]

Then there was the visit on August 8–9 of Elizabeth's brother David, just back from a year of travel in England, France, and Greece. Sherwood took him to Ripshin in midweek so that David could see the farm; they were marooned there for the night by a storm, and they talked endlessly. They agreed that "Americans are wanderers," Anderson proclaiming in his "What Say!" account of the visit that "I myself have been a restless wanderer all my days." They talked of the French, their frankness about sex and their carefulness about money, the French not the Americans being "the real money-lovers." Sherwood praised David as being unlike so many scholars who knew nothing about life outside books; he is a "connoisseur in food, in music, in wine, in painting, in friendship." But considering the closeness of the Prall family and Elizabeth's attachment to her brother, David would have come to Marion for conversation less with Sherwood than with a sister distressed and resentful over a failing marriage.[17]

The months with the newspapers had been only a kind of remission in that failure, and Sherwood had now renewed his hardness toward Elizabeth. She would later recall as particularly symptomatic an episode that she would remember as having occurred during her husband's depression of the previous summer but that actually happened on the thirtieth of the present August. This year one of the features of the Smyth County Fair, which they of course attended, was a ride at two dollars a person in a rickety one-passenger plane, probably left over from the World War. For the first time in his life Sherwood had a plane ride, if only for about twenty minutes. Landing, he asked Elizabeth if she wanted a ride but in a tone implying that "he had seen it all and that it was time to go home." Much irritated at his tone, she took her turn in the plane. When she landed, Sherwood was at the car "staring grimly ahead," and he refused to look or speak to her on the way home. Shortly after this incident, hoping that a temporary separation might help, she suggested that she go to New York to see friends; Sherwood, who had recently "exalted" in New York, brusquely told her that the city was not for her.[18]

Elizabeth knew otherwise. She had never felt at home in Marion. She did not have her husband's ability to make friends easily, and she found the town women dull, opinionated, pious. Noting that "on Sundays ladies wore hats and gloves," she not only refused to conform but sometimes deliberately—deliberately because of her taste for stylish, expensive dresses—appeared at social functions (to Sherwood's irritation) wearing the workaday clothes she wore at Ripshin. Nor did she share her husband's admiration for Laura Lu Copenhaver with whom he had been having long conversations and who often invited the Andersons to Sunday dinner, where the Copenhavers would half jokingly call Elizabeth "a darn yankee" and where she resentfully felt that Mrs. Copenhaver "was instructing [Sherwood] on the ways of the South and that he was eager for such education." That his wife did not like Mrs. Copenhaver's company as he did was another source of irritation. Elizabeth felt trapped by Marion and the newspaper venture, which she had gone into in hopes of rescuing her husband from depression and her marriage from disintegration. That Sherwood seemed tied to the papers by his enjoyment of editorship, by the sense of small-town community they brought him, by the debts he had incurred to buy them, all made the future appear to her doubtful though, she would later insist, she had still loved him despite his renewed hardness toward her.[19]

For the "trouble" between husband and wife had long gone far beyond mutual irritation. Years later Elizabeth would insist that the cause for their coming separation was simply that Sherwood "got tired of me," which was true enough in a sense, yet insufficient. As Burt Dickinson, who subsequently handled Sherwood's suit for divorce, would also years later put it with a lawyer's circumspection, the root cause for the coming separation was "difference in temperament." The difference was not just that Sherwood was emotional and Elizabeth rational in response to life. Nearly two decades after the divorce was decreed in 1932, Elizabeth replied to a query from a scholar with a candid letter but one made condemnatory by her feeling that Sherwood had badly mistreated her. She diagnosed her former husband as "a neurotic, with the further complication of being an artist." Undeveloped morally, he "found it easy to get what he wanted by charm, or if that didn't work, by a trick; and he only felt bad if he wasn't successful." He had much charm and "real warmth" but "was always acting some part." Selfish, "even cruel," like most neurotics, he "had no loyalties if they interfered with his momentary desires," and he "explained and excused anything he wanted to do on the ground that he was an artist and should have special dispensations." Such analysis came after the fact; in the summer and fall of 1928 she was an unhappy wife trying to save her marriage.[20]

Some years after the divorce, Anderson would admit to William Spratling, friend of them both, that he had indeed "behaved really badly" toward Elizabeth; but in the summer and fall of 1928 he had become determined not to live with her longer. The gentleness and refinement that had once attracted him now repelled him as snobbishness. From the first of their living at Ripshin she had made no secret, as William Wright would recall, that she thought Sherwood had too many common people come to the house from the area, probably including Wright himself; and Sherwood resented her attitude of superiority to the Marion people, an attitude more than half implying that she felt intellectually superior to himself as well. He had begun referring to her to his friends sarcastically as "The Lady E." and "The Princess." He resented her expensive tastes and had become convinced that to pay for them she had wanted him to be a "man of letters," that is, for him, a literary hack. He continued to feel that she had been a major cause of his inability to write during the previous year and so was a threat to that to which he was most devoted, his art. For some undeterminable time, too, their sexual relations had been unsatisfactory; and apparently not considering how his debilitating depressions may have affected them, he had decided that, as he would later bluntly assert in a letter to another woman with whom he had fallen in love, Elizabeth

was a bit twisted sexually. She didn't want me or any man in her really.

Fucking for pure joy of skies, river, trees, flesh, man's flesh, woman's flesh wasn't in her.

She was tainted with something with which the modern race is too full . . . liking death rather than life. . . .

The taint he asserted in Elizabeth—though in another letter he merely posed it as a possibility—was an unconscious lesbianism; for, he declared, "her brother is a homosexual and one sister a lesbian." Despite his sympathy for unconventional people, his basic attitude toward homosexuality was the one he had given Aline in *Dark Laughter* when she refuses Esther's advance: homosexuality was quite literally a retreat from life and a seeking for death. Elizabeth's and all her family's gentleness and refinement he now was interpreting to be more than snobbishness, to be the outward sign of an inner "perversity," so that Elizabeth, he would declare to the other woman, "wanted to withdraw from all life. She always seemed to be saying—'Come on. Die with me.'" But Sherwood had used a similar argument, that she was death-seeking, against Tennessee when he wished to be free of her; and for all her gentleness and refinement Elizabeth was in her independent way "life-seeking" enough. There was an added complication. For all his genuine liking of David Prall for his intelligence and learning, Sherwood had distrusted Elizabeth's attachment to her brother,

17

an attachment so close that the astute Burt Dickinson could feel that there was "a real pull" in her between brother and husband. David's early August visit would almost certainly have awakened in Sherwood old resentment against that pull and simultaneously have convinced him finally that Elizabeth was at fault for the disintegration of the marriage and that he must be free of her.[21]

The emotional struggle in the marriage went on throughout the fall and probably contributed to Anderson's having brief periods when, as he openly confessed in his "What Say!" column of August 23: "With me the blues take a physical form sometimes. The black dog is on my back." Partly to throw off the black dog, he began reviewing in mid-August his many contributions to the papers in order to select those which would make up the one-year's sequence of them in his projected book, *Hello Towns!* A month later he was "wrestling" with the book, by September 25 he would be "feeling more sure" about it, and on October 25 he would write Marguerite Gay that he was "just about sending [it] to the publisher." Meanwhile Otto Liveright had sold "Alice" for four hundred dollars to *Harper's Bazaar,* even though the magazine's editor did not like the title and, Anderson not caring what it was called, published it as "Beauty." (When he collected the story in *Death in the Woods,* Anderson himself would retitle it as "Like a Queen.") Continually needing money to run the papers, Anderson kept up his monthly "Small Town Notes" sketches for *Vanity Fair,* but probably in late August or early September to meet the deadline for the October issue he sent in a quite different piece, notably uncharacteristic in content.[22]

Very likely the grim reminiscence "In a Box Car" together with the bleak possible reminiscence "Among the Drifters," which he mailed to Otto on October 2, were of acts of violence recalled or created out of his present feelings. In "In a Box Car," a man accidentally kills another man and terrifies the youthful Anderson who is the sole witness of the act, while in "Among the Drifters," an unhappily married young farmer, now a drifting laborer and perhaps a liar, tells Anderson in his own unskilled worker days how he did not shoot his wife but caused her death in a fire and escaped suspicion. The ex-farmer may actually have told his true or invented tale to the youthful Anderson, or the adult author could as well have invented it; but that the narrator does not, and the reader cannot, know whether the ex-farmer is lying suggests a psychological defense in Anderson himself against the unacceptable but surely desirable behavior, the desirableness emphasized by the unusual extent to which he uses sordid detail to make the ex-farmer's tale at least sound true.[23]

There is no equivocation about the evidence in "In a Box Car," which begins with a blunt question and answer.

Do you want to know how men happen to kill each other? It is because they are irritated beyond endurance, sometimes by the other man, or women, sometimes just by the circumstances of their lives.

As a young fellow out of work in winter in hard times, Anderson is riding freight trains and has crawled into a box car empty except for two other men, one large and heavy, the other thin and tall, whom he perceives as "dopes" gnawed by their craving for drugs. Cold, he falls asleep but is awakened by a pointless quarrel between the two men by the car's open door. The heavy man thrusts out his hand and unintentionally—as the ex-farmer in "Among the Drifters" had unintentionally caused the fire—pushes the thin man out the door to his death, then lies down weeping between Anderson and the door. Anderson, fearful that the man will kill him as the one witness, moves toward the door, terrified that the man might seize him. The man does not move, however, and Anderson the adult artist ends his tale with sudden, powerful objectivity by explaining how to get out of a box car when the train is moving. "IF you are lucky or know how to do it," runs the last sentence, "you land right side up." Technically, then, "In a Box Car" is almost as indeterminate in its conclusion as "Among the Drifters." Both stories, furthermore, are set at a time when Anderson was immature, uneducated, trapped in squalid circumstances, an image of himself such as he sensed "The Lady E" may often have had of him; and in each story a death is done unintentionally but by a man filled with "irritation beyond endurance" who escapes from legal retribution. Writing these stories at this time, one guesses, expressed and so drained off actual homicidal fantasies in an Anderson "irritated beyond endurance" by a wife he was determined to get rid of.

Anderson's thoughts were, of course, not filled solely with violence that fall. Along with "Among the Drifters," he sent Otto Liveright on October 2 another tale, "Fred," a draft of which he was working on as early as late June. In its final version, completed almost exactly six years later, this story is among his most amusing ones. Except in physical description, Fred—not his real name, says the narrator—is Anderson himself, a "well-known writer" who has paid mountain men good wages to build him a house "in his upland valley, a few miles out of town." The mountain folk consider him to be rich, an easy mark, and begin "robbing" him in small ways; but the narrator tells the story of "Felix's" loafing on the job by telling Fred a tale and Fred's writing up the tale and selling it for three hundred dollars, thus showing that for a man without "much money sense" Fred can take care of himself. When Fred's horse strays through a fence around the small hillside cornfield of Tom Case, a neighbor "both mean and generous," Tom demands ten dollars damage, twice what the corn is worth. Tom plays the same trick on the compliant Fred two more times when Fred's horse strays into his cornfield, but òn the fourth occasion he overreaches himself by locking the horse in his barn and demanding twenty-five dollars. Fred gets the sheriff to release the horse and takes the dispute to "a Virginia squire's court" held by two elderly squires, each of whom must receive three dollars for "sitting a case." At the outdoor trial Tom rides about on his big black horse raging, but Fred, who has begun to "get the spirit of the country all right," quietly explains that he has already paid Tom thirty dollars and suggests that a committee assess the actual damage done. The committee decides on three dollars damages, and the squires decide that Fred pay that plus the six dollars costs. Fred, now getting annoyed, asks the committee how much the whole cornfield is worth, is told "About seven dollars," and privately suggests to the squires that he pay them their six dollar costs and Tom get nothing since he doesn't want Tom to get the best of him. They so decide, to Tom's baffled fury. Two months later Tom on his horse and Fred walking meet on a narrow mountain road, stare at each other, then begin to laugh. Thereafter Tom comes once a week to Fred's house to do chores for nothing because, he declares as the story ends, "I believe in neighbors being good neighbors."[24]

In her memoirs, Elizabeth would tell of an occasion when her horse strayed into a farmer's hay field, Sherwood appeared at a trial resembling a squire's court, and despite an eloquent speech on "freedom for horses and good fences make good neighbors" he was required to pay five dollars damage, much to her indignation since she felt that "the farmer had been out to take us because we were not natives." Presumably Sherwood based his original draft of "Fred" on this incident, taking a literary revenge for not actually outwitting the farmer; on the other hand, Elizabeth's memory for time sequences and even details in *Miss Elizabeth* was occasionally undependable, and she may have misremembered a later dispute. Whatever the case, the extraordinary aspect of "Fred" is that in early October of 1928 life copied art. On October 2, Anderson mailed the revised "Fred" to Otto Liveright. On October 5, he wrote a curt note to Charlie Grubb, a neighbor, protesting Grubb's locking up of Anderson's two horses and his unreasonableness about "any damages done," which "can be settled by the court." In his account of the trial in the October 18 *Smyth County News,* Anderson states that he had offered Grubb five dollars damage but that the neighbor, perhaps thinking "we were rich," had demanded twenty. Two squires of Grayson County, where Troutdale is located, decided on three dollars damage and equally shared costs. Since Grubb had to pay three dollars costs, the account concludes, "he was out of money. Had he been more neighborly he would have been $5.00 ahead. Had he been a good neighbor he probably wouldn't have charged us a cent." Revenge in one's life would have been sweeter than in one's fiction, and the cream of it was that Anderson would receive the going price when he sold "Fred" to the magazine *Today,* where it was published under the appropriate title "Virginia Justice."[25]

Obviously Anderson was getting the spirit of the country, all right. "It is education," he had asserted in mid-September in the *Smyth County News,*

here in Marion, being editor of the small town and county papers. Here I am closer to life than I have ever been.

The court, the field, the country road, the farm-house, the street. It is a school when you have a definite place in it.

He was hitting the right notes with the papers, for subscription renewals were "pouring in" in October, "ten, fifteen and even twenty" daily. In early November he wrote an article for the *News* titled "Will You Sell Your Newspapers?," republished in the national *Outlook and Independent* and titled more positively "I Will Not Sell My Papers." Sometimes, he admits in the article, he is bored and sometimes walks the town streets on rainy nights, "sick with disgust of [my] own life, that [I] am so ineffectual in life," but he has walked so in cities; and in the town he has a place, nature is nearby, and "There are a thousand tales in this town as in all towns." He did not mention that he really was becoming bored with the weekly task and restless, exceedingly restless, in his marriage. But soon he was off and away. On November 15 he began the two-week fall lecture tour arranged by Colston Leigh by speaking at the University of North Carolina on "The Creative Impulse," his other prepared lecture being "Modern Tendencies in Writing." On the sixteenth he spoke at the North Carolina College for Women at Greensboro, and thereafter his engagements, usually at two hundred dollars each, took him from South Carolina as far north as Massachusetts. For once he may have disliked a tour somewhat less than usual because he was speaking about writing chiefly to students at colleges and universities, and such students had occasionally written him letters expressing dissatisfaction with a money-oriented society and a desire for new values and ways of life. Then, too, he was away from Elizabeth, who was meanwhile in Marion dutifully overseeing the print shop staff.[26]

Early in the tour he had lectured twice in one day, November 19, in New York, and he arranged to end his tour there. Excited as always to be in the city again, he lunched with Otto Liveright and visited the Emmetts, to whom he boasted of the morality of artists and afterwards apologized since they were "both sweeter finer people" than he and most artists were. Perhaps spurred by that incident he decided to write a play, spent a sleepless night working it out, and then tested its "practibility" by going to Horace Liveright's office and outlining it to him. Horace, he reported to Emmett, "fell for it." During the first four months of 1928 he had had in the print shop a competent and attractive young secretary named Mary Vernon Greer, who was at the moment in New York and may even have arranged to meet him there. (The "several hundred letters" he wrote her "almost every day" over a period of time, she would later recall, she subsequently destroyed at his request.) Picking up from the Liveright office a fresh copy of *Sherwood Anderson's Notebook,* he went to see her and presented it to her, with an inscription, to go with the inscribed copy of *The Modern Writer* he had given her a year earlier. Knowing his interest in art, she suggested that he look up her brother-in-law, Charles Bockler, who painted during the day and at night worked as a bookkeeper in a New York bank. He did so, and the two men went off to revel in some of the collections at the Metropolitan Museum of Art. Bockler would later recall Anderson's heaviness of body and face, his rather long "rough combed" hair, the ring rather than the knot that held his tie, and especially his almost black, very powerful and compelling eyes. As the companions went from picture to picture, Bockler noted that Anderson had an intense interest in painting and a strong sense of color, and especially liked artists who did not "let it get up in their heads," in Anderson's phrase, but put down directly what they saw, as Bockler himself did when some visual impression excited him and he just wanted to get it down on canvas. The two men got along splendidly. That evening at the Bocklers' apartment, Charles and his wife Katharine told Anderson the story of their sudden decision to marry over a Fourth of July; and Charles would much later be wryly amused that, typically of Anderson's way of working as he came to understand, the sudden decision would be the only recognizable fact of the slight tale "Why They Got Married," which Anderson within days built around quite different events and personalities for *Vanity Fair.*[27]

By December 4 he was back in Marion, resolved during his absence to act decisively about his marriage and a future freed as well from the weekly routine of the papers. He began arranging with Robert to leave the Philadelphia *Bulletin* and come to help with the papers, perhaps eventually to run them himself. "I have taken these papers up and played with them for a year," he wrote Bab, adding callously, "I have taken them as I might have taken a woman, have in fact taken women." The unstated decision about Elizabeth was implicit in his self-concerned explanation to Bab that perhaps he was "an artist pure and simple, a man to whom all things feed into a central force."

New loves come and old ones drop away. The land here is lovely. I love that.

Often I look back with a queer feeling. How much I have been loved—by you—by others. How kind everyone has been.

I give little in return. Occasionally, however, something does flow up through me. I produce stories, novels, poems that have a living strength.[28]

Coming to these decisions had released him into a burst of writing after his return from New York—two acts of the play, two short stories, one of them "Why They Got Married," and "About 30,000 words on a novel—The 'Another Man's House' I have wanted to get at for so long." There may well have been an additional reason for such a burst: late in 1928, probably in either the first two weeks of November or the first two in December, Anderson met his fourth wife. At that time Eleanor Copenhaver was thirty-two, small, slim, strong-bodied, energetic, with dark hair and eyes, a quick, friendly smile, and a warm, outgoing manner. This beloved daughter of B. E. and Laura Lu might have grown up to be simply a Southern belle within Marion aristocracy, but she had gone in a different direction. Probably influenced by her mother's literary and religious interests, she had taken a degree in English from Westhampton College of the University of Richmond in 1917 and, after a year of teaching English in Marion, had gone to Bryn Mawr from 1918 to 1920 for a two-year certificate in social work. Then she had gone directly to the Young Women's Christian Association to apply her training, first in rural communities and from 1923 on with the Industrial Program of the National YWCA. Her training and her special interest in the working conditions of women in factories had given her a knowledge of worlds beyond Marion, a strong social conscience, and a sense of independence. Around the end of September 1928, she had returned from a four-month assignment in Italy and Hungary. As always, her occasional visits to her parents were brief ones as she went through Marion to assignments elsewhere. Sherwood and Elizabeth first met her at Rosemont on one such flying visit. Sherwood was drawn to her immediately, rightly sensing in this warm "Italian-looking" young woman, as he would speak of her, a latent passion to match that in what he liked to think of as his Italian blood. (As early as February 2 of the next year he would address her as "Dearest Eleanor" in one of the first of the hundreds of letters he would write her.) He would certainly have been attracted by her independent ways, her knowledge of the world outside Marion, her sympathetic understanding of working-class men and women, and even by her being a Copenhaver. Years later, Eleanor would tell two interviewers half-jokingly that she thought Sherwood "fell in love first with the house, then with my mother, and then with me." She had already read his books, especially liking *A Story Teller's Story*, and here was one of the makers of modern American literature in her own home. For this reason, even if not for Sherwood's ability to charm people, she would have responded to him enthusiastically on their first meeting.[29]

As for Elizabeth's attitude toward this additional Copenhaver, neither in memoir nor interview would she indicate it, and the silence is telling. She knew her husband's moods and responses, and he knew that she was "puzzled and afraid," finding in this meeting another reason for resenting him and her situation in Marion. But the decisions he had made while on his lecture tour were beginning to go into effect. Around December 13, Bob arrived in Marion, and about that time Sherwood suggested to Elizabeth that his lecture fees would make it possible for her to take a holiday trip to California to see her family. She "thought it was considerate of him," she recalled in her memoir; and on or about December 18 she began the long train ride west, and Bob moved into the apartment over the print shop with his father. Very likely Elizabeth had agreed to go to California because she had decided that the marriage must be ended, but one detail in this painful affair remains in dispute. In his original bill for divorce, filed February 1, 1932, Sherwood would state that shortly after her departure she wrote him that she would not return; and Burt Dickinson, who with Andy Funk subsequently arranged the divorce, would recall in 1951 that she had "left him and had told him she would not come back." As Elizabeth recalled some forty years later, a few days after her arrival in Berkeley she received a letter from Sherwood stating "quite simply, 'I just wish you would not come back.'" The letter filled her with "a cold, steady anger that consumed any love I still felt for Sherwood"; indeed, when her philosophy professor friend William Dennes saw her after her return to Berkeley, he was disturbed at how blotched her face was, as he had seen it before when she had been under severe stress. In her memoir she concludes that she burned all of Sherwood's letters, which she had long preserved, dropped the wedding ring, which she herself had purchased, "into a trash can," and deliberately began to forget the marriage. Back in Marion, Sherwood took to his bed with a bad cold and the onset of Christmas. Two days after the holiday, he had recovered enough to write Bab that his illness had come from writing long hours daily for three weeks, that he and Bob were "alone here," that Bob was "getting out the paper," and that he "would like to go away from this place now—for a long time . . . have a year alone somewhere." He made no direct mention of Elizabeth, but he did not forget his treatment of her any sooner than in actuality she did.[30]

2

The Year of the Crash

1.

Anderson began the new year with a case of the flu that was going around Marion and the print shop, but by January 5 he was well enough to head by train for a lecture in Chicago. On the way he dropped off at Indianapolis for a visit to the sympathetic Bab to tell her of his separation from the Princess and of his related decision to sell Ripshin—and then had the ingratitude to write her on the seventh that, like other women, she did not think of him as an artist, "a man working in abstract things." He was through with women, he insisted, except at the times when he needed sex; women "have disturbed too much, spoiled too much" for him as writer. But he wanted Bab as a "friend to the struggling defeated artist" in himself, though only another man could really understand him, and he would be grateful if she could help him sell the house. The kindest thing one can say about so unkind a letter is that it showed his confusion and remorse at how he had broken off a marriage as well as his relief that he had done so. After writing half a dozen letters to Bab over the next three months, often about selling the house, he would send her only seven more in all, at least of those she preserved, before the letters stopped altogether in November 1933. Like Ripshin, which he never succeeded in selling, she apparently seemed too much connected with his old life during the years he was searching for a new one.[1]

He took both relief and remorse with him to a subzero Chicago on January 8, where he lectured on "Modern Tendencies in Writing." He had time to chat with his "feeder" George Daugherty and especially to visit Ferdinand and Clara Schevill in their "warm friendly home." With an echo of his words in *A Story Teller's Story* as he walked out of his mail-order office and his first troubled marriage in 1912, he wrote them that it was, "as though I had been swimming a long time in winter, in an icy river and had got ashore. . . ." In pouring out to them his complaints against

Elizabeth, he admitted, he had overemphasized money and her spending habits: "All of this wild purchasing was purchasing of baubles, of course—to compensate perhaps for love I could not give." After all,

poor E is very very nice—much nicer that I will ever be—and I do not want her any more. C[ornelia] and T[ennessee] were nice too. Why should I not face myself—a wanderer.

Early on the ninth he caught a train to New York, mainly to talk with Horace Liveright about his plan to sell Ripshin. Horace agreed to help where he could and cynically advised him to set the price, not at fifteen to twenty thousand, but at thirty to thirty-five since only a rich man could buy the house anyway and "would respect it more for paying more," particularly since it should be sold as "Sherwood Anderson's house." Before leaving the city, Anderson very likely looked up Charles Bockler again, for his feeling toward the committed young artist had become "half that of a father to a son, half pure feeling of companionship, as brother"; but he needed to get back to Marion to see how Bob was doing with the paper, and by the morning of January 14 he was there at the print shop.[2]

Having already done stints on five other newspapers, Bob was in fact doing a "marvelous" job with the papers, and his father was free to wander where and when he wished; but at the moment he brooded on the linked matters of Ripshin and Elizabeth and began a siege of writing and dictating letters. He must have heard from his wife, for he wrote Bab that "The Princess has made up her mind to be very nice . . . about the property here." With her usual generosity Bab had offered to help him financially as she had his children, but he gratefully refused her offer and suggested that she might have the five percent commission if she could find someone to take the house off his hands. He would send her photographs and a prospectus. For himself he was done with "things." He had already given Bob his editor's office and for his writing was satisfied with "a small kitchen table—3 ft by 2 feet—a kitchen chair," which he could move about the print shop as he wished. The house had become a thing too. When he dictated a long letter to Horace Liveright describing it almost lovingly as "a little gem" with its thick stone walls, its solid native oak floors and woodwork, its situation in a countryside "alive with mountain trout streams" and game birds, he was primarily being the skilled copywriter presenting the house as a summer home or a hunting lodge for a wealthy man. Ripshin was "Beautiful . . . a complete thing" like one of his best short stories, he told Bab, but it was haunted by a dead marriage. He wanted to get back to his "own life . . . the world of my own fancy [which] The Princess almost took . . . from me."[3]

Among his many other letters, he sent one to Jane Heap in Paris answering a *Little Review* questionnaire by saying that he most wanted "not to be professional, smart, intellectual, stupid. I fear most that I will achieve nothing"; and he sent one to an editor at the *Outlook and Independent* who had solicited an article. Since it was a cold winter in Virginia, he wrote, he had been thinking about the South and would "write a piece about what the South means to me." That was on January 15; by the twenty-third he had written "Let's Go Somewhere" in the form of a letter to "Charles," an "imaginary person," he told the *Outlook,* but clearly it was Charles Bockler. Northern cities are "like clenched fists," while New Orleans and Mobile are "like open hands," for these cities will "never industrialize" and clutter people with "things." The South is beautiful with its many colors and soft Negro voices, and even the cockroaches are fun to watch. He doesn't know what Florida is like, "have never been there yet but am going soon." Indeed, Anderson had already arranged to drive south to Florida for a two-week loaf in the sun. Since Bockler could not leave his job, Sherwood had been "absolutely insisting" that Burt Dickinson go with him early in February, but without telling him of his separation from Elizabeth and his need to escape from thoughts of her, which were exacerbated by having to pack up and send off all the things in the apartment she had not taken with her to California. "I have been having sleepless nights," he told Bab, "my house full of ghosts of the departed Princess." Before he fled to Florida in "a highly nervous state," however, he managed to complete and mail to *Vanity Fair* two more of his "Small Town Notes" series and to carry out a plan he had told Bockler about. On January 26 he dictated letters to Otto Kahn, Frank Crowninshield, and Burton Emmett, all of them praising the "straight sensual joy in life" in the work of an unnamed young painter (Bockler) and stating that he was requesting a few of his friends to send him three hundred dollars each in exchange for a painting to be selected by Anderson himself, the total sum to be used to support the young man during a year off from his bank job. He had himself already bought three of the man's paintings—presumably at a much lower price—for he thought the man "has the best chance of any young American painter whose work I have seen." Kahn was so taken with Anderson's letter that he sent his check for three hundred dollars by return mail. Just before Anderson started south, he wrote of this success to Eleanor Copenhaver, whom he had begun seeing whenever she was in Marion and whom he had already begun telling things he did not want known in the town, especially that he and Elizabeth had separated. The separation had been "like a major physical operation," he wrote Eleanor; now he felt "like a convalescent."[4]

At 6 AM on February 3, Anderson and Dickinson headed south in Sherwood's car, driving the first day down through Asheville and along the east edge of the Great Smokies to the town of Murphy in the southwest corner of North Carolina, where, Anderson recorded in his exuberant "A Traveler's Notes" series for the *Smyth County News,* they were "in the real South. More Negroes, the rooms in the hotels not so clean and modern as in the North." The second day they reached Atlanta, where Anderson had arranged to talk with a real estate man about selling Ripshin; at the end of the third day they stopped at Cordele in south central Georgia; and on the fourth day they began rolling along at sixty-five on the wide, flat highways of northern Florida. Here farmers were plowing and planting, and there were mockingbirds and cardinals everywhere along the road in the southern spring. Then came peach trees in full bloom, and farther south the travelers, now driving happily in shirt sleeves, began seeing orange groves, the trees standing in yellow sand, "heavy with the golden fruit," and with the sky blue overhead. "O, what a strange quiet sleepy land this must have been before the northern boomers came," Anderson would exclaim in his "Traveler's Notes." The two companions were duly impressed by the clarity of the lake at Silver Springs near Ocala and then headed for Florida's Gulf Coast, Anderson especially admiring the expensive new cars on the highway, almost as lovely to him as the clipper ship, "the most lovely mechanical thing America produced, before the automobile." Then the rollicking "Notes" came to an end with a brief conversation between the traveler and a middle-aged black bellhop on the mutual problem of women—"how to hold them when you want to hold them—how to unhold them when you want to unhold"—and an early morning rising that reminds him of a description by George Borrow "in that marvelous book *The Bible in Spain,*" and with his desire for hot coffee "as soon as I bounce out of bed."[5]

Of the drive across Florida to Delray Beach on the Atlantic side, of fishing and sunbathing there for a week at the Hotel Casa del Rey, nothing. In response to a letter from Horace Liveright asking how *Another Man's House* was coming, Anderson confessed that he hadn't touched the novel and wouldn't until he had trained Bob to handle the papers and had time "to get over the shock of my domestic break-up." He had not escaped the ghosts of the Princess, was not really "convalescent," and he was further saddened by the news he had received toward the end of January of the death of his Paris friend Léon Bazalgette, "about the most charming man I have ever met," as he had written of him in the papers just before he left for Florida. Memories of Bazalgette had recalled to him his illness during his stay in a wintry Paris with Elizabeth. On the long way back from Florida, he was so depressed and quiet that Dickinson, not yet knowing of his "wife trouble," thought Sherwood was bored with him. Of the return Dickinson could later remember only a very heavy rain in Charleston and Anderson trying for a long time unsuccessfully to phone a woman writer there. By February 20 Anderson was back in Marion "sad," he wrote Bockler, "—made sad by the house, haunted by E. with whom I failed." He was feeling far more guilt for his treatment of her than Elizabeth would ever grant him.[6]

A few cheerful pieces of news were waiting for him. Bob had handled the papers "splendidly," and Burton Emmett had sent three hundred dollars for a Bockler picture, and now with six hundred dollars and some savings the painter could have most of a year free. Proofs for *Hello Towns!* had arrived, and it was a relief to bury himself at once in reading them. Either pleased to see his words in book print or eager to interest Liveright in a volume the author and publisher had originally been hesitant about, or both, he urged Horace that it was "a damn good book—one of the best I ever did": "It is a real picture of life—fragmentary, as I have been lately, but real." It would sell if Horace would push it, and in a follow-up letter after finishing proofreading in four or five days, he suggested—unsuccessfully—"a special signed, limited edition, as you have done with my other books." All Horace had to do was "to jig up your sales force," the verb being the sort Anderson would use when doing his own selling jobs. Most pleasant of all after his return to Marion was that Eleanor seems to have been writing encouragingly to him, though apparently as cautious as he was characteristically impetuous. At the beginning of February she had written that all the Copenhaver family loved him, and he had replied that "I hope you may love me a little specially yourself." Later that month she had apparently commented on marriage as a positive institution, for he replied that it could also be "destructive," as it was to him. "Women, in their moments of loveliness, are as necessary to me as breath," but his and Elizabeth's relationship was definitely over, even though he still suffered "personal remorse" for not being "more wise, gentle, determined" and though as an artist—artists "live in others"—he knew she suffered remorse too. Obviously Sherwood wanted Eleanor to know that he was a caring person but not to fear that he might return to Elizabeth.[7]

But bits of good news were not enough, and he fell further into a "distraught, upset state." Because of her job Eleanor could be in Marion only infrequently, there were the questions of how the reviewers would receive *Hello Towns!* and whether Liveright could sell it, and some bothersome practical matters about the separation had to be settled. With Burt Dickinson's legal assistance, Anderson arranged to pay Elizabeth eight hundred dollars for the piece of land she had added to Ripshin in exchange for a deed in his name, and he initiated the procedure whereby he and she "for the sum of $1.00 cash in hand" deeded her elegant never-occupied house on Governor Nicholls Street in New Orleans to her mother. Since escape to Florida had worked for him temporarily, he continued trying to deal

with his state of mind by frequent physical movement like a sick man trying by changing positions in bed to gain relief from pain. At the end of February or the beginning of March, he spent a couple of days in Baltimore talking with the Marxist writer V. F. Calverton, who had written an approving
article on his work and now proposed, unsuccessfully, a biography—"Let
[biographers] wait till I am dead," Anderson wrote Liveright—and on
the cold, gray morning of March 4 he arrived in crowded Washington to
watch the presidential inauguration of Herbert Hoover, whom he had
talked with a year before. He went partly to write up the event for his papers, partly to meet Baroness Marie-Louise Koskull, who had earlier written him "a very charming letter" praising *Dark Laughter* and subscribing
to the *News*. Later on, she had sent him a piece he had published in the papers titled "Fear," describing a grim experience she had had during the
Bolshevik Revolution. He was now much taken with this "tall, strong, magnificent" Russian aristocrat, whose fair skin Renoir would have wanted to
paint, who invited him to dinner that evening, and who over the next few
weeks would introduce him to her circle of friends.[8]

Back in Marion briefly to write up his "Impressions of an Inauguration," to him a dull, rain-dampened ceremony, he had two unpleasant surprises. Calverton had quickly reported to Liveright that Anderson had
been "knocking Horace Liveright, Inc." for not pushing his books, and
Horace now wrote Sherwood that he was very sorry to hear such a rumor,
especially since Sherwood had not supplied the right book to push since
Dark Laughter, including *Hello Towns!*. Anderson protested in reply that
he had never knocked Liveright and his firm, all of whom had treated him
better than "anyone in the publishing world"; and when he learned the
source of the rumor, he flatly denied discussing his publisher at all with
Calverton. Then Burton Emmett wrote to complain that Anderson had
sent him the manuscripts of only four books and little of the association
material as promised in their contract. In his lengthy reply Anderson was
defensive and apologetic; he had not really understood what of his scrib-
blings Emmett wanted, the past year had been a bad one for him because
he had had to get out the papers while his third marriage was "falling to
pieces," and Emmett could at least have the satisfaction that "I think I can
say to you that owning these papers has perhaps saved me from insanity"
during "this distraught time." Yet he also asserted that by his editing of the
papers "the life of the whole community has been touched and changed"
and even boasted that "I believe that of all the writers living now, at least
in America, I am the only man who has written prose having in it a kind
of singing quality that is necessary to its continued life in the consciousness of others." In a postscript he placatingly told Emmett that he was
dedicating *Hello Towns!* to him and his wife.[9]

The boasting was clearly a way of shoring up his self-confidence in an uneasy time, but he was encouraged to it by having just belatedly read an article in the *Yale Review Magazine* by its young managing editor Dwight Macdonald. The article, though it argued a decline in his writing from *Dark Laughter* on, praised at length the fusion in his best work of objectivity and poetic feelings. In a grateful letter Anderson thanked Macdonald for the "fine intelligence" of his article, mildly protested the concluding "funeral oration," and declared himself to be still "experimentally minded."

Sometimes really I have the temerity to think of myself as a sort of Cézanne in prose, that is to say—"the primitive of the way." I like to think that I have still much courage for new experiments, whether they succeed or not.

He liked the comparison with Cézanne so much that he used it again in a letter to Bab, and then went on to give her, as often before, a taste of the callousness that he insisted was required by his deeper obligation to art than to women.

As for women, to be frank, my dear, our experience has been not unlike others I have had with other women. Much has been offered to me in the way of women, in the flesh. I have taken what I felt clear and clean in taking. When I no longer felt that, I have stopped, sometimes only after much bitterness. I have gone sometimes away from women with fine bodies and fine minds and have gladly taken women to whom I had no obligation, because to do so cleansed me like writing good prose.

Elizabeth would be right in accusing her former husband of forgiving himself much on the grounds of being an artist. For Sherwood to do so now was a way for him to withstand the continuing pressure of guilt.[10]

On the evening of March 13 he left for New York, presumably to reassure Liveright in person against the Calverton rumor, but on the fifteenth he was off to Washington to see the Baroness for a day or so. Then he returned wearily to New York to rest and write. Dreading questions about his "personal affairs," he saw almost none of his old friends and instead hid out in a hotel and in the house of a painter friend, possibly Jerome Blum, in a suburb. He began to write a little prose that pleased him for having "some music" in it; yet his mood quickly changed, as two long pieces in his "A Traveler's Notes" series illustrate. In the first, written shortly after his return from Washington, he is delighted to be in the city, to have interesting chance encounters with ordinary citizens, to respond to the bright colors on the painter's canvases. In the second, written perhaps a week later, he is appalled at the "modern city business rush," which makes the eyes of the young men and women weary, their faces old. A woman bank worker bitterly tells him that the one purpose of a modern business is "to pile up more and more money for those who already have too much [and] the aim of all modern industry [is] to make the individual of less and less importance as an individual." Government used to be of more importance than business; now the businessman is "at the top," and the "growing thousands of submerged ones [are] without meaning in their lives, with no direct connection with the work by which they live." Anderson takes a subway at the evening rush hour and sees the packed-in people as crowds of "automatons" who nevertheless have "a deep, underlying dissatisfaction." Walking the evening streets among apartment houses, he hears radios blaring from all sides. "The voices coming over the radio are all telling the people of the wonder and glory of this modern life of ours. How long" he concludes, "do you think they will go on believing?" The bitter mood of this latter piece is reflected in his report to John at the University of Wisconsin of the "discouraging" day he did bring himself to spend with Karl:

he has got everything a successful painter is supposed to get honors, awards, etc., he is received into the best society and is almost independently wealthy. The result of all this is that he has no truth in painting at all, in fact, I suspect hates it. I don't believe it would be possible for him to love either a woman or a landscape. The more I see of successful men the more I hope you or Bob will not be one.

It would be better for John not to go on with college, as John himself had decided, and then get "a fairly easy living" while painting; instead he might better learn a trade like carpentering and then "work six months and . . . paint six months." In any case he should keep out of "business and industrial life."[11]

2.

Back in Marion on April 2, called there unexpectedly early by a telegram from Bob saying that Gil Stephenson's wife was dying, Anderson soon found that his bitterness at business, wealth, and success might be leading him in a new direction. Within a few days Eleanor Copenhaver was in Marion on the way to observe the labor unrest in Elizabethton, a mill town fifty miles south across the border in Tennessee, at the huge rayon factories of the Glantzstoff and the American Bemberg corporations, three-fourths of whose employees were dirt-poor white mountain girls, many in their early teens. Eager to be with Eleanor as well as to report on the unrest for his papers, Anderson drove her down to the town probably on the weekend of the sixth and seventh or just after, and subsequently wrote the article "Elizabethton, Tennessee," first printed in the April 18 issue of the *News* and reprinted in the May 1 number of *The Nation*. The recently built town, he observed, was already getting shabby, the factory machines were "magnificent," the girls were overworked and underpaid. Shortly before Sherwood and Eleanor came, the American Federation of Labor had sent in an organizer named Hoffman whom a group of townsmen "escorted . . . out of town at the point of a gun" but who returned and had began organizing the women and men laborers into a local of the Textile Workers. In his article Anderson openly declares himself on the side of the workers since, though he now belongs to his "own class . . . the artist class," he came from the working class and is proud to be "accepted by working people everywhere as one of themselves." Let into a crowded organizing meeting in the evening by Hoffman, he observes a new life and joy in the bodies of the union members. Honestly puzzled by his own love of luxury despite his contempt for the rich, uncertain about the possible outcome of a strike, he nevertheless thinks to himself that

"these working men and women have got, out of this business of organizing, of standing thus even for the moment, shoulder to shoulder, a new dignity. They have got a realization of each other. They have got for the moment a kind of religion of brotherhood and that is something."

It is a great deal more than any wage increase they may win from their struggle.

As recently as mid-January, Anderson had written the artist J. J. Lankes that "between the Industrialist and Laborer is no choice for us," that if those in the artist "class" desire closeness, "we have to get it from each other." The further radicalization of Sherwood Anderson lay in the future, but with his visit to Elizabethton the process had begun.[12]

This radicalization would always have a large component of the emotional, and a significant part of the emotion would be his attraction to Eleanor as woman and social worker among the mountain girls with their "straight hard little bodies, delicately featured faces." Although both he and Eleanor were uneasy at being seen together too much in public, back in Marion from Elizabethton they had a drive and a walk together to Walker Mountain on the west and to the cemetery overlooking the town on the east. On the mountain a momentary feeling of separation between them before the loveliness of nature in spring prompted in Sherwood a short story, "Ashamed," later melded into a "Small Town Notes" piece, in which two men—as always personal experience was only the beginning of his creativity—feel separate before the beauty of burgeoning nature because they are ashamed at being unable to find words for that beauty. In actual life, however, the momentary sense of separation had brought the man and woman, Sherwood felt, closer together. Still, the relationship was only in its tentative beginnings.[13]

With Eleanor gone to her job, Anderson had to get along as best he could. While Bob did much of the work, he edited the papers. By mid-April he settled arrangements with Oscar Lewis of the Westgate Press in San Francisco for the publication of *Nearer the Grass Roots* in a special limited edition of five hundred copies, each signed by the author, who would be paid one hundred dollars at once and $150 when Lewis received the two articles comprising the very slim volume. One article would be "Nearer the Grass Roots" from the January 1928 *Outlook;* the other Anderson expected to write as "The Artist's Life," but he gave up and selected instead the *Nation* article, titled simply "Elizabethton." After receiving an early copy of *Hello Towns!* before he left New York, he had carefully praised Liveright for the book's "splendid make-up [and] physical beauty." Now, rather nervously, he had to await the book's unpredictable critical reception and sales after its publication on April 17.[14]

Anderson's old friend Harry Hansen led off the reviews with a brief but enthusiastic recommendation that readers must not miss *Hello Towns!,* and soon Liveright was comforting Anderson with the word that "the critics are being very generous" to the book. Of the seven reviews that appeared in April, six were highly favorable, and the seventh was moderately so despite some dissent. These reviewers admired Anderson's portrayal of small-town life and lives, more accurate than Sinclair Lewis's, two reviewers emphasized, and the way he combined the country editor tone with his own new simplicity of style. (The dissenter thought the style too often falsely naive.) Anderson may not have seen all of these reviews as they came out, but he certainly saw Percy Hutchison's "wonderful" front-page piece in the *New York Times Book Review,* which linked *Hello Towns!* with *Winesburg,* praised it as an interpretation of American life, and ended by declaring that "Mr. Anderson is one of the truly striking figures today in American literature." No longer would he think about sales, he wrote Eleanor; the book "has registered, as a definite thing," which was enough to get out of a bad year. The reviews throughout May and after were another matter. Liveright had shrewdly sent copies of the book to thirty or more newspaper editors around the country, and most of the reviews that resulted were positive, though less for Anderson's unconventional reporting than for his sketches of small-town life. Several of them dismissed the book as dull, however, and the reviews in the more literary publications were now more often than not negative. In his *American Mercury,* Mencken found the book "charming" but written in a childishly naive style and having "little weight"; Sara Haardt in the *Saturday Review of Literature* praised Anderson's understanding of the southern small town but judged his book to be below even his lesser works; and Geoffrey T. Hellman's mocking attack in the *New Republic* so outraged Anderson that he complained to Stark Young, the magazine's drama critic, for the book editor's assigning a serious book by an established author to a "smart, flippant young man" for review. The cruelest treatment came in the July *Vanity Fair*, in which not only another in Anderson's "Small Town Notes" series appeared but also a review in the form of a devastatingly amusing parody of *Hello Towns!* titled "Hello Yourself, Sherwood!" by "John Riddell" (Corey Ford). This second instance of smartness and flippancy probably had something to do with Anderson's decision to send to the "high-class whore house" of an office at *Vanity Fair* fewer of what he had long felt were mainly potboilers done for the convenient three-hundred-dollar payments. As for sales of *Hello Towns!,* they were such that in late April Liveright could order a second printing, but no further ones would be necessary.[15]

A reader coming to *Hello Towns!* in all innocence may find it a "hodge-podge," as an anonymous review called it before going on to praise the volume. Certainly there are few books like it. Its form is dictated by its contents, a selection of news items, editorials, and comment drawn sequentially (with only minor rearrangements in chronology) from the files of the papers for one year, from Anderson's first issues of November 1927 through October 1928. The pieces are marked off by month and within the month by week of issue, each month preceded by a photograph plate showing some place, institution, or person within the community. In addition, ten articles or stories Anderson had published in *Vanity Fair*, half of them before he bought the papers, and the unsold story, "Among the Drifters," are inserted more or less at random except, appropriately, "The Life of a New Country Editor" (in *Vanity Fair* and *News* in February, 1928) is placed in "Second Week of November" with the title "Notes for Newspaper Readers," and the tale "A Criminal's Christmas" (*Vanity Fair*, February, 1926; *News*, December 6, 1928) is placed in "Fourth Week in December," 1927. Likewise appropriately the book ends with the December 1928 *Outlook* article "I Will Not Sell My Papers," the title changed to the more tentative "Will You Sell Your Newspapers?" To organize his book somewhat Anderson introduced several structuring devices. Mostly at the beginning he inserted some brief italicized sections as "Editor's Thoughts" showing his initial uncertainty then growing confidence in his new venture; he preserved from the weekly issues many of his short or long comments on the changing seasons; he included several sequences of developing stories, the departure, return, and death of beloved Nellie the Printshop Cat, for example, or the evolution of Henry Mencken Park. Even so, due to the nature of newspapers, a large proportion of the items are disparate bits about local happenings.

What ultimately gives these bits an overall unity is the town and the editor's relation to it. Unlike *Winesburg, Ohio, Hello Towns!* in its news pieces rarely probes beneath the surface of the townspeople's lives; in his news-gathering activity Anderson somewhat resembles his own George Willard, reporter for the *Eagle*, running like "an excited dog . . . here and there, noting on his pad of paper" the town's outward events. Nevertheless, as he had written Liveright, these discrete items make up "a real picture of life—fragmentary . . . but real," real of course in a quite literal sense. Rather as though putting together a jigsaw puzzle, the attentive reader can assemble the pieces into a portrait of an American small town in the late 1920s with its business establishments and churches, professional people and workers, its mayor, judges, town council, sheriff, and in Marion's case, courthouse with its trials affording local theater and drama, its service and social clubs, fire department band, its social elite and power structure, hinted at by frequent appearances of certain names in contexts, its admirable citizens and unadmirable ones, its customs, celebrations, and catastrophes. More specifically it is the portrait of a particular American small town in a particular part of the upper South, where there had been considerable sympathy for the Union in the Civil War and where there were still relatively few black inhabitants. This was a prosperous community set off in the southwest corner of its state by mountain ranges and foothills good for hunting and fishing, a town especially aware of the neighboring mountain people, soft-spoken and independent up in their one-room cabins in the narrow valleys, scratching out a harsh existence from tiny fields, often making whiskey for sale to the more or less law-abiding citizens in the town and, when caught, stoically serving out their time in the town's filthy jail.[16]

Anderson's relation to the town, part of it at least, comes through clearly, especially his pleasure in being a recognized member of a relatively small human community. His warm sense of belonging is evident in his often jocular presentation of events even when Buck Fever is not doing the writing—no other book by Anderson so displays his rich sense of humor—and evident also is his habit of presenting the facts as required of a journalist in unjournalistic short-story form as though he is telling tales of happenings to a neighbor met on the street. Yet contradictorily, *Hello Towns!* reveals Anderson's sense that he is still something of an outsider in the community and that he is to some extent regarded as such by the townspeople. So with an outsider's eyes he sees and tells about needed improvements in the town such as a park or a new jail; he openly enjoys being a visitor in New York as well as an inhabitant of a small town; often in editorials or the commentary of "What Say!" he suggests alternative ways of looking at American life, the ways of the artist and the wanderer who has known much wider actual and imaginative experience than has been available to most people in Marion, Virginia. Nevertheless, in *Hello Towns!*, despite that contradiction, Marion is obviously his hometown by adoption. The one element of his attitude toward it that is entirely missing from the book, except for one or two vague hints, is that it was the place where, when he was writing most of the pieces collected in the volume, his third marriage finally fell apart, leaving him for awhile unable to live happily in that or any other community.

3.

In mid-April, to "relieve [his] mind" he began writing furiously, turning out "some 15,000 words in a week" on the novel but then got into a "terrible state—not sleeping, nerves all over my body on edge." Trading in his old car for a new one, he left Marion on the twenty-second to loaf northward with the spring up the Shenandoah Valley. The valley was "noble," he would write in his "Traveler's Notes," and the Natural Bridge near Lexington "lovely beyond words," but he was appalled at how all this natural beauty was marred by the number of billboards and tourist homes that had sprung up. Lonely, he drove on to Washington for human company. Apparently he first visited Mary Vernon Greer. Whatever their relationship had become at this point, he was much attracted to her physically; and it may well be that during this visit the two made plans to be together during the coming summer. On the strength of the six hundred dollars Anderson had obtained for Charles Bockler, Charles had decided to put at least the summer into his painting, living with Katharine in an inexpensive place in some small town not too far from the city. Sherwood would help out by sharing the rent, and Mary would stay either with them or nearby. For other company, Anderson visited the Baroness to see her for the last time before she sailed for Germany. He accompanied her to the christening of a child, got volubly drunk on champagne at the postchristening evening party, and met, instantly disliked, and violently argued with another guest named Maurice Long, the wealthy owner of a chain of Washington laundries, a big, handsome, womanizing, life-loving Irishman with "a shock of iron-gray hair," who at their second meeting in the fall of the year would quickly become one of Anderson's closest friends. The next morning, hung over and sunk in a black mood, he walked the Washington streets where, as he would soon write "Dearest Eleanor," "People all seemed ugly to me and I seemed ugly to myself" because, he added in veiled confession of his duplicity with Mary, "I do not at all know that anything I have said to you is sincere."[17]

Driving up the valley, he had been reminded of the tales of the fighting there he had heard told in his boyhood by Civil War veterans, and driving back south he visited many of the battlefields and began thinking out an article for *Vanity Fair* on the special role of Virginia in "the great American War," really fought, he would decide under the spell of the battlefields and his boyhood memories, between his adopted state and his native Midwest. He stopped briefly in Charlottesville to admire Jefferson's Monticello, only recently opened as a national shrine, and to call at Bob's suggestion on one of his teachers at the university, Stringfellow Barr. Anderson arrived in Marion in the evening of April 28, ready to leave the town again at the first opportunity.[18]

That opportunity came early in May while he was finishing "Virginia" for *Vanity Fair*. Donald Freeman at the magazine sent him one hundred dollars expense money and a request that he write a piece about the Kentucky Derby, to be run on May 18. Declaring that "several stories about race people . . . have been flitting about in my fancy for the last ten years," Anderson delightedly left for Louisville early, about the fourteenth, to immerse himself in impressions of "the great horse race of the year." Churchill Downs had grown greatly in size since he had seen the Derby won in 1918 by Exterminator and in 1919 by Sir Barton, who were among the "famous" horses he would name in his article, those three-year-olds who possessed superlatively "both speed and staying power." After explaining the mechanics of the Derby, Anderson begins his description of the 1929 race by distinguishing, rather as in "I'm a Fool," between those among the crowds of spectators "who have come to see the beautiful creatures run and those who have come to gamble." It has already rained "torrents" the morning of the race, the track is "deep in water," the horses walk "daintily in the deep mud"—Anderson must have recalled the muddy track Sir Barton won on in 1919—and it begins to rain again as the "intense nervous creatures" are held in at the starting gate. Blue Larkspur is the bettors' favorite, but the "small trim little" Clyde Van Dusen, running "easily, beautifully, with a long swinging stride," takes the inside track, holds the lead, and crosses the finish line first. For some reason, perhaps a printer's deadline for *Vanity Fair*'s June issue though Anderson had written the piece quickly, "At the Derby" did not appear in the magazine, and he had to be content with publishing it in the *News* for May 23—that and the joy of being at Churchill Downs again, watching his beloved thoroughbreds. Horses, he earlier wrote to Donald Freeman, were better than men.[19]

It was reassuring, of course, that in mid-May Edward O'Brien requested permission to reprint "The Lost Novel" in his *Best Short Stories of 1929;* despite his reservations about O'Brien's annual volumes, inclusion in this one would keep alive his name as a leading short story writer. Then too, Freeman sent, through Otto Liveright as usual, an advance for two more articles after "Virginia," the payment for each article now raised from $300 to $350, Anderson receiving $630 in all after Otto's ten percent commission. A "little cured" also by the particular richness of this late spring from, as he sadly wrote the Schevills, a year of "such depression . . . as I never knew before," he presumably completed the two articles in his "Small Town Notes" series within the two weeks he had projected; but he wrote nothing else that satisfied him. Both the Marion apartment and Ripshin remained haunted by his failure with Elizabeth. He feared further involvement with women; yet he "constantly needed women," as he told the Schevills. In his emotional turmoil he turned, not to Mary Vernon Greer but almost desperately to Eleanor, whom he now sought to be with whenever her work allowed it.[20]

In her cautiously responsive way Eleanor encouraged him. In early June while she was at a YWCA conference for working women at Blue Ridge, North Carolina, just east of Asheville, he drove to nearby Black Mountain, and they had an evening of balked passion together and a happy morning walk in sunlit woods. She had to go on to another conference held near Sapphire, North Carolina, just above the South Carolina line. By this time Mimi, just graduated from the Michigan City high school, had come to Marion for a visit; and on June 20 Anderson, charmed by his daughter's prettiness, good sense, and vigor, brought her with him for a weekend at this second conference at Camp Merrie-Wood in North Carolina. He and Eleanor managed to have part of a rainy Sunday alone together and came near to becoming lovers in "the green close woods." From these meetings on, Anderson's letters became physically passionate in expression. Eleanor, by nature passionate but also as yet inexperienced in sexual matters, more emancipated in mind than in body, had understandable and inhibiting misgivings about their relationship. She was half in love with him; but she had deep love for both her parents, and though she knew her mother's affectionate regard for Sherwood, she also knew that her father and he did not get on well. To the very conservative father, the new owner of the town's newspapers was a semibohemian outsider with a reputation for publishing sex-obsessed fiction and an inclination toward unconventional ideas and dress, a man who had been not once but twice divorced and whose third wife no longer lived with him, a man twenty years older than his beloved daughter, old enough to be her father. Eleanor recognized the disparity in ages, knew, as other townspeople may only have begun to speculate, that Sherwood intended yet a third divorce, and had some suspicions that he might be a womanizer, a man of varying moods including deep depressions. Perhaps most of all she was uneasy about how any close relationship with Sherwood would be viewed by her superiors in her YWCA job, a position and career to which she was devoted. So she went toward him yet held back.[21]

In his way he was holding back too. On the evening of Thursday, June 27, he took the train for New York, where on Friday he talked with Horace Liveright about his writing plans. In Liveright's outer office he learned from a Hungarian newspaper correspondent the explanation for the bizarre item that had appeared in the March 9 *New York Times*: that Sherwood Anderson and the British author Beverley Nichols had been expelled from Rumania for investigating the plight of Hungarians living in the Transylvania part of that nation. Apparently as a hoax two actual investigators identified themselves as these writers to a Hungarian newspaperman, who, taken in, cabled their invented story to the *Times*. On Saturday, the twenty-ninth, Anderson made his way to the village of Dykemans, New York, just across the state line from Danbury, Connecticut. Here in late May the Bocklers had rented a small, isolated cottage outside the village on a side road. The rent was cheap because the place was run down as well as small; but before Anderson had arrived, they had whitewashed the walls, put up red curtains, and made it pretty. Katharine Bockler had arranged one room for him and her sister Mary, for if the two had not already become physical lovers, they were so during Anderson's weeks at Dykemans. He now wrote Eleanor much less frequently; and when he did write, he carefully omitted his return address, explaining that he had "been moving about some & have not been in N.Y." or that he did not want his presence known to "a thin postmistress who may possibly be literary." He even insisted that the poor young painter he was staying with was not Bockler but another one, a rather transparent device that may well have made Eleanor uneasy about him.[22]

Despite some qualms about the deception, he was powerfully attracted to Mary, was probably even testing her out, as it were, for a possible fourth wife; but in any case he had a woman, as he believed necessary for his writing well. In early July he could inform Liveright that he was "feeling like a young bull, in fresh green pastures." While Charles painted all day, Anderson first dashed off a draft of the speech he had agreed to give in August at the Institute of Public Affairs at the University of Virginia, and then got happily into a new novel with "a big theme [which] will give a chance I think for powerful earthy writing." Presumably prompted by his relationship with Mary as refracted through his fancy, the novel was to be a projection of the drastic social and moral effects of the Great War on the generation of Americans that had done the fighting. Some months later he would explain his theme more explicitly in a letter to Bob.

> In *No God*, the novel on which I am now at work, I am telling the story of a man having his roots in the pre-War life, accepting the present day post-War life.
> That is my man's story. He is a man who has had marriage in the old way— memories of it cling to him—and then he comes to accept a woman who is the product of the new world.
> No God—No Love—in the old sense. That is what it means.
> As for the woman, well, I see her every day on the street. I've a notion that she doesn't want and wouldn't take what men used to give women, calling it love. I hope I am right about her. She is the young female kid of today. She has had sex experience and will have more, when she wants it.
> I look at her as my man in the book *No God* looks at her—glad of her, certainly all for her.[23]

At first the writing went well as he worked toward a prose like that he felt he had almost achieved in *Many Marriages,* simple on its "loose rhythmic 'surface' but with laughter under it, buried down under the words." The living circumstances in the tiny cottage, however, began to crowd in on his mood. Katharine had become pregnant shortly before she had come to Dykemans, and through July she suffered badly from morning sickness. Reminded vividly of his first marriage, Sherwood reacted sharply and unsympathetically to her vomiting and "whining voice"; his prose began to "growl," and he saw Charles's summer of painting disrupted as well. He considered leaving, but the Bocklers now more than ever needed his financial assistance. Around mid-July the novel simply stopped on him, and he turned to short stories.[24]

One of these was a first draft of "In a Strange Town," which when finally "inked in" (revised) in late August would suggest the kind of prose he was reaching for, though what is "buried down under the words" in this story is anything but laughter. The rarely anthologized "In a Strange Town" is one of Anderson's subtlest tales. It is told by a first-person speaker, a middle-aged man, in an interior monologue that proceeds by indirection accumulating a final understanding in the reader through repetitions, contradictions, avoidances, and digressions both evasive and revealing. Little "happens." The man has just arrived at the railroad station of a country town unvisited by him earlier, where, he says in one of his many self-contradictions, everything is quiet but there are certain sounds. He says that he has been in the habit of going briefly to strange towns "since that happened"; but instead of explaining what "that" was, he breaks off to ask directions to his hotel and then focuses on three people grouped on the station platform, an older woman, a younger woman who looks so much like the older one that she must be her daughter, and a man who, the speaker decides, is a butcher and the brother of the older woman. The two women are taking a coffin containing the body of the older woman's husband to another town for burial. All three are unimportant people; but when the jolly, loud-laughing conductor and stationmaster pass the group, they fall silent, for the people have become important, the man emphasizes to himself, as "symbols of Death." In narrative terms he has also given them importance by making of the incident the longest scene in the story. He likes being alone among strangers, he goes on to assert, for lives are so much the same everywhere yet, contradictorily, are "of infinite variety." Again he evades the reason for his habitually going on these "adventures" to small towns and instead says that he is a professor of philosophy in a college in his own town. He knows many colleagues and students, but his trouble is that "I know too much and not enough" because "My mind, my fancy, becomes dulled looking at them," as had happened before when he once became curious, felt alive, had "a little jump at the heart" in passing a strange house in his town and then "became dull to it."

Sitting in his hotel room, he reconstructs in his imagination the life of the bereaved older woman he saw at the station and at last says that, as he always explains puzzlingly to his good-natured wife before one of his excursions, he is "going to bathe myself in the lives of people about whom I know nothing," by which he means, not meeting and talking with them, but instead in his imagination inventing their lives and thus "refreshing" himself. Then with his tale two-thirds told he finally admits to himself that he has been suddenly going off to strange towns for a few days ever since a girl, one of his students, was struck by an automobile and killed. This girl, "a woman, really," had been "nothing special" to him, he insists— though in speaking of her as a girl he five times adds "woman"—and carefully protests that he himself is middle-aged and already married. This beautiful girl-woman used to come to his office, and they would talk of philosophy and then lapse into silences looking at each other. After she would leave, he would sit silently for hours, feeling "more aware than I had ever been in my life." He was sitting this way when informed of her death. His reaction was to take a train to a strange town where he forced himself "to observe the little details of life." So now he goes frequently to towns when his imagination has become dulled so that he can become "more aware . . . more alive" again, as he used to feel after "that girl, that woman" and he had talked and then silently looked at each other.

What is "buried down under" the man's, and Anderson's, words is a revelation of a tormented self. He is unable to admit it to himself that he had fallen in love with "that girl, that woman" because she made him feel aware and alive; yet his inhibitions affect not only his sexual nature but the nature of his imagination. Contradictorily he is driven by "curiosity," another word for imagination here, and too readily dulled to that drive. When the girl-woman is killed, he substitutes his "adventures" to small towns, finding temporary awareness, "refreshment" by imagining the lives of strangers, only to fall back into dullness and then renewed need. He is a "grotesque," a crippled personality frozen into and by self-contradiction, obsessed with death, his own physical death and that of others, and the constant threat of death to his always fleeting capacity for imaginative life. What imaginative life is left to him is entirely solipsistic. Unlike an artist he cannot create something outside himself, something permanent; any creativity left him is locked, blocked one might say, within.

Years later Mary Vernon Greer would state that "I happen to know that the strange town was Danbury, Conn.," and the positiveness of her statement suggests some connection among the story, Anderson's own imagination, and his relationship with her. She could well have been the inspiration, even the prototype for that girl, that woman; and Anderson, certainly not sexually inhibited except for feeling some degree of guilt for having an affair with one woman while writing love letters to another, could as readily have created his protagonist out of his own restlessness and love of new places, his sense of age and of aging before Mary's relative youth, his habit and profession of imagining others' lives, and most importantly his all too immediate frustration and despair, his feeling "as low a man as you ever saw" at his block with the novel. More speculative is the possibility that the accidental death of the girl-woman may be not simply a fictional device but a projection of what seems to have been the point reached at about this time in the trajectory of his and Mary's affair. A year and a half later Anderson would recall that there had been "hours with Mary . . . that are shining things. They stay fresh in my mind." But a reliable source would quote Anderson as saying on his return to Marion that, in effect, Mary was insufficiently responsive in sexual embrace, at least to his liking; and in reply to a letter from Anderson the Baroness could write him: "I am very glad you fell in love this summer,—how bad it could not last a little longer." Quite possibly, then, the girl-woman's death masked Anderson's growing conviction that Mary Vernon Greer should not be his fourth wife.[25]

His stay at Dykemans was to last six weeks in all. He had been keeping Liveright informed of his progress with the novel, and on July 25 he went to New York for a day to report in person on it and to request an advance of a thousand dollars to see Mimi through her first year at the University of Chicago, where she was starting in the fall. Around the beginning of August, apparently refreshed by Mary's continued presence though he knew that for him the end of the affair was in sight, he went back into the novel so hard that by the ninth he could tell Liveright that he had written a total of 40,000 words on what he still thought he might call *Another Man's House,* or *A Modern Marriage* or *Another Wife,* but which he would soon title *No God.* By this time he had told Mary that their affair was over. He seems to have had no regrets over the break, but a year later she would understandably still be "rather bitter and resentful against [him]." Probably on the tenth he said his goodbyes to her and the Bocklers and left Dykemans for New York and the South. On the evening of the eleventh he was in Charlottesville where the following evening he spoke at the Institute of Public Affairs at the University of Virginia on "The Newspaper and the Modern Age," describing his purchase of the Marion papers and his method of running them, decrying mechanization, concentration of power, and standardization in modern newspaper publishing, urging the necessity of enjoying one's work and maintaining one's individualism, and concluding, "We have each in his own way to begin to fight to make ourselves figures with at least some of the dignity modern men have built into their machines." After his lecture he went on to Marion. There over the next few weeks he oversaw the finances of his papers in order to meet his obligations to Burton Emmett, wrote a piece for *Vanity Fair,* inked in his draft of "In a Strange Town," and resumed his now more frequent letters to Eleanor.[26]

She and the visit to Elizabethton had aroused his sympathies toward the strikes that had been breaking out since May in southern textile mills. On August nineteenth the *New York Times* carried the story that Anderson, Dreiser, and Fannie Hurst were heading a group of thirty "prominent American writers" who had formed a committee to help the Emergency Committee for Strikers' Relief get funds and public support for striking textile workers. Most recently two thousand workers had been locked out of the Clinchfield Mills in Marion, North Carolina, and were striking under the direction of Alfred Hoffman of the United Textile Workers (AFL) for a reduction in the workday from twelve hours and twenty minutes to ten hours, and for a 10 percent increase in wages. The committee, which included among others Anderson's old friends Floyd Dell and Waldo Frank, had a New York City headquarters, and probably he had only lent his name to a letter that "denounced conditions in Southern textile mills as verging on feudalism"; but his "Elizabethton, Tennessee" article in the May 1 *Nation* and now the headlining of his name in the *Times* story made it publicly clear which side he was on. It was, of course, that of the workers and Eleanor.[27]

Since his return to Marion he had hardly touched the novel. He had long talks in the last half of August with Bob and with Mimi, before she left for the University of Chicago, about the outlook of young people, storing up information and attitudes he could use for the novel, in which he would draw on Mimi for certain qualities in his young woman character Mildred. In the first half of September he seems to have written only *The American County Fair,* one of six boxed "Prose Quartos" by well-known writers that the new firm of Random House was preparing for 1930 publication. Presumably prompted by the Smyth County Fair going on in Marion in the first week in September, this brief piece sketchily describes the fair as "a pagan outbreak," concentrates on the harness races, and ends with a semitale of the love between a driver and his trotting horse Mary Rose, who wins a race for him by going "faster than she could go" without once breaking stride. Too much was going on, including a print shop visit in late August by a woman correspondent from the *New York Times* prompted by his speech at the University of Virginia. (She would shortly publish an admiring article on the "Famous Author" and his papers in the *Times Magazine.*) He could not, he became convinced, work on the novel in Marion. On September 16 he went to Washington and settled in quietly at the Hotel Dupont on Dupont Circle to write.[28]

Quickly he fell into his routine—writing in the mornings, in the afternoon walking about the city, sitting in parks, reading. He saw few people, though he met Maurice Long again and this time liked him immensely. The writing went unevenly. Sometimes he wrote steadily right through the morning; at other times the prose refused to flow. Warm-up letters were easy enough. To Mimi, whom he had found a charming young woman, he began writing advice about university life. To Eleanor he sent "a stream of letters," about the minutiae of his quiet days, about his longing for her presence, about the novel he was slowly developing. By mid-October he began to feel that he had made his central male character, Jim LaForge, aged forty, "come to life in the pages." Jim he understood. He has had a marriage that went bad, he has lived alone since his wife died, he "takes women but is afraid of them," he is "drawn to [Mildred, aged twenty-two] but is suspicious of his own feeling." Now it was time for the author "to bring her more fully into the picture, make her live in it"; but he did not understand Mildred-Mary-Mimi-Eleanor as well as he did Jim-Sherwood, and for the moment the novel would not move.[29]

Questioning whether he had gone "too far, along the road of feeling" both in his marriages and his fiction, he decided to try to be more "objective," as a painter who had gone too far into color might return to drawing. So he broke off from the novel and wrote for *Vanity Fair* "These Mountaineers." (By now he knew that *Scribner's Magazine* had purchased "In a Strange Town" for five hundred dollars and would not want another story from him for awhile.) In the new tale, another attack on the romanticizing of mountain people, the narrator, essentially Anderson himself, loses his way in the mountains while brook fishing. Hungry, he comes upon a filthy old man who takes him to his filthy cabin in a hollow and serves him dirty beans on a dirty plate. A dirty, ragged, wild-looking girl, thirteen at the most, who has run away from home because she is desperate for sex, lives in the cabin also along with a rough, slovenly young man who has impregnated but not married her. She glares with silent hatred at the old man and the narrator, who leaves the cabin, fishes very successfully for trout in the creek in the hollow, and follows the old man's directions back to the main road. Haunted by the look of hatred in the girl's wild eyes, the narrator returns to the hollow another day to fish, taking a twenty-dollar bill, "a lot of money in the hills," as a means for her to escape from the men if she wishes or at least to buy clothes for herself and the coming child. The girl accosts him antagonistically and speaks contemptuously of the young man, who has briefly appeared. Then when the narrator offers her the bill, he senses that he may have "touched her mountain pride," for with a look of hatred and of unexpected maturity in her eyes she tells him to get out and not come back. He can take his money and, the narrator paraphrases her crude remark, "put it somewhere. I won't say where." He gets out and never goes back.[30]

Since the narrator names his feelings while depicting the girl from the outside, the story is not really objective in the manner of, say, Hemingway; but as Sherwood wrote Eleanor, "You will see how much less I am in it as a personality." He had "tried to make [the girl] stand alone, without relation to anyone, a portrait," yet to maintain the reader's sympathy for her. In the story he "bound up something of the new tone I am after now in writing," not to reject feeling entirely but rather to "stand a little aside," to use his hearing and sight more in his details. It was "pretty hard to say what I mean," he admitted to Eleanor, but whatever the limits of his objectivity in "These Mountaineers," he did succeed in making the girl both pitiful and admirable, hardly more than a child, ill-clad and filthy, subject to her body and the two men, yet fiercely rebellious, self-respecting, and independent, and in her perceptions more adult than adolescent.[31]

Apparently his mode of objectivity worked for awhile when he went back to No God, as he had at last decided to call his novel, meaning that the old pre–World War gods, values, were dead and the postwar ones had not yet arrived. Mildred was "sure in it now"; he had got the feel of her from his talks with Mimi. Then came two or three days when he could not write at all, and eager to see Eleanor, he left Washington on October 27 for Richmond, where she was to attend a conference. With a card from State Senator John Buchanan of Marion, he put up at the Westmoreland Club. On the afternoon of his arrival he suddenly broke off from a letter to Eleanor and began writing on the novel again. Having recovered the "tone" of it, he now went on in a rush, on one day getting three long chapters done, "between seven and eight thousand words," and feeling at last that this was "going to be a living book." On November 4, having been assured by an emissary from Liveright of a late February or early March publication, he began "the last movement" of the novel, so jubilant that he was thinking of not selling Ripshin and instead turning it into a small summer community for writers and painters. On the ninth he wired Eleanor, at that point in Durham, North Carolina, that he had finished the first draft of the book. No God would be about seventy-five to eighty thousand words, he wrote Liveright the same day, happily announcing in his ad-man's voice that it was "a corking good tale." The draft would need revisions, of course, but Liveright would surely have it by the end of 1929. Liveright was relieved and delighted, but protested in a telegram that the title No God would be misinterpreted. Anderson then suggested No Love, later proposed The Sacred Service when he learned that No Love had been used already, and would finally settle on Beyond Desire. This would be the title of a novel he would publish in 1932, but the novel would not be the one of which he had just finished a first draft.[32]

4.

Anderson seems to have paid little or no attention to the October stock market crash; although in Richmond he relaxed in the afternoons and evenings by going about with newspapermen, who in any case could hardly have foreseen that this event would mark the beginning of the Great Depression. Very soon this man who had professed not to be interested in causes would become intensely interested in them, but in the remaining week of his stay in Richmond, he was focused entirely on getting his hastily completed draft of the novel typed up for revision and on having some time with Eleanor, brief because of her work commitments and unsatisfactory for both because she became upset by his physical urgency. Then on November 17, he returned to Marion to take over the papers so that Bob could have a vacation. During the next two weeks he did not work at all on the novel. Instead, feeling out of place in Marion, even finding it hard to gather news, he almost daily went pheasant hunting in the hills with a friend, probably Andy Funk, who would habitually joke him for his lack of skill as a bird hunter. Anderson preferred sitting on a log and yielding himself up to "sounds in the forest, a sense of mystery." On December 2, Bob returned, and the next day Anderson boarded the train for Chicago, where he hoped to refresh his impression of the city in which he had set his novel as an aid to revising it.[33]

In Chicago he took a seventh floor suite—living room, dining room, bedroom, and bath—at the Flamingo, an apartment hotel at 5520 South Shore Drive where the Schevills lived. His second evening in the city he dined out with Mimi, and he was able to report to Eleanor that university life had much awakened her; she was strong for socialism, studying and liking American history, and greatly interested in a twenty-eight-year old advertising man named Russell Spear, whom she had met on a blind date and who was out of job, broke, and about to return to his native New England. Getting down to work on revising *No God/Beyond Desire* after the weeks away from it, he realized that it must be "extended, heightened, its points brought out."

> I want to get the consciousness of the two things . . . in the one person. Mildred pregnant . . . wanting to use her pregnancy to make the man marry her . . . at the same time not wanting to take advantage . . . doing it just the same . . . aware . . . rather laughing at herself.
> Jim not wanting to marry . . . afraid of marriage . . . wanting her though.

As he continued to revise, meanwhile nursing the bad cold he had characteristically come down with upon arrival in Chicago, he came to the conclusion that, as he wrote Eleanor on December 12, he would practically have to rewrite the book if it were "to get anywhere near what I want."[34]

He was seeing few people except for Roger and Ruth Sergel and the Schevills, and knew he was poor company even with them. It is not clear whether he or Tennessee was the first to telephone the other (probably she), but they had several phone conversations. From her eager invitations to come see her at her apartment at 153 East Erie Street, however, he assumed that she might be hoping for a remarriage, and he made excuses not to come, a decision he would soon regret as an unkindness. Ferdinand tactfully arranged that he, Mimi, Sherwood, and Tennessee should dine together on the evening of the fourteenth, but at the last minute Tennessee was unable to attend. Overcome by his long-term sense of defeat, of failure with friends, former wives, and most of all his art, sunk in "just plain damn unspeakable gloom," Anderson escaped from Chicago on the seventeenth, by chance just before a blizzard hit the city, heading south by train for St. Petersburg, Florida, the "black dog" so heavy on his back that he would notice little on the two-day trip. He arrived at St. Petersburg on the nineteenth in unseasonably cold weather, took a room at the Hotel Detroit overlooking Tampa Bay, and during the next few days despite his depression struggled with the revising of *Beyond Desire*, trying to get into it the "real movement [and] music" he had already confessed to Liveright the book lacked. But the black dog stayed on his back, and his struggle was unsuccessful. On Christmas Day, the day he had hated since the poverty years of childhood, he wrote Liveright that he would keep at the novel until it became "a living tale," or he would "swim out with it into the deep blue sea and tie a stone to it," as a publisher should, "now and then, take one of [his authors] out into the sea and tie a stone to him." The repeated figure indicates all too clearly that, as he would write the Schevills at a happier time, he "thought of death all the time . . . wanted suicide."[35]

The day after Christmas brought a major decision and a painful shock. The decision was quite simply to give up on the novel. He had been "trying to write another story of men and women in love," he explained to Eleanor, but his heart had not really been in it, for such a story, such a relationship was no longer his "central interest." Instead, as a result of his experience at Elizabethton and his talks with her and her organizer friend Tom Tippett, he wanted to be involved with the labor movement, not as a leader but rather as one who would rescue the rest of a messed-up life by talking with persons on both sides of labor conflict and writing about what he learned. The "central inner story of labor and capital is not being told," and it could "best be told in the simple human tales of people caught in both sides of it," the way he had already shown in *Winesburg, Ohio* and *Poor White*. He himself "came out of the world of workers," but he would be "the artist who wants merely to be open-eyed, to receive impressions and make his pictures, wanting to serve only the central inner story and not one side or the other." Could Eleanor, who had access to both sides, guide him—and, by implication, let him more often be near her? The thought of doing such work was already, he told her, lifting his depression, giving his life meaning, taking away the sense of being nothing in a "nothing real" world he had suffered from on the trip south.

The painful shock that came at the end of that warm, sunny Thursday was the information from newspapermen at his hotel, and from Ferdinand by telegram, that Tennessee had been found dead in her bed that evening. The Friday morning papers carried details. She had apparently died the previous Friday night, the twentieth, but her body was not discovered for six days. Her maid had been unable to enter the locked outer door of her two-floor studio apartment since Monday and, noting the accumulation of mail outside, called the police on Thursday. Two detectives forced the entrance door and found the body in bed, "clad only in night clothing." In the apartment they found two Christmas packages wrapped for mailing, one addressed to Mimi, the other to John. The cause of "the sculptress's" death was apparently "A hemorrhage of the lungs" in her sleep, and it was learned that she "had been under the care of a physician for some time." Despite the newspaper reports, it was quickly known that Tennessee had died of an overdose of sleeping pills, perhaps by accident, perhaps deliberately.[36]

Tennessee's good friend Harriet Welling, who years later would refer to the death as "very likely" a suicide, was in charge of the funeral arrangements. She wired Anderson about Tennessee's death and the funeral service to be held on December 31 in the chapel of Graceland Memorial Cemetery in Chicago. For several days he was in "a rotten state of punishing myself," he wrote the Schevills, for his unkindness in not going to see Tennessee while in Chicago, realizing now that "she really wanted from me there a little love and comradeship and I didn't give it to her." Still he decided not to attend the funeral. On the day it was to be held he finally wrote Mrs. Welling that it would be "a bit absurd" to show kindness now when he had often failed to do so while Tennessee was alive, and besides he "was done up." Privately he worried that his presence might be offensive to Tennessee's married sister, who would be coming from Clifton, Arizona, and that he had an uncertain status as a former husband. Harriet's younger sister Carolyn, who liked Sherwood because he used to listen to what she, the youngest child in the family, said, nevertheless commented wryly on his letter, "and he also saved himself the train fare." Harriet noted that, though dated "Dec 31–29," the letter was postmarked January 5, 1930. Anderson may or may not have seen the *Chicago Daily Tribune* report of the very brief funeral service. No minister officiated; instead the poet Eunice Tietjens read Tennyson's "Crossing the Bar" and Arnold's "Requiescat" to the accompaniment of "violin and cello music" (Mrs. Welling had obtained a string quartet from the Women's Symphony).

Forty or so of Tennessee's friends attended, including Harriet Monroe of *Poetry* but only one family member, the sister. "Even word from Sherwood Anderson, who knew of her death, did not come." As Tennessee wished, her body was cremated.[37]

Perhaps there was another reason why Anderson did not attend. Having telegraphed Liveright on December 27 that he would not have the novel for him that spring—"anyway it is not a good piece of work"—he turned with great relief to writing short stories and forming in his mind for summer a labor book about such little mill girls as he and Eleanor had seen at Elizabethton. One of the stories, "A Dead Dog," was quickly in such shape that he had it typed up for final inking in—it would not be published until the spring 1931 issue of *The Yale Review*—and the speed of composition suggests that Anderson was dealing fictionally with a quite real and pressing emotional problem. He may well have picked up the central incident from his companion in his bird-hunting spree just a month earlier, along with the special language about bird dogs, their trained ability, and the close relationship between them and their masters, like that between horse and rider. A shadowy "I"-person narrator-listener appears primarily at the end, but the incident is told to a group of men by one Tom Hunt, originally from Tennessee, as Andy Funk was, about a Tennessee "attorney-general" (prosecuting attorney, as Funk was in Smyth County, Virginia) named John Wilkins. Tom Hunt, who likes his story "because it had such amazing contradictions in it," first praises the beauty of the dog that is killed, a full-blooded English setter called Bum by his loving master, a lonely widower named Sam Rierdon, and then he describes several cases in which the "hard-boiled, cold-hearted" Wilkins gets maximum sentences against hard-luck hill people to show that in front of a jury he is "a regular man-eater." Still, contradictorily, even many of his victims vote for him as he wins reelection every time, because, as they explain, "he don't have no personal feelings . . . he's just a fellow trying to do his job." As for bird dogs, in Tennessee "a really good one is . . . worth more than anything else in this world." One day John Wilkins borrows the superb Bum from Sam for bird hunting, and when he accidentally shoots him, Bum falls from a ledge and breaks his back. The "icy-eyed" Wilkins carries the heavy, still-living dog in his arms a long way to his car, pleading to him "with a little sobbing sound" not to try to stand and so injure himself further. Bum looks at him, Tom says several times, as the poor defendants looked at him pleadingly in court. Sick at what he has done, Wilkins starts for town, but Bum, never whimpering, dies on the seat beside him. Returning to Sam's house, Wilkins lays Bum's body on the porch, gets courage to call Sam to the door, and angrily, as though an injury had been done himself, tells Sam that he killed the dog. The two men look deeply and silently into each other's eyes, and then Wilkins drives off still acting angry. Tom Hunt repeats that it's the "inconsistencies" that make the story interesting, but when the "I"-person later asks the other listeners, "all men with more or less experience of dogs and horses and men," they refuse to see any inconsistency that Wilkins, in Hunt's words, "could be so hard-boiled about people and be like that about a dog." So the story ends, and the "I"-person has not committed himself either way.[38]

Possibly Anderson, who had recently entered and broken off an affair, and had just received word of his second wife's death after refusing to see her, did not wish to commit himself either way as to whether Wilkins was inconsistent. The cold-hearted prosecutor of luckless people and now a luckless offender himself could have wretched "personal feelings" about killing Bum and nevertheless speak with such inconsiderateness to his owner; even Tom himself says, "He had to." Yet as the story shows Anderson understood, there *is* a larger inconsistency here, the refusal by a human being capable of consideration to accept the responsibility of meeting fully another human being's need. Both Wilkins and his creator could "punish" himself with feelings of guilt and, as Anderson was about to write the Schevills, "wreck myself forever on this shore . . . alive with the jagged rocks of my own unkindnesses"; but Wilkins could protect and preserve himself through his habit of prosecution, Anderson through his practice of art. Never before, it turned out, had he recovered so rapidly from so deep a depression, so painful a shock as he now did at the very end of 1929. By turning life obliquely into fiction he could go on eagerly toward his next life experience with a lighter baggage of guilt.[39]

3

Factories and Speeches

1.

"I have about recovered from my gloom in Chicago and from the shock of poor Tennessee's death," Anderson wrote his daughter on or shortly after New Year's Day; and he shrugged the black dog even farther off his back by informing Liveright that he was putting *Beyond Desire* away for good. That novel had "some gaudy chapters, but she didn't move . . . because I'm through with the ordinary problems of middle-class people in love, etc." Instead he was thinking of a novel about a poor white girl who goes to work in a mill. That would be "living stuff." Mornings now he wrote as usual in his hotel room; afternoons he spent fishing for sheepshead with half a dozen blacks off a pier jutting out into Tampa Bay. He had teamed up with a one-eyed black who supplied him with bait in exchange for any fish he caught. He was fed up, as he had stated, with the middle class, especially the old, diseased specimens in St. Petersburg who stumbled about, played games in the park, talked only of "the Stock Market and the speed of automobiles." He had decided to head north to the Carolinas and "hang around" people in the labor movement, as Eleanor had been urging him to do. The workers, he felt, now were "defeated by Modern American, by the American scheme," and he belonged to them, "the defeated people."[1]

By January 11 he was in Savannah. He had already begun writing sketches, "little flashing pictures" from the life of "a rather naive, good intentioned man, moving restlessly among men and women, blundering of course, getting nothing but life itself, a sort of George Willard of Winesburg become a man of fifty." He was tentatively calling it "A Don Juan's Book of Hours." Afternoons he wandered happily about the many squares of the leisurely paced old city, which reminded him of New Orleans, or sat by the red Savannah River, enjoying the singing of the blacks and the passing of the ships until at sunset the sky flamed red over the red land. Then came night—he had taken to writing occasional "Traveler's Notes" again for the Marion papers, and Savannah made him the poet—night like a slender, naked "high-brown" woman running through the city's streets. The feel of the Old South had "started something down inside him singing again." He was singing too because Eleanor had met him in Savannah, she had excited him further about going into factories and among working people, and they had come close to becoming physical lovers.[2]

On January 16 he arrived by train in Macon, where he settled in at the Hotel Lanier for a stay so that he could begin visiting cotton mills and mill villages in the area. That day he astonished a clerk in the city library by laying his un-Maconlike "Irish thorn cane and his fuzzy black Fedora" on the charge-out desk as he arranged to take out Broadus Mitchell's *William Gregg: Factory Master of the Old South*. A librarian recognized his name and phoned the *Macon Telegraph*, and the following morning it was front-page news that he was visiting the city. He was invited to the next day's annual breakfast of the Macon Writers' Club at the Hotel Dempsey, at which the honored guests were to be his friends Julian and Julia Harris, whose *Columbus Enquirer-Sun* had received a Pulitzer Award in 1926 for crusading journalism. At the breakfast on the eighteenth he was one of the speakers, talking briefly, while he fidgeted with a matchbox on the table, in praise of Julian for his journalism, of his father, Joel Chandler Harris, for his Uncle Remus tales, which "brought the Negro into literature," and of the South for its "charm which is so difficult in this industrial age." The following day's report of the breakfast, which quoted much of Anderson's talk, was headed by a two-column picture of him, "his hair deliberately uncombed," as an adoring young *Telegraph* writer, Susan Myrick, recalled. She wrote how patiently and good-humoredly he dealt with the "rush of aspiring writers" to his hotel room and how he, "so handsome, so witty, so gay," made friends through subsequent evenings of talk with her and other newspaper people, people who could inform him about the local cotton mills.[3]

For a week Anderson drove about the Macon area with his new friends or in borrowed cars. He admired the wide streets and fine old houses of the city, and with his acute feeling for color, as Susan noted, he was enthralled by the contrast between the blood-red clay hills of central Georgia and the dark green of pines, the bright green of winter grain. While he was there the thousands of acres of peach trees around Macon burst into bloom, and as he excitedly wrote Charles Bockler, "The whole landscape suddenly got that light, floating quality you get in Chinese painting." Still, what he most wanted to see were the mills and mill villages. It was easy enough to walk about and observe several villages, "some pretty terrible, others not so bad," he wrote Eleanor, but the mill managers were reluctant to let him into the mills, sometimes to the point of flat refusal, although he was able to win over most of them by his obvious desire to see the machines and the workers—many of them young girls—in action. "I understand what you mean by social sense," he told Eleanor. "I can love whole rooms full of these working girls, the feeling being almost physical in me, without it in the least centering on one of them." Physically he was centered, powerfully so, on Eleanor, who in urging him to go to the mills in the first place, had "done the nicest thing anyone ever did to me."[4]

Toward the end of the month he saw her off and on for two days in Atlanta, where she was busy at one of her many YWCA conferences, and on the twenty-ninth he went on to Columbus, Georgia, to see the Harrises and to visit more mills. Gradually he was beginning to sense what he was after, and as so often he was working his thoughts out in his letters. He had been too "damn middle-class" too long, he wrote Roger and Ruth Sergel, and he was returning to his origins in the working class by living among "laboring people . . . always . . . my first loves" for the present.

The most interesting place in America now is the South.

A great class down here, the poor whites, have been brought into the industrial world in the last twenty years. The Southern towns are full of little mill girls, living in mill villages in the shadow of cotton mills.

I am going to try living among them and telling their story. It is anyway an exciting adventure.

. . . .

I've just a hunch, a feeling, that the story of labor and the growing industrialism is the great, big story of America.

The situation in the South and elsewhere in the nation, as he explained to Ralph Church in England, was complicated by more and more people being "thrown out of work by the perfection of the machines," complicated too by his "notion that half the people who work at the machines are half in love with them." He was trying "to sense [the situation] as a story," which, like the tale of Winesburg's Wing Biddlebaum, "wants a poet." Such a still "groping" approach helped him to gain admission to one among the cotton mills in Columbus. Over cigarettes the owner had asked him what he wanted, and Anderson had replied that he wanted "the rhythm of cotton mills, the machinery, girls and all." The owner and other men in the office laughed at a "guy" who wanted "the rhythm of cotton mills," but they allowed him into the mill for a whole afternoon, during which he made a discovery. In a huge room filled with the clatter of many looms, he talked with a strong-bodied, bright-eyed weaver-woman with "marvelous" fast, accurate fingers. Although she had gone into the mills at twelve and had worked there for thirty years, she was not worn down but rather was "so alive, so young." It may have been at this point that he began moving toward his later conviction that "perhaps women" resisted the dehumanizing effect of machine labor more than men did.[5]

Very likely it was his visit to that particular cotton mill after which "in a moment of ecstasy" he wrote "Machine Song," his first piece to come out of his venture into the factories. A vaguely Whitmanesque prose poem built around an imagined automobile drive by himself from Chicago to Miami, it proclaims that he is "sick of my old self that protested against the machine"; it celebrates the mechanical perfection of his speeding car and the glimpses it affords of the American land; and in a series of rhetorical questions it calls on "singers" and painters to give themselves to the "new age" of the factories. More calmly, during the few days he was in Columbus, he wrote to Burton Emmett, to whom he had sent the manuscript of *Beyond Desire,* insisting that this "patched crippled piece of work" should never be published and expanding on his new "intoxicating" interest in machinery, which, he felt, now more than anything else was influencing life. Beautiful in itself, machinery was "throwing men out of work, making a few men rich, pretty much destroying craftsmanship"; so in order to understand this contradictory force he was going into mills, when he was allowed in, to look at machines and the people working at them, "trying to get the factory feel into me," although "What I will get out of it I don't quite know yet." Following Eleanor on February 5 to Greenville, South Carolina, where he found her sexually responsive to him, though not fully so, he gained free access to any mill in the area, even at night, by talking with disarming bluntness to the lawyer representing the cotton mill association. Then a conversation with a Greenville doctor, William S. Fewell, gave him one key to what he was getting from the factories.

Doctor Fewell told me a marvelous story about a minute man [efficiency expert] brought down here. He followed a woman weaver to the toilet, stood outside the door with a watch in his hand.

Her husband was a weaver in the same room.

He rushed upon the minute man and beat him up. There was a near riot in the room. I have worked it up into a kind of grotesque dance, the looms in the room dancing, the weavers dancing with wrath.

Stomping on the minute man's watch, on his glasses, on him.

All to the tune of the looms.

By February 9 he had written a draft of "Loom Dance," another experimental piece coming out of his factory visits.[6]

"Loom Dance" combines descriptions of mill processes—the way a weaver tends a row of mechanical looms, the way an efficiency expert times the weaver to increase the number of looms tended, with a disproportionately small increase in pay—and a "poetic" attempt to imitate through short, declarative sentences and repetition of words, especially "dance," the "jerky, abrupt, mechanical" movement of the looms. The introduction of new, more efficient machines and the "stretch-out" forced on workers by the "minute-men" throw people out of work, though Anderson maintains that the owners do not intend the result but are merely responding to economic forces beyond their control. Still, when the woman weaver, as in Fewell's account, is humiliatingly timed in the toilet, her weaver husband begins to cry out and dance "the crazy dance of the looms." He assaults the minute man, dances on his body, and is joined in dancing by other shouting weavers, by men and women from the spinning-room, by the lights dancing over the looms, by the jerking, clattering looms themselves, this wild, grotesque dance making "music in the mill." The minute-man is rescued and patched up, but he does not return to the mill, and the piece concludes: "The 'stretch-out' system was dropped in that mill in the South. The loom dance of the weavers stopped it that time." Despite his even-handedness toward the owners in the expository parts of the piece, in the fantasy of the loom dance itself Anderson, rather as in his early futuristic *Marching Men*, sides with the workers, who demonstrate that they have latent power to resist the "river in flood, [the] flow of refined power" which is modern industry.

Although there is no way to tell for certain, Anderson may have written a more sober article, "Factory Town," before "Loom Dance." Probably in early January he had "severed [his] connection with *Vanity Fair*," an act emphasizing his rejection of former interests and his recognition that his new ones would not be compatible with that "whorehouse" of a magazine, where he had been one of the whores. In format, though not in subject, "Factory Town" follows his "Small Town Notes" series. A first section, "Inside the Factory," describes his visit to one cotton mill where the faultlessly precise looms were turning out ugly cloth rather than the "gay . . . joyous" cloth an artist should be designing, and then argues that people who feel superior to factory workers should come to know their "precarious, and every year . . . more precarious" lives. The second section, "Soup Kitchen," brings the early months of the Depression into sharp human focus when, ashamed of his good overcoat and shoes, he talks with individuals humiliated into lying about their actual need to go to charity for food. With the 1930s barely begun, Anderson was already sympathetically aware of the spreading misery and attuned, with Eleanor's guidance, to meeting sufferers one on one as well as in the mass and giving them a voice.[7]

Otto Liveright placed both "Factory Town" and "Loom Dance" in the more suitable, though less well paying, *New Republic*, the first published in the March 26 issue, the second in the April 30 one. Certainly Anderson was already finishing a much longer article when the drafting of "Loom Dance" interrupted, for he had it revised, typed up, and in Liveright's hands by February 13. "Labor and Sinclair Lewis," the article's original title, was in part prompted by his having heard that Lewis, his long-term irritant, was writing a labor novel, and the version of the article he sent Liveright contained a direct extended attack on the author of *Main Street,* who, Anderson was sure, would treat working people with the satirical contempt with which he had treated the people of a midwestern town. Liveright interested the editors of *Scribner's Magazine* in the piece, and it was eventually published in the July issue but only after they had persuaded the author to turn the personal attack on Lewis to a condemnation of a current type of American fiction. After the article was retitled simply "Cotton Mill" by mutual consent, the editors proved their interest by paying five hundred dollars for it, "considerably more," Liveright assured Anderson, "than they usually pay for an article," and by making it that issue's lead article.[8]

"Cotton Mill" summarizes what Anderson had learned and felt at that point about industry and machines, owners and workers. Modern industry is like an irresistible river in flood, "a Mississippi of machinery," he announces, and cotton mills excite him most of all. He "would like to make [his] prose dance with the strange, rapid, jerky movements" of a cotton mill machine and of its attendant, who fits "all the movements of his young body to the rapid, jerky movements of that machine"—as he was about to attempt in "Loom Dance." Then drawing on Mitchell's *William Gregg,* he sketches the socioeconomic situation of the "ruined" South at the end of the Civil War and the way the cotton mill became the basis for an industrialized New South wherein middle- and upper-class white men became owners and managers, black laborers cropped the cotton, and the poor whites supplied the cheap mill labor, becoming the despised "lint-heads" isolated by the thousands in mill villages. Next Anderson describes several of the processes by which raw cotton, brought to the city-block-long mill, is cleaned, spun into thread, and woven into cloth by often massive, always delicate machines attended by "lint-heads," many of them "little mill girls—half children, some of them," all "almost always tired" from doing fast, intense work twelve hours a day, sixty hours a week, earning low wages and the contempt of the townspeople. In a final section he goes on to a discussion of the contempt made popular by "many of our modern American writers" for both industrialism and the small town. As one who likes small towns, is fascinated by machines, and believes that the mill girls themselves are "half in love with the machines they tend," he protests "against an unbalanced view of modern industrial life . . . against the point of view that sees nothing in the small town but Rotarians and boosters, that sees nothing in industry but devils and martyrs, that does not see people [worker and industrialist alike] as people, realizing that we are all caught in a strange new kind of life." Again, as in "Loom Dance"

Anderson tried to be fair to the mill owners, but his heart was with those who worked the machines and danced the machine dance.

Despite his obvious sympathy for the workers, Greenville's mills were all open to him. Owners called him up with invitations to visit their mills, and once at his request he was escorted through a mill after midnight. He continued to respond "to the beauty and wonder of the machinery" like the amazing new Barker Coleman Spooler Warper in the big Easley Mill, which could be operated by one man and put seven others out of work, but two hours spent in the roar and clatter of eighteen hundred looms in the Duncan Mill's huge loom room sent him into his own loom dance and shattered his nerves all the following night. The mill girls somehow stood it, he concluded. At least once, perhaps several times, he was taken through a mill village by a woman who was teaching adult illiterates in many such villages to read and write. His days were so wildly busy that he was forced to do much of his writing at night, when the day had not exhausted him. Still, as he reported to Eleanor, he had "got a new feeling of manhood out of all this . . . man's-sized job," and he felt "basic health" in him such as he had not felt for two or three years before she had persuaded him into it.[9]

Eleanor was constantly on his mind, and he wrote frequently of his physical desire for her, urging possible arrangements for meeting. At last she proposed a time and place to fit her own busy schedule. On February 20 he left Greenville for nearby Asheville, North Carolina, to where John had driven down to visit him, and then a day or two after doubled back apparently to Spartanburg, South Carolina, which Eleanor seems to have fixed on for a stopover on her way by train to a YWCA assignment in Atlanta. They had at least some hours together in a "marvelous little pine grove" before parting, she going on to Atlanta, he heading for Augusta, Georgia, which as an old city he thought they both would like. There he registered as "Will Grove" at the Hotel Richmond, where, returning from her Atlanta assignment on March 1, she met him. Sherwood had rented a car, and that afternoon they drove out into the countryside. Beneath a tree in a pine wood they had their first full sexual union. For the virginal but un-hesitating Eleanor it was a tremendous experience to which she gave her-self wholly; for the skilled but equally ecstatic Sherwood it was, as he put it in another context, "Fucking for pure joy of skies, river, trees, flesh, man's flesh, woman's flesh." Both knew from then on that, whether they married or not, they would be sexual partners, that as Sherwood put it in agreement with Eleanor, they had "something to be treated with delicacy and kept." Characteristically, he the artist would also suggest—"Here is all my mys-ticism"—that in an important sense she had already penetrated him as he now had her, that the things he was writing were the "children" with whom she had impregnated him. Although one of her many attractions for him was and would be that she had her own independent career, nevertheless

I have thought . . . I wonder if I am right . . . that the poet . . . when he is the poet . . . is the ultimate, the final, masculine and that the woman, when she loves, is the ultimate, the final, woman.

The dance that may come, the song, the painting, is the child.[10]

2.

The next day Eleanor left for Marion by train, and the day following Anderson headed for New Orleans. Trains and hotels in his wanderings about the South were costing him money, and now that he no longer received the more or less regular payments from *Vanity Fair,* he was living somewhat hand to mouth, relying on such unexpected windfalls as a check for $180 for *The American County Fair* from Random House. In New Orleans he took a sixth-floor corner room at the Hotel Monteleone looking out over the French Quarter and the river, started writing up his impressions of the night visit to the Greenville mill, arranged a night's visit to a sugar refinery upriver, and began to seek out his old friends in the city. Of these only the gentle, quizzical Julius Friend still seemed "nice" to him at first; most of the others seemed to have gone downhill in one way or another, though this judgment may have been affected by his enduring a bad case of hives and a series of painful visits to a dentist.[11]

As usual, writing letters, especially to Eleanor sometimes twice a day, was a consolation. He had begun to compose bits of poetry again from time to time, and in a letter she asked whether the Bible had influenced his work. His reply was a fuller-than-usual comment on that influence.

Of course the Bible has influenced me, dear. I read it all the time. Where else am I to find such fine dignified prose? Prose means little to me without the quality of poetry buried in it. To tell the truth, dear, I have always been sly about this whole matter. I really want only to write poetry but do not want to be called a poet. To be known as a poet is rather too much like being known as a lover.

I try always I think to shift and change and weave the rhythm of words, trying to have the poetry always alive in it but buried down in what seems like prose forms. The old Hebrew poets did that wonderfully. They have taught me a lot.

I think it is always because the rhythm is so important that I must love to work. Unlove is too terrible. I have to have the whole body in it so that I feel the prose down through my body. Not many of the critics have discovered this yet but I don't care.[12]

He was soon at work trying more obviously to get poetry into his prose. On March 20 he spent a morning in the big New Orleans assembly plant for Ford cars and shortly began to turn his sharp impressions into a piece with the ironic biblical title "Lift Up Thine Eyes." At the "Bogel" plant automobile parts are shipped in by railroad on schedule, by schedule are brought to the great conveyor belt at calculated points and times, by schedule are assembled into completed cars. The men—there are no mill girls here, only strong, quick, young men—"work always on tension" to meet the demands of the moving belt, for "The belt is boss." The men work only eight hours a day and are well paid, but scientific time-motion men, "watch in hand," constantly check for ways to increase speed while maintaining a standard product. (All this is explained in series after series of short sentences, Anderson deliberately attempting an imitative form in his prose to suggest perceived speed and mechanical movement.) Everything is carefully calculated; to save steps the men must walk only along "certain definite white lines" on the cement floor, and individuals are at random given new jobs or fired without explanation. The purpose is to make the central Bogel office at Jointville the unquestioned, all-powerful source of authority.

The thing is to build up Jointville. This country needs a religion. You have got to build up the sense of a mysterious central thing, a thing working outside your knowledge.

Let the notion grow and grow that there is something superhuman at the core of all this.

Lift up thine eyes, lift up thine eyes.

The central office reaches down into your secret thoughts.

It knows, it knows.

Jointville knows.

Here Anderson begins to intermix paragraphs of prose with passages of short, often repetitive statements printed as poetry as an emotional device to prepare for his conclusion that Jointville, not Washington, is becoming the new "center of power, the new mystery," the new Lord, as it were, commanding the prophetic Anderson as Moses is commanded in Deuteronomy (3:27–28) to behold the land his people will inherit, but which he himself may not enter.[13]

Perhaps because the Ford plant he visited was an assembly not a manufacturing one, in "Lift Up Thine Eyes" Anderson makes no mention of any beauty in the machines; instead he emphasizes the central control over the workingmen and the tension instilled in them. The mill girls had worked under tension too, but the "terrible intensity" of the men on the belt helped confirm in him a belief he first elaborated in a letter (probably written on March 14 to Nelson Antrim Crawford, editor of the women-oriented *Household Magazine*), which later published "Machine Song: Automobile." Women, he had become certain, "respond to the machine much better than men do . . . are less afraid of it." Perhaps "the dominant fact of life" now may be "the inadequacy of men and the strength of women." Men give women money instead of love, for they are incapable of love; women, knowing this, have become contemptuous of men. Whatever introspective sources he may have been drawing on for these large generalizations one can only guess at—his suspicion that toward the end of his third marriage he had given Elizabeth things and money in place of love, his admiration for Eleanor's strength and his own frequent feelings of inadequacy—but from his observations, however limited, of women and men in the factories he had come to hold, "very definitely, the notion that we are in a woman's age." Along with two revisions of "Labor and Sinclair Lewis" into "Cotton Mill" and "Lift Up Thine Eyes," he began writing tentatively at an article to be called "A Woman's Age."

He was keeping up his visits to factories in and around New Orleans in his overall purpose, as he wrote Burton Emmett, "to try to humanize modern industry." In one of his letters to John Hall Wheelock at Scribner's concerning continued revisions of "Labor and Sinclair Lewis," he explained that he was writing "Without any social theories" as he had written *Winesburg* without them: "I just wanted to get a picture of life in the small town as I felt it, and I would like to do that for the factories, now, if I can." He would like to go into "all sorts of big, modern industries" such as steel and automobiles, and hoped to get financial help from a magazine to defray travel expenses, the magazine to have "the first look" at every article in a series he would write. Wheelock expressed interest but wanted more details. Anderson was not ready to supply them at the moment, being too busy writing, observing sugar refineries, and seeing friends, several of whom besides Julius had turned out to be nice after all.[14]

One of these was Adaline Katz, his close companion from his 1922 stay in the city, now happily married though still, he wrote Eleanor in an unexpectedly dejected letter, "in an old way" loving him. On March 30 she went with him to a big sugar refinery up river and from her new perspective reversed their old teacher and pupil roles by talking to him on the way about his subjection to moodiness, his tendency to feel "proud and sure," then suddenly to feel defeated, small, ashamed of his life.

She has seen me often with groups of people during this visit here and formerly when I have been here.

She said—"You constantly let yourself be hurt too much. I have watched you with people. I can see you sensing everyone in the room. The expression of your face changes constantly. In one evening you are hurt, you are glad, old, young.

"Thoughts pass through the crowd. People are ugly or nice. Everything registers on you as on a photographer's plate.

"I wonder sometimes that you can stand living at all."

Anderson agreed that "A large part of what she said was true." Most of this time in New Orleans as eight years before, however, he was "proud and sure" of his purpose, his writing, and now Eleanor. Nearing the end of his stay, he had decided that his friends were "really amazingly sweet people," who felt enlivened themselves by the life in him. On April 1 he had the last of his painful sessions with the dentist, at an equally painful total cost of $150, partly offset by one hundred dollars from *Household Magazine* for "Machine Song." On April 3 he sent off the final, satisfactory reworking of "Cotton Mill" to Wheelock and had a going-away lunch with Julius and other businessmen who were also great readers. On the fourth he was invited to early tea at the elegantly furnished home of a wealthy man to see his magnificent galleries of paintings—"a glorious Renoir," he wrote Bockler, "infinitely tender Ryders, fine quality Bonnards and Maurers. But though the man was kind, his wife gentle and nice, "the rich are no good . . . ugly, even when they own beautiful paintings," a remark revealing one of his long-standing "social theories." Leaving that big house, he abruptly decided that he "must have at least one evening on the river." At 4 PM he took passage on the *Tennessee Belle,* steamer-bound upstream for Greenville, Mississippi, the pilot being an acquaintance, old Captain Charlie Barker, to whom he had given copies of *Poor White* and *Moby Dick,* both of which Barker had liked. The two men spent the whole of Barker's watch from 6 PM to midnight talking in the pilot house, Anderson meanwhile fascinated by the land fading away in the darkness and "queer lights play[ing] over the rushing water." In the morning the other pilot landed him near a railroad station, and he took the train back to New Orleans in plenty of time for the big farewell party his friends had arranged for him that Saturday night. On Sunday, the sixth, he left the city for a stay with his former Troutdale friends, the Greears, at Helen, Georgia, a village thirty miles north of Gainesville, where Caroline was running a boarding house and John was a lumber camp engineer.[15]

The following afternoon he was welcomed by the Greears, who had long been urging him to come see them. Depressed at first by the economic depression of the town, the forests having been almost logged out in that area, he became much interested in the operations of the lumber camp up in the mountains to the west, to which he was driven by his favorite among the Greear children, white-haired, bespectacled David, now about fourteen. He was amazed by the logging process, the furiously working lumberjacks, the rough little houses in which they lived, houses moved from place to place on the camp's narrow gauge railroad. He delighted in learning new words like "swamping" and lumber "hicks," not "jacks," and determined to write a piece about lumber camps, including the ugly clear-cutting of the forested hills and the unsettled lives of the men who lived always in temporary places. He was amazed as well during his three weeks at Greear Lodge by the "mountain child" David's adult competence and his sensitivity to nature, by his and brother Josh's mechanical ability, and most of all by David's gift for carving wood. Afternoons when he was not fishing the nearby mountain streams, he often watched the brothers at work in their shop, and he talked frequently with their parents about getting better schooling for them; after leaving the Greears, he sent David a box of fine woodcarving tools, and in July he persuaded Otto Kahn and Burton Emmett to pay for the boy's going to the technical high school in Atlanta to study sculpture. As with Bockler, Anderson was eager to help, and persuade others to help young, hard-working artists whom he thought promising.[16]

As usual, most mornings of his visit he put into his writing. At Edmund Wilson's request he agreed to review *Assorted Articles* by D. H. Lawrence, whose death on March 2 had shocked him. "I did not think he was ready to die yet," he quoted himself as exclaiming in the impressionistic review he maintained he had begun to write while trout fishing a mountain stream with the woods boss of the lumber camp. His review praises Lawrence as "one of the few prose artists of our times," a lover of life, "one of the few clean males of literature," whose *Lady Chatterley's Lover* is "a clean fine book, making everything about you clean and nice as you read." His excitement over Lawrence's 1928 novel had begun at some time during his New Orleans visit when his friend, the philosopher James Feibleman, had given him a copy. He had taken a day off from his writing, according to Feibleman, had read it in a rush, and at lunch the next day had been "loud and robust about his enthusiasm, until the crowded restaurant rang with the timbre of his approval." In letters after the review appeared he again praised this book as "a revolutionary novel . . . clean and nice" and asserted that he and the English writer "stand for something—the bringing back into prose art of the sensual," though at the same time he differed with Lawrence for rejecting, as he did not, "the Industrial Age—the machine." Most of the morning time at Helen, however, he spent on "A Woman's Age," a draft of this semi-Lawrentian account of the decline of love in the American male he was preparing for Eleanor at the same time he was passionately writing her of his love for her.[17]

They were able to arrange a day together, April 22, in Greensboro, North Carolina. Again they made joyous love outdoors in a wood, he in wildly passionate recollection, praising her as being, unlike many women, "a vivid real lover," himself sensing, he declared, "all earth and sky and trees in you, gathered into your woman's body." Ecstatically he insisted in Lawrence-like tones that "Life itself should be the sacred thing . . . Love making, a . . . lovely, strong, tender sacrament to life." It was presumably at this meeting and in response to the outspoken *Lady Chatterley's Lover* that they began calling their genitals "Abner" and "Clarice." He had been right in believing that the "puritanic" upbringing of which she had spoken had not inhibited her deeply. His letters to her in his remaining few days back at Helen were filled with erotic memories.[18]

On April 29 as planned, John arrived at Helen by car, and on the thirtieth father and son left on the two-day trip back to Marion. They stayed in town long enough for Anderson to persuade Bob, who had taken over his father's car, to buy for him a little Chevrolet coupe, and then they drove on to Ripshin. The farm was lovely that spring, and he was again inclining against selling it, especially, he wrote Eleanor, if she might be willing to marry him. She could and should continue with her job, and they could have Ripshin as home base. Eleanor was not ready to commit herself, but he was certain that they could "work out some sort of partnership." Meanwhile the farm was self-supporting, though not profitable, and he was hopeful of getting out of debt with the papers. In early April, Burton Emmett had generously reduced his $5,000 loan by $3,000 with the arrangement that the manuscripts and other items Anderson had sent him remain his property; and between them Sherwood and Bob had paid off all other indebtedness except for about $3,500. He was fairly confident now that he could turn over the paper to Bob in the fall and that Bob could begin sending John and Mimi each a hundred dollars a month until their one-third shares of the papers' value were paid out. Bab Finley had written to say that she could no longer afford to help out the two younger children because of "tighter times"; but the arrangement with Bob would enable Mimi to continue at the University of Chicago, and John, who was already painting away "furiously" on the farm, could continue painting after summer ended.[19]

Satisfied that all was going well, Anderson exuberantly began writing "to the top of my bent," his mind filled with present and future projects. He began a novel so "Rabalasian" in its "pure joy of fields, art, flesh etc." that it might be unpublishable, and soon dropped it. With the farm "fairly teem[ing] with new life"—little turkeys and chicks, two calves, three pigs, even a just-born kitten—he began a series of sketches, some of them rather "pagan," of the personalities of farm people and of their animals; and he considered another series on the hard lives of country folk. By May 19 he had finished for *The New Republic* a review of Margaret Anderson's *My Thirty Years' War* consisting of his random memories of the Chicago days when that "splendid creature" who believed in "unreality" founded *The Little Review* and "got us all together." He was mainly focused, however, on revising to John Hall Wheelock's satisfaction his article "A Woman's Age," which he had sent to *Scribner's Magazine* just before he left Helen, and on working on a long sequel, "Perhaps Women." On May 7 Wheelock had written that he liked "A Woman's World," but he objected to Anderson's much too frequent use of single-sentence paragraphs and suggested omitting certain passages to give more clarity, though admitting the article was "really a kind of poem." In a long reply on the eighteenth, Anderson approved of all but one of the omissions and agreed to restructure his paragraphs, while explaining that he was "essentially a poet," though he'd "much rather sneak poetry across" through his prose.

I break up paragraphs like this sometimes because it seems to me to make a kind of rhythm in the reading that I want. I want the mind of the reader to be singing as it reads without quite knowing what has happened.

In turn, Wheelock the careful editor urged that two more paragraphs be omitted. If Anderson agreed, *Scribner's* would send him a thousand dollars, five hundred for "A Woman's Age"—published in the December issue under the title "It's a Woman's Age"—and five hundred as an advance payment for one of the specifically industrial articles for which he had taken notes only, "Lumber Camp" or "Sugar Mill." *Scribner's* could not take the sequel article "Perhaps Women," but Anderson had already decided to make the two linked articles into a little book. The two final omissions Wheelock had requested, he asked the editor to make himself.[20]

Considering Anderson's recent absorption in the factories and the hard lives of workers, especially of the girls walled in by mill and village, "It's a Woman's Age" seems a curious "think-piece," combining assumptions more suited to *Vanity Fair* with others more suited to *The New Republic*, which published "Loom Dance," combining attitudes held by Anderson in the twenties and now presumably discarded with some he had recently developed out of firsthand observations. The "mystery" of religion, he asserts, has been killed by science, and that of love has been killed by the machine but also, it soon appears, by men's preoccupation with money. No longer making things with their hands like the old craftsmen and thus disconnected from nature, men feel diminished by the beautiful machines, have lost their maleness, and, no longer fit "mates" for women, have surrendered to them. For the purposes of the article "Women" only incidentally includes mill girls and instead refers mainly to middle- and upper-class women who do not work for a living, yet are the "great consumers" for whom most of the goods made in factories are produced. "I am trying," Anderson grandly asserts,

to proclaim a new world, a woman's world.
The newspapers are all run for women, the magazines, the stores.
The cities are built for women. Who do you suppose the automobiles are built for?

Because women, the more practical sex, cannot get love from men, they take things instead. America is "ruled," therefore, by women and the machine. Men have even given up their specific male attribute, "the world of the imagination," before the feminine "passion for possession." What can be done? For an answer Anderson draws in part from his long-held ideas, in part from his ecstatic new relations with Eleanor, in part from D. H. Lawrence. Granted that the machine is inevitable in modern society, men must learn to control it and their money hunger. They must recover the sense of "mystery" by going back to nature more, must create "a new religion, more pagan, something more closely connected with fields and rivers." They must build up "a new and stronger sympathy as between man and man," perhaps finding there "the new mystery." They must cease being afraid of sexuality. "We will have to rediscover the wonder of our own maleness or the women will have no lovers, no mates. There will be no lovers. There will only be husbands."

We cannot know Eleanor's reaction to the draft of "It's a Woman's Age." We can only regret her apparent destruction of her side of the correspondence in this matter. But whatever objections she may have raised, Anderson was not deterred from going on with his long sequel "Perhaps Women." This would be his major project for the summer, for by late June the article had become a book of which he had already written "some 30,000 words." Occasionally he would drop the book to follow other "impulses," so that his desk became covered with unfinished things. One of these he did complete was a short story, "The Flood," written in the last week in June. It was a fictional statement about various kinds of value, a matter he had been thinking about off and on since early April when Burton Emmett had reduced the loan by $3,000. At that time Anderson had thanked him but had protested against treating the fluctuations in a writer's value, his reputation, like the stock market. Rather, he insisted, "real values lie deeper than the surface." In "The Flood" a college professor has long been absorbed in preparing to write a book on values, only to have his thoughts frequently interrupted by his beloved "frivolous-seeming" wife, who calls him "an old stick" and with kisses drags him out of his study to mix with other people. In his thinking he has decided that there is "a divine balance to all values to be found"; a man rich in material things could buy a Rembrandt painting and boast about its cost, but the painting would nevertheless add some immaterial value to his life. When the professor's wife dies, he is terribly lonely; but then the wife's unmarried younger sister appears, bringing again a flood of people into his house and, as his wife had done, calling him an old stick and dragging him out to mix with them. He rejects his theory of a balance of values and advances instead a theory that "Everything in life comes in surges, floods, really," before which the individual is helpless. He proposes marriage to the younger sister, and she presumably calls him an old stick, kisses him, and accepts, in this way showing that life may be both a flood and a balance. In any case, life, a value in itself, is not to be defined by materialists or by the "dry asses," as Anderson was currently calling intellectuals.[21]

That "The Flood" was not marketed to a magazine and was first published in Anderson's 1933 collection, *Death in the Woods and Other Stories* may be a result of the break between him and Otto Liveright. When on June 4 Wheelock wrote that he supposed that the thousand-dollar check (for "It's a Woman's Age" and an industrial article) should be sent as usual to Anderson through Liveright, who would first deduct his 10 percent fee, Anderson replied that it should be sent directly to himself since Liveright "handles but a part of my connections and has had nothing to do with this arrangement." He had, of course, proposed to Wheelock a series of industrial articles back in March. Liveright learned about "It's a Woman's Age" from the managing editor at *Scribner's,* and on June 20 he wrote Anderson, asking about "the situation" concerning the article and concluding that "having originally started the situation with Scribner's [that is, by interesting the magazine in "Labor and Sinclair Lewis"], I would like to be of some service now." Since this would turn out to be the last letter he wrote to Anderson and there is no record of a reply, apparently the two friends simply parted company over the question of agent's and author's rights and recompense. By August 5 Anderson had a new literary agent in New York, Anne Watkins.[22]

Acting for the moment as his own agent, he sent off to the *American Mercury* an article he probably wrote early in July, one that Eleanor definitely disapproved of, perhaps because "They Come Bearing Gifts" prints an arrogantly scolding letter, which he may not actually have mailed, addressed to a woman who had asked him to comment on some sketches she had sent him together with a check for twenty-five dollars. Brutally he told her that she did not know what an artist was and that her "stuff was just plain bad," every sentence over-written, "writey." He was keeping the check, he told the woman, because he was adding good advice: forget about the popular magazines with their trick stories, feel experience directly, treat words carefully. "Fame is no good my dear," he concluded, "Take it from me. I know." *American Mercury* printed the article in its October issue. Later he admitted to Eleanor that he and she "were both somewhat ashamed" of the article since in it he had been subtly trying to sell himself.[23]

Often that early summer he worked afternoons with Mendel the hired man, son of Mrs. Hilton, the wonderfully competent housekeeper at Ripshin, in a campaign to improve the farm; but some of his time was taken up with guests he had insistently invited. In mid-June it was Bentley Chappell and his very beautiful wife whom he had met in Columbus, Georgia; and for a week in mid-July it was J. J. Lankes, whose scenes in his just published *Virginia Woodcuts,* Anderson felt, showed the real, not the romantic, Virginia. Lankes arrived "utterly discouraged" about going on with his work but after talks with Anderson departed with a "new impetus" to push on. Expansively Anderson wrote Bockler, inviting him, Katharine, and their child to come to Ripshin in August and stay for a year in the house across the creek so that Charles could live cheaply and paint; though in the end the Bocklers would decide to go back to live with Katharine's wealthy parents in Bel Air, Maryland. Far better than having guests at Ripshin, of course, were Anderson's June and July trips in his Chevrolet coupe to re-union with Eleanor at the summer camps for working women in North Carolina. They continued their sexual relationship; and although at the July meeting she listed reasons why she should not marry him, he felt that this "little dark-eyed, Italian-looking woman" nevertheless loved him. So, loving her for her courage and willingness to "adventure" with him, he had at last a woman such as he believed always essential to his writing and without whom he would be "a crippled one-sided man."[24]

3.

After the unusually beautiful spring, June and July turned hot and dry, and by the end of July, all Virginia was in its worst drought in decades. Anderson's stand of corn—the best in the county, he had earlier boasted—withered and died, the "bold" spring went dry, Mrs. Hilton quit, and he closed Ripshin and moved into the apartment with Bob in Marion. As though the drought had triggered it, Anderson began to write about the "terrific slump" the whole country was in, a slump that would not end, he had a hunch, for "a long, long time." It was all "tremendously interest-ing," he told Ralph Church, for there would certainly be "a genuine deep-seated shake-up, old gods gone and every one looking for new ones." There will be "tight times . . . ahead," he predicted in a "What Say!" col-umn. Many farmers and middle-class people will go broke this year, and it will be educational to see "how the game of life has been rigged against us," the ordinary people by "the rich and the successful." Politically, at this point, he was essentially a populist. His only other public statement at the time, however, would be an apparently mild-enough address on Sep-tember 5 to the county teachers "on the pupil-teacher relationship; how it abides through later-life."[25]

He continued to work hard on *Perhaps Women*, a summary of which he sent to Tom Smith at the Liveright firm on August 16.

It is an attempt to tell in dramatic terms my notion of present day American civi-lization, what it is doing to people etc.

Out of this I have got what seems to me a rather startling and true statement. It is that America already has begun a matriarchy. Women are in control and should be. The result of the Machine Age has been a growth of spiritual impotence in men, a thing that does not touch women so closely. Women are surviving it better. The spiritual impotence, inevitable to men in a Machine Age, will lead inevitably to physical impotence. Women are beginning to find this out. In every factory I have gone into I have found the women standing up to it better than the men. Every woman has within her something the machine cannot touch.

The argument of my book which I want to call Perhaps Women is that if the present Machine Age is ever brought down it may be brought down by the women demanding the men back.

Despite his apparent confidence, however, the steady push was beginning to tell. He had already sent Charles Bockler his copy of *Lady Chatterley's Lover,* which had helped lead him to the argument of *Perhaps Women,* praising it as "perhaps the great book of our times." On the same day he had outlined his book to Smith, he wrote Bockler that his nerves had "rather got an edge," and he wanted to get away for a week or two of rest at the seashore. He was eager at the moment to simplify his life and so was going back to his idea of selling Ripshin; it was "charming enough . . . but too big and elaborate" for him. Clearing his desk, he then wrote a businesslike letter to Mary Vernon Greer, to whom he had without compunction continued to send his scrawled manuscripts for typing despite her continued bitterness toward him for breaking off their affair. For the most part the letter concerned the possibility of her selling the house, as she had long urged he would be better off doing, even if he had to sell for eight or ten thousand a place that had cost him "about $20,000" to build. Then a day or two later he headed by car toward Ocean Grove, New Jersey, a seaside town apparently selected as a place that Eleanor could visit readily. This vacation had one drawback: he had actually hoped to work more easily on his book but instead came down with a bad sinus condition that gave him a violently painful headache for ten days until a doctor cured the infection. Despite the pain he loafed often on the beach, quite fascinated by the new revealing style of women's bathing suits, but apparently wrote no more than a letter to Mencken congratulating him on his marriage to Sara Haardt on August 27. On the thirtieth he was back in Marion, still weak from his "experience . . . along the road of pain." On the thirty-first he was at work again on *Perhaps Women,* though now only desultorily.[26]

Eleanor had been with him on the two-day drive back from Ocean Grove, saw her parents for several days, and went with him and Mimi (who was also visiting) to the state fair at Richmond to see the horse races. After she went back to her job, however, he felt bored, lonely, restless in Marion, wanted, he complained to Lankes, "to smell the dam horizon." His fifty-fourth birthday came and went with little notice. Why didn't she buy Ripshin, he wrote Blanche Chappell; she could have it for "four or five thousand dollars," for he had a renewed urge to rid himself of property. Eager to leave Marion for anywhere, he arranged with Mimi to drive her back to the University of Chicago by car, and they set off on September 23. Leaving her at the university, he drove over to Michigan City to spend the rest of the month with the Schevills at their summer home on Lake Michigan. This visit was almost a repeat emotionally of the one in December. He had not heard from Eleanor for some days and was seized with the fear that she was ill or might have decided to put him out of her life. Depressed, he walked and talked frequently with Ferdinand, who wisely counseled him to leave her alone to make her own decision and tried to divert his mind by taking him to the current exhibit at the Chicago Art Institute of Frank Lloyd Wright's architectural designs and models; though Anderson in his low mood noted how often Wright's own financial and personal problems had kept beautiful projects from being realized, as he himself had killed so many of his own.[27]

Still distressed, and apologetic for being so again, he left the Schevills on October 1 for the solitary drive home via Indianapolis—where he didn't stop to see Bab—and Cincinnati, but shortly after his return he learned from Eleanor that she had simply been unable to write him because of the pile-up of her work after her vacation and had no intention of turning away from him. Elated, he assured her that although he was not a young man and had made many mistakes out of overeagerness for life—"Life not death is the adventure," he had told her earlier—still "I have had, I presume, more than almost any man of my time, a rather wide, varied experience of American life" and had much left in him to write about. Through their love, and only through that, he would be able to get back to his "materials," life itself, from which he had drawn away. He started a long short story (perhaps an early version of "Mill Girls") and put aside *Perhaps Women* until his sense of its "poetic content" returned. "As you know," he wrote the Schevills in one of his relatively rare aesthetic statements,

poetry—the carrying of conviction to others through feeling through the medium of words—is a complex, difficult thing.

The very color of the words themselves, the feeling in the artist trying to release itself is a part of what must get over to the reader.

As Clara well knows, the notes she sings may be quite perfect at times, but if she cannot get into the song her own inner feeling, nothing happens.[28]

He further postponed work on *Perhaps Women* by readily agreeing to write for *The Virginia Quarterly Review*; by the end of October he completed an article, "J. J. Lankes and His Woodcuts," which the *Review* published in its January, 1931 issue. The article shows clearly why he admired and felt close to the artist. In this "spiritually tired time," Anderson declares, Lankes draws people together by his gift for perceiving "something significant and lovely in commonplace things" and for revealing in his woodcuts how inanimate things reflect the lives of those who have touched them. Because he constantly asserts in his work "the beauty and wonder of everyday life," he is "one of the very significant living artists of our day." One other article Anderson probably took time to write in late October was on an ugly aspect of the South. "Look Out, Brown Man!" was apparently not solicited by *The Nation,* where it appeared in the November 26 issue, but came from his own and the national concern over the sharp increase in lynchings of black men that year over the previous two years. (There had been ten in 1928 and seven in 1929, but in 1930, the first full year of the Depression, twenty had already occurred, mostly in the South: three in August, four as recently as September, the largest number in any month of that year.) Predictably Anderson warns proud black men, whom he rather admires, not "to step too high" in these hard times since many whites, especially the "second-rate ones" who do the lynchings, are out of work and resent seeing "a big proud black man getting along. There'll be lynchings now." Anderson sees no "difference between the impulses and desires of Negroes and myself," he understands how galling it must be to be always in a subordinate position; nevertheless, intelligent Negroes will remain "friends with the intelligent people among the whites," will play the "fawning, polite white man's Negro" only with the second-rate whites, but in any case will walk carefully, not "strut." In other words Anderson advises blacks to accept unprotestingly their subordinate position and endure. In the social context of the time this might be "sensible, realistic" advice, but it was anything but radical, even tended to blame the victim. Where Anderson was advanced in his thinking was in his willingness to identify in his urges with blacks including the proud "Negroes' Negro man, the so-called 'bad one,'" to consider blacks and whites equal as human beings though caught in an unequal situation of long standing.[29]

There were other distractions from the book that fall. Apparently around October 10 he was briefly in Washington to make a speech, perhaps about country newspapers or about small towns, on which subject, he wryly decided, he had become "the conventional authority." Soon after his return home, Laura Lu Copenhaver developed high blood pressure and needed to stop her many activities temporarily and rest quietly. Anderson took pleasure in visiting and talking with her each day, enjoying the play of her perceptions and lively mind, including in his daily letters to Eleanor the progress of her mother's recovery and the subjects they had discussed. He was especially charmed to hear that when the Copenhaver children were young, they had been expected to learn verses from the Bible and recite them at the dinner table, and Eleanor had been best of all at the recitation. It gave him added insight into the loving but restrictive home from which she came, retaining the love but breaking free from so much of the restriction. He was continuously grateful to Mrs. Copenhaver that despite her religiousness she was, unlike her husband, mostly in favor of the relationship between Anderson and their daughter, though she almost certainly did not know how far it had already gone. Probably on October 18, the beautiful Blanche Chappell came to stay for a week at a hotel, not just to consider buying Ripshin but also, Anderson suspected, to get away from her husband and amuse herself with the many attentions Anderson felt obliged to show her. Bob, who was getting along much better with his father than formerly, generously helped to entertain Blanche, but both men were relieved when she finally left. She did not purchase Ripshin. On the twenty-eighth Eleanor again arrived in Marion to stay for several days, and Anderson, struck as usual by "[her] loveliness, [her] feeling about people, the deep kind of real sympathy" in her, asked her to marry him. Her refusal to commit herself to marriage as yet sent him into a brief "nerve break" of despondency. *Perhaps Women* was at a standstill; all he seemed able to write was fragments.[30]

On November 1, despite tight times on the papers, he and Bob paid off the last of the notes held by Arthur Cox, and he wrote Emmett that he expected to pay off the bank loan in a year and Emmett's loan soon after. He hadn't been earning much from articles, he told his friend, perhaps because "I am becoming too radical [for the well-paying magazines] although, God knows, I am not a communist." The winter of visiting factories perhaps "awoke in me anew a sympathy for the under-dog that now begins to show." All artists were feeling that the "general depression" of the times was not just economic. "There is, I think, a kind of general feeling that in some sense our modern industrial civilization has failed to feed men spiritually. Everyone wants something back that seems lost." The announcement (on November 6) that Sinclair Lewis would be the first American to receive the Nobel Prize for literature, he complained, was "very depressing" to him. "The man has never touched American life, except to make it uglier by his touch." The honor should have gone to Dreiser for his "real tenderness."[31]

He was shortly to express other of his ideas publicly. In mid-October he had agreed to preside at a public debate sponsored by the *Richmond Times-Dispatch* on "Agrarianism versus Industrialism" in the South and to introduce two speakers, John Crowe Ransom, poet and professor of English at Vanderbilt University, and Stringfellow Barr, professor of history at the University of Virginia and editor of *The Virginia Quarterly Review*. The debate had originated with an article—"Shall Slavery Come South?," which Barr had written for the October *Review*—arguing that despite the opposition of the "traditionalists," who wanted the economy of the South to remain agricultural, industrialism was already established in the South and so must be accepted but made to conform to traditional Southern "social responsibility" in the treatment of its workers lest it repeat the brutal excesses of the Industrial Revolution in England and New England. Early in October, Anderson had written Barr to compliment him on the article, which had created a widespread controversy. The most outspoken opponents were the "Fugitive" poets centered on Vanderbilt in Nashville and led by Ransom, Allen Tate, and Donald Davidson. They and nine other literary Southerners had just published a symposium, *I'll Take My Stand!: The South and the Agrarian Tradition.* These "Agrarians" attacked the article vociferously, arguing that the South must preserve its traditional "spiritual entity" based on farming the land against invasion by modern industrialism; and the *Times-Dispatch,* perceiving that the controversy was over how the South as a whole should develop, sponsored the debate. In preparation for his role in it Anderson read *I'll Take My Stand!* and recommended it to Charlie Bockler as being "At least . . . an expression of something." He was working out his own idea that he wanted to "spring" on the debaters in his introduction, he wrote Barr. Both sides wanted the same thing, he asserted in the face of obviously opposing positions, and the debate was really over the means of achieving it. "None of us really want communism or even socialism at least until individuality has had another chance." Since Barr had not suggested otherwise, he might have been puzzled as to what Anderson intended to spring in his introduction.[32]

With Bob and Robert Williams, an employee on the newspapers, Anderson drove to Richmond on November 14. By eight thirty that evening the main floor and the balcony of the City Auditorium were crowded with 3,200 people, various dignitaries such as the mayor of Richmond and the governor of the state being seated on the stage behind the speakers. Later Anderson maintained that with his introduction, a speech in itself, he "came near stealing the meeting from the others"; but the *Times-Dispatch*'s report of the debate on the following day gave almost all of its two and a half columns to a detailed summary of the points made by Barr and Ransom. Anderson's "preliminary remarks" received only a brief paragraph paraphrasing his attack on the awarding of the Nobel Prize to Lewis rather than Dreiser and ending with what presumably was an impromptu remark inserted into his prepared introduction: "I am glad to see that in this country there is a movement of young people in favor of the dignity of life on the farm and in small communities." Barr might well have decided that the idea Anderson had wanted to spring on the debaters tended to favor the Agrarian side, beginning with his praise of *I'll Take My Stand!* as a book every young American should read and including his defense of individualism on the grounds that "Communism and Industrialism are really brothers; in both of them there is implicit the same patronism, the same determined regimentation of life, the same determination to wreck individualism." In his rather rambling remarks, which gave considerable time to his being "an illegitimate son" of Virginia, having grown up in the industrialized Midwest, he attacked the American faith in bigness and in success and progress measured by money. "I would like to be, for a change, a little worm, let us say, in the fair apple of progress." Under modern industrialism, he insisted, there is a tendency for "man to lose sense of earth, sun, stars, fellow men and even his own hands. The machine, so blithely accepted by most of us is doing all sorts of obscure and hateful things to men." Industrialism and the machine have given us an unearned vicarious power, dangerous because it makes us proud and arrogant. "Real power . . . imaginative power, creative power, power of the hands and of the head," however, is hard to achieve and humbling, makes for the "real manhood and womanhood" that industrialism has endangered. Barr and Ransom "have as clear a vision of the danger of which I speak as any two men in American could have"—and Anderson at last released them to the audience. The highly articulate Ransom and Barr got directly to the issue of Old South versus New South. In its summary, the *Times-Dispatch* did not indicate how the audience sided but partially tipped its own hand with the headline, which began, "Dr. Ransom Charges Barr's 'Regulated' Industrialism Would End In Communism. . . ." One suspects, however, that the newspaper was more opposed to regulation than to industrialism.[33]

The following evening Anderson spoke to a quite different audience. John Edelman, editor of the Philadelphia-based *Trade Union News,* and leaders of a strike at the big Dan River and Riverside cotton mills in Danville, Virginia, had urged him to come talk to a mass meeting of the strikers and so draw national attention to an important labor conflict which had been going on since September. In the morning of the fifteenth he drove south in the rain with Bob and Robert Williams to the small city of Danville, just above the North Carolina line. Reporters from the city newspapers, which strongly opposed the strike, treated Anderson as a celebrity and insisted on taking the three men to call on the local literary celebrity, the dramatist and critic Laurence Stallings—he had reviewed *A Story Teller's Story* enthusiastically—who lived on a nearby country estate. With his quick sympathetic relation to workers, Anderson would have preferred getting a sense of the strike situation by talking out in the rain with men and women on the picket lines. He had already learned, however, that although the mill managers had introduced the "stretchout" and cut wages 10 percent, the main issue for the strikers was recognition of their own union, which almost all of the original four thousand workers had joined, in place of the useless company one. That Saturday night he gave an impromptu speech to strikers crowded into their meeting hall, owned by the local Ku Klux Klan and built to hold perhaps seven hundred people. The young Danville reporter for the United Press would some years later assert in a supercilious account that what he said was "well-intentioned" but "sadly out of place," since his mill worker audience, put off by his long hair and midwestern accent, found "Only rare fragments of his speech . . . intelligible"; but according to the following day's issue of the antistrike Danville *Register*, Anderson's declaration to this audience that "I am sympathetic with your cause and I hope to God you will win [brought] round after round of applause from the assembled strikers." Sensing the warm feeling of unity the strike had given them in place of what in writing of Danville he would call the "feeling of isolation, so universal nowadays in our modern industrialized America," he told them, as the *New York Times* reported, that he had come to help them.

"I hope that you win. . . . Virginia has a tradition of freedom and right that makes me ashamed to know that there are men in Virginia who are not willing to grant you your rights and deal with you fairly. I came here in the hope that I might be able to write something that would bring your situation to the attention of the country."[34]

Returning to Marion on November 16, he was briefly hospitalized for lumbago, then took to his own bed with the flu long enough to finish reading the first volume of *Further Letters of Vincent Van Gogh to His Brother, 1888–1889*, which Bockler had sent him and which he had begun reading at odd moments on his Richmond-Danville trip. Gratefully he told Charles,

It was very difficult reading the Van Gogh letters. I identified myself with the man so closely. You know he has long been one of my real loves. God, how hungry he was and how, more than almost any man I know of, he saw the need of love as an integral part of work.

Van Gogh's profound sympathy with ordinary life and people put Anderson in the mood to write up quickly his impressions of the strike in "Danville, Virginia," which *The New Republic* would publish in January. The workers there and elsewhere in the nation, his article ended, were in a "heart-breaking" situation. The strikers crammed into that hall had looked up at him with "hope, love, expectation" in their eyes, but even while he spoke encouraging words to them, he was almost choked by his certainty that they and others "struggling for some right to live," were "inevitably doomed to defeat just now." He was already puzzling at some other way he could communicate sympathy and support to the defeated ones. He no longer felt arrogant, as Karl had painted him with Earl and Irwin, he confessed to his brother. More humble now, "I hardly know what I can teach except anti-success. I suppose that is what I mean by a cultural back fire" against what industrialism was doing to people.[35]

As he considered what he could more specifically teach, he drew for his "cultural back fire," not on Danville and the strikers but on the Richmond debate and his expressed pleasure in seeing the movement of young people to farm and small town. His campaign first took the form of an article for *Forum and Century* amplifying the opportunities he had found in running his newspapers. Industrialism in the United Sates, and in the "Russian experiment" as well, he argued in "The Country Weekly," had standardization as its "soul," and "naturally" the big American city daily was standardized also, hence was anti-individualistic. The country weekly could be the much-needed backfire for individualism. Properly run, the weekly is not a newspaper but "in reality a kind of big weekly county letter . . . that would pretty much tell everyone in the county what everyone else was doing." Bright, lively young men and women who abandoned the city daily for the country weekly would be "in touch with life" in the towns and on the farms, "in touch with the people for whom [they] write and about whom [they] write," in touch too "with nature and what nature provides." These young editors, fed up with "the emphasis on money-making in our civilization" would realize the tremendous power of the small-town paper. They need not be reformers but have only "a somewhat decent attitude" toward the community and "a little plain love of life" to accomplish much. They could check "communal brutalities" and the power of the Ku Klux Klan. "I do not believe that lynchings would happen in . . . a town" where a talented young man or woman had taken advantage of perhaps "the biggest, the most pregnant, and the most overlooked opening there is in all American life": today's American country press.

Writing this article encouraged him to look actively for financial backing to further publicize his country press project. On December 11 he left for Atlanta to discuss the role of the weeklies in their communities with Will W. Alexander, who since 1919 had headed the Commission on Interracial Co-operation and in 1930 had become a trustee of the Julius Rosenwald Fund, which was supporting improvements in the status of black people. In the course of his conversation with Alexander, Anderson presumably emphasized his newspaper campaign to build the new school building in Marion for black children. Alexander encouraged him in his project but offered no financial assistance. By coincidence, however, upon his return to Marion on the sixteenth he received a letter from Professor Baker Brownell of the School of Journalism at Northwestern University, asking if he might be at all interested in joining the school's faculty. He replied that he would not, but suggested instead that for three hundred dollars and expenses he would like to come to Northwestern for a few days to give three lectures, talk with students, and answer questions about country journalism's "practical side" and "cultural possibilities." Such an arrangement would eventually, in fact, be worked out for the following April.[36]

Meanwhile, with the Depression deepening and with the Danville strikers still much on his mind, he felt that, as he would suddenly write Bab Finley at the end of the year, "In a way life just now, particularly among working people, the life of reality is more fantastic and strange to me than the imaginative life." He had temporarily lost interest in writing stories or a novel, he confided to Mimi; besides, the magazines—"A Dead Dog" had at last been accepted by *The Yale Review*—had been "hard hit" financially and had reduced payments to authors. Nevertheless, perhaps to match the new fantastic life of reality, shortly before Christmas he was feeling his way toward "a new queer kind of novel . . . a little crazy—romantic—in a new way." This "Crazy Book," which he wrote at off and on for weeks but never finished, he rather vaguely described to friends. In *Dark Laughter*, he wrote to the Baroness Koskull now in Paris,

> I wrote the laugh of the Negro at the white. Now I want white man's laughter, laughing at others and at self.
> I think of a crazy, wild book, half poetry, the jazz of the radios and the talkies, voices, poetry, color—some with warm prose in it, I hope. This I shall strive for now until I get it or die trying.[37]

On December 19 a monster storm buried Marion under more than eighteen inches of snow, but Eleanor was able to get back to town on the twenty-first for Christmas. Nevertheless, Christmas was as gloomy a day for him as usual. He hated Christmas, he explained to Bockler, because family poverty had meant no gifts at all for the Anderson children in contrast with the "flood" of things other children received. Surely his memory was selective and exaggerated, but he was in a sad, subdued mood for the remaining days of the old year. He thought of his impulse toward suicide by drowning off the St. Petersburg pier just a year before and of the little money he had since made from his writing. He was, he wrote Eleanor at the end of the month, "an old theater in which many and many a play has been enacted." She could not get in him "an untouched man"; besides three wives he had had other lovers, "one named Margaret and a Helen and a Frankie. Others perhaps, more faintly," all a part of his remembered life she would have to accept in accepting him. Perhaps she as a young woman might want "new life in a man, comparatively untouched." Nevertheless, he declared, he loved her: "If I hadn't begun to love you I wouldn't be here now."[38] True, but the mixed messages in his current writings and speeches did not clearly define where "here" was for him socially and politically.

4

A Semipublic Figure

1.

New Year's brought him a new sort of year. It began with his push at his satirical "crazy book," an attempt at a form-breaking novel full of "a wild Rabelaisian kind of poetry." Much of it would take place in the "wild dance" of thoughts in the mind of a newspaperman as he and a rich businessman get drunk together in the rich man's house. Whereas the rich man, Anderson explained to Ferdinand Schevill, "is a modern successful, rather vulgar pushing American—a man without cultural background," the newspaperman is one "who has read and dreamed, a defeated hurt, half cynical man," again a persona for the author himself in various moods. Both character and creator know that "Real scientists, like Milligen [Carl Milliken], Einstein etc say—'we can do nothing without the aid of the poet. It is only by the poets road we can go anywhere.'" One "glorious chapter" of the projected book, Anderson proudly told Charles Bockler, was titled "P on Einstein"; but the weakness of the chapter's scatological humor suggests that it was just as well he did not push this experimental novel to completion. On January 8, he wrote a chapter about a procession of faces appearing at night to the newspaper man before sleep, as such a procession frequently appeared to his own half-dreaming self; and after dropping the book for some two weeks, he spent several mornings introducing a woman character, "a rather baffled profane, alive eager person." By this time he had estimated that this "crazy new kind of a book," which on Christmas Day he had dreamed as "Comprehending, in a way, all of our civilization," was "perhaps half done." Fortunately, however, other matters were diverting him, and by the end of January he would essentially put his experiment aside for good.[1]

He had not forgotten the Danville strikers. Back in mid-December, he had drafted a piece aimed at encouraging them by asserting that machines had created a new kind of world and that their strike was a step toward entering it. He had hoped that others, "Dreiser, O'Neill, Sandburg," would write something to show that "artists and writers . . . were with them, in sympathy anyway." On December 26, he wrote out a form letter purporting to come from the four thousand men and women still on strike, the first one addressed to Clarence Darrow and others addressed to "well-known American writers, Senators, educators, famous preachers" requesting that they come speak to the strikers or send some message to be read to them. (There is no evidence that any of these form letters were signed by strikers and sent.) By the end of the first week in January, he had revised and typed his own lengthy piece he intended to read to a mass meeting of the strikers as a full-dress speech rather than the impromptu remarks he had given in November. The revised speech, he declared to Eleanor, "I consider one of the most important things done in my whole life."[2]

In the midst of all this writing he had to deal with an unpleasant domestic problem. During some months in 1930, Bob had been much in love with a young woman named Adelaide who, by late October, had begun putting him into "terrible stews" by not writing him, apparently wishing to end their relationship. Possibly he had been drowning in moonshine his heartbreak and his concern that the papers were losing money, when, according to the report in the December 16 *Democrat,* he was arrested for drunk driving and bound over to the grand jury. Probably Sherwood wrote the account, for he felt strongly that the arrest of any townsperson of whatever social position should be reported in the papers; yet despite his distaste for doing so, he spent much time in the following weeks using any influence he had to protect Bob from receiving a possible jail sentence. He eventually succeeded, and it was with relief as well as anticipation that he drove to Lynchburg on January 7 to spend the day before catching the night train with Eleanor, who was going to Washington.[3]

He was continuing a pattern that became even more pronounced this year. While giving an increasing number of speeches and lectures, he kept closely informed of Eleanor's movements among her various assignments and, whenever possible, followed her about the country in order that they might have as many hours together as she could spare from her duties. While she was occupied, he could keep up his habit of writing mornings in any hotel where he happened to light temporarily, in this way also satisfying his restless need for travel. They both took elaborate precautions to keep these arrangements secret from both her YWCA employers and Marion people by joining each other at train stations away from the town, as at Lynchburg, by customarily registering at two different hotels in the same city, and by his having her send him telegrams addressed to agreed-upon code names. The secrecy was irritating to both and did not prevent gossip about them from occasionally being spread by what he called "small town busy-bodies" in Marion. Meeting her privately this time at

Lynchburg on the night train to Washington, he could go to her sleeping car before returning to his own—he had carefully reserved separate berths— and during his visit presumably repeated what he had already written her during his day in Lynchburg in one of his practically daily letters. He delighted in her having work of her own, he wished to be "an extension of yourself as you already are of myself," in loving her he did not demand that she love him in return, and he "clung to individuality only in the artist's way":

I can't give up my workman's faith in my own word groupings, idea groupings, born out of my own individual experiences of life, out of mistakes and hurts and little victories. That individuality I have to cling to or I would become merely dumb.[4]

In Washington in the morning he registered at the little DuPont Hotel and continued working on the "crazy book," possibly also putting final touches on his Danville speech. Because she was busy, he could see Eleanor only briefly; so he spent considerable time with Maurice Long, whom he had come to love, "man to man." This "flame of a man," as Anderson was to call him in the *Memoirs,* had been born in 1878 in County Waterford, Ireland, and had come to Norfolk, Virginia, at the age of thirteen. He had eventually gone into business there, become active in Virginia Democratic politics, and developed an interest in writing. In the 1920s he had moved to Washington, where he was president of the Pioneer Laundry Company. Even though he had followed the "road" Anderson had long ago abandoned and become rich from his chain of laundries, he was open and honest about his fight to be "a robber chief," Anderson felt, and had "a streak of the adventurer." One of his great talents, Anderson would later declare, was his mastery of storytelling: "Never losing the balance of a tale; catching, in talk, the pathos of lives; understanding, tender, imaginative. . . ." His great defect was that, though married and with a grown daughter and son, he had attracted numerous women into affairs, each woman hoping to make him love her, but he had refused to surrender himself to the love of any. (One of the many women who had failed would describe him feelingly as having "blue eyes—sunlight shining on a glacier" and eyebrows that "grew together across the nose like a murderer's.") Anderson deplored this refusal, this inability to love but admired Maurice's storytelling gift, his tolerance and understanding, his uninhibited gusto for life. Maurice told one of his women friends "many times, that [Sherwood was] closer to him than any man he had ever known."[5]

On January 12, Anderson took the train alone back to Lynchburg to pick up his car and spend the night, and the next day he drove south to Danville to read his speech, now grown to some 5,500 words in length. According to Tom Tippett, a lecturer at Brookwood Labor College in Katonah, New York, who for two years had been observing strikes in Southern textile factories, fifteen hundred strikers jammed into the meeting hall that evening to sing strike songs and hear a Philadelphia labor organizer and then Anderson speak. The reporters who had "surrounded" him that afternoon were there, but none from the Danville papers—the city editor of the *Register,* who had been "nice" to him in November, had been abruptly fired this day for "trying to be a little fair to the strikers"—and these papers would carry no notice of meeting or speech the following day. Anderson carefully organized his hour-long speech around the relationship of human beings to the machine, which has made a "new world." Beginning as tools to extend the strength of the human body, machines have become more and more complicated; capable of making needed goods for everyone in the world, they are controlled, not by the men and women who run them, but by those who own them and now seek profit only, cutting wages and throwing people out of work by replacing them with yet more complicated machines. The present strike is part of a centuries-long struggle to free men from power over their lives. Magna Carta was a successful strike against the English king, the "Boss," the French Revolution was a strike, the American Revolution was a strike. Furthermore, the Danville strike is only one of many now going on all over the world to settle the biggest question in the world today: "Is the machine going to be used to disrupt society, make slaves of men, or are men going to use the machine for the benefit of all?" Strikes are not aimed at creating revolutions, which are destructive, but at preventing them; they are aimed at saving civilization, at making the new world created by the machine a "better decenter" place. The Danville strikers are to think of themselves "as the warriors of the new world": "You are fighting as men and women for the right to stand up, to lead decent lives, to breath deeper, to save your manhood and womanhood."[6]

Although the strikers seemed to him "to drink in every word," and they applauded him at his strong conclusion, he felt "exhausted and blue" afterwards. He had wanted to give the poor white strikers a sense of their self-worth and historical importance, but their whole situation, he admitted to Eleanor, seemed hopeless. Already in late November a thousand National Guard troops had been ordered to the mill village to protect the mills and newly hired replacement workers, and by mid-December the mills had been running again, at more than half force. It snowed the night of the thirteenth, and the following morning Anderson and Tippett stood at the mill gate in the bleak cold before dawn sadly watching the replacements hurry in through the snow past the soldiers with fixed bayonets. No pickets were in sight, and both men knew that the strike was dying. Anderson's speech would be mimeographed for distribution to the defeated strikers, on January 30 and printed in John Edelman's *Trades Union News* in its February 6 issue, but on January 29 the unsuccessful strike ended with the leaders claiming that the owner of the mills had agreed (though he denied such agreement) to allow strikers to be rehired despite their union activity. Anderson was angered at this deception and wrote Edelman protesting that the leaders should have told the strikers frankly that they were licked. They were "good stuff" and could take the licking—"Why, they have never known anything but lickings"—and should be treated unpatronizingly as "grown men and women." Besides, the strike had given them "the satisfaction of feeling themselves something other than cogs in a machine." Since returning from making his second speech at Danville, he found his own satisfaction in knowing that now not only Marion but the whole state knew which side he was on in the labor struggle.[7]

He had driven home from Danville on January 14 in another snowstorm to find that his domestic problem had become even more complicated. The unhappy Bob had brought a "trull" into the apartment and had caught gonorrhea from her. His father called in a doctor to treat him for the disease and a subsequent fever, which kept Bob in bed for nearly two weeks, so that Sherwood had to get the papers out himself and had little time for writing anything but letters. The news was not all bad. *Forum and Century* had purchased his article "The Country Weekly" for $200, his London agent had unexpectedly sent him fifty dollars from the sale of "These Mountaineers" and "Lift Up Thine Eyes," and the last piece he had written for *Vanity Fair,* "Domestic and Juvenile," on the domestic relations court of Eleanor's Uncle "Jay" Scherer, had been translated and reprinted in Paris. It was definite that he was to give the three Harris Lectures on country newspapers at Northwestern University in the spring, and Colston Leigh was offering him a contract for up to forty lectures at a hundred dollars each, all expenses paid, no lectures to be on literature, as Anderson had stipulated. He was not having any luck placing the long Danville speeches in *Scribner's* or *The Nation,* and never did; but his "Danville, Virginia" piece about his first speech to the strikers came out in the *New Republic* within a week after his return to Marion. He began to feel that he had become "a sort of public character," and not just in Marion. There, he received a request to speak on February 3 at the luncheon of the annual one-day Industrial Institute for women workers in Richmond, primarily sponsored by the industrial committee of the YWCA. With Bob slowly recovering, he spent the last days of the month trying to work out the personality of the woman in the "crazy book" and writing a first draft of the Richmond speech.[8]

Late in the month he was interrupted in his writing by a visit from Frank H. Fuller of the Associated Press, who interviewed him about his interest in country newspapers and then published the result in "Sherwood Anderson Comments" in the *New York Sun* for January 26. To Fuller, Anderson reiterated his conviction, that here, as in "The Country Weekly," was "opportunity of escape from the illusion of bigness for talented persons with ambition to write who enter newspaper work to get a start" and that "the weekly press might spring to a place of prominence and usefulness under the guidance of men with courage, imagination and love of life," men who wanted to maintain their individualism. Noting the recent Danville speech, Fuller asked "about communism in the industrial south." Anderson replied characteristically:

"I think communism is a great deal like prohibition—superimposed from the top and just about as hard to make work. . . . I don't know so much about communism but I think Russia should be given a chance if the people are willing to go through the experience."

He expected, he told Fuller, "a period of criticism in American, something of an intellectual renaissance when people would be questioning everything about life," and he was looking forward to telling young college people about the part in this renaissance the country newspapers could take.

He was delighted, he wrote Eleanor, with the way the interview was "running over the country." The day after it appeared in the *Sun,* the *Roanoke Times* reprinted it in full and the day after that printed a two-column editorial, which was friendly, but it urged him to inquire more into improper political influence on the disbursement of county funds. He reprinted two-thirds of the interview and the complete editorial together with his own commentary in his papers; and most satisfactory of all, he began to get letters from young interested men, soon such a "flood" of them that he thought he should have a secretary for writing his replies. It was all good advertising for his lectures, Leigh having just written him that there was a good demand for them and that Anderson could take on as many as he wanted. He felt confident in the outlines of the overlapping lecture subjects he had sent to Leigh: "Women in Industry," on the effect of industrialism on the relationships between men and women; "The Machine," on the new world the machine had created; and "Newspapers," on the city dailies and the country weeklies. He would be willing to give his old lecture, updated, "America—A Storehouse of Vitality," and he especially wanted to speak on "Industries and Modern Machinery"; but he did not wish, he repeated, to lecture on literature at all. "Speaking about writing is a little bit too much like speaking publicly of the lady with whom you are in love." He had found at Danville that he enjoyed speaking on social and economic issues, at least while he was giving his speech; and his dropping of the "crazy book" at the end of January indicates how much his mind had become focused on these issues, how little for the most part on fiction.[9]

Feeling that under Eleanor's influence he was becoming "partly at least a man of action," he took the sleeper train to Richmond on February 2, carrying with him his favorite book of the moment, Charles and Mary Beard's *The Rise of American Civilization.* ("You get what you need," he would tell Eleanor, "A sense of the vast complication of it all. . . . Nearly everybody makes everything too simple.") He had hoped that the speech he had prepared for the next day's Institute luncheon, "Women in Southern Industry," adapted from the materials going into *Perhaps Women,* had "more form and guts," but in the morning he did not feel like speaking because of a cold. He trusted, however, that the crowd would excite him, "as crowds always do," and besides, as he would write to his brother just after returning to Marion, "In some queer way Karl I always see mother in these factory women and want to fight for them." The speech seems to have gone off at least satisfactorily. In celebration, while out walking, he succumbed to his desire for a "swank" grayish-green Burberry coat in the window of an expensive men's shop and went in and bought it. "I do so love my swank," he guiltily confessed to Eleanor.[10]

Despite his love for personal swank, he remained greatly concerned about the "rotten" situation for the impoverished workers in Danville now that the union leaders had ended the strike and "apparently just run out on them." Returning from Danville he had had the inspiration for a short story, "a pretty terrible one," and after seeing his factory women audience at Richmond, he began working on "The General Unafraid." It was to be an attack on the two powerful persons opposing the Danville strikers, the "son of a bitch who runs that paper down there" and especially the general commanding the National Guard troops, a character likewise based on an actual person, a man Anderson had just met at the Westmoreland Club, where he had stayed in Richmond, a man "drunk, and giving himself away terribly." Both newspaperman and general would be made "just what they are, rather nasty boys about twelve years old," the general's one thought, even when put to bed drunk, always being what a brave man he is. If he could keep the right "tone," Anderson asserted to Eleanor, "it will be the most effective possible anti-military propaganda" and would "make the strikers get something out of that mess yet." Perhaps there was more propaganda than "fancy" in the story, for he could not maintain the right tone; and after a few mornings when the writing did not go well, he abandoned his attempt "to get at the use of soldiers to bully workmen"—just as he had recently begun and dropped a novel based on the obsessive desire to own land he had observed in Mr. Copenhaver, a theme that would come to fruition two years later in one of his finest short stories, "Brother Death." Writing to John early in February, he admitted what was happening: "I guess it has become impossible for me to write anything now that hasn't social implications," meaning at this point yet another novel—just begun and quickly dropped—about an advertising man, which drew upon Anderson's as yet unused experience of painful memory in the business world. "It would be a rather terrible but just the same very American story." It was not simply that he was spending too much time on his public addresses; his imagination had not yet grasped a fiction sufficiently charged with what he had seen and had to say.[11]

Eleanor had long since become as necessary for his mind as for his body, and now he could be refreshed by her again. On February 12 he drove to Lynchburg, stayed overnight, and waited to pick her up from her morning train as arranged, though he did not "come down into the train shed, as there may be someone from Marion on the train." They drove south to Greensboro, North Carolina, where Eleanor was to attend a conference, and had two nights together at the King Cotton Hotel. He had accepted an invitation to speak at the Georgia Press Institute at the University of Georgia in Athens, and on the fifteenth, because of their "petty [need] to be so careful" about their relationship, he moved from Greensboro to the Hotel Robert E. Lee in nearby Winston-Salem, where he began working on the speech. Walking among that city's factories, he tentatively decided to finish the last half or more of *Perhaps Women*. He would work out more fully, he explained to Charles Bockler, the theme of "It's a Woman's Age," the article with which the first part of the book would conclude: the machine age is robbing men of their maleness, making them first spiritually, then physically impotent, whereas women, because they are physically creative in bearing children, are not robbed by the machine of their womanhood's strength. Men may well have to turn to women, crying to be saved since they cannot save themselves; women "may have to make the fight to get maleness back into the world." Anderson ended his summary to Bockler with an implied question: "I wonder if you think all this sound."[12]

Such a question suggested some tentativeness in his thinking, as though in reading the projected title *Perhaps Women*, the *Perhaps* should be emphasized. He had asserted to Charles his belief that long working hours and low pay were only "secondary" to "the great harm our present social structure does," that is, the "more subtle way" this structure robs men of their manhood. Yet he knew that the four-months-long Danville strike for union recognition had been called precisely for a desperate fight against long hours and a cut in already low wages; and he also knew from observation what years of demanding labor did to all but the strongest girls and women as well as boys and men. His theory grew from a more personal source than mere observation. That, as he told Karl, he saw their beloved mother in the factory women was the deepest part of that emotion-filled source, and another part, closer to the surface, was his attraction, vaguely sexual as it might be, to the fresh, sometimes lovely young mill girls with their eagerness for experience, this feisty aliveness, their excitement at gaining their first wages, however low, and their first sense of independence, however circumscribed, from the very bone-wearying jobs in which they would slowly lose their youth. But it was Eleanor who had persuaded him to go to the factories in the first place and with whom he had quickly fallen, more and more dependently, in love, and who was the immediate, most powerful part of his theory's source. Just about the time he wrote Bockler about his "hunch" that he would "return" to *Perhaps Women,* he wrote two letters to Eleanor almost paradigmatically condensing the emotion-thought behind "It's a Woman's Age" and *Perhaps Women* into comment on their personal relation. In the first, written on February 14 after the initial night with her in the King Cotton Hotel, he praises her body, in which there is "something" he trusts. She is to some extent confused by "reality," whereas he himself is "helpless in the face of so much reality." Does she "as a woman have any more real grasp of reality" than he has? If she does, he wants her to give it to him "As you would give milk to a child." He is the most inadequate man who ever lived, life is so short, there is "so little real poetry," everyone and everything "is so complicated," he has "muddied his own talents a lot"; in short, he has lost his manhood. (Possibly he had become unexpectedly impotent in their first night of lovemaking.) The second letter, written from Winston-Salem perhaps three days after their second night together, is completely different in tone. He has slept most unusually late this morning, which shows—he is in humorous good spirits rather than melancholy—that she is far better than aspirin for him. The closeness they have had has relieved the tension he feels when they are apart. There are "two beings, fighting in me," he goes on, "as in every man I suppose." One says give up and die; the other says go on "to the last inch . . . for the sake of life itself." Then he tells her happily: "It is this last person you have strengthened, made live, made stronger and younger. That is your comrade, your lover." In short, she— the woman—has restored his manhood and thereby his creativity as writer, as is confirmed by his having just written his Georgia Press Institute speech in two days of steady work. Essentially, then, the theory of *Perhaps Women* recounts his indebtedness to Eleanor for drawing him back into life. One should read that completed book, therefore, not just as sociological commentary, but as masked, symbolic autobiography, an addendum of sorts to *A Story Teller's Story.*[13]

2.

He took his good spirits with him to the University of Georgia. On the morning of February 20, his speech at the Georgia Press Institute urging the revitalization of the country weeklies "went big," and so many people wanted to hear him that he was moved from a small hall where the other speeches were given to a large packed one across the campus. Even more exciting was the stag dinner for thirty-five prominent state personages that evening, where he had "royal fun" defending Russia, its writers and its experiment with communism, so successfully that at the end of the evening the editor of the Atlanta *Journal,* "one of the most reactionary of them all," he proudly wrote Eleanor, toasted him and invited him to come to Atlanta as his guest. Elated, he was up at five the next morning in order to drive to Spartanburg, South Carolina, where he would store his car and catch a train for Marion, leaving time shortly before reaching Spartanburg for yet another lecture engagement in Greenville. Back in Marion, he worked on the first of his Northwestern lectures and pondered his new role as "a semi public figure." Giving oneself publicly was both "poison and health," he wrote Eleanor. Trying to escape from life was wrong, had been "one of the bitter mistakes of my life with Elizabeth"; yet public life would kill the poet in him and the "sensitive, determined, terrible sometimes" boy who lived in him along with the man. He must accept the public role but not let it "coarsen" him. In all things he must avoid "subtly trying to sell myself" and instead try, in Turgenev's beautiful unobtrusive manner, "to sell human life."

I am trying to get at a broad basis for anything I may do—in articles, speeches, stories. I can't be an economist, a politician, a thinker. I would like—always in a subtle way—to insist and insist on the human thing.

It seems to me that every good thing I do has that predominant in it.[14]

Happy at the opportunity to see Eleanor again so soon, he returned by train to Spartanburg on the twenty-fifth, picked up his car, and stayed overnight at the Cleveland Hotel in order to meet her the next day and drive her over to Rock Hill, South Carolina, where she had to attend a conference at Winthrop College. Holed up in the Andrew Jackson House at Rock Hill, he worked hard, probably on the Northwestern lectures but possibly on the second half of *Perhaps Women* as well. Eleanor had gone through her conference ill with flu but had recovered enough by the twenty-eighth to meet him at nearby Fort Mill, thus preserving their secrecy, and to drive with him through heavy rain back to Spartanburg and the next day to Atlanta. They had two nights together in hotels, "the sweetest time yet," he declared. Then on March 2, Eleanor headed west by train for more conferences in Tulsa and Houston while Sherwood set off in his little Chevrolet for Macon, where he had promised the year before to return when the peach trees were in bloom.[15]

He arrived in Macon that afternoon, registered again at the comfortable old Hotel Lanier on "broad leisurely" Mulberry Street, and, as a year earlier sporting his unMaconian "knotty black walking stick with a brass ferrule," went off to see last year's friends on the *Macon Telegraph*—the smart, mannish reporter Sue Myrick, the "keen intelligent" literary editor Aaron Bernd, staff member Ben Johnson, and editor Mark Ethridge, who had sided with him at the verbal free-for-all at the University of Georgia. The blackthorn was a sign of his exuberance, which in turn sparked exuberance in old and new companions. Acidly and approvingly, Myrick would record an anonymous comment: "'If he had never written a book in his life[,]' carolled an ebullient newspaper reporter (feminine), 'he would still be the most fascinating, genial, lovable, enthusiastic, friendly person in the whole wide world.'" He was the center of a social whirl. He dined the first night with the owner of the *Telegraph,* who later brought to his hotel room a gallon of fine whiskey; he was invited to a party at the home of Ethridge, who the next night gave a theater party in his honor; a wealthy lady held a huge reception for him in the former home of Sidney Lanier. He was a guest for dinner somewhere every evening. Afternoons were different. He spent several of them, Myrick would recall, "visiting with the Negro shopowners on 4th Street, listening to his favorite recordings, Cab Calloway, Fats Waller, Bessie Smith and the other Negroes popular in the 30s"; and Sunday afternoon before the reception he and a young Jewish businessman, "the most alive man" he had met in Macon, attended a footwashing at a black Primitive Baptist church, where "the swaying and singing and beautiful prayers" got to him "pretty hard." Perhaps most of all he enjoyed driving out into the countryside with Sue or Aaron Bernd or by himself. The peach orchards were coming into bloom, and he was passionately excited by the acres and acres of delicate pink blossoms, "a swimming sea of color" punctuated by the white spires of pear trees against the blood red of Georgian earth. Whether Eleanor would marry him or another, he wrote in his longing for her, he was certain that his response to nature, color, "all feeling for life" was much richer and more varied than that of other men.[16]

Mornings as always he kept for his writing. At first he worked on the Northwestern lectures, but on March 5, he abruptly went "as deeply as [he] could" into deciding which published articles and drafts of a night visit to a Southern cotton mill should make up a *Perhaps Women* volume and sent them off to be typed for final revision. Then he wrote Julius Lankes asking whether the Virginian artist could provide a woodcut and also could persuade the Ohio artist Charles Burchfield to provide a drawing to illustrate this "queer book," both illustrations to portray the author, not as "an American artist, striving to be of his day and time, a bold strong figure," but rather as a small, shrinking man standing in shadow before a hugely looming cotton mill at night, the suggestion to be "the impotence of so much of modern manhood compared with the potence of womanhood." (Burchfield emphatically declined to be involved since, "something of a puritan" in sexual matters, he had decided that *Many Marriages* proved its author to be obsessed with sex; but Lankes provided a woodcut illustrating Anderson's theme in an entirely different way.) On or about the same day when he had "brought the *Perhaps Women* to a definite head," he received an invitation to give, for a fee of four hundred dollars, the three William Vaughn Moody lectures at the University of Chicago while he was at Northwestern giving the Harris Lectures. He accepted, and putting off further work on *Perhaps Women* temporarily, he went at once into preparing the first of the Moody lectures with the notion that he could use these three lectures on the circuits Leigh was setting up for him.[17]

As his crammed week in Macon drew toward an end, he came down briefly with the flu. Perhaps as a result of his own illness, his initial attempt at the first Moody lecture "exploded in [his] hands" on Sunday the eighth, and he got through the afternoon's reception feeling "like a piece of stone on a seashore." He responded enthusiastically enough, however, to a "lovely" article in the Sunday *Telegraph,* "The Art of Sherwood Anderson," by Joseph Robinson, a professor at Macon's Mercer University, who praised him for his devotion to craftsmanship, his eye for flashes of beauty in American life, his Whitmanesque spirit of democracy, and his ability to inspire affection in those he met. By the following day his flu was mostly gone, he was succeeding better with the first Moody lecture, and finishing or nearly finishing a "Traveler's Notes" piece for the *Smyth County News* describing both the beauty of the peach orchards and the harsh lives of black and poor white tenant farmers, whose terrible poverty he had learned about from talking with a number of them during his drives into the countryside. But he did not, until later, fulfill a promise to Aaron Bernd.[18]

While the literary editor was driving him back to his hotel from the Sunday reception, Anderson spotted on the car seat a copy of Beril Becker's biography, *Paul Gauguin, The Calm Madman,* which Bernd was to review. Anderson insisted on borrowing it, promising to return it the next day or review it himself. He did not return it, read it on his way to New Orleans, somehow lost it; only after Bernd wrote him requesting the book, Anderson sent back nearly a month late what appears a hastily written review. The book "wipes out all the Moon and Sixpence cheapness,"— twelve years of experience had changed his attitude toward Maugham's novel—and shows the close, difficult relationship of Gauguin and Vincent Van Gogh to be "one of the great modern stories" now that "men have forgotten how to love each other."

The book is the story of the life of a man who believed in life and fought bitterly to make it taste sweet in his mouth and other people's mouths. He lost out, of course.

Although he had recently declared himself on Van Gogh's side rather than Gauguin's, Anderson still, if in a different way from twelve years before, read Gauguin's life as a mirror of his own.[19]

On March 10, still dopey with the flu, he drove a long way, going directly south into Florida and then west to Pensacola, passing first through the blooming peach orchards around Macon, where the landscape had "that light, floating quality you get in Chinese painting," then on to the Georgia cotton fields and mill towns, and finally through the turpentine forests of the Florida panhandle, where he had once paused for some time, reading *Paul Gauguin* and listening to the sweet singing of black workers gathering sap from the pines. The cotton fields and mill towns and cities he would soon write about for the *Smyth County News*—the squalor and misery in which the tenant farmers and sharecroppers lived, "hundreds of thousands" of them earning "less than eighty dollars a year"; the cotton mills creating wealth for the owners and the towns, thanks to the low wages paid the poor white workers, better though such pay was than cotton-field earnings; the child labor both on farms and in mills; the contempt of townspeople for the "lint heads" segregated into mill villages at the edges of towns or cities. Whether he was as yet conscious of it or not, what he outlined in the article was about to provide the setting of a novel, one he would actually complete.[20]

From Pensacola the next day he drove the short distance to Mobile, left his car, took the boat across the Mobile Bay to Fairhope, and spent the afternoon with Letty Esherick and her two children—his painter friend Wharton was off in the North—walking on the beach as he had so often done eleven years before. After staying overnight at the Esherick house, he took the boat back to Mobile, got his car, and drove on to New Orleans. Registering at his favorite hotel, the Monteleone, he "renewed friendships" that evening, the twelfth. He had "no particular purpose" in visiting New Orleans, he blandly told a *Times-Picayune* reporter, only that he liked the city; but two days later as arranged he picked up Eleanor, whose Houston conference was over, and drove her, apparently, to yet another conference at Montgomery, Alabama. Enlivened as usual by being near her, he wrote his travel notes on the human effects of Georgia's cotton economy and began his final push at finishing *Perhaps Women*. When her conference was finished, they had six days of living closely together in their own "little world," which seemed to him as real as the world outside. On March 22, he drove her to Knoxville, Tennessee, and after an evening of passionate lovemaking, put her on a night train to her next commitment. For the first time, he would write her the next day, he sensed that she at last loved him enough to marry him. This assertion may well have been another mode of pleading on his part, for she would not consent to marriage for two more years; but it was an assertion connecting a peak in their relationship with an unstated breakthrough in creativity. On the day after he put her on the train and drove back to the Hotel Arnold a "little crazy" with joy and longing, he put in "a good morning of work" before heading for Marion. During that time his public and private interests and emotions meshed in the conception of a new novel under the old title *Beyond Desire,* a novel about a young middle-class man in a Southern mill town who is drawn toward the despised lintheads in the mill village and, when they strike, is drawn toward political radicalism. "I think I have got on something there at Knoxville," he wrote Eleanor after his return to Marion, "that will be closer to everything I feel now than I have found in years. It may be what I have been wanting for so long." Then he immediately made the personal connection.

I always seem to move nearer when I am where you are. Everything I have done for nearly two years I haven't wanted to destroy has had you in it. I feel well-being when I am near you. It is good to live when you are near. Do you wonder I love you.[21]

3.

Much had been happening in Marion during his absence. A couple had driven through town, abandoned their baby there, and although the woman later returned for it, she was, to Anderson's disgust, immediately put in jail; a youth had shot his father dead in a "minor quarrel"; much more happily, the new school for black children was at last being built. Bob and his Adelaide were definitely breaking up, and he had already become interested in Mary Chryst, a small, alert, forthright woman, a teacher of English at Marion College. "In a Strange Town" had been sold for English publication for fifty-four dollars, a welcome sum since Anderson had had only twenty-five dollars left on his return from his travels, and there was the continued flood of mail from young men and women excited by "The Country Weekly" in *Forum and Century,* such a flood that he was sure he had "started something."[22]

Feeling sometimes filled with "inner health" and "manhood" because of Eleanor, other times, when lonely for her or the writing went badly, "just a lost thing floating in some queer kind of emptiness," he pushed himself at several projects—two traveler's notes for the *Smyth County News,* the revision of *Perhaps Women,* the lectures for Northwestern and Chicago, and soon the new *Beyond Desire* novel, which by April 7 he could write V. F. Calverton he was "up to my eyes" in. He worried as to whether *Perhaps Women* should be published, wrote to Lankes that he might not release it, and urged Eleanor that she and her mother look at the manuscript and give judgment during the three days she was about to have at home. In preparation for meeting her train at Knoxville, probably on March 31, and driving her to Marion, he had talked to Andy Funk, who had assured him that he could easily obtain a divorce from Elizabeth, probably in October. With Eleanor nearby, he would declare that it was "all one, touching you and touching the paper here"; and the flow of his writing continued. Still, it was awkward seeing her at Rosemont. Her parents, whom he had by now told that he and Eleanor were in love, were uneasy that the relationship might go too far; even the sympathetic mother, Anderson had written Eleanor, fearing at times that her beloved daughter was infatuated with "some sort of wild man." Her parents lived in a conventional world "like all people not wanting to be disturbed," while she, no longer their child or a model Southern lady, was a grown woman whose true friends were labor people. As for himself, he asserted with some grandiloquence:

My world is my own world. It is, dear, an old and an honorable one. It has nothing to do with respectability, the old South, ladies and gentlemen, etc. I belong with Turgenev, Balzac, Cézanne, Rembrandt.

There's a long list. As an artist I always have been in the tradition. Men like me have gone on for hundreds of years, adding some of us a lot, some of us a very little. If we add anything sound, we belong. I have added sound things. There is work of mine as solid as a rock.

Here, he emphasized to Eleanor, lay "the inner secret of my manhood," that manhood she had given back to him. Ultimately, one realizes, he meant not sexual potency nor "manliness" nor even "maturity" but rather his dedication to being the artist creator of sound work. As with the old writer in the introductory sketch of *Winesburg, Ohio,* that was the young thing inside him that saved him from becoming his own kind of grotesque.[23]

Lovemaking in conventional Marion had to be even more furtive than usual; but probably before Eleanor left on April 3, he knew that in a week she would be in Winston-Salem and they could be together again safely. Apparently she had found time during her brief vacation to read through his *Perhaps Women* typescript and approve it. In a lyrical letter of April 5, he first described a readily interpretable erotic dream in which he had taken away from her father's car wreck the father's companion, "a little slim working girl," who turned into Eleanor and with whom he made love undisturbed on a silent sandy island. He concluded the letter by telling her that he wanted the book to be "a kind of tribute" to her, but not actually a tribute, rather a book "written for you." Nevertheless he felt uneasy about the book, for on the seventh he wrote Paul Rosenfeld that he had it "ready for the press, but rather tremble to let go of it. It seems rather a half-formed thing." It was not until he had gone to meet Eleanor at Winston-Salem, appropriately the industrial city where two months earlier he had tentatively decided to write the remainder of the book, that he mailed the manuscript to Liveright, probably on April 10. That left him free to write the last of his three lectures (he had decided to give the same three for both the Harris and the Moody series since he would address separate audiences), to work on *Beyond Desire,* and to have sweeter hours than ever with Eleanor, he felt, idyllically by a brook in a spring wood among yellow violets.[24]

Absorbed in memories of these hours, he drove back to Marion, on the twelfth "in a queer sort of daze." He spent the following day working on what he now called "our novel" and dictating answers to many of the letters prompted by "The Country Weekly." Then on the morning of April 14, he set off in his car for a leisurely four-day drive to Chicago by way of Indianapolis. There he had lunch with Bab Finley, now Mrs. Vernon Hahn, and an early dinner with her and her young doctor husband, whom she obviously loved. Marriage, he decided, had been good for her, made her "nicer," although he thought the doctor "rather self-satisfied" and both of them "rather foolishly opinionated." There would be no more stopovers for him in Indianapolis to see Bab.[25]

Arriving in Chicago at sunset on April 17, he took a room with a view on the seventh floor of the Hotel Flamingo on the South Side, began making connection with Mimi, the Sergels and the Schevills, and settled down for two days of final polishing of his three lectures as concisely outlined under the general title of "American Journalism and Our Rural Communities":

1. Personal experiences in publishing and editing small town papers.
2. The coming of the machine age. Its effect on the work of every newspaper man.
3. What has happened to our country newspapers. Effect of modern industrialism. An opportunity lost that can be regained. The country weeklies as social agencies.

The first lecture he gave at Northwestern, on the evening of the twentieth, "went off gorgeously," he reported to Eleanor. Despite rain, the audience, mostly students, was so large that the lecture had to be moved from a hall seating some three hundred to one seating hundreds more; nevertheless he felt a closeness between himself and his eager listeners, and he realized that he enjoyed talking about newspapers instead of literature since this subject and questions about it did not "invade the inner life" of his writing and of his love for Eleanor. The following evening, the audience at Northwestern had grown half again in size for his lecture containing "the most dynamite" in its attack on the destructive effects of industrialism on factory workers as well as on newspaper people, an attack that also included a defense, though not an advocacy, of communism. On the twenty-second at four thirty in the afternoon, he repeated his first lecture at the University of Chicago for the Moody series, his old friend and supporter Robert Morss Lovett introducing him, as Schevill was to do for the second lecture. The capacity audience of "alive young men and women" students, he now reported, was "grand" and his "talk went with a swing." His hardest day came on the twenty-third when he gave his second Chicago lecture in the late afternoon and his third Northwestern one in the evening before a huge audience, which he jubilantly estimated at "perhaps 1500 to 1800." The twenty-fourth was an easy day, for he had only to repeat his third lecture at Chicago, where he felt that the audience, restricted to students, was even more responsive than the mixed one at Northwestern to his "general philosophy of smallness as an ideal rather than bigness." Perhaps he was influenced by being told at Northwestern that there were no funds left to print his lectures and then being informed by a skeptical young professor that the real reason for not printing them was that they contained "Too much dynamite." Still, he had a "nice feeling" that at both universities the lectures had gone well.[26]

A reporter who heard Anderson's "dynamite" lecture at Northwestern and afterward interviewed him gave a detailed impression of the writer, now aged fifty-four, and of his lecturing manner. "He is rugged, husky, erect and brown as you would expect a lover of the outdoors to be. He stands at about average height and must weigh two hundred pounds." A "friendly, a very genial man," he had an "open and engaging . . .

smile. . . . A moment ago the face was that dark somewhat brooding one you have seen in pictures." When he smiles, it is different.

Last night Mr. Anderson wore a loose suit of a rough brown material that looked English and expensive, a blue shirt, a dark gray raglan topcoat and a light, almost white cloth hat. He carried a stick that seemed to have been made for him. It was straight, fairly slender, knotted and covered with the natural bark.

You get a feeling of youth and vitality in Mr. Anderson. He seems to be no particular age, though there is considerable iron-gray in the shock of windblown hair that swirls across his head and swoops down over his brow.

When he steps on the lecture platform, however, he looks a little older, partly because he puts on a pair of black, shell-rimmed spectacles and bends forward slightly as he speaks so that his body sags a little and his neck becomes fleshy. And when he speaks the quality of his voice varies deceptively. Now it is strong, young, vibrant, rhythmic; now, uncontrolled, a little shrill, with what you might call a rustic quality, punctuated with a chuckle you would expect to hear around the stove of a country store. He pronounces "further," as "futher"; "were," "ware"; "nothing," "nothun"; "am," "em"; "almost," "a-most"; and "either," "ither."

Off the platform, though, much of his deliberate, homely quality vanishes and Mr. Anderson is young again, witty, vital, well-poised and quite a little urbane.[27]

From the pressure of the six presentations and of the lunches, dinners, parties that surrounded them, Anderson, despite "vitality," had begun to have something like the painful headaches he had had the previous summer during his beach vacation with Eleanor; but a doctor in one visit "cured" him of "a slight [head] infection" and assured him that he was generally as strong as a horse. The rest of his stay in Chicago was equally cheering. Tom Smith at Liveright's telegraphed that *Perhaps Women* would be published; he dined with the Sergels and Mimi, who was working hard at the University of Chicago and looking "very charming"; he met her "young man," Russell Spear, whom she would later marry; and on his last day he lunched for three hours with old newspaper friends at Schlogl's round table. One of the men present recalled his tweed suit, blue shirt and "coral colored tie," his "powerful hands," and his "clear, sometimes dreamy eyes, [which] flattered you by their attention when he spoke to you, or you to him. During most of the lunch Anderson held forth on the Marion papers, country newspapers, and the argument of *Perhaps Women*." Another listener recalled with amusement that Anderson "became so enthusiastic in what he was saying about women that he lost his balance and fell off his chair," picked himself up agilely, and "kept right on talking as if nothing had happened."[28]

On the twenty-sixth he picked up John, who had been living in Chicago, and the two drove to Michigan City, Indiana, for an overnight visit with the Schevills in their house sheltered by a sand dune from the "sea," as Anderson usually called Lake Michigan. For once on visiting them, he was in good spirits rather than despondent. The next day father and son drove to Clyde, where they called on people Anderson had known, particularly his "own special boy friend," Herman Hurd, now the owner of Hurd's grocery and grown fat. They stayed overnight at the Hurds' after Anderson had nostalgically showed John around what he called his "native land," concluding after his many years away that

> The town is very pretty and it's now spring green and has changed little. Fortunately it is one of the towns that has not succeeded industrially. My own fancy . . . has played over and about it so much that it seems all unreal to me.

Leaving Clyde they drove south to Charleston, West Virginia, where by arrangement with Tom Tippett they met and talked with striking coal miners, one of the men guiding them for an afternoon "up strange terrible (hollers) as they call them, where the miners live." Since he sympathized with the strikers, Anderson accepted the fact that Tippett was using him for publicity purposes with the newspaper reporters covering the strike; for his own purposes he was using the strike to get a closer feel for such conflicts into *Beyond Desire*. By the evening of April 30 father and son were in Marion.[29]

But in Marion he could not get back to the novel. Nervous, tense, restless, he found excuses. He was "frightened" by the great accumulation of mail to be answered, including yet more letters prompted by "The Country Weekly"; with both John and Bob in town he must seize the chance to develop greater brotherliness between them; a long telegram from Maurice Long announcing a "yearning for his society" meant that he should visit Long in Washington. What he really wanted was to live for a month in a New Jersey industrial town to get in the mood for *Beyond Desire* and to be near enough to Eleanor to see her frequently in New York since she was essential to his writing well. On May 6, he and John drove north through miles and miles of blossoming dogwood, reaching Washington and Maurice's spacious Rhode Island Avenue house by mid-evening. For two days John visited art galleries while Anderson and Long talked companionably, and on the ninth father and son drove on to Bel Air, where John dropped off to spend the summer painting with Charles Bockler. Then Anderson returned to Baltimore to meet Eleanor and her mother at a warm, pleasant Copenhaver get-together at the home of Eleanor's sister May ("Mazie") Copenhaver Wilson and her husband Channing. On the eleventh, he drove Eleanor to Philadelphia to catch a train to one of her endless YWCA meetings, went on to Elizabeth, New Jersey, a half hour from Manhattan, registered at the Elizabeth Carteret Hotel under the name simply of "S. Anderson," and immediately began writing on *Beyond Desire* "better," he declared, "than I have any time yet."[30]

His sleep that night was made restless by opposing sets of dreams echoing two of his long-held, often expressed symbolic groupings. One set was of seeing "a new kind of sales machine" smashed in a revolt, of hearing a distant roar "as of a thousand factories being destroyed": the other, a "lovely" set, was of beautiful horses racing, "and suddenly you knew that all the drivers were cheats and liars and that the horses weren't." It was as though the complex of dreams were a first unconscious sorting-out for his creative imagination of the materials and shape of *Beyond Desire;* for as he worked steadily the next few days, a form for his novel began to come clearer to him, one related to the book he knew to have been his best.

> It has come into my head [he wrote Eleanor] that what I am attempting really is something like this—a series of what are practically short novels, all built upon people whose lives touch one person—that red-haired young Communist who is killed later in a strike.
>
> You know how *Winesburg* was built up so, out of short stories—all about the figure of George Willard. Red Oliver should occupy something of the same position in this book—or it may be series of books.

The village—the sense of which I tried to give in *Winesburg*—was comparatively simple.

I want to give the impression of something infinitely more complex—modern
life—

Its queer mixtures and futilities now.

It was "a terribly ambitious plan," he continued—"a group of large forms
making up a larger form." Being with Eleanor from time to time would
give him courage to carry it out.[31]

He did see Eleanor fairly frequently for a brief exciting meeting or a
passionate night together when her busy schedule allowed it. Any writing
talent he might have he wanted her to consider hers as well; for as he had
written her earlier from Chicago of *Beyond Desire*: "You happen to be the
father and I the mother in this case. You impregnated me. You are always
doing it." Her "warm out-going energy" was health to him, quieted him,
a fault of his being that "I do force my stroke" in his eagerness "for all
sweetness, all life, all sounds, sights, tastes, smells." When her duties kept
them apart, he relived his own steady intense routine by sometimes going
to see a few other people in New York. He checked out lecture arrangements with Colston Leigh; he called on Alfred Stieglitz at An American
Place and admired an exhibit of Arthur Dove's paintings; he went to the
Liveright offices where everyone was enthusiastic about his plan for *Beyond Desire*, and he readily obtained a thousand dollars advance on it. On
the night of the fifteenth he dined at a speakeasy with Paul Rosenfeld and
then went to a party at Paul's apartment, where two of the other guests
were Edmund and Margaret Wilson. He was delighted to observe their
close relationship, "like two friends," and to talk with Edmund. A month
earlier Anderson had been "deeply stirred" by Wilson's article "Detroit
Motors" in the *New Republic* (for March 25), which first describes the
processes by which massive yet intricate machines produce automobiles,
and then quotes workers' monologues on how the machines and the company managers victimize them. In the longest, climactic monologue, a
Scots-born worker declares that "What we ought to have here is a revolutionary movement geared into the peculiar needs of the American wor-
rukers," one which could be led by the Communists, provided that they
learn "to talk the language of the American worruker." Anderson had
been grateful when Wilson sent him a copy of the article since, he replied,
"I want to refer to it in the story of a young communist I'm working on."
At that time he had "about decided" that Rosenfeld's and Wilson's minds
were "the two minds that my mind most admires." Wilson and his articles
must be counted among the influences moving Anderson slowly toward
his radical gesture of the following year.[32]

Two days after the party, Rosenfeld met Anderson at his hotel in the morning, and the two men spent the day driving the side roads among the spring-blooming hills near the Delaware Water Gap, talking about the early "robin's egg" cultural renaissance of the 1910s broken by the War and prosperity, and about their relations with women. When Anderson told him about Eleanor, the perceptive Rosenfeld understood at once her effect on him as man and writer: "'The Cotton Mill Thing,' he said—'she made that grow in you.'" The day had reestablished their male mind-love for each other, Anderson felt, which had been interrupted when he went "dead" from depression at the end of the 1920s. Repeatedly Rosenfeld told him that "it was the best day out of doors he'd ever had."[33]

A less satisfactory occasion was his speech on May 21 at Purdue University, where he went by train that day. He had not prepared a lecture and instead only entertained his audience with stories about the building of Ripshin and the editing of the papers. He felt ashamed that he had given so little to the students, who, though mostly future scientists and engineers, seemed to him like other students he had been talking to "to have suddenly lost all faith in our competitive, individualistic civilization." Back in New Jersey, he had to face his realization that in the remaining week's time he could not finish book one of *Beyond Desire* as in his usual overoptimistic way he had determined to do. He had already begun having bad days when he tore up what he had written or could not write at all. His prose seemed to him flat, did not "sing" as, he explained to Eleanor, good prose must.

> Prose is a complex thing. It should always, dear, have music in it but the music should not be obvious. I think it would always be better if, in as far as a man is a poet, he hide the fact. The important thing is the poetry not the poet. That is the real glory of prose . . . that down inside these slowly marching lines a man may, occasionally when no one is watching, plant a bit of poetry. It should be like Johnny Appleseed, walking through the wilderness, planting here and there an apple tree to bloom and bear fruit maybe after he is dead.

Living closer to Eleanor might help, and fortunately Burton Emmett invited him to spend at least the night of the nineteenth at Burton and Mary's townhouse in Washington Mews just off Fifth Avenue between Eighth Street and Washington Square, near Eleanor's apartment. This was the first of many times that he and later Eleanor would occupy this "most elegant place imaginable" with rooms filled with the modern paintings and rare prints Emmett had collected. But he and Eleanor had only one brief meeting, and the month was up. On the thirtieth he set off south in his car. By the time he reached Washington, however, he was ill with ulcers in his throat, which brought on an attack of lumbago. After a day or two in bed at Maurice Long's, he managed to leave Washington for Marion on June 2 and by the next day was home recovering. On the morning of the fifth he was at his desk, clearing it of correspondence so that he could get back to *Beyond Desire*.[34]

Perhaps because he would be seeing Eleanor again soon, perhaps also because he looked forward to a visit from Edmund Wilson on his way to West Virginia to cover the miners' strike for *The New Republic,* he went at once "on a grand writing drunk" with the novel. On June 10 he drove Eleanor to Black Mountain, North Carolina, and the following day, after a night together, they drove to nearby Blue Ridge for her first summer-camp assignment. Having rented an "ugly" room in a Black Mountain boarding house, he went back to *Beyond Desire,* more and more convinced as he wrote that revolutionary change would have to come "in the communists' way." On the fifteenth after a morning's writing, he drove back to Marion, found that proofs for *Perhaps Women* had arrived, and welcomed Wilson for his overnight visit. From the intense, constant conversation of the two men, Bob concluded that both were "just about gone straight communist." Shortly after he left the following day, Wilson in a letter to John Dos Passos commented more fully on his host's state of mind.

I found Sherwood Anderson all full of Communism. He doesn't know much about it, but the idea has given him a powerful afflatus. He has a new girl, a radical Y.W.C.A. secretary, who took him around to the mills. He is writing a novel with a Communist hero and I have never seen him so much aroused.

Recognizing that he did not know much about communism, Anderson had asked Wilson to recommend books he should read. He bought "books on Lenin, Stalin, etc." and certainly read in them; but typically he found the biographies of the Soviet leaders "impersonal . . . mak[ing] them seem hardly human." Probably more than the books, Wilson's conversation had convinced him that for a Communist Party to succeed in the United States it must have American members and an American Lenin, must "have its roots in the ground here too." Certainly Wilson's visit had made him "tremendously interested" in going to see what was happening in the Soviet Union.[35]

Having taken Wilson to his train, Anderson was free to work. On June 19 he began the last chapter of the novel's book one, titled "Youth," which deals with the early years of Red Oliver, his "communist hero." The next day he completed reading and mailed to Liveright the proofs of *Perhaps Women.* Lankes had just sent him a sketch of the block print that would be used as frontispiece of the book, and, cropped, as illustration on the dust jacket. It shows a determined-looking woman in trim riding habit sitting astride a powerful horse, which she is walking away from a background of factory buildings below her. In her left hand she firmly holds the horse's reins; in her right she holds as firmly the reins of a mule smaller than the horse and in poorer condition. A man with somewhat slumped shoulders and a worried face sits awkwardly on the led mule, both hands grasping the saddle. In all ways the woman on her horse dominates the print, mule, and man. Perhaps, one may infer from the book, she might be leading the man toward a regained manhood, but the print itself provides no such inference. In sending Eleanor the sketch on the twentieth, Anderson thought it "fine." His back no longer hurt him, he wrote, and he felt confident about *Beyond Desire;* but as though responding to the print showing strong woman and weak man, he confessed that he got "such an ugly feeling of being lost from you . . . as though a part of myself were away off, floating in the air somewhere."[36]

Restless, wanting to be nearer Eleanor though he would still be over a hundred miles away, he drove to Linville in northwest North Carolina on the twenty-first at the invitation of Kirk Rankin, a former friend now grown rich from business enterprises. Although he found Rankin and his wife Sue charming, he could not write about Red Oliver in the room they had carefully provided. They and their friends had, he felt, "chucked" human values too often in making money, and like other wealthy people, with the exception of Emmett and Long, had subtly contaminated for him the atmosphere of their houses now that he was "coming to believe, that, by some method the whole capitalist system must be scrapped." By June 27 he had returned to Marion and was working so intensely that he had written some eighty typed pages and was estimating that a hundred more would finish the "first book," an estimate indicating that he was then planning to include in what became "Youth" much material later placed in the other three "books" of the published novel.[37]

Unlike the drought of the previous July, July 1931 brought such heavy rains that the farmers could not work the sodden fields, and Sherwood and Eleanor, who had the month off in Marion, had few opportunities for lovemaking out in the countryside as they preferred. Nevertheless, he worked steadily on *Beyond Desire* except for a period of ten days or more when both of them were shaken by the unexpected serious, near-fatal illness of Eleanor's mother. Anderson had long been "tremendously fond" of Laura Lu and considered her one of his few close friends in town. In their many conversations they occasionally differed, sometimes sharply as on the value of her membership in the Daughters of the American Revolution, which he once denounced—and later humbly apologized for his extravagant language—as an "evil" group of snobs. Most of the time, however, they greatly enjoyed their talks, and he knew that he could now be open with her about Eleanor's growing love for him while insisting that he recognized her Copenhaver loyalties as well and had no wish to hurt any members of her family. He was, he admitted, "unconsciously pleading" with Laura Lu to be wholly and not just partially on his side in an awkward, unresolved situation.[38]

Presumably he confided to his future mother-in-law one way in which the situation was being slowly clarified, the matter of a divorce from Elizabeth, who wrote him on July 23 "that she had no intention of ever living with [him] again." Probably she was replying to a letter from him designed to obtain such a flat statement; but even so, he did not want to take the usual step of placing a statement of a divorce suit against her in the newspapers. According to Burt Dickinson, who would eventually devise an unusual, less public method of initiating divorce proceedings for him, he apparently felt that a third divorce "wasn't funny," and he was sensitive to what Marion people might think of their editor in an era when even one divorce was sufficiently scandalous. Burt Dickinson would not think of this method until December.[39]

As far as work on *Beyond Desire* went, much of August was a lost month. After he and Eleanor had spent the weekend of August 1 and 2 together, possibly in Charlottesville, she had taken a train for New York, and he had driven back to Marion in a "crazy rush" through a wild rainstorm. Bob was already off to pick up Mimi for a two-week vacation in northern Michigan, and since Anderson had to get out the papers, he had little time or inclination to work on "Red." Out of loneliness for Eleanor he accepted an invitation from the Joseph Robinsons of Mercer University, now summering in Boone, North Carolina, to spend the weekend of the eighth and ninth with them, but in a blue mood he found them much less interesting than he had in Macon back in March. He had hoped to see Eleanor the next weekend at a meeting she was attending in Gastonia, North Carolina, where a textile strike had broken out. He wanted, too, more direct observation of the strike, both through her eyes as well as his own to give life to his book; but his friend Louis Jaffé, editor of the Norfolk *Virginian-Pilot*, was due to visit him that weekend, and Bob and Mimi were also arriving. At least at the moment he had ample money for a stay near Eleanor in New York; an unexpected two hundred dollars in royalties had come in from Viking Press for his books Huebsch had published, and he now had "about $1,300 and all debts paid." Further, Colston Leigh was urging him to take on lectures on the West Coast in addition to his tour to the Southwest in early 1932, and he had decided to accept them since extra fees might take him and Eleanor to Russia. So, eager to "feel the city" with Eleanor and to talk over with her the first book of *Beyond Desire* he had sent her to read, hopeful that he would get back into the mood for the novel when he was near her, he set off on the nineteenth for New York. His four days with Eleanor were "a gorgeous time"; the fourth day, Sunday the twenty-third, "specially stood out as a kind of jewel like day, every hour precious"; yet mornings he wrote little or nothing on the novel in his hotel room. Nor did he write during his subsequent visit to Maurice Long, for the two good friends spent their time walking for miles in the woods around the simple, inexpensive, tasteful house Maurice had built on his farm near Ashton, Maryland, "exactly" Anderson declared, "the kind of house that might be built especially under communism." By noon of the twenty-sixth he was again in Marion and ready, he felt, to "soon really swing into the book of Red." At the end of the month he had begun work on the second book of the novel, but on the last morning of August was worrying that he could not "quite get hold of the mill girls, Doris, Grace, Nell and Fanny. It seems as though I were in the mill myself, too close to them."[40]

To the contrary, this second book, "Mill Girls," would become the best section of *Beyond Desire* precisely because, one suspects, while writing it he could with his empathic imagination be in the mill himself, "too close to them." Here, his imagination worked so creatively because he had observed mill girls through Eleanor's eyes as well as his own; their limited but vaguely desiring lives were suffused by Eleanor's devotion to easing and awakening them as well as by his love and need for her, the unnamed woman in *Perhaps Women* who had brought him back to life.

4.

Published on September 15, *Perhaps Women* by rights should have been dedicated to Eleanor, though its dedication, "To Maurice Long," would in a way turn out to be fortunate. Anderson's long uneasiness about his "little book" is reflected in the two concerns expressed in his brief introduction: that the book is only "an impression, a sketch" to which he wishes he could have given "better form," and his hope that his message will at least arouse thought, discussion, and "real fear and perhaps respect for the machine." As to form, each of the four pieces making up the first, shorter part of the book—"Machine Song," "Lift Up Thine Eyes," "Loom Dance," and "It Is a Woman's Age"—has the form of separate inspiration and publication: a kind of prose poem or "broken verse," description of a process-driven automobile assembly plant, an incident of rebellion in a cotton mill, a personal essay. The longer final part strings together its eight variously titled sections, three of them "Perhaps Women," along a narrative line of a night visit by Anderson to a South Carolina cotton mill, a line frequently interrupted by brief or extended declarations, often rambling, on the theme he had outlined to Charles Bockler and others but here much elaborated.

That theme begins with the observation that America is well into a machine age, which has profoundly affected economic, social, and personal relationships. The machines, efficient and often beautiful in themselves and in their orderly activity, produce floods of goods, needed or not, which are sold by "publicity" (advertising). Men, specifically men, are awed by the machines and have come to worship them and their power as a new god. They try to assume that power vicariously by purchasing goods such as automobiles but inevitably fail; for machines are not only "labor-saving" and put men out of work but, to Anderson, at a deeper level they awe men into first spiritual and ultimately physical impotence. Women, on the other hand, have a fundamentally different relationship with the machines. They of course purchase goods, as "It Is a Woman's Age" emphasizes, but women factory workers, though they may be half in love with the machines they attend, are not in awe of them. Because they are inherently creative with their bodies, can bear children, they may be tired physically by machine work but escape spiritual impotence. It is up to women, therefore, to control the threat of the machines and to restore physical and spiritual potency to men.

For a decade and a half Anderson had frequently maintained that impotence characterized the times, but if one returns to the narrative line of this longer section of *Perhaps Women,* one sees how much his theme, though to some extent based on observation, is an extrapolation from recent personal experience. The narrative begins with his self-confidently persuading a cotton mill owner to let him enter his mill at 2 AM and observe the night shift at work with the machines. That evening, however, as he walks toward the mill gate along the unpaved street of the mill village, barked at by dogs and with the red mud covering his shoes as he goes, he sees—or imagines he sees, for he has "preconceived ideas in [his] head"— a disturbing "grotesque," a hulking, stoop-shouldered figure whom he takes to be emblematic of all American men made impotent by the factory machines. As he and this illusory figure approach the gate, two "erect straight young" mill girls pass laughing, laughing perhaps at the figure and at himself standing like Charlie Chaplin's little tramp. He is further humiliated when he slips and falls into the mud and must clean off his clothes as well as he can with his handkerchief. At the factory gate he is met by a young mill superintendent who is as cold and impersonal, as dedicated to the worship of the machines as a young Communist. Thereupon in a flashback he recalls his past as a writer repeatedly telling to the point of weariness "the story of failure," a time when he had tried to flee the machine, at least not taking refuge in Europe but retreating "from the city to the town, from the town to the farm." There a woman (unnamed but obviously Eleanor) insists that he come out from hiding and go to the factories, where the "new age is to be worked out." Back in the present of this night visit—"Night is the time of love, of strange thoughts, of dreams"—he and his guide enter the mill. Arriving in the great weaving room, he is fascinated by the row after row of machines "going at terrific speed." As he steps onto a small raised platform by himself to watch the men and women working the machines, something in the women seeming to him "still alive," something in the men "going dead," the lights in the great room all suddenly go out, though the machines do not stop. Above their roar, he hears a woman laugh like "a young girl," and call out, "Kiss me while the lights are out." A chorus of male voices respond wearily, "Me? Me? Me?" But the woman's voice replies:

> "No, not you. None of you."
> "I want a man," the girl's voice said. It was a clear young voice.
> There is a burst of laughter from the women, and then the lights come on. Afterward the superintendent explains to Anderson that the women do that sort of thing often.
> "Why?"
> "Oh, they are making fun of the men," he said coldly enough.

So the book ends with an exemplum of how the power of women, a personal power operating "directly on others" in human relations, "is a power the machine cannot touch"—as Eleanor's power had operated on Sherwood to rescue him from spiritual impotence.

Anderson's argument about the differing effects of the machine on women and men is an odd one, and by persisting in it, he comes to resemble a grotesque from Winesburg, Joe Welling, for example, that man of ideas. Yet Joe defends his declaration that the world is on fire by pointing to the burning of decay, and it is easy to overlook the more persuasive insights into the machine age in contemporary America that flash out in *Perhaps Women*. So, for example, although he admires machines, he sees that their increasing complexity and efficiency throw more and more workers into the massive numbers of the Depression unemployed. Again, he observed at Danville the relative helplessness of even unionized men and women under attack by owners and managers supported by local and state governments, the police and vigilante groups, the media, the churches, the courts. (He could not have been surprised when the general strike of 1934 in the cotton mills was brutally and catastrophically broken by such combined enemies.) One of his most fundamental, long-term perceptions is that through the production of goods and the advertising of them the American economy is what is now called a "consumerist" one. For a person who admitted that he was not an economist or a thinker, he had many reliable perceptions.

For the most part, however, the reviewers of *Perhaps Women* focused on his central argument. Only one important review, Mary Ross's in the Sunday *Herald Tribune*, praised the book and the argument fully, the one partly negative remark being that the book "is incoherent in places, yet with that mysterious suggestiveness of the rambling stories of Sherwood Anderson, shot with terror and tenderness." A few reviewers like Laurence Stallings in the *Milwaukee Sentinel* compared this book unfavorably with the earlier stories; a few of his friends and well-wishers such as Harry

Hansen and Henry Seidel Canby excused the book as the work of one essentially a poet. Most on varying grounds rejected the central argument outright, the *Boston Transcript*'s critic dismissing part of it as "arrant nonsense." Very early Anderson admitted to brother Karl that

> I am afraid my new book isn't going to strike. They may not be ready for it and then, again, it may not say it clearly and strongly enough.
> At least I have made the choice—to go with the machine—not to reject it any more.

Still, the few fairly favorable reviews he saw came largely in the second half of September, and by the end of the month, especially pleased by the Ross review, he began to "feel more confidence in the book." Although the anonymous reviewer in *Time* had charged him as being "at times almost incoherent, at times downright silly," he or she had continued, "But he is respected if not read by the U.S. at large, which has been taught to regard him as one of its few genuine home-grown authors," and the review had featured a portrait photograph of him. On the twenty-ninth he modestly wrote Eleanor that

> I am not dissatisfied with the way P W has been received. . . . Again I am surprised. After all, on the whole I am always treated with a certain respect, perhaps more than I deserve. I believe in my soul that the central point of my thesis . . . that industrialism, as at present handled, leads first of all to impotence . . . beginning with spiritual impotence and leading to physical impotence. Of course I laid myself open. It can't be helped. I believe we are in an impotent age. I believe you have never committed yourself as to whether or not you think I am right.
> It pleases me that . . . if I haven't first rate brains but have sincerity the fact of my sincerity is recognized and respected. I am always having a false hope that some day I shall sing some great song that will sweep all before it, like a storm at sea. I am childishly disappointed always for a moment, after every production, that I have not done it. At bottom I have never quarrelled with American criticism. It has always placed me higher than I deserve.[41]

5.

If *Perhaps Women* brought him more respect than approval, he was all the more anxious that *Beyond Desire* be a success. With time out for long walks by himself, mushrooming or brook fishing with friends, talks with Laura Lu Copenhaver, and discreet politicking among his Democratic friends to vote for the Republican Andy Funk for county prosecutor, he worked hard at the novel through the first three weeks of September and found the right way to "get hold" of his four mill girls, to "make the picture," he explained to Eleanor, "so that you sensed and felt" them. Stimulated by seeing Eleanor on her one-day visit to her family on the twenty-second, he was able to stay at his desk almost all the next day and push through the "Mill Girls" section to the end. "Again," he wrote her that evening, "it is full of you and what I get from you."

Alfred Dashiell, the editor of *Scribner's Magazine,* had written him early in the month requesting a long article giving his impressions of contemporary America, but immersed in *Beyond Desire,* Anderson had got nowhere in his attempts at such a large subject and now offered "Mill Girls" instead. Dashiell, "interested in practically anything you write," agreed to look at it, suggesting that it might fit in as one of a series of short novels *Scribner's* was publishing each complete in a single issue. On or around October 2, Anderson mailed fair-typed copies of the manuscript to both Dashiell and Eleanor, telling the editor that "it can hardly be called a complete short novel but it does touch, I believe realistically, a kind of life very common in America now and one not often really touched." John Hall Wheelock at *Scribner's* urged some minor revisions "sharpening and drawing [the piece] together," but both he and Dashiell were enthusiastic: "It gives a picture that has never been given before with such reality." After Anderson had made the revisions, Dashiell accepted it for publication in the January issue.[42]

"Mill Girls" is one of the achievements of Anderson's later career as a writer. Deliberately presenting the lives of Doris, Grace, Nell, and Fanny in apparently disjointed fragments, he firmly organizes these fragments into a subtly shifting dual time scheme. The present is a specific "October, 1929," when "tight times" have already reached the Langdon Cotton Mill of Langdon, Georgia, and is centered on one event, the visit by the four young women to a "fair of shows" on the Saturday afternoon reserved by unspoken agreement for "lint-heads" (mill workers) and blacks. The action of this event is broken into many short passages distributed in mostly chronological order through the piece. Between these passages are placed, in nonchronological order, quick scenes, narrative, and explanatory comment by the implied narrator concerning the girls' lives, present and past, in the "prison" of the mill. Because their lives are so constricted and the focus of the piece is so much on Doris Hoffman, the natural leader of the group, one gradually but readily assembles the various fragments, jumbled though they are in time, into a complex whole: the "exterior" life of mill and mill village, and the girls' interior lives. His method is comparable, Anderson appears to imply, to the way one gradually learns in actual life about the complex whole of a new acquaintance becoming a friend.

The exterior surface reality is primarily of the mill, where, rightly said, Doris, Grace, Nell, and Fanny "live," since "All week nearly all of their waking hours were in there."

The mill at Langdon ran night and day. You put in five ten-hour shifts and one five-hour shift. You had it off from Saturday noon till Sunday night at twelve, when the night shift started the new week.

More narrowly the girls' lives are "walled in, shut in" to the big, light, orderly spinning-room and even more narrowly to a single "hallway," the constricted space between two long rows of machines out of many such rows where hundreds of threads coming down endlessly from the ceiling are wound by the machines onto bobbins. The air is filled with a fine mist of water to help keep the threads from breaking, but even so threads frequently break and the bobbins below them stop. The job on each "side" of the hallway is to run back and forth as bobbins stop and quickly retie the thread. The job requires speed, dexterity, and stamina and is hard on the feet, legs, and back. The settling mist brings dust and lint to the workers' heads, lungs, and especially in the summer the damp heat soaks their dresses with mist and sweat. Now in the "tight times" with wage cuts and the "stretch-out" (the assignment of more machines to each worker to tend) no wonder that the workers are guardedly talking about a union and a strike at the Langdon mill.

Then there is the mill village, rows of cramped identical double houses, forty or more on each side of unpaved streets. Each house is for two families. On one side of the Hoffman house are Doris, her not very strong husband Ed, who works night shifts to Doris's days, their baby son whom Doris nurses, and Ed's invalid mother, who may have contracted tuberculosis from the lint in mill spinning-rooms; on the other side are Grace Musgrave, her unmarried older brother Tom, and their mother. Back in the "good times" before the tight ones, Grace worked with Doris but now has been laid off because she is not strong enough to keep up her "side." Beyond the mill village but separate from it in all ways is the town of Langdon, where the mill girls go only on rare occasions such as the Saturday afternoon when they deliberately pass through on their way to the fair, sensing as they go the contempt the townspeople have for them not unlike the hatred most of the mill girls, except Doris, have for the blacks.

So out of bits and pieces Anderson assembles his picture of one small part of the new industrialized South, a far more detailed surface reality than he usually gave because of his firsthand observations and talks with Eleanor; but as always he was more interested in going beneath that surface into the inner lives of his four mill girls, especially Doris, and their interrelationships. Doris is "a smart, fast workman." With her big head and mouth and short little body she is not at all conventionally handsome, but the implied narrator insists she conveys "a lurking sense of beauty." She is strong, vital, tender, full of fun, "very conscious of people." She likes men yet is firmly faithful to her physically weaker husband. There are days, however, when she is closed in on herself, "quiet and warm . . . like a tree or like a hill lying still in warm sunlight." From the movies, other people's radios, and her own awareness and imagination she has "a dim but ever-present consciousness of a world outside the cotton mill . . . and the cotton-mill village," even though she was born and grew up in a mill village, went into the Langdon mill at twelve (with the full knowledge of the superintendent that she was lying about her age), and is now only eighteen with a husband and child. She feels motherly toward Grace, her pretty but not very strong friend. Back in the "good times" before Grace lost her job for not being able to "keep up her side," Doris used to rub Grace's body all over with her "strong quick hands" to ease the girl's aches and weariness from the day's work, as she rubs her husband's body Saturday nights. While slowly relaxing, the usually silent Grace "likes to describe places," especially the farm in the north Georgia hills where the family lived before the father died, and the little waterfalls in a nearby creek. For Doris, Grace's talk is an outlet through a storyteller into nature. When she massages her husband, he talks of the newspapers and books about famous men he reads or of his wish that he were not so shy and could organize a union and lead a strike. For Doris, who "hadn't been brought up" to read and write, his talk is another window on the larger world of human affairs.

As for Fanny, short, fat, laughing, married but without a child, she is too simple a person for much attention, but Nell, who takes Grace's place in Doris's hallway, is a vivid figure. Tall, long-legged, yellow-haired, she attracts men but, contemptuous of them all as not "man enough," she sticks with the three other young women. She is rebellious, cynical, tough; she swears like a man. If there is to be a union, she wants a Communist one, for she has heard "that was the worse kind." Doris is unlike Nell but almost wishes she were a man so that she could try to get her; Nell once told Fanny that if she, Nell, were a man, she'd want Doris and "be after her."

These fragments of outer and inner reality constantly shifting within their dual time schemes relate to each other and enrich each other's meaning. The little fair of shows, with its stands, its games, its freaks, its dancing girls in not very clean costumes, its Ferris wheel, is gimcrack and tawdry; but for the mill girls it is a welcome break in their walled-in lives. For Doris it is particularly so. When toward the end of the piece the four friends have a ride on the Ferris wheel—Doris and Grace in one seat, Nell, who would prefer to sit with Doris, and Fanny in another—their different reactions to going higher and higher encapsulate their characters. Fanny whoops with laughter, Nell yells, Grace, frightened, closes her eyes to shut everything out and clings to Doris, and Doris "kept seeing things"—the fairground crowd, a man selling patent medicines to blacks, the red-headed young man (Red Oliver, the protagonist of *Beyond Desire*), who has taken a job as a sweeper in the mill and whom she feels attracted to. She also sees from high up for the first time in her life the town of Langdon, its shade trees about public buildings and wide-lawned houses "of people who didn't work in any mill . . . not having any use for mill people." She cannot see the mill village, though she'd like to, because it was behind "a shoulder of land"; but she can see the river,

the river stretching away in a great bend around the town of Langdon. The river was always yellow. It never seemed to get clear. It was golden yellow. It was golden yellow against a blue sky. It was against trees and bushes. It was a sluggish river.

When he slightly revised "Mill Girls" as book two of *Beyond Desire*, Anderson would add the fine echoing detail that Doris also sees distant hills to the north of the town and thinks of where Grace used to live in her happy childhood, "Where the waterfalls were"; but even in the *Scribner's* version his unexpected emphasis by repetition and use of color words in the river passage communicates Doris's sudden surge of emotional expansion, of momentary imaginative release from the prison of her days. With equal skill Anderson then reverts in both magazine and book versions first to further descriptions of that lifetime imprisonment, then to Nell's rebellious anger, and on to the initial stirrings toward a union and a strike, a strike that, as *Beyond Desire* explains, will fail but which gives the mill workers as a whole a sense of unity and a temporary surge of communal release. Without propaganda Anderson shows how, as he had told the Danville strikers, they prove their worth as men and women in their struggle for a new world.

6.

September was full, too, of family matters, some bad, some good. Karl wrote to tell him that their rather feckless younger brother Ray and his son, both out of jobs in the Depression, had appeared at his house to stay, and he was finding Ray's constant cheerfulness and hopefulness maddening. Life, he would write with exasperation three months later, simply rolls off Ray's back—as it had off their detested father's. Sherwood had himself become exasperated when at an argumentative gathering of the Copenhavers he saw the hard-working Eleanor, in her usual self-sacrificing way, allow a sister to take advantage of her and as a result pass up the chance to take a quiet sleeper train to New York, where in addition to her YWCA duties, she was to begin graduate work at Columbia for a master's degree in Political Economy. On the other hand, Mimi suddenly announced that she was engaged to Russell Spear, who sounded to Anderson like "a nice and fine" man, while a happy Bob and Mary Chryst were thinking of marrying in December, though Mary would never forgive her father-in-law for not moving earlier out of the apartment over the print shop, as he had promised to do for them, into a rented room. It pleased him also that John, after a successful summer of painting under Charles Bockler's guidance, would be working in the print shop with Bob all fall and winter.[43]

Filled with confidence at finishing "Mill Girls," he launched immediately into what became the next book in *Beyond Desire*, "Ethel," different from the former, "more sophisticated," and in two days, he maintained to Eleanor, "got perhaps another forty or fifty pages of the book down." To relax from exhausting hours of writing he went fishing, stayed in the cold stream until nightfall, "too much fascinated by the changing light on the water," caught a chill that turned into a nasty cold, and went into a two-week-long depression, when out of extreme lassitude he first wrote badly and then not at all. He felt ineffective and confused. What should he best be doing with his life, he worried, writing things like "Mill Girls" or speaking out publicly as he did to the Danville strikers? He missed Eleanor terribly, ashamed to admit his dependency on her but admitting it nevertheless. "This morning I am not very manly," he wrote her on October 4. "I am a child loving you as a child might love and want for its mother." He felt "marooned" in what he thought of as the tight-minded, self-satisfied middle-classness of Marion, where people might respect him for having his picture in *Time* but in conversation with him had no ideas or interest in ideas. He needed to get out of his absorption with himself, he knew; so he read books, "consumed" them—he was at this point reading Vernon Parrington's *The Romantic Revolution,* the second volume of *Main Currents in American Thought*—and paid almost daily visits to Rosemont to talk with Laura Lu or read Parrington aloud to her as she liked. They had long since become close friends. He admired her traditional "woman's fineness," but equally her "hard good sense," her ability to see "through and around things—[to judge] swiftly and accurately," her delight in discussing new ideas. He had become accustomed to seeking her praise or frank criticism of his own writing—she had much liked "Mill Girls"—and now at one of their talks she announced her determination "to try to make a text book out of [his] comments on writing and the writer's attitude, culled from [his] books." Her responsiveness to him as artist and the frequent warmer-than-usual letters from Eleanor, along with the word he received on October 11 from Dashiell that *Scribner's* would accept "Mill Girls," brought him slowly out of his depression and into some days of hard work on "Ethel"—just in time to receive a shocking blow.[44]

Mid-evening of October 18, a Sunday, Maurice Long's son phoned him to say that his father was dead. Long had set out that morning to inspect his Ashton property, but when he did not return by late afternoon, a search party in the early evening found his body in a ravine near his house. A doctor pronounced that he had died at three o'clock of "natural causes," presumably a sudden heart attack. Devastated, Anderson immediately wrote Eleanor of this "most dreadful thing possible except your own death or your mother's death": "I loved him more than I had loved any man." That night he dreamed repeatedly that Eleanor had brought Maurice into his room to show that he was alive, and the next day he worked at his desk "blindly," trying not to think of his dead friend, "so alive . . . so talented"; but all that day Maurice "haunted" him, and he could not stop grieving. By October 20 he was able to accept the death of "my dearest, my most loved friend" as a bitter loss that must simply be borne.[45]

By the morning of the twenty-first he was at his desk writing intensely about the "queer . . . rather resentful" Ethel, whom, oddly, he had come to like. With her, in a revealing metaphor from painting, he was "trying to put a broad streak of yellow across the canvas," just as "Mill Girls" had been "intended as a grey tone." Then "Ethel" had to be set aside. In the afternoon of the following day he left by train for Charlottesville, where he had been invited to attend the Southern Writers' Meeting at the University of Virginia on October 23 and 24. He had little interest in such a gathering but now saw it as a means of getting away from the nights of Maurice and from the many letters and phone calls from other friends of the dead man who clearly considered his relation to Maurice to have been especially close. At the university, he was pleased at being an honored guest in the home of the acting president, John Lloyd Newcomb, and having a luxurious "whole suite of big rooms, right facing the lovely inner lawn." The next morning at the opening meeting in Madison Hall, he was relieved to find that only a few of the other twenty-nine participants were the "ancients" he expected and most were in their thirties and forties. Among the participants were such well-established writers as the Virginians Ellen Glasgow, who had originally conceived of the meeting, James Branch Cabell, and the popular romancer Mary Johnston; and writers coming into fame such as the Tennessee Agrarians Allen Tate and Donald Davidson, North Carolinians Paul Green and James Boyd, and the Mississippian William Faulkner, who appeared late and only "spasmodically" thereafter. Anderson especially liked the novelists Struthers Burt and Caroline Gordon; his earlier acquaintance Stringfellow Barr; the poet Josephine Pinckney, who, he later wrote Laura Lu, was "one of the nicest, simplest persons there" even though one of "The Pinckneys of Charleston"; the "very, very charming" Irita Van Doren, editor of the *New York Herald Tribune Books;* and Ellen Glasgow, who, though he thought her "quite old"—she was fifty-eight, and he had already turned fifty-five in September—had "tremendous vitality . . . alertness, eagerness and charm."[46]

Glasgow gave an informal opening speech welcoming the group as proof of the diversity and new importance of Southern literature, after which she called on others to speak. Anderson contributed only a few remarks, saying according to one report that "he had moved his home because he is more comfortable in the South, add[ing] that he had the feeling that he was crawling in under the edge of the tent," though other reports have him claiming that it was his "Italian blood" that drew him south to Virginia. Thereafter, he wrote Laura Lu, "suddenly the meeting got bad— long, tiresome speeches from professors. Everyone began to think it was a dentists' convention." Unlike most other of the participants he had no interest in Southern literature as such—Josephine Pinckney would comment that he was "quite undisturbed about letters at any point of the compass"—but others as well found that Mary Johnston spoke at too great length on the spiritual obligations of fiction. Lunch was better since Barr was one of those at table with him at the home of English professor James Southall Wilson, and in the afternoon there was an expedition of the group in automobiles to nearby Castle Hill, the elaborately handsome country house of Amélie Rives, the aging and ill novelist who had married Prince Pierre Troubetzkoy. Feeling that she might be wearied by having so many people conducted into her room, Anderson instead "strolled about the lawn" and the much-admired boxwood walks. Evening was best of all. Dinner was at the moonlit Farmington Country Club, which Emily Clark, one of the participants, called "the loveliest club in Virginia and one of the loveliest in America." One of his dinner companions was Irita Van Doren, whose conversation he found brilliant and intelligent. After dinner, he would tell Laura Lu,

a big crowd gathered about Barr, Ellen Glasgow and myself. We got into an amusing wrangle over some abstract subject, more to hang conversation on than anything else. Presently all joined it. It was the first real thaw-out, fun, going it hot & heavy, good-natured raillery & good talk.

Perhaps it was his part in the discussion that led a reporter present from the *Richmond Times-Dispatch* to comment that "Sherwood Anderson of Marion, Va. has been a dominating figure at the meetings." From midnight until nearly two he and seven or eight other men continued the conversation over drinks at a professor's house. "It was about all the real talking I did," he would comment to Laura Lu.[47]

The second morning he slept instead of taking the automobile trip to Monticello, and though he got as far as the door to the room in Madison Hall where another meeting was convened, he could not stand more speeches, did not go in, and so missed the discussion about the need for more and better newspaper book pages, especially in the Southern press, although in keeping with the deliberately informal nature of what DuBose

Heyward termed this "author's house party," no formal action was taken. After lunch at "another big country house," Anderson "fled" to Baltimore, where that evening he wrote Laura Lu his long, gossipy letter about the gathering, summarizing the events and, tartly, his likes and dislikes among the participants. Although many at the meeting had been eager to see Faulkner because of his recent critical success with *The Sound and the Fury* and his more scandalous one with *Sanctuary,* Anderson saw little of his former close friend, once warning him of the danger of being suddenly adulated by celebrity-worshipers and then as suddenly dropped. In his letter to Laura Lu he sarcastically noted, as Joseph Blotner has confirmed in his biography, Faulkner's intermittent appearances and his drunkenness. Emily Clark's enthusiastic account of the gathering ended with the assertion that it had proved how "the literary field" once held by New England, then briefly by the Midwest, "belongs, by right of the strongest, to the South today." Anderson's letter, addressed, of course, to someone who appreciated amusing literary chitchat, merely stopped with his observation that: "Alice Hegan Rice, who wrote Mrs. *Wiggs of the Cabbage Patch,* looks just like Mrs. Wiggs herself should have looked. A suggestion of the refined washerwoman."

Back at his desk in Marion, he spent four busy days working on his presentation for a public event in which he was one of two star performers. In addition to setting up a two-week lecture tour for him in November, Colston Leigh had in early October completed an arrangement with the Discussion Guild of New York for an open debate between the English philosopher Bertrand Russell and Anderson on the subject "Shall the State Rear Our Children?" Anderson had agreed to take the negative and defend traditional rearing by the parents. (When he later told Mimi of his debate position, she remarked to him with amusement, "What? You?") The time finally settled on was to be Sunday, November 1 at 9 PM; the place, the Mecca Temple at Fifty-fifth Street and Seventh Avenue; the fee to be six hundred dollars for each debater. Midafternoon on a bright, sunny October 29, he boarded the train for New York, excited at the thought of seeing Eleanor soon, and the following noon was happily lunching with her. New York was foggy, and later that afternoon the gloom seems to have made him melancholy during an interview by a *New York Times* reporter. Industrialism is unmanning men, destroying the old craftsman pride in work and making women dominant, he gloomily told the reporter. Many young people, "lost in big corporations," are disillusioned. The bright spot is the American small town with its small-town newspaper; and he remains "a staunch believer in the integrity of the family," for "children [keep] their parents from becoming too 'static and conservative.'" Besides, even if family rearing of children is bad, it's better than letting the state do it. That Anderson had become good copy even in New York was shown by the length of the interviewer's report on the thirty-first and the *Times* editorial on November 2 protesting that, despite his "gift for sound thinking" revealed elsewhere in the interview, Anderson should not have ignored the manly achievements of "industrialized workingmen" during, for example, the World War.[48]

On the evening of November 1, before an audience of 2,600, the two debaters appeared on the stage in tuxedos, though according to the *Memoirs* Anderson had forgotten to change his socks, and Eleanor, to whom he had sent a ticket, was horrified to see that he was still wearing his daytime red ones. Speaking for the affirmative, Russell (as befitted a mathematician and philosopher) organized his presentation around seven points in arguing that mother love was imprisoning for children and that the need of children for "activity and freedom" would be better served by a universal system of state boarding schools. Cannily introducing himself as anything but one of "two intellectual giants," as the debaters had been billed, Anderson argued that any faults of the American system of education were not the result of defective family life but of the present "outworn" economic system of capitalism. What he would like "is not the wiping out of the family by the state but the wiping out of economic fear" and "The family, as an institution, given a chance under new economic conditions." There is already too much standardization of goods in the United States, and taking over children by state institutions would standardize them as well, make them "too much alike." There are after all sensible mothers as well as insensible ones, and children receive much valuable education from "the intimate contacts of family life." In his rebuttal speech in the second part of the program he objected that Russell was laying down "wide sweeping laws," but "Life does not work out like a mathematics problem. At its best it is always strange." Characteristically in his conclusion he appealed to reformers such as Russell to "be reasonable":

At least be reasonable about childhood. Do not take all of the color out of childhood by too grim a regimentation. There is some purpose to life other than that of making automobiles and bath tubs and selling them cheap. Because some parents have failed miserably, do not be too quick to condemn all parents. It seems to me that the whole inner flavor of life lies after all in our personal relations.[49]

Characteristically also in his two presentations he rarely referred to "parents" or "fathers" but almost always to "mothers" only; though at one point he stated that he himself wanted "intimate contact, daily contact" with children and saved himself from falsehood by indicating that he referred to his own grown children. Perhaps he was merely reflecting standard American family patterns, or that of his own family, or perhaps he was thinking of Cornelia's care of their children, or perhaps he knew which emotional strings in the audience to play on. A report of the debate in *The Literary Digest* commented that, "tho radical in literature and in his economic beliefs," he was "very earnest in advocating family life," that he "pounded the reading desk to send home his points," and that when he announced that "I would trust [mothers] as far as I would the average scientist or the average schoolteacher," the audience applauded. Such applause may have convinced him that he had "annihilated poor Russell," and certainly he was fortunate in having the popular side, as was suggested by the printing of three paragraphs from his speech a week later in the "They Say" column of the *Times*. It was surely gratifying too that Leigh should soon write him, "There was so much interest in your New York debate that we have been asked whether you would not debate in New Orleans with Margaret Sanger on Birth Control," he to take the opposing side. Even though the fee (five or six hundred dollars) might have appreciably helped in his still vague plan to take Eleanor with him to visit the Soviet Union in 1932, he passed up this chance to become a talking celebrity. Besides, he was in no position, had no desire, to argue against birth control.[50]

After spending as much time as possible with Eleanor, he took a late afternoon train for Marion on November 2 and the following day was at work on his lectures for the tour, which would occupy a good part of the month. This time he would not be speaking at all on literature but on newspapers and the machine age. He would lecture mainly at colleges and universities and occasionally at men's clubs, but his contracts with Leigh specified that he would not speak at women's clubs because, he explained, they were usually "culture-seeking" organizations and his "subjects not perhaps especially interesting to women," an arbitrary and very "masculine" assumption for the author of *Perhaps Women* and one that a *New York Times* editorial would contradict. The tour began on November 6 when he had a young Marion man drive him in his car through beautiful autumn weather down to Winthrop College in Rock Hill, South Carolina. The man drove Anderson's car back home, Anderson gave an evening lecture on "Journalism and the Young Writer" at the college, and he caught a night train, which brought him into New York the following morning. Here he renewed his acquaintance with Max Eastman, was with Eleanor as much as her job allowed, and on the morning of the tenth took a train to Troy, New York, for a lecture that evening at Russell Sage College. After two days back in New York City and an "altogether lovely" meeting with Eleanor, he took a sleeper on the evening of the twelfth west to the industrial city of Newark in central Ohio, where on the next day he talked his way into a visit to a factory manufacturing fine table glassware as a break in the lecturing routine. He was so charmed by "the glowing furnaces of melted glass, the men moving about, the light shining on the new made glass," amber, green, and yellow, that he almost wished he were a glass worker. That evening he had dinner with a group of students and professors from Denison University in nearby Granville. He was pleased that his lecture there on "America—A Storehouse of Vitality" seemed to go well—he was making a practice of changing and amplifying a lecture each time so that it would not "go dead"—pleased too at the number of students and professors who gathered at a fraternity house to talk with him afterwards, and most pleased by one young professor's grateful remark at breakfast with him the following morning that he was unlike most lecturers from the outside, who were either patronizing in manner or tired and indifferent.[51]

Another break in the tour was the afternoon and evening of November 14 with Frank Lewis and his wife, Mildred, in a Pittsburgh jammed with people who had come to see the Army-Pitt football game. In the afternoon Anderson and Mildred went to see the thirtieth Carnegie International Exhibition of Modern Paintings on view at Carnegie Institute; here he was excited by the "tremendous vitality" of the pictures in the Russian room. They seemed, he wrote Laura Lu, "to shout and dance, full of joy in life, without weariness, as though the Russian had at least found hope." After the exhibit Frank Lewis joined them for dinner and the evening. Frank, the talkative owner of a laundry company, had been one of Maurice Long's oldest friends and was full of tales about him—"Maurice and his adventures, his eagerness, the poet in him." His son, Maurice Jr., who admired and loved his father though not approving of him, had decided to take over the laundry business. So the tales and information went on until Anderson had to take a night train for New York connecting with one for Albany, where he was to speak at the Jewish Community Center. Maurice's friends seemed to hope he would write about Long and his "amazingly fine qualities," as in January he would do in "Two Irishman."[52]

After the evening lecture in Albany on November 15, he took a sleeper to Boston, spent the following day there with his old friend Charles Connick, maker of stained-glass windows for churches, spoke at Dartmouth College the evening of the seventeenth, and on the eighteenth was back in New York, his tour completed. For the next week or so he kept to his routine, writing on "Ethel" in his hotel room mornings, completing at least one "exciting chapter," and in the afternoons and evenings seeing people, Eleanor whenever possible but also Paul Rosenfeld, one of Maurice Long's former lovers Ella Boese, and even Waldo Frank, whom he had not seen in a long time and who was "nice." His last two days were a flurry of visits in preparation for departure. In the morning of the twenty-sixth he called on Theodore Dreiser, recently back from the violence in the strike-torn coal fields of southeast Kentucky. Earlier in the month, as chairman of the Communist-inspired National Committee for the Defense of Political Prisoners, Dreiser had courageously led a delegation of observers, including John Dos Passos, to Pineville in Bell County, Kentucky, and in the face of bitter hostility from the mine owners, the police, and the townspeople had conducted open hearings in which miners described the brutally oppressive, virtually lawless conditions under which they worked and lived. To combat the horrifying publicity from these hearings, the mine owners and local judiciaries saw to it that after Dreiser's return to New York he and his fellow observers were indicted in Kentucky on the charge of criminal syndicalism. (Since he had most unwisely brought with him to Pineville one of the many young women he conducted affairs with, he was also indicted for adultery by the county grand jury; though the lurid publicity over this indictment actually helped spread the damaging publicity from the hearings.) During Anderson's visit, Dreiser urged him to speak at a mass meeting in his defense to be held in New York on December 6, and Anderson rather reluctantly consented because he agreed that Dreiser had been framed, that he owed Dreiser personal support, and that, as Dreiser put it, "other men of the artist class should stand up and be counted." That evening Anderson took his old Lake Chateaugay friend Alys Bentley to the Emmetts' town house to say goodbye, and when Burton presented him with a hundred dollars, he decided to contribute the sum to the expenses of the mass meeting.[53]

On the twenty-seventh after a farewell lunch with Eleanor and a parting visit with Karl and Helen Anderson, he took a sleeper to Washington, where he was to give yet another speech. Arriving at the Ambassador Hotel in the morning, he worked on the speech and then spent much of an emotional day talking with Maurice Long Jr. and an evening talking with a close friend, but never lover, of Maurice's, the tall, "very lovely" Ruth Dove. He must have given his speech at some noon meeting on the twenty-ninth, for he talked in the afternoon with Long's wife and in the evening with one of his mistresses, both of whom he found depressingly "terrible," probably in part because they told him of Maurice's "quick hardness" in business dealings; yet even they felt that Anderson had had a "special and unique" relationship with the man. He was relieved to take a sleeper home to Marion, feeling that he had fulfilled his duty to his dead friend.[54]

In the few days before the mass meeting in New York, he worked mainly on his speech in defense of Dreiser, his duty to a living friend who, he felt, lacked "a sense of words" but whom he continued to admire as a literary pioneer and a man with courage and honesty. "I'm not a communist," he had written to Burton Emmett to explain his standing up for Dreiser. "I'm an artist. We have our own class." Artists had an obligation to speak out as well as create. By December 5 he was in New York at the Hotel St. James on Times Square, but he did not finish his speech until noon of the following day. That evening he faced an audience of three thousand people in the Star Casino at Park Avenue and 107th Street. Actually the meeting had been called by the National Committee for the Defense of Political Prisoners—for reasons of his own Dreiser did not attend—for a public report on their findings by the other observers who had ventured into eastern Kentucky; but no quotations from their speeches were included in the *New York Times*'s column-length account of the occasion under the headline, "Anderson Decries Our 'Speakeasy' Era," while nearly two-thirds of the column consisted of quotations from his speech. (After the meeting he left his manuscript with the *Times* reporter.) Into his remarks he first compressed much of what he had observed and thought about during the past two years—the hard lot of industrial workers in the Depression and before; the sense of brotherhood and sisterhood inspired by that "marvelous thing," a strike; the deft organization of local and state institutions into a powerful strike-breaking force; the "new world" created by machines, often beautiful in themselves but now controlled by "new gods," the owners; the fear in most Americans now that makes them cruel to each other, as fear "is ruling now in Harlan, Kentucky." Moving then to his defense of Dreiser, he praised him as "a story teller" with "a curious hunger for truth," one who "has stood out against . . . the corruption of American writers with money, with promises of social distinction, with all the promises that can be given such men," one who "was the first downright honest American prose writer." Many Americans now have radical thoughts yet keep them carefully private, Anderson asserted, and then declared a major theme: "We are a speak-easy country." But Dreiser and his fellow observers dared openly to go see for themselves the "reign of terror" in Kentucky, and, wanting truth, Dreiser

spoke aloud in a speak-easy country. He said in public what millions of Americans are thinking in private.

For that is he accused of criminal syndicalism.

So that's what criminal syndicalism is? I am glad to know. Now I know at last what is the matter with this country. We need less speak-easy citizens and more criminal syndicalists.

It's time now, Anderson concluded, "for writers, college professors, newspaper men, for every one who has the public ear to speak out." Communists "should be allowed to speak and agitate too." Writers "ought to quit pandering . . . and line up with the underdogs . . . I don't believe we ought to be satisfied or condemned to live all of our lives in a speak-easy country."[55]

With his words at the Star Casino, Anderson was standing up for both Dreiser and himself; he titled his address, "I Want to Be Counted." He was to give one more lecture in 1931, but his defense of his friend was a courageous, rousing, at times eloquent climax to a year as semipublic figure.

5

Radical

1.

After a "so lovely" time in New York with Eleanor on the day after his speech at the mass meeting, Anderson returned to Marion eager to finish "Ethel," since being with Eleanor, he told her, "always sets me off to work." For two days, however, he was busy with correspondence and with packing up his things in the apartment over the print shop preparatory to moving out so that Mary Chryst could move in with Bob after their wedding. Then on the tenth he made final revisions on the "exciting chapter" of "Ethel" he wrote in New York and began sketching in the final book of *Beyond Desire*, "the death of the boy in the communist strike." On the eleventh the influence of Eleanor set him fully off.

A terrific morning—The chapter about the two women in the room at night. One of the most terrible and illuminating chapter[s] I ever wrote. I am shaken.
It is gorgeous writing, dear, but terrible. The book will make a sensation.

The scene was that in which Ethel continues trying to define herself by resisting the attempt by her youthful stepmother to seduce her into a lesbian relationship, as the "exciting chapter" was presumably the one in Chicago when she resolutely escapes from the apartment of a man bent on raping her if she refuses seduction, and as in yet another chapter, she herself initiates Red Oliver into sex and then immediately rejects him. One chapter in "Ethel" remained to be written, that in which she does define herself through a marriage of convenience designed to place herself as much as possible "beyond desire."[1]

Though still shaken by the morning's work, Anderson was able that afternoon to draw up a contract between himself and Bob, signed by both on the twelfth but to go into effect on January 1, 1932. The contract provided for the transfer of fourteen-fifteenths of the newspapers' assets of

$15,000 to his son, who could not contract other debts until he had paid $5,000 each to John and Mimi by 1940, the final one-fifteenth then to be sold to Bob for one dollar. Sherwood would also report to Eleanor that Andy Funk and he had finished all the papers for his divorce, though they would not be filed and the required notice be published in the newspapers until after she had returned to New York from a Christmas vacation home. (His growing concern over publicity would shortly lead to Dickinson's handling the divorce in an unusual way.) The "emotional experience" of the morning's chapter made his night restless and wearying, but at noon on the twelfth he and John started to drive to Savannah for his last lecture of the year so that John could see country new to him. They spent the first night in Florence, South Carolina, and the second in Savannah after an afternoon in Charleston during which Josephine Pinckney, whom he had liked at the Southern Writers Meeting, had taken them to a cousin's home, nearby Middleton Place with its twenty-five acres of elegant formal gardens. On the evening of the fourteenth he gave his lecture on "America— A Storehouse of Vitality" at the Jewish Educational Alliance, and the following day he and John drove the 440 miles home, often over mountain roads, in thirteen hours. By the end of the sixteenth he had written some two thousand words on the last chapter of "Ethel" and found a "large, cheerful" room at Miss Belle Sprinkle's house "with a grand view of the hills," Miss Belle to bring him breakfast daily in his room. He moved out of the apartment just the day before Bob and Mary were married on the eighteenth in the Lutheran church with only himself, John, Eleanor's adoring aunt Miss May Scherer, and the minister present.[2]

At first Anderson felt that leaving the print shop apartment began "another new chapter in my life"; yet things mostly went on as before. After Miss Belle had brought him breakfast, he wrote on *Beyond Desire* until noon, lunched, and then perhaps took Bob's Mary out mushrooming in order to get better acquainted with her or helped his friend the grocer Frank Copenhaver press wine from his grapes or, most often, visited with Laura Lu. He was, to be sure, increasingly determined to go to Russia the following summer, intending to pay for the trip with the fees from his coming winter and spring lecture tours; and through consultations with Dickinson he learned of a way the lawyer could obtain a divorce for him with a minimum of local publicity. So on December 28 a "bill in chancery" was issued with a subpoena to be served on Elizabeth Prall Anderson in California. (The subpoena was delivered to her by her law professor brother-in-law Max Radin at Palo Alto on January 17, 1932.) Anderson surely would have explained the divorce proceedings to Eleanor when she was home for brief visits at Christmas and New Year's. On the morning of the last day of 1931, he completed a letter to her in Marion, as always declaring his love for her but warning that marriage with him would be "a gamble," for "my absorption [in life] involves all my emotions . . . exhausts them at times."

I can tell you what will be hard. I sag terribly but, when I am rested, I begin again. I am terrible. I never get enough of anything, never love enough, work enough. I want everything, absolute beauty, perfection.

He had "tempered that impulse a little in myself"; yet what he wanted was what she would be, not at all just a wife to take care of him, but "a play fellow, a work fellow . . . a lover." That evening at Rosemont, the shutters rattling outside in a howling wind, she sat in a red dress by a dark window and seemed so beautiful to him that he hurt inside. He had already resolved for 1932 to write her a letter every day in addition to his regular ones. These daily letters, usually to be written in the early morning of each day before he began working, would be a kind of journal, "notes of my thoughts," moods, actions, each letter to be sealed and kept secret from her until after his death, when she could revisit "these tangled days" with him from beyond, as it were, the grave.[3]

2.

"Morning in the mountains. . . . It is cold. Now and then there come flurries of snow," Anderson noted in his first Letter a Day on the first day of the worst year of the Great Depression, and he went on to record, as he often would, a dream he had had in the night, this one of being famous. He excitedly revised two chapters of *Beyond Desire* and in the afternoon went driving happily in the hills with Eleanor; but in the evening of the following day he was enraged and humiliated by Mr. Copenhaver's rudeness to him at dinner at Rosemont and the man's insistence that everyone must listen to *Amos 'n Andy* on the radio, a medium Anderson had long detested as dull, materialistic, and corrupt for its shows and advertisements. Then, upset by Mr. Copenhaver's behavior, perhaps a jealous reaction to his closeness to the man's wife and daughter, upset also by his "position" in town while going through his divorce and by Eleanor's departure for New York, he was relieved to take the overnight train to the city on January 4 to begin his eastern lecture tour.[4]

The next morning he registered at the Hotel Carteret at Twenty-third Street and Seventh Avenue, presumably because it was only a short subway ride to and from Eleanor's apartment at 220 Sullivan Street in the Village. As he occasionally did, he gave his name as Beal Anderson of Richmond, Virginia, not, he wrote Karl, because he was "leading any unusual life of vice but to avoid small annoyances—literary ladies, etc." In New York he felt "terrifically excited," as always at such times snapping views as through a camera of "a thousand little things along a street." With John, temporarily in the city, he went to the Metropolitan Museum to delight in art works John wanted him to see—paintings by Vermeer, Cézanne, and Rembrandt, and a Degas statuette of a woman dancer who, he felt, "would live in you forever." He went to see Colston Leigh, with whom he was angry for scheduling his initial lecture to be held at a women's social club, just for the agent's fee, despite his prohibition against speaking to such groups, lunched gladly with Eleanor and John, and had a pleasant visit with Tom Smith at Liveright's. He was still angry with Leigh when on the afternoon of January 6 he gave his "America—A Storehouse of Vitality" lecture before what he perceived as the "fat, well-dressed, self-satisfied upper-middle-class women" of the Garden City–Hempstead Community Club, doing his best in his speech "to upset all these lives," these "dead" wives of businessmen. His lecture fee was three hundred dollars, but he much more enjoyed the following evening dining in a working-class restaurant with a young, self-educated Italian laborer who told him "nice little human stories about himself and his family and friends." His hatred of businessmen and the wealthy had become visceral, as he recognized, but one such couple he exempted from his anger, the Emmetts, especially Burt with his large collections of prints and modern paintings, his generosity and humbleness. He was "nice," one of Anderson's terms of praise. After dinner with them the next evening, he persuaded Burt to show him the prints, and he rejoiced that he had given his friend the O'Keeffe painting he had bought at her show back in February of 1923 and no longer wanted. It was, he thought, "fun to give things to the rich."[5]

Most mornings he worked at *Beyond Desire;* in the morning of January 10, however, he read in the *Times* of the death of his writer friend Frederick O'Brien. Saddened, he wrote in Letter a Day and later directly to Eleanor drafts of his article "Two Irishmen," comparing O'Brien with Maurice Long as two vivid lovers of life, two gifted oral storytellers, O'Brien like "all writers [wanting] some perfect thing—the perfectly balanced immemorial tale told—something that would balance all life—express it all"—as Anderson himself would achieve in "The Untold Lie" and other of his best fictions. He wanted his own death to come suddenly but preferably only after an hour's walk and talk with Maurice, Fred, Bill Faulkner, and "some twenty, thirty, forty men and women known, loved at moments, before complete and final darkness." The rest of that day he felt worthless, but dinner and talk in a speakeasy with his old friend Lewis Galantière revived him as they reminisced about Paris days and discussed the "curious impotence" of American men, the independence of American women, the way beauty "comes like a bird flying," alighting momentarily on some conventionally unbeautiful woman—a motif of the beauty in the commonplace running through Anderson's work.[6]

Perhaps the long talk with Galantière and dinner the next evening in Brooklyn with an Eleanor looking very French in a new hat and coat made him overconfident before his second lecture, to the Institute of Arts and Sciences in Brooklyn's Academy of Music auditorium, and as a result, he felt, the lecture went badly, though Eleanor thought otherwise. The third lecture of the tour, to the Young Men's and Young Women's Hebrew Association in Elizabeth, New Jersey, on the evening of the twelfth, went better because, paradoxically, he had felt "whipped" all day thinking of "the unfairness of bringing so much of the turmoil" of his life into Eleanor's. The words and ideas of "America—A Storehouse of Vitality" seemed to him to "come forth singing," and Karl, who had come in from Westport to accompany him to New Jersey and spend the night in his hotel room, told him "nicely" that it had been "like an orchestra playing." Possibly, the relative youth of the audience had inspired him, since he now felt most comfortable lecturing to young men and women at colleges and universities. At the fourth lecture, for which he had to take a train to Washington, DC, to address the Jewish Community Center on the evening of the thirteenth, he must have felt just right; for he thought he "spoke well," and he read aloud his "Machine Song: Automobile," which seemed "full of strange, lovely music." From Washington the next day he headed north by train to Saratoga Springs, New York, where on the evening of the fifteenth he once more gave his "America—A Storehouse of Vitality" to The Key organization at Skidmore College. Then he returned to New York City, where he and Paul Rosenfeld gave a dinner party for friends, where he spent the next day sick with a cold in his hotel room, and where at 8 PM on the eighteenth he gave his sixth and last lecture of the tour, this time on "The Machine," to Columbia University's Institute of Arts and Sciences in the McMillan Theatre. Since his podium was lighted but the audience was only "a dark mass," he could not see individuals and their responses, he did not speak well and ended up exhausted.[7]

For most of the rest of January he remained in New York, working on *Beyond Desire* mornings in his hotel room, then visiting friends, going to an occasional party, seeing more of Karl than he had in years. In their conversations Karl agreed with him that "the whole key to our American civilization [was] the emphasis on money and things." The peak of any day was of course the time Eleanor managed to find for him from her demanding job and from her graduate studies at Columbia. Characteristically he had a day of "Gloom—intense" after his unsatisfactory lecture at Columbia, but a walk in the city with her the following evening "cured" him immediately, whereas, he wrote her in a grateful note, "These fits of extreme depression used to sometimes hang on for weeks and months." Yet his too frequent preoccupation with "self," which had, he admitted in Letter a Day, "murdered" him so often in the past, would at times, he admitted openly to Eleanor, grow "gigantic out of all proportion" and make him "childishly" resentful toward her and afterwards ashamed of his egotism. Why did she seem more interested in telling him the events of her day than in listening to the events in his? Why was it almost always his hand that reached for hers and not hers for his, he, not she, who said "I love you." Perhaps—this despite all the time she was taking to be with him— she didn't need him as he so desperately needed her, would be better off living only for her job. And yet one day when he urged her to follow him to Russia and marry him there, she agreed, but in his tangle of emotions he still felt he should leave New York even though he was convinced he worked best when near her. On January 30, a Saturday, he did leave for Marion, stopping on the way in Washington, where that night he got staggering drunk with friends of Maurice Long and the next day went by arrangement to the Russian Soviet Information Bureau. Here Boris Skoirsky, the "unofficial ambassador," welcomed him and assured him of assistance in getting the "inside story of the factories over there," which was what he wished to write about. He now hoped to go to the Soviet Union about May 1, after his West Coast lecture tour.[8]

Back in Marion on February 1, Anderson's day was a crowded one— going to the dentist, driving out to Ripshin to plan the coming farm work, calling on the Copenhavers. Most important, however, was his appointment with Burt Dickinson to discuss the filing of the bill in chancery asking for a divorce from Elizabeth. A deposition had been made for the bill by Anderson giving, among the grounds for the couple's separation, Elizabeth's dissatisfaction with living in Marion and her desire to be closer to her family in California. He was confident that Dickinson would not talk to others about a client's affairs; but two other persons had given depositions as well—the cashier at the Bank of Marion (about jointly owned properties) and the typist at the newspaper office (about Elizabeth's work there)—and he became increasingly fearful that one or both might start gossip in the town about his third marriage failure. For much of February the proceedings shadowed his days, were "a little dark valley to pass through."[9]

He was lonely for Eleanor. He dreamed of her often and had other erotic dreams. He had restless nights, some of them his half awake, half asleep "nights of faces"—"The faces snapping suddenly into place before my eyes, looking into my eyes accusing, pleading, smiling. The face stays a moment and then goes and is replaced by another." They wanted him to understand them and tell their stories. Sundays in Marion without Eleanor were as usual the worst times. Townspeople going to church, sometimes quarreling among themselves, had for years seemed to him unreligious. Especially in this beautiful countryside, he declared, "We should return to land worship, river, tree and hill worship," to an "embrace of love with nature." Perhaps impelled by his sensual mood, he suddenly got back to work on *Beyond Desire* by developing the character of Suzanne Graves, a social worker turned Communist, who at the strikers' camp falls in love with Red Oliver, walks out with him the night before he is killed, and later bears his child. In subsequent revisions this figure would become a mountain woman who befriends Red but is not his lover. Here was another false start on the long conclusion to his novel that was giving him trouble.[10]

Having gotten back to "Red," however, he had decided that he would not join the group that the wealthy leftists Charles and Adelaide Walker had assembled to go to Harlan County to oversee distribution of food among starving coal miners on strike. Others in the group were writers Malcolm Cowley, Waldo Frank, Mary Heaton Vorse, Edmund Wilson, and the labor lawyer Allan Taub, ten persons in all. Even when he met them in Marion on the morning train and saw them off to Knoxville on the afternoon one, he refused to go with them on the grounds that he was primarily a writer, not speechmaker, as he would have to be at their destination of Pineville in Bell County, and that he had to "stick to something, to write only when I feel, to let things digest in me a little." He would not have enjoyed the trip, for it turned out to be a frightening expedition into a zone of undeclared war. Mindful of Dreiser's fact-finding visit to their town earlier, the mayor, backed by mine operators and armed deputies who had already ruthlessly shot several miners, forbade the group to distribute their three truckloads of food to the miners or to speak to them. They did manage to hand out most of their food outside Pineville but were seized by deputies and driven at night in a motorcade to the nearby state line at Cumberland Gap, where Frank and Taub were beaten about the head, Frank badly, before the group was released to stumble on foot downhill into Tennessee. When Anderson learned of Frank's head wounds, he wondered if one reason he had refused to go along was his fear of being beaten or killed. Democracy was dead in America, he decided; the country was controlled by a small number of powerful, cynical men. "I think," he wrote in Letter a Day, "there must inevitably be a long terrible war in the world between those who have and won't give up and those who have not and can't get." Still, he had told Charles Walker "politely and nicely" in Marion, "I just have to go on my own damn way and wait until I feel something strongly enough to lash me into action."[11]

Meanwhile, he must write or, rather, try to; for beginning on February 9, the day after the Walker group stopped off in Marion, he went into weeks of slump except for an occasional successful morning. At first his days were shadowed by the wait for the divorce and by twinges of guilt that he was not more the activist, then, as the slump continued, by its continuing. He could not "get the feel" of Red in his last days of life; he had "forced too much—been too much the author." Nor did the block give way, as expected, after he drove to Roanoke to have his eyes "remeasured" and to meet Eleanor's train on the eleventh. Eleanor "was lovely . . . a proud flower," and they apparently made love memorably in the car by "a little waterfall . . . near . . . a tiny town, nice in the evening light" before they went on to Marion for Eleanor's week of vacation. On the nineteenth he drove her to Winston-Salem, where her next assignment was to talk for several days with girls working in the big cigarette factories. He noted how alive she seemed among them, how quickly she gained their trust, but also how the busy, intense work left her tired at the end of the day. He himself felt tired, depressed, futile most of the time, usually writing nothing or working all morning in his hotel room and then tearing up what he had done. He had one satisfactory morning in Greensboro, where he took her briefly for further interviews and where he spent hours listening to the tales of hardship told to him by men and women on strike before an overall plant. On the twenty-fourth, low in spirits, dreading the next day when the divorce would be brought to court for decision, he drove Eleanor back to Marion. He awoke on February 25 "feeling dead on my feet" and worried about his temperature, but the divorce was settled in his favor and he was a free man. In Letter a Day he confessed with jubilation and the striking self-knowledge he was capable of when a personal crisis ended.

A gorgeous day. My illness, like so many of my illnesses, was psychic. It was pure nonsense. Eleanor took my temperature and it was subnormal. I grow weak and cannot face the natural consequences of my own sins against life. I want to be reckless and daring. That calls for constantly facing things. I grow weak-hearted. I become ill.

The matter of Elizabeth and myself—settled in the courts. She was at bottom in love not with me but with her own brother and his life. She wanted, poor soul, respectability and safety. She could not have picked a worse man.[12]

Then, on the twenty-eighth, Eleanor boarded a train on her way west to San Francisco, where she was to study the lives of women workers for a report to the YWCA, which in turn would also be her master's thesis at Columbia. Her departure left Anderson with a "world . . . too empty," and for nearly a week he was sunk in "a discouraged blue mood," again unable to work "successfully." On March 4, however, he tried a different approach to ending his novel.

I have Red up to the last night before his death. There is in my mind a scene, a little farm house of poor whites, just over the hill from the town of Birchfield N.C. Red's night there in that farm house. What happened to him there in Langdon Ga., before he left there, was not as planned at all. It was as though the boy himself had taken hold—"Nonsense. So you have it all planned for me." He is much less noble than I had planned him—nicer I think.

Absorbed in the new ending, he worked steadily each day until the tenth, when thoughts about the talks he was to give took over. On March 11 he too boarded a train out of Marion, heading northward for Detroit for his first lecture on a tour that would take him across Mid-America and the Rockies to the Pacific.[13]

3.

On the train he neither wrote nor thought about his lectures but instead relaxed by reading "for perhaps the twentieth time" Turgenev's *A Sportsman's Sketches,* presumably in his copy of the Constance Garnett translation. As always he admired the "prose—lovely, quiet, assured [with its] color, balance, smoothness," and especially the tale "Byézhin Meadow," to be read "for something perfect in sense of skies, fields, night coming, the mystery of night, the boys—so sharply caught—and the coming of day. It is a rare, a beautiful painting." In February, after reading several Balzac stories, he had reflected that French prose style was "too sophisticated," was inconsequential "beside a prose master like Turgenev," and he had declared that "I have done better prose myself, more earthy than any Frenchman has done." Henry James and James Branch Cabell had that French "slight smack of superiority," which was why Dreiser, for all his bad sentences, surpassed both of them "for manliness and real power." Now on the train, Anderson had also been reading the morning papers he had bought during the stop in Columbus, Ohio, and the activist hankerings of the dedicated writer showed. The papers were

full of murders, kidnapping, robberies. It seems strange, when the effect on everyone of a capitalistic civilization is so very obvious, that there is not a cry out of people's hearts to put an end to it. No cruelty that can possible develop in a communistic society—incidental to getting it under way—can compare to the constant everyday cruelty of our present capitalistic, individualistic society.

The whole capitalistic thing should be fought as long as a man has breath to fight.[14]

He felt the activist even more when he reached Detroit on March 12; for on the seventh, a Communist-organized march of three thousand unemployed from Detroit to the Ford Motor Company plant in adjacent Dearborn to ask for jobs had been halted by armed police who shot and killed four of the marchers. Soon after his arrival he witnessed the fifteen-thousand-strong funeral procession for the four victims through downtown Detroit. As he sat in the comfort of the Detroit Athletic Club, he wondered why he had been invited to speak there that evening on the machine age, for the unusually high fee of five hundred dollars, since he knew he was "gradually acquiring the reputation of being a radical." When he was interviewed by newspapermen, he insisted that working people could not be understood until aspiring writers and artists went to the factories; and that evening, ashamed of his well-to-do audience, he made his speech as "ominous and threatening" as he could.[15]

Taking a midnight train out of Detroit, he stopped over in Chicago for a day to lunch with George Daugherty, who had been hit hard by the Depression, and to dine with Ferdinand Schevill and Mimi, who had decided to leave the University before her junior year was up and go east to marry Russell Spear on April 2 at North Amherst, Massachusetts. To escape Chicago's bleak, depressing cold he headed south toward Evansville, Indiana the day before he was to lecture there on the fifteenth, the train taking him through a series of "sad and dejected" factory towns on the flat prairie land. The Depression was manifest throughout the Midwest, he wrote in a "Travel Note" on the train.

There is a kind of bleakness over most of the towns and cities now. Compared to many of these middle-western industrial towns our own Southwest Virginia towns seem almost gay. Everywhere, in towns and cities, you see factories standing idle and ragged, discouraged-looking men and women walking the streets. Beggars speak to you at every corner. The hotels are deserted and the trains three-fourths empty. Under the train shed on a cold day in Chicago, when I went out to get on a train, I was the only passenger for that train walking on the big platform.

His lecture on "What Has Happened to the American Newspaper," at a dinner meeting of the Temple Men's Club in Evansville did not go well, he felt; he sounded to himself "too pretentious, too faky." He felt much better about his next evening's performance at the University of Illinois in Urbana, where after a banquet put on by the students of the School of Journalism, he spoke on "Doorways to a New World" (on the machine age) to the journalism organization Theta Sigma Phi and noted the many handsome young women students in the audience, "tall, strong and slender like the corn." Eagerly questioning students kept him up until after midnight, and he had to get up at five to catch a train back to Chicago. Here he completed the midwestern section of his tour by lecturing very well that noon at a big luncheon of the Advertising Council on "Doorways to the New World"—at his lowest fee of one hundred and fifty dollars—filling his talk with "dynamite" in reaction to seeing so many of his former companions in the business still engaged

in this senseless money-making civilization. It makes them all such terrible children. There is what Paul Rosenfeld used to call the terrible American mouth.

The heavy face, the cruelty—like boys to one another—the little pretentiousness of those who have made money.

It was a relief to have "good talk" with Ferdinand Schevill, to spend an evening at the Sergels' home, and to have hours of father-daughter talk with Mimi. He found it an "emotional thing" that when he would next see her she would be a married woman.[16]

His last day in Chicago, March 19, was exciting and exhausting. Officials of the Caxton Club, "an organization of rich old men who buy first editions, etc.," he explained to Eleanor, had tried to get him to lecture at their luncheon that day, but he had refused and went instead to Schlogl's with Henry Justin Smith of the *Daily News*. At lunch Smith told him that Bernard Faÿ was talking at the Caxton Club, and the two left Schlogl's for the Club. When they entered, Faÿ was in the midst of an encomium to Anderson as the greatest American writer, about whom he was going to lecture in New York in the fall. In addition, Victor Llond, translator of *A Story Teller's Story*, was at the luncheon and spoke of him with the same enthusiasm. Embarrassed by the "French" extravagance of praise but delighted by the praise nevertheless, Anderson took both Paris friends back for the afternoon to his hotel room. Newspaper and literary people gathered in his room and did not leave him alone until they had taken him in a crowd to board the Golden State Limited in midevening. He was on his way to Tucson and his first lecture in the West.[17]

At the wait in the Topeka station he saw one more old Chicago advertising friend when Marco Morrow, long since a senior editor of the Capper Publications, came to the train with his wife for a talk. Despite the pressures of his job, Morrow had retained what Anderson recognized as his "great personal charm," quite unlike the group of well-heeled, beefy oil executives who, to Anderson's disgust, sat all day in the half empty train's club car, drinking, playing poker, talking loudly of business matters with "the steady thump of coin in their talk." He himself liked "simple poor people," he would muse, but now even "simple poor people want to rise, be as ugly, as stupid as those oil men." It was a wearying trip for him from Topeka southwest across flat western Kansas and the Texas Panhandle through a great sleet-, snow-, and sandstorm. From El Paso across New Mexico to Tucson it was all new American country to him, and he responded to the "fantastic forms" of the trees, the shrubs, the cactuses in the "clear desert light"; but he was relieved to reach "bright, clean, newly painted" Tucson in the afternoon of the twenty-first. Despite the many rich people who were discovering the city as a resort, he liked Tucson, especially its Mexican and Indian populations, and the surrounding cactus desert so different from the sagebrush one he had also liked around Reno.

Before his lecture at the University of Arizona on the evening of the twenty-third, he was twice taken out for long drives in the desert and found it especially exciting and lovely when the light from the full moon made the sand white. Tucson was a city he wanted to revisit.[18]

The lecture, on "What Has Happened to American Newspapers," was to a standing room only attentive audience, and Anderson felt that he was learning the technique of lecturing. It was best, it seemed, to begin with a few informal remarks about his nonprofessional editorship of the Marion weeklies, in which "Local happenings are paramount" but which also "aim to give good reading." Then, by contrast to his independence as editor, he could move to his main charge, that in the large city dailies.

Standardization reigns, even thought is standardized. Centralized power and consolidations are wiping out competition. Newspapers have found that you can control ideas and thought as well as anything else.

Because the business office is now more important than the editor, newspapers play it safe and avoid offending, producing as a result dullness, vulgarity, mere cleverness, as is the case with the movies, the radio, magazines and books. All have especially succeeded in standardizing in our minds one vulgar, perverted idea, that happiness depends on having "money and power." Now he could come to his conclusion by way of machines, the presses in a great newspaper plant, which are "as magnificent as an ocean, as wonderful as a dancing mountain, a singing poem, and run like thoroughbred horses."

We've got to get a revaluation in America. . . . We'll survive the machine age, someday learn to control machines to the benefit of all, money losing its glamour. But those who want to be individualists will have to fight—newspapers, too—and also fight to develop a new social consciousness. We shall have to strive to achieve some beauty and dignity of our machines, gain for our newspapers some of the dignity of the presses that print them.

Perhaps Anderson felt satisfied with his speech in part because "a witty Irish professor," probably Padraic Walsh of the Mathematics Department, came up afterwards and told him, "I've been in America ten years and you're the only American I've ever seen I approve of."[19]

Liking Tucson, Anderson stayed two more days with an excursion each day. On the first, Richard Morrow, Marco's son who was a student at the University, took him on a quietly happy drive out into the desert, while on the second a group of people took him for his first time to Mexico, to the border town of Nogales, where they all ate "marvelous food" and got drunk on tequila, "a most entrancing drink." In the evening of the twenty-fifth he boarded a train going northwest to Los Angeles, then the following morning another going northeast for a day and a night through "magnificent . . . strange" country, up through the Sierra Nevada, down into desolate, already hot Death Valley to Las Vegas—"near where the new Boulder Dam is being built," he noted—and eventually on the morning of March 27 to Salt Lake City. Here at the University of Utah he gave two lectures on succeeding evenings: on the twenty-eighth "America—A Storehouse of Vitality" and on the twenty-ninth "Journalism," on weekly and daily newspapers. He was uncertain as to how well these lectures went; but when on the thirtieth he was driven ninety miles south of the city to give a noonday lecture on "The Machine Age" at the Utah State Agricultural College, he had "one of the best audiences I ever faced, youth, all alive, eager, full of fun. It was a curiously fine emotional experience speaking to them and I spoke better than ever in my life, I think." Although he considered the Mormon religion "even more ridiculous than most religions," he found the people not gray and drab as Mark Twain and Artemus Ward had portrayed them, but gayer than most other Americans; and he quickly came to admire the courage, the farsightedness, the "hard common sense" of Brigham Young, "a great man" who had left his "stamp . . . on everything." When in the evening of this last day two newspaper publishers gave an expensive banquet for him, he was especially impressed that he and various civic and religious leaders present "sat for several hours having fine, rather daring talk," "pure communistic talk." Thinking back over his experiences with the Mormons, he could write Laura Lu that he had "quite remade my opinion of them." Much struck by their "communal feeling," he now felt them to be "one of the nicest people I have been among."[20]

Los Angeles was a letdown after his stay in Salt Lake City, but he liked the day-and-a-night ride southwest on the mostly empty Los Angeles Limited, partway through canyons that were, he exclaimed, "a riot of just those colors that most excite me—yellow and red with all the shading between the two." He had not worked on *Beyond Desire,* as he had planned to do on his train trips since leaving Virginia, and he knew now that he would not until the lecturing was done. Except for his steady flow of letters to Eleanor, he had managed only to keep up with his Letter a Day, that running record of his "moods and feelings," which, in a letter to her of March 21 reveals, she by that time knew he was accumulating for her to read "sometime in the future." In Los Angeles he loafed about for two days. It was, he concluded, "a stupid town," a "fake tin-pan civilization," with its "empty-faced blondes . . . aimless meaningless retired people wandering in streets," and its "rotten" jingoistic newspapers. He admitted he was prejudiced, perhaps by his hatred of the movies made here, which gave such a "false sense of life," but he knew that he couldn't bear to live in this city. At least he could go see the Chicago Cubs play the Pittsburgh Pirates one afternoon; they were professionals doing a professional job. His dislike of Los Angeles was strengthened when on April 4 he plunged back into lecturing by speaking three times in one day: 10:45 AM on "America—A Storehouse of Vitality" at the Institute of Technology in Pasadena; 4:15 PM at the Pasadena Lecture Course; 8 PM on "American Newspapers" before the Jewish Institute of Los Angeles. Upton Sinclair had attended the afternoon lecture and kindly drove him back to his Los Angeles hotel, but Anderson did not warm to him; Sinclair, he felt, was a "soft" Socialist who associated with the rich, and his novels completely lacked Dreiser's great "American tenderness." The true compensation for his bone-wearying schedule—besides his collecting six hundred and fifty dollars in fees in one day—came at the end of his evening lecture. He had attacked the movies without knowing that his old movie friends John Emerson and Anita Loos were in the audience, but afterward they forgivingly invited "Swatty" to rest up later from his ordeal at what he happily recalled as their "lovely Spanish house with an inner garden" and to visit them at the MGM studios.[21]

He had two lectures to give before that visit. On the evening of April 5 he apparently enjoyed speaking to a student audience at the University of Southern California on "Journalism and the Young Writer"; but the next evening when he lectured on "Doorways to a New World" before the wealthy audience of the Los Angeles Book and Play Club, he became indignant that a previous speaker told jokes making artists look foolish or vulgar, and he publicly rebuked the man as himself a vulgarian. The experience reinforced his dislike of the rich, a dislike presumably reinforced further when on the evening of the seventh Upton Sinclair, the "little priest of socialism," and his wife took him to dine at a rich lady's house in Pasadena. The afternoon had been much more interesting, for John and Anita showed him around the enormous MGM complex of studios, explaining how the new "talkies," unlike the silent movies, had to be made under soundproof conditions to exclude outside noises. Most fascinating to him were the many fragments of sets jumbled together, "the prow of a ship—half a street car, a jungle village, a mine, a street in the suburb of a city, an armory," all made of papier-mâché, all realistic fronts but with nothing behind them, to him the very image of "the whole talkie world." Fittingly for his view of Los Angeles, on the eighth he had been booked by Leigh, to his annoyance, for one last lecture, on "America—A Storehouse of Vitality," at the Friday Morning Club. The fee of three hundred dollars was welcome, but the organization was one of the big women's clubs he detested. By this time he had been besieged for several days by "dozens and dozens" of people who wanted to meet him, and after the club luncheon he took refuge from these "herds" in the railroad station to wait for the late afternoon train to San Francisco and Eleanor.[22]

The train arrived in San Francisco the following morning, a Saturday, and by noon he and Eleanor in a rental car were crossing on the ferry to Oakland under a brilliant blue sky, then heading south toward the San Joaquin Valley and "the most delightful two days of my life." Over the weekend they explored the great flat valley aglow with spring flowers, spending the night together in the little town of Patterson. "The two days," he would declare to her in his old bardic manner, "were a kind of testimony from the gods of the poets—as though the gods had said—If after these two days you cannot believe [in your love], then you are no poet and no woman."[23]

After they had driven back to "gracious and striking" San Francisco, so unlike Los Angeles, he had to complete his tour with three more lectures. All three in some way disappointed him. The first—again "America—A Storehouse of Vitality"—on the evening of April 12 at the city's large Scottish Rite Temple drew only a scattering of listeners, before whom he found it hard to be the actor he had decided a lecturer must be. Nevertheless, the entrepreneur of the lecture paid him three hundred and fifty dollars, the highest fee for one appearance he received on the tour. The next evening he repeated this lecture before the Women's City Club of Oakland, another group, he felt, of fat, rich women poisoning the air of the room. For the final talk he had to take an overnight train north to Portland, Oregon, where on the evening of the fifteenth he once more repeated that lecture at the High School for Commerce, unsuccessfully because he was too tired to shake his "dull-faced audience" out of its apathy. The following morning he felt so ill that he could hardly get dressed for his overnight return train; but knowing that the long, hard tour was over and he would be seeing Eleanor daily for some weeks in San Francisco, he soon recovered. After all, the Portland trip had had its benefits besides the lecture fee. To add to his mental pictures of America he had viewed from the train new landscapes in two states and, taken on an automobile drive along the Columbia River Highway, he had been thrilled by the "marvelous scenery," especially the "fantastic" waterfalls from the high river bluffs. Although he had detested being taken to a radio studio, "filthy with noise," to go on the air, he had at some point been interviewed by an admiring newspaperman who had quoted him liberally even on "the present trend in fiction," quite unlike the "reactionary" San Francisco papers, which had, to his irritation, completely ignored him. . . . Mr. Anderson declared he "doesn't see how writers can keep from getting more and more into social criticism in disturbed times like these." Anderson repeated that the machine age was having a marked effect on people, that the style of writing was changing rapidly, and that the type of fiction that only a short time ago was the rage was now among the old, discarded things.

Most importantly, on the train heading north he had clarified for Eleanor and himself his present social-political beliefs as one who wanted "to be and stay on the edge" rather than living safely when millions of people now could not.

Something has been growing in me lately—the determination—hardening in me—to devote the rest of my life to the revolution. I think it's time. I do not intend to go into the communist party for the simple reason that I think the communist party in America is too Russian. I think there has to grow up a new kind of American communist now, out of American life. I think I have the background for it.

I really am, dear, proletarian at heart.

Admittedly a confused man in a confused time, he wanted to accept as one would accept a religion a "belief in a revolution in America, an American revolution" and to devote his life and talent to it.[24]

Returning to San Francisco and Eleanor on the morning of the seventeenth, he was determined that after a month of not working on *Beyond Desire,* he would confirm his talent, so intricately enmeshed in his love for and dependence on her, by finishing the novel. A day later he began tentatively, then for six days was in a "fever of writing—on Red— . . . all I have going into it." During this week and the three more they would stay in the city, he would see Eleanor almost daily, sometimes for lunch, more often for dinner at some restaurant with a dance floor. He was in a temporary passion for dancing and was delighted by her "fine, soft easy grace," though sometimes she was too weary to dance after a day's intense research for the report she and another woman were preparing on the economic and social conditions of the city's working women. Sometimes he lunched or dined with others, with the English writer Elinor Mordaunt (Evelyn May Mordaunt) or the San Francisco bookstore owners and publishers, Leon Gelber and Theodore Lilienthal, who had published his *The Modern Writer* through their Grabhorn Press. At a lunch with these three he ungraciously "managed to say both that [he] didn't much like women writers nor the English." Afternoons he often walked about the city observing such sights as the great-hipped Mother Jordan, who had set up big kettles in a vacant lot to cook stew out of unsold grocery store food to feed for free thousands of unemployed, homeless men. When he was taken by a newspaper reporter, Nancy Barr Mavity of the Oakland *Tribune,* to see what tourists did not—"the truth about how the great masses of the American people live in a time of depression"—he was appalled to observe the numbers of hungry men, women, and children in the "poor little street" and to learn that "there were 50,000 to 70,000 men out of work" in the city; and he was enraged the next day to see the Pacific naval fleet stream in through the Golden Gate, "the great ships moving in ugly threatening grandeur across a grey sea, guns thrust out, the people watching silently."

There was the city with hundreds of thousands of unemployed, all of these terrible modern social problems, and before them strutting this queer neurotic thing—the imperialistic war strength of America—costing more each year than all education in America.

Costing each year enough to feed all the hungry, house all our people comfortably, build great roads—make a new and a real civilization.

He was glad that he had already wired Edmund Wilson to add his name to the list of writers signing the "Manifesto" Wilson had sent him declaring for a socio-economic revolution to establish a workers' state, and had followed the wire with a letter urging Wilson to use his name on any similar statement since "Where you are willing to go I'll go."[25]

His excited work on *Beyond Desire* was interrupted when on April 24 Leon Gelber took him to see Valenti Angelo, a young San Francisco artist who had grown up working in factories and now, while illustrating books for the Grabhorn Press, painted people in relation to machines. Between them the writer and the painter, instant friends, began to elaborate the idea that instead of being owned, property factories and farms should become "the new cathedrals"; making and growing things become religious acts, thus satisfying the need of the times for "a new religious impulse" and creating "the road of the future." Convinced that Angelo embodied this idea in his paintings and that he himself had been groping toward it in *Marching Men* back when he knew nothing of communism yet "felt that march of men toward the factory as a ceremony," Anderson bought one of Angelo's paintings and for the next four days worked furiously at a book to be called *I Accuse,* expanding their joint idea into, as he wrote Laura Lu, "an indictment of all our crowd—writers, painters, educators, scientists, intellectuals in general—in a time when the world so much needs leadership into revolution, we are all such cowards. . . ." Then, having doubts about the new book, which he never did finish, he went back into "a passion of work" on *Beyond Desire;* though he occasionally returned for a morning to *I Accuse* and even contemplated yet another book, this one of "frank" notes about "notable men, so-called, in America" whom he had known.[26]

Time was beginning to run out on his and Eleanor's stay in San Francisco, and he became ever more social in his spare time than before. He kept in touch with Valenti Angelo, for here was another young artist such as he liked to encourage and one with his own interest in factory workers. During a dinner with Eleanor at Angelo's home, he commissioned the artist to sculpt a head of her, first in clay, then in plaster cast, as a gift from himself to her parents. It took Angelo two sittings by Eleanor and two clay modelings since, as Anderson noted lovingly, "her face is extremely sensitive and changes constantly." Even so, he finally selected the first plaster cast to send to the Copenhavers. Eleanor herself was exceptionally busy these days completing her research and in addition had, with three other women, finished a report on YWCA activity among the city's employed women and had spoken before Governor Rolph's Commission on Unemployment on the plight of unemployed women. On May 4 Anderson went to San Quentin Prison with Gelber and Lilienthal to see Tom Mooney, the Socialist organizer convicted, on dubious evidence, of murder in a bomb explosion against a 1916 Preparedness Day Parade in San Francisco. Although he was certain of Mooney's innocence, he was put off by the man's martyr pose—and in mulling over the visit on the fifth stated for the first time in his surviving correspondence his decision that "Some day soon I must begin writing my memoirs." He was put off even more by hearing the muckraking journalist Lincoln Steffens, grown famous for his 1931 *Autobiography,* assert that though Communism would come to America, it would be brought in by some big businessman as leader. When after the speech he protested the businessman notion to Steffens, the latter urged him to come to his home in Carmel for a talk; so on the tenth, with "Flare of life playing in [him]—ideas, self-assertion and just the same great awareness of others," he and Eleanor were driven by Lilienthal down to Carmel for the day to see both Steffens and the poet Robinson Jeffers. He found Jeffers "Cold—wanting to be strong, warm"; of Steffens and their conversation he had nothing to record except that he liked Steffens's wife.[27]

Departure was almost upon them. Eleanor, "as usual trying to do two people's work," found time the evening of May 12 to give a dinner party for the Angelos, the Gelbers, and the Lilienthals at a small Basque restaurant in a working-class section of the city, which for fifty cents served, Anderson noted, "quite wonderful" food and "rather heavy red wine in tin cups." The wealthy Lilienthals felt uncomfortable in these surroundings, but Anderson exclaimed, "How I love life." Up to the last day before departure he worked at getting the "individuality" of the last section of *Beyond Desire* to fit with the individualities of the first three sections into "a kind of orchestration of the whole." It was, he had written John, "a new kind of thing for me and I have been trying to make the prose fit the scene and the people—a baffling but absorbing thing to undertake." Lately his writing, he felt, had fallen into "a new style."

It is broken, jagged, fragmentary. Often a word is made to carry the burden of a sentence. It all hurries forward. Often sentences have no beginning and no end.

But this broken, fragmentary kind of writing seems to be natural to me now. I have tried to reject it, get rid of it. I seem unable to do it.

That was the style of his more recent Letters a Day and would characterize much of the novel's final section, a style perhaps owing something to the rush of new experiences in San Francisco and his unsuccessful push to finish his novel. In the morning of May 14, his last day in the city, he was too distracted to work on the novel and instead quickly converted one of those experiences into the story "Dive Keeper" to illustrate, as the narrator puts it early in the tale, how he wants "to find out all I can about life" and how "often the down and outs, the people out on the raw edge of life, are more interesting than the good people." Two days before, Anderson had spent an afternoon drinking gin with Nancy Mavity in a tough, dirty speakeasy, he not getting drunk, she sorrowing over her husband's death months earlier. In the story, the three-hundred-pound Mexican owner of the dive, who keeps strict order in his place, pays protection money to the police to avoid arrest and admires the unnamed "newspaper woman's" courageous crime reporting, tries to keep her from getting drunk by diverting her and the narrator through telling tales of his own life, including one in praise of his loved and loving wife of twenty-four years. One night, sleepless and worried, he wakes his wife, before marriage the keeper of a bawdy house, tells her that he desperately needs seventy dollars to pay off the police, and goes to sleep. She goes "out in the street somewhere," returns with a fifty and a twenty, puts them under his cup of breakfast coffee, and won't tell him where she got them. The newspaper woman is so absorbed in the story that she forgets to get drunk and urges the narrator to write it.[28]

On the evening of May 14, Eleanor's work at last done, they caught a Northern Pacific Limited train heading east via Washington and Idaho, he relieved not to have met up with any of the Berkeley Pralls—"I had already done that woman enough harm." When not distracted by the "strange and magnificent country" sweeping past, he had time during their three nights and days on the train to St. Paul, Minnesota, just to think about his new style, about accepting Communism on faith as one accepted a religion, about his higher regard now for Edmund Wilson than for Paul Rosenfeld because of Wilson's ability to "carry propaganda into the world of fine art," about his own probable ability in a Communist society to invent ideas and his certain inability to carry them out like an executive, and, because the excitement of San Francisco was wearing off, meditating more gloomily on how his own physical charm and strength were inevitably declining toward decay, a frightening thought for "a life-lover" like himself "whose dream is to squeeze the last drop out of life." His gloom began to recur after he and Eleanor were met in St. Paul by her sister Katherine and brother-in-law Henry Van Meier, a physician in Stillwater. The four-day family visit began pleasantly with two afternoons of river and lake fishing; but Anderson, hypersensitive, felt that Katherine did not like him, and he became unhappy and irritable. He and Eleanor left Stillwater on the same night train, but at Columbus, Ohio, she had to take a train to New York, and he headed toward Marion, depressed that their "long lovely time together" had ended. Although it was dogwood time in Virginia and he realized again how much he loved the countryside in the western part of the state, within hours after reaching home in the early afternoon of May 23 he went to bed for four days with an ugly cold, which he admitted might be—and together with weariness from his tour probably was—his mind's protest against leaving San Francisco and Eleanor.[29]

4.

For several days he convalesced slowly, then rapidly after he met Eleanor's train at Radford on June 3 and drove her back to Marion for a six-day vacation before beginning her stint at the summer camp for working women. On the last day of May, he had tried starting afresh on the last book of *Beyond Desire* by dictating to a stenographer from his first draft—by mid-June she was coming regularly to his room in the Sprinkle house at ten in the morning—and with Eleanor at home he began working steadily, so steadily that after driving her to near Asheville, North Carolina, on June 9 for her first camp session, he drove back to Marion the same day, instead of staying in her vicinity as before, in order not to disturb his "nicely set" arrangement of "outlining the tone and substance of what I want to write rapidly as the thoughts and feelings come to me and then trying to dictate from these notes." In the afternoons he might go mushrooming in the woods or visit at Rosemont, where one day he and Mrs. Copenhaver

tried to name each five great Americans—the greatest—and hit it off pretty well. I named Jefferson, Lincoln, Henry Adams, Whitman, Emerson. She being Southern, eliminated Lincoln. By agreement we later put in Melville and Jane Addams.

(Emerson rather than Twain seems odd of Anderson since he objected to Emerson's "strange stilted style"; but during his recent illness he had read Van Wyck Brooks's just published *The Life of Emerson* and had praised his portrait of the man as "all thought, dreams, intellectual dignity" though without "soiling, lust, sin.") One afternoon he sorted out Maurice Long's expensive clothes, which Maurice Jr. had shipped to him, kept some, and sold the rest to a friend for $125, which he sent to Charles Bockler to help support him as a young needy artist. Generally he participated in the life of the town, and one evening after an unpleasant dinner with Bob, with whom he was usually getting along better, he experienced a kind of epiphany.

I was [sitting] on the court house steps—drawn back into a hidden place where I could look out when darkness came. The town was like an absorbing book and I wanted to make a book called "Saturday Night." It was one of the times when a whole volume writes itself swiftly within you.

There was, as it happened, a sort of band concert given by an organization called the Moose—in the court house auditorium. Very humble people for the most part must belong to it. They came quite close to me, passing in, light falling on them, workers and farmers with their families.

Lovers. Girls in little thin dresses. Families marked by disease, what a procession. I was so excited that I trembled. It was one of the times when I, very lonely for Eleanor, upset about Bob, a bit tired perhaps—when I was most open to impressions. It was one of the moments that will be remembered all my life. What I most hate about this idea of death is that I shall perhaps never be able to distill into work the essence of all such moments.

After all, Marion had indeed become his real life Winesburg.[30]

The writing-dictating experiment was a success. By June 19, he felt that he had finished all of the last book of *Beyond Desire* except the final chapter. He had replaced the woman social worker character of his earlier draft with a mountain woman, Molly Seabright, who has gone out on a cotton factory strike; this action has attracted Red, still puzzled as to his role in class war. Assuming that he must be a Communist strike leader from the outside world, she protects him from the sheriff's search for a "dangerous radical" by hiding him in the loft of her parents' barn. Anderson was especially pleased with a scene he described in a letter to Eleanor.

There is a little scene in a barn—Red lying in the loft above—a woman milking in the light of a lantern down below—he looking down through an opening in the barn loft . . . her hands on the teats of the cow, in the circle cast by the light.

She would like it, he thought, and concluded with self-insight:

It is doing what I like most to do—a glamour over the so-called "commonplace."

Actually it took him five more days to complete the Seabright section to his satisfaction; and before writing of Red's death, for which he could not yet "catch mood, my own nerves, everything," he had to write one more preliminary chapter on Red (chapter 7) and another (chapter 8) giving the history of Ned Sawyer, the young National Guard officer who will shoot him. By June 28 he had written the first of these, and then in one day,

June 29, he dictated his account of the Sawyer family from "rapid notes." On the thirtieth his mood and nerves were such that again in one day he finally "got down the last [chapter] of *Beyond Desire*" in rough draft and "felt like celebrating." On July 1 he dictated "all but the last" of the novel and on the second the last chapter; *Beyond Desire* was finally "all in type." As he had begun doing with shorter pieces, he took the manuscript to Laura Lu for a critical reading. Although she at first objected to the scene of attempted lesbian seduction, she became enthusiastic about the whole novel and returned it to him only with some corrections, which he accepted. On July 11 he finished giving the manuscript "its last reading" and bundled it off to Liveright.[31]

Other matters had been on his mind while finishing the novel, the Depression and the need for social change, for example. He had come back from his lecture tour across the country, "feeling on all sides the social structure cracking and crumbling, men and women out of work, no intelligent leadership anywhere, and most of all, the pitiful fact that no one seems to care very much." Perhaps to prove that he himself cared, he had on June 9 agreed to be the titular head of the Prisoners Relief Fund, which he knew to be a Communist front organization. Granted that the American Communists were too Russian-oriented, he wrote Roger Sergel, whose Dramatic Publishing Company had just contracted to publish Raymond O'Neil's one-act dramatization of "The Egg," still they seemed to be "about the only crowd in America just now who have any guts," the quality the too-sweet Socialists lacked. The ugly and brutal capitalist system, which identified individualism mostly with possessing money, was sure to smash up, and only the Communists, he felt, had the necessary "faith and . . . religion" to lead the country into economic revolution. As for his own economic situation in the Depression, he was already offering to sell Ripshin farm and house, "the kind of house that is built to last a thousand years," for only five thousand dollars. Then there was the matter of marriage to Eleanor, still unsettled after their three-and-a-half-year relationship. When, if ever, would she marry him, and indeed should she? During his recent illness and sometimes afterward in a blue mood, he would write her that, though he loved and needed her, she did not, as a woman with a career, need him and should not risk marriage with a man aging in body and perhaps declining in talent. But soon he would be again pressing her to marry him. Their years of unsettled relationship more and more unsettled him emotionally, driving him to swift shifts in conviction.[32]

With the manuscript of *Beyond Desire* off to New York, he decided to go there himself for a vacation near Eleanor, Burton Emmett having offered him the use of the Washington Mews townhouse while he and Mary were at their country home at Valley Cottage, New York. On June 12 he drove to Richmond for the night and the next day to Norfolk, where he visited with his good friend Louis Jaffé, and then boarded a coastal steamer of the Eastern Steamship Lines bound for New York. On the morning of the fourteenth, he breakfasted there with Eleanor and settled into the luxury of 56 Washington Mews. Here surrounded by Burt's fine collection of paintings and rare prints, and with an unadorned upper room available to him for making last minute revisions on *Beyond Desire,* he was acutely aware that outside unemployed men wandered the city streets and homeless men slept on park benches. "It is interesting being in the city now," he would write Laura Lu, "although terrible too. Here you may lift the lid a bit and see the terror of the depression in a way that has never touched Marion." With millions of Americans out of work, ill-fed, and ill-housed, if housed at all, he concluded in Letter a Day, he was more than ever convinced that the man-woman love problem was "dead" as a literary subject. The "significant young writers who will come will all write about the new economic slant life must take now," will write about hunger and joblessness, about the mass rather than the individual, about life in factories and mills, about a "world coming into a time where history doesn't count any more." He was delighted to find that the Liveright people seemed to like *Beyond Desire*—he was promised a one-thousand-dollar advance on expected royalties—and to hear his enthusiastic editor Saxe Commins praise the book as "the first real American proletarian novel." At an all-day session with Commins on July 22, the two men tightened the book by cutting some ten pages of passages where Anderson "had been rather didactic—fancying myself as an economist, etc." Then his first novel in seven years was ready for the printer.[33]

Meanwhile, he was with Eleanor as much as possible, to have lunch or dinner, to swim at the Shelton Hotel pool, to see a movie, always a Russian one, to be together in her apartment or at Washington Mews. Once he took her to Valley Cottage so that she and the Emmetts could meet and was happy that they liked her, the day bringing out "her charm and theirs." In the evening of July 26, he and Eleanor went to hear young Communists speak on a street corner; he was much moved by their sincerity and hopefulness in contrast to his visits that afternoon to several publishing houses where gloom at money losses hung, he felt, like a Pittsburgh fog, as it did over the whole business world. That day stirred him into activism. Writing Emmett to thank him for giving him the opportunity to enjoy the Washington Mews house, he told Burt that, "I'm running around sticking my nose into all sorts of little holes, dens, Communists gatherings, talking with down & outs on park benches, seeing all I can." He was a little ashamed, he would confess in a brief article in the *New Masses,* at the figure he cut with his "white linen suit, the Panama hat, the swagger walking stick"; but if his class, "the artists' class" must be "submerged" in order to put an end to "a money civilization," so be it. Artists would survive and ought now to endure the hard lot of the workers. He signed a Communist manifesto; with Eleanor he went to see a protest march against war by "30,000 Reds"; along with many other writers and intellectuals, including Dos Passos, Dreiser, and Waldo Frank, he and Eleanor joined the National Committee for the Defense of Political Prisoners; he agreed that he would accompany a delegation going to Washington on August 10 to protest to President Hoover the treatment of the Bonus Army and that he would be an American delegate to the World's Congress Against War scheduled to meet August 27–29 in Brussels.[34]

In the midst of these commitments he found time for an overnight visit to Mimi and Russell in North Amherst on July 29–30. He had known that Russell had lost his job with an advertising agency when the company failed, but now Mimi told him with alarm that she was pregnant. He was sympathetic and concerned about the "finances" of the struggling young couple and had already written Bob suggesting that he send Mimi all the money he could spare. Bob was able to send her the usual monthly check, but the newspapers were having their own financial problems in the Depression. Glad as always to get out of the "cold . . . withdrawn" atmosphere of New England, Anderson had to take more time out during his flurry of activism to read, off and on from August 4 to 8, the galley proofs of *Beyond Desire,* Eleanor helping him as much as she could, though she herself was busy with her job and the writing of her final report on the working women of San Francisco. Rereading the novel, he was satisfied that it was "correct," presumably in outlook; but he had had another complete set of proofs sent to Laura Lu for quick reading and reply since he was "very anxious" to get her reaction to the book as a whole and to know if she caught any "holes in the running story—places where you think I have let down." Clearly he hoped that in her judgment the novel was "correct" as fiction.[35]

Fiction out of the way, he turned to the reality of a cause that had been producing national headlines for months. Back in January, Representative Wright Patman had introduced in Congress a bill to pay immediately and in full the bonus for World War veterans voted in 1924 but not payable until 1945, and the battle between supporters and opponents of the bill spread nationwide. By mid-May groups of unemployed veterans began moving from across the country toward Washington by boxcar, truck, automobile, and even on foot until by mid-June it was estimated that 15,000 had set up an enormous "Hooverville" of flimsy shacks on the Anacostia River flats at the southeast corner of the city. Their protest demonstrations grew, but Congress adjourned on July 16 without taking action on the bonus bill. When on July 28 veterans who had occupied some empty government buildings near the Capitol successfully battled police attempts to evict them, President Hoover ordered Army troops to drive the veterans from the city and destroy their camps. Late that afternoon, under the direct command of General Douglas MacArthur, a column of cavalry, tanks, machine-gunners, and infantry proceeded down Pennsylvania Avenue to the occupied buildings, where the veterans were evicted by tear gas and soldiers with fixed bayonets. The column then moved on to the main camp at Anacostia Flats, and by midnight the veterans, some with wives and children, were driven out and their shacks torched. Order had been restored, President Hoover announced, and no veterans were killed or seriously wounded; but although probably a majority of Americans approved the action, many, Anderson among them, were shocked and outraged by the use of military force against the country's ex-soldiers.[36]

On August 9 and 10 the *Times* ran stories that Sherwood Anderson, "as an ex-soldier, a writer and an American" would lead a delegation of writers and editors to Washington to "challenge" President Hoover. Organized by the National Committee for the Defense of Political Prisoners, the delegation would demand of the president, as quoted from Anderson's letter to him, "whether the treatment received by the bonus men in Washington is what the unemployed or destitute will have to expect in the future." On the tenth Anderson and the delegation of three other writers—Eliot E. Cohen, Waldo Frank, James Rorty—and an editor, William Jones of the Baltimore *Afro-American,* took the early morning train to Washington. At noon they presented themselves at the White House, although Hoover had wired he would not see them; and since he now sent word he was too busy to see them, the writers were received by his press secretary, Theodore G. Joslin. During their five minutes in Joslin's office, Anderson began reading a statement, apparently written by someone else at the National Committee, attacking the use of troops against the veterans; but Joslin almost immediately interrupted him and read a statement defending Hoover's order, blaming Communists for inciting an attack against the police, and urging on the writers their "duty to spread the truth." The frustrated delegation left the White House, Anderson more amused than angered by the nervous Joslin's call to spread what Anderson saw as false "truth." Although a police report declared that the delegation had gone at once to "a Communist headquarters," none of them did. Anderson, Cohen, and Frank went with several sympathetic newsmen to the Press Club for lunch, after which the newsmen helped him get his passport for his foreign trip quickly, and he caught a steamboat for Norfolk.[37]

He spent the next two days at nearby Virginia Beach at the house of Hugh Davis, a lawyer friend of Maurice Long, both days fishing and the first morning writing an open letter to Hoover, which he sent to Tom Smith at Liveright's for release. In this letter, published in the August 31 *Nation* as "Listen, Mr. President," he at some points did directly protest the treatment of the bonus army, but he mainly relied on the technique of friendly persuasion. He was, he wrote, "a story-teller" who had not wanted to come to Washington but was ashamed not to come, not to speak up when people were starving or deprived of their rights. For some years he had been traveling around observing at first-hand factory workers and farmers and the devastating effect of the Depression on them. Perhaps because of personal wealth and high public office President Hoover was "too much separated from the actuality of life." The idea might seem absurd, but if the president could spend three months driving about the country with him—Mr. Roosevelt to govern meanwhile and then having his three months with Anderson—the experience would be "educational" for both public men. They too could observe the actual wretched lives of millions of puzzled human beings and understand why repression on top of hard times was "making radicals in America."[38]

On the thirteenth he drove to Marion, 421 miles in nine hours, he proudly announced, and for the following day and a half had "2000 things to do," principally the "unveiling" with the Copenhavers of Valenti Angelo's just-arrived head of Eleanor. Along with clothes for his trip to the World's Congress, he packed materials for a never-completed project to be worked on aboard ship and to be titled "A Book of Days," a collection of, as he would explain to Ferdinand Schevill, "the most adventurous days and their happenings, thoughts, etc., of the last three or four years." Then in midafternoon of the fifteenth he took the night train for New York, amused by Andy Funk's last minute word that U.S. Secret Service men were watching him. In New York he hid out at the Hotel Albert, close to the Emmetts' townhouse, in order to finish last-minute revisions on proofs of *Beyond Desire,* convinced that it was now "about the soundest thing I've ever done." The eleventh was one mad rush. He turned in the proofs at Liveright's, lunched with the well-to-do lady who had agreed to pay for his ship passage, saw reporters, talked on the radio, said goodbye to Eleanor, and was hurried to the Cunard pier by the Emmetts in a taxi, just in time to dash up the *Berengaria*'s gangplank as it was about to be hauled in.[39]

He had been offered a cabin in first class but preferred being in third class with the eleven other members of the American delegation aboard, mostly representatives from working-class or student organizations, mostly young, "charming" radicals. Several particularly impressed him: Joseph Gardner, a black ex-soldier, the best speaker in the group; James McFarland, a red-haired sailor from Louisiana, who became best friends with Gardner; Joseph Brodsky, a New York lawyer with the International Labor Defense, "a big noisy man," Anderson felt, "but with a quick, intelligent mind"; and Sonia Kaross, a handsome Lithuanian cotton mill worker, "just the Doris" of *Beyond Desire,* who became excited over the book after Anderson lent her a set of proofs to read, and who pleased him by exclaiming, "I would never have believed anyone could know how we feel."

Rather surprisingly he also liked the New England patrician Henry Wadsworth Longfellow Dana, the best-informed of the group in foreign affairs. The delegation knew that Brussels was shut down by a general strike and the congress would meet in Amsterdam. They held daily meetings among themselves, caught the interest of other third-class passengers, a "medley" of nationalities, and on Sunday afternoon put on a peace meeting in the third-class dining room into which passengers from all classes crowded. Anderson often spoke at these meetings but tried to keep the focus on the worker speakers so that he could stand aside, learn more, get sharper impressions of the whole experience. After a quiet voyage the *Berengaria* docked at Cherbourg early in the morning of the twenty-fourth, and by noon the boat train had brought the delegation to Paris, where in the afternoon and evening Anderson raced around with Sonia, Joe, and two others, showing them the sights of the city. The next morning the group boarded a train for Amsterdam and after a long, wearying ride in crowded third class arrived there late in the evening.[40]

On their last free day before the congress opened, Anderson and Joe Brodsky wandered about "the most lovely city" he had ever seen with its tree-lined streets and canals, sidewalk cafés, and streams of people on bicycles. Something about Amsterdam "very quiet, clean and orderly" touched him deeply, evoking one guesses, his old response to the ordered rows of a corn field. The opening of the congress, at 1 PM on the twenty-seventh in the huge building used for the city's automobile expositions, was anything but quiet and orderly. After the 2,196 delegates from many nations had opened the session by singing the "Internationale," they milled about noisily under the red banners lining the walls, occasionally breaking enthusiastically into revolutionary song. As the only writer in the total American delegation of thirty, and one whose books had been widely translated in Europe, Anderson was given special honor by being placed on the hundred-member committee running the congress and by being seated all three days on the rostrum near the presiding officer, the French author and Communist journalist Henri Barbusse. Anderson disliked the verbosity of the intellectuals who gave the speeches that first afternoon and looked forward to hearing the worker delegates speak; but he was flattered that when, at the late-afternoon press conference, his name was mentioned, many European journalists came up to thank him as a writer whose books had helped them "understand America better."[41]

The second day of the congress was the big one. As he sat on the rostrum, he wrote descriptions of the scene before him in a letter to Eleanor and in a short article for *New Masses*. It was "insufferably hot" in this great hall, and he had "never been in a worse bedlam" of shouts and singing; yet the hall was "wonderful," for on this day not the windy intellectuals but the workers spoke, "briefly and with great fire," and when a factory

worker or a peasant took the rostrum to speak, "suddenly it is all galva-
nized into order." Outside the hall thousands of Dutch trade unionists, Socialists, Communists were marching and singing in the streets in solidarity with the delegates; and among the delegates the calls were for solidarity
among workers of all nations, for strikes against munitions plants, strikes
against war. "There is something alive here, glowingly alive . . . a song of
hope," he wrote at the end of his article, caught up with the fervor of
this "mass of workers." By midafternoon, he would admit in Letter a Day,
he was "exhausted with emotions," went to his hotel, and napped for
three hours before he could return to the wonderful bedlam of an even
larger hall, into which columns of singing marchers had begun to pour for
the evening's packed mass meeting. Except for the clamor, he may well
have felt in his excitement that he was in some glorious real-life sequel to
Marching Men.[42]

On the third and last day of the congress—already changed in name
from "Against War" to "Against Imperialist War"—hundreds of delegates wanted to speak. Although feeling that workers, not he, should address the congress, Anderson finally acquiesced to the pleas of American
and English delegates that his words might bring some newspaper publicity to the congress. Speaking for no more than two minutes and as a writer
rather than a worker, he asserted only that "in America the fight now was
all for the imagination, the minds of men and women in America." (The
New York Times did not publicize his words; in fact, it covered only the
opening session of the congress, though its brief account did name two
American delegates, Anderson and Dana.) The final official work of the
congress was to accept its Manifesto, a document proclaiming that capitalism was by nature imperialist and the instigator of wars, that traditional pacifism as represented by the League of Nations was futile, and
that the workers of the world must unite to protect the Soviet Union against
an imperialist "armed crusade" and by strikes and other militant action
oppose governments bent on military aggression. To this end the congress
created a permanent International Committee for the Struggle Against
War with headquarters in Paris. Barbusse and others urged Anderson to
go to Paris as part of this committee, but he refused, though he did lend
his name to the committee's leadership.[43]

His reasons for refusing were several. He had found that the meetings
of the congress's guiding committee quickly made him so restless that he
would simply walk out on them. Then, too, activism was costing him
money out of his own pocket. His ocean passage to Europe and back had
been paid for by the rich lady, but he had to pay for everything else in between. Far more important, of course, was that residence in Paris would
put him impossibly far from Eleanor, from whom he was much too often
and too far separated as it was. Besides, a letter from her arriving on the

first day of the congress indicated that she was going to talk with Lucy Carner, her superior on the national board of the YWCA, about the board's attitude toward her possible marriage to him, certainly a hopeful sign. Most compelling of all was his dedication to the ideal of the artist. As he had told those in New York who had urged him to attend the congress, after his trips to Washington and Amsterdam he must get back to his calling as a writer in America. During this summer he had publicly declared his position in two symposiums. For V. F. Calverton's *Modern Quarterly* he had briefly answered a questionnaire, "Whither the American Writer," by arguing that although the artist "needs to feel himself part of the [revolutionary] struggle," he should "keep clean" of a radical political party and without propagandizing write about the poisonous effects of money and the "possibilities of life" in common men and women. In a longer statement for "How I Came to Communism: Symposium" in *New Masses,* he spoke of his belief that the *Winesburg* tales were "as revolutionary as anything I shall ever be able to write," for they dealt with defeated ordinary people rather than, as in "all the older fiction," the rich and successful; and he declared emphatically that

> I believe and am bound to believe that those of you who are revolutionists will get the most help out of such men as myself not by trying to utilize such talents as we have directly as writers of propaganda but in leaving us as free as possible to strike, by our stories of American life, into the deeper facts.

Again these facts were for him the failure of the rich and powerful to lead happy, successful lives and the right of "down trodden people" to have their stories told. The underlying import of these two pieces was clear: he must be his own person, storyteller rather than protester. Attending the Amsterdam congress, emotionally satisfying as it was, would in fact be his last experience in radical activism.[44]

After the congress ended, he had one more free day in Amsterdam, a rewarding one. All morning he toured the huge and beautiful modern plant of a Social Democratic newspaper, observing, probably with memories of Frank Lloyd Wright, that its form "springs in this simple fine purity out of pure economy of space as it should." In the afternoon he went to the Rijksmuseum and admired a special Rembrandt exhibit. The evening he spent with some Dutch literary people. (He had noted with wry satisfaction that European newspapers had shown much interest in him.) The next day he and Joe Brodsky took a train to Flushing, a Channel boat to Harwich, and in the evening another train up to London. Although ill with a bad cold, he went off the following day to indulge his taste for fine fabrics by purchasing a Harris tweed suit and to walk the streets of the city alone. With Brodsky he next entrained for Liverpool to board the Cunard liner *Scythia,* which sailed in a sleet storm at 1 PM on a bitter cold September 3. The thick, warm, new suit came in handy since it was a rough passage for the most part, including a wild two-day storm, which excited him tumultously. He read books by Lawrence, worked desultorily on his "Book of Days," and spent much time walking on the third-class deck thinking of his past life and his unusual, he felt, "primitive" intimacy with nature, his ability "in fancy" to sink into it and come out "as a part of the whole." Returning from France back in 1921, he had been convinced that America was his future; now a decade later he wrote in Letter a Day a Whitman-like catalogue-hymn to what his country had given him, "It in me. Me in it."

I began to sing to myself. I proclaimed to myself my own knowledge of America.
    Mines, forest, rivers, cornfields, wheatfields, factories, cities, towns, mountains.
    I recited. I sang to myself, trying to make some song of my own life roll in me like the long roll of the sea.
    The hurt, the pain, the shallowness. A life lived, still being lived. Let someone else sing of death.
    Life not death is the adventure.

With this last sentence he almost completely wrote the epitaph that appears on his tombstone.[45]

Thoughts of death and life preoccupied much of his thinking during the voyage. He fell in with an Englishman, an ex-soldier in the British Army and now a newspaperman, and recorded at length the man's tales of "the British way of imperialism," the aerial bombings of border villages in India, a massacre of Indians who had assembled in a city to protest British rule. One day all his fellow passengers seemed to be "going toward death." He almost entered into an affair with a near-middle-aged blonde woman from St. Louis, a "man-hunter" who pursued him but whom he, in part, led on. His final decision not to be "tempted" came after dense fog off the Newfoundland Banks and the wild storm had delayed the *Scythia's* expected landing for two days; and he dismissed the woman from mind with an unkind letter, fortunately not sent, really an essay saying that he pitied "you hungry American women" who through no fault of their own had become poisoned in body and mind with death. When the *Scythia* docked in Boston on September 13, his fifty-sixth birthday, he was relieved that he "lost" the woman in the crush of going ashore. Now, all was life in his thoughts. Going on to New York by train, he went to the Liveright offices and was interviewed by "groups of newspapermen"; for not only was he just back from an international event, but two days before the *Times* had reported that he and a number of other writers had organized a committee of "intellectuals" supporting the Communist candidates for president and vice president. He "entertains a friendly interest in communism," one of the reporters would quote him as saying, a perhaps casual remark that nevertheless accurately characterized the bent and the limits of his independent radicalism. After he had held a pre-publication copy of *Beyond Desire* in his hands at Liveright's and liked its "nice feeling of solidity," he headed back to Virginia by train, joyfully picked up Eleanor at Christiansburg, and went on with her to Marion, where he found his desk "flooded with letters" responding to his open letter to Hoover. Now he had the reviewers' responses to his new novel to wait for, with hope and apprehension.[46]

5.

Beyond Desire, appropriately dedicated "To Elenore," as Anderson always spelled and pronounced "Eleanor," was published on September 19. Unfortunately, of the two reviews that appeared on that day one was by his old friend Harry Hansen, who, Eleanor immediately wrote to warn him, had attacked the novel venomously. Although praising *Winesburg* and *A Story Teller's Story* in a review running the full length of his book column in the *New York World-Telegram,* Hansen called the author of the book "repetitious," "garrulous," unsuccessfully "groping," a "first-rate" writer now filling "pages and pages" with mere "chatter." The second reviewer, Lewis Gannett in the *New York Herald Tribune,* did refer to *Perhaps Women* as "a strange, sappy little book," but he applauded the new novel as "full of . . . brilliant intuitions" and the author's "own uncanny awareness of human beings as individuals." Anderson was delighted with the Georgia-born Laurence Stallings's "gorgeous" review in the September 20 issue of the *New York Sun,* for Stallings had "got" the book. Stallings praised the book's many women, "all of them alive and well-drawn," especially the mill girls, and he traced patterns in the novel's fabric, which like the loom room of a cotton mill had "a thread of blood running through the cloth of it, as all cloth has this thread of blood if it is the machine-made cloth of today." *Perhaps Women* had been "a bad little book," but in *Beyond Desire,* Anderson, again "the balladist of the heart's joys and sorrows," was "showing the young men how to do the stuff he invented; and how!" On the other hand, on the same day the strongly anticommunist William Soskin in the *New York Evening Post* contemptuously dismissed the novel as melodramatic propaganda and its author as "the Harold Bell Wright of the proletarian literary movement." For some weeks Anderson would waver between predicting that the book would not be a public success and, as when it went into a second printing within five days after publication, being confident that it would "make its way" since it was "the solidest piece of work" he had ever done and "a new departure in American writing."[47]

Further reviewers wavered as well, dividing roughly half for and half against, though with somewhat more of them against. Very few besides Stallings praised the book unreservedly, instead favoring it despite objections, as did Granville Hicks, early in his career as a Marxist literary critic, who in his *New Republic* review found some of Anderson's "old incoherence and . . . sentimentality" in the book but primarily a new firmness resulting from his interest in Communism. About an equal number found more faults than virtues in the novel; John Chamberlin, for example, wrote in *The New York Times Book Review* that Anderson was "too rambling, speculative and diffuse to have done well by his theme," though he admitted that the book was "queerly impressive." At least twice as many as those who considered the novel an unqualified success judged it to be an unqualified failure. There was an edge of cruelty in those last reviews as though their authors had felt personally betrayed by the decline of a once good writer. The *Bookman* review called Anderson a "dolefully befuddled naïf who affects the mannerisms of the cracker-barrel sage"; the *Cleveland Plain Dealer* review must have hurt doubly by asserting that of the books published in the week by three "Big Fellows," Ernest Hemingway's *Death in the Afternoon* led as a "remarkable performance," Edith Wharton's *The Gods Arrive* was second as a solid but not superior work, while the "merely vague" *Beyond Desire* flatly "Disappoints." The *Time* review Anderson characterized simply, and correctly, as "nasty." Taken as a whole the reviews were not just a sharp disappointment to him about the reception of the book; too many of them suggested indirectly or directly that he was aging, and losing his talent. Together with the reviews of *Perhaps Women* they certainly threatened a loss of literary reputation.[48]

Now at a distance from 1932 it is easier to see how many of the reviewers failed, as in Anderson's judgment Stallings did not, to fully "get" the book, to perceive what he was saying and how he was saying it. The frequent objection that he was garrulous or wandering or even incoherent in his narrative, however applicable in certain spots, missed the point that he was as usual experimenting with the novel form and with mode of narration. Specifically he was extending the device of dual time schemes that he used skillfully in "Mill Girls" into the other three books of the novel.

The underlying time scheme in books one and three is biographical, though in each case the episodes are not placed in chronological sequence any more than is the mill girls' visit to the fair, but can be easily reassembled in order. Book one, "Youth," traces the life of Red Oliver from his childhood up to mid-summer of 1930 when he is about twenty. He is the son of a loveless marriage between a doctor and a nurse in the mill town of Langdon, Georgia. Neither parent is close to their son, and his warmest relationship as a child is with a black housemaid. As he grows up, he senses that the "better people" in Langdon look down on his parents for the father's heavy drinking and continuing affair with a black woman and for the mother's poor-white background and her finding religion after marriage in a fundamentalist, working-class church. Red becomes a skilled baseball player, and the town is proud of him; nevertheless, he feels "a bit lonely and apart in Langdon," a feeling strengthened by his being sent to a Northern college, where he first encounters disturbingly radical ideas. For the two summers after his two years of college he takes a bottom level job as a sweeper in the town's cotton mill and chooses to play ball, not on the town team, but on the mill village team of despised lintheads, who are pleased but never quite comfortable with the town boy. In the mill he likes the orderliness of the machines, but he does not feel that he "belongs" with either the managers or the workers; though he is silently attracted during both summers to the vital Doris Hoffman in the great spinning room. A rather dreamy, idealistic, puzzled young man, Red is a study in marginality, alienation, ambivalence, and vague desire.

Book two, "Mill Girls," is the story as published in *Scribner's* with some brief additions and deletions, most of the latter being passages Anderson had added at the urging of the magazine's editors, passages emphasizing Doris's unfulfilled attraction to Red and the drift toward a strike in the mill. Apparently Anderson had decided while working on book four to deal only summarily and retrospectively with the Langdon strike, in which Red is not "noble" but ambivalent, the ambivalence helping to motivate his actions in the violence of another strike in another mill town at the novel's conclusion.

With all her socially enforced limitations, Doris is a whole person. Book three, "Ethel," describes a quite different woman whose life and desires interact directly with Red Oliver's. A "fiery child" attracted to "bad boys," Ethel is born into secure social station in Langdon as the daughter of Judge Willard Long, a decent but emotionally immature Southern gentleman. As she grows up, she is in revolt against the "dream of a spotless white Southern woman" and becomes "a modern," a rebel whose cause is personal gratification, especially her passion for expensive clothes. Like Red she is educated in the North, she at the University of Chicago, and though for different reasons feels as "out of it" in Langdon as he does. Her relationship with her father's new second wife, Blanche, a woman only three years older than herself, is a compound of hatred and respect, a relationship her father is too obtuse and fearful to understand. Blanche for her own purposes persuades her husband, against his sense of propriety, to see that Ethel is appointed librarian of the town's new library in order to keep her in Langdon.

Although not "particularly sensual," Ethel has had "adventures" while in Chicago. She has let a man in her rooming house take her virginity and has barely escaped being raped by a cynical womanizer named Fred Wells in his apartment. Now back in Langdon, she is pleased that two men are drawn to her, Red Oliver, younger than she, and Tom Riddle, older. Tom is a shrewd, successful criminal lawyer, a Southerner contemptuous of Southern gentlemen and traditions. Patiently he waits for the stylish Ethel to agree to become his wife as a decorative sign of his success. One night during a furious rainstorm Ethel deliberately tests her attraction to the shy, idealistic Red by seducing him in the library, but immediately after the act rejects him as not what she wants. She returns home, fends off Blanche's lesbian advances, and the following morning goes to Tom's office to accept his standing offer of marriage.

Book four begins in November of 1930 with Red waking up to what will be his last few hours of life. Retrospective narration establishes that he was puzzled and hurt by Ethel's abrupt dismissal of him and ashamed that, though he fought on the workers' side in a strike melee at the Langdon mill later that summer, the townspeople assumed he had sided with them. He could not bring himself to confess his actions openly when Doris Hoffman and the other strike leaders were sentenced to prison. Leaving Langdon he goes on the road and again is ashamed of himself when, while traveling with a group of hungry homeless men, he cannot make himself admit that he has seven dollars in his shoe with which he could have bought all of them food. Drifting toward Birchfield, North Carolina, where National Guard troops have just been ordered out to control a violent strike, Red allows one of the strikers, Molly Seabright, a young mountain woman, to think he has been sent as one of the Communist leaders. She guides him by night over mountain trails to the strikers' camp across a river from the mill and the town. Red has been drawn to Molly, but there is no time to declare the attraction, though he thinks longingly of her as he awakes to his last day.

Into this retrospective material Anderson has inserted a fairly detailed account of Molly's life on mountain farm and in cotton mill. For his next to last chapter Anderson breaks off to sketch the thoroughly conventional, upper-class life of Ned Sawyer, the junior officer in command of the troops just arrived by train in Birchfield. Ned deploys his troops near the town end of the bridge across the river as the strikers leave their camp and crowd onto the bridge. Drawing his revolver, Ned threatens to shoot the first person who steps from the bridge but feels himself "a silly ass" for putting himself in the position of having to shoot. Red, feeling ambivalently that he is "of [the strikers] and not of them," has tried to leave the camp but is caught up in the excitement of the crowd. Angered at himself for letting down the Langdon strike leaders and the hungry drifters, angered at the sight of the troops and by his memory of the Langdon townspeople, conscious also that Molly must be watching, he impulsively steps forward, thinking himself "a silly ass," and is shot dead. The strike is broken, and Red's body is shipped back to Langdon, where many curious towns-people, unable to believe he could be a Communist, attend the funeral.

For the opening of his novel, Anderson had adapted from *Dark Laughter* the device of abruptly introducing a minor character to embody a major theme of the book. In *Beyond Desire* a college friend of Red's, a young Kansas farm man, has been writing him letters about his affair with a Communist woman who has converted him to Communism with her belief that one must "appreciate the wonder of [sexual] desire first" and then must get "beyond desire" to some giving of self to a cause. Red dies still ambivalent, having neither experienced the full wonders of desire nor got beyond them, yet in part influenced by the Communist woman's belief. For the brief closure of the novel, a page and a half on the response of Ethel to Red's death, Anderson seems to have drawn on the second part of "Godliness" in *Winesburg, Ohio,* the composite form of which he had felt he was following. Ethel, now married to Tom Riddle, did not attend Red's funeral; but one evening the following summer during a violent storm, she suddenly leaves her home and, in a "wild, reckless mood" like Louise Bentley in the second part of "Godliness," drives about furiously and dangerously for hours before returning to her separate bedroom in the Riddle house. She and her husband never speak of her outburst again, but the reader realizes that she will never understand, much less get to, what may be "beyond desire." Red had at least been "groping," as Anderson might have said, toward that end.

Decades of modernist and postmodernist fiction have taught the present-day reader that a story or novel need not be told primarily in chronological sequence; and Anderson's mode of narration now seems "natural" enough. As often in his writing the mode in *Beyond Desire* resembles that of the oral narrator, who is privileged to move about nonsequentially in time, recalling a prior incident in the midst of a present one or jumping to a future one, and to move about in space, as it were, by entering at will into the minds of various characters, reserving always and exercising often the right to enter the tale with direct authorial commentary. The result is a kind of narrator's stream of consciousness, yet in this novel, for the most part, not a random but a controlled and directed stream in which the arrangement of events has meaning over and above that of the events themselves. The first curious-seeming placement of episodes in book one is a major example. At the beginning of "Youth" Red is a grown man in 1930 with only a few months to live. After a sketch of his parents' lives and their own ambivalent position in Langdon's social patterns, occurs an episode in which Red, now of high school age, takes a girl of one of the town's better families to a party and is agonizingly awkward and shy with her. Much of this long chapter 2 then describes in nonsequential episode and narrative Red's experiences during his summers in the mill; but the final chapter 3 turns from the "sense of order" he feels in the mill processes to the disorder of the Oliver house and the silent struggle between the black servants and the "Poor White Trash" Mrs. Oliver for the small child Red's affections. In the concluding scene of "Youth," the black maid and her stableman lover have the child with them on the maid's bed at night. Laughing softly, they toss the delighted child back and forth from naked body to naked body until he blissfully goes to sleep with his mouth on the woman's breast. By beginning with Red's adulthood and ending with his very early childhood, Anderson makes, without specifically stating it, an essential psychological point. The one period of Red's life in which he does not feel himself the marginal, ambivalent outsider and is entirely, unthinkingly happy is when he is one with people of low social class and inferior caste. He "remembered these nights," Anderson emphasizes, "as one remembers a fragment caught and held out of a dream." They are, not a picture, more a sense of union with the Other, which, entrapped as he is in ambivalence and alienation, he is nevertheless driven both consciously and unconsciously to seek. Hence his willingness to accept the lowly sweeper's job and to associate with the mill workers, who, though they are white and look down on blacks, are despised by the townspeople as being not only of a lower class but almost of a lower caste as well.

Another example of Anderson's maneuvering of time sequences for maximum effect comes with the ride into the country Ethel takes with her father when the embarrassed judge must query a black schoolteacher as to whether she is pregnant. As father and daughter drive along "Red Georgia roads" past white and black farmers doing their spring plowing, Ethel knows that he would like to dare to ask her about her feelings toward Blanche and, contemptuous of his male opacity, deflects him into telling about his boyhood. As he talks, she recalls the night in her girlhood when he caught her in a field about to experiment with a "bad boy" and, the boy having quietly crept away, she refused to answer his suspicions that she might not have remained a "good girl." On the drive back from the country school—Anderson does not bother to tell the teacher's answer to the judge's query—Ethel keeps her father talking of his boyhood while scenes from her experiences with men in Chicago pass through her mind largely in sequence—her acquaintance with a timid English instructor at the university, her meeting with Fred Wells at a literary party, then "the mess" he and her own desire for adventure got her into, "one of the adventures in her own life that had made her what she was: 'I'm not so damned nice.'" The counterpoint of the ride and Ethel's recollections emphasizes the inability of those, like Judge Long, caught up in Southern tradition to deal with modern reality; indeed, Anderson suggests, the inability of most modern American men to understand women's desire to break through confining stereotypes.

It is only in the following chapter, which describes Ethel's seduction of Red and her resistance to Blanche's attempted seduction, that Anderson provides the brief account of how she had let the man in the Chicago rooming house have intercourse with her once, after which she immediately rejected him, as she does with Red. Other parallels of comparison or contrast Anderson frequently sets up to create patterns that interweave the parts of *Beyond Desire*. The unsuccessful marriage of Red's parents is echoed by that of Judge Long and Blanche, and the loneliness of Red's mother in her marriage echoes that of the judge's first wife in hers. Fred Wells and Tom Riddle consider life to consist primarily of money-making and both money-making and life to be "a game"; both men want to possess Ethel more as an object for self-satisfaction than as a person. Half awake, half dreaming in the morning at the strikers' camp, Red confuses in his thoughts the tall Ethel Long with the tall Molly Seabright, Molly as an Ethel not proud but defeated by life and glad for any love that comes to her, someone with whom he might satisfy sexual desire and learn how to go beyond it. Perhaps the most telling contrast is that between the mill girls Doris and Grace in their loving, kindly, life-enhancing relationship and the upperclass Ethel and Blanche in their hate-like relationship, which Ethel ultimately rejects as, in Anderson's belief, death-seeking.

Although *Beyond Desire* ends with the violent strike at "Birchfield"—some incidents Anderson drew from the violent actual one he had heard about from Eleanor and others at Gastonia, North Carolina, in 1929—he was not primarily writing a strike novel, one of the favorite kinds of Marxian-inspired fiction, which in the first half of the 1930s had a minor vogue. The central purpose, the central pattern of the book is wider and more complex, and provides it with a greater overall unity than at first appears. What Anderson is primarily concerned with is the great socioeconomic development he had been thinking and writing about for years: the effect of the machine and industrialization on American society and American individuals. Now, as Laurence Stallings had understood, he was using his outsider's—but here perceptive and informed—observation of the South as recent resident, small-town newspaper editor, and investigative journalist to make two Southern towns the microcosm of industrialism's manifold impact.

Shortly after the Communist woman's concept of "beyond desire" is explained in the opening pages of book one, Anderson forthrightly announces the theme of industrialization and its effects with two essays in his own voice. The first briefly summarizes persistent Southern folkways, such as a "great deal . . . made of family," the "notion of a peculiar chivalry," and the maintenance of a strict, intricate (and ambivalent) code of conduct to deal with the physical closeness of whites and blacks. The second, longer essay, which merges with narrative, covers Henry Grady's vision of the

New South after Reconstruction, then the coming of the factories, especially textile mills, into this region of cheap labor, and in particular the founding of the Langdon mill by Tom Shaw, who will give Red Oliver a job. As the factories pour out goods, they produce wealth for a few, prosperity for a number—and a further corruption of the community's rigidly Christian ethic, long since perverted by racism, through greed, self-interest, and class hatred. A revivalist minister helps Shaw gain support for his mill by preaching to yearning poor, white congregations the new gospel of material riches. Segregated in the mill village, "imprisoned" in the mill, the white mill workers from the hills and impoverished farms are regarded by the townspeople as hardly better than blacks; indeed Doris and her friends go to the fair on Saturday since this is "a day for mill hands and for poor white farmers and Negroes mostly." When, in book four of the novel, strikes do occur at Langdon and at Birchfield, the townspeople in both communities and their institutions—town government, police, newspapers, churches—are all arrayed against the strikers without any consideration for the industrial conditions of pay cuts, speed up, and stretch out that have provoked the strike. However kind to each other as individuals the townspeople may occasionally allow themselves to be, in the mass they are not their brothers' keepers.

The major characters in *Beyond Desire* would seem to have been created by Anderson to carry out his overall design. Judge Long obviously represents the decent but tradition-bound Old South, and his lack of opposition to the coming of the mill indicates the ineffectuality of that Old South in present-day reality. Ethel and Tom Riddle, whom Anderson presents with a balanced sympathy for their rebelliousness, are nevertheless products of the industrialized South and of the industrialized North as well—Tom says he is a Republican because the "big money crowd in the North" are—and are marked by their greed for money and show, their essential selfishness. Ethel loves expensive clothes and other self-gratifications; Tom asserts that "it is money that rules," and believes that "Some men are meant to be slaves, some masters." Together they make up, in Anderson's view, the spirit of capitalism. Red is one of Anderson's young men who question life, but he is also a type of young American in catastrophic times—puzzled, alienated but honestly searching for the reality beneath the social mask. At every point he is caught between two worlds, one dying, one struggling to be born, perhaps into Communism, perhaps into some other form of change, in any case into something better than the present system. Doris, then, is perhaps so fine a creation since in her—warm-hearted, competent, loyal, fearless, a natural leader—Anderson managed to embody his belief that within the working class could be seen the tentative birth of new values, new relationships, new possibilities for human communication and understanding, a new society "beyond desire."

Five days after the novel was published, Anderson, temporarily convinced that the book wasn't "going to go," wrote to Eleanor a defensive letter, which not only explains what he had been attempting to say but also helps clarify what he meant by wanting "music" buried but apprehensible in a fiction's prose.

To have [the book] go at all there would have to be in people a wide acceptance of some new world. There isn't that, no acceptance yet of the thing as inevitable, no willingness yet to accept responsibility for it, try to go with it.

I have tried, as you know, to catch if even faintly some new music of a new world—

In which the factory is accepted as a part of all life.

It might be—perhaps some day will be—a place to which we will all go—accepting thus, all of us, the responsibility of feeding and clothing these masses of people.

The point will be missed—that all of this is a plea in song for acceptance—acceptance.

Of course *Beyond Desire* has its flaws. Probably too much space is given to Ethel Long's experiences in Chicago; though she is interesting in herself as one of Anderson's major woman figures; and there are certainly passages, often in short, choppy sentences, which verge on or are "chatter," though there are far fewer such than the novel's detractors maintained. (The *Time* reviewer cited the worst as an example of "Author Anderson's prose style" as a whole.) It is easy to overestimate the book's defects, underestimate its sometimes concealed strengths. Reading it attentively now makes Laurence Stallings's assessment seem essentially right. In much of the novel Anderson was still "showing the young men how to do the stuff he invented." Further, with his observer's description of a cotton mill's machinery and processes, and his sympathetic, unsentimental presentation of the workers who ran them, he also helped show "the young men" and their audiences a level of American experience better known now than then, if indeed it is known at all.

6

Unsettled

1.

It was a "black time" for Anderson. The day before *Beyond Desire* was published, Eleanor had returned to New York, having promised to ask Lucy Carner, her YWCA supervisor, whether she could keep her position if she married him; but day after day went by while he waited in anxious uncertainty for the answer, as he likewise waited for the reviews of the book. Repeatedly in his letters to her he linked the two uncertainties, the two fears of failure. "Bob came in," he wrote on the twenty-sixth in his third letter to her that morning, "to tell me that the NY *Times* review of the book was unfavorable. I cannot get you out of my mind." He decided that in fairness to her he must give her up and leave the country for his Russian visit; he decided that he could not bear the loneliness of life without her; he decided that he must write her a firm letter insisting that she tell him once and for all whether she would marry him, and he did write the letter, which he the next day apologized for as "rather arrogant." He worked a few mornings on *The Book of Days* and autographed the copies of a special limited edition of *Beyond Desire* that had been shipped to him; he spent hours outdoors, walking, mushrooming, driving restlessly about; he slept badly at night. Eleanor wrote occasional notes but with no word of a talk with Lucy, although to his "rather arrogant" letter she sent a "sharp, accusing" reply that made him unsure she would marry him after all. On September 29, he felt better after Laura Lu told him that "whatever happens between you and Eleanor, we were friends before you loved her and we will be friends as long as either of us live." That evening two letters came from Eleanor, which sent him wild with joy. She could marry him and for the first time told him "out and out" she wanted to. Although a wedding date must be put off until after she had spent some weeks in Kansas City on a YWCA assignment, she wanted him to be there, near her, as he had been pleading that he wanted to be. At once he felt "all right" about *Beyond Desire*. The black time was over, temporarily.[1]

Writing projects began crowding into his mind. Around October 1 he agreed to Stringfellow Barr's request to do a review article for the *Virginia Quarterly Review* of Aldous Huxley's edition of *The Letters of D. H. Lawrence* and three new books about Lawrence. He dashed off a first draft apparently the day after the books reached him, decided it needed reworking, and then sent off the revised review to Eleanor for suggestions of how to make it less vague. Although she was rushed by her job and was having a painful wisdom tooth out, she quickly complied, as she would often do in the years to come, adding her judgments to Laura Lu's. He reworked the review once more and sent it off to Barr on October 13. "A Man's Song of Life" praises Lawrence for his "Kingship," his "nice clean maleness" standing out, like Cézanne's, in an age of impotence. Manhood, Anderson asserts, "finds its full fruition only in work," while womanhood "comes to full bloom only in physical life—in the reproduction of physical life. . . ." To achieve the "purer, finer individuality" of Kingship and Queenship, one must, paradoxically, give up individuality. So Lawrence, "the finest proseman . . . one of the most truly male men of our times," got by giving. Despite Eleanor's suggested revisions the argument is more impassioned, and abstract, than clear. Casually on the day after receiving them Anderson entered in Letter a Day a more immediate, more "Andersonian" reaction to Lawrence.

The best part of the day was just before dark when I went alone into the country to get mushrooms. It was a cold fall night. The sky was much alive. I kept thinking of Lawrence. There was a kind of life seemed to come up out of the cold ground, out of animals met in the road and out of the flaming sky. The farm houses all seemed very still in the evening light—as though the very houses, like the fields, were at prayers.[2]

Along with the review, he continued working on *The Book of Days*, now half complete, and began to plan a new collection of his tales to be called *Death in the Woods* from the short story's title. Liveright wanted to advertise the book in his spring catalog, and on the seventeenth Anderson sent off to Tom Smith a list of the stories to be included, most of which would appear in the published volume. The morning of the tenth was crammed with writing—more on *The Book of Days*, a short piece on the World Congress for the *New Masses*, which the magazine did not print since it had his report from Amsterdam for its November issue, and a letter on Raymond O'Neil's dramatization, *The Triumph of the Egg*, to be used as a foreword for the 1932 publication of ten one-acters by Roger Sergel's Dramatic

Publishing Company. Admitting that he might in part be imagining rather than remembering the Provincetown Playhouse production of the play back in February 1925, he described and praised that version of the ending as closer than O'Neil's in making "the whole point of the play . . . that the audience stays balanced between laughter and tears." An even more exciting morning at his desk, however, was October 8, when after a sleep "filled with sex dreams" of Eleanor, he began a letter to her, which soon turned into an attempt at a new novel, *The Family,* based with some masking on the Copenhavers. By the seventeenth he was well into the project and could describe its structure and theme in the letter to Tom Smith. An uneducated but imaginative working-class man has come to believe in absolute individualism and the uselessness of worker organizations. When he is close to the age Anderson was when he left Elyria, he loses wife and child, leaves his factory town, and goes to work as yard man for a country doctor and his family, "an American family of the present day," whose interrelationships he observes from the outside but is also drawn into. "I want to show in the novel, if I can," Anderson wrote Smith with his Lawrence review in mind, "how this man, living by a purely individualistic philosophy, comes out at about the same place as the man who goes through life struggling to give up individuality." Clearly the book, which in this form he soon abandoned, would in respects have been masked autobiography as well.[3]

Almost as abruptly as his explosion of writing occurred, it died away. A letter from Ruth and Roger Sergel upset him with the news that they might separate, and he became increasingly tense and worried that Eleanor was writing him infrequently. On the twentieth she wired him that she could not leave New York for Marion as planned. The next morning he received her letter explaining that she must have an emergency operation, which in a phone call she specified as for a possibly cancerous ovarian tumor. Almost frantic that he might have injured her in their sexual relations, he took the afternoon train for New York, arrived there the morning of the twenty-second, registered at the Hotel Albert, and got to the Harkness Pavilion at Presbyterian Hospital just in time to see her for a few minutes before she went into surgery. She came through this major operation successfully, and the tumor was found not to be malignant; but her recovery was slow, and for four days, to his anxiety and resentment, only Eleanor's brother Randolph, who was completing his medical studies in Washington, and later her sister Mazie up from Baltimore were allowed to see her. Anderson had moved to the St. James Hotel near Times Square for better subway access to the hospital in upper Manhattan and went there daily so that he could at secondhand report her progress to her parents in Marion. Unhappy at feeling shut out, he wrote Sergel to see if he could come visit him in Chicago and if Roger could send him money for the trip. Finally on the afternoon of the twenty-sixth he was able to see Eleanor, looking "entirely lovely," and on the same day began a new novel to be titled *Thanksgiving* to celebrate her recovery. It was to be "full of earth, sky and trees . . . a simple story of a family in the hill country of Kentucky and what happens to the children of the family—the intense drama of family life." Apparently a new attempt at the focus of the abandoned *The Family*, it would be, he wrote her, "different and clearer than any story I ever wrote. I am happy."[4]

Greatly relieved that Eleanor was on the mend even though she needed to stay at Harkness for two more weeks, he invited Karl to dine with him at a little French restaurant he and Eleanor favored, was struck by his fifty-eight-year-old brother's air of both youth and maturity, and sensed a new closeness between them. Mornings now he was absorbed in the world of *Thanksgiving*, refracting as it did Eleanor and her family, and by the end of his stay in New York was over halfway through the novel's first book. Back during his black time in mid-September he had thought tentatively, if Eleanor refused to marry him, of joining the staff of the *Daily Worker* or being in some other way active with the Communists, whom, he wrote her, he liked best of "all the Americans" for their devotion and humility. He had already gone entirely public as to his political position by becoming, along with Dreiser, Waldo Frank, and Edmund Wilson, one of the fifty-two members of the League of Professional Groups, which had issued the signed pamphlet *Culture and the Crisis* announcing support for William Z. Foster and James Ford, the Communist Party candidates in the coming presidential election. Now living within his new novel, however, he realized that he had come to a basic decision. He would not, he wrote Eleanor on the thirty-first, go into "active communist work" such as speaking to meetings but could and would "do most" for the cause "by story telling." The next day he expressed even firmer conviction.

I believe I'm going to take the point of view now—have suddenly come back to it stronger than ever—not that the communists are not right, or that I want individualism, but that I ought to go, with all my strength, my own road. Even if we had a revolution I'd think that about everything in personal relations we have in the world now would carry over.

If you tell the story of lives lived in any civilization I guess you tell your whole story of the civilization.

I just mean I'm going back wholeheartedly to story telling now.

Whatever new turns it might take, he would keep to his own road thereafter.[5]

Since Eleanor's mother was planning to come to New York to be with her and since Roger Sergel, his business prospering even in the Depression, had sent him money for train fare, Anderson went to see Eleanor for the last of his daily visits in the evening of the thirty-first, and shortly before midnight he boarded a train for Chicago. The week's stay with the Sergels was half a failure because his impulse to be among old friends was cooled by tensions between the couple, half a success because he felt a new comradeship with Roger and because, after the first day, he was absorbed again for hours at a time in *Thanksgiving*. Here, Anderson was attempting the "delicate and alive" task of entering the feelings and thoughts of "Little Mary Grey," who at twenty-five has never had a lover, though one night she had almost given herself to a man not bold enough to take her. Instead she has grown close to her brother Ted. One summer evening when she has brought him home from a dance almost dead drunk, she holds his head in her arms out in a field most of the night and, the next morning in her room, thinks how she has separated herself from the rest of the family, from "all life really . . . on account of Ted." That same morning Ted dies suddenly in the yard of the house as he plays with a dog, leaving her feeling terrified at losing the one male in her life but also liberated to center her emotions on some lover. (One sees in the names and sister-brother unit separate within the family the faint but certain adumbration of the short story the novel would eventually become, "Brother Death," one of Anderson's greatest tales.) "There is so much of woman in this story that I will have to check with you," Anderson wrote to Eleanor late in the afternoon of November 9 after he had been at the novel all day. That evening after farewells to the Sergels he left by train for Marion.[6]

On the tenth he arrived back in town, again took a room in the Sprinkle house, and Eleanor left the hospital for her New York apartment. Anderson worried about her recuperation, felt frustrated that he could not see her daily, was angered at Mr. Copenhaver's refusal to let his wife spend the money to go to New York to be with their daughter, and deeply resented the man's dislike of his wife's pleasure in conversations with Anderson. Marion seemed a desolate place with its trees naked of leaves in the bitter early November cold. He felt temporarily shut off from Laura Lu and soon was even unable to write to Eleanor because, he learned, her apartment mate, Lois MacDonald, became spiteful at seeing letters from him arrive in the mailbox. It was no help to his spirits to read at this time Clifton Fadiman's article in the November 9 *Nation*, "Sherwood Anderson: The Search for Salvation." In all of Anderson's work, Fadiman asserted, there were two movements: a search for individual salvation and "a sense of evasions, retreats before the overcomplicated spectacle of contemporary American life." These were, to be sure, the "type-experiences of the post-war generation"; but though in *Winesburg* and the racetrack stories he "made certain undeniable contributions to American fiction and to the interpretation of American life," his art now has little appeal, his reputation has declined since 1925, and "Like Dreiser he seems to be slipping into literary history." Anderson's reaction to the article was disgust that "So many critics go on performing funeral services over a man." Coming on top of adverse reviews of *Beyond Desire,* Fadiman's pronouncements probably persuaded a number of readers that Anderson was indeed a literary has-been.[7]

Often miserable, distracted, even "sunk in gloom so thick that there [was] no light at all" and it hurt just to be alive, he began fearing that he might lose Eleanor, on whom he felt a dreadful dependence. Nature was some relief. He frequently went mushrooming—the yellow, orange, red bricktops glowed "like miniature sunsets"—or he went bird hunting with Andy Funk and his dogs as companions. Funk recalled that Anderson was a poor shot and preferred to spend his time watching the landscape, as he did one rainy day looking up a mountain valley and seeing in the mist rolling majestically down it a recurrent vision, a romantic image of his poet-person self as "a white boy—always present in me—who runs singing through green forests and tall grass in the moonlight." Infrequently came the greater relief of that poet-self singing in his writing, but it did come on at least two mornings during which his imagination discovered a part of a central story element-symbol for *Thanksgiving* and later "Brother Death." It was the Mary Grey character's reaction to a story she had heard as a child on the Grey farm, "a question of authority in the matter of cutting down two young oak trees, near a barn." On the afternoon of the following day he was mushrooming in sunny woods and saw, almost as a concretizing of his imagination's work, "two trees such as I had been writing about during the morning, trees standing very red and alive, with all the leaves clinging in an open field." The great relief, however, was when Eleanor came home on Thanksgiving Day, November 24. Now that she could assure him in her presence that she loved him and would marry him, he broke off his Letter a Day journal except for four random entries in December, largely prose poems by a "heavy-bodied man" wanting to be "a slim boy [running] over the hills naked, through the mist, never tiring." Wanting to be and being, he assured her, and himself: "The running poet's just as real as the heavy man."[8]

2.

On some day while he had been in New York anxiously waiting for Eleanor's recovery from her operation, he had gone to a drinking party at Horace Liveright's apartment. There he talked with a lively, red-headed young man from Memphis who, after a career as a vaudeville actor and press agent for a movie company in New York, had teamed up with another publicity man to write *Wonder Boy,* a comedy lampooning the movies, which had been a stage hit the previous fall. At the party this Arthur Barton spoke of

Winesburg, Ohio admiringly and of his dream of making a play from it, and seems to have urged that the author and he collaborate on the dramatization. At first Anderson was skeptical; he had never collaborated with anyone or written a play, and he felt that, with the exception of O'Neil's *The Triumph of the Egg,* previous attempts by others to dramatize individual stories had not caught the spirit of them. In mid-November, however, Barton sent him a copy of the *Wonder Boy* script; and apparently impressed by the loose episodic structure of the play and the sympathetic presentation of a naive young man trapped among high-pressure movie-producing businessmen, he decided that he and Barton could work together as playwrights. When on the day after Eleanor's homecoming he received from Barton what he considered a "workable" synopsis of *Winesburg* as play, it was as though a door had been "jerked open" for him. Greatly excited, he abruptly dropped *Thanksgiving* with a draft of its second book just begun and dived into three weeks of work "night and day" to turn *Winesburg, Ohio* into *Winesburg.*[9]

On November 26 he responded to Barton's synopsis with a long analysis of the theme and characters of the book and of the projected play. The central theme that unifies the stories into a book, his letter asserted, and which should be the theme of the play as well "is the making of a man out of the actual stuff of life." George Willard is "An American boy . . . growing up in an American village." All the "queer, interesting, sometimes essentially fine, often essentially vulgar figures" of the town represent "influences . . . playing on his own character, forming it, warning him, educating him." Emphasizing the symbiotic relationship between George and the other characters, Anderson concluded:

What the book says to people is this—"Here it is. It is like this. This is what the life in America out of which men and women come is like."

"But out of this life does come real men and women."

That it seems to me is the essence of the theme of the book and the thing we have to put across.

Taking off from Barton's synopsis, Anderson proposed that the dominant characters in the play should be George, his mother, his father, Helen White, and, to a lesser extent, Seth Richmond. The entirely self-centered Seth, a foil to George, wants material success and the upper-class Helen as a decoration to it. By contrast, George "should be of the rather poetic brooding dreaming type," unformed as yet but "holding on to some idea of decent manhood and respect for other people and their lives." The mother should be not just the "rather tired defeated woman" of the book but also capable, when excited or angry, of showing the "inner fire" of her girlhood when she dreamed unsuccessfully of finding in her lovers the "fine manliness" she is determined George must achieve. In opposition, the father, or, Anderson declared, "at least the man who thinks he is George Willard's father," is a "mean spirited . . . cheap tricky man," defeated in his desire for wealth and "some kind of showy success," who "like the mother . . . has transferred his dream of what he would have liked to be to his son but the dream is essentially a cheap dream." Helen White, to be given more prominence than in the book, has been brought up in a protected situation unlike George's mother, but like the mother at Helen's age is "full of fire and spirit . . . ready to break through conventions whenever she thinks she has found what she wants in a man," not Seth Richmond but George, provided "he can make a man of himself." In sum, the play as Anderson sees it is "the simple story of what happens to a boy with these ordinary forces of life playing around him, how he handles them, and what the audience feels he becomes."

Perhaps remembering his recent changing of O'Neil's ending of *The Triumph of the Egg*, Anderson began having a "rather gorgeous time" developing scenes for *Winesburg* out of Barton's synopsis and sending them to his collaborator. Within a week he had nearly finished the scenes for the first act, often using minor characters like Dr. Parcival and Joe Welling to help develop the three struggles providing "the whole central feeling of the play": that between Seth and George and their opposed views of life, that between the equally opposed views of George's parents and the desire of each to influence their son, and that between the two boys for Helen White. Like the book, he assumed Barton agreed, the play should not be "a neat hard package but . . . create its own form." By December 7 he was finishing the scenes of act 1 and had thought out those of acts 2 and 3. Already he was diverging from Barton's synopsis. Whereas, for example, Barton had had the mother kill the father at the height of their struggle over George, Anderson would have her attack him with scissors but, rather than killing him, collapse herself dead at his feet, this to be the "big scene" ending act 2. The final scene of the play would be George's departure at the railroad station, but Anderson was planning a final conversation among minor characters suggesting that George has "in him the making of a man," in this way providing more explicit closure to the play than does the book.[10]

On December 14 he took to his bed with what he thought was the flu but which his doctor diagnosed simply as overwork, and the next day he was back at his desk. This was a happy month for him. Made "all alive and a workman" by the presence of Eleanor, he kept pouring out scenes for the play mornings, and every afternoon, as she began recovering quickly, they took long walks out in the country. Evenings they often danced together to a phonograph at Rosemont. Before her operation he had hoped they could have their wedding at Christmas time; but Eleanor now insisted that, as she had promised, she must first return to New York and then in mid-January go to Kansas City for two months to carry out her YWCA research assignment, and he had accepted her resolve to continue her career after marriage. She urged him to go to Kansas City to stay near her and assured him enough times she would marry him that he escaped his usual Christmas depression and worked much of the day at the "new medium—the theater" he had become convinced was "the most real of all mediums" to him. Apparently even Mr. Copenhaver—"Be-YEE," as Anderson angrily referred to him when talking to Andy Funk—was beginning to grudgingly accept as inevitable the unpleasant fact that he was to lose a beloved daughter and gain a son-in-law he would much prefer not to have.[11]

3.

On New Year's Day, Eleanor left for New York and her job, and almost immediately afterward, at Anderson's invitation, Arthur Barton and his pleasant wife, Miriam, came from New York to Marion. For nearly two weeks the two men worked so intensively "polishing off" the *Winesburg* play that, Anderson would recall, he never had time to look at a newspaper; though he did manage to send off to Liveright's office the typed copy for *Death in the Woods*. He had been uneasy that Barton "might want to New York smart my people," but the young man was "O.K." Because of his stage experience, Anderson declared, he "really helped a whaling lot in making it all good theater." On January 14 the Bartons left for the city, Arthur to try to interest the Theatre Guild in the script. The next day Anderson met Eleanor's train, probably at Lynchburg, and together they headed west in his car to Kansas City.[12]

In motion across the eastern third of the nation and with Eleanor beside him, he was in an expansive, Whitmanesque state. "I had," he exulted to Charles Bockler,

a grand ride, over mountains and rivers and out onto the prairies, crossed the Cumberland, Tennessee, Ohio, Mississippi, and Missouri Rivers. It rained, the wind blew & the sun shone. Again I got in love with America. What a land! O, Charles, if we can but begin to love it and treat it decently some day! It is so violent and huge and gorgeous and rich and willing to be loved, like a great, fine wench.

Arriving in Kansas City on the eighteenth, Anderson took Eleanor to the Pickwick Hotel opposite the YWCA and himself found lodging six blocks away at a little tough hotel where "no one very respectable could stay," named, to his amused delight, the Puritan. Here for $5.50 a week he had a big clean corner room with a bath, a view out over the city, and a long table for his writing. The Puritan was "full of little actors, prize fighters, auto salesmen out of work, and whores, also out of work." He loved being among these disreputable, often drunk people, for there were enough characters among them, he felt, to write about "forever." He was especially charmed to meet one night at the elevator his own Doctor Parcival "—soiled white vest, cheeks red from drinking—and just the extreme politeness of the real Parcival." To support himself during his winter in Kansas City and the following spring he had had to beg Tom Smith at Liveright, Inc. for the $500 still owed him from the $1,500 advance on *Beyond Desire* and for a $500 advance on *Death in the Woods*. That Arthur Pell, the company's treasurer, had promised him $2,000 but he now must beg for half that amount, might have suggested to him that Liveright, Inc. was also having Depression difficulties.[13]

While Eleanor energetically began her investigation of the conditions of the city's working women, Anderson spent two days walking about the city, reading, and writing "worlds" of letters to various friends, including one to Paul Rosenfeld in an effort to regain the warm friendliness they had had before he had moved toward Communism—to Paul's dismay. *Winesburg* and possible other plays still danced in his head, he wrote Karl, though he was trying to get back into *Thanksgiving* and soon did. Then, by the twenty-fifth, he came down with a recurrent kind of flu from which until well into February he would recover for several days and relapse back into illness for several more. On well days after the morning's writing he would often wander the city, "so American it hurts," talking with out-of-work men, sitting with them on park benches and railroad embankments or standing with them in breadlines, struck repeatedly by their puzzlement over why their hands had been made idle. Occasionally he would meet the busy Eleanor for lunch or she might dine with him and spend a mutually satisfying night at the Puritan. Since they both loved dancing, they fairly often went to a dance hall the size of a city block, complete with a large orchestra and a smooth floor where a couple paid forty cents admission and danced as long as they wished. Analyzing a pamphlet about unemployment for Eleanor as one of several ways he tried to help her in her industrial survey, Anderson out of personal experience agreed with the writer that when people are out of work, they go to the dance halls in order to feel "a part of something" if only temporarily. "I have been out of a job myself and know what it means—the curious feeling of isolation and uselessness in the social structure—without which it is difficult for any man or woman to live." The local YWCA should be practical, Anderson declared, and start up such halls to provide the huge number of unemployed people in the city a sense of community rather than, as both he and Eleanor had observed, "spout[ing] endlessly about love and internationalism and working for world peace . . . large loose sweet sounding generalities that don't mean a thing." The "more level headed" Eleanor went ahead steadily with her assigned work; the "more emotional" Sherwood—the two terms were his—exploded in a letter to Dreiser that "what's needed is one big smashing revolution."[14]

About the first of February he received galley proofs for *Death in the Woods and Other Stories.* He had already become concerned that only some of the stories he had originally selected were "fine," and now reading the proofs he decided to omit two of the weak tales and add three stronger ones, "These Mountaineers," "A Meeting South," and "The Flood." Still not satisfied that the book had sufficient "distinction," he, in a few days before February 7, "took the heart" out of the unfinished *Thanksgiving* and "condensed it" into a new story, "Brother Death." Writing to Ferdinand Schevill that he was dedicating *Death in the Woods* to him, he declared with self-confessed cockiness that this story would be placed last in the collection and would "make the book. It is, I'm pretty sure, one of the finest stories I've done, and I even dare say one of the finest and most significant anyone has ever done." Because he had considerable right to be cocky, the story deserves fuller than usual attention here.[15]

"Brother Death" is set in "the Blue Ridge country in southwestern Virginia" in the wide Rich Valley, the valley by that name that in actuality lies just over Walker Mountain visible across the Holston River from Marion. The incidents of the story seem outwardly simple, but in narrative form Anderson rejected the mainly linear one of most of his mountain tales and adopted that of "Mill Girls" with its shifting, achronological time scheme and apparently rambling tone. It is a complex story complexly told, and the incidents and their sequence must be assembled from bits and pieces as one reads. John Grey is a hardworking, successful cattle raiser who as a young man inherited his father's farm lying next to the Aspinwahl place. The Aspinwahls were rather a "fast lot," who thought of themselves as Virginia aristocrats, bred racehorses and bet on them heavily, though on the other hand they were "naturally sensitive, really first class" people. John Grey knew beef cattle and land and how to acquire and hold onto land. Over the years he slowly acquired the Aspinwahl land, the Aspinwahl house, and one of the Aspinwahl daughters, the nicest one, as his wife. Anderson makes the contrast between the nature of an Aspinwahl and that of a Grey balanced and fair, however. John Grey has made every penny count, yet he is not a miser, he is not mean or dull, and he is known for his absolute honesty; he is, however, driven to possess land and have power over others, and he has always been contemptuous of the Aspinwahls' improvidence, of their dashing style of living, and of their sensitivity to beauty.

By the time the main event of the story occurs, John and Louise Grey have had five children, and the story is as much about three of the children as it is about the parents, Anderson exploring, as in his unfinished novel, the intricate personal relationships that grow up among the members of a single family. The oldest son, Don, is eighteen, big and strong like his father, like him a natural cattleman and land lover. The next child is Mary, already at fourteen very perceptive for her age, a mixture of child and grown-up. Then there is Ted, eleven, who has a heart disease and, according to the doctor, might drop dead at any moment. (The two other children are too young to count in this family constellation.) Mary might "normally" have most admired Don, the strong older boy, but because of Ted's precarious health she is drawn to him, and the two have formed themselves into a little unit within the larger family group. Ted wants to live a regular boy's life, to "learn to drive one of the two family cars, climb a tree to find a bird's nest, run a race with Mary," but the parents and Don are always cautioning him to be careful because of his weak heart. Mary, however, understands that this overprotectiveness infuriates Ted, who refuses to live a life of constant carefulness; so she does things with him, like wading in the creek, that he is forbidden to do. One day the two children are playing boisterously in the rain, and again Mrs. Grey cautions Ted that he mustn't do this. Ted runs off angrily, but Mary confronts her mother. As though she were as an adult, Mary tells her mother she ought to have more sense than to be so overprotective of Ted. At first the mother is angry at what she considers her daughter's impudence, but then realizes what Mary is getting at without saying it in the words that Anderson as narrator supplies: "Life, what is it worth? Is death the most terrible thing?"

One obvious meaning of the story's title is that brother Ted lives so close to death all the time that death itself is like a brother to him and so to Mary as well. Another meaning emerges from the symbolic images with which the story actually opens, in time some months after Mary's confrontation with her mother and even after the main event of the story (yet to be discussed) has occurred. Playing in a field near the Grey farmhouse, Ted and Mary keep coming across the stumps of two oak trees, which are "knee high to a not-too-tall man and cut squarely across." To the children they look like the stumps of amputated legs, of a man's legs, and Ted insists from hearing war stories that only men have their legs cut off. Mary argues that women can have their legs cut off too, in automobile accidents, but Ted won't listen. In terms of the main event in the story, Ted will turn out to be right.

Originally the stumps were trees planted on the Aspinwahl land by Louise Grey's grandfather, who had set the trees exactly where they were so that in the autumn their dark red leaves would show up against the blue of the distant hills. One day John Grey half decides to have the trees cut and says so to his wife. She objects because she has always loved their autumnal color, whereupon John thinks how like an Aspinwahl it is to waste an area where hay might grow just for a beautiful effect. This thought makes him obstinate, and he decides to have the trees cut that day. What finally fixes his determination is that Don unexpectedly sides with his mother. The son has no interest in the beautiful color of the trees; but like his father he wants possession and power, and this makes him oppose his father in a struggle to see who controls the farm and the family. If the father has the trees cut, Don asserts, he will walk off the farm forever. Thereupon John Grey orders two farm workers to begin cutting the trees, and Don walks off the farm. In only three or four days, however, he returns, perhaps after telephoned pleas by his mother. Young Mary is in the barn when her older brother enters to submit to their father; she has crept into the driver's seat of a car parked in the barn, "her hands on the steering wheel, pretending she was driving." She watches as John Grey accepts Don's return matter-of-factly and says, "It will be yours soon now . . . You can be boss then." Not immediately but eventually Mary will understand her father's full meaning, a meaning that Anderson, breaking the usual rule of modern narrative, explicitly supplies: the son will soon be in possession and in turn will command others meant to obey, but only after something in him has died.

Thereafter whenever Mary and Ted play in the field, they often discuss the stumps and keep on doing things Ted is forbidden to do; but no one protests, and a year or two later Ted dies in his sleep. The story concludes with Mary's thought about him.

But while he lived, there was always, Mary afterwards thought, a curious sense of freedom, something that belonged to him that made it good, a great happiness, to be with him. It was, she finally thought, because having to die his kind of death, he never had to make the surrender his brother had made—to be sure of possessions, success, his time to command—would never have to face the more subtle and terrible death that had come to his older brother.

Part of the controlled power of "Brother Death" comes from Anderson's getting into concentrated form the contrast between what he saw as two basic human types, the lover of beauty and the lover of possession and power, the risk taker and the calculator, the open-handed person who experiments with life and the closed-handed one who accepts "a kind of death," or to put the contrast in his usual terms, the artist and the businessman. Another part is his willingness to enter with sympathetic imagination into the psyche of an individual almost completely different from himself. At the crucial point in the story when Don is about to side with his mother, Anderson "digresses" into a short paragraph, each sentence of which helps explain the complex of feelings and attitudes motivating a man like John Grey.

It would have been such nonsense to think of the father of Mary Grey as a man without feeling. He had struggled hard all his life, perhaps, as a young man, gone without things wanted, deeply hungered for. Some one has to manage things in this life. Possessions mean power, the right to say, "do this" or "do that." If you struggle long and hard for a thing it becomes infinitely sweet to you.

A third part is the amount in this fiction of much-masked biography-autobiography. Like John Grey, Bascom Copenhaver, who had a hunger for land as Anderson had perceived, felt strongly his position and power as head of his family. Ultimately, despite her firm self-respect, Laura Lu accepted her husband's authority. The Scherers from whom she came were not at all "horsey" people with a dashing life style—her father was a Lutheran minister—but she was a literary person with her own love of beauty and an aesthetic sense Anderson often relied on. Within the family constellation, Sherwood plays the "insider" role of Don only in his "outsider's" threat to Bascom's authority because of his close friendship with Laura Lu and his probable marriage to Eleanor. Her brother Randolph was no threat to his father but was like his father in having no interest in or understanding of literature and art, and in being as much, or even more, conservative. As for Eleanor, Anderson had already portrayed her in *Beyond Desire* as Ned Sawyer's sister Louise, "a passionate little thing" who is doing graduate work in economics at Columbia and has radical ideas about the collapse of capitalism and a coming class struggle. In "Brother Death" despite much altering of circumstances Eleanor is the sensible, perceptive, strong-willed, loving child-woman Mary Grey, who seeks, uncertainly because of her youth, the way to be independent in action and outlook—she observes Don's submission to his father from the driver's seat of the car that she is pretending to drive—and to be a risk taker in life. In his aborted novel *The Family*, predecessor of *Thanksgiving*, Anderson had drawn on his own situation with the Copenhavers in describing an early middle-aged workman who has the opportunity to observe a family from both outside and inside. Here in "Brother Death," much transmuted, he is the imaginative, risk-taking Ted who together with Mary has created almost "a new family" within the larger family, "a little inner world" from the security of which "they could suddenly look out at the outside world and see, in a new way, what was going on out there in the world that belonged also to others." "Brother Death" is, then, a contrast of basic human types but as well a statement in nonsexual terms of Sherwood and Eleanor's present relationship as he felt it to be and a vision of their hoped-for life together. Ted's early death, then, might represent Anderson's occasional concern that because of the disparity of their ages he would probably die first after too few years with her; but certainly in "Brother Death" he successfully encapsulated his firm conviction, except when he was "heavy" with depression, that life was an adventure and that there were far worse deaths than death.

Greatly happy at having written a fine short story, he sent off a copy of "Brother Death" to Theodore Dreiser, who for weeks had been urging that he write something for The *American Spectator,* the monthly literary newspaper that Dreiser, George Jean Nathan, and Ernest Boyd as chief editors had begun issuing in November and with whom Anderson would later join. He knew that his new tale was not the "short short story" Dreiser had asked for, but apparently he wanted to show Dreiser that he was still the storyteller. In this brief happy period before he went down before a brief resurgence of flu and depression, he also made the important decision not to leave Ripshin vacant and for sale but to move back into it in the spring. Now that good roads were to be completed between Marion and the farm, he could bring Eleanor there after their marriage, and invite writers and artists for stays in the summer.

By February 12 he was again at his desk, working now on a new book under the old title of *Thanksgiving.* Drawing at last on his years in advertising, he slowly developed the scheme of a novel about the life of an advertising man named Frank Blandin, son of a truck gardener in a small town near Indianapolis; in fact, Anderson's last known letter to his old friend Bab Finley was primarily a request for information about the possibility of a public market having been in her city around 1900, which his character could go to with his father. Interspersed among sections of the novel were to be short tales about advertising, largely critical, to provide a sense of "the life going on about the central figure . . . as his own life story develops," the novel together with the tales "to give a picture of the growth of advertising in America, its vast influence in making our civilization, effect on our newspapers and magazines, our habits of life and thought, and incidentally its tragedies." Printed by themselves, the tales might be a *Winesburg, Ohio* of business life. Meanwhile some of them might also satisfy Dreiser's desire for short things for The *American Spectator.* The combined project would help send him into one of his few comparisons of the novel as a genre and the short story. To his old advertising friend Marco Morrow he would write:

. . . the problem of the novelist is not lack of material. It lies everywhere about. The great problem always is to make the prose remain prose and yet sing. The novel, in a true sense, is a great canvas. It is an orchestration. As in all real orchestration there is a basic rhythm running through the whole and then the picking up of the theme in little side songs—that come floating in to carry and give variety to the whole. I have succeeded only a few times perhaps with the greater form . . . [*sic*] my own natural tendency being the single song—the swift rush of the short story for example.[16]

Through February until mid-March he kept at the never completed new *Thanksgiving* until he became uncertain whether the novel had "possibilities of bigness" or was "N.G." [No Good]. Around March 20 he abandoned the novel but continued to write the short things that he thought might become "a kind of Winesburg of advertising." Other projects had already begun crowding into his mind. Probably soon after Dreiser, Nathan, and Boyd wired a request on February 15 for "an article on the social revolt as you now personally observe it," he wrote and mailed off to them his first contribution to the *Spectator*. "To Remember" is a chatty piece on how he loves his car and driving about in it; how all the jobless people he picks up on the road blame themselves for being down and out rather than "blaming capitalism, the machine, our American overlords"; and how "silly" it is to be in a Depression in this gorgeous, big, varied land when "we" could take possession of all of it. Toward the end of February a letter from a man named H. S. Kraft fired him up somewhat as had Arthur Barton's synopsis of a *Winesburg* play. Anderson had first met Kraft, a freelance writer and literary promoter, a year earlier in New York and later had bluntly turned down his written suggestion that Anderson could make lots of money, with Kraft's help, by providing plots for movies. Toward the end of February, Kraft again wrote Anderson to say that Louis Gruenberg, the American composer whose operatic version of Eugene O'Neill's *The Emperor Jones* had successfully premiered at the Metropolitan Opera in New York on January 7, was much interested in collaborating with him and Kraft on an opera based on some of Anderson's machine pieces such as "Loom Dance." Excited, Anderson replied that he had for months been thinking vaguely of something called *Awake America* to be a novel or, better, a play or now "infinitely better" something like an opera, "a kind of dance of men and machines." It would be "nice," he wrote impulsively, if Kraft and Gruenberg could come to Marion in May for a working session. Anderson's immediate enthusiasm suggests that, as with dropping the first *Thanksgiving* for the *Winesburg* play upon receipt of Barton's synopsis, he was beginning to feel uneasy about the second *Thanksgiving,* was perhaps beginning to feel that he was going stale with fiction and wanted or needed to try a new medium and a new writing system: collaboration. He seems not to have noted in Kraft's delighted reply with its request for an outline of *Awake America*'s theme that there might be risks in collaboration. Chester Erskin, a producer for the Theatre Guild, Kraft reported, had made some kind of deal with "the fellow who dramatized 'Winesburg.'" Barton seems already to have begun misrepresenting his share in that dramatization.[17]

When Kraft again asked for an outline, one to be worked on at Marion, Anderson picked up on his suggestion of Henry Ford to propose as central figure, a combination of the Lincolnesque Hugh McVey of *Poor White* and Ford to show the development of an agricultural town into an industrial city, "the splendor of the machines and the factories contrasted with the growing degradation of the life of the people." Then almost immediately Anderson sent Kraft a somewhat dithyrambic letter, the more discursive part of which presented the argument developed most fully at about the same time in "Sherwood Anderson to Theodore Dreiser," his second response to the Dreiser-Nathan-Boyd wire of February 15. Published in the June issue of the *American Spectator,* this piece asserts that he has found no desire for a violent social revolution among the many unemployed he has talked with and that the Socialists and Communists have misunderstood the American spirit, which is different from the European one. What puzzled, out-of-work Americans want is the opportunity to work, to rebuild their neglected country. If the Socialists and Communists "shift their entire emphasis over to building-working," the revolution will come peacefully, "incidentally." To Kraft and Gruenberg he declaimed his "theme" with an echo from his early novel *Marching Men.*

> Listen! Listen!
> Do you hear the feet of the marching men coming!
> The builders!
> The builders!

His vision of an industrial opera as well as his conversations with workless men were beginning to reshape his political ideas. On January 25 he had written Dreiser that his drifting about and looking at America had convinced him that the country needed "one big smashing revolution." Now in mid-March in a letter to Marco Morrow, he confirmed his new belief that thinking of such a revolution was a waste of energy and that instead individuals should, as in the early Christian and Communist concept of "cells," go toward others whom they "can work with" and so forming voluntary groups with a common purpose, as in fact he hoped to do this coming summer at Ripshin.[18]

It was time to be leaving Kansas City. Eleanor's research was nearing completion, and he was thinking not only of the opera but also of the future of *Winesburg.* Barton had already argued the Viking people into dropping their permission fee for the use of *Winesburg, Ohio* to 25 percent of any profits from the play. Ten percent would go to "the play agent" (Frieda Fishbein, who had placed *Winesburg* with the Theatre Guild), while Anderson and Barton would split the remaining profits fifty-fifty, "so I won't get rich," Anderson wryly commented to Roger Sergel, who had read the play in manuscript and liked it. Chester Erskin now wrote that "the drama is all there" and the only change needed would be some re-arrangement of scenes. On March 26 or 27 Anderson received word from Barton that the Theatre Guild would probably take *Winesburg,* and he realized that he might soon have to go to New York to work on revisions. Clearly, too, Kansas City had become injurious to his health, for in mid-March he went to bed with a severe chest cold followed by a resurgence of the flu. One wonders if these afflictions were not to some extent the result of his having become a grandfather, certainly a reminder to him of both his advancing age and his past as rebellious family man. When Mimi's first child, a daughter named Karlyn, was born on February 28, he began writing Mimi frequent, for him, cheery letters; but on March 24, probably from his sickbed, he wrote her somberly of her childhood that, "As you know, my dear, I never did domesticate well."

I have always been pig-headed like that—self-centered and determined. I hope I may have done some good and lasting work in prose. It is the only justification I shall ever be able to find for the inconvenience and suffering I have brought on others—as well as on myself.

How his and Eleanor's relation would turn out he still did not know; he feared putting a fourth woman "through the ordeal of marriage with me." Still, he wanted Mimi to bring Karlyn up "into the new cooperative world. Women are going to be powerful and important."[19]

4.

On March 26 or 27, recovered from the flu, he left for Marion by car, Eleanor perhaps taking the train in order to get a few days rest at home before returning to New York. On the morning of his departure he took time to write a long letter to Kraft and Gruenberg, first to assure them that they three could work together successfully on the opera, and then to describe in detail a fanciful opening scene adapted from chapter 5 of *Poor White.* Here, for the character of Hugh McVey inventing a machine from the movements of cabbage planters, Anderson substituted the figure of Abraham Lincoln similarly inventing from the movements of farm workers a machine that introduces the many machines of the industrial age, Lincoln "working now, not just to free the blacks, but to free all labor, the heavy, brutal labor that for ages has tied men to the soil." Very likely he conceived other scenes for the industrial opera on the long drive east; but shortly after he arrived in Marion around the thirtieth he received word that *Winesburg* had been acquired by the Theatre Guild for fall production, and he began excitedly planning for a stay in New York both to meet and talk with Kraft and Gruenberg about the opera and to meet with Barton and the Guild people on revisions of the play. He was set on having Gruenberg and his family live at Ripshin in the summer for work on the opera and the Bartons coming so that he and Arthur could start a new play. He wanted to try out his notion of a "cell" of like-minded men who would give him companionship. Ideas on his several projects swarmed in his head. "Why," he wrote Roger Sergel, for example, "can't the [opera] be done now in the talkies?"

Get real & poetic stars and do your machine things actually in factories. Great dinamos—as at Mustle [Muscle] Shoals—delicate intricate machines—big newspaper presses—insides of cotton mills.

Music made to fit the dancing and whirling of all this—an orchestration with song of the new day to come.

This from the man who had wanted nothing to do with the movies.[20]

Then another reason, in fact a necessity, for going to New York broke in on him. He learned, probably from Tom Smith, that Liveright, Inc. was in deep financial trouble and that employees were being laid off. Anderson needed to come to the city at once. By April 19 he was there being interviewed by reporters from the *Times* and the *Herald Tribune*. Apparently he could not comment directly to them on Liveright affairs, but he did insist that writing books was "a dead business" and that young writers should turn to the moving pictures since Americans now were more interested in them. What the country needed was "a great American movie and not a great American novel."

Movies should be simple. I am not sure I believe in propaganda movies, though Eisenstein's 'Potemkin,' with that wonderful scene of the terror on the long flight of steps, was a great work. But the movies I have in mind should be simple stories of life in this country, in America. I believe it would work, though I'm not entirely sure.

After asserting that he was going to try writing scenarios, he maintained rather oddly that his new enthusiasm for film came from talking with unemployed men in Kansas City who had no interest in political revolution and only wanted work. Perhaps the connection was that, as he told the reporters, he could best write his simple stories "about people who are a little hungry, a little ragged," when he was closer to being poor himself.[21]

With these interviews he launched into a two-week whirl of activity, which, he complained, hardly gave him time to breathe. He had an encouraging conversation with Theatre Guild people, who were "enthusiastic" about *Winesburg*, and a discouraging one with Tom Smith about the confusing Liveright mess. Apparently he did see at Smith's office for the first time the file to date of reviews of *Death in the Woods,* which had been published unadvertised on April 8, and was delighted to learn, as he put it, that his stock was up. Lewis Gannett in the daily *Herald Tribune* and Harry Hansen in the *World-Telegram* praised the book highly though with objections to the weaker stories, while Fred T. Marsh in the Sunday *Herald Tribune Books,* though dismissing Anderson's novels, commended the collection almost unreservedly and its author as "the supreme story teller of a significant period, now passing." (With only a few unfavorable exceptions subsequent reviews would also welcome the new proof that Anderson's true talent was for the short story, and only one, in the *Boston Transcript,* would find the book almost totally without redeeming aesthetic value.) Seeing Eleanor as often as her work permitted, Anderson spent the next two or three days talking with Gruenberg and Kraft about the opera and with Barton about *Winesburg* and ideas for a new play. Since he found Gruenberg afraid of "the machine theme," he urged instead an opera about the Mississippi River. On the twenty-fourth he and Barton had a conference with Theatre Guild representatives, who told them that *Winesburg* was "grand stuff—fine character drawing but not a play." Obviously when the Bartons came to Ripshin, the collaborators needed to work hard on revision. Anderson may have begun having doubts about Barton when on the twenty-fifth he and Eleanor went to the opening night of Barton and Don Lockbiler's comedy *Man Bites Dog,* which he along with the drama critics thought "pure horrible." The next evening, at the urging of the Theatre Guild that he look for actors who might be suited for parts in *Winesburg,* he and Eleanor saw Maxwell Anderson's *Both Your Houses* and concluded that the play's Sheppard Strudwick would be perfect for George Willard.[22]

By the twenty-seventh it was clear to Anderson that Liveright, Inc. was "going on the rocks" and would soon fail, for most of the employees had left when no money was available to pay them; and in fact a week later three of the company's creditors filed an initial petition in bankruptcy against it. The approaching failure of his publisher was a catastrophe for Anderson, since except for sending out review copies, no effort at all was being made to sell *Death in the Woods* despite its generally enthusiastic reviews. Liveright, Inc., Anderson wrote Roger Sergel, had done him "dirt of course—issuing my new book when they knew they were bankrupt—I must presume just to tie it up as an additional asset." Not only would he receive no income from royalties on the book, but the critical success coupled with even a moderate advertising campaign might at least have checked his declining literary reputation. Further, he must now find a new publisher as other Liveright authors were forced to do. Fortunately his name still carried power. Quickly he was approached by several publishers— Knopf, Simon and Schuster, Scribner's, and Viking—where Ben Huebsch was willing to let bygones be bygones. He was especially attracted to Viking, for at a lunch Huebsch assured him that with this company he could get all of his books under the same publisher with more favorable contracts than Huebsch had originally offered. Viking might even bring out, as Anderson wanted, a volume of his collected short stories. Since the whole situation was confused and confusing, he asked the capable Luise Sillcox of the Authors League to handle any actual negotiations.[23]

Other elements entered the whirl. Probably prompted by the newspaper interviews, an agent from Paramount Pictures took him to lunch and told him that the company "wanted a story," and Anderson suggested that the agent consider the "picture possibilities" of *Marching Men*. Frieda Fishbein, the agent who interested the Theatre Guild in *Winesburg*, now wanted to "handle [his] books with the movie people." It was a relief on the twenty-seventh to have dinner and the evening with Dreiser, whom he found as impressive as ever; and he had the good fortune one day to meet on the street his old artist friend Jerome Blum and see his new paintings, which led him to begin writing a piece on "the rich sweet feelings" they gave him. His praise for the "ripe, alive, glowing" new quality of Blum's canvases would appear as "Communications" in the September *American Spectator*. For the most part his days were too busy for writing, but he sold two of his advertising sketches from *Thanksgiving* for two hundred dollars each to the *New Yorker*, which in its May 27 issue printed "Pop," Anderson's first appearance in that magazine. Pop Porter is the fat, amiable manager of the copy department at the Griver-Wharton advertising agency who tumbles drunk down the marble staircase of an advertising club and breaks his neck, thus adding to the record of violent death and suicides of employees in that department over the years. "Off Balance," to be published in the August 5 issue, tells of Alonzo Funkhouser, vice-president of Griver-Wharton, who made big money during the war, whose son "Got his head blown off" in battle, and who always refers melodramatically to his son's death in his many speeches to business associations. Billy Moore, an alcoholic copywriter, trains Alonzo in melodramatic presentation but hates him, and one day punches him flat yet is retained in his job by Alonzo, who likes, and needs, him. Both rather slender pieces illustrate Anderson's desire, like Billy's, to "show . . . up" the "advertising racket."[24]

His last few days in New York were hectic. He talked on radio on Sunday, April 30; he visited Ring Lardner during his last stay in Doctors Hospital before his death the following September, and in Lardner's words they "got to talking why we'd ever left our small towns"; he talked about movie contracts with the playwright Sidney Howard, who advised him that if he sold anything to the movie people, there was no way to control what they did with it. Somehow he had met the stage and screen actor Paul

Muni, who was about to star in a "Special Return Engagement" of Elmer Rice's *Counsellor-at-Law,* and he spent a "fine" evening with him and his wife discussing Muni's idea for a "mining story," on which Anderson could collaborate with him after spending some weeks in mining country to get a feel for the life there, Kraft to turn such a story into script form for a movie. Nothing would come of this proposed collaboration, but the weeks in New York when he was "flirted with by movie people, actors and the sort of small play carpenters with which the town is full," had fed his sudden brief fascination with the film world. Preparing to leave the city, he collected what advice he could get from any source, including Sergel in Chicago, about the failure of Liveright, Inc., where his book was "just lying dead," and about the best publisher for him to go to. He decided on Viking. Probably one of his last acts, however, was to respond to a request from the publishing firm of William Morrow to join other American authors in writing letters to condemn the Nazis' public burning of books by and about Jews scheduled for May 10. The *New York Times* of that date listed five authors who had written open letters of protest—Anderson, Faith Baldwin, Irvin S. Cobb, Sinclair Lewis, and Lewis Mumford—and after quoting from Lewis concluded: "Mr. Anderson referred to the anti-Semitic crusade in literature as 'utterly stupid' but cautioned against becoming overalarmed as to its importance." If Anderson was in this instance a poor prophet of the future, he at least recognized and openly condemned an outrage in the present.[25]

5.

On May 5 Anderson was back in Marion and almost immediately began dashing about for days collecting beds, bedding, chairs, dishes, and other household goods for settling the Gruenbergs and the Bartons at Ripshin for the summer's experiment in cooperative living. On the seventeenth the Gruenbergs—Louis, wife Joan, their baby, and Joan's mother—arrived in Marion and were driven to the farm in convoy with Anderson in lead car, the Gruenbergs in Andy Funk's, and a truck following with their baggage. They were put up in the "green house," part garage, part apartment; Louis had Anderson's writing cabin on the hill for his composing, and a piano borrowed from Marion College was shortly trucked to the cabin. Anderson found Gruenberg temperamental, one day "sunny," another "terrible," sometimes kindly, sometimes rude, devoted both to art and to popular success, deeply versed in music and theater, an expert technician but definitely different from himself: "Art to me is an adventure. To him it is a profession." Together, he felt, they complemented each other, and he could learn much about stagecraft from him. When Anderson wrote a complete story line for *The Mississippi* for him, Gruenberg during the rest of that single day worked out the "theme" of the opera and its presentation through pictures, actors, and an off-stage chanting chorus.[26]

Frequently sparked by Gruenberg's theaterwise suggestions, Anderson worked off and on at a revision of *Winesburg* while waiting for Barton's arrival. On the morning of May 23, however, he wrote a short introduction to Charles Cullen's illustrated book of selections from *Leaves of Grass,* for which the publisher, Thomas Y. Crowell, paid him a much-needed one hundred dollars. Emersonian "Self-Reliance," fixed in the American mind, the introduction characteristically asserts, helped produce industrialism, the flight from the land to the cities, and the notion of money as the measure of success. But Whitman "is in the bones and blood of America . . . is the real American singer." Americans must return to "land-love, river and sky-love" in order to "begin again to get brother-to-brother love of which Whitman sang and dreamed." Such love was about to be tested by the arrival of Arthur Barton and his family in the first week of June.[27]

Anderson had had two tents with wooden floors set up "charmingly" among the apple trees behind the house, one for Arthur, Miriam, and their five-year-old son to live in, one for Arthur to work in. Almost immediately Anderson realized that inviting Barton there had been a mistake. The recent attacks on his second play had destroyed Arthur's cockiness but had also left him pitifully afraid of Sherwood and blocked from making any but "trifling" suggestions for revising *Winesburg* either when working with him or by himself. By contrast Anderson fell into a schedule: up early, into the creek for a dip, breakfast at his desk, and five or six hours of solid work. Resolved not to make further mistakes, he wrote Kraft that he would be collaborating only with Gruenberg on *The Mississippi,* and he began steeling himself to tell Barton as kindly as possible that further collaboration with him on *Winesburg* must end. His resolve was strengthened by Eleanor's arrival in Marion on the twelfth. Her master's thesis, "Working Women in San Francisco, California," had been "approved and delivered" at Columbia on May 19, she had received the Master of Arts degree in the Faculty of Political Science on June 6, and had that part of her life behind her. She now assured Anderson that she would marry him after she completed her two-week YWCA assignment to Camp Merrie-Wood near Hendersonville, North Carolina. On the eighteenth he ecstatically drove her to the camp and the following day returned to Ripshin filled with "a marvelous new feeling of courage." The next evening Barton forced the issue by asking Anderson how he felt about him. Putting it as gently as he could, Anderson told him that he had not understood the people in *Winesburg,* that he had been no help at all on the play while at Ripshin, and that he and his family should leave soon. The evening ended with a sometimes weeping Barton consuming a quart of Anderson's gin and pouring out "hours of drunken talk" about his sexual exploits. Perhaps he himself would learn from the whole experience with Barton, Anderson wrote Eleanor, "that you can't really help secondary people in the arts, etc. Poor lad."[28]

The strain between the two men increased with the arrival on the twenty-first of Roger Sergel and his eighteen-year-old son Chris for a welcome four-day visit. Suspicious of Barton, who claimed that he had copyrighted *Winesburg* in Anderson's and his name, Sergel drew up a transfer of copyright to Anderson alone and made him sign the transfer. Roger then insisted that they all go to Marion, as they did, and have Andy Funk draw up a new contract changing the equal sharing of profits to 65 percent for Anderson, 35 percent to Barton, a contract both men signed. Even more cheering to Anderson was Roger's enthusiastic praise when Anderson read aloud to both Sergels and Barton the first two acts of *Winesburg* he had completed revising. Although Laura Lu Copenhaver had been reading the scenes as he revised them and making suggestions, he even more trusted Sergel's judgment based on long experience reading plays for his publishing business. At the reading Barton as usual had no helpful comment. On the twenty-sixth after the Sergels had left, Anderson received in the mail a voluntary loan of five hundred dollars from Burton Emmett and, feeling rich, bought a beautiful saddle mare for Eleanor for one hundred; but he also received the sad news from Ferdinand Schevill that his wife, Clara, had died. Upset, he decided that night, as abruptly as in his youth he had stamped on his own straw hat, to "boot [Barton] out" before Eleanor returned from Camp Merrie-Wood. For several days he buried himself in revisions of the third act of *Winesburg,* and then on the Fourth of July, not having the courage for another confrontation with Barton, he got up early and wrote him a letter flatly stating that he wanted him and his family to be on the way to New York by the time he himself returned from a two day absence. "In your work on this play," he continued bluntly,

I have felt that you never at all grasp the real story of the play, the meaning of these lives with which we are working here. What you have got to do, to learn to do, is to feel about the people of whom you are writing as tender as you are now rather in the habit of feeling about yourself. When I have done a really good bit of writing, the reader should never be left feeling that I have been doing good or clever writing. The entire absorption of the reader should be rather in the people written of. I thank God that no one yet has ever thought to call me a smart or clever writer.

Rather as he had abruptly driven away from Tennessee back in 1922, he drove south for Hendersonville "most of the time at 60," wildly eager now to pick up Eleanor as soon as she was free to come home and marry him.[29]

They did drive home together on July 6, and that evening they were married at Rosemont by the Lutheran pastor "in a quiet ceremony before a small group of relatives," after which, according to the brief *Smyth County News* announcement of that date, "Mr. and Mrs. Anderson left on a motor trip to a Virginia resort," that resort, one suspects, actually being Ripshin. No more did he talk of selling the farm; with Eleanor there as wife it was at last home, and he settled down happily to finish the revision of *Winesburg*. Eleanor was happy with Ripshin and, she "guessed" in her diary, with Sherwood, but her feelings were indeed more complicated. She loved him; yet as she confessed to Mary Emmett, she had married "against my better judgment" and at least at first found that "marriage doesn't solve anything." The problem was her job with the YWCA. Although it was strenuous and wearying, she was committed to social work, got satisfaction from it, and enjoyed the sense of independence her small but steady salary gave her. Now she was concerned with how to harmonize "the two professions of wife and worker" since after his morning writing her husband wanted her with him the rest of the day. He complicated matters in another way. He kept urging her to resign, but when she spoke seriously of doing so, he became "frightened" about their financial future. What if *Winesburg* should not be staged by the Guild or staged and failed? Then there was the question of her name. Her mother and the Y wanted her to keep her last name as Copenhaver whereas Sherwood repeatedly urged her to make it Anderson on the grounds that keeping one's maiden name after marriage "was a sort of half refusal to face a fact." She soon persuaded the Y that she should sign herself Eleanor Anderson, but the job was the main problem. On the seventeenth she had to return to New York for a ten-day assignment. She offered to resign, was refused as being too valuable to the organization, and, though her salary was cut, eventually accepted the arrangement of working ten months a year with two months off. As the years of their marriage passed, it would prove better for them both financially and psychologically that she kept her job.[30]

Although lonely for Eleanor away in New York, he kept busy at *Winesburg*, completed the revision by the twenty-fourth, and had copies made for sending off to the Theatre Guild and to such friends as Roger. He had discovered from correspondence with the Copyright Office in Washington that Barton had lied to him and had actually registered *Winesburg* as by Arthur Barton only, and he mailed to Luise Sillcox at the Authors' League for action the transfer to himself only, which he and Barton had both signed. Momentarily convinced that his future lay in playwriting, he started a "mountain play"—never finished—based on "Brother Death" and "These Mountaineers," and he definitely decided not to collaborate on *The Mississippi* with Gruenberg, who increasingly seemed to him obsessed with the desire for money and fame. Collaboration had turned out to be "a delicate matter." If he collaborated with anyone, it should be Sergel, he wrote his friend, for they understood and complemented each other. But already he was thinking of doing a book of memoirs Roger had suggested to him during his Ripshin visit, to be called *I Build My House*—

the story of a man's experience building a house in the mountains with native labor . . . really the study of a mountain community and the relationship between the mountain people and the man coming in from the outside. This could be a very fascinating human study of people and would be great magazine stuff.[31]

While he was puzzling which project to turn to next, Sillcox urged him to come to New York immediately since the publishing situation was in disarray, and he arrived there on the twenty-eighth to cope with it as well as he could. The many creditors of Liveright, Inc. had organized and brought another bankruptcy suit against the company, and on July 12 it had been declared bankrupt, with, as Anderson had surmised, an income "for the past month's sales . . . held for the benefit of creditors." On the twenty-fifth the assets of Liveright, Inc. had been sold for $18,000 to one Victor Gold, but since Arthur Pell had retained ownership of the largest number of shares of company stock, he would be able shortly to gain control of the firm and reorganize it as the Liveright Publishing Company with himself continuing as the now all-powerful head of the business department. During Anderson's two-day stay in New York, however, he was released from any contract with the company and was sought after by Viking, of which he had become distrustful, and Scribner's, where Max Perkins pleased him by saying that he was "the best writer in America" but had been mismanaged by Horace Liveright as "being a sex writer." When he and Eleanor left the city, he was leaning strongly toward accepting any Scribner offer.[32]

On August 1 Perkins mailed him a formal offer to join Scribner's, stipulating that his next book would be "a continuous narrative," either a novel or something like *A Story Teller's Story*. Anderson had already "plunged into" *I Build My House* and had decided that the stone house must be extended to symbolize "American earth, American men & women met . . . the house that is a man's self built." As he went at it in a rush—5,000 words in a few days, 20,000 in some three weeks—he decided that the narrative must be "a story of my own experience in the American literary world, people met, what has hurt and what has helped me in my own particular effort to produce beautiful literature here." It would be an extension of *A Story Teller's Story* into the present—and a first tentative reach toward what would become the *Memoirs*. Having written about 20,000 words, however, he felt the need for a fresh start among all the recollections crowding in on him, and he momentarily put aside the project with what Eleanor called its "glorious prose."[33]

Considering the distractions going on about him at Ripshin, it is something of a wonder that he managed to write as much as he did of *I Build*

My House. On August 2 his New Orleans friends Marc and Lucile Antony arrived for a brief visit, during which they read aloud the final installment in the August *Atlantic* of *The Autobiography of Alice B. Toklas*, Anderson "beam[ing]" at Stein's praise of him and Eleanor "thrilled" that he should "get a good critical word for a change." Stein, she noted in her diary "is evidently a great thing in his life and to him." There was a birthday party for Louis Gruenberg, a Copenhaver clan picnic, and a constant stream of visitors, many seeking Anderson's help on some project; and on the tenth Henry Wallace, President Roosevelt's new secretary of agriculture, who had wanted to see Anderson, arrived with his son for much talk and an overnight stay. At this his first chance to size up a "New Dealer" directly, Anderson found Wallace "keen and sensitive" and began feeling drawn toward the hopefulness of a New Deal for America. In the midst of this activity, an enthusiastic letter arrived from Viking on the fourth with a better offer than Scribner's had made; but after some indecision Anderson, at least by the twelfth, committed himself to Scribner's primarily on the basis of his strong liking for Max Perkins, and he turned the Viking offer down. Even more exciting was a letter from Mary Emmett inviting the Andersons to live in the Washington Mews house while the Emmetts were in Europe for Burt's health. The deep pleasure both Andersons felt at the prospect of a winter in the city at their favorite place helped to offset their uneasiness when, later in the month, the Theatre Guild wrote that they did not like the revised third act of *Winesburg*. What the Andersons presumably did not know at this point was that by early August the Guild had accepted Eugene O'Neill's *Ah, Wilderness!* as the first play of their season and had immediately begun production. Subsequently, Anderson would learn that the Guild had already decided against accepting *Winesburg*, not wanting to do in the same season another "small town" play besides O'Neill's comedy.[34]

While Eleanor was away for a week in early September, Anderson suddenly found his fresh start for *I Build My House* and began writing with "new force," this time going back in more exact detail than in *A Story Teller's Story* to his childhood and the coming of the industrial age to Clyde. He now wanted to tell, he would write the Emmetts on the fifteenth,

in story form—half story and half reflection—the tale of what happened to a young American business man, that reversed everything in him—attitude toward his fellows, toward sex—toward society—his turning toward the arts and his adventures in the American field of intellectuals and artists. . . .

By that time, he had written, he claimed, "nearly 40,000 words" about how his house of self was built. Meanwhile he was beginning to pack for the winter in New York, preparing to close up Ripshin, and firmly and directly telling Gruenberg that he was taking him and his family to Marion on the ninth and putting them on the 8:50 PM train. Since he had learned some dramatic technique from Louis during the summer, the cooperative experiment, he felt, had not entirely failed; but he had become increasingly irritated with the whole family as "slaves to little pieces of money" and was immensely relieved when they were gone. For years he had attacked individualism in the American businessman, but he had to admit that as an American writer he was too individualistic himself for collaboration with another.[35]

Eleanor had barely returned to Ripshin on the tenth when she had to leave for Chicago where, on the thirteenth, she was to represent the YWCA at a meeting of government officials. This time Sherwood insisted on going with her. They stayed at his favorite hotel, the Auditorium; and it may have been to celebrate his fifty-seventh birthday that they spent an evening at the Chicago's World's Fair, "A Century of Progress," which he thought a mixture of the wonderful and the cheaply gaudy. He was more excited by the city itself—"amazing, changing, undisciplined, odd flashes of a new world, remnants of an old." The peak experience for them both was his taking Eleanor to the old rooming house at what used to be 735 Cass Street and, under the pretext of their looking for lodging, to the room on the top floor, the one with the window looking down toward the Loop, the one where he wrote "Hands" and many of the other tales of *Winesburg, Ohio*. In his later account of that visit in "The Finding" in the *Memoirs*, he had earlier told her of the grandeur of the room and was now shocked by the shabbiness of the house and the actual smallness and tattiness of the room; nevertheless, it was in this room that on one exalted night he wrote "Hands" and so discovered his vocation. Hurrying his wife away from room and house, he recalls that discovery but also the failures that had preceded it and those in both life and art in his succeeding years. But in a letter he wrote Burt and Mary Emmett one or at most two days after the visit, he gives an account differing sharply in tone, details, and outcome.

> I took E[leanor] with me and we went—pretending we were a couple seeking rooms—I think the landlady was suspicious—she may have thought I had made a pickup on the street—
> We went to the old rooming house, and to the room where I wrote Winesburg.
> Afterwards she wanted to go there—sleep there while we were here but I wouldn't. Our going was such a success—old dreams coming back—faces popping up.
> "No," I said—"let me have it just as it is."

The contradictions between the two accounts must be examined in context at the end of chapter 12 in order to understand the nature of *Sherwood Anderson's Memoirs*.[36]

Returning to Ripshin, the Andersons packed quickly and headed north in the Chevrolet, arriving at 56 Washington Mews in the evening of the eighteenth. Happily settled into a quiet, comfortable studio room on the second floor, he started again on *I Build My House,* then endured a four-day "awful slump" (Eleanor's phrase) probably caused by his growing concern that the Theatre Guild would not produce *Winesburg* and by worry that he had "made nothing" from the year's writing, though in actuality he had received $400 for the two *New Yorker* sketches and $100 for the Whitman introduction. "With me," he confessed in a letter to the Emmetts, "the blues take the form of a kind of dreadful humility . . . I want to crawl and debase myself before every man or woman I meet on the street." He pulled out of the slump by seeing the many people he knew in the city. When Horace Liveright died of pneumonia on September 24, intestate and almost penniless, Anderson loyally attended the funeral service for his flamboyant former publisher in the morning of September 26, lunched with Max Perkins, and in the evening took Eleanor to dinner with some of his New York friends. "Sherwood," Eleanor soon decided, "has lots of friends, too many sometimes, who drop in. He likes it when they come to help him pass the afternoon but loathes it when they interrupt his morning work." Frequently he saw Dreiser, who repeatedly urged him to become an editor of the *American Spectator.* Liking Dreiser "tremendously," Anderson (at a dinner with him, George Jean Nathan, and Ernest Boyd) accepted, knowing that the editorship was unpaid but feeling, as he wrote the Emmetts, that the connection "would give me an outlet and association with some very interesting men."[37]

On October 3 the Andersons drove to Washington. Eleanor was to observe the American Federation of Labor convention, where there were mixed signs that the organization might be overcoming its long lethargy; but the real excitement was in the atmosphere of the still new Roosevelt administration. They were invited to dinner at the home of Jerome Frank, whom Anderson had known as a Chicago lawyer and who was now head of the legal division of Wallace's Department of Agriculture. Wallace and his wife dropped in later that evening, and during a long conversation Wallace offered Anderson a job as a publicity man for the department. Feeling unsuited for the job, he turned it down; but having "taken a violent liking to Wallace, a very very human man" and being exhilarated by the two New Dealers, he began thinking over succeeding days of ways in which he might help them, perhaps traveling about the country and reporting people's reactions to the new role for government being planned by such men. They seemed to him to be establishing "an entirely new principle in American life" he himself was for: the treatment of human beings—not as objects as in the usual factory—but simply as human beings. Eleanor too was offered a job in a large experimental plan for worker education. She turned it down, but the stir, the excitement, the heady spirit of Washington stayed with both after their return to New York on October 7 and would soon influence Anderson in making another kind of decision.[38]

Just before leaving for Washington, Anderson had written and sent off to the *American Spectator* a satirical sketch of a man he presumably met on a train out of New Orleans whose emphatically expressed attitudes reveal him to be a superpatriot. He apparently has become "the rat [muskrat] king of the South" by organizing "a lot of selfish individual men," the independent muskrat trappers, into a strictly rationalized and profitable business. He detests all reformers and especially those who pushed through the law prohibiting the shooting of egrets for their beautiful feathers for women's hats: Those "damned foreign birds" fly here from South America each year to gobble up "millions of native American fish"; egrets should all be shot and their bodies sold at profit. Since this piece suited the temper of the *Spectator,* it appeared in the December issue along with an announcement welcoming Anderson to the board of editors and their "editorial wrestlings." Now just after returning from Washington, he sent off to the *Spectator* two of his tales about frustrated advertising men from the second *Thanksgiving,* which Mencken had earlier turned down for the *American Mercury.* The first of these, "I Get So I Can't Go On" is more substantial than the two slight pieces the *New Yorker* had taken.[39]

One night four employees of the Griver-Wharton firm go to a small, cheap restaurant for dinner. Frank Blandin, through whose consciousness much of the story is presented, tends to escape from his job inward into his thought-world, including snatches of remembered poetry. Al, a salesman, always drinks too much as does Bud, a commercial artist, who longs to become a painter but never will. Little Gil, a copywriter with a "little girlish face," must grind out ads to support his mother and sisters. "Nothing happened that night"—except that Frank, meeting the eyes of the proprietor's alluring wife in an "embrace," looks up, sees Little Gil gazing at him in the way he had gazed at the woman, and understands that Little Gil is "a fairy" who constantly fears that his sexual orientation may be discovered. Frank does not condemn his friend, indeed sympathetically intuits his emotional crucifixion, but he suddenly imagines hearing in the future two men approving of Little Gil's being knocked down by a man he had approached and being fired from his job. At home that night alone Frank tells himself that he must stop thinking of Little Gil and his probable fate. "Jesus," he concludes, the exclamation ambiguously echoing the crucifixion motif, "I better be thinking about something else." Anderson's own sympathy for the tormented Little Gil is as obvious as it was for the confused, tormented Wing Biddlebaum in "Hands," but Frank's exclamation of necessity lacks the abrupt force of the earlier story's final image fixing the sacramental quality of Wing's hands. Predictably, too, the prose of the later story for the most part gives no sense of carrying poetry in it, as Anderson wanted for his prose. It tends to be flat, explicit even to the bluntly disparaging "fairy," the snatches of poetry Frank thinks of having too much the effect of self-conscious ornamentation. Of course, Anderson was not trying to write another "Hands," but "I Get So I Can't Go On" suggests some of the limitations of the advertising *Thanksgiving*.

"Harry Breaks Through" is an unconvincing tale about an awkward middle-aged advertising man who in "his change of life" in the late 1920s rebels against his job and respectability, tries to commit suicide but out of awkwardness fails, and so is somehow prepared, with occasional financial help from his son, to treat the Depression as a laughing matter. Of these two stories Anderson sent him, Dreiser wrote back that he liked "I Get So I Can't Go On" but felt that "Harry Breaks Through" needed to "be made just a little more poignant." Fortunately, Dreiser did not write until after he had celebrated Anderson's becoming an editor of the *American Spectator* by inviting him to a weekend, October 14–15, with a Sunday afternoon party at "Iroki," his house in Mount Kisco, where Anderson saw his old friends Floyd Dell and, most joyfully, Wharton Esherick, and where he learned from George Jean Nathan why the Theatre Guild had definitely decided against doing *Winesburg*. When Dreiser's letter about the two stories came a few days later, Anderson raged to Eleanor, "Who is Dreiser to tell me what a short story is?" He told Dreiser he would resign as an editor, and Dreiser said that would be fine; but there was no resignation, and the two men were reconciled. Anderson withdrew the two stories, however. "I Get So I Can't Go On" appeared in the December issue of *Story*, while "Harry Breaks Through" did not come out until 1936 in the *New Caravan*. Dreiser, and Mencken, were right about Harry after all.[40]

October 16 was in two ways a day of new directions for Anderson. First, he arrived back in the city from Mount Kisco that Monday morning, just in time to have lunch with Raymond Moley who had written asking to see him. Moley had advised Roosevelt in the beginning of his administration but now was founding the pro-administration political weekly *Today*. "I have often said," Moley wrote, "that your own remarkable stories have done more to enlighten the reader than many books on politics." Both Ohioans, the two men liked each other at once and worked out an arrangement whereby, for his expenses and $300 a week, Anderson would travel around the country as "a kind of super reporter" examining the impact on people of Roosevelt's policies. His first commission, Moley urged, would be to do an article on Henry Wallace, which Anderson jumped at since he had been trying to think of some way he could help Wallace; in fact, he was delighted with the whole arrangement. Here was a reliable source of income when he wished it, and he could earn it by doing one of the things he most enjoyed, driving around the American land, talking with people, and writing about them. Besides, *I Build My House* had for the moment "stopped dead still." That same day he wired Wallace's office to find out when he might interview the secretary, and about midweek was again in Washington to see him.[41]

The second change of direction that October 16 came from his talk with Benjamin F. Kamsler, a play producer whom Frieda Fishbein had urged him to see. At their first meeting Anderson thought him "a swell guy." He was "alive, a man of culture and so overwhelmingly sold on [*Winesburg*]"; but a day or so afterward Kamsler pressed for a share of Barton's percentage of any profits, and Anderson dismissed him as a "chiseler." By the twenty-first, however, he had found another producer, Sigourney Thayer, who back in February 1925 had staged *The Triumph of the Egg* in New York. He liked Thayer "tremendously," for the man seemed to have "good taste, knows a lot of theatre and has enough money to go ahead." Thayer had "good ideas" about changes in *Winesburg* and had already given Anderson "more help than anyone who [had] worked with him," so much so that after completing the article on Wallace for Moley, he put the first half of November into "racing day and night" at a second complete rewriting of the play, rather to Eleanor's dismay since she saw playwriting deflecting him from writing stories. Despite the shock at learning that Barton had deceptively copyrighted *Winesburg* solely in Barton's name, he very scrupulously had had him come to the first consultation with Thayer, had urged him to take to the producer any suggestions he might have for the play— Barton suggested nothing—and as he himself rewrote each scene, he sent Barton a copy of it. On November 18 he took the final scene to Thayer and began waiting for his decision whether to produce the play.[42]

When the Wallace article "No Swank" appeared in the November 11 issue of *Today*, it was to Anderson's delight much praised. Moley told him that it "made a bigger reaction" than any other piece the magazine had published, and Anderson's friend Saxe Commins, who had left Liveright, Inc. for Random House, effused, "[I]t's a marvelous piece of writing—giving the setting—full of poetry—indirect—yet telling all." Very indirectly indeed, with many remarks about his own closeness to common people and his own belief that the Depression is bringing Americans out of self-centered individualism into a greater sense of community, Anderson comes to an admiring portrait of Wallace as an uncommon man, a man of superior mind but quite without self-importance, without "swank," an undeviatingly honest, "very sincere and human civilized" man, the sort who can help "lift a whole race of so-called individualists out of individualism and into civilization." Moley sent Anderson $350 for the article and called for more. Although Eleanor worried that Sherwood might have "gone pro-administration completely," he obliged Moley with "Explain! Explain! Again Explain," the first of a planned series of letter-articles to the editor, this one suggesting that President Roosevelt, who "has made us feel close to him" by several radio talks explaining New Deal policies, continue to convince "us of his good intention" by giving the talks weekly. This piece, written between November 13 and 18 just as he was completing his second rewriting of *Winesburg*, appeared in the December 2 issue of *Today* along with "The Editor's Reply to Sherwood Anderson," praising his writing for its "sensitiveness to the deep emotions and ideas of people" and exhorting him to "Go out through the states as Walt Whitman used to and talk to people and write what they say and what you think of what they say, in the form of letters to *Today*." Just after doing "No Swank" he had also written two pieces for the *New Yorker* at $200 each: "Meeting Ring Lardner" (November 25 issue), a memoir of his brief acquaintance in New Orleans with Ring, who had died on September 25; and "Delegation" (December 9 issue), a recounting, now more amused than indignant, of his attempt with others to protest the treatment of the Bonus Army to Herbert Hoover, a president, he pointed out in "Explain!," isolated in office as Roosevelt—by his use of radio—was not. It is no surprise that Eleanor should write the Emmetts that Sherwood was "going like mad working much longer than I have ever known him to each day." He was "plugging to get free," he himself told Sergel, for a "treck" into America after Christmas.[43]

6.

In the morning of November 21, Arthur Barton telephoned Anderson to say that everything Thayer and he had done in the rewriting of *Winesburg* was "wrong." Shocked and angry, Anderson told him on the phone what he thought of him and that afternoon wrote him in more measured words, detailing his dishonesty about copyright registration and his failure to contribute anything substantial to the original version of the play and anything at all to the two revisions, concluding that he could not depend on him any longer. Three days later Barton telephoned again, this time offering "to get out." Anderson offered to give him 20 percent of his own royalties, and Barton's name was not to appear on the play. Barton agreed to have an attorney draw up such a contract, but on the twenty-ninth he wrote reneging on that agreement, and insisting that he be present at any conference with any possible producer. Sending this letter to Sergel, Anderson wryly commented that Barton had "changed his mind." Meanwhile, Thayer had approved the second rewriting of *Winesburg*, but before a production contract could be drawn up Anderson learned from someone he trusted that Thayer was in financial trouble with two other playwrights. Much upset by this information and by advice that legally Barton's name would probably have to appear as co-author in any production, he temporarily withdrew the play, unhappily aware that up to this point much of a year's concentrated work had brought him nothing but experience with writing drama and a conviction that he had something to say in this form.[44]

He had another, quite different cause for concern. Shortly after the Andersons' September trip to Chicago, Eleanor had begun to feel ill; though she resolutely kept up with her busy work schedule. In mid-November she was sick in bed four days with the flu and finally agreed to have a complete medical examination. Presumably she had written of her illness to her sister Katharine in Minnesota, for Katharine wired her to read the report in *Time* for November 20 about the epidemic of amebic dysentery among World's Fair visitors stemming from infected food-handlers at the Congress and Auditorium hotels. Like a real life *An Enemy of the People*, the existence of the epidemic had been kept from public knowledge for more than two months so that attendance at the Fair would not drop off. It had been unfortunate that the Andersons had registered at the Auditorium Hotel—Sherwood escaped infection—but now, doctors having been confidentially warned, Eleanor could be treated specifically for a disease that had already stricken a hundred or more people and killed sixteen, including the famous nightclub hostess Texas Guinan after a misdiagnosis of her infection. For days thereafter Eleanor's doctor gave her the prescribed treatments, but they did not work, and by December 11 he persuaded her to enter Presbyterian Hospital "to get her bugs killed."[45]

Early in December, Anderson was distracted from concern over Eleanor by a telephone call from Moley asking him to go down to the West Virginia coalfields to write a letter on the situation among the miners. In mid-morning of December 13 he registered at the Ruffner Hotel in Charleston, and for the best part of three days he talked with miners, out of work or still working, and was driven about the coalfields by a one-legged ex-miner to observe the grim poverty of the ramshackle mining towns. Despite the near destitution of most of the men, women, and children, he reported in his letter "At the Mine Mouth," there is a new feeling among them, quite different from that of two years earlier when there was open warfare between miners striking to organize a union and the police and company "thugs." Now Roosevelt, the first president to say so, has openly stated that workers have the right to organize, and the miners have at last a sense of hope. Not interested in a Communist revolution "yet" or Fascist hero worship, they regard the president as a man like themselves, "smarter maybe, that's all," who could lead them into a new deal that would let them "give this democracy thing another whirl yet." If "you ain't [for Roosevelt]," Anderson is told, "you'd better get out of this town . . . and damn you, if you're again' him, you'd better stay out of here." Anderson's letter was clearly pro-miner and as pro-administration as Moley could have wanted.[46]

By the sixteenth Anderson was back in New York to welcome Ferdinand Schevill for a visit at 56 Washington Mews. Excited by his "grand week" in West Virginia, but distressed by Schevill's being unexpectedly ill during the visit, worried about the fate of *Winesburg,* and by Eleanor's hospitalization, he was unable to work on any long project and instead continued to do "short things . . . make smaller pictures." Soon after its premiere on November 29, he and presumably Eleanor had seen the Theatre Union production of George Sklar and Albert Maltz's antiwar drama *Peace on Earth;* for on December 4 he wrote a letter to the *Times* praising the radical play as "vital and alive . . . full of the curious dramatic realism of everyday American life right now." (His letter would be reprinted as the "Foreword" to the published play in 1934.) Probably later in December he "made" for the January and February issues of the *American Spectator* three minor pieces: semi-stream of consciousness impressions in "Winter's Day Walk in New York"; commentary with vignettes in "Cityscapes"; and a snippet juxtaposing the unemployed and empty-headed popular magazines in "American Spectator." In whatever time was left between visiting Eleanor in the hospital and "flying about" for *Today,* as he wrote the Emmetts, he was finding it fun to begin bringing together "the little book of people we are making up for you two," a first reference to the collection of impressions of various individuals, which in final form would be published as *No Swank.* Besides this "special edition" for the Emmetts, he was already planning, with much help from Laura Lu, a projected volume of pieces from *Today* and elsewhere, which he might persuade Max Perkins to accept for Scribner's despite the editor's insistence on a "continuous narrative." This project eventually appeared two years later as *Puzzled America.* In these unsettled and unsettling weeks Anderson was scattering his energies.[47]

He and Eleanor had hoped to leave for Marion well before Christmas, but it was not until Christmas Day that tests showed her cured and she was discharged from Presbyterian Hospital. They just managed to catch a train south. At Rosemont, Eleanor celebrated what was left of the holidays by staying in bed as her doctor had ordered, while Sherwood, to her relief, at last went "deep in work." He hoped to write a long "joyous book," full of moments of intense response to nature; but he could not find the right "kind of tone, melody, chord" he was after, and shortly abandoned the attempt. On New Year's Day of 1934 they returned to New York, she to her job, he to the exciting prospect of soon being on the road fulfilling assignments for *Today* and his own "philosophy, to live, feel, taste, smell, see all I can of life."[48]

7

On, and off, the Road

1.

Shortly after returning to 56 Washington Mews, Anderson wrote Moley proposing articles for *Today* based on New Deal developments he would observe on a tour of the South: the Civilian Conservation Corps camps for unemployed young men; the Tennessee Valley Authority, created by Congress in the previous May, with administrative offices in Knoxville; and cotton mills and mill towns he had visited in 1930–31, now under the industrial codes of the National Recovery Administration established in June. In his reply Moley agreed to the proposed subjects, set no deadlines on the articles but a limit of eight of them, and contracted to pay $250 each and his tour expenses. It was everything Anderson wanted.[1]

While these arrangements were being made, he was also dealing with literary matters. He worked a few last mornings on the "joyous book," and he sent off to Albert Maltz the "Foreword" for the book publication of *Peace on Earth*. In reply to B. G. Braver-Mann, editor of *Experimental Cinema*, who had written him proposing to make a film from *Poor White*, he wrote at length in a detail probably influenced by his unhappy experience with Barton his understanding of Braver-Mann's project. The latter was to "prepare the scenario, subject to my approval," employ the Russian camera man Joseph Houdyma and an American cast primarily of real working-class people, obtain financial backing for the production, and direct the film, which was to keep to the spirit of the novel, now become "a kind of classic" illustrating "the destructive influence of present-day uncontrolled industrialism." The film was definitely not to be "a typical Hollywood picture."

It is my own understanding that the entire effort is to do something new and worthwhile in the picture field. No one of us is entering into this project with any idea of making it primarily commercial. The hope is that something so real to

American life in the curious situation of America may be produced as to attract attention and achieve its success in that way.

At about the time he wrote to Braver-Mann of the filming of *Poor White*, he learned from Frieda Fishbein that a successful New York producer, Courtney Burr, had suddenly become enthusiastic over the *Winesburg* play, and Luise Sillcox and Max Perkins were arranging a contract between Scribner's and Anderson for his next book. On a busy January 16, in addition to packing for the southern tour, he managed to sign the contract, talk with Burr, and then discuss with William Stewart, managing editor of *Today*, final plans for his articles.[2]

The following day Sherwood and Eleanor, who had several YWCA assignments in the South, drove to Washington, he to look in on a conference on "The Cause and Cure of War," she to attend a meeting on "Group Conscious" made awful by the "hypocrisy of Christians." Both of them enjoyed an evening at a speakeasy with the brilliant and capable New Dealer Jerome Frank, then general counsel for the Agricultural Adjustment Administration. Eleanor got drunk for the first time ever, found it "delightful," and decided she would "do it again if [she] thought it would be as good the second time." Anderson spent much of their two days in the capital talking with AAA men about southern tenant farmers and with people in the Department of the Interior about CCC camps, then struck off to visit a number of the camps in the Appalachians. On the twenty-fourth he mailed to Bill Stewart his first article from the trip. "Tough Babes in the Woods" shows his enthusiasm for this New Deal innovation—the orderliness of the temporary camp towns, the competence of the army men and foresters in charge, the chance the CCC offered thousands of mostly high-school-age boys from factory cities not only to escape unemployment and perhaps petty gangsterism but also to learn, through the work of their hands, the usefulness and the beauty of restoring woods and fields where the ruthless clear-cutting of mountain forests had left barren eroded land and fouled streams and rivers. The CCC was "a kind of revolution in many lives that goes both backward and forward," forward to "a possible conception of an America that shall belong essentially to all Americans," backward to a time and land when the Ohio River ran so clear that swimmers could see down to the bottom, a time to be restored from nostalgia to reality. It is unlikely that many administrators of the CCC intended the kind of "forward revolution" that Anderson enthusiastically, if vaguely, foresaw; but he was certainly right that the CCC was committed to the restoration and preservation of "great stretches" of ravaged country and in making "new land" make "a new kind of American man."[3]

Arriving back in Marion on the twenty-fourth, he spent the next morning catching up with correspondence, the most important matter being a new legal agreement sent from Frieda Fishbein's office between him and Barton concerning the play now titled *Winesburg, Ohio.* Anderson's share of royalties would be 75 percent, Barton's 25 percent; copyright of the play would be in Anderson's name, but Barton would be named as co-author in contracts for production and in presentations. Wanting an added clause allowing himself to make production agreements on his own—he was "sure Barton will have no objection to this"—he forwarded the legal agreements to the ever-helpful Luise Sillcox for the addition and her approval of the document. Letters done, he drove to Ripshin to consult with John Sullivan, who was now farming the land, and then was off to the hill country of Tennessee, just over the Virginia line, to observe small tobacco farmers at a big tobacco market for his second article for *Today.* In a couple of days he was again back in Marion organizing his observations into "Blue Smoke."[4]

This article, which he mailed to Stewart on the thirty-first, is skilled journalism carrying Anderson's trademark of sympathy with people at the bottom of the social and economic scale. Much of it is description of processes—how tobacco markets function; how tobacco is grown on two- or three-acre patches by small farmers, who, as one of them explains, must "mess and mess" with this demanding crop all year long; how the baskets of harvested tobacco are brought to the market, graded, and priced by expert "pin hookers" and bought by the shrewd buyers of the "four or five big tobacco companies in America," who by their offers determine the year's income for each farmer. Anderson personalizes the processes by the comments of a particular group of farmers waiting in their patched overalls for their meager yearly incomes to be set. Viewing the big tobacco companies as their overpowering enemy, they have lost their suspicion of government men and are convinced that the government in Washington, personified in President Roosevelt, has "got to help us or we're lost." Their situation is dramatized at the end of the article by the pricing of Fred's tobacco. His friend Jim explains to Anderson that a family can live on eighteen-cent tobacco, "but your five- or your six-cent stuff . . . it's starvation." A third of Fred's crop goes for nine cents, the rest for two and three.[5]

In the midst of writing "Blue Smoke" he found himself ready, probably on January 29, to write a quite different kind of piece, one in defense and praise of Gertrude Stein's work. Such an article had been forming in his mind since the Christmas vacation when, apparently at the urging of his daughter-in-law Mary, he read in the January *Atlantic* B. F. Skinner's "Has Gertrude Stein a Secret?" Skinner argued that in *Tender Buttons* Stein had returned to her interest at Radcliffe in experiments with automatic writing, where she had consciously avoided the creation of a true second personality doing the writing, and where much that was written, though grammatical in form, had been unintelligible in content. Likewise, *Tender Buttons* must be automatic writing, for any implied second personality doing it is of "superficial character" and most of the writing is indeed unintelligible. Hence, unlike *Three Lives* or *The Autobiography of Alice B. Toklas, Tender Buttons* can be dismissed as unimportant. Anderson's rather oblique answer to Skinner actually came in two parts, one private, the other public, both reflecting his tremendous excitement upon first reading *Tender Buttons* as described in *A Story Teller's Story*. Around January 28 he wrote to Mary Anderson that "I have always known I was essentially the poet," and where Stein rejected the "secondary self," his secondary self *was* the poet, to whom could be attributed "all of the more beautiful and clear, the more plangent and radiant writing I have done." Since "Suppose [Stein] taught me to recognize the second person in myself, the poet-writing person, so that I could occasionally release that one," he believes she is "a genius." The public part of the answer was a short, somewhat disjointed article titled "Gertrude Stein." Here, his defense of her is essentially that she understands the "color" of words. As in painting, Anderson insists, "Color lies in the word, form in the color." It is word *color* that produces "the unnameable overtone" in prose, as achieved by the really great writers, "writer's writers" like Melville, Borrow, and "Turgenev superlatively."

Stein is great because she is a releaser of talent. She is a pathfinder. She has been a great, a tremendous influence among writers because she has dared, in the face of ridicule and misunderstanding, to try to awaken in all of us who write a new feeling for words. She has done it.

Rejecting Skinner's condemnation of automatic writing as "nonsense," Anderson concludes that

Stein is a revolutionist. If we ever get again a world that knows what pure writing is, the sense and form of Stein's work will come through. She also will stand as a restorer of "the word."

When Sherwood read the Stein piece to Eleanor and Laura Lu, they both thought it "good" and urged him to send it to the *Atlantic,* but he insisted on giving it to the *American Spectator* as he had promised. Apparently he felt a special obligation to the *Spectator,* since early in January Dreiser had resigned from the editorial board, adducing the press of his own writing and his opposition to Nathan and Boyd's lack of interest in articles on social and economic matters. That obligation now discharged and "Blue Smoke" finished and sent to Bill Stewart, Sherwood and Eleanor drove out of Marion on the last day of the month headed for other obligations in Tennessee and the Deep South.[6]

In Nashville and then Knoxville, while Eleanor worked, Anderson talked with TVA people and viewed construction on the great Norris Dam, the first in the series planned by the TVA for the multiple purposes of flood control, improved navigation, production of cheap electric power, stimulus of industrialization, and conservation of agricultural and forest lands. While Eleanor went on to Macon for an assignment, Anderson completed his third *Today* article, "Price of Aristocracy," and then drove watchfully about among the mill towns of the Carolinas and Georgia. The tragic price of aristocracy, he had concluded from his years in the South, was in part the cruelty toward blacks, but even more the creation over many decades of a permanent white underclass, "millions of Southern poor whites, tied to the poor land, long dispossessed, so often living on land that should be given back to forests, again slowly enriched in that way," an underclass slowly becoming convinced that it could be saved, not by individuals, but by a new form of government, "bigger, taking everyone in." His initial report from his visits to the mill towns was another *Today* article, "Tom Grey Could So Easily Lead Them," an account of a dreary, inconclusive meeting of a mill union, most of the members of which had been fired after a failed strike; yet the hopelessness of the meeting is offset by an introduction praising the NRA (National Recovery Administration) for bringing hope to mill workers fearful of losing their jobs, the NRA having established industrial codes that, among other effects, were intended to decrease work hours, increase wages, end the child labor prevalent in the cotton mills, and support the workers' right to organize and bargain collectively. Reunited in Winston-Salem, Sherwood and Eleanor spent a week at the Carolina Inn "much in love," she noted in her diary. By February 13 he had finished the "Tom Grey" piece and had mailed it to Bill Stewart, and on the seventeenth they were back again in Marion.[7]

While using Rosemont as a rest stop for a few days, Anderson put in his customary mornings of writing. By the twenty-first he sent his fifth article to Stewart, a collection of sketches of people met on his recent travels, titled "Personalities": an independent woman wanderer who had left her husband when he had scabbed, as she had not, during a cotton-mill strike; a panhandling man, an unemployed electrician, cheerfully optimistic about getting a job again; an older man who, like many Americans in the Depression, apologetically regarded his loss of a job to be his own failure "in this American scheme" and who had lost, in Anderson's words, "that sense of being some part of the moving world of activity, so essential to an American man's sense of his manhood"; and a group of Tennessee "hill billies" disproving the stereotypes by becoming skilled workers on a government-financed archeological dig of a mound-builders site, disproving also the anti–New Deal charge, "If a man is out of work, it is because he's no good." Anderson's firsthand observations of the New Deal in operation and its effect on people had in fact changed, he realized, a kind of stereo-typing of his own; for while he was writing "Personalities," he also began (though apparently never finished) an article called "Moonstruck,"

an article that attempts to bring out the essential and rather pathetic romanticism of the radical.

I dare say a good many of the radicals won't like it, but most of them are es-sentially such children face to face with the facts.

Seeing some of the facts of the New Deal had shown him a future that was working because it was putting Americans to work, fulfilling their basic need. His own conversion away from the romantic revolutionary was completed.[8]

Rested, he and Eleanor drove off on February 22 to an assignment for her in Richmond and then, "through [a] strangely beautiful frozen world" treacherous for driving, to another assignment at Duke University. During a four- or five-day stopover in Durham he worked on his sixth piece for *Today,* "a labor article" based in part on a conversation with a middle-aged unemployed machinist, though he would not complete a final draft of it until the second week in March. "I Want to Work"—Anderson's own title would be "They Can Take It"—tells "the old story of a man whose civilization had got through with him before he was through," the story illustrating Anderson's old concern with the "devil" in the machine, the machine beautiful in its steel complexity and efficient in its motions yet that beauty and ever increasing speed and efficiency throwing "American workmen, so often now . . . out of their place in our social and economic scheme." The unemployed machinist, who with time on his hands reads much in the public library, hopes and hunches that, as Grant was the one Northern general to see the Civil War as a whole, President Roosevelt, who has recognized the right of labor to organize, may see the problems of the workers and of the country as a whole. With a first draft of this article fin-ished, Anderson on March 1 drove Eleanor to Greenville, South Carolina, she to attend her last Y assignment, he to get material for a later article on the Deep South, which he "want[ed] to call the Nation's Sweat Shop."[9]

Later, when Eleanor left by train for New York, he wanted company on his last trip, drifting through the Deep South's back roads to observe the plight of the tenant farmers. After an exchange of telegrams with Roger Sergel, the two men met on March 8 at the Farragut Hotel in Knoxville for Anderson's last and Sergel's first views of the TVA project before begin-ning their drift south toward New Orleans. Having just left what Ander-son in his article on the TVA would call "the land of new hope, men busy, the strikingly charming government-built town of Norris, at Norris Dam, going up, men laughing at their work," Sergel the northerner was appalled by the southern back country as a "land of desolation, of no hope," the roads rutted, the bridges decayed, the poor tenant farmers, white and black, "getting poorer every year," their wives with tired eyes, their children undernourished, their "little unpainted cabins half fallen down." To both men it was a relief to get to New Orleans, another kind of South, where they were grandly entertained by the Feiblemans and the Friends. On the fifteenth they drove to Mobile, where Sergel had to take a train for Chicago. Three and a half days of hard driving got Anderson through Atlanta and up the Eastern seaboard to New York and to 56 Washington Mews and Eleanor.[10]

After a few days of rest from weariness and a cold, he went into "a rage of writing." He wrote, rewrote, and finished the article on the TVA, "A New Chance for the Men of the Hills," sweating over it, he told Bill Stewart, because the "story is so damned big." To demonstrate that the TVA is a multipurpose "sphere of influence," he focuses on two population groups who could benefit most immediately. The first are the Appalachian hill people, from "the oldest American stock we have," who barely but independently exist on tiny, worn-out farms; the second, the southern tenant farmers whose impoverishment so shocked Roger. Both can be brought into the modern world by the electric power to be generated by the dozen or so dams soon to be built along the winding Tennessee River, power available for homes and new industries working in conjunction with conservation to restore the land. So at the end of the article the newly converted Sergel is reported as exclaiming that the TVA may be the beginning of "something new in American life . . . and it mustn't be stopped." The TVA article went to Stewart toward the end of March, and on April 5 Anderson sent in his eighth and last piece, "New Tyrants of the Land." Insisting that there are many Souths, not just one, and that all are changing, he argues that despite the industrialization primarily of the upper South, "the South as a whole is still essentially agrarian," and here a new class is rising into power. These are new land owners, unfunny Faulknerian Snopses made brutal by having grown up in desperately poor families and, having been driven themselves, make money off cotton land by driving other desperately poor families and keeping them in virtual economic slavery, even turning them off the land when no longer needed. As the subtitle of "New Tyrants" in *Today* puts it: "Merciless 'farm sweatshop' is the latest problem to plague the South." Anderson had intended this article to be "a sort of general rounding up of the series," he wrote Stewart, but it made a grim, angry conclusion to the hopefulness of most of the others.[11]

Even before these last two articles came in, Moley praised the series to Anderson: "I want you to know that the several articles you have sent in from the South constitute, to my mind, one of the most valuable commentaries on present-day American life that *Today* has been privileged to publish." Anderson was also pleased that two publishers had suggested to him that he make the series into a book. When he began writing the articles, he had enjoyed doing them, but, Eleanor noted, "every now and then he bursts out against them, saying he doesn't want to write anything but pure poetry," that is, the poetry he wanted buried in his fictional prose. Working on the final article in late March, however, he found himself uninterested in turning to a novel; the account of an individual now seemed to him unimportant. "I believe," he wrote Sergel, "I'd rather remain what I have been these last six months—a kind of reporter of feeling and moods." Yet traveling through the South, he had thought from time to time of the Civil War, and now he temporarily decided on spending the next winter in Washington at the Library of Congress working on "a big history of the Civil War with all its implications," something, he wrote the Emmetts, "I have wanted to do since I was a boy," which if true might well have come either from excitement over his father's endless tales of the War or in reaction to them from a desire to get at the true story. Actually he was uncertain what to turn to next since he felt in "a hopeless jam" with the *Winesburg* play. While he was on his last southern trip, Barton had appeared in the Dramatists' Guild office of Luise Sillcox and refused to sign the contract Anderson had sent her; and by March 23 Anderson had withdrawn the play until Barton gave in.[12]

Early in April things began to look more certain, and he was full of projects. On April 5 he sent Stewart his final article on the South with the suggestion that *Today* next send him to some industrial city of the Midwest, such as Cleveland, to see how the Depression had affected some of its economic leaders. On or just before that date Barton, after much "fussing and bluffing around," signed the new contract giving him his name on the play as co-author and twenty-five percent of production profits but leaving Anderson free to find a producer for the play on his own. He was also thinking seriously about making a play from *Dark Laughter* using experimental devices such as, he wrote Sergel, having "sound come from all sides of the audience . . . the idea being to give a sense of another life going on around the audience and the players in the theatre. . . ." Probably on the tenth he talked again with Courtney Burr, who was so encouraging about producing *Winesburg, Ohio* that soon he began again "playing with the play." Early in the month he had even discussed with Sumner Blossom, editor of the *American Magazine,* a plan "particularly fitted to what talent I have got and to my experience," a series of eight stories, each set in a different sort of town in a different part of the United States. Obviously he had not after all given up wanting to write the "poetry" of fiction.[13]

On April 12 or just after, a set of circumstances began to shape Anderson's life for months to come. He and Eleanor had gone to Philadelphia to attend a session of the American Academy of Political and Social Science, where nationalism and high tariffs were attacked, and that evening went to a performance at the Hedgerow Theatre, founded and directed by Jasper Deeter in nearby Rose Valley. Very likely they went as guests of Wharton Esherick, who had been a supporter of Hedgerow since its beginning in 1922 and who may have brought Anderson and Deeter together that Thursday evening or during the ensuing weekend when the Andersons were at Esherick's house in the Philadelphia suburb of Paoli. Deeter had heard of the *Winesburg* play from Esherick, read a copy of it, expressed interest; and on May 3, while Eleanor was at a ten-day YWCA convention in Philadelphia, Anderson arrived at Paoli ready to revise his script once more, this time at Deeter's suggestion, after reading the play aloud to a group "in a rather corking way," that the ending be changed. During the following week, sometimes at Esherick's home, sometimes at Hedgerow, Anderson reworked his too "literary" ending into a "reflective epilogue," giving the conclusion of the play, he wrote Laura Lu, "a thing you might call horizon—the lives of the people in the play passing into other lives of the town and life going on." (When he sent her a copy of the epilogue, she praised it, proving to him, he wrote her, that she was his "ideal editor.") After Anderson, working intensively with Deeter, had completed other revisions, the director was convinced that *Winesburg* was "actable" and, according to Eleanor, in his excitement over it, was "sure it is the great American play." By the time Anderson returned to New York on May 10, Deeter had decided to stage it in the summer.[14]

Anderson was excited. For the first time he had been receiving expert advice from someone totally immersed in directing actors in a theater. Stimulated by that advice and his success with the epilogue, he went further "up to [his] eyes in work" at Esherick's by starting on the dramatization of *Dark Laughter,* "the prologue of voices, etc.," completing a second one-act play to go with "Mother," and at least thinking about a third one-acter to make up an evening of drama. To put together "They Married Later," the second one-acter, he borrowed from *Poor White* a reticent, insecure inventor, a rebellious young woman, and several exploitative businessmen, some of whose crude, drunken voices at the party after the wedding of inventor and woman are heard from offstage, probably as another experiment in the use of sound. The woman regrets marrying the inventor, but when the man, feeling unworthy of her, steals away from her like Hugh McVey on their wedding night, she exults that he is not like the businessmen and resolves that the two will after all have "a real marriage." In comparison with the episode in *Poor White,* the play is as predictable and wooden as this synopsis suggests. It would be turned down when Anderson submitted it to *Scribner's Magazine,* and when published in *Plays: Winesburg and Others* along with "Mother" in 1937, it was understandably not noted as having been acted. No third one-acter would appear in *Plays.*[15]

Back at 56 Washington Mews, Anderson was informed that after weeks of delay Burr had bought *Winesburg,* and though he had signed no contract, he had "promised to put into it an absolute guaranty of production in November." So the matter stood for days, both Andersons expecting, then hoping that Burr would sign the contract for a Broadway opening. At some point late in the month, however, it became clear that Burr had not bought the play, was in fact, as Eleanor put it disgustedly, "scared to buy it after having practically given his word and kept off others for a month or more." Burr's final decision not to produce, she noted solicitously, "bruised" her husband's "ego." That nowhere in his surviving correspondence does Anderson mention that decision may indicate that the bruise was too painful for him to discuss. At least he had the Hedgerow production to look forward to, and he could drop the play and try to keep his mind off Burr's reneging by working on his commitment of "two little stories" for the popular *American Magazine,* at three hundred dollars each, and two "A Reporter at Large" pieces for *The New Yorker.* The first in each pair would be amiable and unmemorable. Although introduced editorially in *American* as "a little story of real human folks," "Mr. Joe's Doctor" comes as close to a folksy O. Henry tale as Anderson ever produced: in essence a wealthy city surgeon wishes that he had the opportunity to be like a poor country doctor, while the country doctor regrets not having had the opportunity to be like the surgeon. "Stewart's, on the Square" for the *New Yorker* is an amusing piece of journalism, a description of the all-night cafeteria on New York's Sheridan Square that swarms with customers at noon and even more so at midnight when the eccentric regulars and "the little children of the arts" crowd in in "a blind desire to be with others, the more others the better." Katherine White, E. B. White's wife, had suggested Stewart's to him; both pieces show Anderson's ability, when he wished, to write at least competently for different magazine audiences, for money.[16]

Life in New York for the Andersons, when they were not off traveling, had not been simply YWCA office work and writing. Occasionally they saw plays and especially liked the Theater Union's production of Paul Peters and George Sklar's antiracist *Stevedore.* Plays were a kind of practical school for Anderson, who had admitted that "my own difficulty, as regards playwriting, is and will always be a matter of structure. I believe I could make people live and can build character." Perhaps the outstanding theatrical event for both was the return engagement of Gertrude Stein and Virgil Thomson's *Four Saint in Three Acts,* which Eleanor and her mother had seen while Sherwood was in the South and found "tremendously" exciting, so much so that she insisted on going with him again on his return. Feeling it "a master stroke, having it done by negroes," he thought it "unbelievably charming—delightful. . . . The whole thing got utterly out into a world of fancy—carried you along like a bird flying." He urged Stein to come back to the United States for a visit. Now, there were visitors at "56": Eleanor's sister Katherine came for a week's visit in early April; Charles Bockler spent a weekend later in the month; and early in May Mimi appeared, partly to talk with her father about running a small-town newspaper, since toward the end of May she and Russell did buy the Madison, North Carolina, *Messenger*. (The "great thing," Anderson advised, was "to keep in mind that the paper belongs to the community as well as to you.") Then there were the increasing number of invitations to dinner and to literary teas and cocktail parties. Anderson was a drawing card for such affairs; on one occasion a tea was given for him with the purpose of making money "at $1 a head" for the Authors League. "I could write a book," Eleanor commented, "on an author's wife at cocktail parties." By this time she had acquired her own kind of fame; for she was invited to the White House to talk with Eleanor Roosevelt about helping unemployed women but could not go because of an assignment and instead had to content herself with tea with the Norman Thomases in Philadelphia.[17]

By mid-May both Andersons were tired of working and seeing people, and wanted to get back to the country. Although Burton's health was much improved, the Emmetts were not yet planning to return from Europe; still, Sherwood and Eleanor decided to leave New York around June 1. Their remaining days in the city, crowded with packing and social engagements, were "strenuous but fun," Eleanor wrote in her diary. On May 29, Dreiser took them to dinner at Lüchow's, where he seemed to her "gauche and crude" but possessed of "a grandeur and virility that makes him for me a great figure." Their last night they dined at Ticino's, where Mary Heaton Vorse, who had reported on the Gastonia strike and had written a novel, *Strike!*, about it, restored Anderson's bruised ego by praising *Beyond Desire* as superior to her novel by catching "the real essence of the whole thing in poetic form too." At the end of the month they headed out of New York toward Marion and Ripshin by way of Paoli and Hedgerow.[18]

2.

When in 1922 Jasper Deeter, at the age of twenty-eight, left a promising acting career with the Provincetown Players because he felt the group was going commercial, he searched for and found an unlikely but good place for his dream of an experimental repertory theater. It was an abandoned stone mill at the end of a tree-lined dead-end road in Rose Valley, Pennsylvania, a small community some twenty miles southwest of Philadelphia. (His letterhead would read Moylan-Rose Valley as the post office address.) Reconditioned, the mill had room for a small stage and 167 seats for the audience. Close by was an old farmhouse, which became home for most of the regular repertory actors, who took turns doing the chores of house and theater. For some years after opening in 1923, the Hedgerow often had to struggle to survive, but long before 1934 it had begun attracting aspiring young actors, had built up a trained group of professionals, and had become one of the best-known little theaters in America. Leader and director, Jasper Deeter, known as "Jap," believed in acting and the theater as a way of life. Careless of dress, uninterested in comfort, he demanded much of his actors and gave much in return. He was dedicated to experiment, repertory, and Hedgerow. He was the perfect person and Hedgerow the perfect place for the staging of *Winesburg, Ohio*.[19]

He was known for starting rehearsals at any time of day or night and driving them onward relentlessly for hours. The first rehearsal of *Winesburg* went through the entire day of Sunday, June 3, Deeter urging the actors on by repeatedly telling them, to Sherwood and Eleanor's delight, that the play was "the best material they ever had." Whether or not a Hedgerow production might encourage a Broadway one, and Eleanor doubted the play could be popular in New York, she was convinced it was "beautiful stuff," and she marveled at how Deeter grasped her husband's intent even to the most minor detail, unlike Barton whom she had spotted on first meeting as of no use at all for this kind of play. (She had begged Sherwood to drop Barton at once, but he would not. Sherwood, she wrote in her diary, "is so naive and trusting. I must protect him more from such people.") At Hedgerow he needed no such protection. He was happy with the place, the actors, and their director, and they were happy with him. In the years to come he would feel at home in the repertory community.[20]

They were back in Marion and at Rosemont on the fifth after a long drive from Esherick's home, and the next morning Anderson began a running correspondence with Deeter, suggesting cuts and acting details and settling business arrangements—Anderson to receive 10 percent of gross receipts of each performance of *Winesburg, Ohio,* now in the Hedgerow repertory—and assuring mutual admiration. Within a week the Andersons were settled in at Ripshin, and in the farm's quiet he revised his earlier story "Fred" (discussed near the end of chapter 1) which Stewart and Moley thought "swell" and published as "Virginia Justice" in the July 21 issue of *Today,* paying Anderson three hundred dollars for it. He had already repaid Burton Emmett the five hundred dollars he had borrowed the previous fall and now felt, as he put it, "nigger rich." Despite the casually used phrase, he had become more sensitized to racism from his year of radicalism, as shown in a review of two books he probably wrote at this time for the *Nation.* He likes, he wrote, Carl Carmer's poetic title, *Stars Fell on Alabama,* but feels that Carmer, a northerner, is too eager to ingratiate himself with southerners and makes the Alabamans too "cute, even in their cruelties," particularly to blacks, but for Anderson, "Give me the Bill Faulkner." Carmer is not even a good storyteller, whereas Langston Hughes in *The Ways of White Folks* is "an infinitely better, more natural" one. Yet where Carmer too readily accepts the white man who "stinks with old prejudice" against blacks, Hughes in effect says "Damn the whites," each writer not really understanding the race of the other, each in his way paying for America's original sin of slavery.[21]

It was the opening performance of *Winesburg* set for the evening of Saturday, June 30, that was most on his mind, however; and as early as the twenty-second he was back staying with Esherick in Paoli, going often to Hedgerow to watch rehearsals for the big night and urging friends to attend. Eleanor and her mother arrived in the morning of the thirtieth, followed through the day by, among others, Dreiser and his Helen and the Emmetts, back from Europe, who brought Karl. That stifling hot evening all 167 seats of the theater were filled. Eleanor, sweltering with Sherwood in the small balcony, thought that the performance dragged badly; he insisted it was all "beautiful" but was depressed by the complaints of many that the script needed cutting. A New York reviewer would agree with Eleanor, writing that the play ran "for an unconscionably long time" and was much too repetitious, and concluding acidly that "Only the intermissions served to relieve the tepid tedium." Although most of the Philadelphia reviewers would have objections, such as the play's looseness of structure or its need for cutting, at least one would comment that, considering the applause, the audience "liked the play enormously." Dreiser, Eleanor happily noted, praised *Winesburg, Ohio* as "pioneering in dramatic art" and predicted that even though it might not be "popular on Broadway," it would influence future Broadway. After the performance the Andersons, their friends, and some of the cast spent the night at the Eshericks'. Sunday morning there was what Eleanor called "a long breakfast," with Dreiser sitting throughout "exhibiting his genitals," apparently through an unfastened dressing gown. "Fortunately Mother didn't notice," Eleanor added. The Monday evening performance of *Winesburg* was shorter and much better, as a third one on Tuesday, July 3, seems to have been also. Although Anderson had still not recovered from his depression over the demand to make cuts and other objections by reviewers, he knew of Deeter's resolve to stage *Winesburg* once a week, he still felt the play was beautiful and beautifully acted, and he responded gratefully to the repertory group's adoration of him. The "whole experience was nice," Eleanor concluded.[22]

Very shortly after the three performances, Anderson wrote Deeter from Ripshin to insist, somewhat disingenuously, that his depression had been caused only by weariness and constant thinking about the play and that he would soon be making helpful cuts. He had actually accepted one cut after opening night—a question about sexual experience by one young Winesburg man to another ("did you ever have a piece?"), which some in the 1934 audience had found particularly shocking. This question would be restored in the text of the play published by Scribner's in *Plays: Winesburg and Others* in 1937. Otherwise, however, this published text would follow the acting script with the minor cuts made by playwright or director and so may be examined here.[23]

In a prefatory "Note" to the text, Anderson warns that he has "not tried to follow exactly the theme of the tales" or to include all the book's characters but rather "tried to capture again the spirit of the tales." To the question as to whether he succeeded in his attempt, one must answer yes and no. Recognizing the limitations of drama, he of necessity had to select from among the tales, their events, their characters, and the characters' relationships. Eventually he concentrated the action into nine scenes instead of a conventional three acts—"I find my weakness in playwriting to be the structure rather than dialogue," he confessed to playwright Laurence Stallings—reduced to half their number the characters listed as "concerning" in the book's "The Tales and the Persons," and gave new emphasis to relationships. Further, of the nine scenes seven have different settings, and all the settings except the first are in rooms or just outside houses, the first being set in the Winesburg cemetery at the funeral for the old reprobate Windpeter Winters, smashed to "sausage meat" while defying a railroad engine. This funeral, the play's one public event, enables Anderson to introduce many unnamed townspeople and all of the play's thirteen major characters, except for the sickly Elizabeth Willard, and thus create a sense of Winesburg as a community. In sum, by such devices of episode and setting the play does produce a dramatic equivalent of the separate tales, externalizing for the stage an essentially internalized book. A New York drama critic, who admitted that he had not read the book, began his review of the August 16 production by asserting that the play is "Curiously chaotic . . . openly defies each law of craftsmanship . . . bumps casually along" for nine scenes; but then he chided "an entire row of protesting Pennsylvanians [who] arose and departed in a huff" when young Winesburg men discussed their "amorous adventures"; and he ended by declaring that the play "is not to be taken lightly," for "Out of its chaos, its lack of coordination, there emerges a portrait of a town," not a "pleasant portrait [but one] worthy of study and contemplation." If, as is probable, Anderson saw this review, he may well have felt that the critic despite his formal training had grasped an essential point.[24]

At the center of *Winesburg, Ohio* are two sets of relationships: George Willard's involvement with three different women, and Elizabeth and Tom Willard's bitter struggle over the direction of George's development. While Dr. Parcival drinks and excoriates respectable society in scene 1, George takes notes on the funeral for the newspaper and worries about the rumor that he is responsible for the pregnancy of Belle Carpenter, milliner and loose woman, admires Helen White as does his rival Seth, and receives an inviting note from Louise Trunion. In scene 2 Belle admits to Dr. Reefy in his office that she was impregnated, not by George, who did have his first sexual experience with her, but by Helen's highly respectable father, Banker White. Elizabeth Willard, coming to see Dr. Reefy, is distressed by hearing part of his conversation with Belle but is reassured by the doctor that George is not the father of Belle's child. Having also been reassured by Dr. Reefy, George in the third scene goes to see Helen, who had agreed with George that it was better to die defiantly like Windpeter and is now rebelling against her family's respectability. The two young people are on the verge of declaring their love when, misunderstanding each other, they quarrel. In scene 4 George, still angry at Helen, goes to see Louise, who is Ed Hanby's girlfriend. Becoming "bold," he draws her away to have sex with him despite her protests. Scene 5 begins with George in his room in the New Willard hotel writing a poem to Helen, while his friend Fred scoffs at poetry and says he is going into business. Subsequently, Tom Willard enters and urges George to be like Seth, who works in Mr. White's bank and regards it as "almost like being in a church." Tom wants George to be "a big man—a rich man." He leaves when Elizabeth comes in and urges George to oppose his father's wishes and listen instead to all kinds of people and understand how they live—one of Anderson's own rules for the writer. In Scene 6 Helen shows her dislike for Seth and her sudden liking for Belle, who has come to the White house hoping unsuccessfully to see Mr. White before she leaves town. When the banker returns, he continues to conceal from his daughter the truth about his involvement with Belle and suggests that he walk with Helen as her "beau" for the night, to which the pleased Helen says, "Oh, daddy, I'm crazy about you!" In front of Louise's house in scene 7, Ed Hanby roughly tells Louise that he is going to marry her and make her behave; and when George appears, Ed beats him up. The climactic scene 8 takes place in Elizabeth's room in the hotel where Dr. Reefy is visiting her. She describes her frustrated, sickly life and has Reefy take for George the eight hundred dollars she has secretly saved for her son. Leaving when Tom enters the room, the doctor warns her as before not to become excited. Tom angrily insists that up to now George has been *her* son but now will be *his* and that he will make him, not a poet, but "a snappy, alive business man." Confronting Tom for the first time, Elizabeth tells him that she was pregnant with George by another man when she married him and that she will not allow George to accept Tom's "cheap pretense of bigness"—whereupon, overexcited, she falls dead. Scene 9, Anderson's wholly invented epilogue, takes place two or three years later in Ed Hanby's saloon. Ed has married Louise, Tom has married a rich widow, and George is in Cleveland "making up stories about people" for a newspaper. While Dr. Parcival drinks especially to achieve oblivion from thought and dreams, Tom boasts of George's success, all the result, he claims, of his influence, and boasts of his plan to refurbish the New Willard House and put Winesburg, Ohio, on the map. Joe Welling, who at times throughout the play has burst volubly on the stage with imaginative ideas, now bursts into the saloon with the news that the hotel is "all afire." Everyone rushes out except for Parcival, who continues to drink to drown his belief that people are "all Christs and they will all be crucified."

Such a synopsis demonstrates that, contrary to the New York critic's academic judgment, the nine-scene structure of the play is not "chaotic" but coherent if unconventional in development, rather like the nontraditional Anderson short story. The Hedgerow productions had other experimental devices. Presumably Deeter, with Anderson's approval, worked out the notion of simple stage sets that allow quick scene shifts with the theater in darkness. The effect, as Anderson claims in his "Notes on Production," is to give the play "a rapid flow." Almost certainly it was Anderson with his recent interest in off-stage sounds who developed the use of popular tunes, voices, and other sounds usually between scenes, sometimes during the action, and often with the effect as of symbolic echo details in his stories. So at several points throughout the play beginning with the end of scene 1, the off-stage voices of Bun Grady and his wife quarreling over his attempts to hit an alley cat with a milk bottle replicate in part the antagonistic marriage of Elizabeth and Tom, her death coinciding with Bun's final success and having the dual reference to her as victim of Tom and as his conqueror. Again, at the end of scene 3, during which Helen has shown her desire to break with family respectability by offering to go with George to the town racetrack early some morning to watch the horses, the recorded "clattering sound of horses' hoofs trotting and pacing" fills the dark theater, symbolizing, as in Anderson's racetrack stories, the possibility of a liberated, more honest life. But when that sound is repeated at the end of scene 6, after Helen has twice declared, "Oh, daddy, I think you're grand," the clattering hoofs are an ironic comment on the chance for liberation lost.

In light of decades of dramatic experimentation since *Winesburg, Ohio,* Dreiser's pronouncement that this play was "pioneering in dramatic art" seems apt, and to this extent Anderson's attempt to "capture again the spirit of the tales" succeeds. In his treatment of Helen and more importantly of George, however, he failed seriously to recapture that spirit. To be sure, Helen is fleshed out more fully in the play than in the book. Belle Carpenter specifically says she is beautiful, and in her own speeches Helen shows an attractive yearning to be an independent person. More explicitly than the Helen of "The Thinker" and "Sophistication" she is "sick of . . . this darn respectability," wishes she were a boy or a "tough" woman, one free to go to tough places, meet unconventional people, and she does make the brief belated friendship with Belle; yet where in "Sophistication" she shares an enlarging sense of "maturity" with George, in the play she gets into a quarrel with him, childish on both sides, lapses back abruptly into respectability and her role as daddy's girl, and disappears from the action. For the reader of the tales and the viewer of the play as well, it is saddening and puzzling to observe Anderson impose so arbitrary a fate on so vital a person.

Equally serious as a departure from the spirit of the tales is the presentation of George Willard, the object of the struggle between his parents who, in play as in book, do represent in Anderson's mind the opposition of two fundamentally different views of life. Other persons in the play declare that George is, in Dr. Reefy's words, "imaginative—sensitive—alive," he loves words and writes poetry, and he is clearly his mother's son and shares, if rather vaguely, her hope for his future; yet aside from his dislike of his father—reminiscent, as Anderson acknowledged to Deeter, of his own dislike of his—and his liking of Windpeter Winters and Dr. Parcival, the George Willard of the play shows too little of the quality the writer must possess or develop: an understanding of people. This is especially evidenced in the difference between his relations with the women in the play and the highly significant relations with those in the tales. In the play he has already had his first sexual experience with Belle and has presumably felt, Dr. Reefy suggests, the normal reaction of the young Winesburg male, the mixture of fear and wonder at "possessing" a woman, any woman. As the play begins, this brief ecstasy is lost in his nervousness over the rumor that he is the father of Belle's unborn child. No doubt his reaction is "normal" enough in Winesburg and elsewhere, but it is a self-centered one; he shows no concern for, no understanding of, Belle herself. After his insensitive quarrel with Helen, he goes to Louise for a second sexual experience, not his first as in "Nobody Knows," and as in that tale thrills to his entirely self-absorbed dominance over her protests. Because the Belle Carpenter of "An Awakening" is a quite different person in the play, there can be no indication that he learns anything from his later brush with Ed Hanby and Louise as he begins, vaguely, to do in the tale. Finally and most tellingly, of course, since Helen in the play has relapsed into being daddy's girl, there is no equivalent of the climactic illumination of maturity achieved in "Sophistication" by her and George. Hence, when in the play's epilogue Ed Hanby reports that Louise has read "some of George's pieces" in the Cleveland newspaper—"stories about people . . . good ones, too" adds Tom the pathological liar—George is simply *said* to be a writer; in the book Anderson with subtle skill *shows*, through the sequence of three tales about three women and George, how the young man develops the essential understanding of others that makes him at least capable of becoming a writer. Despite the play's virtues, this externalizing of an internalized book diminishes it.[25]

3.

On their drive back from Paoli to Ripshin, which they reached about July 6, the Andersons brought Esherick with them as the first of a stream of visitors for the rest of the summer. It was probably during his July-long visit that Wharton Esherick carved from a log the half-length, Cubistic statue of Buck Fever with the right hand unmistakably thumbing the nose at the observer. With his vigor and wild sense of ribald humor the sculptor was delightful company, but Eleanor the social worker feared that his lack of concern with serious social matters was beginning to blunt her husband's interest in them. "I must keep S in touch with young labor people, etc.," she wrote in her diary. The many visitors were distracting, too. Mimi and likeable little Karlyn, whom Anderson had dreaded seeing since she was proof that he was a grandfather, arrived in mid-July, followed by Bill Stewart and his wife, Bill reporting a letter from the historian Charles Beard asking why *Today* "didn't have more things like Sherwood Anderson about people." Then before the end of the month the Emmetts, much occupied with a new diet, came briefly, and Braver-Mann settled in to work on the script for the *Poor White* film. By this time Anderson was smoking too much and having trouble sleeping, though Eleanor could comment that "We are very happy and adjusted so that it's too bad." They had their worries. Both were concerned that she did not get pregnant; yet Eleanor particularly wondered whether they ought to have a baby since without her independent income he would have to do hack work to support them, which, she feared, "would probably crush him." She continued to face the dilemma he put her in with her job: "Sherwood is afraid for me to stop for fear we starve and yet wants me around all the time." As for Sherwood, he was troubled about the fate of *Winesburg* with some Broadway producer and the fact that though guests were fun, he was getting little writing done.[26]

Around the first of August he suddenly began writing again, quickly producing two impressive stories about the same subject, a man's death and its effect on others. "Jug of Moon," which the *American* returned to him for revision and which *Today* snapped up unrevised, is not quite in a class with "Death in the Woods," with which it has a distant affinity, but it has been too little examined as a short story, perhaps because "buried" in the *Memoirs*. It flows easily from narrative form to narrative form, even the interruptions soon seen as purposefully placed. It begins like an essay with a description of the poor, independent hill men as being not stereotypes but "just people," whom the city person may look down on but who himself might look foolish among. Essay blends into tale as a first-person narrator, like Anderson a townsman and a writer, takes a city sculptor— Esherick and the artist part of Anderson—walking on mountain roads, where the sculptor, who "knew something," exclaims at how beautifully the barefooted hill women walk. "But I sat down this morning to write the story of the death of an old mountain man named Bill Graves," the narrator interjects as though his essay-story has been a kind of digression, and he moves into a biographical sketch of the man, who died a year ago at the age of seventy-five. After his first two wives have died of hard work and child-bearing, Bill meets and within hours marries Hallie, a tall, young, mountain woman who bears him four children. Bill is "an impressive sort of a man," hard-drinking, hard-working, trusted and relied on by men, admired by women, and generous—one late fall he threw six loads of firewood into the yard of a widow and cursed her for improperly letting her husband die before she did. Abruptly, but to set the climactic scene, the narrator introduces a description of the old-fashioned method of mowing a mountain grain field with scythe and cradle, a group of men marching, swinging across the field, each trying to get ahead of the others as a test of manhood, women and children shouting, laughing, following to bundle the cut grain into sheaves. The afternoon Bill dies, the narrator and the sculptor are out walking and see over the rail fence Bill leading a line of mowers swinging across his big hillside rye field, he taunting the laughing men to keep up with him, a sight which "grip[s]" the sculptor as being a rhythmic dance. Seeing the two watchers, Bill runs down to the fence, cursing, laughing, challenging "you city and town fellows" to join the line. He has been drinking heavily from the customary jug of moonshine to dull the two-year pain (the writer later learns from a town doctor) of stomach cancer, about which he has told no one, not even Hallie. At that moment, standing at the fence and laughing, he begins to die before the watchers' eyes. Calling Hallie to him, he quietly says he is dying on her "wrong," before she does, and slumps to the ground. The other hill men carry his body to his house with the women and children following; but Hallie, wanting to be alone in "the first storm of her grief" at losing a man who "had really got her," goes to sit on a little bridge across a stream, making a figure of loss the sculptor tells the narrator he will never forget.[27]

Anderson had got his story told right without further revisions. By having in effect two narrators—a "regular" one, the writer, and an "adjunct" one, the sculptor who "knew something" and who enlightens the writer— Anderson establishes patterns of repetition that help create the tale's form and meaning. It is the sculptor who instructs the writer, and the reader of the story, to observe how beautifully the barefooted women walk in the mountain road, enabling him to notice especially the walk of "one tall dark woman" among them and so to see how Hallie resembles that woman who at Bill's call comes "tall and barefooted, down the hillside, through the grain stubbles," and finally to understand that Hallie's figure as she sits on the bridge is an unforgettable representation of grief, she being ennobled simultaneously as artwork and as grieving human being. It is likewise the sculptor who perceives the mowers led by Bill to be in a rhythmic dance but who also laughs unalarmed at the laughing curses of Bill challenging the two outsiders; he understands Bill, that is, as a particular human being as well as part of an aesthetic action, this understanding symbolized in the detail that the sculptor puts his hands on the top rail of the fence, a sign of communication despite separateness. Such a conflation of ennobling art objects and admirable human beings justifies by exemplum the opening essay's claim that hill people are "just people," in the case of this man and wife admirable "just people." In this context the death of Bill Graves is that of a heroic, even monumental figure in a traditional society still living close to the earth; indeed, Bill becomes the protagonist in a small Greek tragedy—a noble person living by the code of his society but who, by his personal code of "right" dying, is defeated, as is his wife, by a mighty antagonist—death.

The second tale, "The Corn Planting," which *American Magazine* did accept for its November issue, is a lesser but still fine one, further proof that Anderson had not lost his storytelling talent. In a simple, conversational style, which occasionally becomes lyrical, a man of "our town" tells the story of Hatch Hutchenson, now nearly seventy, whose small nearby farm is "one of the best-kept and best-worked places in all our section." When nearly fifty he marries a schoolteacher of forty, and both seem "to fit into their farm life as certain people fit into the clothes they wear." They have one much-loved son, Will, who is strong, bright, and popular, and whose talent at drawing leads him to study at the Chicago Art Institute. In the city he becomes good friends with another young man from "our town" named Hal Weyman, who studies at the University of Chicago, returns to the town as high school principal, and tells the narrator about Will's many invitations to parties and his good income from the sale of his drawings "used in advertisements." Often Hal walks out to the Hutchenson farm to talk with Will's farm-bound parents about the letters he sends them describing life in the city. Late one spring evening a telegram for Hatch comes to the railroad telegrapher announcing Will's death, a random one unlike Bill Graves's, in an auto accident, and Hal and the narrator are prevailed on to take the telegram to Hatch. Walking slowly through the lovely spring moonlight, hating their errand, the two reach the farmhouse, where Hal, uncomfortable, rouses Hatch and blurts out the terrible news. Hatch merely shuts the door of the house silently. Soon the two messengers, now hidden, see Hatch and his wife come out in their white nightclothes and begin planting corn, kneeling together silently at the end of each row.

Anderson's ending is a delicate combination of assertion and qualification, of the definite and the indefinite. Up to this point the narrator has been primarily only a reporter of facts. His first reaction to the ritualistic behavior of the old couple in their nightclothes is characteristically visual, that it is "ghostly" enough "to curl your hair"; but then, shocked into the more self-probing, he declares that "It was the first time in my life I ever understood something," though he's not sure he can verbalize that something. The old couple's planting of corn is "a kind of silent cry, down into the earth . . . as though they were putting death down into the ground that life may grow again, something like that . . . asking something of the earth, too." But it's useless, the narrator concludes, to try to put into words how the old couple connected "the life in their field and the lost life in their son." It is not useless, however, to speculate as to the meaning of Hal's comment with which the story ends as with a diminuendo after the crescendo of the narrator's words: "'They have their farm and they have still got Will's letters to read,' Hal said." Such a remark might appear rather cynical, but in the context of the story it is merely realistic. In actuality Will's bright promise was fading. That his drawings "were used in advertisements and he was well paid" sufficiently indicates that he has commercialized his art, has sold out his talent. His parents' grief at his death is as profound as that of Hallie Graves, but they have their connection with the earth to sustain them as well as their image from his letters of a good, uncorrupted son. Hal and the reader know the double tragedy—the death and that corruption.

In the same letter in which he informed Anderson that *Today* would print "Jug of Moon," Stewart also wrote that Moley had approved Anderson's proposal of a fall and winter trip through the Midwest. Yet another kind of cheering letter had come back in mid-July when Harold Mason, co-proprietor of the Centaur Book Shop and the small Centaur Press in Philadelphia, invited Anderson to contribute a collection of essays or stories to a planned series of limited-edition books. Although interested, Anderson had decided that the proposed financial arrangement was unprofitable for him; but after Mason increased his offer in late September— $150 advance and higher royalties—Anderson accepted enthusiastically, for here was an opportunity to publish a gathering of his numerous essays about writers and artists he had known.[28]

Meanwhile after finishing "The Death of Bill Graves" and "The Corn Planting" in early August, he spent much of the month writing what Eleanor called "luscious stuff . . . very witty sort of reminiscences and reflections on persons" and which he would call simply "Notes on Living." Company continued to arrive—first Ferdinand Schevill, a formidable opponent at croquet, Anderson's favorite game, which he played seriously to win; then Marc and Lucile Antony, who at first exhilarated Anderson and then annoyed him by staying on and on. By the end of the month he stopped writing altogether at the chance to oversee needed work done at

Ripshin—a well dug, a pump installed, a stone wall and a bridge built—Eleanor wryly commenting that his delight in the "vocation of being a boss thus raising reflections on his democracy, etc." Company and vocation, however, did not keep him from thinking of his contractual obligation to Scribner's and urging Max Perkins to look at his *Today* articles as material for a book, and he mailed Perkins the whole series.[29]

By September, Eleanor had become almost as happy with the rural life as Sherwood, and both were dismayed when she received word from the YWCA to be back in New York on the seventeenth of the month. Already packed to leave, however, she learned from the Presbyterian Hospital in New York that her amoeba had shown up again in a test. Since she had to stay in Marion for treatment, Anderson set off by himself on the seventeenth or eighteenth, going first to Hedgerow to see another performance of *Winesburg,* which had "improved . . . wonderfully," and then on to New York, where he settled in at the Hotel Chelsea to put together two books for publication. He talked about the *Today* articles with Max Perkins, who had been "delighted" with them but had tactfully suggested more were needed to make up a substantial book. After accepting, on September 26, Mason's financially improved offer on the Centaur Press collection, Anderson had to see Perkins again to make sure that he had no objection to the limited-edition book. He had none, and Mason began urging the early deadline of November 1 for the entire manuscript to go to the printer so that the still-untitled book could be issued during the first week in December in time for the Christmas trade. With the help of Eleanor back in Marion, Anderson began assembling the pieces, mostly already published, he wanted on various people. At the same time Perkins was pressing for more articles for the untitled Scribner's book in hopes that it could be brought out early in 1935.[30]

Through the rest of September and most of October, Anderson busily juggled his two commitments. By early October, he had a final table of contents assembled for Mason with one piece, a "letter" to Jasper Deeter, yet to be written, and was tentatively calling the book *Flashes.* Mason thought that sounded too much like the fast-talking columnist Walter Winchell saying "Flash!" on his radio program and suggested instead *No Swank,* the title of the included *Today* article on Henry Wallace. Within a week Anderson had agreed on *No Swank* and written the Deeter letter, the book's epilogue, praising him for "mak[ing] the theater a way of life" and for being "an educator—one of the few we have had in the American scene, in the American theater." Then within two or three days he rewrote his old celebration of Dreiser in *Horses and Men* into a new celebration of him as a man "often rough, browbeating those about him" but inwardly possessing "the gift of infinite tenderness, always reaching out to the others." To Perkins, meanwhile, he was sending various other pieces for his consideration, some of which Perkins rejected as not relevant, others he liked, for example "The Nationalist" and "Please Let Me Explain." In the latter, each of two out-of-work hitchhikers Anderson picks up is a typical American in not blaming "society" for his joblessness but himself for not being "a good American because he has not risen above his fellows." The second young man believes that the government will and should pass a law requiring that the poor and the unemployed, like himself, be killed for not succeeding. As for the rejected pieces, Perkins was right, Anderson agreed, for they had been written "in a different mood."

I think that perhaps, for a year or two, I did rather go over to something like a communist outlook. Now again I am rather uncertain about all that. This attempting to touch off the lives of human beings, in relation to the world about them, is much more healthy for me. I have no solution.[31]

It had been a full month's work. With *No Swank* going to press, the Scribner book well on its way to completion, and even a dramatization of *Dark Laughter* started, Anderson took the night train for Marion on October 25. Eleanor had been able to return to her job early in the month, they had been together in New York at "56" for two weeks at midmonth, and she had leave to go with him on his Midwest tour for *Today;* but in the meantime he had another assignment for the magazine, an article on Rush Holt, West Virginia state legislator who at the age of twenty-nine was running for the United Sates Senate. Anderson drove into West Virginia on October 30, interviewed Holt the next day, spent three days in Holt's hometown of Weston and elsewhere talking with people who knew him and his career, returned to Marion on November 4 with a "good story," and on the fifth mailed the completed "Young Man from West Virginia" to Stewart in the midst of reading proof for *No Swank,* which he returned to Mason on the sixth. It was as though he had caught energy from the young man along with the admiration that the article shows. In a state marked by quick riches and enduring poverty, Holt is the working people's candidate and, like his doctor father, a fighter for progressive causes. A university-trained student, "his power in the state [is] due largely to his knowledge"; he has an unparalleled command of facts and a gift for explaining issues clearly. He will go to Washington, Anderson predicts, and "will go as a fighting young student, a smiling and warm young man." On November 6, the day after Anderson sent off his article, Rush Holt was in fact elected to the Senate, although he would not be seated until he reached the required age of thirty.[32]

There was further proof of his West Virginia–caught energy. In the intervals between talking with people there, he worked out an outline for an article on "the old age pension thing" and wrote and sent to Stewart one titled "The Princess and the Creeping Fear," based on a dinner conversation while in New York with the Baroness Koskull, who was in the United States again, looking for a job. In Europe, she told him, people wanted a dictator, and now has begun their "creeping fear" of that dictator "in Germany, in Italy, in Russia." America must keep free of a dictator, no matter what social class supports him, and must again be "the hope of the world." Because Anderson himself seemed to link the Soviet Union with two fascist nations, the article, when Eleanor read it, "made [her] sick" that he seemed to be becoming unconsciously more conservative in politics, though he insisted that he was "just against dictators." For whatever reason, Stewart turned it down for *Today*, but Anderson would use it, retitled "The Return of the Princess," as the conclusion to the Scribner book.[33]

4.

Despite Eleanor's dislike for the Princess article, both she and Sherwood loved being on the road again together. On November 9, they drove westward from Marion through the mountains of Virginia and Kentucky. They spent the next night in Cincinnati and on the eleventh headed north into early-Anderson country—lovingly described by Eleanor in her diary—to College Corners, near which his mother had been "bound"; to New Englandish Morning Sun, Karl's birthplace; to Camden, Sherwood's birthplace, which she thought "charming" with its "old beautiful trees." Here they were guided about by Steve Coombs, a young man who had written Anderson about his researches into his family, and by Steve's doctor father. Eleanor was especially delighted by a visit to the present occupant of the house her husband was born in; the house was "perfect!" for him. When Steve reported his finding that Irwin Anderson had been "very talkative," Sherwood added, "Yes, and drank a lot." Eleanor thought him "disappointed that no one remembered his mother," his differing reactions to his parents indicating that his love for his mother and dislike for his father remained unchanged. There was still enough time in that "day of Andersonia" for them to drive to Springfield, see Wittenberg College, and find that Mrs. Folger's house had been torn down. On the twelfth they drove through remembered Anderson country, through Caledonia, and then to Clyde. Here, Eleanor wrote in her diary, "S knows and loves and remembers everything," and he happily showed everything to her, including "the hotel around which he built *Winesburg*." With Anderson telling stories about his childhood, they drove on to Elyria where, Eleanor wrote by contrast, "he showed me the factory he walked out of and the street he thought he lived in, but reluctantly. Says he doesn't want to think of that awful period."[34]

A three-day stayover in Cleveland was more in his Elyria mood than the Clyde one. At a dinner party a guest savagely attacked him for being no radical and indeed no good as a writer at the same time that the wildly anti-Communist Elizabeth Dilling, author of *The Red Network*, was publicly declaring him "one of [the] worst communists" and Eleanor was continuing to feel sick over his uncertainty about Russia. After reaching Chicago at sunset on the sixteenth and settling in with the Sergels, her concern about him became stronger. "I find S is in a real reaction—puzzled and uncertain about Russia and everything. I can't tell yet whether it's the need to make money." Nevertheless the visit with the Sergels was an entertaining one. There were two lively dinner parties, the guests for the most part being cynical commentators full of Washington gossip; on the twentieth Sherwood and Roger went to Springfield at the governor's invitation to stay overnight at the mansion, conversation at the breakfast table being about the Civil War even more than about present-day legislative corruption; and after days of simply absorbing impressions, Anderson began writing, though he seemed to Eleanor to be curiously uninterested in developing leads for *Today* articles.[35]

Almost certainly while at the Sergels he wrote a nonpolitical piece that had, he hoped, the Midwest feeling. "Sherwood Anderson Goes Home" is a largely fabricated account of reaching "the land of the long cornfields in central Ohio" on his November tour, of having to get his car repaired, of becoming "a little poetic" at length about the corn, of being invited to stay overnight with a farmer and his family—Eleanor was not along, it seems—and of telling a fabricated dream, which ends a misunderstanding between the farmer and his tenant. "I may not be the poet of the cornfields," he thinks, "but as a talker—an itinerant maker-up of tales of dreams of the land—I am pretty good"—which the account proves is not a fabrication. It is certain that in this brief period of puzzlement about "everything" he also, at Max Perkins's request, wrote an introduction to the Scribner book urging the reader to "imagine the writer as going about, constantly puzzled as you are." Going about in this naturally rich land, but a land despoiled by greedy individualists, he has found that Americans "do not want cynicism. We want belief," a belief that government should not "go on just being a meaningless thing" and that democracy can be made to work. He also sent Perkins two suggested titles for the book: *Puzzled Americans* and *We Want to Believe*, at first favoring the second, later opting for *Puzzled Americans*.[36]

On November 24 the Andersons set out for Stillwater, Minnesota, but stopped in Madison to watch the second half of the game between Wisconsin and Minnesota's "greatest team in history"—Minnesota won, 34–0—so they did not reach the Van Meier home until the following day. They found Henry enjoying his growing practice but Katharine very eager to continue their rise in Stillwater society, even though she did invite in some of the leaders of Minnesota's Farmer-Labor Party, recently victorious in the state elections. On the night after the Andersons' arrival or the next, the kindly Henry took Sherwood to one of the new sort of dance hall that was appearing at the edges of small midwestern cities, where debt-ridden farmers and their wives and unemployed factory workers with theirs, many of the couples surviving on relief, met to drink sparingly, dance, and socialize. In "Village Wassail," the Today piece he quickly wrote afterwards, Anderson sympathetically concludes that any minimal spending of relief money in such pleasure by couples hard hit by the Depression is acceptable; such dance halls provide a necessary stay against despair. Having written this "good article" (Eleanor's phrase), Anderson went briefly into his own form of despair. On the twenty-eighth the Andersons attended a Farmer-Labor victory celebration at which Sherwood was introduced "with gusto," they listened to speeches, and they had a long talk with the lieutenant-governor about the history of the radical movement and party. In this and later conversations was political material for Today articles, but Eleanor soon noted that she was "terribly puzzled by S's difficulty in writing now." On the evening of December 3, while workers were digging out streets after a storm, the third in four days, had dropped a record eighteen inches of snow on the Twin Cities, the Andersons and the Van Meiers made their way to the St. Paul Athletic Club as dinner guests of the dean of the University Medical School and Governor Floyd Olson, who had just been elected to his third term. Olson began "courting" Anderson, urging him to come to Minnesota to edit a Farmer-Labor newspaper; but from too many martinis and too rapid eating Sherwood became ill and the guests had to leave, though not before he had learned much from Olson's animated stories about the campaign and had come to admire the "big laughing," open, working-class Governor greatly.[37]

For the next two days at home Katharine pressed her own campaign for social advancement. She had learned that Gertrude Stein, who back in October had arrived in New York for her American lecture tour just as Anderson was leaving the city, would be speaking in St. Paul on the night of December 8; and she insisted that if possible Eleanor should get her and Alice B. Toklas to dinner at the Van Meier's as "the one thing that would give her [Katharine] prestige." Reluctantly Eleanor agreed to try, but with her husband she had a quite different sort of discussion revealing his present state of mind.

S and I had a long talk about his special problem—whether he should expect or want (as K[atharine] says recognition here and now). We mentioned Dreiser and Sinclair Lewis. S says he believes he is more significant than either, but it won't be known for 50 years. In spite of this feeling once in a long time, he is torn by doubt and a sense of failure most of the time.[38]

Apparently his feeling of failure had become acute since their visit to Elyria and the Cleveland dinner party at which the guest had attacked him with what Eleanor called the "cruel blow" that "he had let down his generation," and she may have deduced that his lack of interest in leads for *Today* articles showed a growing concern that he was writing for money instead of for art. Still, since he had contracted to write the articles, he must now go to the towns to assess the effect there of the Farmer-Labor movement. Leaving Stillwater at noon on the sixth, they bucked the snowdrifts west to the "small frozen Minnesota town" of Willmar, where he probably went to the political meeting that helped shape his belief that the Scandinavian inhabitants of the state were not afraid of experimenting with bold radical ideas. The next day they drove through lessening snow to Albee, South Dakota, where they talked with a young Scandinavian farmer who was leading marches to the county courthouse to prevent foreclosures on farms, and then on to Brookings, South Dakota, where Anderson was "rushed" by reporters from miles away "saying they hardly ever got a real writer out there and just wanted to talk." On the eighth the Andersons attended a huge political meeting of farmers, which Sherwood, probably reassured by the reporters' rush, left to write his article "Northwest Unafraid," praising the Scandinavian Minnesotans for their "determined belief that some kind of a good life is possible for more people, through governments," and praising Olson: "This man knows, he feels, and it is his knowing and feeling that has made him what he is, the outstanding and the best loved leader of the radical Northwest."[39]

Since Henry Van Meier had confirmed that Stein and Toklas, overjoyed to see Anderson at last, would be coming to dinner on the evening of the ninth, the Andersons set out for Stillwater at 3 AM, he driving all the way and arriving in time, Toklas recalled years later, for him to pick up the guests at their St. Paul hotel for "that lovely evening." There was "much hugging and kissing" on arrival, Eleanor wrote in her detailed account two days after the event. Although she resented Alice's customary taking of her, the wife, away from Gertrude and Sherwood, she managed to overhear bits of the stream of talk between them. Not wanting "to talk down to people," Gertrude had prepared her lectures carefully; she was "thrilled by everything . . . her audiences, the publicity." (For her St. Paul lecture there had been a sell-out of five hundred tickets.) The two old friends talked a lot about French and American farming, about one of their favorite subjects, Grant and the Civil War, and of course about writing, Gertrude commenting that "if you stop to think what you write it's not direct writing." Because Alice had "immediately nailed" her and because she wanted to record Gertrude's talk, Eleanor did not record any of Sherwood's; but she did note that "S condemns homosexual tendencies so and yet thinks it all right in her" and that "She dotes on S and wants to take an automobile trip with us in the South." As an afterthought, Eleanor recorded that Gertrude greatly admired Katharine's rugs made by Virginia mountain women and wanted some for herself. (Sherwood later sent her one.) So it was a successful evening even for the captured Eleanor.[40]

A day or two later the Andersons left Stillwater for a swing first through central Iowa, getting a sense from people they talked with that, after Minnesota, Iowa tended to be conservative. From Des Moines they headed southeast to stay overnight at Hannibal, Missouri, where the next morning they got up early to stand on the bank of the Mississippi watching Twain's and Anderson's river flow and later to visit Twain's boyhood home. Then with Sherwood talking for miles about his sudden notion to write a new kind of life of Twain, they drove down along the river to St. Louis, registering at the Mark Twain Hotel. Here they found waiting a letter from Roger Sergel praising *No Swank,* which had been scheduled for publication on December 3 but which did not appear until the eighth, "too late for the Christmas trade," Eleanor noted. On the morning of the fifteenth, with a reporter who had left the *Daily Worker* rather than join the Communist Party, Anderson crossed the river to observe East St. Louis, which he was appalled to find "one of [the] most absentee cities in the world," and to take notes for a *Today* article. Later that day the Andersons drove northeast to Decatur, Illinois, where at a cocktail party Sherwood, within Eleanor's hearing, explained why he wrote so simply.

S accounted for his style by fact that not having had high education he relied on Anglo-Saxon words rather than Latin derivatives and used Anglo-Saxon sources— influence of King James version—fact he and Dreiser rebelled at getting their America through England by way of New England.

On the seventeenth they drove through Indianapolis to Columbus, Ohio, where at a university business school luncheon "Everybody [was] terribly flattering to S" and Eleanor was introduced by the school dean as "Mrs. Dreiser." Then it was southeast through Ohio and West Virginia and on the nineteenth "over icy roads with gorgeous fog" to Marion, where, weary from the trip and probably depressed by the approach of Christmas, Sherwood immediately went to bed with the flu for the holiday season.[41]

Lying ill for several days, he had time to think over his two tours into twenty states and come to some conclusions about what he had seen and heard and about himself, conclusions he summarized in a letter to Ralph Church at the end of the month. If, back in 1932, there may have been a "big push toward some sort of revolution," that push was gone. Despite what he had observed in Appalachia and Minnesota, he now felt that people in general "dread[ed] change of any kind" and would simply settle for a lower standard of living. "They will stand for a lot and at bottom are not revolutionary minded." As for himself,

I've been about with the revolutionists a good deal and being with them always intensifies my own individualism.

Then I go with the rich and see how, generally, riches make life ugly.

Repelled equally by left and right, he now saw little as center. Given, as he had long believed, that American lives were dominated by a "curious loneliness, separateness," perhaps they needed some sort of religion, but he himself had no interest in places such as churches "where people were engaged in the corrupt business of trying to save their souls"; nature's beauty lying about him was his church. At the moment, all he could offer was "a kind of idea," though he did not himself "live up to it very well," that the true center was the continual reaching out among isolated individuals, especially men, toward closer personal relationships. It was a limited sort of offering.[42]

En route to a peace conference in Amsterdam, 1932. Used by permission from the Newberry Library.

In Central Park, June 5, 1937. Photograph by Carl Van Vechten.

Eleanor Anderson, Sherwood, Katharine Van Meier, Bascom E. Copenhaver, Laura Lu Copenhaver, and Eleanor Wilson at Ripshin.

At Ripshin Creek, 1935.

At the mouth of the Rio Grande, 1937.

Sherwood and Eleanor at Rosemont, Marion, Virginia, 1937.

Sherwood, Laura Lu Copenhaver, Bascom E. Copenhaver, and Randolph Copenhaver at Rosemont, 1937.

The house at Ripshin farm. Used by permission from Greear Studio.

The library at Ripshin.

Sherwood and Katherine Ann Porter, Olivet College in Michigan, July 1939.

At the writing cabin, Ripshin. Used by permission from Greear Studio.

Aboard the SS *Santa Lucia*, February 28, 1941. Used by permission from the Newberry Library.

Sherwood and Thornton Wilder on the ship to South America, 1941.

Sherwood Anderson's grave in Marion, Virginia, monument designed by Wharton
Esherick. Used by permission from Greear Studio.

8

Looking for an Art Form

1.

Not only did the lateness of *No Swank*'s publication slow its sales, but it was issued by a small press with limited distribution facilities, it was at best a pleasant but minor addition to Anderson's works, and it was noticed by few reviewers. Lewis Gannett spoke kindly of it in the *New York Herald Tribune* the day before Christmas, but his conclusion was moderate in its enthusiasm: "If you are desperately looking for a last-minute Christmas present for a real American you could do worse than 'No Swank.'" Late in January, Ernest Boyd would write in *Today* that the book and Anderson's articles for the magazine "show no lessening of his power; instead, we like to think, an increasing depth." Two reviews at the end of December, however, were more negative. A brief notice in the *New Yorker* judged that Anderson "spoils [his essays] by enlarging too much, but his impressions are often canny and perceptive." Under the heading "Anderson Embers," *Time,* while agreeing that he would be in "a U.S. literary pantheon" for his best work, quipped that in this book he "goes on talking when he is no longer on the air." These four were the only reviews, and unfortunately by early January the Andersons had apparently seen only the two "not too good" ones with the clear suggestion in *Time* that the essay collection showed their author's decline in both reputation and talent.[1]

Despite his disappointment at the reviews, he managed to finish in two days of shaky recovery from the flu an already half done, cleverly organized, vividly observed article for *Today* ironically titled "Revolt in South Dakota." Although this agricultural state was in the middle of the Dust Bowl where from great sections of its land the drought-parched topsoil had been blown away in dust storms by high winds, where for flat miles around these storms had killed all the trees, and he "had seen places where the sand and dust drifts had all but covered fences, had seen the corn in cornfields, cut and shocked, the shocks far apart, standing up hardly

higher than my knees," where the surprising lack of snow meant no mois-
ture for next year's planting, here nevertheless he had found farmers sensitive to slights against their state, cheerful about the future, politically
conservative, not in the least interested, unlike North Dakotans and Minnesotans, in revolt of any kind. Probably in the next few days he also wrote
the last of his three stories to be published in *American Magazine*. "Feud"
with its happy ending and too manipulated first-person narrator would
seem to be a tale deliberately designed for a popular magazine. An adaptation of the Romeo and Juliet situation to a hill country setting, it first
sketches the friendship and then lasting enmity between John Lampson
and Dave Rivers. Both men marry. John has a son, Jim, who grows into "a
sensitive, rather slender man"; Dave has a "slim, lovely" daughter, Elvira.
After John has died and Elvira has reached sixteen, the two young people
fall in love. Transferring his anger against John to the son, Dave threatens
to shoot Jim if he continues to court Elvira. Enraged, Jim is tempted to
shoot Dave in his house at night but instead returns to do so in daylight.
Dave has killed a pig and has it "in the scalding barrel filled with . . . boiling water." When Jim faces Dave with rifle leveled, Dave quickly heaves
the pig's body out of the barrel for some unexplained reason—to use the
body as a shield or weapon, to demonstrate his fearlessness before death,
or simply to help the author achieve the happy ending?—but his act tips
over the barrel, which floods his own body with the boiling water. Jim
drops his gun, takes out his knife, and cuts the man's clothes away to prevent further scalding. From the way Dave looks at Jim the narrator knows
that the feud has ended. Anderson could hardly have been proud of this
tale, but it would have added $300 to the *Today* article's $250 to help pay
for the vacation in a warm climate he had been wanting for himself and
Eleanor for some weeks.[2]

The Andersons had decided to head south through New Orleans to
Brownsville, Texas, on the Gulf, which promised warm weather, closeness
to Mexico, low costs, and much fishing. Sherwood having mailed to Max
Perkins the last of his pieces for *Puzzled America*, they happily drove off
on January 9, reaching Knoxville in time for him to show Eleanor the progress on the Norris Dam and for them to spend an exciting evening with
some TVA officials. On the tenth they went on to Tuscaloosa, Alabama,
"S thrilling at getting in the South and swearing he will go south every
year." The next day they saw the Civil War sites at Vicksburg, some of the
fine old houses in Natchez, and Huey Long's new thirty-four-story state
house in Baton Rouge. They arrived in New Orleans on the twelfth, put
up at Anderson's favorite hotel, the Monteleone, and at once were surrounded by reporters and old friends—the Feiblemans, the Friends, the
Antonys, and others. Eleanor especially liked Julius Friend, "an exquisite
sensitive person with fine brain," and found "Jimmie" Feibleman "very

entertaining [but] dogmatic and arrogant." All his friends "adore" Sherwood, she noted, which "should help his ego," but they gave him no time to work on a new novel he had already started or on the plays he now wanted to write. So they needed to get on to Texas.[3]

The last of their four days in New Orleans was a busy one. Anderson was interviewed at length for the *Times-Picayune* on the present situation in American literature. Today, he asserted, writers must deal with political and economic subjects. "I am not," the reporter quoted him as saying, "essentially a politically minded man, but I suppose I could be called a Socialist. In everything I write that deals with the social question, I find myself unconsciously on the side of the working people." Current American writing, he went on to explain, represents a second literary rebellion. The first, which began just prior to World War I, was slowed by the war but became a major movement in the 1920s, was essentially a rebellion against "the rigid moral standards imposed on [writers] by the existing puritanism" and made the twenties "one of the most creative periods of American literature." Now a second rebellion is rising out of the economic crisis of the Depression "which will probably result in a new burst of writing equally as vital" as that postwar literary renaissance. That evening, at Marc Antony's urging, he spoke to a "huge crowd" at the local Group Theater's workshop on experimental theaters. After making Eleanor nervous by at first pacing around the speaker's table, he "perched," the reporter wrote, on a corner of it, "a characteristic, straggling gray lock over his forehead and his wrinkled coat caught over something in his hip pocket" and kept his audience "on the edges of the chairs" with his insistence that experimental theaters must become popular by encouraging young playwrights whose best plays "probably will have social and economic implications." He may have surprised his audience by urging that art should be self-supporting and that the Group should make its theater "commercial as quickly as possible"; but he used as his example of success "fantastic Jasper Deeter" and Hedgerow, "which made money out of Shaw to play Chekov." The busy day ended with a party at the Antony home at which he was adored as usual.[4]

On the sixteenth, they drove west to New Iberia to call on the odd painter Weeks Hall in his lovely old colonnaded plantation house and then on to Texas and down the Gulf Coast. By the following day they had reached Corpus Christi and temporarily taken a small furnished house on the bay. Immediately Sherwood went "madly" into his new novel, "a queer but, to me very moving book," he informed Perkins guardedly, and the rest of the time went enthusiastically into fishing. Despite his remarks in the *Times-Picayune* account, Eleanor noted bluntly that he had become "more interested in writing as writing and less in economic, causes, life, etc. We have a perpetual fight about Russia." For Sherwood, Corpus Christi was beautiful, the weather was mostly pleasant, his writing was going well—"any place is beautiful if you work," he wrote Bockler—and he happily loved his wife, who nevertheless confided to her diary that, "Obviously, he more and more loves a simple setting with me as the drudging little wife." When proofs for *Puzzled America* arrived in the mail late in January, he read and returned them in a single day along with directions that the articles be arranged according to his two tours, "In the South" and "In the Middlewest," and with some suggestions of persons who should receive copies and might "boost" it. Already, he had decided that the dedication should read "To Roger Sergel."[5]

Happy as he was during their two weeks in "Corpus," both he and Eleanor wanted to get closer to Mexico, and probably on February 1 they drove down to Brownsville, where he was even happier, the happiest Eleanor had ever seen him. Living was cheap—they had "a very comfortable room" at the Miller Hotel close by the Rio Grande for eight dollars a week—and the fishing was superb; in half an hour one day he caught five big redfish, each a six- to seven-pound fighter. Even Eleanor caught the excitement, and together they roamed the Gulf shore north and south of the Rio Grande's mouth, Sherwood celebrating his blissful freedom by growing a beard, amusedly described by a friend as "an Imperial—just a few rust hairs sprouting a bristly path down the center of his chin, with scarcely growth enough to leave a perceptible fringe hanging goatily below." For the beard Eleanor began calling him "Conquistador." Afternoons, presumably after the fishing, they regularly went across the river to the still untouristed Mexican town of Matamoros, where they could shop in the old market for "lovely glass, hand blown, so dirt cheap," and have venison and quail dinners for fifty cents. The town and its ways delighted them, made them reject as "pat popularization[s]" some of the current American books about Mexico.

S adores the square. Two fiestas were amazing revelations of mores or something. The men in blocks of two hundred or more march 3 or 4 abreast around and around the square. The women in the same formation head in the other direction—on and on with a beat into the earth almost like the dances D. H. Lawrence describes. This is the system by which the boys meet the girls and later pursue the matter. The latter behind the iron grill on each window, the former before.[6]

Mornings, of course, Anderson wrote. Besides a few letters and the new novel he had worked on at Corpus Christi, he produced only a brief contribution to a symposium on lynching for *The Crisis*. Condemning lynching as "such a rotten and stupid way to get a justice," he explained it as part of "the story of what has been done to the poor whites . . . the meagerness and ugliness of life . . . this occasionally breaking forth in a

Negro lynching. The whole mess is bad." At Brownsville he switched from the novel long enough to do two more articles for *Today*. By the tenth he had written the first, "Nobody's Home," a grim, angry report on East St. Louis as "the most perfect example, at least in America, of what happens under absentee ownership." A city of 80,000 people and many factories, it is black with smoke, dirt, and dust; an ugly, broken-paved street of prostitutes is in the center of the business district; homeless men, the drifters, the unemployed wander the city. The owners of all the factories live elsewhere; at night even the clerks in the stores return to their homes in St. Louis across the river, leaving only the factory workers in their homes in mean, dirty streets since they cannot leave. The only hopeful sign is that the federal government has taken over a huge dilapidated factory in the middle of the city, and it has become "the hotel, the club, of the down-and-outs, the wanderers," who themselves have set about cleaning it up, putting it into shape, establishing a laundry, a kitchen, a bakery, a hospital. Otherwise, Anderson decides, absenteeism is in "almost every human relationship" in the city, indeed in the country as a whole, for the owners, the rich keep themselves far away in every sense from the poor, the unemployed, and the workers.[7]

Within a week after writing this article he had finished the second one. "Valley Apart"—in the Southwest the Rio Grande Valley is spoken of simply as "the Valley"—is as cheerful as "Nobody's Home" is gloomy. He admires the vast flat, rich Texas farming country; he is equally fascinated with the often homemade "houses on wheels," predecessors of the mini-homes and RVs, and with the process by which the Mexican women make tortillas from shelled corn; he feels comfortable with the big wheat and corn farmers from the Midwest who happily winter in Texas along the Gulf and possess "a kind of hardiness, a native kindness and shrewdness." The Valley, he comments, "is the one section of America I've been in during these last two years of wandering, in which I have heard no talk of a new age coming, no talk of politics or economics at all. They all seem to think and feel that what's here is all right as it is." Finally, he is interested in the many Mexicans, whom he sees both as, stereotypically, shy, cruel, and readily dangerous, and as the source in the Americans of the Valley of "the kindness in their eyes, the relaxed easy walk, the neighborliness in them that is soothing like a caress." He knows that the Mexicans do the hard work in the vast fields for low pay but is willing to accept the notion that "it is maybe O.K. with them." He is aware of hatred between the people of the two nationalities but describes a friendliness, which is even stronger. Anderson appears to have become as relaxed as other visitors to the Valley; yet at one point he abruptly interrupts his praise of the friendliness of Midwest vacationers with his usual nonvacationing cry: "Oh, the lonely American! I wish someone could tell me why we are such a lonely people!" It is a brief sudden eruption of his social consciousness, of such powerful feeling, as lies behind "Nobody's Home."[8]

Most mornings during the month on the Gulf, however, he had "gone writing nutty" on the novel, and in mid-February he could estimate that he had put down "some" 25,000 words. Two weeks later it would be "about" 35,000, and he was willing to give Max Perkins a brief summary.

I think I can tell you, in a general way, that it is the story of one of my own brothers and I am calling it Brother Earl.

He was a strange chap, very talented, rather silent. He was born of a woman who did not want him. He felt that. He could not make his own living.

People were always trying to help him. They couldn't.

He became a wanderer, in the book because of a crime committed, not intended, took up with all sorts of so-called queer people, died young, after a good many odd adventures.

Admitting to Perkins that this was "but a sketchy outline," he added that he was "having great fun with the book. It is the kind of book I would write for the sheer joy of writing it even if no one ever read or published it."[9]

The writing flowed daily, the fishing was grand, Matamoros was a constant delight, the other visitors were friendly and kindhearted; except for a few cold days the weather was beautiful, and both Sherwood and Eleanor had rarely felt so healthy. Only one problem marred their happiness at Brownsville. With increasing concern she noted in her diary that early in their stay there they had "several fights" over his "glee" in reading William Henry Chamberlin's *Russia's Iron Age,* published in the previous October at the end of the author's twelve years as correspondent for the *Christian Science Monitor* in the Soviet Union, to which he had come as an enthusiastic supporter. Focusing on industrialization and collectivization under the First Five-Year Plan of 1928–33 and on the great famine of its last year, Chamberlin now wrote, for the most part, as a severe critic of Soviet policies. Further convinced by Chamberlin of his own antidictatorship position, Sherwood charged Eleanor with being "romantic about Russia"; admitting that Chamberlin was convincing, Eleanor noted that "nonetheless I hate for S to go terribly anti-revolutionary and pro-democracy and pro-Roosevelt." By mid-February their fights over Communism had become "terrific," and she noted seriously, "I have taken it as a joke, but we may develop real incompatibility." Such fights may partly explain why, leaving him to write and fish, she went alone to visit Monterey and found it, though more Americanized than Matamoros, "one of the most beautiful cities I ever saw."[10]

They did agree on another book. Gertrude Stein had written that she and Alice would be in New Orleans on February 18, where she lectured that evening at Newcomb College on "The History of English Literature As I Understand It," and the Andersons had somehow learned that they were staying over for several days to enjoy the city Sherwood had praised. In preparation for this second meeting, he and Eleanor had been reading *Three Lives* and had decided that "The Gentle Lena," not "Melanctha," was "the good one." On the nineteenth they set off for New Orleans, driving the length of the Gulf shore to Orange, Texas, the first day and arriving in New Orleans on the twentieth in time to spend the evening with Stein and Toklas at the home of the author Roark Bradford. "Gertie effused over [Sherwood] and his new beard," Eleanor wrote of the occasion, and coolly noted that "Lovey" (Toklas) usually won arguments with "Pussy" (Stein), who struck Eleanor as "an awful prima donna." The next day, while Eleanor began tests at the hospital to determine whether she had recovered from her second bout with amoebic dysentery, Anderson showed Stein and Toklas around the French Quarter and Market and the Garden District, and that evening the four dined together. Since Stein and Toklas had to take a plane early in the morning of the twenty-second to get to a lecture engagement in St. Louis, farewells had to be said that evening. Although Anderson and Stein would maintain their friendship through occasional letters, they would not meet again. In an interview in New Orleans, she had already declared that he was "a much more original writer" than Hemingway; and in New York before she sailed for France at the end of her tour, she would give him parting praise in a long, open, memorable interview on May 3 with a young writer, John Hyde Preston:

STEIN: And there is another [besides Robert Frost] whom you young men are doing your best—and very really your worst—to forget, and he is the editor of a small-town newspaper and his name is Sherwood Anderson. Now Sherwood—
PRESTON: He was the only man she called by his first name, and then affectionately
STEIN: Sherwood is really and truly great because he truly does not care what he is and has not thought what he is except a man, a man who can go away and be small in the world's eyes and yet perhaps be one of the very few Americans who have achieved that perfect freshness of creation and passion, as simple as rain falling on a page, and rain that fell from him and was there miraculously and was all him. You see, he had that *creative recognition*, that wonderful ability to have it all on paper before he saw it and then to be strengthened by what he saw so that he could always go deep for more and not know that he was going.

It was the tribute of one American original to another.[11]

Life in New Orleans for the Andersons continued to be "always exciting but too strenuous." On the twenty-third Eleanor spent the entire morning at the hospital finishing her tests, which indicated that she was free of the amoeba, and in the afternoon they were interviewed at length by a *Times-Picayune* reporter, their accompanying picture the next day showing them both handsome and healthy from vacation. Asked about his findings "on the human side of the New Deal" in his forthcoming *Puzzled America,* Anderson told the interviewer that on his two tours he had found strong support for Roosevelt and very little for fascism, Socialism, or Communism, and that the two government projects, which had impressed him most, were the CCC camps and the TVA. At the latter, he declared, "in the midst of the depression and general uncertainty, we found a big body of men working with the feeling they were building something." Rounding out that day, they went to an evening party at the Antonys where he got into a bad squabble with another guest and where, to his dismay over their capabilities, the Group Theater members seemed bent on doing *Winesburg.* "These New Orleans people make over S tremendously, but I guess a little praise won't hurt him," Eleanor set down as her last entry for 1935, perhaps because for her the vacation was ending.[12]

Well before she left on March 1 for Marion and then New York, Sherwood was busy mornings at his desk in the apartment they had taken in the Buena Vista Apartment Hotel on St. Charles Avenue. First he read added proofs for *Puzzled America* and designated "The Return of the Princess" under the new caption, "What the Woman Said," as the conclusion to the book. Then he went back to *Brother Earl,* an experiment "unlike anything else I have done," he wrote Perkins on February 24. As soon as Eleanor left, he came down with the flu—she had it in Marion—but he was so rested from the vacation that he recovered in three days; the night before the height of Mardi Gras he danced until four in the morning. Then it was back to his desk. In a letter to Karl in mid-March he wrote again about this "rather crazy book . . . an attempt to get at something in [Earl's] life, what it meant, etc.," though he was most interested in how his sentences flooded from him unendingly. In two months, he estimated, he had written about 50,000 words.

And, alas, it has only begun. It is one of those things that, it now seems, may go on forever. Of course, I have given him a new background, different parents, in a different position in life, but yet in some way, I hope, having the essence of his background too. It is the sort of thing in which a man just lets himself go, not thinking: "Will anyone ever care to read this? Will anyone understand what I am driving at if he does read?" Just, you see, letting it flow like water. It is a most satisfactory feeling anyway.[13]

For some time he had been wanting to spend a few days fishing at Grand Isle, a town on an island, at the end of a peninsula jutting out into the Gulf, south of New Orleans. Waiting until he had given a talk on the promise of country newspapers on March 14 at a press luncheon for the triennial convention of the National Council of Jewish Women—he had found that "Most of the intellectuals and the most entertaining people [in New Orleans] are Jews"—he set out, probably on the sixteenth, for a second vacation. Grand Isle suited his love for the raffish and unconventional. The inhabitants were an intermarried mix of French, Spanish, Indian, and African American; and he stayed in a ramshackle hotel with an outside privy and a hard-drinking woman manager who decided she was in love with him because he was "so refined." He fished nights in the moonlight on the deserted beach, wading far out in the dark water in his hip boots to cast for redfish. Although his catch were mostly small ones, he exulted in his "mysterious" isolation in the moonlit dark with large porpoises occasionally swimming close to him. "It gets you kinda crazy," he summarized, "the beauty of things sometimes."[14]

Refreshed, he returned in the evening of the twenty-first to New Orleans, to his social rounds with intellectual and artistic friends, and to *Brother Earl*. By the twenty-seventh he had finished book one of this experiment. Immensely happy that Eleanor was arriving from New York the next day, he was concerned only that, because she had a YWCA assignment in the city, she would be working even harder than usual to meet the already too many demands on her, and also that Roger and Ruth Sergel were arriving for a visit and must be entertained. As he feared, the ensuing social life became demanding, so much so that at a party at the Antonys, Eleanor disappeared; Sherwood found her curled up asleep on a settee in another room, and he left her to sleep through the party. Despite the constant socializing he nevertheless kept his mornings free to "rite right wright write," as he informed Laura Lu, the "novel expand[ing], spread[ing] out like a balloon" while he also contemplated writing a third one-act play to make up an evening of three to be called "Short Stories."[15]

2.

As though there was not enough excitement already, Max Perkins wrote on March 29 that *Puzzled America* was published on this day, and the wait for its critical reception began. Presumably Perkins would have made sure that the advertising department at Scribner's, which had capacities far exceeding those of Harold Mason at the Centaur Press, distributed review copies widely to literary editors at magazines and newspapers across the nation; and surely he would have seen that his author received clippings of reviews as soon as possible, especially favorable ones. Fortunately, of the seven reviews appearing in New York newspapers at the end of March only two were unfavorable, and it would have been possible for Anderson to have received clippings of them all in the mail before he and Eleanor left New Orleans early in April. Very likely he would at least have seen Lewis Gannett's in the March 30 *Herald Tribune* with its encouraging assessment that Anderson was "a true rural American" whose report on "the byways of America . . . rings true." Not until later could he have seen Sterling North's proclamation, in the reassuringly headlined "Sherwood Anderson Stages a Comeback" in the April 3 *Chicago Daily News,* that "Anderson proves himself to be as good a reporter, poet and story teller as we have in America . . . with a book which takes your breath away." Few other favorable reviewers would be quite as euphoric, but between three-quarters and four-fifths of some seventy reviews would be strongly or largely positive, to Perkins's and Anderson's great satisfaction. There were, of course, negative reviews, though very few as much so as Louis Adamic's "A Puzzled American" in the April 13 issue of the *Saturday Review of Literature,* an attack so thoroughly damning both book and author as unredeemably "puzzled" that one suspects some kind of personal grudge. Most of the objections raised by negative reviewers were made by Ernest Sutherland Bates in his yes–no assessment, "The American Countryman" in *New York Herald Tribune Books* for April 7: Anderson had "deliberately excluded" the city proletariat; he reported nothing on such important matters as southern textile strikes or "the terrorization of the Negroes"; most importantly, though he had "intuitive insight" into individual lives, he was incapable of generalizing adequately. Others complained that he offered no solutions to a Depression-puzzled America. The many enthusiastic reviewers obviously judged otherwise, including Gertrude Stein, who in the *Chicago Daily Tribune* for May 4 reiterated the word "puzzled" to assert that puzzled America and puzzled Anderson cannot "really and truly" be puzzled. These majority reviewers maintained that Anderson's purpose was to report, not predict, that his generalizations were for the most part both persuasive and illuminating, that, as Bates himself pointed out, he powerfully and movingly described "the whole picture of rural America . . . a picture of wasted land, wasted natural resources and wasted lives."[16]

With all the individual *Today* articles brought together, it could be seen that of its three sections, the much longer one on the South is the strongest part of the book. Anderson knew and understood many of the South's problems. Congenitally disenchanted with southern aristocracy, he tended to see these problems from the bottom up, and one of the cements for these separate pieces is his sympathy for the unemployed, the down-and-outs, the drifters, for all those like the coal miners, the small tobacco farmers, the white and black sharecroppers living in poverty from birth and now in the Depression at the edge of destitution or beyond. There is nothing puzzled or puzzling about his sympathy for these. Nor, with his long-held attitudes, is he puzzled or puzzling about his dislike for, his anger against, such persons as the "New Tyrants" who "would make money in hell," against those who pervert the concept of individualism and the "American Dream" to mean getting rich at the expense of and without regard for others, against the just plain rich since, he is convinced, most are not really aware that there's a Depression on. He is himself puzzled, he claims in the introduction—if this is not a former ad-writer's device to get on familiar terms with his readers—because he has no *specific* remedies for the ills he sees or learns about. From his travels, interviews, and observations, however, he has come to a number of not-in-the-least-puzzled conclusions, desired goals rather than quick, definite answers. America, he consistently maintains, is a country of vast national wealth that could and should be the source of jobs for all and of the good life for everyone. Americans do not, yet, want revolution; they want a government that is truly democratic and that works. Among their benefits, the TVA dams will control floods and provide power to homes and new industries of an entire region, bringing many of its inhabitants into the modern world; working together, the young CCC men reclaim both wasted land and their own potentially wasted lives. Most of all, Anderson decides, he and the people he has talked with want, not cynicism, but "a new birth of belief": "Can we find it in one another, in democracy, in the leadership we are likely to get out of a democracy?" To ask a question is not necessarily to puzzle. "We" know in general where "we" want to be, Anderson reports and thinks; our problem is how to get there. Although Stein's reiteration of "puzzled" irritated one reviewer of *Puzzled America* into a fit of lame parody, it would seem that she shrewdly got the point behind that rather misleading title. To quote her more fully:

> It is a puzzled America seen by a puzzled American and it ends up by its not being possible to really puzzle America or as Sherwood Anderson is an American. In his introduction he explains all that without telling you makes you realize that a puzzled American is not a puzzled person that a puzzled America is not puzzled land, and he makes all that come out so clearly and so truly that it makes any one glad that he Sherwood is an American and that America is that land.

The book does "end up" with an unpuzzled America and American. The second section, "In the Middlewest," is much shorter than the first for obvious reasons. The second tour was shorter in time, and Anderson produced fewer articles from it; in fact, for the most part it provides much less "in-depth" journalism. Nevertheless, in late January he had established an order for the pieces in this section different from that of their composition or of publication in *Today;* in late February he had taken out "The Return of the Princess" from the second section, where he had originally placed it first of five pieces, and put it by itself under a new caption, "What the Woman Said," as his conclusion. The reordering suggests deliberate design. "Revolt in South Dakota," last to be published in *Today,* now comes first. Although the "surface" point of the piece is that there is no stir of revolution at all among these conservative farmers, the point beneath the surface of their lives is that they have a stubborn, even fierce pride in their state and a stubborn, even fierce faith that there will be a crop next year and a better one. In the most admirable sense these human beings are part of the land, part of nature—as Anderson felt all human beings, especially Americans, ought to be. In "Village Wassail," third to be published in *Today* and second in the book, much of the piece is devoted to an argument between two close friends watching the dancing, one liberal, the other conservative, over whether unemployment relief payments by the government, here being spent on pleasure, are corrupting the recipients into lazy people unwilling ever to work again. Though Anderson gives both contestants fair time, he obviously feels that the amount of money spent is small, that the dancing is a way of coping with the despair of joblessness, and less obviously that the springing up of such dancehalls about the country is an illustration of how people will on their own create institutions designed to give, even if only temporarily, a sense of community; in the case of the dancehalls the bringing together of two frequent opponents, town folk and country folk. From land love and community Anderson goes next to the necessity of close individual relationships in "Night in a Corn Town," first in the Midwest series to be published in *Today*. Closer to fiction than to journalism, form following function, the piece gives an instance of how art influences two estranged men, farm owner and tenant farmer, to establish a fair economic relation between themselves and to regain their former friendship.[17]

Each of these pieces is concerned with a way of dealing with the Depression primarily in human terms. The fourth and climactic one in the series, "Olsonville," was second to be published in *Today*, where it was titled, to Max Perkins's confusion, "Northwest Unafraid." (Anderson changed the title without explaining the old term for the Upper Midwest.) Here in Minnesota with a large percentage of Scandinavians in the population and its nontraditional Farmer-Labor Party, Anderson had found "a restless growing and determined belief that some kind of a good life is possible for more people through government [a readiness] to go off at almost any experimental tangent." Does this approach to the massive problems of the nation through pragmatic, experimental government puzzle Anderson? On the contrary, it exhilarates him and should exhilarate others, for it is the way to get to where "we" want to be in America, the way in which, he had come to believe, President Roosevelt and the New Deal were leading. Repositioning "The Return of the Princess" as the only piece in the final section, "What the Woman Said," thus gives it great emphasis and makes it a kind of coda to the book, juxtaposing the United States to Europe where "the creeping fear" has begun to pervade nations under dictatorships. Americans, the woman tells him, must keep the creeping fear away by preserving and strengthening democracy. "You in America, in spite of all the desperate position you may now be in, may be again what you were. You were once the hope of the world, the place to which the oppressed came. You may be it again."[18] Whatever its limitations, *Puzzled America* remains among the best contemporary accounts of ordinary people caught in the Great Depression, of their devastations and their hopes.

3.

The busy social life of the Andersons, and Eleanor's hard work on her New Orleans assignment, continued up to Thursday, April 4, when late that afternoon they set off in the Chevrolet on the two-day drive to her next assignment in West Palm Beach, Florida. From there he drove her to speaking engagements before local Y groups, first in Miami Beach and then north to St. Augustine, which Anderson thought the "most charming town yet," Jacksonville, Macon, and Greenville, South Carolina. Between St. Augustine and Jacksonville they took a side trip to Sea Island, Georgia, for a few hours visit on the fifteenth with Eugene O'Neill, whom he found ill but working on a series of eight interconnected plays and perhaps from whom he learned definitely how favorably the reviews of *Puzzled America* were running. In Macon, while Eleanor spoke on problems for women caused by present industrial conditions at Wesleyan College and, in the morning of the eighteenth, at YWCA hall, he visited with Sue Myrick and his other friends on the *Telegraph*, Sue reporting tartly that he was in high spirits "'glorying in the American failure' [and] mourned that success had ruined everything in America that it touched—even Dreiser and Eugene O'N[eill]." Late on the nineteenth they arrived in Marion, where he continued in high spirits because the reviews he now was able to read seemed pleasingly "extra fine."[19]

During the Y tour he may have worked a little on *Brother Earl*, but he had been primarily occupied with imagining and then starting to write another play, an adaptation of *Poor White*, and he now decided to get a room near Hedgerow early in May and complete it in that hospitable environment. First, probably on April 22, he had to drive Eleanor to Greensboro, North Carolina, for a week's assignment, taking with him a new Scribner's novel Perkins had sent him as a book he "would appreciate beyond almost anybody." The novel was Thomas Wolfe's *Of Time and the River*. He was so impressed by it that on or just after April 23, he wrote the novelist a note praising him for "such a gorgeous achievement" and adding a comment possibly explaining why he himself would "lay off" *Brother Earl*, not just for "a month or two," as he had told Perkins, but permanently. Wolfe's achievement makes me a little sad too. Here I've been struggling all these years, trying to write novels, and along you come and show me, very simply & directly that I'm no novelist. Some things I can write but you—you are a real novelist.

Wolfe's grateful reply, delayed because he had been traveling in Europe, must have pleased Anderson in turn.

I want to tell you how proud and happy your letter made me. You are one of the American writers whose work I have admired most and whose work has meant a lot to me. It seemed to me ever since I first began to read your books when I was a kid of twenty that you got down below the surface of our lives and got at some of the terror and mystery and ugliness and beauty in America better than anyone else.

With this exchange began a friendship that lasted for several years but ended unhappily.[20]

Anderson's main occupation while at Greensboro, however, was putting on paper first scenes of the play. "I have a hunch," he wrote Sergel with his characteristic enthusiasm over any new project, "that this playwriting thing is really my meat." He loved "the whole idea" of the theater, even its "stink." He would not abandon *Brother Earl* but keep it by him "perhaps for two or three years, as a big, difficult job to fall back on." After driving Eleanor back to Marion at the end of the week, he left on Monday the twenty-ninth for Hedgerow. He had barely got settled in a hotel room in nearby Media and seen the first May performance of a vastly improved production of *Winesburg* when he received the bad news that the sixty-three-year-old Burton Emmett had died in his sleep on May 6 while he and Mary were visiting a friend in Virginia. On May 8 Anderson attended the funeral service at the Church of the Transfiguration on Twenty-ninth Street in New York, and later wrote feelingly of the to him unsatisfactoriness of the Christian forms and the need for "a new funeral ceremony written for the modern man" in a changing world, a ceremony appropriate to this friend who had dignified the lives of all his friends by his "gift of belief in others." Throughout May he was back at Hedgerow but went occasionally to New York for a day or two to see Max Perkins or to give emotional support to the grieving Mary. Occasionally he did work on the play he had come to Hedgerow to write, and once, perhaps once only, he lost all sense of self in the ecstasy of composition, at his desk "for hours with no consciousness of time passing, completely lost, the words and sentences with a fine rhythmic flow, ideas coming like flights of birds. . . ." Most of the time, however, he would confess to Sergel, he did little at Hedgerow, "just hung around and absorbed theatre, under [the] rather corking conditions" he reveled in.[21]

There was one break in his hanging around, an important one, for out of it would eventually come his last completed and published novel. Back on February 9 or 10 while he and Eleanor were vacationing in Brownsville, he had received a phone call from Washington and subsequently a letter from Herbert E. Gaston in the office of Secretary of the Treasury Morgenthau asking whether, as the secretary had suggested, he would be willing to go to Franklin County, in western Virginia and report on a massive, highly organized illicit whisky operation, which had brought that county the notoriety of being labeled in 1930 by a presidential commission as "the wettest spot in the nation." Gaston had explained that a federal grand jury had just, on February 7, brought indictments for conspiracy to evade taxes on liquor against thirty-four persons, including county and state officials, a federal Prohibition agent, and even a grandnephew of Robert E. Lee, now the Commonwealth's attorney for Franklin County, who would be acquitted in the subsequent trial. Anderson had replied that he could not travel to Franklin at the time but would be glad to do so in the spring, emphasizing that he was not a newspaperman trained to get facts quickly but that "The human side of such a tale I can I believe often dig out." He probably had not known that a lengthy Associated Press story on the indictments printed at least in the *Washington Post* and the *Richmond Times-Dispatch* listed also the fifty-five persons named as "co-conspirators" but not indicted, and gave special attention to one Mrs. Willie Carter Sharpe, "the driver of liquor pilot cars whose diamond studded teeth caused a sensation in the courtroom." In a separate box about "Franklin's 'Outlaw' Heroine," the *Times-Dispatch* termed her "Almost a legendary figure among the hill people" of the county for her skill as frequently the driver ("pilot") of a "block car" preventing federal Prohibition officers from capturing the caravans of cars running the cases of liquor ahead of her.

> Her thrilling races over the tortuous mountain roads and down the main streets of Roanoke, Rocky Mount and other mountain towns are credited as deeds of a devil-may-care valor which her male companions seldom venture to duplicate.
>
> Local legend, aided and abetted, no doubt, by the imaginative credulity of her mountaineer neighbors, has made a sort of super-woman of her and neither the nature of her calling nor the fact that she has served a term in the Federal Women's prison at Alderson, W. Va., has detracted from her fame.

As Anderson later indicated, he would base the protagonist of *Kit Brandon* on Willie Sharpe.[22]

When on April 22 the trial of the indicted persons opened in Roanoke before a special session of the Federal Court for the Western District of Virginia, Anderson began making a scrapbook of almost daily reports of the court's proceedings in the *Roanoke Times* as background for his own investigation. Sometime in mid-May he was quite willing to drop his stalled play project for a fresh journalistic one. He drove the five hundred or so miles to Roanoke, observed the trial "for a few days," thought it made "an interesting, human story," and decided that he needed to return in June. It is possible that on this first visit he met and talked with Willie Sharpe, one of the stars of the trial who was in Roanoke for its duration; but if he did, it is odd that he did not stay for the three days (May 23, 24, and 25) when she was at some time on the stand as the 165th witness for the prosecution. On May 22 he was definitely in New York, and he was back at the Hedgerow the next day when Sharpe, the *one* diamond filling in a tooth having been extracted a few days earlier, began her testimony before a crowded courtroom. The gist of that testimony he could get from the *Roanoke Times* report and would add to from later conversations with Sharpe, whom he described in an article on the trial as "a rather handsome slender black-haired woman of thirty."[23]

She was born a mountain girl in rugged Floyd County, just west of Franklin. In 1918 at about age seventeen, she had left the hills to go to work first in a Roanoke cotton mill, then in a Lynchburg overall factory, finally in the Roanoke Kress five-and-ten-cent store, a job she left after three or four months to marry Floyd Carter, son of John Carter, then the "bootleg king of the city." Like her husband she became a bootlegger, and after their divorce in 1925 she hauled moonshine from dozens of Floyd County stills for her own business until the following year when, already a natural, superbly skilled, utterly fearless fast driver, she moved into the big Roanoke operation, first as hauler, then as pilot. Almost every night for the next five years she piloted runs out of Franklin County to the city, most often in her favorite roadster, which was specially built for high speed and equipped with steel fenders to prevent law officers from shooting out her tires. She buzzed like a bee, as another witness described piloting, around, before, and behind caravans of four or five to a dozen whiskey-laden cars traveling the dark, twisting roads bumper to bumper "like coupled railroad cars" at speeds over sixty miles an hour, sometimes roaring into the city at speed with officers firing at them. Piloting a total of nearly 200,000 gallons of moonshine out of Franklin county, "perhaps more than any man," a reporter commented breathlessly, she became the legendary "queen of the Roanoke rum runners." But federal officers caught up with her in May 1931. She was tried, sentenced to three years in federal prison, and on the day of her release was subpoenaed by the grand jury. Having testified, she was worried that she might be convicted, went to St. Louis and took a new job, but was brought back by marshalls to the Roanoke trial, where, Anderson later wrote in his article, she was a "romantic figure," liked and admired by all the spectators, obviously including himself.[24]

Actually Anderson had driven to New York from Roanoke via Washington, where he spent at least a day and a night and wrote his next-to-last article for *Today*, "Give Rex Tugwell a Chance." Through friends at the Department of Agriculture he interviewed Rexford G. Tugwell, economics professor, undersecretary of agriculture, and one of Roosevelt's chief "brain trusters," whom on May 1 the president had named as director of the just-created Rural Resettlement Administration. Typing out his article in his hotel room, Anderson declared that Tugwell was a man "I like and respect," a representative of those bright, young experts who would have been hired by a big American corporation in former years and now are working in the big federal government necessary to deal with the Depression. Tugwell had spoken before a large audience of conservationists—in Albany, not New York City as Anderson had it—urging his program of combatting soil erosion, replanting forests, controlling floods, resettling farmers off worn-out or dust-ruined land in an attempt more massive than the TVA Anderson so much admired "to fight back at the land destroyers," natural and human. "We have to begin to think more of America as a whole," Anderson put it enthusiastically.

There are all sorts of big new things to be found out concerning the land . . . and what is America but the land? Factories, towns and cities go but the land stays. If we are to live on the American land as a great people, we will have to preserve it, feed it, manage it.

Businessmen and politicians will speak against him, but Tugwell, the "intensely practical man," must be allowed to accomplish his mission. Raymond Moley could not have hoped for a more pro–New Deal piece. Since Anderson's friend Bill Stewart had left his position as managing editor of *Today* in early April (for unspecified but "good enough reasons"), Anderson may have driven from Washington to New York to deal with Moley directly.[25]

Six months earlier, Anderson had written his agent Frieda Fishbein that he would leave *Winesburg, Ohio* with her for half a year for placement. Since she had found no other producer during this period, and since he was rejecting the Theatre Guild's wish that "a Broadway technical man" work on the script, he withdrew the play from her, resolved to handle it himself. Perhaps because he enjoyed feeling liberated from both connections, he felt "hot" for his long-delayed new play. The first week in June he spent at 54 Washington Mews (Mary Emmett's address after Burt's death), giving a "new slant" to the play and providing emotional support to the grief-stricken Mary Emmett, whom he would urge not to "try to lead the old life [but to make] a clean sharp break . . . new faces, new impulses, new awakenings." Almost certainly it was such advice coming at such a time that would lead to Mary's years-long emotional dependency on him and Eleanor. Around the ninth he left New York for a brief stay at Hedgerow and subsequently went on to Washington. Here at the secretary's own request he had "a long interesting talk" with Morgenthau, who wanted him to write from the "human" side one or more articles on "the present bootlegging industry." Anderson decided to do one on the Roanoke trial. Returning to Marion on the fifteenth and then on to Ripshin, he had his writing cabin moved down from its hilltop to a more convenient position along Ripshin Creek near the house. There he completed the first half of his play, which he now called *They Shall Be Free,* with "the same theme as the novel *Poor White,* but different—new characters, etc." By June 25 he was in Roanoke absorbed in the last day of the liquor conspiracy trial, beginning to shape an article on it, and this time definitely meeting and talking with Willie Sharpe.[26]

In an account in an October 1939 lecture, "Man and His Imagination," Anderson stated that he was in Franklin County and at the Roanoke trial for "some weeks" and implied that he spent much of that time having "many long talks" with the "young woman rum-runner" who, later, became Kit Brandon. In actuality, both of his visits together could hardly have amounted to more than a week and a half, and it is fairly certain that his acquaintance with Willie Sharpe lasted no more than his week-long second visit. It cannot be known how much he learned of her life directly from her, how much from newspaper accounts of her testimony, how much from the work of his imagination; indeed, he makes the believable point in his lecture that through his imagination "She became . . . completely another person." Clearly, however, she told him much in their conversations as he "rode about with her in a car, dined with her"; for in the article he would write, he noted that after she had given her testimony, she "talked freely," emphasizing, for example, that as with Kit "It was the excitement [of piloting which] got me." Almost a fifth of the article would be given over to her, the only witness referred to by name, and her story forms much of the article's climax. Anderson had arrived in Roanoke on the forty-fourth day of the long trial, a day too late to hear the captain of the Roanoke police be quoted as saying of Mrs. Willie Carter Sharpe that "while [she] was a notorious violator of the law he knew nothing to impeach her truthfulness"; yet she must have passed on her truthfulness and her sense of excitement to Anderson. In her story he would at last find the art form for which, over many months, he had been searching.[27]

4.

Presumably Anderson stayed in Roanoke, at least until shortly after 4 PM on July 1, when the jury announced its verdict of twenty persons convicted of conspiracy, three acquitted. The unindicted Willie Sharpe was free to return to St. Louis and her new life. By July 3, he was back at Ripshin and at once at work on his article about the trial. The title of the published piece, "City Gangs Enslave Moonshine Mountaineers," is lurid but accurate as a description of his central point as to what the trial revealed. Moonshine, from the traditional little homemade stills of poor mountain men who ran the risk of a destroyed still and jail time, was picked up at only ten cents a gallon by haulers; for a dollar or so a run, these haulers faced the risk of prison sentences. This wide network of illicit liquor production and transportation was organized like a legitimate business into higher levels of management, involving some of the solid citizens of the county who did the bribing of county and state officials to look the other way and who, themselves, collected enormous profits.

It was evident that something new had sprung up in the mountains—big business, mass production, introduced by a few shrewd determined men, the plan being to make the little fellows work at a dangerous occupation—prisons staring at them—for little more than a day's wage.

At the trial some of the mountain men, the "cobwebs" as the owners of larger stills called them contemptuously, and even some of the "big shots" in the business testified for the prosecution as though they "wanted to go back to the old ways," the new big business way being "too cruel. It brought out too many ugly things in men." So in his article Anderson subsumed his old rejection of business, his ingrained sympathy for those at the social bottom, his recent trust in the New Deal when he praised the two government prosecutors, and his abiding admiration for the rebel when he made Willie Carter Sharpe the one named witness among many whose stories revealed to him, and the court, what had grown up in the Franklin County mountains. A part of that massive operation due to her skill, courage, and love of excitement, she is a redemptive figure because of these qualities and the frankness of her testimony. She is the heroine of this human drama—and typically Anderson tells a tale through a storyteller to prove it.

A Virginia businessman at the trial, full of admiration, whispered of her accomplishments: "I saw her go right through the main street of our town and there was a federal car after her. They were banging away, trying to shoot down her tires, and she was driving at seventy-five miles an hour.

"She got away," said the businessman. He liked her, as did every one in the courtroom.

In effect, he was already beginning to write *Kit Brandon,* the idea for which, he wrote Gaston, "has been dancing about in me ever since I went [to the trial] and met those people. . . ."[28]

Eleanor, who was conducting much of her husband's business correspondence, had tried to sell the unwritten article to the *American Magazine* even before he had gone to Roanoke the second time, but the magazine was not interested. On the day he began writing the article, she wired
queries to the editors of the *Saturday Evening Post* and *Liberty*. The *Post*
too was not interested, but Fulton Oursler at *Liberty* was. On the ninth
she sent the completed article to him, suggesting a payment of five hundred dollars, "about what Mr. Anderson has recently been getting," which
was actually "about" three hundred. Oursler offered four hundred, which
Sherwood accepted because of *Liberty*'s wide circulation. Apparently neither Anderson had any qualms about misrepresentation when dealing
with the mass media market, though Eleanor scrupulously sent Fishbein
$8.98 as Arthur Barton's share of the $27.91 sent to Anderson as his receipts from performances of *Winesburg* at Hedgerow. Fortunately for all
concerned, "City Gangs" was one of his best pieces of journalism; and
when he inquired of Gaston about the possibility of reimbursement for
one hundred dollars in travel expenses to Franklin County, he was obligingly appointed ex post facto a "Consulting Expert in the Office of the
[Treasury] Secretary" at twenty-five dollars a day for four days beginning
July 23. So he had the reimbursement, payment for the article, and the idea
for "a very absorbing novel," he wrote Gaston, joking that he shouldn't
take the reimbursement.[29]

He had "plunged" into the novel as soon as he had finished the article,
wrote "hard every day," and was "deep" in it by the end of July. Through
August as well he kept going "hog-wild" at what, he wrote Max Perkins,
had become "a romance of all things," and by midmonth he had a title:
Kit Brandon: A Romance. "It is something quite different from anything
I have ever done," he told Perkins. He was having fun and expected to finish it in September. Besides the steady writing, always reason enough to
make him happy, other things made it a banner summer. The house, the
farm, the season were gorgeous, the weather and crops fine. As usual, invited guests came for long or short stays to be talked, walked, driven, and
croquet played with in the afternoons and the long light of summer evenings.
In July, Paul Rosenfeld came for a three-week visit, which reestablished his
and Sherwood's old friendship, while early in August the Friends—Julius,
Elise, and their two children—arrived from New Orleans to stay in the
guest house until late September, Julius to "polish" the manuscript of a
philosophy book. With Paul and Julius, Anderson would have had especially good talk. Recognition by others came as well in these two and a half
months. He could have learned and been pleased that in the just-published
Creating the Modern American Novel, Harlan Hatcher began the chapter
on him with "Sherwood Anderson belongs with Theodore Dreiser and
Sinclair Lewis as the three most stimulating and influential authors in the

creation of the modern American novel, and most of the significant work of the twenties and thirties stems in one manner or another from their work." He certainly did receive Thomas Wolfe's admiring letter of July 8, however, and he listed as an achievement of the summer that Percival Wilde would be publishing his one-acter "Mother" in a collection of short plays. Knowing that play was selected for printing may have stirred him to find time, as he did this same summer, to add scenes to *They Shall Be Free* along with, as he later reported to Ferdinand Schevill, "two or three short stories, an article or two." The articles were of course "City Gangs" and probably at least a draft of "The Right to Die—II: Dinner in Thessaly," in praise of suicide were he faced with "old age, decrepitude, with incurable disease the final evil," his contribution to a four-part "Debate on Euthanasia" in *Forum and Century*. Although he did not identify the short stories, one was certainly "Playthings," a grim tale set in a small southern town about Pinhead Perry, a poor, "simple-minded" man long married to Hallie, a woman with a twisted foot, from a rough, disorderly family. During a dull summer some "smarty" townsmen looking for fun play a cruel trick on Pinhead, Hallie, and their simple-minded daughter, which leaves all three crying. When one of the men tells a drugstore audience about the outcome of the trick, "nobody laughed." For Anderson, with all this "Scribbling" it was a summer to remember.[30]

Having to leave Ripshin on September 3 to go back to her job, Eleanor had invited Mary Emmett to come down and "keep house" for Sherwood while he finished *Kit Brandon*, a task for Mary made easy since there was "a real good maid and Sherwood lives very simply." Mary did come to Ripshin for two weeks, and Sherwood finished a first draft of the novel. On September 8, while he and Mary were driving in to Marion, he "quite innocently" began to tell her about his dislike of having to interrupt artistic work to earn money from journalism pieces and of his desire to do a book on the Civil War, which would require research during the winter at the Library of Congress. Thereupon Mary offered to give him three thousand dollars a year, the book to be a memorial to Burt. Her husband, she pointed out, had made much money in advertising, and it was appropriate that some of it should come to "one hurt by advertising." Both Laura Lu, when he consulted her, and subsequently Eleanor opposed his taking the money; but in a long letter to Mary, written to clarify his thinking, Anderson showed that he really wanted the money because he dreaded the interruptions and would accept if Mary could feel that she was giving it to him as artist rather than to him as friend. With the question thus loaded, he turned it back to Mary to decide.[31]

Probably on the fourteenth the two drove to New York and then the thirty miles to Valley Cottage, the eighty-acre farm where Mary had invited the Andersons to stay with her until, in the late fall cold, the three would move to Washington Mews. At the Emmett summer home Eleanor had an easy half-hour commute by train to the city, and Sherwood could enjoy daily, rather than on brief visits, the Ripshin-like seclusion of the low, white, comfortably renovated farmhouse. Sitting at his desk before a window, he could look out on an apple orchard and across a little lake to hills beyond which flowed the Hudson. While finishing the draft of *Kit Brandon,* he had felt that it was "more outside me and impersonal" than his other work and that perhaps he had "created a rather nice, hard-boiled but yet very decent woman"; yet rereading the draft he found it "not very complete . . . rather ragged and sketchy," and began a slow, thorough revision, almost a rewriting. It would be hard, absorbing work; for he was attempting to remain "impersonal," trying, as he would later explain to Perkins revealingly, "a new approach."

I have, almost always, tried to work out of pure feeling, having the conviction that if I got the feeling straight and pure enough, the form I wanted would follow. I am trying to make this job more objective, keep the whole story definitely on two or three people, the whole centering upon one—in other words, being more objective, trying, you see, to use mind as well as feeling.[32]

There were, of course, various interruptions to the work of revision and to his seclusion. Almost certainly he went to New York on September 23 for a lunch with Perkins to tell him about the Civil War project and to suggest the publication of his collection *Plays;* and again almost certainly it was on the night of September 30 that he and Mary were in New York to attend the opening of a show at the Contemporary Arts studio of paintings and prints from Burton Emmett's collection of old masters and contemporary artists. (Quoting from Anderson's praise in his *Colophon* tribute of Burt's gift for friendship, an art critic also emphasized his generosity to both artists and other collectors.) At the beginning of October, Anderson spent three days at the Hedgerow, where he was warmly received by the actors and admired the acting. Then he took time off from revising to write a review praising Edgar Lee Master's biography of *Vachel Lindsay,* who was, Anderson asserts, "one of the three or four important American poets," a man living his life "in a kind of religious ecstasy," trying always "in his flaming days . . . to lay the foundation for an American culture." Suddenly lifted into fame and as suddenly dropped, Lindsay eventually committed suicide after a week of physical and emotional torment described in detail by Masters and quoted fully in the review. That Anderson felt a considerable degree of sympathetic identification with Lindsay when reading and writing about the biography is confirmed by his summarizing judgment that "To me it is a story of a writer, by a writer, for writers, but I may be wrong about that. It may be a story for all young Americans."

He would explicitly call the sometimes eloquent piece reflecting some of his own ideas and attitudes not a review but an article.[33]

On October 3, Scribner's wrote him that in its first six months since publication *Puzzled America* had sold only 1,411 copies with total royalties of $522.28. "Not bad for a book of essays," Anderson commented to Laura Lu cheerfully; but he had obtained a thousand-dollar advance on *Kit Brandon* to give him the past summer free for doing the first draft, and he had already been concerned about ways of getting further money. Late in September, he had arranged with Raymond Moley for a *Today* piece on the American Federation of Labor convention to run in Atlantic City from October 7 through 19. Probably on the thirteenth, Eleanor, Mary, and he went to what promised to be, and was, a much livelier convention than it had been formerly. It was more than lively, he discerned; it was a major event in labor history. He begins his article, "Boardwalk Fireworks," with a recollection of a previous convention he had attended, where the entrenched old guard of craft union leaders had seemed to him more interested in the stock market than in labor organizing, while his travels in mining and manufacturing towns were showing him the hard life of unorganized workers. Now since the stock market crash and the coming of Roosevelt and the New Deal there was "a new assertiveness, new consciousness of dignity in labor" manifesting itself among younger labor leaders, especially among those in favor of organizing a whole industry, such as automobiles or rubber, rather than by the various crafts in it. Anderson was in the hall, he notes, when on October 16 the five hundred delegates to the convention furiously debated all afternoon and much of the evening the minority resolution defended by the "roaring voiced" John L. Lewis, head of the United Mine Workers, that the great mass-production industries be organized only industry-wide. In the vote on the resolution the old-line craft unionists defeated the "rebels" nearly two to one and retained control of the AFL; but Anderson records that they "were uncomfortable," were "shaken up a bit . . . wondering what's coming." Obviously he could not have foreseen what was coming—the expulsion of the industrial unions from the AFL the following year and the CIO's massive organizing successes in the second half of the decade—but he had accurately sensed "the rather amazing new feeling in the air at this year's labor convention."[34]

He was so excited by the battle between the old and the emerging new that he wrote "Boardwalk Fireworks" while still in Atlantic City, had it typed for submission to Moley, and sent the manuscript to the helpful Laura Lu for filing. Doing what would turn out to be his last piece for *Today* sent him into a flurry of further writing. Late in September, Whit Burnett, editor of *Story*, had asked him to inaugurate a series of notes on American short-story writing planned for the magazine since "the American short story as we know it, has pretty well stemmed from Winesburg, Ohio." Apparently, Anderson now rapidly wrote a piece by hand and mailed it to Burnett, who had a typed copy sent to him, presumably to see that the typist had read his scrawl correctly. "Why Men Write" illustrates Anderson's ability to write well quickly. Reviewing yet again his career as advertising copywriter and businessman, both occupations seeming to him even then marked by forms of dishonesty, he describes how he gained "a kind of nice inner honesty" by putting imagined characters in his own situation. Writing, then, is "a kind of giving out, a going out"; if done not for money but "from a healthy point of view," it is "merely a tool a man can sometimes use to get at this business of living." The flurry of writing continued after he, Eleanor, and Mary returned to Valley Cottage on the eighteenth; for he had one day at *Kit* and on the next, suddenly inspired about *They Shall Be Free,* created a whole new scene to make six out of a projected seven. Then he was back at *Kit* again on the twenty-first, finishing his revision of the first section of the novel before he and Eleanor went to New York that evening; on the following day he prepared notes for two lectures he had been invited to give at Columbia. The first of these, on the twenty-third, was to a class of some fifty students and was, he thought, "pretty swell." He had attacked the notion that the writer should aim at money-making success, since the true writer's purpose was to bring the world of the imagination "over into life" without "selling out," betraying that world. The second, on the evening of the twenty-fourth, was on the same subject, but he felt that he did not "get [it] across . . . although I think they liked me." He was liked well enough that he was informally approached about the possibility of teaching one day a week at Columbia, but no formal offer would be made. On the twenty-fifth he returned to Valley Cottage and his steady three or four pages of revision a day. The writing flurry was over.[35]

During one of the three days he was in New York he went to the Weyhe Galleries, where he found the three volumes of *Letters of Vincent Van Gogh to His Brother,* which he had been trying to find for some time and which Erhard Weyhe, he emphasized to friends, sold him for $17.50 instead of the retail $22.50. "They are worth it," he wrote Dreiser, "They are really great literature." For days he read little but the *Letters* and began referring to Van Gogh often in his own letters. To John, whom he was deliberately trying to make more communicative in the manner of Vincent to Theo, he wrote:

> To me it seemed, reading the Van Gogh letters that the writing of them must also have been a tremendous help to that painter. I know that writing my own thoughts, about my own work, to men, often helps me tremendously to get at something I may be trying for. Would it not be so with you.

Again, when Laura Lu wrote of her Lutheran concepts of God and the church, he referred her to pages 267 to 315 in the first volume and aligned himself with Van Gogh in having his own similar form of religion:

> If I can look through the window here, really see the little lake out there, trees and the bare bones of the hills—not be too blind—if I can see and feel people—feel and see down into them some, a little with understanding—do I not approach God so?

"It seems to me," he told Charles Bockler, "that I began closer to Gauguin but have come around until I am closer to Van Gogh." The *Letters* had "become a kind of Bible" to him, as he went on to illustrate:

> What fools to think that man a fool. He was shrewd and real. He had this sense of going into nature and growing out of nature. He must have loved nature as a man would love a woman.

Certainly his absorption in this bible was intensified by the great one-man show of Van Gogh's drawings and paintings, most never seen in New York before, which opened at the Museum of Modern Art on November 5 and attracted so many viewers that a *New York Times* editorial described how, on the first Saturday afternoon of the exhibition, the Museum was "packed like a popular store on the Saturday before Christmas." To Anderson, who saw it as soon as possible, the exhibition was "simply gorgeous . . . something very stirring and beautiful." John must come to New York to see it.[36]

Even his absorption in the *Letters* did not keep him from his steady morning absorption in *Kit Brandon*. Around November 10 he finished the second "book" of the novel and sent it to Laura Lu, who was overseeing the typing of the manuscript; apparently about a week later he sent her an additional part that dealt with Kit's sexuality and so, he thought, might shock her a bit. He was, after all, "trying as you know to show the development of a modern." He was also trying technically, he wrote Jasper Deeter, not to "trust too absolutely to feeling" as formerly when he had "avoided structure" because too much concern with it had spread the rigid plot story "like a disease" through American fiction. He was attempting to be less "difficult," to be more like "Chekov and Turgenev, to name two masters, [who] managed to give free play to feeling but always, also, to let mind come in and more or less control." Dostoyevsky, he now felt, "perhaps went rather the road I have been inclined to take." His new "interesting technical challenge" was making him work more thoughtfully and slowly than usual.[37]

Abruptly, on the morning of November 23, he dropped the novel temporarily and wrote a short story titled "Mrs. Wife," which, he told Sergel, "was aching to get itself done" and might be "pretty good." A subtle, intricately told tale, it deserves extended discussion for its excellence. To tell "Mrs. Wife"—the redundant title emphasizes the wife's significance—he used one of his favorite narrative devices, one he was adapting for *Kit Brandon:* the double narrator. A first-person speaker, a writer, introduces and comments on personal experiences told him by a capable country doctor alert to "human relations" with whom he develops a close friendship, as together they visit his patients and fish trout streams. In a necessarily long introduction, the writer tells much about his friend. His wife is very beautiful when she smiles, but she has suffered much from the deaths of their two sons from the infantile paralysis that also left their daughter crippled for life. The doctor, a handsome, vigorous man, has readily rejected the advances of many woman patients, especially those of a rich one who offers him money and the chance to be a wealthy city physician. With another woman, however, things were not so easy, the doctor admits; and one day as the two men rest by a trout stream from an afternoon of fishing, he begins to tell of this experience, whereupon Anderson interrupts the tale with a digression into the writer's thoughts, which is essential to understanding "Mrs. Wife." The writer has come to admire the doctor for his ability to accept life's misfortunes with something the writer calls "inner laughter" and so has attained true maturity. Then the "digression" extends into the explanatory example of a farmer whose crops and livelihood have been destroyed by the uncontrolled forces of nature. Instead of lapsing into despair, the farmer laughs quietly inside himself at his misfortune and thereby achieves maturity.

Now the doctor resumes his tale. A city family comes to the area for a summer stay. The parents have only one child, a daughter likewise crippled by infantile paralysis, who is cared for by a nurse. When the doctor comes to the house, he meets the nurse, a statuesquely beautiful Polish woman of thirty and instantly is overwhelmed, as he senses she is, by a sexual desire powerful as a force of nature. For a week, despite his recognition of the suffering he and his wife have gone through with their children and of the close bond of their daily lives together, he is distraught with what he admits is "pure lust" for the Polish woman. Late one moonlit night he leaves his home after telling "a terrible lie" to his wife, who, he guesses, may perceive the truth, and not giving her the customary kiss even though her face is beautiful in the moonlight. He drives to the city family's house and takes the Polish woman out into the country, where they walk for hours in the moonlit roads. Although she is passionately ready for him and is also extraordinarily beautiful in the moonlight, he cannot forget either his wife's beauty or their life together. He does not touch the woman, and she unhappily understands that he will not. His refusal of her seems to him "the great moment" of his life, the moment when he begins to be mature. He drives her back, returns to his home, and loving his wife even more fully than he already has, gives her the kiss he withheld. Before the doctor finishes his tale, the two men get up from their rest and prepare for "the great moment" of trout fishing, "the quivering time, so short a time between the last of the day and the beginning of the night"—the brief time, in other words, before life ends. Then the doctor finishes his story. After he kisses his wife, she tells him of her fear that they might have lost each other, and she laughs. "'It was the nicest laugh I ever heard from her lips. It seemed to come from so far down inside." By enduring suffering without despair Mrs. Wife has already attained maturity.[38]

As in *Kit Brandon* Anderson used "mind" in writing "Mrs. Wife," but judging by many of his other stories, "feeling" was enough to create the web of motifs that give this apparently loose tale its controlled shape. The two major motifs are fishing and moonlight. The second paragraph of the story emphasizes stream-fishing as one of the grounds for the two men's friendship; the doctor tells of the Polish woman during an afternoon by a trout stream, and as he finishes his story, he is absorbed, in the tale's last sentence, in playing a trout he has hooked. Fishing is not, however, just a neat repetitive detail; it means something in the tale as a whole. Somewhat beyond the midpoint of the story, a fishing episode reveals something of life's misfortunes the doctor has had to contend with even before he begins to learn inner laughter. While he is explaining that he wanted the Polish woman "with a kind of terrible force," his mind "goes off at a tangent . . . into a side tale of a fishing trip taken alone, on a moonlight night, in a very wild mountain stream, on the night after he had buried his second son." Wading and casting in the swift water—rather like the solitary Anderson wading out under a full moon into the dark water off the Grand Isle beach to cast into a deep hole—he feels himself in a strange "perfectly primitive world." Hooking a big trout, he plays it, feeling at the other end of the thin line the trout's fight for life and at his end "the fight to save himself from despair." The writer thinks, "Was it the same thing between him and the Polish woman?" So this lust is something to fight against, to control, and his refusal of sex with the woman is not a simple, conventional decision to be faithful to his wife but the end of a successful struggle to maintain his and her lives together. As for the moonlight motif, which, significantly, first appears in the "side tale," it obviously links and enforces the special beauty of the wife and the opulent beauty of the Polish woman, but it also links both with the doctor's struggle in that "primitive" place of external and internal nature to dominate both trout and despair. Fishing/moonlight becomes a complex, condensed metaphor for the way true maturity is to be achieved and maintained and for its beauty and value.

"Mind" does appear in "Mrs. Wife," though perhaps not in the sense of the term Anderson used in his letter to Deeter, for the tale is a remarkably clear example of how he often dealt with ideas by first imagining them in fiction before organizing them in more logical, nonfictional discourse. After he had written the story in the morning of November 23, he took a long walk in the afternoon alone "in the late fall woods," thinking about the responsibility of the artist and explicitly about "inner laughter" and "maturity." Later that day he typed out some of his thoughts in "Notes . . . for Mary," and the next morning he wrote more of them in letters to John and to Miriam Phillips, one of his favorite actors at Hedgerow, who long afterwards said, "I loved Sherwood. He was the only man there who never tried to make me." All three letters deal in some way with the specific nexus of ideas imbedded in "Mrs. Wife." In the "Notes" he criticizes an acquaintance who writes nonfiction books out of research and scholarship, for in such writing "The mind is involved without the heart. The terrible responsibility of life escapes from under your hand." By contrast the artist, "trying to create the very feel of life," takes on that responsibility; for if he tells the truth, he will at first inevitably hurt others. Over time, however, truth also "heals." Telling the truth seems to the artist "the only road to maturity," that which "we all, knowingly or unknowingly, are seeking." In his letter to his son he asserts that not taking "the responsibility of entering life" in one's writing and as well "not taking responsibility in relationships, in life, [is] a kind of way to death." He prefers an old man in the neighborhood, a compulsive thief who steals flowers from the gardens of the rich and gives them to people without flowers. "He is such a grand old thing, crippled, old, unmoral, a kind of grand inner laughter in him." He himself has a little of such inner laughter in him. When *Winesburg* "was almost universally at first called dirty"—one recognizes the old grudge—it "hurt like hell but afterwards the laughter came." His fullest expression of his thoughts while walking was in his letter to Miriam Phillips, to whom he also speaks of his "very moving experience" of reading Van Gogh's *Letters,* which are "so terribly close to life."

If in any art you really attempt to take the responsibility of your art, you have to suffer. Why not. But isn't it also true that the taking of that very responsibility is the only road to life?

I was trying to think what happened to people, and why, during the walk. . . . I think it's like this. The hurt affects people in two ways . . . they become silent or resentful . . . this probably from the notion that they and they only have been so hurt . . . or they get what I like to call "inner laughter," and I wonder if that isn't just maturity.

Feeling that his letter was "inadequate," he added a long postscript with an exuberant ending.

The idea I did try to express is perhaps sound enough, that the protection we must always seek is that inner laughter . . . that is to say, I presume, to try to take it also as a part of the total picture, this damn fascinating thing . . . life.

Jesus, even at its worst, I wish sometimes I could have a thousand years of it . . .

That Anderson was so concerned at the moment with the responsibility of the artist in his art and in his personal life, with "inner laughter" and maturity, suggests the possibility of some autobiographical subtext in "Mrs. Wife," which perhaps not incidentally he wrote the day before Eleanor's return to him from a weeklong conference in Chicago. It is not necessary to suppose with one-to-one literalism that during her absence, he might have been suddenly attracted to the Italian woman servant in the household. This woman, at his request, he reported to Laura Lu, read the section of his novel on Kit's sexuality to see whether he had caught Kit's feeling accurately and told him that although she was a Catholic and a virgin, she might have acted as Kit did—though he could have drawn on this recent incident in creating the fictional foreign woman. Rather, a subtext seems likely to lie elsewhere in the tale. Leaving out the writer, who is hardly characterized at all except as a fisherman and an intelligent, sympathetic listener, there are indeed certain resemblances between the doctor and his wife and Sherwood and Eleanor. Besides being, like Anderson, a dedicated fisherman, the doctor is "a great reader" and rereader; he rejects a success defined by money; like the Anderson of 1935 he prefers writings about "human relations" to, as now fashionable, the "economic slant" of capitalists and proletarians, and he is a skilled storyteller. Like Eleanor, the wife is "rather small and dark," although Eleanor's beauty was always evident and not simply when she smiled, she is sensitive to her husband's ways and to their marriage; while the wife has suffered from the deaths of their sons and their daughter's affliction, Eleanor had come to very much want a child and was saddened by her inability, because of one partner or the other, to become pregnant. More essentially, "Mrs. Wife" is centrally concerned with the responsibility of the artist and of individuals in lived life. As artist, Anderson must tell the truth about human relationships; a husband or a wife may indeed obliterate thought of the other through passion for a third person, and the doctor's hurt to the Polish woman in the refusal, which constitutes *his* "great moment," is manifest. Anderson would not let his tale become just a romance of true love—as indeed it would become when Laura Lu revised it and made it acceptable to the mass-circulation "woman's magazine" *Redbook*. As powerfully as the doctor is motivated in his refusal simply by love for his wife, he is equally motivated by a responsible recognition of how their sufferings together had bonded them. In his own life, Anderson had of course not lost sons; but he had known suicidal despair late in 1929, and as he wrote Eleanor ten days before he wrote this story, he knew how she had then "put me back on my feet," knew how "terribly important" she was to him. He knew also that in truth neither he nor she had yet attained "inner laughter," the attainment of which he felt distinguished her mother; so he settled for something else. The subtext of this story that was "aching to get itself done" would be a celebration of his love for and debt to his own Mrs. Wife. Perhaps for this reason he would think the tale "one of [the] most beautiful short stories [he] ever wrote." The modern reader might well think it yet further proof that the short story was the art form in which Sherwood Anderson excelled.[39]

9

The Year of *Kit Brandon*

1.

The days were getting shorter, the nights colder, the skies more often clouded and gray. Anderson's usual winter sinus infection had slowed his work on *Kit Brandon,* and he looked forward to a vacation after Christmas in the warm, dry climate of the Southwest. It was time to leave Valley Cottage for the city. He and Mary moved to 54 Washington Mews in the afternoon of November 24, while Eleanor returned there that night from her Chicago conference. She had already resigned from her job, apparently with the understanding that she might return to it a few months each year, and so was free for the Southwest trip. Within a day or two after the move, happy to be in Burt's study with the paintings on its walls, he was back steadily at work revising the novel. Afternoons and evenings, however, were filled with engagements. On December 3, for example, he and Karl drove up to Middletown, Connecticut, where he talked at Wesleyan University twice without notes in two hours, first on country newspapers to a student group, then on writing to a large audience, both talks, he felt, "quite a success." On the eighth, John came to New York as his father had urged, and they were off to the Van Gogh exhibit and other delights of the city. The three Andersons spent an evening with Stieglitz and O'Keeffe, during which, to Anderson's irritation, O'Keeffe announced that she felt *Many Marriages,* more than his other works, represented the real Anderson. The following morning he wrote her to protest that she had misunderstood the book, for it "was written to bring flesh, the feel of flesh, as far as I could go with it, into prose." Besides, he insisted, it "was a book written in purity and in innocence, and I am neither pure nor innocent; so it is not me." Still the Andersons had had a good evening. More on his mind was his unfinished *Kit Brandon,* which he had decided to subtitle *A Portrait.* "It's what I want," he wrote Sergel, "—one life, outside my own, standing stark against its time." Around the ninth he took the typescript of about half of it to Max Perkins for him to read and comment on, and discussed the Civil War project with the always supportive editor. Anderson would be delighted later when Perkins found the manuscript, except for a couple of minor objections, "extremely moving and exciting." The final engagement was an afternoon and evening party on the twelfth at Dreiser's house in Mount Kisco to which all three Andersons were invited. Early in the month, Anderson had suddenly begun writing Dreiser about the need for writers to communicate with each other more frequently, and now he hoped to talk of this idea directly with him, but there were so many guests at the party that he had little opportunity to speak to his host. He would have to elaborate on the idea later in a letter.[1]

Since Eleanor had to stay at her job until just before Christmas, Sherwood and John decided to head south on the fourteenth, going by way of Hedgerow where they had a joyous visit with Jap Deeter and the actors. By the evening of the sixteenth they were at Rosemont, where the quiet, reclusive John, exhausted by the New York social scene, went to bed for the most part of three days. Meanwhile, his father had gone back to *Kit Brandon* and had one day driven out to Ripshin through a "glorious" snowstorm, the wind-driven snow thick as a heavy fog on the mountain road. At the farm, he found that in the preceding mild weather a terrific flood had poured down Ripshin Creek and swept away big stones supporting the bridge across to the stone house. As he and his hill man farmer John Sullivan walked the creek bank to inspect damage, they came upon the body of a calf that had been staked out in a grassy spot and had drowned in the flood. The two men looked at the dead calf for a moment, and then Sullivan thoughtfully commented: "Take God Almighty up one side and down the other he does about as much harm as he does good." It was a remark Anderson treasured as speech of the common American.[2]

At about this time he celebrated another form of "poetry out of a people." When he had talked with Perkins in New York, Max had given him a copy of a newly published Scribner's book of stories and sketches about trotting horses, their owners, and their drivers on the circuit, Evan Shipman's *Free-for-All*. Reading the book gave him such a "grand thrill" that he wrote Perkins an ecstatic letter of gratitude, urged such friends as Dreiser to read the book, and arranged to review it for the *New Republic*. Young Shipman's book has made his "older American writer's heart jump with joy," he declares. Ignoring both "the current fad of romanticizing the proletariat" and the wealthy world of the "running horses," beautiful as the thoroughbreds are in themselves, Shipman writes of one of "the sweeter sides of our American life," the world of harness racing still existing at state and county fairs in the farming states. That world has not changed since the days of such "master reinsmen" as Budd Doble, Walter Cox, and "the great master of them all, Pop Geers," and Shipman has caught it all.

Going all out with praise in his nostalgia and admiration, Anderson ranks the book "with the best of Hemingway or Faulkner and even with Chekov and with the finest of Turgenev, his glorious 'Annals of a Sportsman.'"[3]

Then for the rest of December it was back to *Kit Brandon,* the writing going well before Christmas, poorly afterwards. He was relieved when Perkins set fall, rather than earlier, for the publication of the novel and, as requested, sent the thousand-dollar advance, which would cover vacation expenses; but Christmas was for him the usual bad day. He detested "the fake generosity," he exploded in a letter to Karl, and the "talk of love [is] balls . . . I myself got drunk early in the day & stayed comfortably so—to avoid going about saying sarcastic insulting things to the innocent." His head ached almost steadily from the sinus infection, and the house during the holidays was crowded with Copenhavers, both afflictions making it hard for him to work. For days he was angry and unreasonable toward Eleanor, who, already concerned that her resignation might damage her career, saw herself caught between her husband and her family, felt lonely and confused, in her words "like a violin string drawn to the very breaking point." He would "spit out poison at her," then write her a contrite letter. The new year started badly with quarrels flaring between them, she deeply hurt afterwards, he ruefully deciding that "I seem able to be a son of a bitch and pop right out of it as gay as a lark." Both wanted their marriage to work, however; their much needed vacation was approaching, and the quarrels stopped. On January 14 he would write her in the "Mrs. Wife" mode to say she must not always be thinking of things to do for others. "You've got sometimes to realize that you are you and that your natural loveliness has its own value and that you are not a servant destined to spend your life running errands. / So I love you very much."[4]

The first three weeks of January before they were to leave for the Southwest via Chicago were an unsettled interim. Some mornings he managed to work on *Kit,* more mornings not, often putting his whole desk time into letter writing. As though in antidote to his quarrels with Eleanor, he made January 1 and 2 a New Year's celebration of communicating ideas to other men. To Stieglitz, for example, he wrote familiar encouragement: "You are old enough and wise enough to get the inner laughter that I call maturity and that is the only thing that can save any of us." To Karl he described a "formula" he was working on: "For a long time now I have thought that the man artist in America needs his fellow man artist much more . . . than he needs any kind of woman we seem to produce." His main effort, however, was the long letter he had been brooding over to Dreiser elaborating on that "formula," that problem. What could be done about the loneliness of writers and artists scattered over a vast America with no cultural center like Paris for France or London for England to bring them together? Insisting, as he had repeatedly done before, on his odd fixed sexist position that "the imaginative world is naturally the male province" and that a woman really wants instead the "personal beauty, one might almost say showered down upon her, that can only come out of the imaginative life," he proposed that men "working in the imaginative field" in this politically confused time must build new man-to-man relationships through—his solution to the problem seems rather anticlimactic—writing letters to each other. He was considering, he wrote Dreiser, expanding his thinking into a pamphlet perhaps titled "American Man to American Man." He held his letter for a few days, adding "Notes," but never did mail it, very likely because on the third or fourth he would have received Dreiser's response to a previous letter of his own attacking science and technology, Dreiser defending them and concluding that he would prefer discussing philosophic ideas directly with him to writing of them in lengthy exchanges. Anderson's response to that response was that writers served best not as philosophers but as storytellers trying to give "the simple story of lives." He continued to believe that all American writers and artists felt lonely, indeed that Americans were the loneliest people in the world. As they always had been, letters would continue to be for him a means of trying to break through the walls of human separation.[5]

To help fill in the interim before vacation, he drove Eleanor to a several days Y assignment in North Carolina before she left on the tenth for New York, relieved that she had worked out an arrangement with her office to allow her a total of some seven months a year free. He sent off "Mrs. Wife" and "Playthings" and an article, "Give a Child Room to Grow" to Charlotte Barbour, a New York literary agent specializing in women's and popular magazines, noting that "Mrs. Wife" might just possibly go in a popular magazine. He read Hemingway's recently published *Green Hills of Africa* and detested it. The book showed, he wrote Ralph Church and Eleanor, that the man could not work in the imaginative world, turned to what he thought the real world of hunting and killing, and "romanticized" even that "all out of focus." Then Anderson had to prepare for two speeches he was to make, in Richmond and Baltimore, and a third later in Chicago. The interim was about to end.[6]

Rejoicing that he was a "born wanderer," he drove with son Bob in Bob's car on the sixteenth to Richmond, where that evening he told the assembled members of the Virginia Press Association that country newspapers were much improved now that able young editors, obviously such as Bob, had begun taking them over. After spending a day talking with press friends and a night drinking too much with them, he took the train to Baltimore on the eighteenth, still recovering from his spree but ready for his lecture on "The Theatre and the Writer," given prior to an amateur production of his one-acter "Mother." Eleanor and Mary had driven down from New York in Mary's big new Packard touring car, in which the three would travel west, and Eleanor would note that "S in grand mood for speech—audience responsive." "S" would note only, "Rotten play," a comment on play rather than production. On the nineteenth with Mary at the wheel—she usually preferred speed to caution—they slowly negotiated ice-covered roads with wrecked cars along them, arriving in Marion late in the evening. Then on January 21, after a day of packing the three "citizens of the vast unknown," as Sherwood put it expansively, set off westward.[7]

The trip to Chicago in midwinter was hair-raising. The first day it was over dangerously iced mountain highways, and on the second they ran into a record snow storm, the temperature falling to 20 below zero, a hurricane-like wind so blocking the roads with drifts that at Lebanon, Indiana, Eleanor and Mary had to put Sherwood on a Chicago-bound train and stay the night at a crowded hotel. Safe and happy at the Sergels' home, he gave a newspaper interview on the twenty-third, cheerfully praising contemporary writers, especially midwestern ones, many of these being as good as Mark Twain, but declaring that "Our playwrights aren't turning out anything that's good enough to produce." That night he spoke to the Friends of American Authors about his findings in *Puzzled America* in a lecture, which he felt went "very very badly." Eleanor, who with Mary had managed to get to Chicago in time to rush to his lecture, judged only that he had been too serious for his audience. For the remaining days of their visit, Sherwood saw old friends while Eleanor did YWCA work; the most memorable event for her was a dinner party at the Sergels' made successful by an "amazing 5 hours talk on civil war" between Sherwood and Lloyd Lewis, newspaper columnist and Civil War expert, "with Ferdinand chiming in and also Roger." On the twenty-eighth, the three travelers headed the Packard southwest over highways still so treacherous with ice and snow that often they drove at ten miles an hour, through, as Anderson listed them Whitmanesquely to Karl, Illinois, Missouri, a bit of Kansas, Oklahoma, across the Texas Panhandle, then northwest into New Mexico, and through "the most inspiring" (Sherwood), "the most beautiful" (Eleanor) country they had ever seen to Santa Fe, where they made a two-night rather than the usual overnight stop. "Such strange towns, strange places," Anderson summarized to his brother. "I really think sometimes I shall travel always. Even the worst of hotel life is so good compared with family life . . . so impersonal, nice, free." On February 1, their one full day, they drove up through "gorgeous country" past the Rio Grande Canyon to Taos, "still full of [D. H.] Lawrence," saw the museum, the old Spanish church, the Pueblo, which Eleanor found "still strange and moving," and at lunch ran across an old friend of Sherwood's from the Cass Street rooming house where he began the *Winesburg* tales. Back in Santa Fe they had dinner at the luxurious home of the wealthy poet Witter Bynner, where, Eleanor noted, Sherwood "made a big hit" with the host and other guests, and Bynner gave her a lovely necklace of Indian jade. On February 2, the travelers headed south through New Mexico to Las Cruces, and the next day with Mary at the wheel they raced due west across "the warm and inviting desert" at such speed that, to Sherwood's disgust with her driving, a tire exploded. They were delayed in getting it repaired, but by late afternoon they had reached the outskirts of Tucson and the end of their long journey. Late that evening Anderson "in a state of exhilaration" walked out of their tourist cabin into "a clear moonlit night—the white sand like snow—the rare clear air—great cloud forms, mountains seen in the distance. I understand why the indians danced. I wanted to dance."[8]

An immediate conflict marred this desert Eden. During the enforced closeness of their traveling, Sherwood had become increasingly angered, Eleanor merely irritated by Mary's hyperenergy, her dogmatic judgments and bossiness, her exultation in small triumphs over them. The exploded tire was the culmination for him. After they had moved permanently the following day into the St. Paul Hotel, across from the elegant facade of the Cathedral of San Augustín and close to the Mexican quarter, he blew up furiously at Mary. Eleanor effected an uneasy peace; but although Mary left a week later for Palm Springs, the plan having been that she would on return drive back East with them, Sherwood promptly purchased a little secondhand white Ford truck not only so that he and Eleanor could "scoot" about in the desert by themselves but so that Mary would see that they intended to return without her. Hurt and confused, she drove off on the eleventh, leaving them as placation a number of hotel-room conveniences, a commitment to give Sherwood two thousand dollars to buy Civil War books, and a check to reimburse him for the truck. Eleanor sadly noted that "We will miss her as a troublesome child," and all three realized that they must work out a new relationship during the years ahead.[9]

With some other exceptions, however, the nearly six-weeks stay in Tucson was a joyous and productive one. By the morning of the fifth Anderson was back in the swing with *Kit Brandon*, and by the end of the stay he had almost completed his revision of the novel. Days when he did not feel like writing, he read books purchased or borrowed from the city library relating to the Civil War, Eleanor frequently helping by typing up his scrawled notes. When he talked of the War, she was impressed that "S's enthusiasm is marvelous—like a young boy's—goes on for hours over one episode. Marvelous!" He had already decided to devote one volume to each year of the great conflict, deal as much as possible with individual human reactions to be searched out in diaries, letters, firsthand accounts, and to emphasize that the War was to Americans as the Trojan War had been to the ancient Greeks, a historical turning point; for American society it was the speed-up out of the old individualistic agrarian era into the new standardized industrial one. Other writing matters were of lesser importance. Either he or Laura Lu, or both, had earlier reworked a portrait of his father in *A Story Teller's Story,* which was printed in the decidedly popular *Reader's Digest* for February under the title "The Magnificent Idler," his first appearance of four in that magazine. On the tenth he and Eleanor learned that the literary agent Charlotte Barbour had sold his article "Give a Child Room to Grow" to *Parents' Magazine* for twenty-five dollars. Sherwood did not enter the information in his diary; but Eleanor did in hers, noting later that both she and her mother were angry at the agent for not trying *Woman's Home Companion,* which would have paid much better. Presumably both Andersons were annoyed when Barbour wrote that she could not sell "Mrs. Wife," which Eleanor noted, "S thought one of [the] most beautiful stories [he] ever wrote." Sherwood was happier to learn from his Viking Press statement that sales of his pre-Liveright books were better than expected and that *Winesburg, Ohio* was continuing to sell about five thousand copies a year, though his royalties continued to be small. At the beginning of March, the Andersons bought a copy of the March 2 issue of *Time* to see in its colored supplement, "Mural Painting in the U.S.," the portrait of Sherwood in one of the paired frescoes "Tragedy and Comedy" that the midwestern John Stewart Curry had painted on the walls of the Westport, Connecticut, junior high school. In the crowded stage scene of "Tragedy" Anderson is depicted in a place of honor at the front of the lefthand box overlooking the stage with Eugene O'Neill and Dreiser behind him. The faces of O'Neill and Dreiser are partly turned as they observe a spotlighted pair of acrobats, the woman falling as her outstretched hands fail to grasp the hands of the man. Anderson looks full front while below, among the actors, Little Eva lies on her deathbed and Hamlet gazes at Yorick's skull. Anderson's left hand rests upon the edge of the box, and his chin rests on that hand. His face is somber; his eyes look directly into the eyes of the viewer.[10]

Afternoons and evenings and some whole days when the writing would not go, the Andersons explored Tucson and its area, Sherwood much relieved that the dry climate had quickly relieved his sinus problem. Clustered on its desert plain, encircled by sharp-edged mountains, Tucson was "very bright and alive"; and delighted by the colorfulness of street attire, Sherwood bought clothes to match—"a ten gallon hat, mauve pants, snake belt." He and Eleanor often took long walks in the Mexican section to enjoy the adobe houses, the crowds of dark, often beautiful children, the boys flying kites, the leisurely pace of life. Very early he got in touch with two professors he had met during his 1932 lecture tour—Melvin Solve of the English Department at the University of Arizona, who gave large cocktail parties to which the Andersons were invited; and Padraic (Paddy) Walsh, "a little black Irishman" in the Mathematics Department, whom he had much liked in 1932. Walsh and his wife, Mims, Anderson

would write Laura Lu, were "very well read and intelligent but not literary, and when we want someone to play about with we play with them."
The Andersons had already done the usual tourist attractions, winding
Sabino Canyon to the northeast and the Mission San Xavier del Bac, "The
White Dove of the Desert," to the south. Now they could drive with the
Walshes to Nogales, just over the border in Mexico, to walk about and eat
spicy Mexican food. On that expedition by a new route over a high park-
like plateau, which both Andersons thought incredibly beautiful, Sherwood was moved to talk of his early books and stories, Eleanor would
note, "of what S, Dreiser and western group did—why they had to insist
on sex in order to get away from New England—flesh needed—rich middle
west versus frozen rocky New England." Although not literary, those
"grand people" the Walshes were eager to talk about and listen to anything. In Tucson there was always something to see or do—parties, boxing matches, polo games, a big parade, and rodeo days. Anderson found
the bronco riding brutal but was excited by the calf and steer roping with
its speed and the "technical beauty" of both cowboy and cow pony. The
best part of the rodeo, though, was its setting—"the grandstand, the colorful crowd, the Indians, Mexicans and then the grey sand of the desert
going away in front and always, in the distance, the fantastic mountains."
Most of all the Andersons enjoyed taking the little truck out together into
the desert to see the saguaro forests, the delicate desert flowers just beginning to bloom, the intense blue of the sky and the cloud masses, the great
ring of distant mountains clear in the dry air, the flaming sunsets. They
understood why Indians and pioneers came to love this part of America.
Huge, lonely, "gorgeous beyond belief," the desert became for them "a
kind of companion." [11]

With *Kit* finished, Anderson thought, it was time to leave for a visit to
New Orleans, where Eleanor had to begin a long stint for the YWCA. Starting early on March 15, they took the southern route to El Paso, Alpine,
Del Rio, and San Antonio, driving through deserts, then mountains, then
rough country, then rich, flat farmland. From San Antonio they went on
to the town of Columbus, where Laura Lu's ancestors, the Scherers, had
settled and she was born. After pausing for Eleanor to hunt out family
gravestones and Sherwood to decide quite on his own which house was
Laura Lu's birthplace, they drove on to Houston, Beaumont, and with
Sherwood relieved that he was completing "nine hundred miles of just
Texas," to Orange at the Louisiana line. On the twentieth, they reached
New Orleans and at once were "fairly drowned in social demands" by
such favorites as the Feiblemans, the Antonys, and the Friends, Eleanor
amazed as before at how much and how long the group had "adored" her
husband. She was amazed also to learn that the Group Theatre's production of *Winesburg* had shocked its audience "terrifically" even though one

word about sexuality had been circumspectly changed from "Did you ever have a piece?" to "Did you ever have a woman?" She made a running start at her YWCA duties by addressing the business "girls" of the Y at their annual national banquet, exhorting them to realize that the underlying causes of war were economic rather than idealistic and to work for political candidates committed to the peace movement. She also had to deal in her firm diplomatic way with a characteristic race relations "mess," as Sherwood put it, resulting from young white southern Christian women's desire "to be nice to the young intelligent negro working woman" and their real terror lest such a woman might want to be treated as a social equal. Meanwhile Sherwood was sinking into "a ghastly period of blues," as always happened to him, he explained to Sergel, after he completed a lengthy work—partly because he had grown close to his imagined characters and now they had left him, partly because as always the work had not attained "the real splendor I want." He decided that the last two chapters of *Kit* needed revisions after all, and he struggled with them during the hot, sticky New Orleans mornings. Up to March 30 when he and Eleanor left the city in the little white truck, however, he had not yet found "the tone . . . or rhythm . . . don't know what to call it . . . the music" for them.[12]

Dogged by depression, frustrated by his unsatisfactory attempts at revision, gloomy at the thought that Eleanor must leave him for more Y assignments, he became half ill with disappointment and anger when they reached Birmingham and learned that Roger Sergel, whom he had urged to ride with him for companionship, was sick and could not do so. In the morning of April 2 Eleanor took the train for Chattanooga, and he drove on alone to Macon, Georgia, for his fourth and last visit to Sue Myrick and Aaron Bernd. This time it was an unhappy one. He stayed at Aaron's pleasant house out in the country, but the weather turned cold and then rainy, and he was in no mood to be pleasant to others. As Literary Editor of the *Telegraph,* Bernd had invited him to attend a Writers Club breakfast at which the guest speaker was Margaret Mitchell, who had just finished reading proofs for *Gone With the Wind;* but Anderson had already replied "I've had my breakfast" and now refused to come. Sue thought Mitchell a hilariously witty speaker, but when Anderson met her later in the day, he inevitably found her a "vain . . . wise-cracking authoress." At a big drunken party for her in the evening, she amused the other guests with, Sue noticed, the "gay chatter" of her monologue while Anderson "retired to a corner and kept silence throughout . . . the evening." At a dinner the next evening, he would note in his diary, he was still "a bit irritated so tried to irritate others by saying things against the South"; and he would frankly note even more self-destructive behavior in a conversation on his last evening in Macon when he "made an ass of myself by my arrogance. Talked of things about which it is best with most people to keep your mouth shut." It took him two days to drive back to Marion through weather as miserable as his thoughts, arriving there on April 9 just before Eleanor returned from her successful tour of southern cities. Three weeks later he would contritely write Aaron and Sue that his visit had been "a failure, due to my own fault. I gave nothing. I came. I took from you and went away. One is that way at times."[13]

2.

Eleanor's brief presence at Rosemont cheered him, but on April 12 she had to return to New York. The next day he stirred himself to drive out to Ripshin to make summer plans with John Sullivan, and later he mailed off to the *New Yorker* a short story, "Nice Girl," which he probably had written while trying to revise the final chapters of *Kit*. Like Joel Hanaford, the young man Kit meets at the end of the novel, the brother of Agnes, the "nice girl" of the ironically titled tale, has been gassed in the war and drinks heavily, like Joel getting his liquor during Prohibition years at a filling station. Agnes, however, is the exact opposite of the frank, open, adventurous Kit. Secretive, manipulative, scheming, totally self-centered, she reveals herself as nice only in her nasty-nice choice of language, as when she remembers seeing her brother playfully slap the handsome housemaid "on the place where a person sits down." She tips off the sheriff to raid and close down the filling station, and she is jealous of her plain, intelligent younger sister, who is close to the brother and who has married a handsome man. Eavesdropping on her parents' conversation, Agnes is pleased to hear that her sister's husband wants a divorce but is displeased that she herself has not been told the news. She is certain, however, that her sister, whom she considers "a fool," will accept divorce without even asking for alimony. As the story ends, Agnes, knowing the husband's attraction to herself, is happily planning revenge on her whole family by luring the husband into a marriage to her, which she is confident she can control. Although a reader wonders as to the ultimate cause for Agnes's malignant behavior, Anderson liked his story about a "bitch" and so would the *New Yorker*. The magazine paid him three hundred dollars for it—he would later claim that this was "$100 more than their usual fee"—it was published in the July 25 issue, and it brought him the invitation to contribute a profile of Jap Deeter.[14]

The spring in Marion had been cold and bleak, but on the fifteenth came fine spring weather, and he put in the first of two mornings again revising the last chapter of *Kit Brandon*. Then, though he hated to leave "the grand time of the year" at Ripshin with its "planning, planting, earth smells," he set off by car for the Hedgerow on the sixteenth, arriving the following afternoon and after a long talk with Jap and some actors "feeling," as he recorded in his diary, "that this is the one place in America

I feel at home." The Hedgerow people seemed to him completely uninterested in money success, completely dedicated to their artistic work. Before leaving Marion he had arranged to have the first half of *Kit* fair copied and sent to Perkins, and on the twenty-second he mailed in the finished typescript of the other half. Now supported by the Hedgerow spirit, he threw himself almost daily into completing his second long play, *Man Has Hands,* which he had dropped in order to write the novel. On the last day of April, he had the much-revised final scene finished and went briefly through the "usual" reaction "—the thing done seems so trivial. So much to be said and so little said and so badly"; but the next day, under the Hedgerow spell, he began planning a comedy of family life about a goodhearted poor-white southerner grown rich and his varied involvements with the southern adulation for its "best families," and shortly he started a long (unfinished) tale about a ballplayer and two women, one a prostitute. The disparity of subjects suggests his indecision as to what he should turn to next; his recovery from the blues, however, was completed by visits from Eleanor and a highly encouraging letter from Perkins praising *Kit Brandon* as

extremely interesting, exciting, and significant. It tells ever so much about America. It has plenty of the proletarian angle in it, and much more rightly than the proletarians give it. It makes you realize what a strange country America now is.[15]

During May and early June, Anderson shuttled back and forth among Hedgerow, "54," and Valley Cottage, sometimes with Eleanor, sometimes alone. He worked on various projects such as "The Good Life," another uncompleted attempt like "I Build My House" at a memoir, and the profile of Jap Deeter, which he began late in May and sent off to the *New Yorker* on June 11. In "The Good Life at Hedgerow" he first sketches Jap's early experiences, his move to New York, his joining the Provincetown Players to satisfy his love for the theater, his success as an actor, and his rejection of such success—this a special reason for Anderson's praise of him—in order to establish Hedgerow as an experimental repertory theater, the best school for training young actors. Much of the article, however, concentrates on the hardships of the student actors in this "cooperative venture," their dedication individually and as group to learning to act, and Jap's ability as "a born teacher" patiently and persistently building acting skills in young people and convincing them that devotion to the arts of the theater constitutes "the good life." The *New Yorker* would reluctantly turn this admiring profile down as not having "their tone," a tone, Anderson would surmise to Deeter, of debunking, "rather [making] fun of in a nice subtle way ... people of distinction." The editor of *Esquire,* Arnold Gingrich, learned of the article and accepted it for $150, though Eleanor, in agreeing for Sherwood to that sum, politely protested that it was "less than half of what he is accustomed to get for articles this long." It was published in *Esquire*'s October issue.[16]

Throughout much of May, however, Anderson was most preoccupied with adding new scenes to *Man Has Hands* and reworking others until he had put together a kind of dramatic adaptation of *Poor White,* which shows his strength and weaknesses as a playwright. Like the Lincolnesque Hugh McVey, the play's Tom Lincoln invents machines to lighten the drudgery of farm work, and he and his devices are exploited by the slick promoter, Steve Halliday and the unscrupulous banker Jim West. The three scenes making up the first of the play's two acts are arranged in a condensed but coherent order of development. In scene 1, while the members of a farm family are setting out cabbage plants in a field at night, crawling like "crippled beasts" across the land, Ike the father and Fred his son quarrel bitterly over Fred's desire to leave the farm and work in the factory where Lincoln's machines are to be manufactured. To stop the quarrel Ike's wife tells the children of how her father had killed her brother in a similar quarrel; and when Lincoln appears, imitating the "grotesque half dance" of the plant setters' motions in order to replicate them in a machine, she perceives the tall figure as her father's ghost and runs with the children from the field. Despite some unnecessarily long speeches, the scene has its power in compressing the agrarian-industrialism opposition and, at the end, suggesting symbolically through the mother's perception the harm that Lincoln will unintentionally cause through the exploitation of his inventions. Scene 2 has the power of vituperative language. Rather like Colonel Sherburn facing down the Bricksville lynch mob in *Huckleberry Finn,* the rough Sylvester Hagen, journeyman harness maker in the town of Median, contemptuously taunts a crowd of townspeople as "rubes," "rabbits," "worms," "cowards"—first, for putting their savings into the hands of Halliday and West to build the plant-setting machine factory, and then, when Lincoln's machine fails to work, for letting the pair cheat them by buying the factory at a low price for the production of Lincoln's workable corn planter. When a preacher, who one night had knelt and prayed before a big machine in the factory, begs Sylvester not to taunt the townspeople, Sylvester, who has declared that he will happily accept machine-made harnesses, tells the preacher he was right to pray to the machine: "The machine's the new God. Your old God's dead. Jim West and Steve Halliday are the disciples of the new God." The crowd becomes angry, and Fred, who has lost his job at the bankrupt factory, calls for the crowd to lynch not just Sylvester but also Halliday, West, and Lincoln. The "town epileptic" Willy Hurt protests against violence and falls with a seizure. Sylvester picks him up in his arms, demands that the crowd give way, and strides through the now-silent mass with the final gibe that Willy is "worth the whole kaboodle of you." In scene 3 Tom Lincoln is alone in his room, the stage dark except for a floodlight on his work table and a spotlight on the back wall. He soliloquizes on his unhappy childhood and a self-blocked attempt to kill his brutal father, influences that have kept him separate from people and living "in a world of things, of steel and iron and wood." Recently, however, he has been deeply troubled by the effect his inventions and their exploitation have had on the factory workers whom he has heard complaining of long hours, low pay, and the loss of jobs through labor-saving machines. Using a stage device reminiscent of O'Neill's *The Emperor Jones*—in which Jap Deeter had achieved great success as Smithers—Anderson has a "chorus" of figures moving about in the darkness or the spotlight, voicing Lincoln's troubled thoughts and asserting his inability and that of other thinkers and leaders to "work with life," to understand that "man has hands," wants satisfying work but is deprived of it by "machines, machines." Although Lincoln now understands that he should not keep separate from people, he defensively retreats into his habitual refuge in "wood, steel, iron." The figures continue to chant "Man has hands"; and as the scene and act 1 end with the stage in darkness, there come "a shuffling sound, as of men marching" and the chorused cry, "There is a way. / There is a way." [17]

Considering this echo from *Marching Men,* one might assume that the play's second act would now develop directly toward some affirmation of social change through a working-class movement; but what is presumably the first scene of this act, though originally labeled "Scene Four," is instead a revised but not improved version of Anderson's earlier one-acter *They Married Later.* Without any preparation for the event, Tom Lincoln is presented as having just married Banker West's daughter Kate, who after the ceremony has fled to her bedroom in disgust at the drunken ribaldry of the men guests and in concern that she knows the shy Tom so little. After her mother has tried unsuccessfully to persuade Kate to accept her situation, Tom enters the bedroom, but like Hugh McVey in *Poor White,* he soon escapes through a window rather than consummate the marriage and so "make a whore of her." Thereupon Kate decides that Tom is not like the other men and she can love him. (Just after he abandoned the play, Anderson would write Sergel, on May 26, that this scene constituted in itself "a very beautiful one-act play"; in the typescript "Scene Four" is crossed out and the title "Marriage, A One Act Play" is printed in his hand.) For *Man Has Hands* Anderson apparently wanted to counterpoint the marriage scene with two quite different ones adapted from yet another section of *Poor White.* In the first, which takes place in the evening of the day after the wedding, a crowd gathers outside the harness shop, eager to view where the owner, Pilly Smead, crazed by Sylvester's insistence that machine-made harness be displayed for sale, has cut the journeyman's throat with a harness maker's knife, an act vividly described to the crowd by Willy Hurt, who has witnessed it. In the second scene, set later that night, Lincoln lies in bed in the West home, wounded by Smead, who has already killed Halliday. When Smead is captured, the crowd turns into a lynch mob intent on hanging him in West's front yard as a bizarre way of honoring this accomplice of Halliday—and so demonstrating that the townspeople still hold their mistaken faith in the two men who have cheated them. Not realizing the mob's purpose, West is terrified and helpless, but Kate braves the mob, disperses it, and preserves Smead alive to stand trial.

Setting this scene in the West home obviously presented Anderson the unsolved problem of how to incorporate it into the whole play; indeed, in scene 5 Tom Lincoln lies wounded in a bedroom of his own house. While a nurse tries to quiet him, he prophesies that "Until we men find each other we will keep making whores of our women." Kate and the gruff misogynistic Dr. Gray enter, and to them he declares that he had wanted his work to "give life" but that something needs to be resolved. Thereupon the shadowy figures of scene 3 reappear, crawling in the plant-setting dance, and Lincoln exhorts them to stand up, to recognize that machines can be beautiful as birds, factories can be the new churches. He commands them to use their hands, for "Life can be beautiful! / Life, not death, is the adventure!"—this last phrase now one of Anderson's favorites. In the first version of this final scene the figures stand briefly, then sink back into their crawling dance as the doctor laughs at the failure of men "to worship life and not death." If the first ending is histrionic and vague, a revision attempting to unite two themes Anderson was struggling with is sentimental and vague, a makeshift conclusion in the mode, even to the language, of a popular romance. With man and wife alone on the stage, Tom asserts a link between his refusal to crawl before her after the wedding and so make her a whore, and men's need not to crawl before "life." Kate understands that women need real manhood in their men; Tom understands that the two of them must work together for, in the trite phrase, "something bigger than us." Neither ending resolves the issues of *Man Has Hands* satisfactorily.

Desiring both assistance and praise, Anderson had the play read by Deeter, who judged it "a little too personal . . . too far out and away from any public." Sherwood sent a typescript to Roger Sergel, who advised him to cut down on the long speeches and to clarify his theme. He read the play to the Hedgerow actors, who liked its "music, the poetry" but didn't grasp its meaning. His own final decision came when he read the play aloud to Paul Rosenfeld during Paul's May 24 visit to Valley Cottage. Both thought the first act "splendid," but he himself felt that the play then went to pieces because of, he wrote Sergel, a "great fault."

Which is in the theme, the handling of it. I have been trying to tell, in the play, the story of the creative inventive man, working in the factory, that is to say machinery, and realizing how his creativeness, intended to be a help for others, has ended in what seems to be hurt.

My difficulty is that I have been trying to find the answer. That got me muddled, because, as yet, no one, least of all yours truly, knows the answer.

Now I am going to attack in a new way, simply making the play tell, in action, the story, making it a simple tragedy.

But he was still muddled. Was it to be the tragedy of "the unusual man," as he wrote in his diary for the twenty-fourth, or as he wrote the next day to Laura Lu that of "the modern man"? Sensibly he decided "to put it away and do some thinking."[18]

He had to do some thinking also about his and Eleanor's relations with Mary Emmett. Already in mid-May he had suggested to Mary that he not accept money from her after all, and seeing her, often daily, at "54" and Valley Cottage was making him increasingly critical of her. While he and Eleanor were out walking with her on her farm the last Sunday in May, they came on a pair of lovers lying in the grass of a field. When Mary angrily ordered them off her land, Sherwood empathetically identified with the young man, some young factory worker with his young woman looking for a place to make love, and became so furious at Mary that he wanted to drive away and never come back. It was, he realized, a small incident; but after a "day of thinking " on June 3 he wrote Eleanor that he would not accept money from Mary, indeed that he could no longer work or live at either "54" or Valley Cottage since she seemed maddeningly attached to the Emmett possessions at both residences. Nevertheless he stayed on a few days longer, and on June 8 he and Mary set off from Valley Cottage for Marion by car, stopping briefly at Hedgerow where he learned details of Arthur Barton's suicide. On the fourteenth he was much relieved when Eleanor arrived from New York—"Find I only half live when she is not about," he noted in his diary—and the three settled in at Ripshin for the summer. Or so it seemed; but within a few days Sherwood's irritation with Mary returned, and though he had earlier urged her to come to the farm and she had worked "like a horse" getting the flower gardens and croquet lawn in shape, he ruthlessly, despite her and Eleanor's hurt feelings, insisted that she leave and saw that she did. So his and Mary's unstable relationship would continue, predictable only in that periods of pleasant friendship, during which he could write her warm, perceptive letters, would be broken abruptly, as now, by his intense dislike of having her physically present too long in his and Eleanor's daily lives.[19]

Even before Mary's departure he was at work on writing projects. He began a one-act play, *Tobacco Market,* a dramatization of "Blue Smoke" from *Puzzled America,* and was almost immediately deep into his autobiographical "The Good Life," which he now tentatively titled *Rudolph's*

Book of Days. It interested him much more than the Civil War book, he wrote Perkins enthusiastically on June 18. He would be remembering his life "as an American writer [with] a peculiar experience," including varied occupations as a young man, a coming into writing during the pre-war "Robin's Egg Renaissance" with personal acquaintance of Chicago and New York writers and artists, and a broad knowledge of the United States from his "persistent wandering." Not developed chronologically, the book would be an unusually rich "impression of a world of publishers, artists, actors, painters, musicians, sculptors, etc." All this was, he repeated confidently, "very rich material and I am loaded with it." Very likely his enthusiasm over the autobiographical possibilities of *Rudolph* overflowed into the messages of praise for Maxim Gorky he telegraphed that same day to *Soviet Russia Today* and the Soviet Tass Agency in New York on learning of the Russian novelist's death. "With what excitement," he messaged Tass, "I, as a young factory hand in America, read his tales of defeated people. I lived among them and knew them." Gorky, "this great master," wrote of them with the unsentimental "tender understanding" for which Anderson even then, he asserted, "hungered."[20]

He did not finish off *Tobacco Market* to his satisfaction, but in one piece or another he worked for a number of weeks that summer on what eventually became the posthumously published *Sherwood Anderson's Memoirs*. Other matters crowded in. On the twenty-third he drove Eleanor to her week-long YWCA conference for factory women at Camp Merrie-Wood at Sapphire, North Carolina, and returned on the twenty-fifth to find that the first batch of proofs for *Kit Brandon* had arrived. He was delighted to get a "grand" letter from Deeter ecstatically describing the audience's rapt response to the "entirely beautiful interpretation" of *Winesburg* on the thirteenth in a new, simplified setting, which speeded up the play. That letter, more proofs of *Kit,* a single day's good writing, and even the purchase of a new Chevrolet did not much dispel his intense loneliness without Eleanor; and it was a relief when he could bring her back to the farm late in the evening of July 1. The next day, however, a "pest of people," Andersons, Copenhavers, and other assorted guests began flooding Ripshin for the Fourth of July weekend, starting with Mimi, Russell, and their two small children. "Awful day," Eleanor noted in her diary for July 5, adding acerbically, "S can't take his grandchildren and son-in-law— left before breakfast," holing up in his writing cabin to read more proofs of *Kit*. She herself had learned from her sister Mazie the devastating news that their mother had been diagnosed with arteriosclerosis; yet she appears to have handled the pest of people with clear-eyed competence.[21]

The interruptions continued. On a furnace-hot July 9, Sherwood and Eleanor drove the 490 miles to Hedgerow to see on the next evening a performance of *Winesburg* with its new, almost bare, stage settings, which made possible only brief pauses for set shifting between scenes, and a new, effective amplifier for the interscene sounds. These innovations gave the play "a flow, a music, a rhythm" that, he ecstatically exclaimed, was "very, very beautiful," and he remained in a state of rapture during the long, hot journey home the third day. Immediately the next morning he began an introduction to *Plays: Winesburg and Others,* which Perkins had agreed to set for publication in the spring of 1937, and he left it to Eleanor to drive to Marion to pick up Paul Rosenfeld at the train, the next in the usual summer series of visitors, for a three-week stay. Paul was no trouble mornings since he worked for hours on a novel, which, Anderson observed, he wrote like a critic with his head not with his emotions, unlike himself for whom "each book is a kind of love affair." Afternoons or evenings they often went for walks and talks or played Sherwood's favorite game, croquet. Apparently not considering his own fierce desire to win every game, he began to note frequently Paul's tense need to win; but there developed a far more important rift between them in their many discussions of Communism and Fascism, a rift that made Anderson "believe in [Rosenfeld] less." As he outlined the problem in two separate letters, neither of which he sent, he had come to believe that except for the Nazis' treatment of Jews, Rosenfeld, himself a Jew, might favor Fascism because it put down strikes, "suppressed the troublesome workers and gave [him] security in [his] own way of living," as Anderson put it in his long, second August 14 letter. Paul frequently insisted that workers were "a sullen and ugly folk" who "hated us," and as though from an ivory tower, he looked down on them as incapable of sensitive feelings. By contrast, Anderson declared that he was not a revolutionary but was convinced that no one "can interpret American life and remain so aloof." Then in an emotional outburst he concentrated the experiential basis for his own "keeping at the task of telling the story of the common man."

> You must remember that I saw my own mother sicken and die from overwork. I have myself been through the mill. I have worked month after month in factories, for long hours daily, have know the hopelessness of trying to escape. I have seen my own mother stand all day over a washtub, washing the dirty linen of pretentious middle-class women not fit to tie her shoelaces, this just to get her sons enough food to keep them alive, and I presume I shall never in my life see a working woman without identifying her with my mother.
>
> At any rate, I know that there are among workers men and women as sensitive and as easily hurt as you and me.

On this second letter Anderson would write, "Not sent. Too smug." The two men remained friends, but friends with an ideological strain between them.[22]

Before and during Rosenfeld's visit Anderson kept busy with his own work. As proofs for *Kit Brandon* continued to arrive, he not only checked for typos and the unnecessary repetition of details he had asked Perkins to catch, but he also made revisions in the text. One significant change was urged by Max. In the version Anderson had sent him, Kit's hill country father forces incest on his fourteen-year-old daughter, an act that causes her to flee the one-room cabin in the East Tennessee mountains and so to enter on her later career. Sherwood accepted Max's sensible argument that Kit's undergoing this "horror" might well make her "repugnant" to readers this early in the book, and he invented a scene in which the father only begins to bathe Kit as, after a day's work together in an upland cornfield, they stand naked in a mountain stream. Frightened, she runs from him and that night steals away from her father's house for good. Pleased with this revision and impressed with the book as a whole, Perkins wrote encouragingly that, "It might almost be called a portrait of America, or a portion of a big section of it, a kind of adumbration of the American nature different from any I have read." Anderson agreed that "it is not just a story of Prohibition but, really, a story of America. I am myself convinced that it [is], by far, my best long story. It is more objective than any other novel I have done." By July 21 he had finished reading and revising the galleys himself, for two more days Eleanor, who was "crazy" about the novel, went over the last of them with him, and on the twenty-fifth he sent the proofs off to Max. He was dedicating the book to Mary Pratt Emmett for, he wrote her, "our friendship and the many, many kindnesses you have done."[23]

Meanwhile, he was working almost daily as well on *Rudolph's Book of Days,* the title of which he had changed by the end of June to *Cousin Rudolph,* still using the name as, he hoped, an objectifying device for his autobiographical material. In mid-July he began a "new start . . . new conception," developing two new characters, Fred Wescott and Kate, into what soon became a never-finished novel titled *How Green the Grass;* and on July 25 he exuberantly told Laura Lu that "I am writing . . . with a kind of gaiety I never knew before. Except when I wrote *A Story Teller's Story.*" *Rudolph* continued to "march" until August 2 when Ripshin became flooded with guests for nearly simultaneous two-week visits. Paul left that day, but Marc and Lucile Antony, Roger and Ruth Sergel, and Y. K. and Julie Smith had just arrived—along with the first batch of the revised galleys. Anderson seems to have found time that guest-filled day to begin reading the galleys, and two days later, he noted, there was "in the house an outbreak of proof reading—on Kit." Besides himself at least two others read the proofs: Marc, who liked *Kit* partly because he could follow the story better than in most of Sherwood's novels; and Roger, who wrote a piece so praising the book and author that it would be published in the November issue of the *Book Buyer,* Scribner's promotional magazine. On August 7, five days after the revised galleys arrived, Anderson mailed the last of them to Perkins. Then he was free to "play" with his guests and to return joyfully to *Cousin Rudolph*.[24]

For a few days he reveled in that joy; but on August 13, the day the Sergels left, he noted ominously in his diary, "It was the end of a writing period," and the next day's entry begins, "In a writing slump." The Antonys and Smiths left on the fifteenth, Ferdinand Schevill arrived on the sixteenth for a week's visit, and on the seventeenth, after having put down some 25,000 words of *Cousin Rudolph*, he dropped the project abruptly, not to return to it for months. Instead, mornings he worked on the introduction to *Plays*; afternoons he walked and talked with Ferdinand; evenings he found this "treasure of a man" a stimulating match at croquet. Even before Schevill left, however, Anderson was in trouble with the introduction, for it had become too disorganized and rambling, too personal when he wanted it to be "outside self and objective." The more he struggled with it, the longer his slump persisted, and by late August writing slump predictably turned into physical illness with stomach pains and fierce headaches. For Eleanor, still "dead tired" from all the visitors and concerns about her mother's health, the night of September 3 was "the most horrible night of my life." When Sherwood's temperature rose sharply and he became delirious, she called in the Troutdale doctor, who on the possibility of appendicitis took him to the Memorial Hospital at Abingdon some thirty miles southwest of Marion. Learning that his illness was intestinal flu, Anderson began to feel better, and in his fourth day in the hospital he defied the protest of the doctors, discharged himself, and went to Marion, where for the most of two weeks he remained ill in bed. The illness climaxed in his second break that summer with Mary Emmett. After he had insisted that she leave Ripshin in mid-June, he had written her a long letter strongly critical of her dislike of Jews—a Jewish woman had been one of the lovers she had harshly commanded to leave her Valley Cottage property—but his later letters had been as usual affectionate, and both Andersons had urged her to return to Ripshin. He did write her a partial explanation of his fluctuating attitude toward her.

> I presume I am selfish, Mary. I love to have you with us and it is only when you get so tense and restless that something happens. . . . I guess there is something very finely balanced about any artist at work. While he is at work he goes often completely out of himself. At such times he goes very clearly into others, lives in them, so that if you are restless and driving, driving, driving the restlessness comes out of you and goes into him.

Mary returned to Ripshin just before his hospitalization; in fact, it was she who drove to Troutdale through night and rain to fetch the doctor. When on September 14 Eleanor had to return to New York and her job, however,

Sherwood noted in his diary: "Mary in charge. She is hard to take." In his illness the "assertive, dogmatic," even tyrannical side of her personality got progressively on his nerves until, as he had often done before, he escaped physically from the problem, this time taking the train to Knoxville on the twenty-first after inventing the story that he might be away for some time and hoping that she would leave. Overnight he made some decisions and returned to Marion the next day: he would directly "shake her off"; he never would accept the three thousand dollars a year he and she had discussed; in New York he and Eleanor should try living in a hotel "—not too close to 54." Mary departed that day, and at once he began feeling better.[25]

3.

On September 28 he left Marion for the Hedgerow, spent two days there talking and seeing plays, and on October 1 drove to New York and registered with Eleanor at the Royalton, 44 West Forty-fourth Street, the hotel she had found in the middle of the theater district. For sixty dollars a month they had a big, luxurious room and bath on the eighth floor, hence above street noise. It was the best hotel room they had ever had, they happily decided, good for his writing and within walking distance to Eleanor's work. Immediately his afternoons became crowded—lunches and dinners with Karl or with friends like Paul Rosenfeld and, from his Chicago past, Ben Hecht, cocktail parties, talks with Max Perkins and other publishing house or magazine editors or with Harold Freedman, his knowledgeable new play and movie agent, who was trying to find a producer to bring *Winesburg, Ohio* to Broadway. Other activities were varied enough. On the morning after he moved into the Royalton, he and Amelia Earhart spoke on WABC's radio program, *Magazine of the Air*. In the evening of October 9 he was one of the prizefight crowd who saw Joe Louis knock out the Argentine champion Jorge Brescia in the third round; on the fifteenth he lunched with Ben Huebsch and presumably talked about the possibility of Ben's waiving publisher's rights to *Winesburg, Ohio* (the stories) for the publication of *Winesburg, Ohio* (the play) in the projected *Plays: Winesburg and Others* and the possibility—there was none—of Anderson's purchasing the rights to his books under the Huebsch imprint for a long hoped-for omnibus volume of his short stories and a uniform edition of his works. In the evening of the twenty-first he, Eleanor, and Paul had dinner and then saw John Gielgud star as a "strange new homosexual Hamlet" in Shakespeare's play. Fairly often they went places with Mary Emmett, who to their pleased surprise had become relaxed and agreeable after the tense encounters during his illness.[26]

Mornings, however, continued to be almost always saved for writing. Soon after settling in at the Royalton he went back to *How Green the*

Grass, but he noted in his diary that it was "little use trying to work on the long thing here." Although later that month he would finish another chapter of the novel, he spent many October mornings doing short pieces. Of the published ones, three were done in a day or two. In "The Story-Teller's Job" (*Scribner's Book Buyer,* December 1936) he asserts that the storyteller should not be a thinker or reformer but should deal "with life, in his own time, life as he feels it, smells it, tastes it . . . wanting only the story, to tell it truly, with some grace. . . ." "Belief in Man" (*New Masses,* December 15, 1936) celebrates the twenty-fifth anniversary of the *Masses*—*New Masses* by describing the exciting time in the arts in the American 1910s when the old *Masses* was founded and flourished and "belief in life" was "in the very air you breathed." It was, Anderson nostalgically recalls, a time of "laughing boldness," which dismissed as "bunk" the accepted notion that success meant "getting a lot of money—no matter how you got it." World War I grimly ended that lively period; yet—here his one, oblique reference to the *New Masses* itself—"belief of man in man" must always "be at the bottom of what you are trying to do." For *The Writer* he produced "Why I Write" (December 1936 issue), a two-day piece he liked. As he recounts it, "Last year"—read "Last summer"—he wrote much on a book about his experiences as a writer, but "chucked" it as being too much about himself. Similarly, when he originally began writing because dissatisfied with being a businessman, "self" got in the way until he "began to invent imaginary figures, tried putting them into positions in life I have been in. I was close to them, yet separated." Now he writes in "an attempt to give life form and meaning" and to gain what everyone wants, "understanding." For him this means understanding people, in whom he has long been "interested, absorbed." The brief essay is vintage Anderson, only apparently rambling and casual, using self-deprecating humor as a kind of "laughing boldness" to provide a serious rationale for his art.[27]

His most substantial short piece was "Brown Boomer," which took him three days, October 13–15, to complete to his aesthetic satisfaction. In one sense a journalistic report on the Louis-Brescia fight he had watched at the Hippodrome theater near the Royalton, Anderson gave it some of the quality of fiction. For example, he may have gone to the match with a man named Fred; yet Fred may well be/might as well be, an invention, for he functions throughout as a foil, even an alter ego, to the "I" narrator, obviously Anderson, though in part an invented Anderson. Fred knows boxing as "I" at times does not; though in fact Anderson had attended many boxing matches and had been following Joe Louis's career for months. Fred's part is surprisingly like Buck Fever's; for he twits "I" as being a tightwad wanting cheap seats, as writing "sad short stories" and "bad" ones at that, as favoring Brescia because the program states that he is "versed . . . in literature." His deprecating—Anderson's self-deprecating—

humor implies that this is not really a skilled literary man's account, though under the mask it is indeed. In a straight journalistic account the attention given early to a mix-up in seats would seem excessive, literalistic, but Anderson's emphasis on it is meaningful. Fred and "I" have bought two seats in the top row of the top gallery, farthest of all from the ring, just in front of a "fence," that which protects, separates, shuts out; behind which the black workmen standees are packed. A "kind-hearted usher" has already given their seats to two one-legged war veterans, one white, one black, both drunk. It is a tense situation watched by other whites and blacks nearby. The soldiers stand up, so unsteady that "a big Negro man" reaches across the fence to keep the white one from falling, another black man to steady the black, who saves the situation by saying they will leave, being too drunk to see the fight anyway. As the soldiers "painfully" go out on their crutches, a liquor bottle drops from the white soldier's pocket, and a black man returns it to him. Then Anderson writes (reports?), "'Come on buddy,' said the white to his Negro companion . . . 'Let's get out of here and be on our way.'" By such details and language Anderson the storyteller turns a minor occurrence into a parable.[28]

The seats in the top gallery provide another kind of socio-moral geography. A dentist sitting beside "I" reveals his middle-class anxiety about money and social standing by saying that he could afford a ringside seat; a middle-aged woman with worker's hands has climbed up to the top gallery despite a heart condition because, as "we all felt," she wants Louis "to have another chance at that Schmeling." Below them are more expensive seats occupied by black couples and some white ones. Far down at the ringside sit those Fred calls the "millionaires," while behind them are seats "probably" occupied by small businessmen. During the fight the ringside people rejoice when the white Brescia lands a right on Louis, whose skin Anderson describes as a "quite shiny silky lemon yellow," the kind of blow that had given the German Max Schmeling his victory over Louis back on June 19. The true American patriots are the whites and blacks in the top gallery, those who are "we" and "us" in backing Louis. "I" just happens to have in his pocket a clipping from a Nazi magazine, which asserts, in convenient translation, that Schmeling's victory was a "'Cultural Achievement' for the white race." "We" in the top gallery are angered by "that way of putting it" and are united by their admiration for the twenty-two-year-old Louis, not because he has already made much money from matches but because "he was a man doing brilliantly, superbly, the thing he could do, was born to do." He was "one of ours"—like the great artist, Anderson might have said, but "I" does not.

The brief description of the first two rounds emphasizes Louis's crowding attack on the tall Brescia, "very swift-seeming and cat-like . . . all grace," Louis as an artist of the ring, as it were. In the third round comes Brescia's sudden Schmeling-like right, which sends the ringside people dancing and shouting and sickens the gallery into nervous silence; but Louis recovers, breaks free, and lands a right and a left, which "I" does not see but reads about later in the papers. Brescia goes down like a dynamited rock. Inexplicably for Anderson the boxing fan, the "I" character does not see the referee counting, but he does see Louis, "so strangely gentle and boyish-seeming," courteously help the referee carry Brescia to his corner while the top gallery, black and white, explodes with joy. Anderson the journalist has skillfully enough described the prize fight; through "I" Anderson the storyteller has put the fight into a context that "says" something without its being said: it is ability rather than race that should count, that on occasion blacks and whites can unite, that—here the parable—it is possible and admirable for human beings, white and black, like white and white, black and black, to be close friends, "buddies." Considering racism in the United States in the 1930s, Anderson had come quite a distance from using the Negro as mere symbol in *Dark Laughter.*

4.

While he was writing "Brown Boomer," Anderson was eager and anxious to know how *Kit Brandon,* a much more ambitious attempt to unite fiction and journalism, was being received by reviewers and the book-buying public. Scribner's published the novel on October 9; Anderson had received and liked his six "handsome" bound copies before coming to New York, and he was delighted when Perkins mailed him two favorable reviews before they came out on the eleventh. That Sunday morning, he and Eleanor read the reviews in print and thought both of them so "sympathetic and even glowing" that they celebrated with a big breakfast at the Algonquin Hotel across the street from the Royalton. Stanley Young praised the novel in the *New York Times Book Review* for its "uncompromising interpretations of American life" yet its "affirmative attitudes" and praised the author as an "honest poet" combining "romantic sensibility" and realism; Alfred Kazin praised *Kit* in the *Herald Tribune* for its "new application" of Anderson's distinctive qualities and its method, "seemingly no method at all, a matter of shuffling time, memory and place [revealing] an artisanship that is so subtle that it appears imperceptible." Already, on the ninth, Lewis Gannett in his *Herald Tribune* column had judged the novel to be Anderson's "best-rounded story in a decade, and perhaps his sharpest criticism"; on the other hand, Anderson's old friend Harry Hansen, writing in the *New York World-Telegram,* saluted his earlier achievement as "enough for one lifetime" but dismissed *Kit* as inferior. (Anderson's explanation for Hansen's judgment was that the reviewer had indirectly learned of Anderson's comment that his *Midwest Portraits* was inaccurate and dull.) As reviews came in—three-fourths of them in October, more than sixty in all—Anderson could have been heartened, if he read each of them, that well over half were in general favorable. Some, like Young's, were emphatically so, more seemed favorable despite reservations, but the only other review he would refer to in his diary was that by James Rorty in the labor union publication the *Advance*. In this "Amazingly fine review" Rorty, who had been with Anderson, Frank, and the others in their attempt to protest directly to President Hoover in 1932, did object to the ending of the novel as a "sentimental" solution by an individual to a problem solvable only by a group, but he commended the novel for not having "a single phony line" in it and Anderson as being "an honest man, and by and large, one of the few really good writers we've got—still good, and still growing at sixty or thereabouts. A lot of us younger writers have talked a good deal about 'proletarian literature.' Anderson has written it." The unfavorable reviewers were equally enthusiastic in condemning book and author. The story was melodramatic; the author's excoriation of American business was merely, as one reviewer put it, "pet peeves"; the fictional method was confused and confusing; the style was the usual Anderson style, clumsy, repetitious, choppy, naive. Mark Van Doren even put his criticism into the form of a parody of the style, a parody now seeming as inept as he felt the novel to be. "Still Groping," the title of Van Doren's piece, sums up the opinions of the very considerable minority.[29]

Since later critics, more often than not, have slighted or misread *Kit Brandon,* it deserves detailed consideration. In approaching the novel it is essential to recognize that, as Anderson wrote Perkins, "the purpose of the book, as you know, is to give not only a picture of the girl's life but a sort of picture using her as a spring-board of American life." To effect that dual purpose, he adapted from some of his tales the technique of telling his story through two narrators. In his new attempt to be "objective," he has Kit, the first "I," recount her life's adventures in her own words to a "subjective" narrator, the second "I," who questions her, gives his impressions of her and her story, increasingly puts into his own words what she has told him as the novel proceeds, and, often in little essays, presents a "picture" of American civilization as a whole as revealed through her life. For basic elements in that first "I's" life, Anderson drew on what talks he had had with Willie Carter Sharpe and on his scrapbook of *Roanoke Times* reports of the bootlegging trial; for his second "I" he drew openly on his own experience and ideas. On the first page of the novel, the fictitious Kit comes to him to tell her story in winter (for Anderson read early December) as he drives (with Eleanor, like Kit a strong, independent woman) through drought-ravaged South Dakota to write an article (read "Revolt in South Dakota") for a magazine (read *Today*). Later this "I" will state that he has lived among mountain people, from whom Kit comes, for ten years

(1925–35), and "I's" analysis of American civilization is, to reemphasize, that which Anderson had been making in such books and essays as *Puzzled America*. Unlike the "I" in "Brown Boomer," however, the second narrator (hereafter referred to as "the narrator") is Anderson in his own self as journalist and, as he writes in a commentary, one of "us novelists." In this latter capacity he is also a character in his own fiction, responding as he himself imagines he would respond to his invented Kit. A novel with a dual purpose and double narrators, one himself doubled, complexly and for the most part successfully combines fiction and fact, story and commentary, biography and autobiography. Despite such complexity of form any attentive person can read the novel with ease.[30]

As the tall, slender, darkly handsome Kit skillfully drives the narrator's car, he notes that she often tells her story "in fragments," natural enough in the situation and a warning to readers to expect leaps back and forth in time; indeed, in the opening chapter and largely elsewhere in the novel Anderson fluidly manipulates, just as skillfully as Kit drives, a variety of time sequences, and he smoothly interjects relevant, knowledgeable commentary. In this first chapter he describes the mountain people from whom she comes, their impoverished, isolated lives, yet their intense love of their rugged land and their fierce independence, which makes them almost a nation within a nation. Kit sketches her childhood in a slovenly cabin in the East Tennessee mountains with a lazy mother and a father who can "bend men to his will." Moving easily back into the present, Anderson-narrator has Kit, now a well-groomed, self-possessed woman of thirty, speak of her acquired sense of life as a game, of her willingness to use men to her purpose, with sex if necessary, a willingness, he thinks, and thus casually initiating a theme to be developed, which might have made her one of "a certain kind of Americans . . . our successful ones, another Rockefeller, a Harriman, a Gould." Returning to her childhood, Kit tells how she had to do the house chores, tend the garden, milk the cow, drag her to be serviced by a neighbor's bull. Each winter she gets a few months in a one-room school, and very early she must stand lookout against the sheriff when her father makes a run of moonshine in his still. At thirteen, she acquires a lasting love of fine clothes from touching the flashy ones of a bootlegger who tries unsuccessfully to seduce her. Speaking to the narrator, she refers briefly to her later job in a cotton mill, her work in a factory, her months as a clerk in a five-and-dime store, where she meets the man she eventually marries, the son of a famous bootlegger, and her increasingly notorious career as the daring "pilot" of rumrunning car caravans—the same sequence of experiences lived through by Willie Sharpe. In jail once, Kit introduces indirectly another of Anderson's themes when she tells of being visited by the beautiful daughter of wealthy parents, who, bored by their dullness and hypocrisy, pleads with Kit unsuccessfully to be taken into the gang for the excitement and danger—this being one of several examples in the book of the rebellion in the 1920s, as Anderson saw it, of the younger generation against the money- and success-oriented older one. Anderson then has Kit drop back to her childhood, and in preparation he describes, like a good journalist, first the ravage of Appalachia by lumber and coal companies and then, for the chapter's climactic scene, the process by which Kit's father makes a new patch of ground for corn by "ringing" (girdling) some trees and, when the trees die, planting seed among the dead roots. In language as lyric as that of *Winesburg,* the narrator tells his version of a decisive experience Kit reluctantly describes one evening. She was fourteen. After a day of planting corn together, her father takes her to a secluded stream, strips, tells her to undress, and begins bathing her. Suddenly recalling the bootlegger's fondling of her, she becomes alarmed, runs from him, and that night steals away from the cabin, never to return. As Kit finishes that story-revelation, she suddenly begins driving the car at wild speed without its lights on through a town, past cars, until, "turning on two wheels," she stops, her long horror over the incident exorcised. It is a shocking end to her tale and to a first chapter proving that, given a right focus, Anderson's narrative talent was still abundantly available to him.

Equally shocking and adept is the beginning of chapter 2 with its unexpected leap in time from Kit as mountain girl to woman rumrunner. "Boy, God," exclaims an admiring businessman, echoing the one in Anderson's *Liberty* article, "she's a tornado." He once saw Kit driving her pilot car at eighty along a quiet residential street, well ahead of a caravan of liquor cars pursued by a big car full of federal men trying to shoot out their tires; she doubled back through side streets, deliberately crashing broadside into the federal car, and then played the distressed young woman who had simply lost control of her car. Since this had happened early in Kit's piloting career before she became known through the newspapers as the "Queen of the Bootleggers," she is taken to court and merely fined for reckless driving, though the businessman now thinks the judge had been fixed. This "flash forward" episode is followed by brief movielike cuts to Kit's departure from home and her first job in a cotton mill. Much of the rest of chapter 2 deals with the story of Jim, a young college man who rebels against his father, a wealthy manufacturer of cheap furniture, and joins Tom Halsey's gang (the one to which Kit belongs) for the fun and excitement of fast driving. Kit and he become not lovers but close friends, and he opens her eyes to the larger world of industry and business, a world of bold unscrupulous men like the Rockefellers and Morgans, the Al Capones and the "little big shots" like Tom Halsey. In this way the narrator introduces yet another theme in *Kit Brandon:* the parallels between legal and illegal business make them much the same. As Kit now explains Jim's understanding of Tom Halsey, the gang leader seems to the narrator more and more an American figure. He became more and more an earlier American, one of our pioneers, a pioneer of business, of industry. . . . He was like a man building a railroad across the continent in an earlier day . . . stealing land along the railroad as he went . . . corrupting legislatures of States as he went. He was like a fur trader, of an earlier day . . . breaking down the morals of Indians. He was an organizer in steel, in oil, he was a chief.

As for Jim, once a driver of a faulty car in a caravan piloted by Kit, he is pursued by federals and crashes up against the stone steps of a town's courthouse, his face and body so crushed that he cannot be identified. Such is one kind of fun and excitement the business of rumrunning may hold.

   With another abrupt jump in time, in this case backward, chapter 3 describes Kit's months in the spinning room of a North Carolina cotton mill. Into what she tells him of her life in mill and mill village, narrator/journalist Anderson interjects brief comments, little essays, Whitmanesque "machine songs" drawn from his knowledge of and articles about southern mills. Each of these is in some way relevant to Kit's growing ability as a young mountain girl, bred in isolation, to relate to other workers and her job, to machines "with a strange new kind of beauty" that make one want to dance, and to townspeople, whose contempt for the millworkers, she perceives, reflects the self-contempt of those "who lived by buying and selling." Among the workers she feels closest to two: the massive, raw-boned, red-headed Agnes, a tough, idealistic fighter for the rights of labor, and pale young Frank, embittered by his slow dying of tuberculosis contracted from mill conditions but an imaginative talker. Agnes instructs her in the need of workers, of everyone, for fair treatment and self-respect; Frank, her "first beau," likes to tell her his ideas, observant, questioning ideas that, she tells the narrator, "make her a little grown up." In a later chapter, she tells the narrator how she lets Frank take her virginity because he wants to know sexual intercourse once before he dies.

   More than half this third chapter is taken up by a long conclusion, which several reviewers rightly recognized as being in itself among Anderson's best tales. One moonlit summer night Kit, Frank, and Agnes together with Frank's visiting cousin Bud, "a little dark squat man from the mountains," take a walk out in the country. As they sit in a farmer's field, Frank tells the story Bud had told him of taking a truck trip north through Virginia and stopping along the road by a big horse farm to watch a party going on, "the people, beautifully dressed, and horses more beautiful than the people." Since Bud loved horses but couldn't afford one, he made a pair of leather hoofs for his hands and on all fours "became a horse." In the field that night he straps on his hoofs and demonstrates, shambling like a bear, walking like a dog, but most of all catching perfectly the horse rhythms of prancing, trotting, racking, single-footing. Kit is both amused and shocked at Bud the horse, and Agnes, hurt by what she sees as Bud the workman's humiliating rejection of manhood, starts a long impassioned speech about the gap between workers with their needs and the rich with their possessions. When she stops, the four walk along a road until they come to an estate where, in a big country house, a dance is going on for "beautiful young women and tall young men in evening clothes." As the dance ends, Agnes throws a brick she has found smashing through the "large plate-glass window that separated those outside from the revellers." The four run away to hide nearby, and men from the dance come out in search of the brick-thrower. As the men are about to discover the mill-workers, Bud down on all fours rushes toward them growling uncannily, shambling like "a huge dog . . . a bear . . . a horse," and they are frightened away. When Bud returns, Agnes embraces him, crying "you darling little son of a bitch." On the way home across fields, the four stop by a creek where Frank, ill from excitement, begins to hemorrhage. Kit, holding his head over the creek, sees his blood gush from his mouth into the moonlit water.

The final paragraph of the story, in summary here condensed to two sentences, is a telling example of Anderson's art at its best. Stated almost wholly in impersonal, matter-of-fact sentences, it shifts in the last sentence with shocking effectiveness to the personal. Further, this final paragraph is an unresolved ending—is Kit seeing Frank die?—which ends the story by placing it, without comment, within the overarching human condition of life and not-life. The whole tale is at the same high level. It is technically adept; the frame of two different rich people's parties is kept from being mechanical by the differing uses of Bud's horse hooves as longing and aggression, and Agnes's long appeal for "love, understanding, respect" for workers is not intrusive and "propagandistic" but comes naturally from this future labor organizer, a woman both life-hardened and tender. Equally impressive is Anderson's capacity for conveying understanding of working people not as stereotypes but simply people, his evenhanded imaging of "have-not" resistance against "have" and its limitations yet its persistence, and his ability to combine the odd and strange with the everyday, "poetry" with realism.

Given such success in this tale and in the first three chapters of *Kit Brandon*, it is all the more unfortunate that in his fourth chapter Anderson temporarily faltered. The purpose of this chapter, crucial and well-carried-out in itself, is to show how Kit, who has become a close friend of Agnes, nevertheless begins to develop toward a different personality and way of life from Agnes's. Whereas Agnes, experienced in strikes, warns Kit away from churches since in a strike "the preachers always stood by the mill owners," Kit, who is "fast becoming a woman," dares to attend the wealthy town churches, not to worship but to see how young women "dressed, walked, held their heads," and to notice "the shining beauty" of the cars they drive. In this way her early fascination with fine clothing is strongly reinforced, and her love of fine, powerful cars begins. From now on such cars and her driving become a constant motif in her life and in the book. The action of chapter 4 begins with the two friends walking from the mill village to a speakeasy in the town through the snow of a wonderfully described winter evening. The time is "the period immediately after the World War," and Frank has died "only a few weeks earlier," the unresolved ending of chapter 3 now being resolved in a single flat sentence. At another table in the speakeasy are a group of men, one of whom, a pale young man, reminds her of Frank, and she recalls for the narrator at this point her and Frank's one sexual union. As Agnes and Kit start to leave, one of the men, against the protests of the pale young man, pushes the unwanted Agnes aside and tries to detain the desirable Kit. Agnes punches the man to the floor, and she and Kit go out into the snowy night, which seems beautiful to Kit, ugly to the hurt and angry Agnes.

Up to this chapter, except for slight slips, the narrator's commentaries have been clearly pertinent to Kit's story, but here they are of a different and less successful kind. They are impressionistic essays only tenuously related to her, crammed with a medley of detail and written in a self-consciously "jazzy" style with slang, many commands ("Flood the market," "Quick, buy copies"), and at times sentences separated into their segments by the ellipses that irritated Mark Van Doren into parody. Anderson's intent is obvious enough: to give an impression of the swift postwar changes in American society that Kit is not yet conscious of but which are beginning to affect her unconsciously. Anderson touches rapidly on new modes of dress design created in Paris but duplicated in cheap cloth, the advertising and romantic fiction in women's magazines, new words in the American vocabulary, the "new mystery inside houses" of electricity, which also enables factories to turn out fast cars speedily, and back to his beginning, "nice slick foxy little gowns for women . . . just like the top-notch dames . . . wear." The clothes Kit admires and later will wear, however, are well made and expensive, not cheap imitations; later she wants to drive a fast car for a highly personal reason, not just because she wants to get somewhere like narrator-Anderson's postwar Americans, but because "the machine . . . seemed beautifully alive to her," because "In a sense she loved it," as though it were a man, something like "a husband." So here, and from time to time in later chapters, Anderson uses Kit arbitrarily "as a spring-board of American life," in a few instances into a not-too-well-connected stream of ideas. Most of the narrator's commentary, however, remains relevant and revealing.

Such is the case with the following chapters, which deal with Tom Halsey, head of the bootlegging gang and father of Gordon, the man Kit later marries. Since the actual John Carter, Willie Sharpe's father-in-law, had died several years before the Roanoke trial, whatever Anderson learned about him would have come from his conversations with Kit; and Anderson would have been essentially free to make Tom come, like Kit, from mountain people and to use his own ten years experience with them to create the early years of this "pioneer, a bringer of a new and modern world into the mountain life." Anderson devotes most of a whole chapter to tracing the history of the southern Appalachian highlands from their settlement by, often, whiskey-making Scotch-Irish, through the disastrous invasion of their mountain forests by the "great lumber kings [with their] ruthless cutting and slashing," to the Prohibition era when whiskey, the distillation of corn into moonshine, became "the money crop of the hills." It is the adult Tom who, feeling himself "in the American business tradition," organizes and draws together under his headship "a scattered industry of thousands of small units" as other captains of industry had organized oil or steel, his business goal being to "control the illicit liquor business, control and organize crime." Even as a boy he shows his ability to control men when, assisting his father in getting a wagonload of moonshine to a lumber camp for sale, he breaks mountain tradition by quietly asking his father for, and getting, a fair share of the profits. In a fine chapter, which Anderson would later excerpt as a short story: Tom as a young man marries a mountain girl of fourteen, who bears his one child, falls ill, and dies while the frantic husband is away from home threatening a physically powerful man into giving him money for her hospitalization. In the following melodramatic but powerful chapter, Tom, needing a woman to breast-feed his baby, rides to a nearby revivalist meeting led by a preacher "adept as an interpreter of God's wishes" in his own favor. His wife, Kate, has just suffered the death of her first child. Before the astonished husband and his followers, Tom confronts Kate, unbuttons the top of her dress, places his baby at her breast, and rides off with her, half-dazed by his personal force, to his home to become the mother to his child and the completely devoted accessory to his bootlegging business.[31]

With Tom's career established, the narrative returns to Kit, bridging her life from her cotton mill years to a further development away from Agnes. While still at the mill she has become friends with the "alive pert little" Sarah, whose motto is "Life's a game," whose plan is to get as much out of men with her good looks as she can, and who is happily carrying on an affair with a married man. Sarah, "a gold-digger," has learned to drive a car, and when the man gives her a key to his runabout, she teaches Kit to drive, Kit learning "quickly, instinctively." Caught up in Sarah's "American restlessness," Kit leaves the mill town by train, takes a job briefly in a larger town in a shoe factory; when picked up in that town by a young man with a car, she, Sarah-like, persuades him to let her take the wheel to drive them in her fast, skilled way to a hotel in a North Carolina city, where, not Sarah-like, she skips out on him.

Lying almost exactly half way through the novel, the following chapter 10 begins abruptly with the sentence, "Tom Halsey, the man old enough to be Kit Brandon's father, was destined to be the big figure in her life," and continues being an example of Anderson's effective "post-Modern" interweaving of time sequences. Kit is about to meet Tom, brought to him at Kate's house by Gordon, now at twenty-four a big, handsome, weak, self-centered "young sport, a woman-getter he hoped, a rich man's son." At once the narrator shifts to Gordon's finding Kit, now eighteen and a clerk in a five-and-ten-cent store, and trying unsuccessfully to break down her mountain-bred reserve for an affair. Having had to rely on his father to get him out of a first marriage to an unfaithful wife, he must get Tom's approval of Kit if he decides that to have her he must marry her. The narrator returns to Kit and Tom's meeting long enough to describe in detail the isolated farmhouse, which he bought as home for Kate and headquarters for his bootlegging operations; but there follows a brief retrospect of Gordon's lonely childhood in fear of Kate, who adores him as Tom's son but whom he thinks of as "rather a woman of stone." Then after an assertion that "Kit Brandon was and is a real person, a living American woman," the narrator ends with by far the longest scene in the chapter showing how Kit, walking in spring with Sarah along the same route as her winter walk with Agnes, came to a moment of revelation, "a whole new viewpoint on life," that for her and Sarah's youth and beauty there was a "market." By such interweaving of past and present, Anderson signals the importance of Kit's first meeting with Tom Halsey, sketches in Gordon's unstable character and his "campaign" against Kit, and ends emphatically on Kit's "new-viewpoint," which will enable her to marry Gordon, less for himself than for the fine clothes and fast car he will give her. That viewpoint is indeed Anderson's implied and forceful comment on the 1920s as a period when a commercial culture ranked money and things above human beings and their close relationships.

That Anderson meant such a comment is reinforced by the dating of Tom and Kit's meeting as a summer day in 1920—"The prohibition law had been passed the year before," that is, ratification of the Eighteenth Amendment in January 1919—and by one of the narrator's longer comments in the form of sketches illustrating the class nature of the amendment: no saloons for the workers, good bootleg liquor for "the rich and the well-to-do." The bootleg business is "in its first full flush of success" when Gordon takes Kit to meet Tom at Kate's place. The event reveals the sort of dangerous toughs in Tom's gang, including one Steve Wyagle, who will attempt to overthrow Tom, and Gordon's uneasiness before them and his father. Walking together alone, Kit and Tom, both from mountain folk, approve each other. Tom sees her as someone he could trust and talk to and as a suitable wife for Gordon through whom Tom hopes to achieve one of his basic aims: respectability for the Halsey name, impossible for him as a gang leader, possible for Gordon, probable for a grandson. At this point Kit feels that the quiet, confident Tom has the quality of genuine manhood and that she may be able to make Gordon something of a man while getting the money to buy things and the "swell fast car to drive."

So she accepts marriage to Gordon, briefly. They live in a comfortable hotel suite with separate bedrooms; she buys any number of beautiful clothes, including many expensive pairs of shoes for her trim feet; Gordon gives her a fast, sporty little car, which from the beginning is "the best thing she got from her marriage." Despite all this ease, luxury, and pleasure, the former mill girl begins to wonder vaguely about her right to them when other people live in want. Having begun her reading with *Sister Carrie* in the public library of the shoe-factory town, she now tries to "improve the mind" by taking the *New York Times Book Review* and buying and reading recommended books. Particularly she enjoys Tom's frequent visits to the suite, she mainly to listen while he talks of his early life and his bootlegging organization. Having found that she dislikes Gordon's sporty crowd and his presence in her bed, and having discovered that he is having an affair with another woman, she insists on his moving out of the suite. Tom's visits stop after a showdown with her in which he blames her for refusing pregnancy, and she, eager for a life of danger instead of her "queer half-dead false life" with Gordon, asks Tom to use her as a liquor-driver in recompense.

Slightly more than the final third of *Kit Brandon* covers Kit's "new life" as driver of liquor cars, then as a pilot, and finally her escape from the bootlegging business. It is a lonely life, dull periods of waiting in cheap hotel rooms for someone to drive her to isolated farm houses to pick up a loaded liquor car and then the too-brief excitement and danger of getting the car to its next destination in the wide bootleg network. In her waiting days at a hotel, she drives about the surrounding countryside learning the highways, roads, lanes as shortcuts to a destination or escape routes if pursued; and she always wears her fine clothes as a way, she has learned, of keeping the rough men of the gang or bribed deputy sheriffs at a distance, of creating the "half-mystical romance" surrounding her as perhaps some new kind of big shot. Feeling separated from others, she at times "terribly wanted a man, not primarily as sex comrade, but as real comrade, someone to creep close to, feel close to, perhaps even a little to command her, direct her." She lives for high speed, reckless driving to show Tom, who she thinks now distrusts her, that she is his best driver, and almost always gets the liquor through. As the months pass, she begins to take on the even more demanding job of piloting caravans of liquor cars; and newspapers, especially after she has been briefly jailed, begin to romanticize her as "a desperate character, bold, beautiful, dangerous," as the rumrunning queen with "diamonds set in her teeth." More and more hiding out in her rooms in small-town hotels, she takes to reading books about early settlers in America, pioneers heading west, builders of railroads, bridges, telegraph lines binding "all of American together," and sometimes feels herself to be like one of these "early adventurous American men"; still, she feels increasingly lonely, separated from others, increasingly desirous of a man who would not be "a buyer or seller, not an exploiter, merchant, lawyer, not a schemer of any kind." Despite her isolation, she hears that Tom is becoming more and more greedy—"It was the story of every big American industry," the narrator comments—arranging with local officials to jail the little moonshine makers in the mountains and getting them out on condition that they work in the new big stills filling the demand by industrial workers and coal miners for the cheapest, rawest moonshine.

Tom is beginning to rule by terror, as Kit is about to find out. For some time she has been teaching the tricks of piloting to Alfred Weathersmythe, a sensitive young "college boy" already a skilled driver. As her earlier friend Jim had rebelled against his businessman father, so Alf, also bored with respectability, has rebelled against his hypocritical father, a state politician from an old Virginia family who votes as Bishop Cannon and his Anti-Saloon League direct and who is privately an alcoholic on bootleg liquor. Instead, Alf made a hero of his aristocratic grandfather, who in the Civil War was one of John Mosby's Partisan Rangers and has so filled his grandson's mind with stories of guerrilla exploits that the boy has romanticized war and killing. The lonely Kit has taken a motherly sort of interest in Alf and listens for hours half fascinated, half repelled to the tales of the young man, "a born story teller," about his grandfather's adventures. Piloting for Tom's gang, she realizes, is Alf's attempt to have his own such adventures. She has heard rumors of dangers to the gang, that the gunman Steve Wyagle is cooperating with federal agents in his scheme to take Tom's place. After Alf leaves Kit, possibly to become a bodyguard for Tom, she is summoned to Kate's place and forced by Kate to watch as Tom makes Alf a killer by forcing him to shoot the captured Wyagle. In reaction Alf runs away hysterically, and Kit, filled with hate for Tom for his cold-blooded use of the young man, follows. Anderson then pulls the whole Weathersmythe episode together quickly and dramatically. In his flight Alf has cut his head, and Kit leads him to a creek in a field where he lies down ill. As she washes blood from his cut, she remembers one of his tales when his grandfather rode down and shot some Yankee prisoners out of a sense of duty, an act Alf had admitted he could not have done. Washing away Alf's blood, Kit has a flash recollection of holding Frank's head while his hemorrhage colored another stream. Abruptly Alf leaps to his feet and dashes away. She does not see or hear of him again.

From this point on the action of the novel, deliberately on Anderson's part, it would seem, runs quickly until the ending, where it as deliberately slows. A few reviewers charged him with turning this part of his book into a popularized thriller; yet necessarily he had to extricate Kit from a gang grown dangerous to her since Tom, whom she now hates, is openly hostile to her. It is also notable that from this point on the narrator's paralleling of legitimate and illegitimate business essentially disappears, his longest attack being against "success-ridden" American men, such as painters and writers, who tell themselves they will first get rich from doing cheap, popular work and only then do something worthwhile. Gordon, almost paralyzed with terror, comes to her hotel room and urges that they run away together out West, but Kit, resolved to confront Tom, instead drives her shaken husband to Kate's place. Thinking that Kit might talk to federal agents, Tom is setting her up for execution gangland-style when the agents attack the farmhouse. In the confusion Kit escapes, Tom runs out, Gordon rushes after his father and, "gone half insane with fright," shoots him. The action now slows to follow Kit as she hides out for three days, first in a shabby hotel, then in the surrounding countryside to avoid capture as the notorious "Queen of the Rumrunners." Continuing to feel lonely with what Anderson frequently called "the loneliness of many Americans," increasingly desiring a human relationship to which she could in some way give herself, she rejects the excitement that held her to piloting and longs for work "that has some meaning." She decides that she must get out of this part of the country and goes to a roadside filling station, one that, as many did in Prohibition times, dispenses gas and liquor, and where two motorcycle policemen are searching for her. Luckily she is accepted into a car by a young man about her age named Joel Hanaford, who recognizes who she is but agrees to drive her away. With Joel, Anderson rounds out the pattern of generational revolt, which is one of his devices for organizing *Kit Brandon*. That pattern in one sense is hinted at in the first chapter when Kit rebels by flight against her father's attempted sexual exploitation of her, is defined, to repeat, during the wealthy young woman's visit to Kit's jail cell, and is clearly established by Jim's rebellion against his businessman father and Alf's against his politician one, Anderson carefully differentiating among circumstances not only to avoid mechanical repetition but also to suggest how widespread is revolt among youth. Joel, who came home from the war wounded and gassed, a hard-drinking "wreck," has also rebelled against an exploitative father, a successful lawyer, politician, and eventually judge. At political meetings the elder Hanaford used to seek the ex-soldier vote by declaiming, "I gave my son to my country," until Joel told his father that if he so exploited him again, he would denounce him publicly or "simply kill" him. Although Kit rejects Joel's offer of an affair or marriage, she is exhilarated by his "bitter resistance to life. . . . He had been defeated but he was mature." She leaves him, resolved to find both work that did not "so separate her from others" and "some one other puzzled and baffled young one with whom she could make a real partnership in living."

The novel seems to end openly, unresolved, with Kit's hope for a new "adventure," not her experience of it; yet returning to the present of the book's beginning it becomes clear that something has been resolved in Kit's life. She may or may not have found the work she wants, work that joins her with fellows, and she certainly has not yet found the whole man she wants rather than Joel's self-styled "half a man." She has told her story to a sympathetic listener, deliberately reaching out to another person, honestly confessing the bad as well as the good, and in doing so has proved that because of her own not bitter "resistance to life," she is *not* defeated and *is* mature. She justifies the narrator's remark about her at the end of the book's first paragraph: "She had her knowing, her way of knowing, and it seemed to me more real than most of the ways of knowing most of us have." Her path to such maturity and way of knowing has not been direct or, as an adult, admirable. She has adventured into "Sarah-ism," marketing her beauty and youth for money and things in a bad marriage, and lured by the excitement and her almost erotic feeling for fast cars, she has become deeply involved in an illegal, violent, corrupt and corrupting business, in pursuit of which she has used men with her body as Tom has used them with power and terror. Throughout, however, she has maintained a sense of self, a large capacity for affection and loyalty, at least an awareness of ethical issues, and, as the narrator puts it, "a kind of basic common sense." In Anderson's "portrait" she emerges, taking the light with the dark, as an attractive, complex, even admirable person. She is certainly one of the best-conceived characters in Anderson's long fiction.

Anderson's portrait of the 1920s as revealed doubly through Kit's career and the narrator's commentary is, by contrast, neither attractive nor admirable. He rightly assesses the only recently repealed Prohibition Amendment as having been a social disaster, which encouraged the widespread hypocrisy of public abstinence and private drinking, and the rapid formation of gangs with gang violence, massive corruption in the legislature and legal systems, and quick illicit wealth. Against such a background Kit's participation seems almost virtuous. As for the twenties as a whole, Anderson's analysis is selective, as any novelist's must be—he ignores, for example, the decade's outburst of creative energy in the arts—but he is perceptive in his untheoretical way in viewing the period as a culmination of industrialism in a commercial-consumerist culture marked by the desire for things and more things, by a thirst for money and success, which overwhelms the desire and need for human community. It is this culture to which Kit the mill girl responds by entering a loveless marriage, as it is the hypocrisy and thirst for success in the older generation that creates such rebels in the younger one as Jim, Alf, and Joel, men to whom Kit is attracted, in the pattern that helps define her personality, link characters and commentary, and unify the novel.

Kit Brandon is not, "by any standard, a great novel," as Roger Sergel declared it, but except for minor slips it is a successful blend of fiction and journalism, an experimental form occasionally adopted in the 1930s and developed more variously in the postmodern time. One of the many indications that Anderson was, for the most part, in firm control of his novelistic material throughout is to return once more to the book's beginning. That Kit starts telling her story in cold, bleak, dust-stormed South Dakota is not only to set the time of her narration as the depths of the Depression but also to assert symbolically that this mid-thirties view of the twenties is the view of a chastened nation forced to search, as a chastened but hopeful Kit is, for better modes of individual life and of human relations than the destructive ones of the previous decade. "I want my story told," Kit insists to narrator-Anderson, who knows that it is not just her story, but in its aspiration, lawlessness, violence, accomplishment, and hope it is a story of America.[32]

10

Slippage

1.

Late in September, Anderson had had Max Perkins send advance copies of *Kit Brandon* to Henry Morgenthau, Jr., by ways of thanks for asking him to find "the human side" of the Franklin County trial where he conceived the idea for Kit and her bootlegging career, and also to Raymond Moley because, as he wrote the editor of *Today*, "I got a good many ideas for the broader theme of the novel out of the trips you sent me on." He also had a copy mailed to Rexford Tugwell, who had been interested in his work, and in a favorable review of *Dark Laughter* back in 1925, had understood its cultural critique. Possibly Anderson hoped for another such review of the new novel to boost its sales, for he was now urgently asking Perkins to keep him informed as to how the reviews went. In mid-October Max reported that *Kit* had sold "not much beyond 2,000 copies," enough, however, for a second printing. His really good news was that the British publisher Hutchinson wanted it, and it had been offered to Jonathan Cape as well. Although small reorders began coming in from American booksellers still cautious in the Depression, sales slowed until by early December Anderson was complaining to Laura Lu that the novel "seems to have fallen pretty much unnoticed." The exact figure is not known, but total sales of his three books published by Scribner's—*Puzzled America, Kit,* and *Plays* (1937)—would be an intensely disappointing 6,500 copies. The British editions were a consolation prize. On November 4 Scribner's received a cablegram from each firm, Cape offering advance payment of 70 pounds (about $350), Hutchinson 120 (about $600). Without hesitation Anderson took the Hutchinson offer, which with deduction for agent's commissions and British taxes would be somewhat under $500. Taken together with payments for some of the short pieces he had been writing in October, the prospect of this advance would allow the winter vacation in Brownsville both Sherwood and Eleanor wanted because they had been so healthy there.[1]

Toward the end of October he went for a week to the Hedgerow to see four new productions and talk with his friends. While there he was notified that as a veteran of the Spanish-American War with 10 percent disability, he would receive a twenty-dollars-a-month federal pension for which he had applied in June. Back at the Royalton he began writing an article, perhaps for *Scribner's,* about building Ripshin, rejoiced in Franklin Roosevelt's triumphal reelection, and in the afternoon of November 7 went to the International Building of the developing Rockefeller Center where he and other "well-known writers" spoke on problems in writing. Before a huge crowd he talked for two minutes on the "problem of writing as the problem of living," the latter being how "to draw closer to others and to find out more and more about others," a process more easily accomplished through imagined figures, hence his reason for writing. On the twelfth, he and Eleanor headed south by car to carry out her YWCA assignments in several cities on the way to Tampa, where she was to report on the annual convention of the American Federation of Labor. Without the rebellious John L. Lewis and his Committee on Industrial Organization leaders there, Anderson found the meetings sad and repulsive, the AFL representatives "just nothing . . . frightened old men," only small businessmen, "life and the struggles of the workers, such a real and bitter thing, all about and they so unconscious, so concerned with hanging on to small advantages acquired." For relief he walked often in the Spanish-speaking section of Tampa, which he thought "by far the most alive & interesting part" of the city. He talked, went to the beach, and dined with newspaper reporters, went with them and Eleanor to talk with some sailors jailed for picketing in a strike, wrote a petition for their release, and got the reporters to sign it. "I tell you," he wrote Sergel, "more and more one feels that if there is ever anything done to make a better society, it will have to come from the dispossessed." Nights, probably in reaction to the meetings, he frequently dreamed, sex dreams, a dream of being in a strike against the AFL, and once when he could not sleep, yet another "night of faces. In semi-conscious state they kept coming—all women, all sad, all hurt."[2]

Besides his conversation with the sailors, two events were strongly emotional for him. He and Eleanor met Isabel de Palencia, newly appointed ambassador to Sweden from the Loyalist government of Spain, and they gladly went to hear her speak on Spanish labor and the Loyalist cause in the Spanish War before a huge crowd of working people in a football field with few AFL men present. She spoke so forcefully and eloquently that he sat weeping openly. The other event was more private and greatly satisfying to him as artist. In the November 25 issue of the *New Republic,* Robert Morss Lovett gave a glowing, perceptive, but not uncritical revaluation of Anderson's achievement, beginning with assertion that he possesses "in truer balance than any other of his contemporaries, of three qualities marked by

Maeterlinck as requisite for great literature: a sure touch upon the world of our senses; a profound intimation of the mystery that surrounds this island of our consciousness; and the literary technique comprehended in the term style." Praising *Winesburg, Ohio* as "a masterpiece" marking "an important date in American literary history," Lovett emphasized Anderson's dissatisfaction with mere realism and his ability to relate fact to the imagination with "an emotion which is the essence of poetry."

It is in thus seizing on scraps of reality and projecting them beyond the small range controlled by the senses that Sherwood Anderson's imagination brings fiction to the enhancement of life, and enlarges his art beyond the limits of naturalism into expressionism. Not the fact, but the emotion with which the artist accepts it, is the essence of living.

Citing Anderson's interest in his short stories in "states of consciousness which eventuate in moments when the unconscious wells up and overwhelms personality with a sense of completion in the larger unity of life," Lovett went on to discuss the social concern of the later books beginning with *Poor White* and reaching its peak in *Dark Laughter,* "undoubtedly" his best novel with its "thoughtful" weaving together of two major themes in his work—"freedom through craftsmanship, and through love." That Lovett judged *Beyond Desire* and *Kit Brandon* to be inferior novels seems not to have spoiled the revaluation for Anderson. After he read it, Eleanor noted in her diary, "S very much moved."[3]

Glad to be leaving the "dead timber" of the AFL, the Andersons headed north on the twenty-eighth for the three-day drive to Durham, North Carolina, where Eleanor had a week's work lined up with the local Y. Mornings in their room at the Washington Duke Hotel Anderson tried a fresh start on *Green Grass,* his diary name for the new novel, in "sharp reaction" to the Tampa meeting, meanwhile writing a report on that convention for the busy Eleanor and rough drafting two or three stories. Roger Sergel telegraphed and then wrote him of the possibility that the Federal Theatre Project in Chicago might stage *Winesburg,* and there was a flurry of letters and telegrams as Anderson got together from various people a complete copy of the final version of his play, which he now insisted was "essentially one of character"; but nothing came of his and Sergel's efforts. On the evening of December 5 he and Eleanor dined at the home of Howard Odum, sociology professor at the University of North Carolina in Chapel Hill and a national expert on southern farmers, and there met and were charmed by the playwright Paul Green and his wife, who invited them to dinner the following evening. Another guest at the Greens' was the novelist James Boyd, whom Anderson also liked as an artist, despite his wealth, and who had driven the sixty miles from his estate in Southern Pines to tell Anderson what Thomas Wolfe had said of him to Boyd recently.

"So, I see," Boyd says he roared, "that the smart boys are after Sherwood Anderson. Ha! He is the only man in America who ever taught me anything. Anything I know of writing I have from him. He is our one sophisticate. He knows life, all of its ugly and [its] sweet side, better than any of us, but he is not soured. He takes life as it is and loves it, and they will be reading him long after all these smart boys are forgotten."

Delighted, Anderson relayed praise to Laura Lu the next day, adding that it gave him needed courage now that *Kit Brandon* was selling poorly. A farewell dinner to the Andersons on the seventh was at the Boyds'.[4]

Despite the friendliness of his various hosts and the report of Wolfe's praise, *Kit*'s failure to sell seems to have been a trigger, for by the time the Andersons reached Marion on the eleventh, after stops to complete Eleanor's assignments, he was as gloomy as the three days of rain on the road, able to write little except letters. "Nothing in me sings," he noted, "Can't really approach anyone." When Eleanor left with her report for New York, his gloom became even darker, for he missed her "terribly," dreamed that his mother was trying to get him as a boy into a factory job, his mother being surely, considering her original rescue of him from despair, a dream close to truth. He played cards rather cheerlessly in Andy Funk's woodworking shop, walked by himself in the countryside and the Marion streets, where "All the people . . . seemed sad and hurt," fiddled at "correcting" his two short plays, started but never finished a short story. The gloom, one of the worst he had had for years, he wrote Sergel, cleared when Jap Deeter, Mims Phillips, and Ferd Nofer (who had played Tom Willard in *Winesburg*) arrived in Marion for almost three straight days of talk about theater problems. Their visit, together with the arrival of Eleanor and Mary Emmett on the twenty-fourth got him through the "usual Christmas disorder." On the day itself Eleanor seemed to him particularly lovely, and the next day he recorded a tribute: "She remains the best one, of all living people I have known." In the last few days of 1936 he got back to work on *How Green the Grass*, reread *Madame Bovary*, had a friendly talk about money with Mary, and approved the enthusiastic request of his Dutch translator Waldie Van Eck to translate *Kit Brandon*. Writing on December 30 to Max Perkins to ask him to negotiate the best advance possible with the Dutch publisher, he sounded as though the "beast" of gloom had never leaped onto his shoulders. He knew that he should be writing the short stories and articles, "a kind of modern 'Winesburg,'" which the new editor of *Scribner's Magazine* had asked for, "but here I am plunged instead into a new novel and I am having such a good time with it that I cannot let it go." One wonders how many, quite possibly fine, stories may have been lost in his pursuit of a novel never finished to his satisfaction. Tactfully Perkins replied on the last day of December that he was pleased to know the novel went well, though he hoped Anderson could do the stories for the magazine "in the interests of all of us." Anderson's last contribution to *Scribner's,* however, would be only a late 1936 letter celebrating the magazine's fiftieth anniversary, a letter ending: "Hurra for the new SCRIBNER'S and a greater and greater closeness to the reality of living in the old 'These States' that Walt Whitman always talked about." It was hardly more than a gesture toward the interests of anyone.[5]

2.

The Andersons and Mary Emmett celebrated the first day of 1937 by driving to Asheville, North Carolina, for Eleanor's last assignment before vacation, a two-day conference with leaders of her industrial girls and women. Back in Marion on the fourth, Sherwood came down with a four-day flu, unable to write much but able to play cards with Mary and to come to an agreement with her about money. Early every month, starting with the present one, she would give him $150 "to live and work on," making the arrangement so considerately that when she left, Andersons and Copenhavers felt "a great tenderness" for her: "She is such a force, so wrongheaded at times, so warm and generous." Sherwood felt less tenderness for the official notification, which he received on the ninth, that he had been elected a member of the National Institute of Arts and Letters in the Department of Literature along with nine other writers, including James Branch Cabell, John Dos Passos, Robinson Jeffers, Robert Sherwood, and Thomas Wolfe—but not Dreiser, he noted, and he wryly joked to Eleanor that "now all he needs is [a] tombstone." Nevertheless, he replied, accepting his election but indicating that he could not attend the ceremony on the twentieth. At that time he expected to be well on his way to Texas.[6]

On the twelfth, the Andersons began their vacation journey by driving to Southern Pines for a three-night visit at the elegant eighteenth-century-style house of the Boyds, "the best I've ever seen the life of a rich man done," Anderson noted, "but wouldn't want it." The two couples quickly became friends. Eleanor enjoyed the luxury of breakfast in bed without, as always, having something that had to be done at once. Sherwood much liked but was somewhat puzzled by the thin muscular Jim with a permanent sinus infection far worse than his, who delighted in the "absurd" pastime of riding to the hounds in his scarlet coat with rich friends, yet loved his horses and big pack of foxhounds, had many liberal political ideas, and was a dedicated artist in his fiction. The two men talked writing, and Boyd admired Anderson's remark that an artist "must be in love with the world." Eleanor found their host "brainy and nice," he and Katherine "unspoiled by money." One day he took them to see the end of a hunt and talk with the hunters, the next day to a harness-racing track to watch the trotters and pacers. It was a memorable visit, and Anderson had a new correspondent.[7]

Reluctantly they left on the fifteenth for the long drive via Mobile to New Orleans for a rather different visit, three days and evenings of much eating, talking, and drinking with the Friends, the Feiblemans, the Antonys, Lucile's sister Elma Godchaux, and others in their closely knit group. Sherwood, always alert to whether people were Jews but normally a defender of them, irritably found his two philosopher friends Julius and Jimmy to be, as he wrote Sergel, "terribly provincial in the worst sense. Can it be," he speculated of the largely Jewish group, "that to be a Jew, in our civilization, is to be, inevitably, provincial? They seem to live and move so much in just that little, rather tight New Orleans circle." He did manage to get in two mornings on *How Green the Grass* and told Eleanor that his protagonist, Fred Wescott, was "a lovely guy . . . somewhat like Faulkner." It was probably at this time that he answered a query from the *Literary Digest* for his opinion on sit-down strikes such as the one going on in defiance of a court order at three General Motors plants in Flint, Michigan. He defended the worker occupation of plants as an appropriate nonviolent tactic against a corporation blocking unionization. Weary of drinking and talking, the Andersons were glad to be off to Texas on the twentieth, although they invited the Antonys to visit them wherever they landed. The first day was over rain-flooded roads to their old stopping place Orange, Texas; the second was south in glorious warm sunshine along the Gulf through Port Arthur, Galveston, Aransas Pass to Corpus Christi, where they settled in at a cottage in the Yacht Beach Court, an "auto camp" at 2700 Rincon Street where they had stayed two years earlier. This cottage was for them a bit expensive (sixteen dollars a week), but it had a gas stove for cooking their meals, was only three steps from the bay with a long pier in front for fishing, and had, by a window looking out over the water, a big table for his work. Eleanor felt that the small house would take some getting used to, but Sherwood, eager to fish and write, found it all perfect.[8]

Overnight, however, the weather turned bad and stayed bad for days, dark, rainy, the coldest in years. Unable to write the first day there, he worked to exhaustion on the second, tried fishing, got a chill that turned into a fever and subsequently a terrible cold with a racking cough. Fearing he had pneumonia, the worried Eleanor finally persuaded him to see a doctor she was referred to who, like a bad joke, turned out to be a blind chiropractor and was no help. Over several days Sherwood was able to go for occasional walks and even to do some fishing, but he was gloomy from making little progress in writing and concerned when Eleanor became half-ill with flu herself. Since the cold, gray weather persisted, they stayed much of the time inside reading, Sherwood appropriately enough *The Brothers Karamazov*, Eleanor *Of Time and the River*, where she found (on page 670) Eugene Gant-Thomas Wolfe's two-edged assessment of Anderson as the writer who most "suggests the strangeness and variety of [American] life" although "he's got too fancy since he wrote *Winesburg, Ohio*." On February 3, Sherwood did manage to write Max Perkins to say that he was not working at his best but wanted Scribner's to publish *Plays* in the spring. Max quickly replied, urging him to send copies of the plays as soon as possible; but before that letter could reach him he became seriously ill, awaking on the seventh doubled up with cramps and in the worst pain he thought he had ever been in. Alarmed, Eleanor called in a Dr. Jerome Nast, "a Jew and a surgeon," Sherwood noted, who diagnosed him as having, not the appendicitis he feared but a severe case of intestinal flu. While Nast was still at his bedside, the Antonys and Elma Godchaux arrived for their visit and added to a confusing situation by instantly, along with Eleanor, disliking the doctor as secretly wanting to operate on his patient. After two days of "great misery" Sherwood on the tenth finally agreed with Nast to let Marc drive him to Spohn Hospital, a Catholic institution, where he asked a sister to pray for him, Eleanor noting "(Marc says this to be nice to sister—I think he's desperate.)"[9]

For several days Eleanor had been in anxious touch with her able brother-in-law Henry Van Meier for medical advice and had become angry that Dr. Nast would casually prescribe nothing more than bed rest for Sherwood. Now she was upset and furious at him for refusing to consult with Henry by telephone and, with her, only bragging of his own accomplishments. A "vain pathetic little Jew," she exploded in her diary, "& yet he has S's life in his hands"; but somehow she persuaded him to have her husband fed intravenously, as Henry prescribed, with glucose and saline solution. Slowly the solution would help, but at first he remained, as she put it, "horribly ill." Even so, he was pleased to have been put in a double room with a poor, young oil-well driller named Rush Weatherby, who was recuperating from an operation, read Wild West pulps but who was a natural storyteller and who told "wonderfully well" tales of life in the oil fields. For four days, despite Anderson's frequent violent vomiting, he talked with and listened to Rush until the night nurse would tell them to keep quiet. By the time Rush went home, Sherwood was feeling somewhat better and began to be interested in hospital life as though it were a miniature Winesburg. There was the full-figured Thelma Landig, "a treasure," whose rubdowns with her powerful hands he looked forward to all day. There was tall, slow moving Miss Conrad, a private night nurse Eleanor insisted he have despite her "hatred of special privilege." Although this nurse was habitually silent, he soon had her telling him about growing up on a great wheat farm near Amarillo; and he talked the intern, Dr. Goode, into telling him about each new patient. By the fifteenth he could dictate a few letters to Eleanor, and after days of being unable to eat, he could take a little tea and even oatmeal. Though tired and worn, Eleanor had begun coming at dawn to talk and read to him from Boswell's *Journal of a Tour to the Hebrides,* Sherwood praising Boswell as "a good writer because so detailed." On the twentieth he was discharged from Spohn, after giving Thelma of the marvelous hands a copy of *Kit,* but for days afterward he felt weak and dragged out. He and Eleanor, weary from strain and sleeplessness, took short walks, played cards, and read; on the twenty-fifth he began dictating to Eleanor, first recollections of his brother Earl, then another attempt at an introduction to *Plays,* which sounded to her too much like more autobiography. She tried to persuade him to omit "Mother" from the book, but he insisted that the one-acter "plays badly but reads well." They visited the oil fields, "a wild, strange and terrible place," he thought, where workers risked their lives to produce the oil wealth that was turning Corpus into a crowded, planless boom city. He went to Dr. Nast daily for shots of iron and arsenic; and when he grew stronger, they had three days of boat fishing, once with Weatherby, and on each of the last two days Sherwood hooked and landed a huge basslike drum, one weighing fifty-five pounds. After settling with Dr. Nast—gentile got Jew "down from $125 to $75," Sherwood commented—he and Eleanor on March 6 left the cottage and city she had come to loathe because of his illness, the doctor, and her fear of a relapse, and began the three-day trip back to New Orleans.[10]

The four-day visit there was much like the previous one except that Roger and Ruth Sergel had come down to spend time with them. Despite the constant socializing, Anderson managed to dictate a draft of an article, "Friend," on Burton Emmett, trying out a new procedure of dictating what he roughly wanted to say and subsequently reworking the stenographer's typescript. Relieved to be alone and in motion, the Andersons left New Orleans on March 13 for the two-day trip to Atlanta, Sherwood driving most of the way, though his legs were "still rubbery" from the flu. In Atlanta, while Eleanor worked at a Y convention, he stayed in their room at the Winecoff Hotel reading and pouring out to a stenographer recollections of his varied "adventures in American life." *Kit Brandon* had been published in England, he cheerfully wrote Mary, enclosing its first review, presumably favorable, from the London *Post.* On the nineteenth they left for Knoxville and the next day were back in Marion, Eleanor only briefly before dashing off to an assignment in Nashville.[11]

After catching up with local happenings from Bob and Andy Funk and with John's striking progress in painting while spending the winter at Ripshin, he caught up with his correspondence. The most important item was the invitation from Edward Davison to participate in the Eighth Annual

Writers' Conference in the Rocky Mountains at the University of Colorado at Boulder from July 28 to August 11. Davison, the conference director, explained that he was not to teach a course but give two evening lectures, take part in some round table discussions, and help out in daily workshops by reading some manuscripts, all for a fee of four hundred dollars. Although a little uneasy about the new experiences, he accepted the post of general advisor and wrote that he would also bring Eleanor. On the twenty-sixth, he sent Perkins the manuscript for *Plays* so that Max could start getting it into type and later explained that the introduction might be turning into a whole long book about his life. He had put in mornings dictating a half-hour radio play, *Textiles,* and finished it on the twenty-ninth from the stenographer's typescript, along with "Friend."[12]

This article on Emmett resulted from an invitation to contribute recollections of his friend to a memorial issue of *PM,* a magazine for, among others, advertising men. After emphasizing again Burt's gift for friendship and his ability to combine a career in advertising with collecting prints and paintings, Anderson, conscious of his audience, declares that were he to be placed on an island, he would want to have as companions some of the advertising men he had known in his early career instead of most of the intellectuals, writers, and artists he has come to know later; for the former, along with certain day laborers, had been honest, kind, helpful, whereas too many of the intellectuals and writers scorn businessmen as commercialized yet jump at the first chance to go to Hollywood and sell out for the big money. *Textiles,* a considerably more important piece, likewise resulted from an invitation. This one had come in the previous October from a social worker-actress-musician named Lucile Charles, who was coordinating an ambitious project to dramatize through a series of half-hour radio plays the conclusion of a recent engineers' National Survey of Potential Product Capacity that the United States was indeed a land of plenty. Already convinced, as in *Puzzled America,* that the country had rich unused resources and excited about the possibilities of radio as a medium for the experimenting in sound he had wanted to do since dramatizing *Winesburg,* he had agreed by mid-October to do the play on textiles—weaving. For weeks thereafter Lucile worked with various dramatists, actors, and radio technicians completing a proposal to the Columbia Broadcasting System to air through its experimental dramatic workshop "Land of Plenty," a series of thirteen one-act plays by such "socially progressive" playwrights, besides Anderson, as Lillian Hellman, Langston Hughes, Albert Maltz, Elmer Rice, and Irwin Shaw. By January 15, 1937, CBS agreed to broadcast one play in the series each month as soon as the first six scripts were ready, stipulating that each play be reviewed for suitability. Much wanting Anderson's to be among the six, Lucile sent him a contract and the set fee of $250 on February 15, just when he was beginning to recover in the hospital from his flu,. On March 22, the second day after his return from Texas, he made his first draft of *Textiles;* presumably, on the twenty-ninth or very soon after, he mailed the completed script to Lucile Charles.[13]

In the play, he later explained to Deeter, he was trying to give "a kind of panorama of the industry done partly in songs and chants. I don't know how it will play." Eleanor, who had been supplying him with background material, described it as "a sort of group choral speaking thing—Very beautiful, I think and hope." Combining brief speeches of individual men and women with choruses spoken in unison, the play briefly describes the historical beginning of weaving on hand looms, and then concentrates on the first power looms and the coming of the cloth factories. At each stage of mechanization the voice of Croaker, "a cracking complaining voice" of anger and fear, urges the workers to destroy the machines and return to the old ways of the hand looms before the machines destroy them by taking away their jobs; but counterpointed against his preachments and the sound of the machine-wreckers, the chorus declares that the machines and factories will produce "a Mississippi of cloth" of all descriptions so that in the coming "age of plenty" everyone everywhere may be clothed.

At about this point, the first version of the play ended, short of the requisite half hour. By April 13 he would add, as he wrote Charles, "a most striking ending in the song and march of the workers."

"Listen to the song of the day of plenty. Listen to the song of the factories," calls a voice, and the chorus sings a much-adapted first stanza of "The Battle Hymn of the Republic," in which the glory is the coming not of the Lord but of "the Day," when "We have loosed the mighty power of the factories grim and grey." As the workers are heard marching "to the mills . . . toward the age of plenty," factory whistles begin blowing with the *"effect,"* Anderson's note explains, *"of one of the circus calliopes that used to go in circus parades through the streets of American towns,"* the implication being that each factory will become, not a focal point of class strife, but a joyous center of restored village community. Over a "din" of sounds—the whistles now playing "The Battle Hymn," the heavy tramp of marching feet, the cheers of workers—rises the voice of a woman singing the often repeated chant of the weavers of many kinds of cloth, but now with a new appeal.

> We are not afraid of work.
> We are not afraid of the factories, of the machines.
> Help us thinkers.
> Planners, plan for us.

So, unlike the Marching Men of Anderson's early novel, these workers do not simply march in threatening silence at the exhortation of a visionary labor leader, but march, men and women, in holiday mood toward a goal, that of being happy, busy producers in factories like small towns under the hoped-for direction, not of any bosses, managers, or owners, but as the woman's song urges, of the benign New Deal and New Dealers.[14]

A reference to *Marching Men* is not casual. Different as it and *Textiles* are, they do provide an unexpected kind of frame to Anderson's writing career; they are linked as his two works most focused on labor as subject and as his only works belonging, at least in part, to the fantasy of the future as genre. The novel, now powerful, now clumsy, was written by a former blue-collar workman and soldier, troubled in occupation and marriage and seeking to express a personal need that could well have made its author feel at times as out of place, even "grotesque" emotionally as Beaut McGregor is physically. The book ends, of course, in personal, perhaps deliberate failure. The play, which effectively exploits the aural resources of a relatively new medium, summarizes and distills the experience of an older, more skilled man who has observed, on the one hand, the human devastation of the Depression and the ossification of traditional labor, and on the other hand, imaginative governmental efforts to alleviate the devastation and the stirrings of a new, rebellious labor movement. Out of the latter he projects a wish-fulfilling public success as unreal in contemporary actuality as in subsequent history. *Textiles,* it might be said, conveys symbolically the despair and hope of America in the mid-1930s. The fact remains, however, that Anderson's resort to fantasy of the future, once near the beginning of his writing career, once near what would turn out to be its ending, confirms his relationship to organized labor as being, despite his manifest sympathies, that of romantic observer rather than informal participant.

3.

Eleanor had barely returned from Nashville before she left on March 30 for conferences in Louisville, Chicago, and Des Moines, and Sherwood the same day took the night train to New York for a week crowded with activities. Mornings he dictated reminiscences to a skilled stenographer at 54 Washington Mews, where Mary, he observed, was "getting command of herself"; but afternoons and evenings he saw people. Having been impressed with the beauty of John's painting of a mountain girl, he had brought it with him and now showed it to Paul Rosenfeld and Stieglitz, who praised it, to the father's delight, for its freshness and color. On the third he dined on Italian food with Dreiser, and on the fourth at Cherio's restaurant with Perkins and Thomas Wolfe. From the start Anderson and Wolfe liked each other; the younger thought the older wise and perceptive, the older thought the younger "one of the few real ones." He talked with Lucille Charles, now on the CBS staff, about revisions of *Textiles,* which the oversight committee of the series much liked but wanted lengthened. He spent most of his last two days in the city talking with Jap Deeter and the Hedgerow actress Rose Schulman, and on the seventh he took the train with them to Hedgerow, where he talked for another day with Jap and all the players before reaching Marion on the eighth.[15]

Randolph Copenhaver, Eleanor's brother, had just returned from Army Air Force medical duty in the Philippines bringing gifts for the family. Anderson's was a tan camel's hair coat, which with his love of fine fabrics he inordinately admired as "grand . . . very swank" and strutted about in; but the next day he was hard at revising *Textiles* in accordance with the committee's suggestions and this time giving it the required length with his "most striking ending." Then he turned to dictating his life "adventures." Spring had come to Marion, and the cherry trees, he noted, burst into bloom in just hours. nevertheless, Eleanor had another month's work to do in New York and they must head back north. On the twenty-second, the Andersons with B. E. Copenhaver and Randolph drove to Washington, where the Andersons dropped off father and son, stayed for a day to see newspaper friends met in Tampa, then drove on to the Hedgerow, where they saw a superb production of *Twelfth Night,* which sent Sherwood into a longing to write more plays, a reaction suggesting on his part both a continuing interest in experimenting with new forms but also a growing inability to fix, as with *Kit Brandon,* on a single major project.[16]

Settling in at "54," he began dictating on "the big book" to a goodlooking, skilled stenographer, broke off for a two-day visit to Hedgerow seeing plays and talking, dictated again for a couple of days, and on May 8 drove with Eleanor and Mary to Wells College in Aurora, New York, to see a production of *Oedipus Rex* at the invitation of his old friend J. J. Lankes, who was then teaching in the Department of Fine Arts. Back at "54," he wrote and dictated busily on "the long book" for a week, went abruptly into a slump on the seventeenth, and two days later tore up much of that week's work as having been "a side path." Feeling "in a jam" on the book, he turned to writing an account of his 1932 trip with the American delegation to the World Congress Against War in Amsterdam, but he soon abandoned it and any further work because the end of Eleanor's month at the YWCA was approaching. Afternoons he went to many major league ballgames, lunched and talked with friends, did errands and frequently played cards with Mary, all as though killing time until Eleanor's month was over. Evenings he did fairly often go to the theater, the best performances being, he judged, those of Katharine Cornell in *Candida* and Maurice Evans in a "very absorbing—beautifully staged" *Richard II,* and there were other pleasures. On May 6 he picked up at the Chase National Bank the sum of $249.15 in royalties from Russian translations of his books and felt "prosperous. Russian money always seems coming out of the skies." At least by now Perkins must have received and given him the mostly favorable review of the British edition of *Kit Brandon* in the *Times Literary Supplement*. Despite "the rather chaotic narrative," the reviewer had grasped Anderson's dual intent.

His portrait of Kit Brandon is inextricably woven with a penetrating study of American sociological conditions. Kit Brandon in many lights is symbolical of the rise of non-morality attendant upon the heyday of the "get-rich-quicks" who, making swift capital out of land and people, drove the land and people to destruction.[17]

There were also the parties, Mary's huge, successful one with "a flood of food and drink" for fifty or sixty old friends of Burt early in the month, and near the end a much smaller farewell dinner party at "54" including among others Paul Rosenfeld, Max Eastman, and James T. Farrell, already famous at thirty-three for his *Studs Lonigan* trilogy and *A World I Never Made*. Seventeen years later Farrell recalled that evening and his first impressions of Anderson, who had "influenced and inspired me, perhaps more profoundly than any other American writer." Farrell found him "a sweet and simple man, but [with] much of the actor in him." Immediately they were on a first-name basis "as though we were friends already." Although Jim had recently met Leon Trotsky at Trotsky's home in Mexico during the hearings there of John Dewey's Commission on the Moscow Trials, Sherwood was not interested, unlike many New York intellectuals, in Trotsky or the hearings; instead the two men talked especially of writing, Sherwood, sounding like the teller of *A Story Teller's Story*, insisting that writers "told lies, not the truth," by lies meaning "fantasies and stories." Jim, the more logical and analytical, "saw Sherwood as something of what is called a 'natural.' He was direct, simple, and spoke with feeling. His talk was personal and every so often there would be a sly flash of wit." Jim concluded that "The evening was pleasant, rather than stimulating. What I carried away from it was a sense of the sweetness of Anderson as a man." No doubt partly because Jim told Sherwood "something of my feeling for his work and of its influence on me," the older man noted in his diary that it had been "a really beautiful dinner party" and despite much talk about Trotsky, "the evening really fun." He had in fact heard the talk of other guests about Trotsky, "rather the new god," he wrote to Lankes the next day, marking his own distance from his radicalism of 1932 with his comment: "I guess the Stalin crowd rather overdid it in the so-called Moscow trials. Its pretty discouraging. They remake the world etc and then it is as full of the old evil and hatred as ever." Nearly a month earlier he had admitted to Sergel that he was "a bum revolutionist." His "great difficulty . . . in all this matter of going somewhere is that I am not terribly interested in arriving. My chief interest is what happens on the way."[18]

4.

Leaving New York on May 29 with a stopover at Hedgerow, the Andersons arrived in Marion on the thirty-first. Early the next morning they were at Ripshin, eager for the two-day task of cleaning and opening it for the summer; and by the late afternoon of the second day he was happily dictating to Margaret Fry, the newly hired live-in stenographer, the talk on Realism he had agreed to give at Colorado State College at Greeley, prior to the Writers' Conference in Boulder. He had never seen the house and the countryside more beautiful with azalea and purple rhododendron blooming, laurel to come, and the promise of a rich fruit year. Rejuvenated, he felt ready, he wrote Sergel on June 2, to plunge again into telling "as honestly as possible, the story of my own adventures in living," of which he had "done nearly two hundred pages," though the whole book would need a great deal of editing by Roger and Laura Lu after the dictation process. Two days later, however, he shifted to writing "Personal Protest" for the *Canadian Forum* in response to an article by an acquaintance, Earle Birney, on "Proletarian Literature." Rejecting his early 1930s radicalism, he protests that writing to praise the proletariat for a sociopolitical purpose should not be the artist's intent. He himself came out of the working class and has written mostly about the poor because he finds them more interesting than the rich, but he could write of the rich as the rich Turgenev could write with beautiful tenderness of the "obscure lives" of the poor. The real challenge to the artist is to respect his own imaginative life and the imaginative lives of others, for in this way he "will best serve all men." His protest made, Anderson went back, not to working on his "adventures," but to dictating speeches for the upcoming conference and correcting incoming batches of proofs of *Plays* from Perkins until June 14 when he noted in his diary, "Got back to the novel [*How Green the Grass*]. It was fun working on it." He wrote on the novel for only two more days that week, and then on June 23 in a single morning he finished a short story called "Two Lovers" and again took up the novel as his one project, which he would work at, but only off and on, until shortly before he and Eleanor left for Colorado a month later. The energy was there—but only intermittent and scattered.[19]

"Two Lovers," a spin-off of the novel, begins slowly but builds to a conclusion that is pure Anderson. John Wescott, father of the Fred Wescott of the novel, is a successful but shy, self-doubtful Chicago realtor who has never ceased wondering why his much better-educated wife, whom he "thought . . . beautiful," should have married him. After her death, he spends an evening in a bar drinking with a friend, "A. P." Grubb, head of an advertising agency. As they drink, Wescott, who feels he is uneducated and "dumb," silently admires A. P.'s ability "to throw words about," words that the reader perceives to be a web of clichés. A. P. declares that he has never been unfaithful to his wife but inadvertently reveals that when entertaining clients, a diversion he professes to dislike as much as Anderson really did with client Bohon, he and the clients have gone to prostitutes. The nearly silent Wescott, made talkative by several drinks, admits that he had been faithful to his wife and describes how, walking with her in a lakefront park one evening, he had been emboldened by the lashing of the waves to ask her to marry him, and to his delighted surprise she agreed. Coming back with her to the street, he saw, parked by the curb with the driver inside, "the grandest, the most beautiful car he had ever seen." Still insisting that he doesn't have A. P.'s "gift of words," he tries to tell him how he was feeling, and his words come out unconsciously as the superb equivalent of that feeling.

"It was as though, as if that man . . . as if he had suddenly got out of the car and walked over to me . . . as if he had said, 'Do you want this car? You can have it. Take it away.'

"As if . . . just like that . . . he had given it to me. I felt like that about her saying she would be my wife."

"Two Lovers" is not one of Anderson's finest stories, but it demonstrates that he, from the working class, could write about the rich, or at least the well-to-do, could let the advertising world he had hated reveal itself as corrupt in language and character, could show how the uneducated person might turn the ordinary into poetry.

Liking this tale, he sent it to the *New Yorker*, which turned it down as "too long," whereupon he sent it to his new literary agent, Jacques Chambrun. Long since dissatisfied with Charlotte Barbour's inability to place "Mrs. Wife," he had talked with Chambrun in New York, probably on May 13, and had arranged with him to handle his stories and articles. Within days Chambrun wrote him that the popular magazine *Redbook* was now "reprinting stories published in the quality group a few years ago" and that the editor wanted to reprint one of his. *Redbook* declined "Brother Death" as "very beautiful but too sad" but accepted "I Want to Know Why" for five hundred dollars. Realizing that by contract with Huebsch, who had published that story in *The Triumph of the Egg* and had since joined Viking, Viking was entitled to take 50 percent of the $450 left after Chambrun had deducted his 10 percent fee, former businessman Anderson wrote complaining that he himself would receive only $225 and pleading that Viking take only 25 percent as a one-time concession. When a Viking representative agreed to the commission, whereby Anderson received $337.50, Anderson replied, thanking him for the concession and now urging that the concession be extended to all future reprints. Chambrun continued to apply his skills. In the summer of 1936 after Barbour had returned the unsold "Mrs. Wife," the disappointed Sherwood had turned it over to Laura Lu for possible revisions. As Eleanor would put it in her diary for July 6, 1937, her mother "doctored [it] up, renamed" it "A Walk in the Moonlight," and "made S send off," as he did to Chambrun on June 22 after retitling it "A Moonlight Walk." Chambrun liked the story very much, and he and Laura Lu apparently knew the popular market better than Sherwood did; on July 6 he and Eleanor returned from celebrating their fourth wedding anniversary in Marion to find a letter from Chambrun reporting that he had sent the check for "I Want to Know Why" to Viking and that, provided Anderson accepted a few minor editorial revisions, he could sell "A Moonlight Walk" to *Redbook* for around $750. It was, Anderson noted, a "very exciting day." It was also pleasant later that after he accepted the revision, the price paid was $800, "my price," Chambrun noted.[20]

As usual there were summer visitors. Ferdinand Schevill and Mary Emmett arrived on June 9, Ferdinand for a two-week round mainly of talking, walking, and croquet playing, Mary staying until the Andersons left for Denver and occupying herself energetically with reworking all the flower gardens. John arrived for a long stay bringing Mrs. Eleanore Jubell, whom he would later marry, and her eight-year-old daughter Ann. Sherwood found the mother "intelligent and charming." He was, Eleanor noted with irritation, "happy as a country gentleman," while she, with the help of only an unskilled housemaid had "to do 4–5 hours of housework a day" in addition to entertaining these and other guests, and preparing for her yearly Y conference at Camp Merrie-Wood. Sherwood did get involved in running farm errands and happily helping to rebuild the two tent guest houses with roofs and bark siding, so much so that by early July he found it hard to keep at the novel and shortly dropped it completely because three plumbers, at Mary's expense, were putting in a new water main to the house and throwing the house into an uproar. It was something of a relief to be packing for the trip west; though Sherwood had complained to Eleanor earlier that he regretted agreeing to go to the Writers' Conference "as he loves Ripshin so." July 17 was a busy day. After more packing in the morning, the Andersons and guests drove into Marion, where between Sherwood and Andy Funk's bottling of their joint wine—Sherwood's share was two hundred bottles—and a big family picnic, he signed his last will and testament to provide "financially for Eleanor as well as he could."[21]

On the nineteenth they headed for Chicago, stayed that night in Louisville, and the next day reached the Sergels' house, where they left their car expecting to go on together by train, a trip both looked forward to. Unfortunately, Eleanor fell briefly but violently ill with dysentery, and on the twenty-second, in order to meet a speaking appointment at Fort Hays Kansas State College, Sherwood had to take a Santa Fe day train down to Kansas City and a night Union Pacific train to Hays, arriving only two hours before his nine thirty engagement on the morning of the twenty-third. The next day, weary and missing Eleanor, passing the time on a slow Union Pacific train by reading, surprisingly, about "Tibetan mysticism," he reached Denver where a recovered Eleanor joined him. "Life," he noted in his diary, "in unlivable without her." Eleanor noted in hers, "Swell to see him." On the twenty-sixth they rode by bus to Greeley in time for his afternoon talk on Realism at Colorado State College before a large, attentive audience, after which a student drove them to Boulder and the Chi Omega sorority house, where they were to stay during the conference.[22]

Although he later wrote Karl that the two-week conference had been, "on the whole, a pretty pleasant" experience, one would not have expected it from many of his diary entries. Having spent his first morning reading conferees' manuscripts, which were "universally without the spark," he decided that nothing was sillier than trying to teach writing at a school; a discussion of "The Limitations of the Short Story" in which he partici-pated on the second day was "terrible," and he was already sick of "this eternal talk of writing"; a two-day session on regionalism in literature in which he later took part was "very dull" and (twice) "stupid." Two of the three evening lectures he listened to were very bad, but Davison's on po-etry was "fine"; his own first lecture, "The Impulse to Write," to a large audience because it was open to the public, was, on the other hand, "pretty good." Eleanor agreed; his voice was "good," his talk "gorgeous—Real quality tone—People moved." One of the conferees who heard him, Martha Monigle, who did become a writer afterward, wrote of him thirty-seven years later as performing quite differently. In her "Sherwood Anderson in Boulder" she begins with a description of his "shy and nervous" appear-ance at the short story discussion the day before.

To the students packed in the large high-ceilinged room, Anderson looked and acted nothing like the dashing photographs and blurbs on the book jackets at the campus bookstore. His eyes were obscured by thick glasses his round face was red and puffy; his fingers were twiddling constantly across his paunch, drawing atten-tion to the perpetual tremors of his hands.

When it was Anderson's turn to speak at the round-table discussion, everyone was forced to lean forward to catch his faint and aged voice. Though only sixty he looked ten years older.

Monigle seems to have been able to hear well enough to take careful notes, however, quoting him as saying, for example, "My stories are what I picked up. What I saw other people do. What my own feelings were from observing them." On his delivery of "The Impulse to Write" she casts a very cold eye.

Again the author showed signs of extreme distress at having to face an audience. He shuffled to the podium and spread out his notes with trembling fingers. Frequently his words were blurred and indistinct as he read from the sheets of paper, rarely looking up at the spectators.

In his "faint voice" and "a rambling way" he described the life experience that led him to become a writer; yet again Monigle heard and took notes. "'The theme in all my stories,' he told the audience, 'is how a man tries to recapture his lost innocence.'" Asked for his philosophy, he answered musingly, "I guess it's a pagan one—to feel more, see more, think more, hear more, and taste more." Monigle goes on to admit that later he became less shy with the conferees and then alludes to the weather in a way which may explain the disparity between her and Eleanor's accounts. "That summer at Boulder was unbearably hot with air conditioning still in the future. Occasionally thunder storms rolled down from the surrounding Rocky Mountains. . . ." In her diary Eleanor makes the odd statement that "S used the thunder for his talk tonight." Possibly he did begin speaking faintly and then to make himself heard over the thunder was forced to speak loudly and so lost his "shyness."[23]

At any rate, Anderson was so praised and lionized at the conference—Whit Burnett, editor of *Story* magazine, "heralded him as second master, Checkov being the other," Eleanor noted—that "S worried that he gets too much attention and praise." Among the other instructors at the conference both Andersons especially liked Burnett; John Peale Bishop, novelist and poet; Evelyn Scott (novelist); Davison (poet as well as conference director); despite a "wisecracking" lecture, Howard Mumford Jones (poet and scholar, who had just completed his first year as a distinguished professor of English at Harvard); Sherwood's old University of Chicago friend Robert Morss Lovett (lecturer); and Margaret Mayorga (dramatist). They saw little of the famed novelist Ford Maddox Ford, who was ill and lectured almost inaudibly, and they were put off by their impression that the poet John Crowe Ransom had Fascist tendencies, which he denied. There were dinners and cocktail parties, at one of which Eleanor was greatly amused to see a lady "who looks like an Egyptian hieroglyphic and poses." When Anderson had to discuss a conferee's writing, he liked to drive up in a borrowed car to some high point overlooking the city and, as in the *Kit Brandon* situation, talk it out with that person; otherwise he tried to keep away from the everlasting chatter about writing. When interviewed by a reporter, he amiably refused to talk about his own writings, published or in progress, though admitting that he continued to write some part of most days. For both Andersons the happiest days were those when Davison or some other Boulder resident drove them on excursions to the deep canyons behind the campus or on the "long and magnificent" circle ride northwest to Estes Park through Rocky Mountain National Park, across the Continental Divide down to Grand Lake on the west slope, and back through Central City to Boulder. Equally satisfying was the visit on the last day of July to Central City's annual drama festival. Although Anderson was disappointed by the play—Thornton Wilder's revision of Ibsen's *Ghosts*—he was "excited by the aspects of the old mining town" and especially by the square dancing performed in a livery stable in the center of town by Lloyd ("Pappy") Shaw's Cheyenne Mountain School couples, the men in dark trousers, bright western shirts, and cowboy hats, the women in gaily colored, full-skirted, ankle-length dresses, Sherwood so delighted by the whole scene that, as Shaw later recalled, he "took part in" one of the "old time" dances. The dancers, he later wrote to Shaw, had "a kind of rough grace, sincerity, feeling of fun; joy in living," brought back "a more authentic old western life" as opposed to the clichés of romantic novels of the West, and gave "the feeling of an early America and its joy in a huge new land." Such excursions helped to carry him through his first Writers' Conference. On the evening of August 10 he brought it to a close with his second lecture, "The Obligations of the Writer," "very serious," Eleanor noted, "but I think people liked it." Summing up the conference for Perkins afterward, Anderson would write, "it turned out better than I expected." Besides the mountain drives and drinking "more than usual I met some pretty nice people. It wasn't bad."[24]

In the afternoon of August 11 the Andersons left Denver on the Burlington Zephyr, luxuriated in the train's smoothness and speed, reached Chicago the next morning, spent two days mostly in talk with the Sergels, and left in their car on the thirteenth for the two-day drive through a heat wave to Marion, Eleanor sad at approaching assignments, Sherwood joyful at returning to Ripshin. He had trouble getting back into *How Green the Grass,* however, and instead on the twentieth wrote a story-article, "Ah, There's the Rub," admitting that the "dream world" presented by most movies does provide viewers temporary escape from their daily lives, yet asking why there could not be more films making these daily lives "more real." For example, he tells of observing how a farm family copes with the son's bitter disappointment at not being able to go to college because of his father's illness, his getting drunk for the first time as a momentary protest, but recognizing that he must accept the destruction of his hopes. As Anderson was at last getting back into the novel and was admiring the "beautiful" book design of *Plays,* six prepublication copies of which Perkins had sent him, he had his own hopes seemingly destroyed by the arrival for a week's visit of Mimi, Russell, and their two young children, Mimi pregnant with her third. Insisting that he was "allergic to kids" and these were "simply a pest" to him for disrupting the household, he, as Eleanor put it, went "all to pieces" and took refuge as often as he could in his writing cabin to have the peace and quiet he maintained that as artist he deserved. Mimi and the children, he complained to his wife, brought "back the days when Cornelia tried to kill the artist in him again and again by insisting he make money for the children." His extreme overreaction to his daughter and grandchildren was further proof of how deeply imbedded in his emotion-charged memory was his conviction as to why his first marriage broke up and why, by corollary, he must so intensely dislike business, so unswervingly dedicate himself to art. Caught in the middle between her husband and his daughter, Eleanor could only try to keep the peace, but it was a relief to everyone when the visit ended.[25]

Upset by the children, he nevertheless accomplished quite a bit in his cabin during that week. On August 24 he received a letter from Norman Holmes Pearson, professor of English at Yale, who with William Rose Benét was editing *The Oxford Anthology of American Literature* in which they were printing a story they much admired, "Death in the Woods." Would Anderson send a note on how he wrote it? By the twenty-sixth he had the note written and in the mail. In retrospection he could state flatly that "the theme of this story is the persistent animal hunger of man," a hunger fed by certain women all their lives. In his several attempts to write the story he had deliberately made the old woman "tired out, sexless" in order to "definitely lift that hunger . . . out of the realm of sex" and to imbed the story "in the whole life of a community," these "flashes out of a community life" to give "a certain effect [which] is a little hard to define. What is wanted is something beyond the horizon, to retain the sense of mystery in life while showing, at the same time, at what cost our ordinary animal hungers are sometimes fed." The note opens up ways into the story, but even its author could not hope to open all the ways into this remarkable fiction. As the philosopher John C. Danto has put it, "With great art one never touches bottom."[26]

Grateful for the note and certain that "Death in the Woods" was "a completely satisfying realization of form," Pearson later wrote Anderson about the problem of form, and the latter would reply with one of his few summaries of his aesthetics. All artists "begin out of a great hunger for order," out of which form grows expressionistically.

You see, Pearson, I have the belief that, in this matter of form, it is largely a matter of depth of feeling. How deeply do you feel it? Feel it deeply enough and you will be torn inside and driven on until form comes.

But form does not come to exist in the absence of "morality," which has two aspects. Any artist must strive unceasingly to create form or he "betrays this morality," the code of the artist, which is so important that it "may be the only true morality there is in the world." For the story writer

there is a special application in the use of human beings as characters—
and Anderson makes his familiar adjuration.

> And what is so little understood is that, in distorting the lives of these [people]—
> often imagined figures to be sure, to achieve some tricky effect, you are betraying
> not only this indefinable thing we call form but that you are betraying all of life . . .
> in short that it is as dirty and unworthy a thing to betray these imagined figures as
> it would be to betray or sell out so-called real people in real life.
> And so this whole matter of form involves, for the story writer, also this
> morality.[27]

On that August 26, the day he sent off his note to Pearson, he probably
realized that the Spear family visit was in its fifth day and the house would
soon be free of his grandchildren. That morning he wrote "rather well"
for the first time since their coming on *How Green the Grass* and the next
morning prepared his story "Playthings" for mailing to Chambrun. (Four
days later he would learn that his agent could not market the story because
it was "too grim.") The following morning in a burst of relief at being
alone with Eleanor again, he began one story and finished another, "We
Little Children of the Arts." The first third of this piece is a memoir of
some of the nameless inhabitants of such Chicago rooming houses as Anderson's 735 Cass Street, people who yearn to create great art yet fail for
lack of talent or of perseverance; the last two-thirds is the story of big,
rough Ben, married and with children, who goes on a Sunday painting excursion into the countryside with two other painters and the narrator. Enraged by his inability to paint a field right, Ben smashes his easel, throws
his canvas and brushes into the grass, heads with the others for the evening
train into the city, then runs back to pick up the brushes for his next attempt, successful or unsuccessful, to create art, a conclusion perhaps
replicating Anderson's own series of failures before getting "Death in the
Woods" right. He was "feeling tops" after finishing this tale, ready for
more congenial house guests.[28]

Letty Esherick was first, but what she really wanted was for him to tell
her to leave Wharton. Then on September 5 Paul Rosenfeld came for ten
days of mainly the usual walking and talking. In the midst of his visit Tom
Wolfe arrived for an overnight stay, filling the house with his "gigantic"
six feet six inch frame, booming voice, and "flood of talk." After spending a day with Wolfe, Sherwood assessed him as "generous and big, in every
way, but a good deal the great child," though in letters to Perkins, whom
he knew Wolfe was leaving, he praised the writer as having "tremendeous
gifts" and being "quality." Eleanor could not decide whether he was "a
great one of the earth or a gigantic adolescent—gusto he has and warmth

and so American." More metaphorically Paul declared that "Sherwood is like the people of the U.S. and Wolfe the soil." Paul's own departure was marred when, during a pleasant dinner Laura Lu insisted on giving Sherwood for his sixty-first birthday on September 13, Paul attacked workers as uneducable and Sherwood attacked him furiously. The parting of the two old friends the next day was strained.[29]

From then on, by chance, the stream of guests dried up, rather to the relief of Eleanor, who was continuing to find it a constant strain to run the house with only the unskilled help of John Sullivan's daughter Ruby. Besides, the weather was getting too chilly for Sherwood to write in his cabin even with a fire in the fireplace. He had worked occasionally on *How Green the Grass,* and he wrote to Perkins on September 9 that he had "seventy or eighty thousand words down and it keeps prancing along. I think of it," he explained,

as a novel without a purpose not intended to reform anyone or make any new world . . . just the story of a rather shy little man and his half amusing, half tragic adventures. Most of the time as I write I sit giggling.

When Max asked if it would be ready for spring publication, he admitted that he thought probably not; and in fact on the eighteenth he told Eleanor that the novel's characters had "suddenly left him" and he must "let them rest." He started three or four short pieces but completed none. Since he seemed temporarily adrift, Eleanor began going through his great mass of unfinished or unsold manuscripts, searching for pieces to revise, found an old speech titled "The Younger Generation," with her mother "did [it] over," and sent it off as wholly his to the *Richmond Times-Dispatch,* which published it as the lead article in its October 3 Sunday Magazine Section. Whichever of the three wrote most of the opening half, presumably Sherwood, provided one of the best summaries of his concept of American historical development: first, the period of exploration and settlement; next, the Industrial Revolution; third, the present age, "a time of pause" when Americans are beginning to understand that they have become the servants of the machine, not the masters, and so must make a tool of it rather than be made a tool by it. The second half of the article, on what the younger generation must do, is often eloquent with, surely, Anderson's form of poetry.

Can you tell me that Mark Twain when he wrote "Huckleberry Finn" did not love life? How otherwise did the wind, the sun and the rain get into that book? The whole book is a song, an American song. It is full of slanting rains, starry nights, the silk-like wash of the Mississippi River cutting its way down through our American Middle Western empire.

But this second half is also too often disorganized by Andersonian false starts and repetitions that Eleanor and Laura Lu should have cut and re-arranged. The message is of a piece, however. The next generation, by which Anderson actually means its artists, must refuse to cheapen their work for profits and must become craftsmen, true workmen in "the materials of American life . . . the American scene, the American speech, the American customs"; for, "To be a good workman, a good craftsman is the only thing in the world that I know anything about that is worth striving for." Still, refurbished old work is not as good as new, and Anderson continued unsettled in direction.[30]

Such a state of indecision might help explain something curious. Nowhere in his diary entries for September or thereafter does he refer to the publication on September 9 of *Plays: Winesburg and Others* or to any review, favorable or unfavorable, of the last book he was to publish through Scribner's. If, as probable, Max sent him a clipping of the first review, in the *San Francisco Chronicle* for September 5, he could well have been depressed by its beginning: "Of late Sherwood Anderson hasn't been writing with his old time prolixity, so the more rabid members of his cult—and their number has diminished appreciably—will no doubt be cheered with this collection of his plays. Calm onlookers, however. . . ." Many reviews were short, a few hardly more than notices, and not until the end of October did the first of two reviews in New York newspapers appear. Walter Pritchard Eaton's completely negative one in the *Herald Tribune Books* blamed Anderson's "inexperience with the dramatic medium"; on the other hand, Peter Monro Jack in the *New York Times Book Review,* which did not appear until November 14, found that the "interestingly dramatized" *Winesburg* "retains the taste of a small town in Ohio," though the "sketches," Anderson's two short plays, are "slight and unimportant." At least half the reviews were on the whole favorable, some southern newspapers—the *Richmond Times-Dispatch,* the *Raleigh News,* and the *Durham Herald*—strongly so. The only reviewer in a magazine, *Theatre Arts Monthly,* liked the short plays but complained of the "dislocated and bedraggled" structure of *Winesburg* and of the characters, who "rant and rave in a bold and frequently embarrassing manner." Understandably, the total number of reviews for *Plays* was much smaller than that for *Kit Brandon,* but the relatively small number of them was another sign that Anderson's popularity had indeed "diminished appreciably."[31]

He did receive a kind of consolation prize as dramatist at this time. Back on April 19, he had received a telegram from Lucile Charles saying that *Textiles* was much liked and she would inform him just as soon as CBS gave final approval. Around the first of May, she sent out an undated seven-page mimeographed "Bulletin To All Friends," stating that CBS would be airing on May 9 only the first of the projected series of six *Land of Plenty* radio plays, Irwin Shaw's "Supply and Demand," on Food; meanwhile she would be trying to persuade CBS to air another and then another. Her only other communication to Anderson was a handwritten letter dated November 29 explaining that the rest of the series had, to her dismay, been definitely canceled. Two months earlier, however, he had already noted his prize, this one in his diary for October 5: "My short radio play is to be in a book." And there it is, *Textiles: A Play for the Radio,* the opening piece in William Kozlenko's *Contemporary One-Act Plays: Radio Plays, Folk Plays, Social Plays* (Scribner's, 1938), a play reaching a far smaller audience than the one a CBS presentation in the summer of 1937 could have reached, but reachable permanently.[32]

5.

Summer was ending. The Andersons spent nights and work-mornings at Rosemont and went out to Ripshin afternoons. After the characters of his novel "left" him, he started several short stories but finished none, occasionally worked at pieces for the future memoirs, or wrote letters. After Bob had proudly told him that he had been asked to be president of the state's conservative Young Democrats, Sherwood, upset by his son's desire for political power, firmly wrote rather than told him that "Power is a disease Bob. Don't let yourself think Bob that there is any real family honor to be got by the road of Virginia organization politics." For Bob to take that road would "Mean the building of a kind of spiritual wall between [son and father], a kind of spiritual divorce." He wrote entirely differently, encouragingly to Wolfe, who had taken, as he expressed it to his son, "the only possible road, for the modern man . . . to try to chuck all of this surface stuff and to try instead to do, as well and beautifully as he can, the more simple job before him." Gratefully, Wolfe responded with a characteristically long letter agreeing that, as Anderson had suggested, he did indeed throw himself fully into both life experiences and writing. Now that he was leaving Scribner's as publisher, he had to find another since he was simply "starving for publication." He concluded with enormous praise for Anderson, not as in any way an influence on him, "save in the ways in which it has enriched my life, and my knowledge of my country."

I think you are one of the most important writers of this country, that you plowed another deep furrow in the American earth, revealed to us another beauty that we knew was there but that no one else had spoken. I think of you with Whitman and with Twain—that is, with men who have seen America with a poet's vision, and with a poetic vision of life—which to my mind is the only way actually it can be seen.

311

Expressed in terms Anderson would have thought appropriate for his poet self, it was welcome homage to him in his uncertainty of directions.[33]

On September 15 he had received a letter from John Paul Cullen, a student at the Boulder Writers' Conference and an employee in the Veterans Administration in Washington, generously offering assistance in his application for an increase in his twenty-dollar-a-month Spanish-American War pension, a matter that would take up a certain amount of time and correspondence over some weeks, beginning with a prompt letter of thanks to Cullen and visits to two doctors for physical examinations. During many of his afternoons at Ripshin toward the end of September and the beginning of October he painted the inside walls of the refurbished guest houses or watched John Sullivan and a crew strip off the leaky old wood shingle roof of the house and replace it with green composition shingles. On October 13, he and Eleanor drove into North Carolina in his newly purchased Dodge, she to Durham on a Y assignment, he to Chapel Hill for long talks with Paul Green. They returned to Marion in time for a last trip to Ripshin on the seventeenth before leaving together in the Dodge the next day for the "East," by which, as usual, he meant New York. Stopping for a day in Washington, they visited John Cullen, and Sherwood, as Cullen had assured him he could, was officially examined by several doctors at a government hospital in preparation for a possible pension increase. Then they drove on to Hedgerow, where Eleanor took the train for New York and Sherwood stayed over to see the company "beautifully" perform Shaw's *Misalliance* and to talk happily with the players far into the night in a display of their "adoration" for him which, Eleanor was convinced, made Jap jealous. On October 21 the Andersons were settled in together at "54."[34]

After two or three days of heavy gloom, during which he decided that the themes he had been working on were not for him "true themes," he turned again to his "Book of Days" (the *Memoirs*) and immediately began putting in many good mornings on "Pick Your War," his experiences as a soldier. On the morning of November 4, "Days" led him into making a first draft of a short story, "Not Sixteen," which, he thought, might or might not fit into the long work. Still working mainly on "Pick Your War" for three weeks, he finished revising the story on November 27 and mailed it to Laura Lu for fair copying, an arrangement indicating that he had not returned to dictating to a stenographer. It is easy to see how, as he wrote Laura Lu, he "ran on into the story while writing the adventures in the Spanish War"; for though he dates the tale as just after World War I, he transfers to his young protagonist John much of his own early experiences. As a youth, John has been a swipe for a trotting horse and caught "the race-horse bug." Later he enlists in the AEF, not in order to be a "hero" but to escape a factory job he detests and to see "strange places." Returning from the war to his Michigan small town—he later wanders to Ohio for the major event of the tale—he and his fellows have the parade, the banquet, and the praise as heroes that Sherwood and his had setting off to war. Anderson had been writing of how his going deprived Stella, now that their mother had died, of the share of his warehouse wages she needed to bring up his two younger brothers; John has brought back some money he has won in crap games during the war but does not share it with his likewise burdened sister. Both men briefly feel guilty, but John wants to save his money for the education he, like Sherwood, is certain he must have as a "ladder" out of life as a workman "with his feet in the mud." Both young men envision themselves as a prosperous businessman, "a man risen in the world, money in pocket, good clothes to wear." John rides freight cars from town to town looking for work, as Sherwood had done before his war, and, having used up his money, takes a job on an Ohio farm as Sherwood did in the summer after Cuba.

At this point the John-Sherwood similarities change in nature, become more an inward resemblance, and add a new dimension to what has clearly become a story. On the farm lives Lillian, a frank, pretty, passionate fifteen-year-old girl who may or may not have some origin in Bertha Baynes, the young girl Sherwood had loved but turned from when marching with his company through the Clyde crowd. Despite John's and her physical attraction for each other, she insists, as in the story's opening scene, that she will not marry or have sex with him until she is sixteen, when she will do both in either order. She likes best to have him hold her and talk to her, and what he tells her has echoes of Anderson the author. After cutting corn with her in a field and putting it into shocks, he points out how the shocks stand in silent, orderly rows like drawn-up soldiers, both corn shocks and human ranks long being symbols of order for Anderson; the dry leaves racing across the open field are like "living things running along," not unlike the dancing leaves in "Brothers"; and when John talks, he, like Anderson in the *Memoirs,* cannot "tell what, of all he told her, was real and what invented." His repeated urgings for sex, however, she meets with the reiteration "When I'm sixteen" until the refrain becomes for him a "wall." She can wait; he cannot. One night he simply walks away from the farm, proudly assuring himself that "I have controlled myself"; though it is she who controlled him, and dismissing her with the final thought, "After all, she is not sixteen," a rejection paralleling Sherwood's of Bertha and George Willard's of Louise Trunnion at the end of "Nobody Knows." As Anderson repeatedly insisted, the storyteller must be honest with his characters, especially those who are dishonest with themselves. He was honest with his art, too, for despite the John-Sherwood similarities, he decided that "Not Sixteen" did not fit into "Days" and sent the fair copy to Chambrun to be marketed as a story.[35]

Even before he went back to work on his "Book of Days," Anderson as usual began looking up New York friends and acquaintances. One of the first was Chambrun, who told him again that his stories could now be sold to the big circulation magazines since these wanted to include a younger audience and hence like *Redbook* must have some "class," and who on December 3 would write him that he had sold "Ah, There's the Rub" to *Photoplay Magazine* for $150. (*Photoplay*'s editor would change that title to "Listen, Hollywood!") Together Sherwood and Eleanor went out to Westport to admire Karl's just completed mural for a Bedford, Ohio, government building and were excited to learn from him how much Charles Burchfield's painting had been affected by his discovery of *Winesburg, Ohio* back in 1919. Both Andersons wished that Viking would bring out a special edition of the book with Burchfield illustrations, a project Sherwood would unsuccessfully urge on Huebsch just before leaving the city in late December. He several times lunched or had drinks with Max Perkins, who told him stories about Tom Wolfe, Hemingway, and others, and on November 6, he noted in his diary, he and Tom spent a long afternoon at the Brevoort happily drinking and talking in "a story telling bout." At other times he saw such friends as Rosenfeld, Stieglitz, O'Keeffe, and Dreiser; and twice he lunched with an admirer, Edward Dahlberg, novelist and essayist, the two talking nonstop about literature and writing. Years later Dahlberg still remembered Anderson's insistence that Americans were the loneliest people in the world. His most unexpected meeting with an old friend was with William Faulkner. In mid-October, Faulkner came to New York to talk over his affairs with Random House, stayed on at the Algonquin, began drinking heavily; one drunken night, as Joseph Blotner described the event in his *Faulkner,* he burned his back seriously on a bathroom steampipe and collapsed on the floor of his room, where he was found by a friend, Eric J. ("Jim") Devine, who brought in a doctor to treat him. Asked by Devine on November 7 whom he might like to see, Faulkner replied, "Joel Sayre or Sherwood Anderson."

Devine could not find Sayre but reached Anderson, who soon appeared. Sitting down at Faulkner's bedside, he began to talk in his easy way. To Devine he seemed quiet and soft, almost saintlike. What the doctor had not been able to understand [—why Faulkner drank so heavily—] presented no problem whatever to this other storyteller. Anderson was warm and solicitous, but he made no mention of his one-time protégé's illness; he was just visiting.[36]

Since Devine had definitely gotten Faulkner back to Oxford, Mississippi, by train by November 10, it is at first curious, then puzzling, then ultimately very revealing that in his diary entry for this date, immediately following "Worked O.K.," Anderson writes of visiting Faulkner and of bringing in a doctor and a nurse for him, and also that in a November 11 letter to Laura Lu he expands that entry, dating the visit "yesterday" (November 10), naming the doctor "Dr. Joe" (his friend, Dr. Joseph Girsdansky), and stating that Faulkner may be sent off to Oxford "today." It would seem certain that the storyteller was already in diary and letter trying out a section for "days" and fictionalizing the facts of an event that had occurred only three days earlier. The fictionalizing about himself and Faulkner did not end there. About three and a half months later, on February 25, 1938, during a productive period for what he would now begin calling "the memoirs," he wrote "Faulkner and Hemingway" with its conclusion describing how, as with Hemingway, he did not again see Faulkner "for years" after some to him inexplicable break between them. So,

... when, after a good many years, I was, one day, in New York, at a cocktail party and saw Faulkner there, I avoided him.

"It will be better," I thought, but presently, as I did not approach the man, he came to me. He took hold of my coat sleeve and pulled me aside. He grinned.

"Sherwood, what the hell is the matter with you? Do you think that I am also a Hemy?" he asked.

It's a good ending, but an invented one. Quite possibly Faulkner had made some such remark to Anderson during his visit out of gratitude for his coming; but the record shows no meeting of the two men at a cocktail party in New York, certainly not, as has been suggested, between Anderson's arrival there on October 21 and November 7, the only cocktail party noted in Anderson's diary for that period being one given on November 1 by Eleanor for "mostly her radical friends." Indeed, there is no indication in a diary, correspondence, or other record of any event at which both men were present after their break in New Orleans early in 1926, none except for the Southern Writers' Meeting of October 23–24, 1931, after which Anderson commented only disparagingly to Laura Lu on Faulkner's drunkenness without any suggestion of some conciliatory remark from him, something Anderson would surely have mentioned to her. As for Faulkner's reference in his 1953 "Sherwood Anderson: An Appreciation" to one final meeting with Anderson at "a cocktail party in New York," the best explanation for the conclusion to this article—in which he had just created the impression that Anderson had not read a word of the typescript of *Soldiers' Pay*—is that he had read, or reread, "Faulkner and Hemingway" and adopted Anderson's fiction as a device for paying homage to him as "a giant in an earth populated to a great—too great—extent by pygmies, even if he did make but the two or perhaps three gestures commensurate with gianthood." So storytellers tell stories because they are storytellers, and the not-unexpected revelation of this apparent digression in the Anderson manner is that in writing nonsequentially the episodes to be collected as the *Memoirs,* Anderson drew on remembered and misremembered fact but also actively on the truth of the imagination and, as with his transformation of private visit into public reconciliation, the truth of the heart.[37]

6.

By the time he began fictionalizing his visit to Faulkner, he had received two pieces of good news from John Cullen at the Veterans Administration. Although both John and he had hoped that his pension would be increased to fifty dollars a month, it at least was to be raised to thirty-five, and his various physical exams in Washington had proved him to be, as Cullen put it, "too damned healthy for your age," sixty-one—pulse, blood pressure, heart normal; pyorrhea, which he should have checked; astigmatism and presbyopia corrected to normal vision by his glasses; no sign of sinus infection. He was "in excellent shape." In good spirits he left New York on November 11 to add lecture fees to pension increase, spent the evening happily at Hedgerow, drove on to Philadelphia the next day, admired a Daumier exhibit at the Art Museum, and that evening spoke "OK" at the Academy of Music on "The Obligations of the Writer" before a small audience. Joined by Eleanor, he drove to Baltimore, where at Mazy and Channing Wilson's home he learned, by telegram, that John and his Eleanore were married. Late in the afternoon of the thirteenth, his own Eleanor took a train for a week's Y conference in Chicago and he took one for Charleston, South Carolina. After three mornings spent in his hotel room improving his lecture on Realism and then talking and dining with Josephine Pinckney, a poet and novelist he had liked at the Southern Writers' Conference, he gave the lecture successfully the night of the sixteenth before a large turnout of the South Carolina Poetry Society. Then, after a three day vacation-visit at James Boyd's estate in Southern Pines, during which Jim took him to see some beautiful horses, he returned by train to Baltimore, met Eleanor's train from Chicago and Washington, and on November 23 drove with her back to New York and "54."[38]

Mary Emmett had returned from a European tour on the day Anderson left for Philadelphia, and with her also at "54" the social life of the Andersons became a seemingly endless round of going out to lunches, cocktail parties, dinners, evening events. The three saw Joseph Holland and Orson Welles in a modern dress version of *Julius Caesar,* which Anderson noted as "extraordinarily vivid and alive. The best show I have seen for years"; but he had some reservations about Steinbeck's *Of Mice and Men* and Clifford Odets's *Golden Boy.* He fairly often relaxed by going to sports events; within a few weeks he watched boxing, football, a horse sale (twice), ice hockey, and a six-day bicycle race. Since there had already been telephone calls and other morning interruptions at "54," he had, on the day of his visit to Faulkner, engaged a room for his morning work at the nearby Broadway Central Hotel below Eighth Street, to which he had been brought by a Jewish poet he met accidentally in the street. The hotel was an old, inexpensive, "very very Jewish . . . really wonderful place," he wrote Mims Phillips. "Think of a place where the hotel clerks begin to talk with you about one of your stories and where the manager comes shyly to you and asks you if he may send his son to have a conversation with you." He was "quite in love with the place."[39]

The morning after his return from his lectures, he first worked there and the next morning, Thanksgiving Day. The third morning, the twenty-sixth, he wrote "The Writer and the Woman," which he sent unsuccessfully to Chambrun and which would appear in the *Memoirs* as "Woman at Night" (1969, pages 449–50). Prompted by a letter from an admirer, Carrow DeVries, who had written of his preference for sleeping apart from his wife, this brief lyric piece celebrates watching his sleeping wife, an instance, as he explained to DeVries, of his theory that beauty in women must be "fed" by the male imagination. He liked the piece so much that he sent a copy that same day to Laura Lu, explaining that "at present" he was "just letting myself go . . . am trying to put down, just as they come to me, impressions out of a life." Obviously he was continuing work on what he would shortly call his *Memoirs*.

I am really, Mother, trying to achieve a new looseness and a new reality of experience. How it will all come out I don't know. My thought is that I will just let the thing flow, as it seems to be doing, and then later try to limit and arrange. There will be, in the end, an editorial job that I may try to get you to help me do.

The wonderfulness of the hotel seemed to be working, for on the fourth morning he completed "Not Sixteen." On the fifth, November 28, however, his attempt to revise "Pick Your War" did not go well, and he quickly slid into what, in his diary entry for December 4, he termed "one of my stale periods [when] I write and tear up. Nothing I do has any meaning. Such times are insane times." This particular time went on for about two weeks, the words not seeming "to march [and] a kind of flow, a cadence" not attainable; and when the cadence did begin to return during his last week in New York, most of his diary entries were of "some," not good, work.[40]

Just why he should have gone into writer's depression at this time is not clear—because "Pick Your War" had "gone quite dead" on him, because he was becoming fed up with the constant press of the city's social life, or/and some other reason. It could have been prolonged, however, by the destruction of a warm friendship. On the evening of December 1, the Andersons gave a dinner party at "54" for Mary, Tom Wolfe, Ella Winter

(Lincoln Steffens's widow), the Max Eastmans, and another couple. Wolfe, who had been agonizing over leaving Scribner's and drinking heavily, arrived, in Anderson's words, "late and, in many ways, ruined the dinner." At some point in the dinner occurred what Eleanor would call in her diary an "Incredible clash with Wolfe" and was apparently still so upset by that she broke off beginning an explanation in the middle of a sentence. Years later she would explain.

We were talking about the South, noting that when you were too liberal they never blamed you for the liberal sentiment or act, but found some extraneous point. Without thinking, I said to Tom that I had heard the week before in North Carolina that he was Jewish.

Enraged, Wolfe leaped up and began shouting at her that he was not Jewish and that she had no right to say so. Sherwood and some of the guests shouted back at him that he had no right to attack her and that by reacting so violently he was being anti-Semitic. Eventually the uproar calmed down, and at the end of the evening Tom hugged Eleanor and said, rather inappropriately, that he forgave her. Subsequently Sherwood, concerned for both his wife and his friend and also desirous of giving Mary an outlet for her "terrible energy," persuaded her to give a large cocktail party on the twenty-first, each guest to contribute two dollars to the support of the Loyalist government in Spain embattled by General Franco's fascist armies. He himself typed an invitation note to Dreiser on the fourteenth and telephoned, apparently on the same day, an invitation to Wolfe, who was then trying to decide on which new publisher's offer to accept, still drinking heavily, and from time to time brooding over Scribner's and over the Anderson dinner party. Because of the phone call to him, Anderson did not send off until the morning of the seventeenth a typed invitation beginning tactfully, "I do hope Tom you didn't take seriously the queer row we seemed to have got into that night at Mary's house," and ending, "Dreiser and a lot of others are coming and I hope you can come, as I'd like to see you again." In a handwritten afterthought he made another peace gesture, "Why not have dinner with us afterwards, at some nearby resturant." Unfortunately Wolfe did not receive the letter until well after lunch that day.[41]

Lunch for Anderson on December 17 must have seemed to him one of the strangest he had ever had. He had arranged to meet at the Hotel Brevoort at noon with, as he noted, "French newspaperwoman Miss Chaney," actually Claudine Chonez, who later wrote an extended account of her interview with him for *Les Nouvelles Littéraires*. Entering the dining room, he assumed that a woman sitting alone and apparently waiting for someone must be Chonez, sat down at her table, and, not at all surprised by her perfect English, patiently waited perhaps ten minutes for her to begin interviewing him. (Actually the woman was the artist wife of the Iowa poet Arthur Davison Ficke, whom he knew but not the wife.) When Chonez appeared, as she wrote, she recognized the *poëte* Anderson with his dreamy (*rêveurs*) eyes and robust body and clarified the misunderstanding. As Anderson burst into enormous laughter at his mistake, a young man came to the table, took him by the sleeve, and pulled him away— into, as Elizabeth Nowell's standard account has it, the hotel lobby. The young man was Wolfe, who had glimpsed Anderson by chance and now "'told him off,' saying that *Winesburg, Ohio* had meant something very important to him and his entire generation of writers, but that Anderson had 'failed them' in his later work . . . and that he was 'washed up.'" Wolfe ended his tirade by praising Anderson's early work "as the best writing that had been done in America in the twentieth century" and insisting that they must always remain friends. Anderson's private reaction was that Wolfe was "drunk and insulting." When he returned to the lunch table, his expression was so dark, and he so silent, that Chonez kept urging him to explain. Finally he told her that the man was

a young novelist, not yet known by the public, but with originality and an exceptional future. Unfortunately, the boy, as everyone knows, is losing himself through drink and girls. He comes to show me his terrible moral situation. I know him very little, but it is no less horrible, horrible to see a man of rare worth destroy himself with his own hands.

For the rest of the interview nothing really cheered Anderson up, but, chain-smoking, he answered her questions in detail: that his father was a born storyteller with a limitless imagination was the reason why he writes as he does; although Jacques Coupeau, and now Chonez, thought him a European, his roots and writing are imbedded in America; he always wants to understand and be fully open to life; he is not really a mystic but instead feels that the life of the imagination is more real than "real life," and he is fascinated by looking behind what is expressed for what is not expressed; he knows nothing at all about Freud or God. He thinks his greatest success was *The Triumph of the Egg,* "a collection of stories which tries to show the clumsy brotherhood of men, their clumsy ambitions also, and their failures." *A Story Teller's Story* was a success because it defends craftsmanship against standardization. The interview went on so long that he drove Chonez home.[42]

When Wolfe got back to the Hotel Chelsea later on the seventeenth, he found Anderson's invitation, regretted his tirade, and began writing a letter of explanation, apology, and self-defense, which he seems never to have mailed. On the morning of the eighteenth Anderson, hurt and angry, mailed a curt note to him:

When I wrote you yesterday, suggesting that you have dinner with me Tuesday evening, I had no notion how you felt. As you have expressed such a hearty desire to chuck our acquaintance—why not.

On the evening of the twenty-first, the guests to Mary's party filled "54." Anderson introduced Dorothy Parker to make another of what he thought effective pleas on Spain. Afterwards Sherwood, Eleanor, Mary, Karl, and Dreiser dined at a nearby restaurant; Wolfe of course was not with them. He and Anderson did not meet or correspond again.[43]

The Andersons with Mary headed for Marion by car on the twenty-third and arrived at Rosemont the following noon in time for Sherwood to be "much put out" as usual by the holiday preparations. As usual also he found it so "very hard . . . to get past the Christmas morning with the attempt to push back into childhood" that he was depressed and gloomy for three days. Recovered, he visited Bob and Mary, and for the first time in years saw Cornelia, "looking," he noted, "very well and very grey. It seems impossible that I ever lived with her." When 1937 wound down to its last day, he drove Eleanor to Knoxville for a conference on Camp Merrie-Wood, felt ill, got to bed early in their hotel room and, despite the New Year's Eve racket outside in the street, went to sleep.[44]

11

Going toward Pieces

1.

He celebrated the new year with an attack of intestinal flu, which kept him in the hotel room for two days "reading and running to the toilet." It was an unpleasant beginning of 1938, which despite happy interludes would have as unpleasant an ending for him as any year since 1929. After he and Eleanor returned to Marion, he worked half-heartedly at *How Green the Grass* and prepared to drive her to Chicago, where in mid-January she had to begin two heavy weeks of a difficult Y assignment. Leaving on the ninth, they reached Louisville without trouble; but the next day they ran into icy highways, saw two wrecks with three people killed, crept as far as Lebanon, Indiana, the place where they and Mary had given up driving through the blizzard two years earlier on the way to Chicago, left the Dodge in, to Anderson's wry amusement, the same garage where they had left Mary's Packard then, and went on by train. Chicago was gray and cold; Eleanor had to take a room many nights at the Palmer House in order to keep up with problems she gloomily feared would make her assignment a "dismal failure"; Sherwood, staying with the Sergels, sensed tensions in the family, which made him depressed and unable to advance the novel or even revise a short story he called "A Fast Woman." He did receive word from Chambrun that *Coronet* magazine had offered $150 ($135 to him) for "Virginia Country Squires," a very funny sketch of the since defunct system of informal country courts for trying misdemeanors. These courts were so well attended that they became "the theatre of the countryside," especially on the occasion when a known chicken thief, an artist in his trade, succeeds in getting off with a light jail sentence. Anderson visited friends in the city and went to numerous dinners and parties, at one of which a professor at the University of Chicago urged him, if he and Eleanor decided to go to Mexico, to visit the quiet town of Acapulco on the Pacific for fishing and a warm climate. Still he felt that he was wasting work time in Chicago. On the twenty-fifth, before Eleanor could leave, he told her that he didn't like the city's weather and, in her phrase, went "tearing off" by train for a visit to the Van Meiers in Stillwater, Minnesota, where the snow was drifted deep, roads were icy, and the temperature stood at ten below zero. The visit, however, invigorated him. He wrote a "good story" and spent much time following Dr. Henry on his rounds, being passed off by him to his patients as a doctor from New York. The conscientious Eleanor, certain that this assignment had been a "professional failure . . . one of the most definite I experienced," managed a two-day visit to Stillwater, after which she and Sherwood returned to Chicago on January 31.[1]

The next day they took a train back down to Lebanon, retrieved the Dodge, and headed south for somewhere in Mexico. They stayed two nights at the old Hotel Gayoso in Memphis, long enough to spend an evening walking in Beale Street, to pick up Laura Lu on her way to visit Randolph in San Antonio, and for Sherwood in the one morning to do "a story of the woman on the stairs—3,000 words reeled off." Driving south, the first day to Natchez, the second down the Natchez Trace to New Orleans, they put up at the Monteleone in time to go to a huge party "with the entire New Orleans crowd" at the Antony house. Although the party went on until 1 AM, he was up after a brief sleep and began writing, switching abruptly back to what he at last was beginning to call "the memoirs." This morning he wrote of his visit to San Quentin prison when in California in 1932 and the contrast he found between, on the one hand, two men convicted of a lethal bombing who had accepted their guilt and life sentences, had worked as capable mechanics in prison, and had remained intellectually alive to the point of reading books by Anderson and other current novelists. On the other hand, there was Tom Mooney, innocent, Anderson believed, of participating in another lethal bombing and so regarding himself as a martyr, who, dressed in a white suit with a flowing black tie, advanced on Anderson at their meeting "a bit [like a] bad actor" playing Napoleon and commanded him to drop whatever he was writing and become the American "Zola" for him, the "American Dreyfus." After the meeting Anderson raised the question whether Mooney's sense of outrage might have produced his self-dramatizing conduct; but by reiterating at the end of this piece the contrast between the warm, pleasant guilty men and the cold, self-obsessed innocent one, he leaves the latter merely diminished and finesses the sympathetic examination of psychic distortion, which one thinks of as typically Andersonian.[2]

After another evening party, the three left on February 7 for the two-day drive to San Antonio, where Sherwood rented a room in a separate hotel for an unbroken week of good writing mornings on "the memoirs." Afternoons and evenings he joined Eleanor and Laura Lu in socializing with Randolph and his fellow officers and wives. He was mildly aston-

ished to find the officers "very nice fellows," not eager for war but for adventure. "It is one of the puzzles of life," he wrote the Sergels, "that most
of the rather rotten things, like inventing poison gas and all the rest, is
probably done by perfectly nice and kindly people." He would not protest,
however, "all notion of really changing anyone rather gone out of me."
Surprisingly, when at the end of the visit the three went to see Randolph
take off on a long medical mission, Laura Lu, happy at having seen her
beloved son, was unperturbed about his flying and "brave" at his departure, while Eleanor, deeply affectionate toward her brother despite his
conservative views, was frightened by his flying and wept. The visit over, her
mother took the train for home and, as arranged, Mary Emmett arrived
with a friend, Winona Allen, who was still shaken by Mary's wild driving,
which had left her car needing major repairs. Traveling with Mary would
continue to be alternately exasperating and delightful for both Andersons,
and she never forgot the generous monthly "slip of paper," the check for
$125, especially welcome now that Sherwood had learned from Max Per-
kins that his income from Scribner's for 1937 had been only $260.16.[3]

Leaving San Antonio on February 16, the party of four in two cars
drove south into Mexico for three days via Monterrey to Mexico City, often through wild, always "the most magnificent," strange country, Anderson wrote Laura Lu, he had ever seen, with great mountain vistas, tiny
Indian villages where the agriculture was biblical in its primitiveness,
desert wells where women carried water jars on their heads like Rebecca
or huge packs on their backs like "pure beasts of burden." Mexico City
was much different. They settled in at the "very bourgeois, very comfortable" Hotel Geneve, 7A De Londres, where he and Eleanor had a roomy
parlor and bedroom for only ten pesos ($2.80) a day. At their first oppor-
tunity, all four went to a bullfight where eight bulls were to be killed, a
spectacle Eleanor found "horrible and beautiful." Both she and Sherwood
became absorbed in the technique of the matadors to put themselves in
maximum danger of death, yet escape and kill their bulls, but in the end
Sherwood decided that he preferred watching good baseball. Most mornings he worked in their parlor on parts of the memoirs, often so excited,
he told Mary, that he wrote two thousand words a day. (It was on the
morning of February 25 that he did the piece on Hemingway and Faulkner.)
Afternoons and evenings the four explored the city and surrounding towns,
which he much enjoyed, the city seeming to him lovely, the towns colorful;
and they were invited to lunch at the American Embassy by Ambassador
and Mrs. Josephus Daniels, an occasion both Andersons especially liked
because Daniels turned out to be a gifted storyteller. Nevertheless, Sherwood became increasingly restive at so much female, so little male, company, so much social life, so many well-off American tourists, so bourgeois
an atmosphere at the Geneve. Not knowing Spanish, he felt frustrated at

not being able to chat with ordinary Mexicans in the streets and the cafes. Then too, the altitude of well over 7,000 feet was making him, he complained, "high strung and nervous, unable to sleep." Abruptly on March 3 he decided that he and Eleanor must get away by themselves to quiet, sea-level Acapulco. The next day his decision to get away from it all was reinforced by his receipt of a letter from a lawyer representing Arthur Barton's widow threatening suit for his omitting Barton's name as co-author of *Winesburg, Ohio* in *Plays*. So "knocked out" by the letter that he could not sleep that night, he put the next morning into composing a long letter to Luise Sillcox at the Authors League, describing the whole history of his relationship with Barton. Eleanor had not been surprised at the lawyer's letter, for she had strenuously argued against the omission, which Roger Sergel had favored; but knowing her husband, she now resolved "in the future when I feel as strongly about anything as I did about this to have it down in writing so that S signs it to be sure he listened." For years after Sherwood's death, she would have to deal with what he called "one of the most unpleasant affairs I was ever in."[4]

Leaving Mexico City on March 7, the four and *Detroit News* reporter Sam Marshall found it "one hell of a job" to get through the spectacular mountain country in two days, what with two hundred miles of primitive road construction, breakdowns of Mary's poorly serviced car, and a couple of major rows between her and Sherwood about her bossiness and his refusal to stop in Taxco lest he run into Elizabeth and William Spratling, both now settled there. At the end of the bad road, however, was Acapulco, a "paradise" as he called it ecstatically. They put up at the El Mirador Hotel, a scattering of separate little houses high on a bluff among rocks and tropical trees and flowers overlooking the warm Pacific and its beaches. As soon as Mary, Winona, and Sam had left after two days for Mexico City, Sherwood and Eleanor relaxed into a blissful routine—breakfast at nine, writing for him until one, lunch and siesta, the beach from three to seven, dinner in the town at nine, sleep. Eleanor wrote her parents that except for the daytime heat, the place was "divine." Sherwood thrived on the heat, she noted; he "never has been so well, sinus gone for the first time since I knew him." He himself declared that his head felt clearer than it had for years. The one disappointment, which he felt sharply, was that John Emerson, who had written of joining him in Acapulco, could not come. Still, from the first morning at El Mirador, the words flowed freely from his hand into the memoirs. Then on the fourteenth and fifteenth he broke off to write a short story, "His Chest of Drawers," apparently prompted by a morning visit on the fourteenth to the Andersons' little house by an advertising man he had formerly known. Sherwood thought the story "beautiful," Eleanor, "a gem."[5]

Read without its background, "His Chest of Drawers" seems to be no more than an anecdote, presumably about that visitor, expanded into a mildly amusing tale. Beside the desk of the "I" narrator, an advertising copywriter, is that of another copywriter, a small, narrow-chested, self-deprecating man of Spanish descent. (Sherwood told Eleanor that the real man was actually Irish, but he was "disguising it so the man's family wouldn't know.") Married and with four daughters, this insignificant man frequently tells the narrator that women should be honored; and since in fact he has a small salary and lives in a small house, he confines his clothing to a single chest of drawers in order to give his family of women more closet space. When one day he does not appear at his desk, the narrator is sent to hunt him out and finds him drunk in a saloon, buying drinks for a group of men and "delivering a talk on the position of small men in a civilization that, as he said, judged everything by size." After the narrator sobers him up, the little man tells him of "a greater tragedy in [his] life" than being just an underpaid copywriter. Over several days the oldest daughter, about to be married, preempts the top drawer of his chest for her new clothing; his mother-in-law on a visit preempts the second drawer; and his wife's sister, also visiting, preempts the third, or rather, he admits since he must be fair to and respect women, his wife reserves half that drawer for him. So he gets drunk among men and addresses them as a way "he could get temporarily the illusion that he cut some figure in life."

The story is slight but sufficient for showing that Anderson was "disguising" more than his protagonist's nationality, was actually using the man to reveal the author hiding behind the apparently nonjudgmental narrator, himself surrounded by women who exasperated him yet must be treated with at least outward respect, women who press in on him, make him feel "obligated" to them, as Eleanor had observed in her diary concerning Mary and Winona—Winona "instead of proving a relief as S hoped is a drag," and Mary, whose "behavior . . . has been perfect" but who creates "strain" for the Andersons who must "drag her around [to social occasions] and explain who she is." These two are the immediate targets but also, one guesses, so are the women crowding Rosemont at Christmas or perhaps, more remotely, the audiences at women's clubs on Anderson's earlier lecture tours who irritated him into finally refusing to accept such engagements. By contrast, the protagonist's getting drunk with the men and talking to them masks Anderson's own desire to have male companions to talk with such as Andy Funk, or write his thoughts to such as Roger Sergel and Dreiser, or to request photographs of as he was beginning to cover the walls of a room with at Ripshin. Physically, of course, the broad-chested Anderson was the exact opposite of his narrow-chested protagonist; but opposites have their own congruence, and in what the little man talks about to the men he exactly parallels Anderson's growing insistence that now was the time to "think small," locally, individually rather than "large," nationally, in big generalizations. For the author to call this story "beautiful" was to use the word so oddly that it seems more likely he thought that, under disguise, he had "beautifully," perfectly, expressed his own state of mind. When Eleanor called the story "a gem," she almost certainly used the word in a similar way; for her diary entries show that, as with her comments on Mary and Winona, she clearly understood her husband's feelings, attitudes, and needs. As early as the third day after they registered at the Geneve, she noted that he was "Over fed with females." Two days later she wrote, almost prophetically of the tale, "S so hungry to talk to men [that he] enjoyed a few minutes with men in saloon." On February 25, Sherwood showed "determination to leave [Mexico City] to get away from 'too many females.'" When the telegram came from John Emerson on March 3 saying he would be in Acapulco on the seventeenth, "S very delighted." Then on March 13, with word that John would not be coming, the entry records a sudden connecting insight on Eleanor's part: Sherwood's "disappointment over John lets me see that mother was right in attributing S's nerves [at] Christmas to humiliation over too many women." Since his "Christmas psychosis" began long before he began displaying it at Rosemont, Laura Lu's word "humiliation" seems not fully adequate to explain his annual reaction, though the pressure of a "houseful" of women could and did exacerbate it. At any rate Eleanor had all the information and understanding she needed to see through the "disguising" of "His Chest of Drawers," to perceive what the chest stood for, and to grasp the whole fiction in its minor gemness.[6]

A second old friend appeared by chance in Acapulco. While the Andersons were at dinner at El Mirador, the night of March 15, Sherwood recognized William Spratling dining at a nearby table with another man, who turned out to be the young actor Mel Ferrer. According to Spratling's account, he and Ferrer decided to play a practical joke on Anderson. When Sherwood "rushed over to speak to him," as Eleanor recorded the incident, Bill baffled him by pretending to be Mexican and speaking Spanish. A few minutes later, however, he admitted his identity, greeted Sherwood warmly, spoke of being a "button manufacturer" in Taxco, and invited the Andersons for a sail the next day on his yacht now anchored in the Acapulco harbor. In Eleanor's account, Spratling "begged us to go to Taxco but S said he didn't want to see Elizabeth—that such an experience left a scar." Eleanor does not mention a day's sailing, and may not have gone along; but Sherwood records it, and Spratling, writing many years later and strongly on Elizabeth's side in the divorce, gives him a different response.

Sherwood, seminude and flabby, seemed to me suddenly very vulnerable and almost senile. However, he had the same mental exuberance as ever. As we lay there on the deck I said, "Sherwood, now that you're in Mexico . . . I can tell you

that Elizabeth still cares for you and it would give her great pleasure, heartfelt pleasure, if you would drop in and visit her there in Taxco for a few days . . . Elizabeth
would love it."

Sherwood looked out to sea and said, "Bill, I simply couldn't face it. After all,
I guess that was one time I behaved really badly." So that was that.[7]

On March 17, the day that John Emerson was to have arrived, the Andersons left Acapulco for Mexico City, Eleanor "very sad" at going, Sherwood reluctant but, in a characteristic attitude swing, worried about their
obligation to Mary. Because of the torn-up highway the return took them
nearly three days; but the last morning—it was March 19, the day after
President Cárdenas announced the nationalizing of the American and
British oil companies—they did stop at Taxco to have breakfast and walk
about the town, without seeing Elizabeth. By late afternoon they were
back at the Geneve. Almost sleepless for the three nights afterward because of the altitude, he could not work and was able only to send off "His
Chest of Drawers" to Chambrun. Although they were delighted by Cárdenas's act of Mexican economic independence and convinced that he was
supported by most of the Mexican people, they were uneasy about the rumors filling the city that gasoline soon might not be available. Since, also,
Eleanor had become increasingly worried and Sherwood desperate about
his sleeplessness, they decided to say goodbye again to Mary, who wished
to stay in the city, and to head north to Brownsville to be alone and to get
in some fishing during what remained of Eleanor's vacation. Leaving on
the twenty-second, they made the trip in three days, the only disappointment being getting to Monterrey too late on the second day to see the "gigantic parade of 50,000" labor supporters of Cárdenas. By the end of the
twenty-fourth they were through customs and comfortably settled once
more in Brownsville's little old Miller Hotel, where they could look through
a window of their two-room suite (two dollars a day, he wrote in an affectionate letter to Mary) "across the Rio Grande and into Mexico."[8]

The morning after their arrival Anderson was happily at work on a
story, "A Mexican Night," which Eleanor thought "delicious" but Chambrun would never be able to sell; and on subsequent busy mornings he wrote
two pieces for the memoirs, finished the story, and did a brief, concentrated
article he called "Mexican Impressions." Eventually appearing in the
Southern Literary Messenger for April, 1939 under the title "An Impression of Mexico—Its People," the piece summarizes Anderson's belief that
the future of Mexico probably lies, not with its "upper classes," but with
its Indians. Exploited, enslaved for generations, they are capable of savage
cruelty; yet through their enforced closeness to the earth they have gained
a dignity like that of the earth itself and an ability to "do without," both of
which have been lost in "our own complex civilization." Granted Anderson's

liking for the "primitive," the piece nevertheless indicates that he had not been the usual vacationer passing unobservantly through a strange land. But if his writing went well, the fishing did not, and on April 6 they drove on to Corpus Christi to their old place at Yacht Beach Court, where the fishing went only a little better and the writing went not at all. So on the eleventh they headed home, arriving in Marion on the fourteenth.[9]

2.

After spending three days catching up with correspondence and getting Eleanor to a train for the YWCA National Convention in Columbus, Ohio, Anderson faced up to a dental problem he had been "putting . . . off and off," as he wrote Mary—"a lot of jagged, bad teeth, in my lower jaw that I have to have out." On the eighteenth he had the bad teeth pulled and on the twentieth the remaining lower ones pulled in preparation for a plate; but although the dentist had given him a local anesthetic to block the pain he had long dreaded, he felt "knocked out" for days afterward, had trouble sleeping, and could record in his diary only occasional mornings of writing. Presumably he was working on personal recollections; for *How Green the Grass* was "about half done," he reported to Perkins at the editor's request about progress on a book, and in effect put aside, while he had written much during the winter on the memoirs but could not say when it would be finished. "It seems to be such a rich field that although I have written many thousand words I seem just at the beginning." He did not tell Perkins that he was filling in the time trout fishing, making preparations for the summer at Ripshin, talking by the hour with friends like Andy Funk and Laura Lu, and, once, going to a movie, Walt Disney's *Snow White*, which he unexpectedly declared "the 1st entirely satisfactory movie I've seen." Not unexpectedly of him, however, was his reason: "It is gorgeous fantasy."[10]

During the last two weeks of April and the first two of May he had three surprises, one pleasant, one distinctly unpleasant, one at first pleasant but eventually quite the opposite. The first came around April 23 when he discovered a nearly complete manuscript of *Winesburg, Ohio* that he had years earlier put into a box of other manuscripts and half forgotten about. Written in longhand and mostly in ink, though with two or three of the tales still in pencil, the manuscript appeared on the backs of the "print paper" sheets he had used when writing advertisements for Critchfield, the front sides having already been covered with sections of unfinished novels. Because most of the stories were in ink, he could write Sergel that the manuscript was "the last draft corrected for fair copy to go to a stenographer." One story in the sequence was missing, "Nobody Knows," although he found at least one other penciled copy (version?) of it, perhaps separate in the box; and in a May 1 letter to Mary, he requested that she send him yet another copy he had given Burt so that he could compare them for possible stages of writing. On May 5 he wrote Roger asking if he could get an estimate of the manuscript's worth; for it might be, he wrote pathetically to Mary, something to give Eleanor, he having "so little to leave her" at his death.[11]

For whatever reason he made no mention in his diary of finding the manuscript, but he did note on both May 7 and 8 the (for him) unpleasant surprise that Eleanor had been offered "a big job" in the YWCA administrative structure, and noted as well the cold, which probably in psychosomatic reaction sent him to bed for a few days afterward. The position was the headship of the Industrial Division of the National YWCA. In a letter to her on May 26, Sherwood outlined his objections to her accepting. They would have to live mostly in New York and in effect abandon Ripshin; the work requirements would be extremely demanding on her energy and time; it was essential that she remain physically close to her parents, who were aging and ill. As for his own feelings, he disliked the idea of living mainly in New York as contrary to his nature.

If it is true, dear, that there is, as you sometimes say when I am closest to you, when I am making love to you, that I am a poet, it is also true that I am a mystic. I can't figure on what will happen next year. I was, as a boy, in the country. Most of my life has been spent in the country or in small towns. More than I can say without sounding silly, I get something from the sky, the trees, the silence of country nights by which I live. I presume for me the city will always be connected in my mind with those years in business. I do not much like the present day intellectual and radical crowd with whom, in the city, we seem destined to be. They choke and kill something in me.

Although I have always, even though not much figuring on the future, managed to live, I can't naturally superimpose my point of view on you.

That is as near as I can say what I feel. I can't, naturally, ask you to take risks that any artist who remains alive must I guess take.

He did not in this letter, of course, comment on how much they depended on her salary, to be higher because of her increased responsibilities, especially since this year his writing was bringing in little money, nor on his wish to have her around for companionship afternoons and evenings after mornings at his writing, a conflict of needs that understandably often exasperated her, nor on her own need for career and service to society, though surely these concerns came up in their discussions about her decision. In July she accepted the offered position, and there began a subtle readjustment in their relation. To be with her, as he craved to be, he must accept and be limited by the demands of her occupation. In their small universe, where her star, as it were, had tended to circle around his, now they would be two stars circling each other.

The third surprise came in a May 12 letter from Chambrun, who wrote of suggesting to Edwin Balmer the possibility of an Anderson novelette for *Redbook* and of Balmer's enthusiasm about it. If Anderson would submit an outline of such a long story and its characters, Balmer would, if it was acceptable, "order" the story, which should not exceed thirteen thousand words, and would pay "between twelve and fifteen hundred dollars." Chambrun added that Balmer "feels that some sort of romance should be in the story, and of course the characters in this and the other large magazines are in what might be called 'moderate circumstances.'" Ordinarily the author of the epilogue to *A Story Teller's Story* might have turned the offer down promptly—"order" was certainly as commercial a term as possible—but since it had been so thin a year financially, he accepted. He did not get at the novelette at once. Eleanor was in New York during May, the spring was a rainy one and he did not want to stay at Ripshin, and he had things to do in Marion such as his two last visits to the dentist. (Chambrun wrote, on May 16, that Balmer, editor of *Redbook,* had turned down "His Chest of Drawers" on the grounds that "there wasn't quite enough to it.") On June 1 Eleanor returned in time for her and Funk to go with him to the little town of Ivanhoe, some fifty miles east into the mountains from Marion, where, as he wrote Mary, he "delivered the graduation address for the country boys and girls.

Am afraid my speech was quite contrary to what the superintendent and the others were telling them, they all telling them to work hard and succeed and me telling them not to go for success but to play a lot, try to get really acquainted with people, try to understand others etc.

After making Ripshin ready for the summer, he and Eleanor got settled there on June 5, and on the morning of the seventh he was in his writing cabin starting the novelette, which he called "A Late Spring." From reading or hearing him talk about his first day of writing, Eleanor was certain that he was naive to think the story fitted *Redbook*'s requirements, but he went on happily with the story and on the ninth quickly completed an outline, which she mailed to Chambrun stating that the story was already half completed. On the sixteenth the agent took the outline to Balmer; yet, as Sherwood wrote Karl, by this time "the people of the tale got out of hand, got completely away" from his outline and from what Balmer wanted, and he thought he might be heading for a novel. Chambrun reported on June 30 that Balmer and his associates considered the outline to be "rather gloomy," by which time, however, Anderson would reply that he had "probably written about 20 or 25 thousand words," well over Balmer's limit. He was now asking Funk for information about law school, since "A Late Spring" had turned into "a long story about a country boy, of a very poor family, who became a lawyer and finally a judge," along the way, he would later tell Max Perkins, "trying to learn to live, to get belief in himself, to feel himself a man with a man's right to live." The artist in Anderson had won out over the lure of popular success; though the winning would have its consequences.[12]

That summer Eleanor went with another YW administrator to her annual week-long Conference of Southern Industrial Girls at Camp Merrie-Wood near Sapphire, North Carolina, while Sherwood stayed at Ripshin writing at "A Late Spring" fairly steadily, painting the woodwork of his cabin, and longing for her, especially at night. When she returned on June 30, they had two days at Ripshin before setting off together by car on July 3 for her next assignment, a Business and Industrial Girls Conference at a Y camp on Okoboji Lake near the town of Milford in the northwest corner of Iowa. Going by way of Cincinnati for the first day and on the second to Michigan City for dinner at Ferdinand Schevill's home at Duneland Beach, they had a long drive on a torrid third day around Chicago to Milford, where, weary, they found a pleasant cottage by the lake. Sherwood loved the countryside with its low hills, big prosperous farms, broad cornfields, and beautiful lake filled with fish he had no luck in catching; and it inspired him, as he would write Max Perkins, into wondering why a writer wants to write. Since Eleanor was at the conference from seven in the morning until near midnight most days of the week with a hour off for a late afternoon swim at the cottage, Sherwood worked "furiously," detouring from "A Late Spring" into a long essay on that question as a kind of introduction to the novel and finishing on the thirteenth, the last day of the conference, before speaking briefly on Mexico to the participants. The next day he and Eleanor started on a return southern route, stopping along the way in Kentucky at Owensboro to renew old friendship with his former advertising client, W. A. Steele, and at Louisville where another friend, Mark Etheridge, publisher of the *Louisville Courier-Journal,* took them to a party of millionaires, whom, Sherwood noted, he had "a good time shocking." Barely back to Ripshin again, Eleanor left on July 19 for a short visit to New York where he knew she would accept the Industrial Department headship, he, as he put it, "wanting her not to work but knowing he could not support her."[13]

Abruptly the next day he decided that telling "A Late Spring" in the form of letters written by his protagonist to a boyhood friend was "too cumbersome," and he began the novel all over again, telling it now, he explained to Perkins, "straight out." For the rest of July and well into August he kept at the novel most mornings; on August 5 he not only "advanced the novel" but also wrote a draft of a short story first titled "The Writer" and ultimately "Pastoral," all this work accomplished despite the usual parade of visitors, mostly welcome ones. It began on July 24 when Eleanor returned from the decisive New York visit in a huge second-hand Rolls-Royce driven by its proud owner, Bill Stewart, the managing editor of *Today* whom Anderson had worked with while doing the articles that became *Puzzled America.* When Bill and his wife Bern left after five days of walking, talking, and driving about, Sherwood noted that they were "Very satisfactory guests." On August 7, the recently married Lewis and Nancy Galantière arrived for a two-week visit during which Mary Emmett also appeared and promptly went to work with her usual energy rebuilding and planting the Ripshin flower beds. Nancy was both beautiful and intelligent, and the diminutive Lewis was as brilliant a talker as he had been when Anderson saw him in Paris in 1921; both Andersons felt that they were two of the finest guests they had ever had, a real tribute, since toward the end of their stay Sherwood went suddenly if briefly from delight to despair with his writing.[14]

On August 18, he spent the whole morning happily drafting a long letter about writing to George Freitag, a young Ohio writer, a piece linked both to the introduction to "A Late Spring" and the "Writer's Book" he would soon suggest to Perkins as a "text-book" for young writers, but would never finish. Drawing largely on his own early career as a storyteller, he restated in the letter's final form, sometimes ramblingly, often eloquently, his long-held convictions. He had wanted to write, he told Freitag, not the "nice little packages" demanded by fiction editors of the big commercial magazines, but rather "simple little tales of happenings, things observed and felt," finding his "milieu [in] common everyday American lives." Believing that really "what was most wanted by all people was love, understanding," he wrote, not for success, money, acclaim, but "to develop . . . my own capacity to feel, see, taste, smell, hear. I wanted, as all men must want, to be a free man, proud of my own manhood, always more and more aware of earth, people, streets, houses, towns, cities. I wanted to take all into myself, digest what I could." But when he wrote the stories of *Winesburg, Ohio,* some critics asserted that they were not stories or—the old conviction again—condemned the book as unclean. The young writer must not blame publishers for being the businessmen they are, but instead remember that "if you are by nature a teller of tales, the realization that by faking, trying to give people what they think they want, you are in danger of dulling and in the end quite destroying what may be your own road into life." Anderson was so elated by his morning's work that Eleanor recorded the moment in her diary.

S came up from his cabin this morning wistful and in a glow. "Why couldn't everything like this last so perfectly. He was working well, liked the people etc.—but of
course everything has to end. Why can't we hold the now?"

Yet August 19, Anderson himself recorded, was "A bright clear cool day
but a day of utter gloom and misery for me—the novel at which I was at
work seeming suddenly to fall to pieces under my hand." (Eleanor's only
entry was "Novel went to pieces.") He was so sunk in depression that
evening that when John came to show him new paintings, he "could see
nothing." Unable to face the 350 completed pages of manuscript during
the last two days of the Galantières' visit, he bounced back from depression enough on August 22 to start the novel all over again from the beginning for, counting the earlier Okoboji introduction, the fourth time. A
week later, on the twenty-ninth he happily noted in his diary, "I found a
new form for the book—returning to the Winesburg form"; and on September 7 he cheerfully wrote Perkins that he was going back to this arrangement of individual stories bound together into a whole. He felt "curiously
at ease in the form," he told Perkins. "It seems to relate itself to life as I
feel it." (Writing to Sergel of his reverting to the *Winesburg* form of "really a novel," he became possessive: "I invented it. It was mine.") Clearly,
however, this "new angle" of approach was producing a new novel. Now
his theme was "American men, in relation to their women and now the
title I have got for the book is 'MEN AND THEIR WOMEN.'" He was
"taking a related group of people, their lives touching, never quite touching, what they do to each other, the growth of missunderstandings." (How
uncertain he was about the direction of his novel is suggested by his hand-
print in ink: the "miss" in that final word over the original crossed-out word
"men's.") The conclusion of this letter to Perkins was the proposal of the
new kind of college textbook, one that unlike the usual college professor's
book of sample writings would, like the letter to Freitag, draw from his
own experience to describe "the life of the writer, what difficulties the
young writer has to face, what the real rewards are for the writer. . . ."[15]
    Briefly Anderson was full of confidence in his new group of tales. Dur-
ing the first week of September he completed two of them while much of
the time also entertaining a young writer, Millen Brand, whose novel,
The Outward Room, had been published the previous year and who was
grateful to Anderson for "'opening up' writing to him." Sherwood found
him honest and talented but also slow and boring. On the day he finished
a first draft of the third tale, September 10, his old friends Ferdinand
Schevill and Robert Morss Lovett arrived for a week of pleasant walks,
fine talk, fine croquet, and the celebration at Rosemont of his sixty-second
birthday. An indelible mark of his aging was the immediate cause that in
the following two days, while Ferdinand and Robert were still at Ripshin,

he faltered with the tales, then stopped completely, then predictably spent half of each of the subsequent two days in bed with a cold. Schevill left on the seventeenth, and after Lovett's departure on the eighteenth, Anderson ominously took his emotional pulse in his diary: "Very blue all day, hated the coming of the summer's end . . . Life seemed to be closing in on me. . . ." On the twenty-second he touched bottom: "Sunk deeply into the blues—the black dog constantly on my back, hating the summer's end, feeling my own inefficiency. It seems to me that I have done nothing."[16]

The underlying reasons for his descending into the acute, enveloping pain of depression are obvious and interlocking. By taking "A Late Spring" out of the constricting *Redbook* frame of novelette into a potential novel, he had followed his artistic impulse, but even after this fourth beginning the novel was not going anywhere. Not only had that impulse failed, sufficient reason for discouragement, but he had also lost the large payment offered. This money would have given him the satisfaction of knowing that his work was still salable and, much more important, might have persuaded Eleanor that she need not accept "the heavy job" of directorship, which, aware of the emotionally damaging effect of her job on her husband, she in part dreaded. Both felt all too strongly that summer was ending and they must leave the farm they both loved, especially Sherwood, who disliking New York had come to feel more and more that he was a "countryman." There could be no long summer vacations together at Ripshin after this one, he feared. Possibly, though one suspects Anderson of exaggeration because of his hatred for his father, memories of childhood may have made autumn a melancholy season for him. Eleanor noted in her diary: "S very blue, says he thinks its the fall when he remembers each year his father going off and leaving his mother with no money for food or anything." Certainly one event coming at the end of this summer did affect him sharply. On the sixteenth he learned that Thomas Wolfe had died the day before in Johns Hopkins Hospital in Baltimore, and he was, as Eleanor put it, "terribly cut up" by the news. "I was terribly upset by Tom's illness and death," he wrote Perkins. "The loss to literature is just a bitter fact. It hurts. We don't get many in Tom's class." He did not go to the funeral, he confessed, because he hated funerals. He did not tell Max that for him the death of the man who had once said that he was through as a writer was a step downward into depression. He could not have known that, with intermittent days of relief, this attack by the black dog would be one of his worst since 1929.[17]

3.

As the last days of summer and the first of autumn went by, Anderson carefully noted daily whether or not he had worked in the morning. A writer, he would tell one correspondent, "only really lives when he is writing," and he was really living only infrequently. On a dark rainy September 29 he wrote too long in his chilly cabin, walked too long in the rain, probably brooding over Eleanor's impending departure, and caught so bad a cold that he soon went to Marion to recover. He was still sick in bed when she left for New York on October 2 to take up her new position. After a week more of illness and no work he drove to Ripshin through beautiful fall weather for a final visit and on the thirteenth left for Hedgerow, where Eleanor joined him for a weekend of seeing plays and talking to all hours with Jap and the actors. Driving to New York and "54" on the sixteenth, he was unable to work for a week, being, one "terribly depressing day— sunk in deep gloom . . . The sun was shining but I was all black inside." Soon he was admitting to Eleanor in a letter that he was "really in a bad state," blamed himself for living off her and Mary, could not "produce the glamorous stuff now wanted." (He had recently had from Chambrun the discouraging news that *Household Magazine* would pay only $75—$67.50 to him—for "His Chest of Drawers.") His letter ended abjectly, "I am like a child clinging to you and want rather to be a man, standing on my own feet with something to give. My darling."[18]

Slowly he began working, "living," again, and on the twenty-ninth he recorded that "I have begun to come out of my bad time, one of the worst I was ever in." He even started a new long story and took it with him when, on November 2, he drove to Niagara Falls, where Eleanor had preceded him by a day in order to attend a weeklong Y conference. She had registered for them both at the Cataract House overlooking the rapids below the falls, so old a hotel that a placard outside their room announced it had been occupied in 1857 by Mr. and Mrs. Abraham Lincoln. He was amused by having breakfast "in solemn splendor" in the four-hundred-seat dining room alone, it being out of season, except for two bowlegged waitresses. He was not amused but resigned that, as he told Mary, Cornelia had written of Mimi and Russell's losing the *Messenger,* the newspaper they had contracted to buy in Madison, North Carolina, unless they could come up with a final payment of nine hundred dollars. Cornelia would pay half that amount if he would pay the other half, and he felt he in fairness must; so he must go on accepting the monthly $125 check from Mary. "I know now," he wrote her on November 3,

that I shall probably never make much money. I missed my chance. I had the one successful book, *Dark Laughter,* that built my house and, had I been wise, should have pushed success. It is the way it is done. I should have played literary politics, having written a book that sold, I should have written another in the same tone, should have quit experimenting.

I didn't. I couldn't. Because I couldn't I missed the great opportunity. It is too late now. I have gone too far on another road, can only try and keep trying to find something better, more honest, more real.

He was "quite cheerful about it," however. The weather was warm and beautiful day after day at Niagara Falls, and he happily worked hours daily on the long story—until the last day of the conference when the weather turned rainy and cold, the blues descended on him again, and he became discouraged with his work. Returning with Eleanor to New York on November 9, he daily forced himself to do his morning stint on the long story, "chucking" that for another tale and many days recording his work as "ineffectual." Not surprisingly, such a feeling of ineffectuality carried over into his perceived relationship with Eleanor. "I find myself," he wrote Sergel in mid-November, "more and more, I'm afraid, in the position of the man who has no very definite place in the scheme of things, while his wife keeps taking on more and more responsibilities." In their small universe he seemed now to be the lesser star circling around her greater one.[19]

Despite being a countryman and a depressed one, he was readily sharing in the pleasures of the city. He saw old and new friends—Max Perkins, Paul Rosenfeld several times, the Galantières, brother Karl, "old Stieglitz," who was exhibiting John Marin's recent paintings, O'Keeffe, who had the Andersons to tea, his admirer Edward Dahlberg, Paul Green, visiting New York, and, also visiting, Marco Morrow, companion from advertising days. Frequently the Andersons were invited to cocktail parties or dinners, most of which he seemed to enjoy; and when Dreiser was about to move to Los Angeles, Sherwood, Eleanor, and Mary gave him a big farewell cocktail party and afterwards dined with him and O'Keeffe. "It was an evening of good fun," he recorded. His writing had gone "better" that morning, too. Quite often he, with the busy Eleanor or someone else, went to plays, which he usually assessed in his diary—Orson Welles's revival of Georg Büchner's *Danton's Death* (Anderson lunched with Welles, liked him, asked Perkins to send him a copy of *Plays*); John Stokes's *Oscar Wilde* (Anderson did not accept that Wilde was "a great man"); Clare Boothe's *Kiss the Boys Goodbye* ("the last word in the rather tiresome wise-cracking style"); Maurice Evans's uncut *Hamlet* (which he mostly liked); Robert Sherwood's *Abe Lincoln in Illinois* (at first "a fine thing . . . but later fell to pieces"). As often, he found spectator sports a release, especially the newly popular, extremely fast Basque court game of jai alai, which he delighted in as "very beautiful" and took others to watch. On Thanksgiving Day, as in the year before, he went to the Old Glory Horse Auction at Squadron "A" Armory, where he thrilled to the many beautiful yearling trotters and pacers, and added impressions for "Here They Come," an article celebrating harness racing he would write about a year later.[20]

Through much of November, however, such diversions could not keep his mind for long off his "ineffectual" writing and his lack of success in publishing profitably. After many failed attempts to place "Two Lovers" with large circulation magazines, Chambrun finally sold it to Whit Burnett's *Story* for the usual $25 ($22.50 to Anderson) but still had several unsold Anderson pieces on his hands. Developments in Nazi Germany in this year of European crisis also troubled Anderson deeply and, for a while, reinforced his depression. Although he seems not to have commented in writing specifically on the forced incorporation of Austria into the German Reich the previous April, or on Neville Chamberlain's acceding at the Munich Conference in September to Hitler's demand for the annexation of the Sudentenland part of Czechoslovakia, he was certainly aware generally of Nazi aggression and opposed it, wryly suggesting to Sergel on November 1 that his long depression might come from his being "allergic to Hitler, to the ugly thing going on so rapidly, apparently growing." Wholly serious was his condemnation of totalitarianism in his letters as brutal, savage, driven by nationalistic hatred; equally serious was his belief that "Democracy is man's only hope." The event that appears to have shocked him most profoundly, however, was the infamous *Kristallnacht* of November 9–10 when, at the instigation of the Nazi government, mobs in German and Austrian cities wrecked and looted Jewish homes, businesses, and synagogues, killed nearly a hundred Jews, and injured hundreds, after which "night of crystal" (glass from broken windows) new repressive measures were carried out against Jews. Appalled by reports of the event and by "this horrible anti-Jewish feeling run over the world," he declared to a correspondent in mid-November that "The thing makes it impossible to work." Optimistically he declared that "Germany has now, I'm sure, overreached itself"; yet he wondered "how long it can go on—I mean the dominance of hate as a motive for action in the world." Sharing in the widespread outcry against the abuse of the Jews, in mid-November he suggested to Sergel and wrote about it to Eleanor Roosevelt, "a new movement for the protection of our democracy," best led by women, a "kind of world's Gentile committee against totalitarianism," Jews to be excluded in order, as he put it elsewhere, "to show the world that others besides the Jews are interested in putting down race hatred."[21]

Perhaps being shocked into "thinking big" instead of "small," of the single individual as he preferred, helped him to begin turning outward from depression's obsession with "self," that disease as he thought it. At any rate, when he drove to the Hedgerow on November 30, had a "long real visit" with Jap, and was joined there by Eleanor, his mood changed abruptly. His diary entry for December 2 was almost lyrical, as though he had risen well from a sickbed. "Worked beautifully—the Great Man theme—W. F." (Very likely the initials were those of Waldo Frank, whom years before Anderson and Rosenfeld thought overly concerned to be recognized as a Great Man.) The evening's play he saw was "very stirring and fine. I was full of my new theme and very alive all day." Back at "54" on the fifth with "Many ideas in my head about the new book," he wrote for ten days straight, eight of which he recorded some variant of "good morning of work." Exuberantly he wrote Laura Lu on the fourteenth that "I seem to be really at work again," since he may have found the form he had been "feeling for . . . a loose flow." Very likely he was encouraged by receiving a December 7 invitation from Joseph Brewer, president of Olivet College in Olivet, Michigan, to spend some part of the winter term at the college as a writer in residence. On the twelfth he accepted the invitation, suggesting three weeks in January at the "modest" (the delighted Brewer's term) salary of three hundred dollars and "necessary expenses." He accepted, he wrote Mary, quite flatly because he could "make a little money." Even after he and Eleanor had returned to Marion for a Christmas break, he spent most mornings writing well. On the night before Christmas, Rosemont was, he noted, "a hubbub," but the holiday itself disturbed him less than usual, for he had found the way to deal with the problem: "Much Xmas fuss in the house," he recorded in his diary, "but I stayed in my room at work." Then his writing streak broke. December 26: "Work—not very effectual—off wrong. Work to be chucked," and the next morning was "no good." For three days out of the four left in 1938 he managed to work fairly well, even started another section of the "Great Man" novel; but he would never finish the book; in fact, he never worked at it again after the last day of that brief spurt. It was one more failure in a year marked by failures. He had not exactly gone to pieces in 1938, but he had spent a good deal of time and effort going in that direction.[22]

12

A Sort of Rescue

1.

At least he was not ill New Year's Eve and Day as the year before. On January 4 he started by car toward Olivet and a new experience, recollecting old ones as he drove north through Ohio. In Athens he dined the next day with Helen Dinsmoor and her parents, Helen needing help from him in preparing one of the growing number of master's theses on him, hers being on his life and its relation to his writings. In Springfield he went to City Hospital to call on Trillena White, his longtime "great friend . . . the first person to really introduce me to literature," who was now "condemned to death of [stomach] cancer." He was much shaken, he wrote Eleanor in New York, to see her "suffering constantly but doing the job nobly." (She would outlive him by two months.) In Clyde he spent an evening with Herman and Jennie Hurd. Herman, his best boyhood friend, had grown "broad and fat and 60," he told Laura Lu, but remained solid and honest, "a very lovable, shrewd, capable man of no pretensions for whom I have a great affection." Although the town had changed little, he was still shaken by the visit to Trillena and was saddened to learn that three-fourths of the townspeople he asked the Hurds about had died. On the eighth, he drove into the pleasantly wooded village of Olivet (population 500) in south-central Michigan and located the small campus, shaded by oaks and maples on a hill overlooking the community. He was to stay at President Brewer's home. Probably at a faculty reception that evening he found out that he now held the title of Resident Lecturer in Creative Literature.[1]

Olivet, then a coeducational college with three hundred students, had been a conservative Congregationalist institution until the lively minded Brewer became president in 1934 and began introducing such progressive programs as a summer Writers' Conference and an artist- and writer-in-residence designed to develop in all the students an awareness, as he had written Anderson, "of the function of the arts and the artist in society, but

339

particularly in present day society." Anderson had known that he was replacing the English writer Ford Madox Ford (on campus part of 1937–38)
and had in fact been recommended by him. The day after the reception he
arranged for a room in the college library in which he could write undisturbed mornings "experimenting," he told Paul Cullen vaguely, "trying
to get at something I want." He learned that he would have his meals in
the Commons in Dole Hall, the women's dormitory, and soon settled his
teaching program. Two afternoons a week he would be available in his office to talk with any student interested in writing, twice a week he would
hold a one-hour class, once a week he would give an evening lecture open
to all students, and he would give a one-time public speech to which
townspeople would be invited. Unfortunately, he did not prepare his first
evening lecture, on contemporary literature, and was so chagrinned by not
doing well that he wrote out his later ones so that when he gave his next
week's lecture, on "Personalities," his large student audience "seemed to
enjoy it." Although he liked seeing individual students—he spent a whole
afternoon with one Carrow DeVries, a nonstudent officer in the state highway patrol—he especially liked talking and drinking to all hours on free
evenings with male faculty members from various departments. "While
underpaid and overworked," he wrote Mary, they "are fine fellows and
sincerely interested in education." In his diary he noted, "There is good
talk and good company here."[2]

Still feeling that he had been too much surrounded by women, he saw
a great deal of three young bachelors who rented a house in town: George
Rickey, the artist in residence, Charles Parkinson, biology teacher, and
Glenn Gosling of the English Department, with whom he became best acquainted. Two decades later, Gosling remembered Anderson vividly as
plump, though not fat; he customarily wore handsome, rather dark Harris tweeds with bright-colored socks and necktie; he generally rose at five
thirty or six in the mornings and wrote until ten or ten thirty, at which time
he liked to go down to the village and talk with farmers and the townspeople about crops and the like. The people he talked with still remembered him years later. Easy to get along with, "vital . . . the sort of person
who seemed capable of living forever," he delighted in telling funny stories out of his experience. Gosling recalled that one of his favorite tales

was of meeting Ford Madox Ford in Paris at a party and of being given Ford's routine. At each meeting at the party Ford would say to Sherwood, "So you're a writer.
I always like to help young writers. Now I have a winter home in Florida that I
don't use. You're welcome to go there to live at your convenience." Next time it
was a summer home in Maine, then an apartment in New York, then two other
things. Finally Sherwood asked someone what was up, and the person replied:
"Oh, Ford's a writer just like you and doesn't have a damned nickel either."

(In his later "Legacies of Ford Madox Ford," Anderson elaborated on the story with Ford's own elaboration on the view from his house in Pennsylvania with its staff of servants whom he had not discharged, Anderson's understanding finally being that Ford "was a man who lived in a splendid world, created in his own splendid imagination, and the world he had created was gloriously real to him.") Other writers, Chekhov and George Borrow, he praised to Gosling highly, very highly. What he liked about Borrow, he told the young man, was his "just writing along casually about people he had run into and talked with." After Anderson had gone back to New York, he picked up at a secondhand bookshop *The Romany Rye* and *Lavengro* and sent them to Gosling, who years later still had them in his bookcase.[3]

Life at Olivet was so satisfying that by the end of his second week he was considering the possibility of teaching at some college for the whole school year regularly as, he told Laura Lu, "the answer for E and me." He had been particularly encouraged by the reception of his public address the night of the twentieth to a packed audience of students and people from all over the region. In "A Writer's Conception of Realism" he announced to his listeners that he did not know what reality was since his and everyone's "touch with life [was] influenced by our imaginations." Drawing as usual on elements of his own experience and as usual in no chronological order, he described his "nights of faces," the procession of faces that in his "half dream state . . . seem to snap into place before my eyes," each face as though imploring him to tell its story and—the apparent digression preparing for a point he would insist on later—each face that of an individual he had actually seen. Then sketching the influences that made him want to be a writer, he spoke of his early admiration for his father's skill as a storyteller—the author of *Windy McPherson's Son* had long since singled out that one "quality" in his father for praise—and spoke also of his departure from business as caused by "a particular reason," the realization that in the "accumulation of possessions" he was losing a sense of the richness of the imagined world. To try to enter other people's lives through the imagination as the writer does, he told his audience, is enriching for anyone, for it takes one out of one's self, makes life more interesting. So in his roundabout way Anderson drew his listeners to the points of his announced subject. For the writer, he insisted, the "Life of the imagination will always remain separated from the life of reality"; yet paradoxically, "the imagination must constantly feed upon reality or starve." And yet to attempt to restrict one's self to realism, to be "the writer with a notebook in his hand," is to distrust one's own imagination and to produce bad art. "The life of reality," Anderson concluded, "is confused, disorderly, almost always without apparent purpose, whereas in the artist's imaginative life there is purpose. There is determination to give the tale, the song, the painting, form—to make it true and real to the theme, not to life." So, Anderson had declared, the faces which appeared to him at night were those of real, observed individuals, but their stories came from his imagination and followed its demands. Likewise his account of the influences which made him a writer had its contour in reality, but, as he knew, it was highly selective yet, as he hoped, would lead his listeners to his conclusions. As in many of his stories, the apparent rambling of his lecture had its aesthetic as well as its explanatory purpose.[4]

Despite a touch of the flu, during which he finished rereading *Moby-Dick,* his last days at Olivet were busy. He gave an "anti-Fascist," pro-democracy speech to a meeting of men's clubs in nearby Battle Creek and an account of running his papers at a state convention of newspapermen at Lansing; but he had much "good talk" with students and faculty members. An appreciative Brewer soon wrote him that "Your being here meant more to the kids than you will ever know, and to the rest of us." For Anderson, his three weeks stay at Olivet had been a stimulating experience; he would have agreed with a student who subsequently declared that "under the presidency of Joseph Brewer, Olivet College had an extraordinary life as a center of education in the arts." Even before he left on the twenty-eighth, he readily agreed to teach at another of the president's innovations, the Olivet summer Writers' Conference.[5]

From Olivet he went on to Springfield, Ohio, for another visit with Trillena White and then to nearby Yellow Springs where he spent three days, again as a self-styled "college professor," at Antioch College. Since he had been invited there as one in a series of writers speaking on "the writer in the political world of 'today,'" his long talk on the evening of the thirty-first, which he had written out and, he thought, "went well," probably argued against "thinking big" and advised the practice of writing down one's thoughts and experiences as a way of getting to understand other people and their problems. As at Olivet he was happiest talking with faculty members and students, and he was pleased to find that at both colleges the students were generally more disillusioned about the drive for success in the world than his generation had been. As he responded to both faculty and students, they responded to him. Fifteen years later Jessie Treichler, assistant to the college president, recalled, "All of us remember Mr. Anderson's visit vividly—he was a joy to have on campus for the three days he was here." Again, as at Olivet, he seemed to himself "to open out," as he had written Eleanor; perhaps a regular appointment for him at a college could give them "a life together."[6]

On February 2 he began a two-day drive to Philadelphia, where he picked up Eleanor for a visit to Hedgerow, and on the fifth they were back in New York at Mary's townhouse. The following day he reached a conclusion significant enough to enter in his diary: "I have come to a deter-

mination to get away from my present situation as soon as possible."
While still feeling "opened out" at Olivet, he had succinctly explained that
situation in a letter to Eleanor.

As when you first knew me, I find that I have been drawing more and more within
myself. It is, darling, partly because of the Mary arrangement that is not, at bottom, sound. As it has turned out, it is you now who are constantly meeting and as-
sociating with people while I am in some way shut out.

Alert to her husband's moods and what lay behind them, Eleanor seems to
have made a special effort throughout February to please him, to spend as
much time with him as her work allowed, to make him feel included. As
usual he found most solace in his writing.[7]

Very likely sparked by his speech to the newspapermen at Lansing, he
began on the seventh an account of running the Marion newspapers and,
as he noted, "Enjoyed it." Working off and on, he finished it on the fifteenth and put it aside temporarily for final revision. One can see why he
enjoyed writing it. Whatever "How I Ran a Small-Town Newspaper" may
lack in factual information, it is one of the liveliest, most amusing, most
imaginative of his articles. The first half describes the circumstances of his
purchasing the papers and poses the problem of how through them he,
both newcomer and writer, could become an accepted member of the community despite its suspicion that he was really just looking for fictional
material. Neatly reversing the argument of his public lecture, that the
writer takes persons from real life and lets his imagination play over them,
he straight-facedly explains that, since he could not afford to hire a reporter, he invented Buck Fever, who through his reports "presently became in the minds and imaginations of the readers of my papers . . . I'm
sure, a pretty good sample of a high-grade mountain boy . . . a distinct
character in the town life [whose] adventures in life took place right in the
streets of the town." Further, Anderson found that Buck could say things
about townspeople he as editor could not, even make fun of them just as
long as nothing he reported would "rob any man of his self-respect." Buck
did give him trouble, however, for this star reporter—here Anderson writes
as though Buck *were* a real person—kept wanting a salary raise, but the
editor refused to give it to him lest he fall into town ways. But it "wasn't
all play," for "we"—Buck, the invented Mrs. Homing Pigeon, and "even"
the editor—went after the filthy jail and made the townspeople so conscious of it that they had it cleaned up. The great triumph of the trio was
to make the vacant lot eyesore outside the print shop into a park by simply
assuming that the park was actually there for people to stroll or rest in until
the fact that it was not there "became unendurable" to the townspeople

and they made the park a reality. So the real became the imagined, the imagined, real. Moral: a country newspaper should not go in for "big thinking," but instead encourage the use of the imagination in "our daily lives."[8]

The solace of good writing did not continue, however. For two mornings after finishing the newspaper article, he searched unsuccessfully for a theme, and after dining with a friend and his family, all "full of flu," he went to bed on the eighteenth with an attack of it so serious that for most of two weeks he was in bed, Eleanor coming down with it badly too. When the fever allowed, he read—Kipling's *Kim* ("too damn British") and Matthew Josephson's *Zola and His Times*—and brooded over his "situation," made even worse by his request, for income tax purposes, of the total amounts of payments for his writing in 1938. Scribner's reported $251.53 and Chambrun $224, for a combined year's total of only $475.53. Slowly recovering from the flu but still weak, he sent off his newspaper article to the agent in hopes of better sales in 1939 and decided to escape from his "situation" by taking the winter break in a warm climate he had become accustomed to. He chose New Orleans, where two experimental novels had poured from him with little or no block; he would be surrounded by long-admiring friends, and he might be able to show the city to his closest friends at Olivet, Glenn Gosling and Charles Parkinson, who were considering a spring vacation trip to New Orleans. Weak and very despondent, he set off by car on March 7, bypassing Hedgerow, and spending the night in a Washington hotel, where he wrote an abject letter to Eleanor, apologizing for "running away" while she still had the flu and with her mother coming to visit. He "had to."

It has been very hard for me this year. I have seen you working harder and harder, showering presents and money on me and, in the midst of this, it has been for me, as you must know, a time of absolute ineffectualness. The only time for a year now that I have felt a little useful in life was the few weeks up there at Olivet.

Mary's kindness, Eleanor's working too hard, his own living expensively "beyond what I deserve"—the "whole set-up" was hard for him. His love for her, he assured Eleanor, was "the most real thing left in my life"; it was simply that at this "cross-roads" he "wanted to be by myself, think if I can—try to face what I am and why." In self-abasement, he added a note: "I hated asking you to attend to the income tax but was too horribly ashamed that I had earned nothing." Momentarily he had again touched bottom.[9]

Although he felt weak and sick the next day, driving south through endless sunny days cheered him, and by the time he reached Mobile, he was well enough to stop there to write successfully for two mornings and to revisit Fairhope. On the twelfth, he drove into New Orleans and took a corner room on the tenth floor of the Monteleone with a wide view of the river and the French Quarter, as he told Eleanor in a newsy, perfectly "normal" letter. The next morning he "worked at top speed until 1 PM" and most mornings of the remaining eight days of his stay worked steadily, probably at this time writing, revising, typing up, and sending to Chambrun a short piece, an "editorial," titled "I Live a Dozen Lives." Drawing from his Olivet and Antioch lectures, he argued against "big thinking" and instead for the proper use of the imagination to lead one out of one's self and into the lives of the many others around one, thus enriching one's own life and gradually increasing "understanding of men by man." The rest of the time he was seeing old friends and the new ones, the "Olivet crowd," which turned out to be Glenn; Laura Marshall, his wife-to-be who taught physical education; and another couple. Years later the Goslings would nostalgically recall how Sherwood in great spirits "took charge of them" during the whole of their four-day visit—coffee at the coffee houses, lunches, dinners, the sights of the city, get-togethers with his New Orleans friends. They remembered how he took the four of them to an elaborate dinner "with gardenias in fingerbowls" at James and Dorothy Feibleman's new elegant house just decorated by Marc Antony "in the modern style" with chartreuse color throughout. At dinner Sherwood demonstrated how one could shake up a bottle of fizz water with thumb on the neck. Unfortunately his thumb slipped, and water sprayed all over one wall, just missing a huge Rivera original, an eight-foot section of a mural on canvas. Although the Feiblemans were upset but tried to pass it off, Sherwood was "not in the least perturbed." Fortunately the Antonys arrived and assured everyone that the water would dry right off and wouldn't stain the wall. That was the evening of March 16. In the afternoon of the eighteenth, the Olivet crowd's last day in the city, Lucile Antony and her sister Elma Godchaux joined Sherwood and his friends for a drive in two carloads up the river to the town of Reserve to see the big refinery at the Godchaux family's enormous sugar plantation. Glenn, who drove one car, recalled how Sherwood, driving the lead one with Laura in his group, would from time to time stick his hand out the window, whereupon both cars would drive up onto the levee so that Sherwood could look at the river, then down again onto the country road. At the plantation Sherwood announced that first they should go up to the big house, unused but kept staffed with black servants, for drinks. The party sat around drinking planter's punches until near sunset and never did get to the refinery. Then they drove back to the city, everyone including Sherwood singing all the way. That evening he had a farewell dinner with the Olivet crowd.[10]

2.

As soon as the four had left, taking away his Olivet feeling of belonging, a morning cough he had developed turned bad; and for his last two days in New Orleans he stayed in his room too ill to work, cut down on his excessive smoking, and, depressed, suddenly decided to leave the city. On the twenty-second he headed home via Vicksburg and Knoxville, feeling stronger and better as he drove. Reaching Marion on the twenty-fifth, he felt even better after reading Chambrun's March 23 telegram reporting that the *American Magazine* had purchased his newspaper article for four hundred dollars ($360 for him). Characteristically feeling wealthy, he traded in his old car and bought a new Dodge as a surprise for Eleanor. He was pleased also to find in his mail a handsomely printed and bound copy of *Five Poems,* a reprint of five from *Mid-American Chants,* just published by Quercus Press of San Mateo, California, which he sent to Mary Emmett to show to Burt's friend Elmer Adler, an expert in fine printing. Furthermore, Chambrun soon wrote that Balmer of *Redbook* still very much wanted to have an Anderson novelette in the magazine. After two mornings of "no good" work, he began writing well. When Eleanor arrived home on April 1 in a heavy rain, she found him in the best of moods.[11]

Between April 3 and 7, happy to be with her, he drove Eleanor on a YWCA mission to three North Carolina cities, where he worked well in their hotel rooms. One day he began, he noted cryptically, "a really dangerous story that I have always wanted to do," saw and liked a Marx Brothers movie, and went to all baseball games within reach. During their brief return to Marion he struggled one morning at his desk to write a useful response to a young correspondent who had described his desperate reactions to his homosexuality, one of which was deep depression. Pointing out that many other people, including himself, had periods of depression, he urged the young man to talk openly with his father, if possible, about his "perversion," as Anderson "presumed it is" because it "does strike at the source of life," and to deal with depression in the only way he himself knew, by finding "some work that may absorb you." Although Anderson apologized that his response was "so inadequate," it was highly sympathetic, entirely opposed to the "ugly" reaction of the so-called normal man. When the man replied that it was impossible to talk with his father, Anderson responded that were he his father, he would "stand by" him; that considering the many letters he received from troubled young people, the man must not consider himself "abnormal"; that "I guess morality is outside sex, outside everything but work"; and that for what it was worth he offered the young man "friendship." Considering the ugly homophobia pervading American society then, and to a somewhat less extent even now, the real life response of the author of "Hands" was as sensitive, understanding, and enlightened as his fiction.[12]

After driving Eleanor to a mission in Tennessee, Anderson stayed in Marion while she prepared to go off to Nashville alone. April 15 was an exciting day for them both. Word came from Chambrun that *American Magazine* had purchased his editorial "I Live a Dozen Lives," for the unexpectedly high price for its short length of three hundred dollars—in less than a month Anderson's income just from this magazine was a third higher than in all of 1938—and a letter from the agent arrived with the news that the editor of the *Reader's Digest*, DeWitt Wallace, had "a very keen desire" to have from Anderson a two-thousand-word article to be titled "The Most Unforgettable Character I Have Ever Known." Chambrun had persuaded Wallace to offer the unusually high price of fifteen hundred dollars if the article was accepted. That same morning Anderson returned for his unforgettable character to a tale, "The Writer," he had first drafted the previous August and now retitled "The Letter Writer," about a doctor who over the years writes many letters to a woman but never sends them. Working "intensively" that day and "passionately from 9 to 2 PM." the next, he completed a new draft, feeling then so "high and tense" that he got into the new Dodge and just drove until he was relaxed. Two days after his "big splashy" April 16, he again wrote so intensely that in the evening he picked up Andy Funk and drove for hours on country roads. On the twenty-second he put the final touches on what he was convinced was a "fine" story.[13]

This simply written, meaningful story, which in its final form would be published in *Redbook* under the title "Pastoral," is indeed a fine one. An advertising writer, the tale's first-person narrator, makes extended visits to a town to work up advertising for a manufacturer there and becomes acquainted with a local doctor through their mutual admiration for "an old and little read author" (George Borrow perhaps). The doctor, a small man, is highly skilled and liked by the townspeople; he rarely speaks to anyone and even when he looks directly at his patients seems not to see them. Taking the narrator with him for his round of patients, he is usually silent but reveals his intense love of nature by giving learned lectures, without looking at his passenger, on some unusual bird or wildflower or mushroom he sees. By contrast he is married to an outgoing, handsome woman, a civic leader without interest in nature, supports her and their two daughters in style, and has provided for them financially after his death. Having always "found it difficult to make a direct contact with people," he often spends his evenings alone in his office where he carries on a "secret life." After he dies, his lawyer finds in the office safe some two hundred letters addressed, but not sent, to "a small and a seemingly rather colorless woman" whom the doctor had frequently seen going to work as a clerk in a drugstore across the street. The lawyer calls in the narrator that evening to look at the letters, which not only show the doctor's love of nature but also reveal in their many "tales of people" that he had actually been "a close observer of others." The letters even have "a kind of hidden poetry," which moves the two readers, but they decide to burn them. Afterwards the two go to the drugstore, where they see the woman talking gaily to the customers. The narrator, however, glimpses her concealed for a moment from the customers whereupon she becomes "a figure expressing infinite weariness" and then goes back to them in her gay manner. He and the lawyer go out into the empty street, look into each other's eyes "much as the doctor had always looked at people," and part.[14]

That he should have written this story so "passionately" that he had to bring himself down from a "high" afterwards suggests there were other impulses at work besides his usual exhilaration from creativity. One impulse might be that the tale was bringing into unstated but clear relationship some of his firmest convictions: the profound difference between the outer and the inner self; the isolation of human beings, especially Americans; the capacity of the imagination to begin with a close observation of reality and thus lead one out of one's self into the understanding of others. It is through his imagination that the "unseeing" but actually seeing doctor writes tales about his patients; the narrator elevates his glimpse of the "rather colorless" woman's "figure" into generalization of an art work, so he and the lawyer can look into each other's eyes and presumably penetrate momentarily each other's secret life. Indeed, Anderson was not an ideologue, but a storyteller aware of ambiguities. The imagination's work may be only momentary or may fail, the individual lapsing back into isolation. The doctor does not mail his letters, and they are destroyed; the woman, whose inner life could well have been enriched by them, resumes her mask of gaiety; the narrator only *thinks* he and the lawyer see as the doctor would see, and in that *Winesburg*-like setting of night in an empty street they say good night and go their separate ways. And yet the narrator does remember the unforgettable character and tell his story.

A second impulse behind the story was that, though hardly a happy tale, Anderson was writing it out of a flood of happy memories of his several visits to Owensboro to lay out advertising programs for W. A. Steele, as the narrator of "The Letter Writer" does for a nameless manufacturer in a nameless town. His first visit had been in mid-May 1919, immediately after the publication of *Winesburg, Ohio,* that "classic" by which he knew two decades later he would best be remembered. Remembering his jubilation at that time, he could celebrate his book by making the doctor's secret tales about the men and women of a town told with "a kind of hidden poetry" a condensed description of *Winesburg.* Nearly twenty years later, he thought fondly enough of Steele to have taken Eleanor to visit his old friend on July 16, 1938, and just three weeks later, on August 5, he drafted "The Writer." When Steele wrote him of his pleasure in this visit, Anderson replied, "Indeed Mr. Steele I do not remember the particular story of which you speak but do remember the trips we used to take together . . . and how I used to love to come there." In "The Letter Writer," of course, the narrator and the doctor take trips together, though the latter is hardly the conversationalist Steele was; but there is some evidence that obliquely suggests that a doctor with at least such outward behavior may have lived in Owensboro. Whether Anderson met this "unforgettable character" or was told about him by Steele can not be known and is irrelevant anyway. What is relevant is that when he was writing his tale, Anderson was immersed in memories, which he knew were helping to bring out all his talent. It should be no surprise that on the happy morning when he decided to turn "The Writer" into "The Letter Writer," he started the day by editing a manuscript sent him by Steele's daughter Phyllis. The flood of memories had begun again.[15]

Then, of course, there was the impulse of the money offered. His payment, $1,350, would be more than twice the income already received from the two *American Magazine* pieces, and the total would already be a sizable increase over the humiliatingly small income for the previous year. He again seems not have been concerned that his present income was from the mass circulation magazines he had attacked through much of his career, though he justifiably felt that in such a story as "The Letter Writer" he was not compromising his art. Probably even more than the money itself was its psychological effect. The *Digest* offer and his response to it would wipe out, or at least offset, the lost chance of last year when the novella requested by Balmer of *Redbook* turned into a novel that he could not finish, a failure damaging to his self-confidence about writing and his relation to Eleanor. Now his confidence in himself about both was being restored.

3.

Back in February he had refused to be concerned at being listed as a dangerous radical in *The Red Notebook* by "the Idiocrat woman"—he got the word from Sergel—Elizabeth Dilling, who had said "that in fifteen minutes she could prove Roosevelt a communist." He did become concerned, however, when on April 16 a Department of Justice man, acting under the Foreign Registration Act of 1938, called on him to inquire about his being listed—along with John Dos Passos—as the American members of the Presidential Council of the Paris-based World Committee Against War and Fascism, headed by the French novelist and dramatist Romain Rolland. Disturbed, he wrote his State Department friend Herbert Feis for advice, protesting that he had casually lent the use of his name, had never acted in any way in the organization, and was "just an ordinary old-fashioned liberal Democrat and certainly with the same impulse against Fascism, Communism, or any other sort of dictatorship that most of us feel." Leaving for New York in the new Dodge on the twenty-third, he and Eleanor stopped for a day in Washington, Sherwood to see Feis, who took him to the Justice Department, where no one could advise him whether the act required him to register as a foreign agent. Anderson settled the problem by writing Rolland that he was "essentially a story teller," knew nothing about the Comité Mondial because he neither spoke nor read French, and, not wishing to have to register, in effect wanted to resign.[16]

After they had settled in at "54," one of his first actions was to give "The Letter Writer" a final review on April 27 and, before sending it to Chambrun, change its title to that of the *Reader's Digest* series, "The Most Unforgettable Character I Have Ever Known (He Was a Letter Writer)." Then he launched into a weeks-long flurry of uncompleted projects interrupted by a second drive to Wells College, at J. J. Lankes's invitation to give a lecture on May 10 on *Perhaps Women,* which, because he had not bothered to prepare it, was, he admitted, "rotten." He began a story, "Black Night," about "night life," drafted "He Built the Boat," part of the *Memoirs* reminiscence of Jack Jones and the death by drowning of Ann Mitchell, and started a novel. After a week down with a bad chest cold and a cough that shook him "to the toes," he wrote erratically through the last week in May until on June 2 he had a day with the black dog on his back and decided to drop attempts at the novel and to do only "short things." Most likely, however, his depression was caused by Chambrun's May 31 message that the *Readers' Digest* had turned down "The Most Unforgettable Character" because, the agent guessed, the magazine wanted "more of a 'story'—which means, I think, more anecdotes; 'something,' they say, 'which the reader will want to tell his friends after he has read it.'" Chambrun suggested that Anderson send him a short list of other characters he could show to Wallace and assured him that he himself liked the story and could place it elsewhere. Anderson's answer was apparently to change the long title of the story to "Pastoral," a suitable title for a tale written "passionately" out of happy memories, and to return the typescript immediately to Chambrun, who on June 3 thanked him for sending the story "which I think deserves a good place in the body of your work."[17]

"New York is all right until they find you out," Anderson wryly complained to Sergel in the midst of these weeks. In Washington, he had been told, there were "seven hundred dinner parties" nightly. "Here it's cocktail parties," though he and Eleanor went to enough dinner parties, and the number of people at various parties began getting him down. His favorite diversion was going to major league baseball games, seven of them in May alone. He and Eleanor went to a few plays: Jack Kirkland's drama-tization of Erskine Caldwell's *Tobacco Road*, now in its sixth year of con-tinuous run, Sherwood seeing it for the fifth time and still liking it; Lillian Hellman's *The Little Foxes* ("Fine acting."); and the all-black *The Hot Mikado* with Bill Robinson ("Wonderful dancing."). The New York World's Fair opened on April 30, but he recorded only one visit, in mid-May, in the "rain, rain." Obviously he had little confidence in the fair's insistence, just four months before World War II broke out, on the bright future of man-kind through technology; for only a few days before the opening he had written Henry Van Meier: "Sometimes . . . I think the whole mechanical age has ended in guns and little else. It's certainly a time of pretty gloomy outlook for the young. My mails are full of it these days." The fair did, however, bring to New York a number of visitors from South America, among them several writers whom he met toward the end of May. He was especially taken with María Luisa Bombal, a free-spirited and gifted young Chilean woman, then living in Buenos Aires, already well known and admired in Chile and Argentina for her innovative novels and stories about women trying to escape the bondage of a male-oriented society, writings that showed, as did Anderson, that she responded intensely to na-ture and believed that one's real life was lived in the imagination. At their first meeting on May 24, she had intended to interview him about his work and ideas but found him mainly interested in the reception of his books in South America. Afterwards they met several times before he left New York, once at the Galantières', "a very fine evening," he noted, "the con-versation of the best." That morning he had written a note of introduction for her to Max Perkins and an enthusiastic letter about her to Max urging him to talk with her.

Max why wouldn't it be worth while for some American publisher to try to do something with the South American writers. I am sure the interest in South Amer-ica is bound to grow. Why not. We certainly should know more of the life down there and how get it except through the writers.

Almost certainly it was Bombal who introduced him to Carlos Davila, for-merly Chilean ambassador to the United States, briefly president of Chile in 1932, and in 1939 director of Editors' Press Service in New York. By September Anderson was writing to Davila, whom he now regarded as a good friend, to thank him for information about books by Anderson pub-lished in South America and commenting on "my dream of going to Chile . . . and spend some months in your country." Clearly, meeting Bombal and writing the letter of recommendation for her were the beginnings of a process that would end with this North American writer's death outside his homeland.[18]

The Andersons drove to Hedgerow on June 11, and on the next day, after putting Eleanor on a train back to New York, he reached Marion. On the fifteenth he began a new story, which he first called, perhaps in a glance at Turgenev, "Father and Son," since he was recollecting his feeling about his own father. For four mornings he worked well at the story until he had to put it aside to help Eleanor prepare for her annual week with factory women at Camp Merrie-Wood, to drive her there, and to spend the week running errands for her, working on speeches for the approaching Olivet Writers' Conference, reading, and again becoming "sick of females in the mass." Back in Marion and then settled in at Ripshin on July 1, he picked up the first guests of the season, the Galantières, and the next morning finished the new story, now titled "Unforgotten," which was, Eleanor wrote Chambrun, "just right for the Readers Digest." Chambrun had just gladdened Anderson's Fourth of July with a check for $450 from his sale of "Pastoral" to *Redbook,* and now, delighted with this new "memorable" piece, he sent it to DeWitt Wallace at once. On July 18 Wallace telegraphed Anderson that the *Digest* had accepted "your article Unforgotten with enthusiasm" and would "pay their absolute maximum of fifteen hundred dollars." "Unforgotten" would be published in the November issue of the *Reader's Digest* under yet another title, "Discovery of a Father: The Most Unforgettable Character I Ever Met," first edited, however, with many deletions and some sentence rearrangements, which maintained the Anderson style and actually improved his somewhat rambling and repetitious original.[19]

Both Chambrun and, apparently, Wallace described "Unforgotten" as an "article," which suggests that they, and some others after them, were willing to believe that Anderson's portrait of his relationship with his father, particularly the concluding reversal in it, might be in large part factually accurate. Anderson, however, knew that he was writing a "story"; for in each of his five references to the piece in his diary he specifically called it that, and in a long unnecessary digression early in "Unforgotten," wisely deleted in "Discovery," he too obviously foreshadowed the son's final revelation by commenting that writers "are after stories. We jerk people out of the lives in which they live . . . and put them into a world we invent. We use our own lives so." The true fact behind "Unforgotten" is that from boyhood and throughout his life Anderson detested his father as a talker, a show-off, and a poor provider, but otherwise in this story factuality is literally displaced by fiction. To present the father as a show-off, Anderson revamps the celebration scene early in *Windy McPherson's Son* in which Windy rides impressively on a white horse into Caxton's main street, but to his consternation and the crowd's jeering laughter fails to blow the bugle. In "Unforgotten" the father mounts a hired white horse but "couldn't ride for shucks," falls off, is laughed at by the people, and, seeming to enjoy being ridiculous, laughs back at them. Constantly the boy wishes he had "a proud silent dignified" father and is especially ashamed that his father loves telling stories about himself to groups of men, even preposterous ones that make him look foolish, such as his tale (presented as a tale within the tale) of being so close a friend to General Grant that on the morning of Lee's surrender at Appomattox, Grant could not be found because he was in the woods drinking from a bottle with "Irve." The men know he is lying and laugh at him, but "Major" just likes their attention. (Sherwood himself liked this inner tale so much that a year and a half later he expanded it into the sketch "Tim and General Grant.") In "Unforgotten" he then draws briefly on *A Story Teller's Story* for the son's anger that during hard times the father would leave the family in poverty and go off to enjoy himself at surrounding farms.[20]

For the conclusion of "Unforgotten," in which the boy comes to view his father differently, Anderson returns to *Windy McPherson's Son*, revamps the ending of chapter 6, indeed turns it upside down, and fabricates one of the most powerful scenes in his writings. In the novel as his wife lies terminally ill one rainy evening, Windy comes in drunk, goes to sleep in the kitchen, awakes and begins complaining, whereupon the son, seeing his "coarse and sodden" face, chokes him unconscious, carries him outside into the rain, and dumps him into the street. In "Unforgotten" and the more concentrated "Discovery," Anderson pulls out all the romantic stops. As the boy sits alone in the kitchen one rainy summer night, the strong healthy father, his clothes dripping, comes into the house strangely silent, looks at his son with "the saddest look I have ever seen"—shades of the Byronic hero!—and speaks only to command the boy to come to him. With the always-talking father now not talking, the son feeling that he is with a "stranger," they walk out of the town to a large pond, strip at the father's command and, naked, walk into the pond. As lightning flashes and thunder "peals" in the darkness—"Discovery" omits the thunder and the cliché—they swim back and forth across the pond, the father, a powerful swimmer, keeping one hand of his son, a poor swimmer, always on his own muscular shoulder. Since Anderson was skilled in the use of symbols, one readily perceives that the emphasis on water and nakedness, on the strength of the father and the weakness of the son beneath the natural tumult in the dark skies, stands for a baptism of the son into a strange new understanding, into a relationship with his father that has been purified and transformed into an acceptance of his father as, in the son's upside-down thought, "blood of my blood." When they return home, the "discovered" father, still silent, leaves the room "with a new and strange dignity," while the son goes to bed knowing for the first time that "I was the son of my father. He was a storyteller as I was to be." A storyteller, the reader realizes, need not necessarily be ridiculous but is, of necessity by nature of his trade, like the father a kind of liar, yet in this climactic scene a splendid liar, capable of persuading many readers to the incorrect conclusion that toward the end of his life Sherwood really was reconciled with his detested father.

4.

After two weeks of enjoying Ripshin, entertaining the Galantières, writing desultorily, enduring the tension that the visiting Mary Emmett brought him, and deciding to take no more of the monthly checks she had generously and promptly given him, he was ready for the Olivet Writers' Conference. On July 15 he and Eleanor set off in the Dodge, the next day visited Trillena White in the Springfield hospital and drove around the streets of Clyde before Eleanor took the train to New York. On the seventeenth he reached Olivet, settled into his room at the Dole Residence Hall on its oak-shaded hilltop where the conference activities were held, and that evening participated in a memorial service for Ford Madox Ford, who had died on June 26. It is unclear how much or little of Ford's writing he had read, but his tribute was to him as "the very type of the artist man" in terms he himself believed in. Ford

understood what a man undertakes in becoming a writer. He understood the obligation taken on. . . . He was a professional writer who didn't soil his tools. He was unashamed, firm, a real workman, a man who understood what it is that gives a man's own life some significance.[21]

Anderson's first major contribution to the conference was the opening lecture the following evening in a series given by each of the specially invited writers, his, he noted with satisfaction, going "off with a bang." Of the three other writers he liked the Irish poet Padraic Colum for his sense of humor and the poet and novelist John Peale Bishop, whom he had long admired; but he was less attracted to Katherine Anne Porter, although he had praised her recently published *Pale Horse, Pale Rider,* thought she had "real ability," and on the back of a photograph of the two of them, sitting by one of Dole Hall's columns on the morning he would leave the conference, wrote, "At Olivet with a lady I much admire." She seemed to him a rather cold woman who perhaps resented the way he tended to be starred at Olivet. Her private comment was somewhat more generous; to a friend she wrote that the four "assort rather nicely: Sherwood Anderson supplies the rough-diamond note." An anonymous newspaper reporter interviewing the writers came up with a different view of Anderson on the day after his first lecture. He

wanders around Dole Hall . . . like a sheep dog. He spoils the shaggy effect by using a cigarette holder and wearing an aggressively clean panama hat. But he paces
back and forth like a high strung dog, and paces back and forth when he doesn't
like what you're saying. And the rest of the time he just sits around comfortable
and wise.[22]

He found the workload lighter than when alone at Olivet in January,
so light that he was able to spend the first weekend visiting Schevill at
Michigan City, Indiana. "Personal Interviews" with attendees submitting
writings were scheduled for late afternoons in Dole Hall, but he later told
his frequent correspondent Carrow DeVries that he preferred to take such
an attendee in his car and talk of his or her writing problems while driving about. He was not interested in "quibbling over words and sentences"
but invariably had to point out that the writer had forced a character "to
do something you knew the character could not do in real life" and in this
way had done "horrible violence" on the imagined life of the character, the
result being, he would tell the writer (one assumes gently), not just "bad
art [but] a display of immorality." Twice he lectured publicly on the short
story, once on a subject that makes one long for a stenographic report: "on
sources of the writer's material, using 'Untold Lie,' 'Death in the Woods,'
and 'Man of Ideas'." For the first, he presumably spoke of seeing from the
train a man running across a field; for the second, Glenn Gosling would
recall, probably the account in the *Memoirs* of seeing dogs run at night in
a circle about him in the snow; for the third, unknown. Once he filled in
for another writer by repeating "A Writer's Conception of Realism," and
twice he read from his own work, the second time being his last night at
the conference when, substituting for a no-show Carl Sandburg and disgusted by a previous lecturer's confession of having sold out the writer's
art for money, he read the epilogue of *A Story Teller's Story*. This concluding act "particularly delighted" President Brewer when he wrote
gratefully to Anderson that this had been the best of the four Olivet Conferences and "You were marvelous . . . and just made the whole show."[23]

Buoyed up by learning on the second day of the conference that "Unforgotten" had been sold for fifteen hundred dollars, Anderson swam
ebulliently in the parties and proceedings of the two-week gathering; but
though Glenn Gosling was on the staff, he apparently saw little of the
young man and did not have with him the long talk he had originally
suggested concerning a project he had first written Gosling about back in
April. Laura Lu had been urging on him "a new kind of text book for
young writers [not one] much concerned with the actual technique of
writing but rather with the building of an attitude toward writing, the
art of learning to use the imagination etc." Would Glenn be interested in

collecting and editing such a book out of already published material? When Glenn expressed interest as long as the material be collected and edited from Anderson's own writings, Anderson had replied that the book should be "something fresh, original and all of a piece." Gosling should come to Ripshin after the conference to talk about it with him and with Laura Lu. From the exchange of letters, it is clear that the nature of the proposed book was at this point unclear to both men, and, as is turned out, always would be.[24]

Leaving Olivet on July 28, he met Eleanor's train from New York in Sandusky and learned of the trip she probably would have to take to the Pacific Coast and the Southwest from late October into mid-December. By the time they had reached Ripshin on the thirtieth, they had decided to drive out together; the next day he wrote to Clark Getts, a New York lecture agent who had just arranged a speaking engagement for him in the following February, asking him to try to set up others along their way west. Then on August 2 he launched into "a new and quite terrible story . . . the Primitives," a first draft of which he finished in the four days before Paul Rosenfeld arrived on the sixth and Glenn Gosling shortly afterwards to restart the flow of summer vacationers.[25]

Now in August, while the Andersons entertained sometimes housefuls of guests despite the unseasonably heavy rains, Sherwood's determination to write only short stories gave him, he told Laura Lu, "a new rush of what people are fond of calling inspiration"; yet on the seventh he began a first rewriting of "The Primitives" and kept with it so many mornings that on the nineteenth he wrote Chambrun it would go over twenty-five thousand words. Toward the end of the month he took three days off to do a "dream fantasy" titled "Fred Griffith's World," which Chambrun called "unusual" when he acknowledged receiving it and which he was never able to sell. Returning to his "long story," Anderson decided on August 29 that it had to be entirely rewritten a second time. After trying twice to do another short story and twice failing, he would go back to "The Primitives" once more on September 13—he had forgotten that it was his sixty-third birthday—but completing the pattern of the year before set by "A Late Spring," the novelette for *Redbook* that turned into an unfinished novel, he abruptly dropped it permanently. Meanwhile visitors came and went. Paul left after two weeks, but Glenn, who had learned from Laura Lu that she thought the proposed textbook could well be made up of selections from Anderson's writings, stayed on through the end of the month, so long that Sherwood tired of him and decided that he was too immature to work with. Not wishing to face him directly with his decision, Anderson wrote him after his departure to say that since he was an aspiring young writer, he should put his time into his own work and that he himself had not thought out the nature of the book, so Glenn should forget the matter.[26]

Infrequently thereafter he would think about the book, but its nature never did become clear to him, and the "Writer's Book" never became more than a few disconnected pieces. In Martha Mulroy Curry's edition of it, the first piece, "Prelude to a Story," which occupies nearly two-thirds of the text, is obviously based on Anderson's experience with "A Late Spring." Needing money, he agrees to the proposal of a literary agent (read Chambrun) to write a story to fit the requirements of a mass circulation magazine (read *Redbook*), chiefly that it be about people in "comfortable circumstances" and contain nothing sordid. At the end of this semi-story about trying to write such a story, he feels that he has been "a slave to these people of my imagination," attempts to force them to serve him, laboriously and joylessly completes the tale, but, realizing that the true artist must not impose his will on his imagined characters, burns the manuscript. The long middle of this tale, however, is a somewhat rambling account of experiences in his past life—his mother's courageous battle against poverty, his sordid, unsuccessful encounter with a prostitute, his life as a businessman—experiences that convinced him he must write of ordinary people, not in "comfortable circumstances," sometimes caught in sordid situations. These episodes are too often punctuated with little essays on his beliefs and opinions, especially his customary attacks on business and businessmen, on Hollywood, on success defined by money, these being abrupt "textbookish" intrusions into the narrative episodes where the connections usually are those of association, contrast, echoes, motifs, the structuring devices of his fictions. There is no objective evidence for the emotional-artistic crisis concluding the "Prelude"; Anderson of course did not burn a laboriously finished manuscript, "the people of the tale got out of hand," as he explained to Karl, and the story turned into a novel that was "destroyed" only by being one of a growing number of uncompleted projects. As for the six pieces making up the rest of the "Writer's Book," one, "The Writer," is an early, perhaps the first and certainly an inferior, version of "Pastoral," while the other five are brief "Notes" on various aspects of writing arranged in no particular order. Obviously Anderson had no compelling interest in what Laura Lu had envisioned, and the "Book" would remain yet another uncompleted project.[27]

At the end of August he still hoped to have a book of stories ready for Max Perkins for late winter or early spring publication, but there continued to be too many distractions. On the twentieth, Augusto Centeno, who had translated *Dark Laughter* into Spanish and was now teaching in the Department of Modern Language and Literature at Princeton, wrote to invite him to lecture there in October as the first of four American artists in a program on the "intent of the artist" for the Spencer Trask Lectures. Pleased by the invitation, he "hastened" to accept and shortly began sketching out a lecture. A quite different, far more serious distraction was his deep concern that a European war was "in the air," literally so since whenever he was at Rosemont he could not avoid hearing reports on the radio, which was kept on all day by "Bee *Yee*," as Anderson generally called Mr. B. E. Copenhaver to Andy Funk. When on September 1 German armies drove into Poland, he noted in his diary that war "will now invade everything. There will be nothing else thought of or talked of. It will be a great sickness in everyone." When on September 3 Eleanor brought back to Ripshin news that Great Britain and France had declared war on Germany, he "had to flee the house to be in darkness," his mind very likely filled with recollections of the propaganda that "sold the country" on the first World War. A third distraction was his commitment to speak at Roanoke College in Salem, Virginia, a speech he hoped might test out ideas for the Princeton lecture. The morning after his birthday and his final abandonment of "The Primitives," he turned, not to another short story, but to an article, which he hoped would be more immediately marketable.[28]

Wanting very much to go to Kentucky at the end of September for the Lexington Trots, the most important harness races of the Grand Circuit season after the Hambletonian at Goshen, New York, he had already written Arnold Gingrich, editor of *Esquire,* to ask whether he would like an article "about the harness horse people and the horses." When Gingrich replied that he would like an article not just about the Trots but about harness racing generally, Anderson had an outlet for a nearly lifelong enthusiasm. In one day he drafted a piece on the trotters and pacers and the next day polished it. "Here They Come" is one of his most attractive articles, for it is a carefully worked out amalgam of memory, observation, anticipation, and nostalgia. He begins with memory and nostalgia. Back in the "horse age" before the automobile threatened to kill harness horse racing, before the stables behind houses were torn down or turned into garages, "almost every man you knew owned some kind of a horse," and every town had a few men training prospective colts for the harness races at county and state fairs, perhaps even for the national Grand Circuit races. "Men and boys knew the blood lines of horses as now they know the various makes of automobiles," and they idolized the harness drivers like Ed Geers and Budd Doble. One could see a horse race almost daily, even in winter after a snowfall when—Anderson must have been happily remembering Clyde—a sleigh race would be run down the main street of "an American town," the "street cleared of farmers' teams, men and boys standing in crowds on the sidewalks before the stores, all business suspended for the time." But harness racing, which "many men had thought the noblest and most beautiful of all forms of sport," did not die; rather it has come back strongly. One reason is the American love of technique, for driving a trotter or pacer has always required extraordinary skill to press the horse to its maximum speed without letting it break its stride and be disqualified.

Another reason is one "we Americans understand, big money involved." Sports writers now come to the outstanding races such as the Hambleton-ian—Anderson persists in calling it the "Hamiltonian"—and the Trots and report them to big city newspapers. Furthermore, harness racing is "adjusting itself to the modern age." Horse sales, like those of the Old Glory in New York, are crowded by breeders and buyers; great new horses are constantly setting new speed records unbelievable to the men of the horse and buggy age; new drivers replace the old heroes, drivers like Doc Parshall at the reins of Peter Astra, the Grand Circuit winner, or the eleven-year-old girl Alma Sheppard who at Lexington in 1937 drove the trotter Dean Hanover to a new world's record for the mile; and new technology has been introduced like the modern bike sulky and quick starting machinery. As always, most of the crowd even at the big races are still small-towners and farmers, and still, unlike the owner of a running horse who must hand over the actual racing to a jockey, "The harness horse man can, if he wishes and has the courage, the nerve, the gift of the hands holding the reins, get up there himself," feeling in his own body "the curious accord that sometimes grows between man and horse." This, Anderson anticipates, is what is bringing back the harness horse and harness horse racing.[29]

The Lexington Trots were only a few days away, but first, because of the cold weather, he and Eleanor had to move from the farm to Marion on September 19, and that evening he drove her north to Roanoke to catch the midnight train for New York and her job. The next morning he drove to the small suburb of Salem to read at the opening exercises of Roanoke College an address, "The Modern Writer in a World of Realism," a somewhat revised version of his Olivet lecture, "A Writer's Conception of Realism." A guest at the convocation and the private luncheon at the president's house, Pendleton Hogan, a novelist and weekly columnist for the *Washington Post,* described Anderson on this formal occasion on a "bright-gold" September day.

He had a rugged quality as if made of such solid ore that even the rubbing of time could not wear him away. He was sixty-three years old. His dark hair had grey in it, his eyebrows were dark and thick. His eyes were clear behind round horn-rimmed glasses and, though his lips were thin, in general his features were "heavy." His strong hands were expressive and he used them as he spoke. He was not a man of sparkle, wore humor on his sleeve; rather, I felt here was a man who had brooded, dreamed and searched. . . . His strong face showed, I felt, little tolerance for the absurd, none for the lazy. I believed that he detested pretentiousness and I suspected a core so tender it could drown in emotion. His dark suit had not lately been pressed.

More relaxed at luncheon in the president's house, Anderson was willing to talk of his intention in writing, as Hogan summarized it.

"The people I write about are part of the American experience living their every-day lives. I just describe them as I see them."

Because the American experience was everything to him he wanted, more than anything, to leave behind a recording of it, an honest interpretation of at least his own spectrum of it and he well knew how difficult, how complicated, how virtu-ally impossible this was. He had worked tirelessly toward this end and, no matter what the critics said, he would keep on trying as long as he lived.[30]

Having given "Here They Come" a final revision, he drove on the twenty-fourth to Harrodsburg, only thirty miles from the Lexington track, and settled into an inexpensive, quiet, comfortable room at the Hotel Har-rod, where he used to stay when working up advertising for Dave and Hanly Bohon, their business and themselves now dead. He could write here mornings, he told Laura Lu, and then afternoons drive in to see those "beautiful creatures," the harness horses, at the Trots, for which he had obtained a press pass on the strength of Gingrich's letters. In the morning of the twenty-fifth he "fixed up an article called 'So You Want to be a Writer,'" a revision of his opening lecture at the Olivet Writer's Confer-ence; and that afternoon from the press box in the grandstand he excitedly watched Doc Parshall, trainer and always the driver of Peter Astra, guide that three-year-old trotter to an easy victory in the Kentucky Futurity, man and horse having also recently won the Hambletonian and seven other races on the Grand Circuit. Anderson was in his element, or one of them. At the Trots most of the day on the twenty-sixth he was, as he wrote Eleanor, "quite a boy." First he was asked to help present the Futurity cup, and when the two-year-old Gentleman Jim, on whom he had made one of his customary small bets, won the Kentucky Stakes, he was again called up over the public address system to help present the silver cup and to say "4 words" to a huge crowd. Then when Ann Domian and her driver raced against time and, as the *New York Times* reported, "lowered the world record for 2-year-old pacing fillies to 2:02½," he had his picture taken with the horse and her owner, and a reporter from the *Lexington Leader* inter-viewed him for a story, which pleased him when printed. He ended his "horsey" day by dining with wealthy harness racing enthusiasts and watch-ing the beautiful yearlings at an auction. After two more glorious days at the Trots, he headed for Marion.[31]

Back at Rosemont he sent off "Here They Come" and "So You Want to Be a Writer?" to Chambrun. Although the latter in its Olivet version was successful with its audience and DeWitt Wallace would find the hu-mor of the revision "irresistible," the piece now seems only mildly amus-ing in its advice to writers on how to deal kindly, or occasionally unkindly, with persons who profess to just love their books but clearly have read none of them, or in Anderson's case confuse him with Maxwell Anderson or Robert Sherwood. "Tremendously complimentary" about Anderson's work, Wallace paid eight hundred dollars for this article and arranged to give it to the *Saturday Review of Literature* for first publication before abridging it in the *Reader's Digest*. Gingrich at *Esquire* would purchase the superior "Here They Come" for two hundred, the two articles reinforcing Anderson's self-confidence. Already on the day he had sent the two articles to Chambrun, he began work on another of Chambrun's ideas for enhancing their incomes. At a lunch with Mrs. William Brown Meloney, editor of *This Week*, the magazine section of the Sunday *New York Herald Tribune* and published also "by twenty-four national newspapers," Chambrun suggested that Anderson might well contribute to the magazine's weekly editorial, and he subsequently urged him to send him proposed topics. After two mornings of unsuccessful work, Anderson on October 5 replied to a letter from an angry young man, David Virgrin, who declared that his talents were too great for Elkhart, Indiana, and he intended to go to the big world of New York where these talents would enable him to move and direct masses of men. "Why do you have to leave Elkhart?" Anderson asked, when "if the large doesn't grow out of the small it will never really be large." Here, indeed, was his editorial. On the sixth he wrote and mailed to Chambrun "Why Not Oak Hill?" an argument that one should first, like Lincoln, know and understand the individual lives of a small community in order to be "effective in the larger place." Shortly Chambrun reported that *This Week* had accepted the editorial so enthusiastically that he was trying to raise the offered payment of four hundred dollars, and eventually did win a hundred-dollar increase. As Anderson wrote Roger Sergel in mid-October, "I keep working on short things, as it seems impossible now, the state of the world being the state of the world, to stay on any long thing but have been doing rather well with the short things." The short things, however, were not short stories such as might have helped reclaim his failing reputation.[32]

5.

The editorial out of the way, he set off on the eighth for New York to rejoin Eleanor at "54." Since Mary was in Williamsburg, Ontario, having an eye trouble treated, they had the place to themselves; but after a morning perhaps on the *Memoirs*, he felt himself "ineffectual" at that kind of writing and instead worked on the Princeton speech and others he might give during the approaching long trip. It was a week or more of waiting. He saw old friends like Paul Rosenfeld and, three times, the Galantières, had a "night of faces," possibly in anticipation of his Trask lecture, and then on the morning of the nineteenth drove to Princeton, where he was to stay at the Centeno house. That evening he gave his lecture on "Man and His Imagination" to a large audience with what he felt was "good success." The major part of his lecture, to be published later with those of the three other artists in the Trask series, consists, occasionally in the same language, of the ideas he had expressed in his big public speech at Olivet back in January, such as "the imagination must constantly feed upon reality or starve," yet its life "will always remain separated from the life of reality"; but he made significant additions as well. Near the beginning he quotes an appropriate passage about the difficulty of telling the truth from *War and Peace,* which he had finished reading while at Harrodsburg; he recounts, though not with complete accuracy, the circumstances of his meeting with the original of Kit Brandon and of his conceiving *Marching Men;* he explains his dislike of the southern way of categorizing people as hillbillies or aristocrats; and toward the end he condemns big thinking, urges as in the editorial "trying to think small, to stay closer home, to use our imaginations at home," and defends "the right of the story teller, of any imaginative worker, to lead his own life, to build up and maintain his own attitude toward life." Anderson's "Man and His Imagination" is a good summary of many of his leading ideas at the end of the 1930s.[33]

The morning after his lecture, he left Princeton early and drove to the Hedgerow for a day with Jap. That evening he met Eleanor's train from New York, and they stayed the night in Paoli at the home of Wharton Esherick, the next in the series of friends they would see on their way across the country. On the bright morning of October 21, "beautiful [with] fall colors," they set out for Denver, where Eleanor had her first assignment, driving toward it as nearly in a straight line as the highways permitted. Day one, to Wheeling, West Virginia; day two, to Terre Haute, Indiana, after "a nice hour's visit" in Springfield, Ohio, with Trillena White; day three, 491 miles in ninety-two-degree heat to Topeka, Kansas, for an overnight stop with Marco Morrow and family; day four, just to Goodland, Kansas because of a bad tire; day five, only two hundred miles to Denver and the Brown Palace Hotel.[34]

Since Eleanor had to attend meetings and interviews during each day and most evenings, Sherwood was left to himself to get used to the altitude, work on lectures, and write many letters advising people with personal problems. Gilbert Wilson, a young radical artist who had begun but not finished a mural at Antioch, had visited him at Ripshin and bored him with constant talk, and now puzzled and dismayed by war in Europe and the just-completed Nazi-Soviet Pact, was, Anderson felt, too filled with self-pity. He should go back to Antioch and as an artist think about the mural rather than himself. For entertainment Anderson went to one of the few movies he ever liked, *All Quiet on the Western Front,* "very fine antiwar propaganda," and with Ted and Natalie Davison saw a college football game, "Denver-Utah—7 to 7." Having been invited by Ted to give two lectures at the University of Colorado for seventy-five dollars, he left Eleanor to finish her Denver work, drove to Boulder on October 30, and the next day gave an afternoon lecture to a journalism class and an evening one to a general audience, which Eleanor arrived too late to hear. On November 1 they began the last leg of their transcontinental trip, heading south into New Mexico and taking the old Santa Fe Trail to avoid mountain snowstorms, "the country," Sherwood noted, "more and more strange and beautiful as we went." The next day they drove five hundred miles across uplands to Williams, half way across northern Arizona. The third day he recorded as a "remarkable" one—first north from Williams to see the Grand Canyon, back to Williams and due west to Kingman, north again to Boulder Dam, which struck him, he would exclaim to Sergel, as "grander and gaudier" than the Grand Canyon, "I guess because you feel the human in it, man struggling with a really gigantic thing and bringing it off, something outside of the bigness of big guns and big battleships, real achievement. It got me in a big way." Before evening they had driven through a small part of Death Valley and had stopped in Tonopah in southern Nevada. On day four they easily reached Reno, where Judge Bartlett, who in 1924 had declared Sherwood divorced from Tennessee, insisted that they stay in his house; and on the sunshiny fifth day they had a "beautiful" drive through the High Sierras to San Francisco and the downtown Hotel Canterbury.[35]

Although Eleanor's evenings were usually free, she had a full schedule most days, and Sherwood would roam the city in the brilliant San Francisco Bay sunshine, liking, as he would write the Galantières, "the hills of that town, the good restaurants, the tall beautiful women, a kind of aliveness in the people in the streets." Learning that Chambrun had sold his first editorial to *This Week*, he characteristically felt "quite rich" and also characteristically bought "an expensive and beautiful new Italian hat." He saw old friends—Leon Gelber and Ted Lilienthal, who had published his essay "The Modern Writer" back in 1925—and made new ones— Joseph Henry Jackson, book critic for the *San Francisco Chronicle*, and John Terrell of the *Chronicle*, who took him to the Bohemian Club, which since its founding writers and artists had begun taking in wealthy businessmen and was now as little bohemian as any place he had ever seen. He gave a "very stupid interview," which appeared in the *Chronicle* along with a "very stupid" fat-faced picture, one of the least attractive ever taken of him. Asked who seemed to be an outstanding author today, he replied: "I guess this fellow who wrote 'Grapes of Wrath' is making the most stir, but I don't know his work. I haven't read the book yet." Either the interview or Jackson alerted Steinbeck to Anderson's presence in the city, and he insisted that Anderson come see him at his secluded house in Los Gatos in the high hills south of San Francisco, halfway to Monterey. Driven there by Lilienthal on November 14, Anderson spent the day with Steinbeck, whom he found "a big man, giving rather the impression of a truck driver on his day off." Although not "quite figuring him out," he liked the author of the best-selling novel, but he did not like his wife, who he suspected might push her husband too hard to be successful. Apparently the two men had talked "of the danger he was in from money and popularity that has done such evil things to so many writers." The following afternoon, a busy one, he noted in his diary: "Went to [Lilienthal] to send a book to John Steinbeck. Liking him." Then, cryptically, "Saw a man about doing a book on the American small town." The man is not named, but here is the first reference to what would be his next published book, *Home Town*.[36]

Despite diversions, he spent more mornings than not in his hotel room writing. He finished one unnamed story on November 10, on the twelfth rewrote "You Be the American Zola" (his article on Tom Mooney published as "Backstage with a Martyr"), and on the fifteenth started another new story, "For What?" working on it so hard and long that by noon he was exhausted. The story was still unfinished when, on the seventeenth, he and Eleanor left San Francisco for Fresno, where she was to meet with more women industrial workers. Here in their room at the Hotel Sequoia he first dashed off a short piece requested, probably by Jackson, for the *Chronicle,* "San Francisco at Christmas." Beginning his "little paean to Christmas" by questioning how much, with war abroad and hunger and joblessness at home, Christianity is truly practiced, he ends with a celebration of the beauty of the city and its air of friendliness. San Franciscans should dance gaily in their streets, glad that "we Americans may still, some day, if we can stay off wars, get into our daily lives with one another a bit more of what the figure of Christ really stands for." His day-long conversation with Steinbeck seems to have stuck in his mind, for after a second morning of work, probably on the "For What?" story, he drove a group of Eleanor's "factory girls" to see some of the migrant labor camps among the fruit groves and vegetable fields stretching around Fresno. These camps were "horrible enough places," he exclaimed in his diary, and to the Galantières he wrote:

I'm sure of this, having gone to take in several of these labor camps, that what goes on in them is in no way different from what is going on all over the country and am convinced also that one of the reasons for the great popularity of [*The Grapes of Wrath*] is that it localizes a situation that is universal. It seems we have got back about the same standard of production we had in '29 and have a million and a half more men out of work. That looks like a more or less permanent situation, not just a California one.

Not all California nor the United States was like his picture of San Francisco, nor was all of San Francisco, as Eleanor could have and probably did tell him.[37]

The third and last day in Fresno he put in a long session on "For What?" very likely getting through the first draft of it. Then as though worn out by the push, he caught a bad cold that evening and felt so miserable on the drive to Los Angeles that when they got settled in the Hotel Figueroa, he was too unwell to dine with his good friend Anita Loos. For a full week he was confined to his room or at most the hotel with a kind of flu, unable to work and passing the time reading *Anna Karenina*. On the twenty-eighth, however, he had recovered enough to go to the Loos-Ross Clinic for the complete check-up that Eleanor had long been urging and received, as he admiringly noted, "the best and most intelligent medical treatment and advice [he had] ever experienced." The next day he had bounced back, the flu was gone, and he had "a wonderful time" watching some dances at a Spanish restaurant. Best of all was that in the morning he had inked in any changes he wanted in "For What?" and had it ready for typing and mailing to Chambrun, who on December 4 would acknowledge having just read it "with enjoyment."[38]

While putting in long, concentrated hours on "Why Not?" Anderson reexperienced his desire to write his memoirs and in a new way he would describe to Sergel two weeks later.

I am trying to do a series. The idea is really, Roger, to do an autobiography in a new way, not in the life of the teller but in lives that touch his life . . . much as I used the figure of George Willard in Winesburg but carrying the idea into more mature years.

Although he would often deviate from this plan in the following year when he would spend so many mornings on the *Memoirs,* this particular piece exemplifies the combination of fiction and recollection he felt comfortable with. "For What?" asks "What is it keeps stirring in a man, making him want to do something out of himself?" The first-person narrator, who wants to be a writer, and three friends, who want to be painters, spend a summer Sunday in the fields west of Chicago, free for the day from entrapment by marriage, dependents, or job. Sitting by a sluggish stream the writer tries all morning to get down a story he has been trying to write for months, and in the afternoon he tears up his pages and throws them into the stream. As the afternoon wanes, Jerry, a big, profane German comes to sit with him and, for once speaking without profanity and in words reminiscent of *Mid-American Chants,* explains that he had wanted to paint the cornfields stretching beyond the stream in such a way as "to give men new confidence in life . . . to make people believe in the land";

for the "real significance" was not in the artifacts of the machine age, but in "the tall corn growing. There was the real American poetry." Swearing at his unsuccessful painting, however, he throws it into the stream, and as the return train to Chicago approaches, he throws his easel, paint tubes, and brushes into a field of weeds near the station; yet as the other three men board the train, they last see Jerry on his knees among the weeds picking up his painter's materials. At the Chicago station the two painters with their own failed canvases leave at once, but the narrator waits for the next incoming train, remembering how in his boyhood farmers near his midwestern town showed a "kind of deep patient heroism" after a disastrous crop year in plowing their fields again the following spring. "I wanted to see what I did see, keeping myself unseen, the arrival of Jerry, most of his painting traps again collected," ready to try again some other weekend. When Laura Lu failed to see the point of this story, Anderson explained that Jerry "didn't surrender when he found his dreams were fading," showing rather "something I have always felt in farmers [displaying] something heroic, not in a big showy way but in a kind of heroic patience with failure." What makes anyone, artist, farmer, or other, want to do "something out of himself," why, Anderson might well be indirectly asking, had he himself persisted in failed attempt after failed attempt to write "Death in the Woods"? Fundamentally, he answers in this story-recollection, to achieve "that curious happiness that comes sometimes, fleetingly enough, with accomplishment."[39]

Escaped from the prison of the flu, Anderson was filled with energy. The day after the final revising of "For What?" he reworked an old story, "There Are Such People," though a month later he would find the whole piece badly written and throw it away, and another morning he started a new story. Although Eleanor had a touch of the flu, she refused to slow down, dining one night with the Dreisers, another with one of Judge Bartlett's daughters, Gene, who had married a likable rich young "running horse man." Also a guest was Gene's sister "Monte" (Margaret), whom Anderson had liked during his year in Reno but who on his and Eleanor's recent stopover there had irritated him with her insistent overpraise of him. Nevertheless, he had written her friendly letters in which he explained why since "I perhaps live only in affection . . . Eleanor is so terribly important to me."

She's never assertive, as I am and as I suppose I like being. We've always been good for each other. When we are not together, often I try and try to find out something personal about her. I can't. She'll give me all the news I want of the doings of everyone about, none of herself, while with me everything is personal. It may be the real reason I write, to occasionally escape out of myself and into others in that way. The truth is that I think the Judge and I are a great deal alike. Both of us would like, really, to make love to all the world.

Besides the dining out he made two special visits. One afternoon he visited Anita Loos, who had also invited Aldous Huxley and his wife. Although Anderson thought that the English writer's "work is too clever, that he is always making rather a display of his erudition," he found the Huxleys "charming people," the wife very attractive, the husband gentle and quiet. He had a hunch, however, that Huxley felt somewhat uncomfortable in the "movie atmosphere"; and when shortly afterwards he wrote "An Open Letter to an English Writer," he called him hypocritical for satirizing Hollywood in his new novel, *After Many a Summer Dies the Swan,* while he was drawing a salary of $1,500 a week as a scriptwriter for Metro-Goldwyn-Mayer. The second visit was anything but pleasant. Flu-struck his first evening in Los Angeles, he had nevertheless phoned John Emerson, his old friend from Clyde days, whose situation he had earlier described to Laura Lu. His parents being poor like Sherwood's, John had developed an acute, lasting fear of poverty and an obsession with money; although he and Anita had made much of it in the movies and he had an annuity of some fifteen thousand a year, he was now apparently manic-depressive and lived most of the time in a sanitarium "in constant terror of poverty." Since Emerson had sounded very depressed during the phone conversation, Anderson may have put off his visit to the sanitarium until two days before he and Eleanor left Los Angeles. He was deeply saddened by the day with John, observing his "tragedy . . . the end of all his scheming, charm, money-getting," a fit subject for "a terrible novel to be called 'American Money.'"[40]

On December 5 the Andersons left Los Angeles—"an unhealthy city," he had decided, "in spite of the fine climate"—and began their backtrailing eastward across the continent, first through the "wonderful" desert country he loved to Phoenix, where in the evening he worked at slightly expanding "Man and His Imagination" for the book publication of his and the three other Trask Lectures, and then south to Tucson, where he, and Eleanor when free, talked and partied for three days with Paddy and Mims Walsh, and he finished the first draft of "Letter to an English Writer." It took them two days to get east through Arizona and New Mexico to San Antonio, Texas, for a visit to Randolph and a stimulating afternoon being guided about the city by its young New Dealer mayor, Maury Maverick, who was happily fighting the dominant conservative interests, putting men to work, arranging clearance of the terrible slums of the Mexican workers, building new housing for them, restoring historic houses, beautifying the banks of the river, trying to make San Antonio a magnificent city of which all Texans could be proud. Excited by this "young alive man" and his accomplishments, Sherwood and Eleanor drove on to Houston, a fast-growing city like an "early Chicago," he thought, where on December 14 they settled in for a week of work at the Sam Houston Hotel. While Eleanor held her last meetings on the long trip, he drafted an enthusiastic article, "Maury Maverick in San Antonio," had "good mornings" of other writing, and in letters to Paul Cullen and Sergel described more of his activities in that busy second week in Los Angeles. He had had an offer to be a movie writer but had no interest, and in any case he expected to return to the Olivet Writers' Conference. He did sign a contract, as had such figures as Albert Einstein, Thomas Mann, and Eleanor Roosevelt, to give a "Dramatized lecture," he to talk on "the passing of an American town from an agricultural to an industrial community," pictures to be flashed on a screen meanwhile to illustrate and dramatize what he was saying. "Then," he wrote Sergel,

there is another stunt on. I am to go to Washington for that. There is to be a series of books, on American cities, communities, etc, largely made up of pictures and they want me to do the American small town. The government has some 35000 photographs to select from.

As far as Anderson was concerned, nothing came of the condensed *Poor White* lecture, but its opposite in praise of the continuing hometown was about to move from idea to action.[41]

In midafternoon of December 19 they headed east through familiar territory, pausing in New Orleans only to talk for an afternoon with the Antonys, dine at the Feiblemans', and sleep that night at the Monteleone. Then, after an overnight in Chattanooga, they reached Marion on the twenty-second to find Rosemont, as Anderson noted irritably in his diary, "in the grip of babies and Christmas . . . The house more or less a bedlam." He survived the day itself, possibly because of a cocktail party in the afternoon, but for the following four days was depressed and unable to work. Suddenly on the twenty-ninth he exploded into a streak of writing, excitedly putting "An Open Letter to an English Writer" into final shape in an all-day session at his desk and the next day finishing the Maverick article. On the last day of 1939 he celebrated by writing "The Finding," which he thought "may be good."[42]

It was and is good, along with "Discovery of a Father" one of the finer episodes in the *Memoirs*, but how factually accurate is it? The contradiction between this account of the visit, in September, 1933, to the rooming house in Chicago where he wrote "Hands" and that in a letter to the Emmetts—the one written more than six years after the event, the other no more than two days afterward—must be examined and their implication understood. The differences are immediately clear and are striking. In "The Finding" it was explicitly a "mistake" for Anderson to take his wife to the house; in the letter the visit was "such a success." As they enter the shabby, run-down house in "The Finding," they come upon a young couple, possibly married but more likely not, quarreling loudly, she with her hair "in disorder" and smoking a cigarette, he "accusing her of taking money from his pocket," the suggestion being that at best he is her lover, at worst one of her customers. When the landlady appears, she is a slattern "in a torn dirty dress" and shows no concern over the quarreling. In the letter she is "suspicious" that Anderson has picked up a woman on the street, suggesting that she wants no misbehavior in her presumably well-run, not noticeably unclean house. In "The Finding" the room is "a shabby little hole . . . all tawdry, the room so small, the wallpaper so dirty"; yet in the letter Eleanor, habitually a well-dressed woman, wants to stay with him there while they are in Chicago, indicating that the room is large enough for two and not unpleasant. To be sure, the two accounts are somewhat similar: in "The Finding" he recalls at length the exaltation of writing "Hands," his own kind of story uninfluenced by other writers, this surely being what he means by "finding" his vocation, while in the letter the room is where he "wrote Winesburg," the book that confirmed his vocation and established his reputation. The room brings back to him happily "old dreams" and "faces popping up," as it were like a daytime occurrence of a welcome "night of faces," and he does not accede to Eleanor's wish, for he wants rather to keep the room in memory "just as it is." In "The Finding," however, the visit is a "mistake" because while he stands by the door without entering the room, he not only remembers how writing "Hands" was "the greatest moment of my life," but also remembers "all my failures" before that moment; and taking his wife's arm he hurries out of the house, "feeling deeply the shame of my many failures" after that moment.[43]

One notes admiringly the skill with which in his brief, packed conclusion Anderson interweaves and balances achievement and failure, shame and exaltation; but good writing does not conceal the obvious, that on the evidence "The Finding" is an imagined reconstruction of the visit, turning it, except for the impassioned parts on the writing of "Hands," from actual success to its opposite. It is a well-told tale but a misleading autobiography or even memoir. Granted that one tends to remember things as one thinks they were rather than as they actually were, granted that one may change one's mind after years of retrospection, and granted that Anderson's memory was often burdened by a sense of failure in life and art, still one must place "The Finding" with its reversals of actuality beside "Discovery of a Father," that adept fabric of fictions, as a reminder that many, possibly most, of the episodes he would write for the *Memoirs* draw to an extent on creative imagination as well as factual memory. On the other hand, it is not

necessary to accept as immutable truth his clever warning in his "Foreword" to this posthumously published book that "Facts elude me . . .
When I try to deal in facts at once I begin to lie." As he warned in "Man
and His Imagination," the "imagination must constantly feed upon reality or starve." To some degree—much, some, little—reality, truth, factual
accuracy exists in the episodes. The truth and fact in "Discovery of a Father" is that throughout his life Sherwood detested his father, a storyteller
or no, and could describe a reconciliation with him only as a fiction. The
basic truth, facts, in "The Finding" are that in September 1933 in Chicago
he did indeed visit the room where he exultantly wrote his own new kind
of story and parts of a groundbreaking book, and many times in early and
later life he experienced a sharp sense of failure. One goes to *Sherwood
Andersons' Memoirs* for *both* autobiography and storytelling.[44]

13

Home Town, Memoirs, and Others

1.

The streak of writing at the *Memoirs* continued briefly into the new year with "Sherwood writing at top speed," Eleanor noted in her diary. He started a portrait of John Emerson on January 1 and switched the next day to one of the Italian poet Emanuel Carnevali, which as "Italian Poet in America" he finished in two more work mornings. Such portraits, she explained, "will also tell his own story (what he has thought)." Before he completed this second piece, he probably felt rich by receiving two checks, one from Chambrun for $450, his share of the sale of "Why Not Oak Hill?" to *This Week,* and the other, amount unknown, in an unexpected and flattering letter from DeWitt Wallace, who wrote: "In surveying the past twelve issues of the *Reader's Digest* we feel that 'Discovery of a Father' was notably the strong feature in the November number. May we therefore, as a gesture of appreciation, make this additional payment?"[1]

One can only guess why he so abruptly dropped the story of Emerson for that of Carnevali. Perhaps he was still thinking of John as the subject of a "terrible novel," whereas Emanuel, whom he had known briefly in Chicago in the late 1910s, would be a portrait quickly written; but his shocking visit with Emerson and his view of him as a self-destroyed man may have made him think of the other, more dramatic self-destroyer. The piece about John Emerson he eventually completed for the *Memoirs* under the title "Money! Money!" would cover only their friendship as boys and as young men in Chicago, and emphasize his admiration for John's skill at getting his way with people, his ability to attract women, and his single-minded drive toward money success, qualities Anderson himself, then a futureless day laborer, was certain he lacked. Even then, however, Sherwood was disturbed that John, frightened by poverty and obsessed by making and keeping money, hated people who failed, contemptuously regarded them as "cattle," whereas he, Sherwood, though also wanting money, was

already making up stories in his mind about people he was passing in the
street and most wanted instead "Penetration into other people's lives. /
Understanding." Carnevali, on the other hand, was in Anderson's portrait
obsessed with women and poetry, a woman's love enabling him, he would
assert, to be "a really great poet"; yet ferociously hating his father back in
Italy, filled with anger and a compulsion to violence, he frightened as well
as attracted women and treated them brutally as objects necessary for his
own sexual and poetic release. Afflicted with syphilis picked up from one
of the many prostitutes he had earlier visited, he showed a gentler side by
living with another of these "women outcasts" who worked in a whorehouse and by loving her as she loved him. Apparently his disease had been
of long standing, for he now became wildly erratic in behavior and maintained that he was near death, "that the beautiful poetry he had hoped to
write would never be written." He appeared once at Anderson's apartment
"thinly clad" on a bitterly cold and snowy night, refused his offer of an
overcoat, ran out in the storm, and was found kneeling in the snow in front
of the house where his lover worked, shouting to God to save his and the
woman's souls. He was taken to a hospital, and so passed out of Anderson's life; but the writer remained convinced that in this night "adventure"
Carnevali was taking "a way of suicide." What Anderson presumably
"thought," as Eleanor put it, was that by presenting these two linked portraits, obsession became a mode of the "grotesque" leading toward or to
the loss of one's talent and one's self.

He had made a New Year's resolution: he and Eleanor must spend the
winter not at "54" but at the Royalton. Unwilling to face Mary, as usual at
Rosemont for Christmas, with this upsetting news, he waited until she left
and then "composed" a letter explaining that, with Eleanor at work all day,
he needed the solitude of a hotel room in which to write intensely and to recover from such intensity, though of course they would see much of her. The
same morning he explained his feeling more fully and exuberantly to Roger
Sergel. He found it "too disturbing to live in a house belonging to another"

And, then, besides, I adore hotel life. There is a grand freedom to it. I find that,
when a man works intensely, as I always must to work at all, he is likely to be irritable, and even nasty, until he recovers. You simply pick up the phone in your
room and tell the girl at the switch board that you are out for 2, 3, 4 hours as you
choose. Then you read, walk up and down, take a drink, do whatever you can to
try to make yourself human again.

Leaving Marion on January 5, they drove to Lynchburg, where Eleanor
had two days of work and he completed "Italian Poet in America." From
there they drove on to Washington, where on the ninth he talked with Edwin Rosskam, editor at Alliance Book Corporation, and Roy Stryker, head

of the Historical Section, Division of Information, of the Farm Security Administration. Stryker wanted him to write the text of a semidocumentary study of American small towns, the photographs to be selected from the huge and growing FSA file of them by such skilled photographers as Ben Shahn, Marion Post, Dorothea Lange, Russell Lee, and Walker Evans. The volume would be one in Rosskam's "The Face of America" series. Anderson had been interested in the project when he had first been approached about it in San Francisco by, presumably, Rosskam, who would have known that few writers had his knowledge of small towns across America. Now having spent nearly a whole day going over possible photographs with the two men, he became so excited about the project that after reaching New York on the tenth and getting settled with Eleanor in a big comfortable room at the Royalton, he gave his first work morning to making notes for what would become his last book published during his lifetime, *Home Town*.[2]

His excitement over a new project turned his January mornings into almost a frenzy of writing a miscellany of pieces. In the second day at his desk he "resurrected" a tale out of *A Story Teller's Story*, "In a Field," his recollection during a boring advertising conference of an incident in his youth when, one night lying in a field, he witnessed two brothers knife-attacking their sister's lover but then amicably settling for his marriage to her, the tale William Rose Benét in his review of the 1924 book had praised as "one of the great short stories of our generation . . . great with the greatness of Homer." The following morning he apparently resurrected part of an old manuscript, "Other Men's Houses," for the *Memoirs*, and for several days thereafter he did more work on *Memoirs*. On the seventeenth he lunched with Stanley Young and others from Harcourt Brace for a talk about doing a children's book, a project that interested him so much, briefly, that he agreed to write the thirty or forty thousand words of "Mountain Boy"—he could do that "off hand," he assured Laura Lu—with an advance of $750. Besides he had only to picture Dave Greear as a "tow head kid," and he might be able to have John do the many required illustrations. On the twenty-first he finished his short piece, "Legacies of Ford Madox Ford"; in response to Chambrun's message that the *Ladies Home Journal* would pay "from four to six hundred dollars" for an acceptable short article by him, on the twenty-sixth he wrote such an article. On the thirtieth he wrote another, "Oh, the Big Words!" in which he asserted his now-frequent theme of escaping world affairs, that "big words" such as "the people" or "the middle class" are empty generalizations preventing real communication, which can best be achieved by thinking "small," understanding individuals, and so grasping "the intimacy of life, its charms, its strangeness, its terrors, its accidental qualities." Probably because it was too short, the *Journal* did not accept the piece, but Chambrun eventually sold it to *This Week* for five hundred dollars. On January 30 he signed contracts to do the two "small books": the "mountain childhood" book for Harcourt Brace and the one about present day life in American small towns for Alliance Book Corporation. The total advance for the two books, he boasted to Laura Lu, was $1,150. Besides, "I think they will be quite simple to do. They should be fun."[3]

Another reason why he could write so many and so varied things in January and contract for more was that from the fifteenth onward he had the services of one of the best of his many secretaries, Miss Jean Black, a senior in high school planning to go on to college and already skilled at taking dictation and typing. Both he and Eleanor found her delightful as well as capable. At the end of the month he wrote Laura Lu that

There was some question when E got her, about her coming here to work, in the hotel room. She is a tall long-legged girl. Some of the things I am doing now are rather intimate revelations of men and women. I said to her—"How about this. Some of the things I will be wanting to dictate are pretty intimate. You may be shocked."

She grinned. "Im from Iowa," she said. She seemed to think that would explain.

"I know you are a realistic writer. I have read your stories. You do not need to be afraid of shocking me."

These modern kids are grand. It saves me a lot if I can just scribble, as I am doing here, then dictate, editing as I dictate.

That he had "turned out a lot of work here" proved he was right in insisting on the Royalton rather than "54."[4]

The big hotel room was indeed the right place to work on the many projects he had; but since the Royalton was close to Forty-second Street and Broadway, "in the heart of things," he and Eleanor, he complained to Laura Lu, were "just now . . . going out too much, [seeing] too many people." Even more than usual there were the lunches with talk, cocktail parties with talk, dinners with late evenings of talk, only occasionally plays to see, infrequently films. During the nearly five months of their stay in New York this time, he saw only six plays, three of them—Clare Boothe's *Margin for Error,* Moss Hart and George S. Kaufman's *The Man Who Came to Dinner,* William Saroyan's *The Time of Your Life*—he dismissed as inferior; but three he admired—James Thurber and Elliot Nugent's *The Male Animal* ("a fine amusing show"), Elmer Rice's *Two on an Island* ("amusing . . . keenly observed"), Ferenc Molnar's *Liliom* ("beautifully done"). All three films he saw he quite liked—a group of Chaplin comedies, Marcel Pagnol's *The Baker's Wife* ("fine French movie"), and especially Pagnol's "wonderful . . . very simple and moving" *Harvest.* Praising this "beautiful French movie" to Laura Lu, he asked, "Why can't our people do some of these simple things? It was like one of my own best stories."[5]

During this New York stay he was occasionally asked to speak. At a dinner of the Euthanasia Society on January 16, he gave a short talk; despite the fact that his name appeared on the letterhead of the society, presumably as a result of his article, "Dinner in Thessaly" in the *Forum*'s Right to Die debate, he noted "They thought I was Maxwell Anderson so I let it go at that." He had reluctantly agreed to speak the next night at a dinner of the National Institute of Arts and Letters, which Eleanor insisted he attend and, to see that he did, even rode there with him in a cab. Although he sat with his old friend Van Wyck Brooks, after ten minutes of listening to the "Old blow blow" president fulsomely praise the members, "second rate men" in Anderson's opinion, he walked out of the "dead" place, disgusted. Brooks also felt that the Institute had become "the elite reward for conformity" but stayed because he was trying to make it "a vital force." Two days later Anderson relented—"who am I to chide the poor fakes"—and wrote an apologetic letter claiming that he had had diarrhea. On March 27 he talked about country newspapers at a luncheon of the Overseas Club, an organization of newspapermen who were or had been foreign correspondents; the next evening he spoke briefly at a dinner of the PEN Club (Poets, Playwrights, Essayists, Editors, Novelists); and the following evening he conversed on radio with some newspapermen at 6 PM, after which he admiringly watched Joe Louis, an "artist" in the ring, retain his heavyweight title by knocking out Johnny Paycheck, "a calm beautiful quick job." Then on May 21 he found it "very amusing" to give a short speech as guest of honor on Whit Burnett's weekly radio program, *Tonight's Best Story*. In sum, Anderson could almost always be relied on to say a few words at an occasion.[6]

The center of his life remained his almost furious burst of writing, which lasted, with interruptions, into mid-February. By the fifth he had switched from the *Memoirs* to the "small town book" and was in Washington with Eleanor, he to talk with Rosskam about text and pictures, she to attend a conference on "the special problems of unemployed young women" and to speak at a session held in the White House, doing "a great job" according to the organizer of the conference. Although Sherwood was unable to hear her speak, he did attend the final meeting of the conference where Eleanor Roosevelt gave the closing address, and he "fell hard" for the president's wife for her "poise, dignity and infinite good sense and courage." Otherwise he did not like the Washington atmosphere with its "seemingly necessary bureaucracy-newspaper men peddling gossip, eternal conferences, etc, etc. It's better to be where people just go along, earning a living." Back in New York, he worked hard on the town book and saw such people just going along as Stieglitz, Perkins, and George Jean Nathan. For an article on Nathan in *Life* he had his picture taken with him at the Ritz bar and again at Club 21; and another night he was a guest along with several painters at a men's dinner at "the famous '21'" given by Ben Hecht, where a "nice thing happened" to him, pleasingly out of character with the milieu. "Here we were," he wrote Laura Lu, "in the most expensive resturant in town, full of the sons and daughters of the rich, movie stars, etc and during the evening eight of my books were brought to me to be signed, not by the rich and fashionable but, in every case, the hard working waiters."[7]

He was writing away at "American Town" all morning and dictating letters to Jean Black in the afternoon on February 13, after which he took an evening train for St. Louis with a connection to Oklahoma City, where Clark Getts, his lecture agent since 1936, had booked him to speak at a luncheon at a convention of the Oklahoma Education Association on "What Makes an American Writer." Despite heavy snows and train delays, he reached Oklahoma City in the morning of the fifteenth in time to learn that he was to give *two* lectures and to put together the extra one for an evening meeting of rural teachers, which he managed to get through. The following noon he gave his expected speech to a congratulatory audience of state high school and college English teachers. He was up early the next morning, when snow had turned to heavy rain, in order to catch his train east; and again he came down with a miserable cold, which soon turned into a "slaughtering" one. Worn down by the lecturing after weeks of hard-driving writing, missing the long trips to the warm South he and Eleanor had once been able to take, he had collapsed by the time he was back in New York into what became, with occasional respites, a two-week siege of full-fledged flu. Not until March 4 did he get back to work on the small-town book, but then he wrote at it fairly steadily throughout that month, finding as he went along, he told Rosskam, "that writing of just the phys-ical aspects of the towns doesn't satisfy me. I keep wanting to people the towns, fill them with town characters. It may be the only way I can work. It may be because I can only think and feel in terms of people." By the first day of April he could note in his diary, "Coming to the winding up of 1st draft of Home Town book"—he had found his title—and, he added, "Have enjoyed writing it."[8]

From the first he had been deeply interested in the many photographs of small towns and their life that would accompany and illustrate his text, and he was full of suggestions of shots that should be selected from Roy Stryker's huge files or should be taken for *Home Town*. To Stryker he sent a two-page list of them, including

Before the coming of the movies, every town had its opera house where road companies used to come. There must be some of these in existence and I would like a shot of the front of one.

I want to bring out how the radio and the movies have changed life in the towns. It has pretty much broken up the little assembly of citizens that used to gather at the back of the drug store, the hardware store, the harness shop, or some other place. These would be country lawyers, doctors, and so forth discussing national politics. I would like such a shot.

And so on and so on, even though none of these suggestions would be taken. Filled with energy, willing to take on other tasks, he dictated a note to the editor of the *Writer,* a small professional magazine, on the morning of April 5, agreeing to try to send him an article as soon as he finished the book "within the next two or three weeks," though what he did eventually send was only the text of his Olivet speech, "A Writer's Conception of Realism," shortened through omissions by about a third. The same morning he wrote Rosskam that only a few short sections of *Home Town* remained to be done and that he would be heading south for a brief change of scene. On the sixth he went up to Mary's Valley Cottage by train to pick up his car, left there as usual to avoid the expense of a city garage; and the next day he and Eleanor drove to Atlantic City where she was to attend the ten-day YWCA national convention. By the ninth he was in Marion for two days, seeing that Ripshin had withstood the winter well, working on *Home Town,* and sending off to *This Week* "American Small Town," a version of section 3 of the book, at Meloney's urgent request for something from him for her editorial page. Then he drove on south into North Carolina to see Mimi in Madison and approve of the way she was running the newspaper, spend a night with the Paul Greens in Chapel Hill, and finally on the fourteenth farther south, "the whole country in bloom" with dogwood, to Southern Pines for four days with his now special friends, James and Katherine Boyd. Here he went most days to the trotting horse tracks at nearby Pinehurst to watch the "many lovely fast animals" being trained, and twice he and Jim talked long into the evening. His last day there Eleanor came by train from Atlantic City, on the eighteenth they headed north by car, and on the twentieth they drove through cold, heavy rain to chilly New York, where he arrived with the beginnings of a three-day attack of flu.[9]

When he was able to write again, he worked on the sections near the end of *Home Town* concerning two central institutions of the small community, the churches and the schools. As before, he and Eleanor were pulled back into the lunches-parties-dinners routine, and he went to watch the Giants win over the Red Sox and the Yankees over the White Sox; but with part of the book's last chapter yet to be written, he came down on May 4 with another slaughtering cold, which quickly developed into a two-week stretch of a most enervating flu and fever. Too weak most of the time to work, he could do little but lie about the hotel room and read Frederick Jackson Turner's *The Frontier in American History* and *Moby Dick.*

Worried about his repeated attacks of illness, he called in a doctor, who was, he noted, "woman—very charming—said I was too fat and hurt my pride." He briefly recovered enough on May 14 to finish *Home Town* and presumably to have Eleanor mail the whole manuscript to her mother to arrange for a quick typing up of a fair copy, but the effort exhausted him. Still, the next day he made a start on the "Mountain Boy" book, perhaps thinking that a new project might get him over feeling "weak and floppy," perhaps also because he had become concerned about son John's finances. For some months his son had been supported with thirty-five dollars a month as an artist on the Works Progress Administration payroll, but whatever he painted must be turned over to the WPA. Sherwood had persuaded John to accept fifty a month from him so that he could retain his paintings for some future exhibition, and Sherwood, counting on Mary Emmett's generosity and eagerness to help any Anderson, then suggested she might take over the payments. Meanwhile, until this day he had done no work on the children's book, which he had originally thought of as "a realistic story" when back in January he had asked John to begin making illustrations for it. More recently he wrote John that he was going to "just play with it, make it a fantasy," and on May 20 he would tell a newspaper interviewer that he was "thinking about 'a fantastic child's book'"; but realistic or fantastic, he would make little or no progress with "Mountain Boy" after this one morning's work. As for the monthly payments to John, Mary readily took them over.[10]

After two visits to the woman doctor, Dr. Eugenia Ingerman at 27 Washington Square, and a letter of medical advice from Henry Van Meier, he began slowly to recover from his distressing sickness, which at times seemed to him to be part of a "world sickness" caused by the daily bad news of the invasion of the Netherlands and Belgium by the German armies, news, he wrote Trillena White, he could not "get . . . out of my mind." By May 20, however, he began getting back to his desk in the mornings. The fair copy of *Home Town* having come from Laura Lu, he sent it off on May 22 to Henry G. Koppell, head of the Alliance Book Corporation, which was publishing Rosskam's "The Face of America" series, sending it to him rather than directly to Rosskam as editor so that the second half of the four hundred dollar advance, due upon delivery of manuscript, could be mailed to him quickly. That same morning Anderson wrote a draft of a piece for the editorial page of *This Week*, "The Dance Is On," which reflected his sickness over the war in Europe by arguing that machines, capable of producing "a proud rich new world," a dance "of joy and new life" for every one, were now an "inanimate monster," loosed on the world with a horrible destruction of towns, cities, countless human beings. "It is up to man who made [the monster] to control it. Is it all to end in a dance of death or in a dance of new rich life? / The dance is on." After dictating a final draft to Jean Black, he mailed it on the twenty-fourth to Chambrun, who had just sent him a ninety dollar check from the sale of "You Be the American Zola" to *Coronet*. The same morning he dashed off at DeWitt Wallace's telegraphed request "an amusing true anecdote" for the next issue of the *Digest*. Both editorial and anecdote would subsequently be turned down, but for the moment his brief flurry of writing for the renumerative mass market was over. He wanted desperately to get away from the city to the country, since, as he wrote Paul Cullen, "The whole terrible mess in Europe now seems too close to me here." At one farewell dinner where Paul Rosenfeld was a guest, he was irritable, even "grew angry and spit at him, spoiling the dinner party." On May 29, after a much pleasanter dinner the evening before at the Galantières, he and Eleanor, much to his relief, set off by car for Marion.[11]

2.

Since Eleanor had to return to New York almost as soon as they reached Marion on May 31, and since John Sullivan and other help had much yet to do to get Ripshin ready for summer, Sherwood spent much of the next three weeks at Rosemont, "renewing" as he put it, "touch with the town," occasionally driving to the farm to work with Sullivan, occasionally writing in the mornings. He started a never-finished story, "Who's Your Friend?," which as often happened with him, he admitted, turned into another story, also unfinished, and put in a few mornings "on book," presumably the *Memoirs*. It was an unfocused, in-between time. Although he had wanted to keep away from newspapers and radio reports as much as possible, he could not shut out news of the collapse of the French armies before the German assault and, on June 14, occupation of Paris, which, he noted, "left everyone stunned" and himself in a day-long depression. As always he missed Eleanor greatly, and his mood improved when she arrived in Marion on the nineteenth on the morning train from New York, which may also have brought in the mail a welcome note from Chambrun with a check for $450 from his sale of "American Small Town" to *This Week*. The next day the first guests of the summer arrived, Augusto Centeno with his American wife, Myrtle, who, as arranged, were to have the run of Ripshin while the Andersons were at Camp Merrie-Wood in North Carolina for Eleanor's annual week with women industrial workers.[12]

Annually also, when they arrived there on the twenty-first, Anderson delighted in the lake and the mountain country but found that the camp held "Too many women." Quickly he got into the habit of leaving after breakfast to drive the mountain roads, "banked with laurel, now in full bloom" until he found a good spot to sit and write all morning. He started and dropped a new novel, but most of the time, he wrote to Sergel, "I work on notes—something I call—'Notes for Troubled Times' . . . I've an idea Roger that, after all our democracy has been a thing run by business—by money. Now we shall have a world run by soldiers." Afternoons, however, he could stand women in small groups and happily took five at a time on long drives, for them unusual and unexpected, around the highlands of the southwest corner of North Carolina and the northwest corner of South Carolina. At such times he could shut out thoughts of a Europe at war. "It is impossible," he commented to Roger, "to think or feel beyond a little circle—Outside that all is blank. A man listens to scraps of conversation, of factory girls here. How little it all changes when you do that—the same human impulses, hates, loves, desires." It is impossible to know the nature of the unnamed short story he wrote beside a mountain road during one midweek morning, but that of the section of the *Memoirs* he was about to write is explicit, and one surmises that he may have been prompted to it by his awareness of the various girls and women in his car, and perhaps something in their scraps of conversation.[13]

Back at Ripshin with Eleanor at the end of June, he went almost at once into a series of long work mornings on the *Memoirs* beginning with "the story," as noted in his diary, of his "first attempt at love making with a woman—its ridiculous ending." The account, titled "Second Woman," is one of the few written examples of Anderson's reported skill at ribald oral storytelling. Almost every evening two girls used to walk the streets of Clyde enticing men and boys for free sex. One was the daughter of a drunken tailor, the other that of a man who lived by going from town to town exhibiting a stuffed whale on a railroad flatcar. One evening, a bolder boy than Sherwood arranges to go with the tailor's daughter, Sherwood to go with Lula, "the daughter of the whale," as Anderson puts it in the 1969 text (*Lily*, in the 1942 edition). Eager for a first full sexual experience, but uneasy about sexual competence and ashamed at violating the moral code, Sherwood goes along. The foursome stroll across the railroad tracks and into a moonlit field where Lula takes off her white panties and lies down. Eager, frightened, ashamed all at once, Sherwood stands with his "own short pants" dropped and suddenly feels on his bare buttocks the sting of a handful of coarse railroad gravel thrown by a man who has quietly followed the four and spotted those "little buttocks shining in the moonlight." Clutching up his pants, Sherwood runs off in panic, hysterically calling out repeatedly, "Get your pants, Lula." Word of the incident spreads, for days afterward townspeople call out or whisper to him, "Get your pants, Lula," and for some time he is "terribly afraid of women and girls."[14]

True recollection for the most part or mostly invented story? There is evidence that the diary entry favors essential truth, with the usual allowances for the storyteller's embellishments; and one bizarre minor detail can be confirmed: years later Karl, though his memory was failing, could firmly recall that there was indeed a Clyde man who exhibited a stuffed whale on a railroad flatcar. But other kinds of "truth" besides the literal enter here. The incident and those immediately following illustrate Anderson's conviction that sexuality is a powerful force in people's lives and must be dealt with by writers honestly, in this case as having its hilarious side. (Even in 1942 a few reviewers of the *Memoirs* would object to such material as merely sordid.) There is the "truth," which most memoirists need to establish as early in their books as possible, that the narrator is essentially dependable, and surely one ought to be able to trust a memoirist who can make fun of himself or herself, even though that trust can be seriously tried as in Anderson's case by such a fine if untruthful piece as "Discovery of a Father." Then there is the truth in Anderson's direct picture of the contradictions in small town sexual mores, a picture that he had given with such brilliant indirection through George Willard's "adventure" in "Nobody Knows." So the boy Sherwood knows the overt code of sexual conduct, the taboo against premarital sexuality, and feels shame at intending to break that taboo, while also driven by his adolescent urgings and the covert code stipulating that one becomes truly a man only when he has had full sexual experience with a woman—a code tacitly recognized even by the overt one in that the activities of Lula and her friend go on unhampered except in the single instance of the man with a handful of railroad gravel, who may of course simply be playing a prank, using the taboo rather than enforcing it. In fact, the calls and whispers of "Get your pants, Lula" by the townspeople, which drive Sherwood into being "terribly afraid of women and girls," is a form of using rather than enforcing the taboo, having a community joke rather than inflicting punishment for a moral lapse. Anderson understood his own and other home towns.[15]

The memoirs-writing Anderson had three more intense work mornings after the beginning one, and it would seem likely that he used them to continue "Second Woman" with the "Third Woman," which immediately follows it in the 1969 *Memoirs,* in this way obviously forming a developing sequence in his sexual adventures. In "Third Woman" he first refers to subsequent undeclared crushes on school girls and describes how one winter's night he watches though a house window as a naked girl inside turns her body around slowly before a stove for warmth. The main part of this section concerns a period when he, at fourteen, is drawn into an affair with a beautiful girl staying with her grandparents in Clyde. After days of rapture in this "paradise" of the flesh, he begins to fear that she might become pregnant and stops seeing her; yet he now feels superior to other town boys who talk about sex, "but who among them had known, had been privileged to know such an adventure as that of my own?" The reader is left to wonder whether this account is actuality or daydream or something of both. At least Anderson is announcing, in this last, long episode in the series on his early sexuality, the end of his fear of women and girls—except as they might in some way interfere with his "great plans" for the future, at that point "to be a businessman and grow rich." Subsequently, of course, it would be his writing that ultimately needed to be protected.[16]

That he seems to have written of the two women in sequence was atypical of Anderson's usual practice in composing his book. In the section of the 1969 *Memoirs* titled "What Time Is It?" he explicitly rejects chronology as his framework: "I cannot do my book in that way, checking off the days, months, years by the calendar. They do not come into my mind so." Rather, his "method" usually was to begin writing on any particular morning about any memory that came strongly into his mind, an erratic but effective approach to his material. He had gone directly into "Second Woman," but he had prepared the reader for a "First Woman" episode, turning the pair into an ascending series of three in sexual knowledge: "The incident of the little girl under the porch did not count. Now [with Lula] it was to be real." Possibly the incident had not warranted full development into a story, but on some earlier or later morning when he was working on "What Time Is It?," he illustrated his own sense that "Time is slippery."

Was I a boy of ten when that little neighbor girl got me to crawl with her under the porch of the house? How hot still and strange it was, lying so close to her under there, tasting, for the first time, of the fruit of the tree. We were merely nibbling at it. Was I ten then or was I fifteen?

So he ends this section repetitively for emphasis:

Time is a slippery thing. Time sequence is meaningless. I have to tell my stories of the people and events of my life as they come into my head.

Whatever may have happened in that hot intimacy it was clearly not full intercourse, but at least it was the beginning of sexual knowledge.[17]

During the four days devoted to two women he was "in a good splash of writing," as he called it in a letter to Stanley Young urging him to come visit and talk about the book; but then he was stopped by events, first by a gathering at Ripshin over the Fourth and fifth of July of all available members of the Copenhaver and Anderson families, during which on impulse he offered to have one of Mimi's children stay all summer. Fortunately she did not accept the offer, for, as he noted realistically, "I am not good with children." Then Myrtle Centeno found some letters written to Augusto by another woman he loved, and after two "stormy" days of tears and anger she left Ripshin—and her husband. Then John Peale Bishop arrived from New York on Anderson's invitation to come for a few days before driving with him to the Fifth Annual Olivet Writers' and Readers' Conference. On the thirteenth the Andersons and Bishop set off for Olivet. After driving through Clyde the next day and putting Eleanor on the New York train at Sandusky, Sherwood and John reached Olivet in the evening of the fourteenth in time for the General Assembly with which the conference opened.[18]

For almost all his time there he found this summer's conference not as pleasant as the previous one. Unlike his light workload in 1939, this time it was heavy, and the manuscripts he had to read were all bad except for a "fairly good" novel-in-progress by a nearly blind woman, Marian Judd of Fanwood, New Jersey, whom he would continue to encourage by suggesting publishers who might be interested. He liked Robert Penn Warren as a person but again found Katherine Anne Porter a "cold woman"; and where he had enjoyed the late-night partying before, he now went to bed early. He objected to "a little clique of the more precious ones"—Porter and even Warren and Bishop and others—"who get away with it [in their lectures] by analyzing everything," whereas he tended simply to tell stories, entertaining his audiences but, he suspected, not teaching them much. Usually his classes and lectures seemed to go "O.K."; when at the All Star evening midway through the conference several of the speakers read from their work, his reading of "The Egg," he felt, "went big." Still, he had no time at all for his own writing because of many interruptions, early in the two-week period it turned and continued "blistering hot," he missed Eleanor greatly, and he wrote her about the conference that "probably the whole thing doesn't pay—a waste of time." Then, possibly on July 26, his last morning there, Mary Colum, whom he had liked at the previous conference, announced during her lecture on criticism that, as Eleanor would record, "If you want to know what an artist is its Sherwood Anderson," and in one of his abrupt reversals in mood at this praise, he ebulliently decided that the conference was a success. He later wrote Joe Brewer that he had enjoyed it even though he felt he had not contributed much to it and would not come to the next one.[19]

With the summer temperatures rising to record heat, he drove away from Olivet that afternoon, picked up Ferdinand Schevill at nearby Marshall, and the next morning met Eleanor's train in Sandusky. Heading south, they stopped in Clyde to introduce Ferdinand to Herman Hurd, that "sweet" man, as Eleanor noted in her diary, adding Herman's story of how his father had bought a barrel of olives for the grocery store. "Clyde people didn't buy. S & Herman reached in & got a handful each til whole barrel gone." The next visit, to Trillena White in the hospital at Springfield, was a sad one, however, for this woman who had awakened the young Anderson to good literature was nearing death. It would be the last time he saw her. On the twenty-eighth, with the heat at its peak, the three reached Marion and on the following day got to Ripshin in time for the first of several record rains.[20]

Driven by his pent-up need to get back to writing and by word that Stanley Young would be arriving on, literally, a flying visit, Anderson in the morning of July 31 drafted "One by One," an article arguing that those who use abstract expressions like "the masses" are unable to look "beneath the big empty words to what is right next to them, to what is all around them, to the individuals who are 'the people,' to the adventure of their days, the ever-varied texture of their lives, the dreams and hopes that, slowly, they work to make into reality." That afternoon Eleanor, Ferdinand, and Sherwood drove south beyond Bristol to the Tri-City Airport just inside North Carolina to meet Stanley's plane and thus begin two evenings and a day of constant talk among them all. Stanley, Eleanor noted, "thinks S one important remaining figure and thinks his memoirs would sell—Wants them for Harcourt." Young was a powerful persuader, and when on August 2 the three drove him to Tri-City for his return flight, he had assured Anderson that a contract would follow. Even before the contract arrived, Anderson wrote him, "I am sure your fellows are the one I want for the book."[21]

That visit, as he exclaimed to Young, started him "throwing ink all over the place." One noon he brought in from his cabin a story, "Henry & 2 Women," which he told Eleanor he had "dreamed in the night" and written entirely that morning. She thought it "Good, but no one will publish it and if they do will say he is sex obsessed." The next day he "came in with story for memoirs—Woman whose husband wore her out with constant intercourse. S pushed me to know if I liked it—I said yes but no one would believe it happened. He swears it did and that he never felt so sorry for anyone as the woman as she talked." On August 11 he began a childhood story, "Big Fish," one safe for inclusion in the *Memoirs* and which *This Week* would buy for the usual five hundred dollars and ask for more pieces from the book. This amusing tale is worth summarizing for its unexpected relationship to "Second Woman." One day at school he wishes that he were out fishing like a neighbor boy who has "inflammatory rheumatism" yet can go fishing; so he complains to the teacher of aching all over, such a symptom being what he imagines that disease produces. Sent home by the kindly teacher and to bed by his busy mother, he sneaks off with his fishpole to the town pond. Here he hooks a huge carp, nearly half as big as himself, leaps into the pool, wrestles it to shore, and runs home clutching the still-struggling fish. (The storyteller pauses to explain that during "a big spring freshet" a dam to a private pool breaks, releasing carp in that pool into the stream feeding the pond.) He is praised by the whole family as a "big hero" until his father, who by chance met the teacher after school, asks what had ailed him. Without thinking, Sherwood replies that he had had the inflammatory rheumatism, whereupon the family bursts into jeering laughter. Beginning to cry, he insists that he does have it and runs upstairs, knowing "it would be a long time before I heard the last of the inflammatory rheumatism." Soon afterward his mother comes upstairs and, as Anderson puts it with an indirection neatly relating both end of story and beginning, makes a new part of his body ache because of his lying and skipping school.[22]

Despite their obvious differences, "Second Woman" (written shortly before the unproductive Olivet break) and "Big Fish," (written shortly after), have the same overall pattern: Sherwood as a boy rebels against standard social constraints, at first achieves something (Lula wants him, he catches the carp), but from his own inadvertent speech is humiliated. The puzzling questions, perhaps unanswerable, are why the pattern exists and what it may mean, if anything. Perhaps it was only to use twice the technique of assuring readers that Anderson is being essentially truthful, if not in detail, about his life and is willing to tell all, the admirable and the unadmirable. The fact of self-inflicted humiliation, however, would seem to confirm that at times in his boyhood he had had a sense of insecurity within town and family and, as a result, some resentment against both. That he could now write of this insecurity and resentment with such amusement would show that in maturity he could look back on them without acute discomfort, merely accepting the pattern as representing a part of his boyhood feelings. Of course he may have simply been playing with his readers in the manner of Fred in "The Persistent Liar," the very first piece Chambrun acknowledged receiving from him, on September 9, after getting "Big Fish" on August 26. In "Liar," this rather manipulated and reader-manipulating tale, very likely prompted by a now-amused recollection of the Centeno blowup, Fred tells a listener that he came into the bedroom one night to find his wife, Carrie, reading a love note to him from Mabel, which he had carelessly left on the table thinking she was out for the evening; but before he tells his listener more, he digresses into a barely believable account of how he and Carrie had got married after accidentally having to spend a night wedged side by side in a boys' unfinished tree house. Returning to the present situation, Fred tells how, while the stunned Carrie looks out their bedroom window, he takes the note into the bathroom and flushes it down the toilet, so that "now there wasn't any note." Then he begins to test out "scientifically" on his stormily weeping wife his long-held theory that "If a man lies and keeps on lying presently people will believe." For several years he persists that there was no note until Carrie is convinced that she had had an hallucination. "And now," he tells his listener, "when I come to speak of all this, I am myself in a very strange state. I may be lying to you. I may just be amusing myself . . . There is nothing in the world so powerful as persistence."[23]

3.

While Anderson was working on "Big Fish," the occasional heavy rains became all-day, every-day ones until in a storm on August 14 Ripshin Creek flooded, temporarily wrecking their spring-fed water system and bringing down from the hills huge logs that tore out both their bridges and left the cars marooned by the house. In spite of continued rain John Sullivan and friends began building a new bridge for the cars that day, and Anderson soon abandoned writing for the excitement and interest of bridge building out of logs from the woods. Five days later the bridge was finished, "better than the old one," he noted; but equally exciting was the arrival in the mail on the twenty-second of a contract for the *Memoirs* from Harcourt, Brace. He continued nevertheless to work fairly steadily on pieces for the book, one, "I See Grace Again," describing a brief chance conversation during his 1926 lecture tour with a plain, self-doubting woman who had comforted him with an affair during his disturbed last months in Elyria, a recollection demonstrating again that he was writing not by chronology but as person or event might suggest itself. Such a mode of composition would have been accentuated at this point by his actual continuing indecision whether to stick with Perkins and Scribner's or go to Young and Harcourt. When Scribner's delayed a long time in forwarding a letter inquiring about rights to publish his works in Chile, he complained to Max that "This is the sort of thing that convinces me that the house of Scribner's is not much interested in me." Perkins, trying to placate him, wrote back, calling Anderson a master of his craft. Replying to Max on the sixteenth, Sherwood asserted that such praise did not help him financially, and only Horace Liveright had understood that, as Anderson firmly believed, "the American people do not buy books. Books are sold to them." Scribner's should have done "a better job of selling my books than I got." On the twenty-third, the day after he received the Harcourt contract, he wrote Young that its "main provisions . . . are O.K.," though of the $3,000 advance offered he wished to receive only $2,000, the remaining $1,000 to be paid when he delivered the manuscript, since he wanted the cancellation of the mountain childhood book contract upon his return of the $750 advance on it in order that he could be wholly "absorbed" in the *Memoirs*. In addition he wanted the right to sell short pieces from it to magazines. On that same day just as he went to his desk to write Young, he received a letter from Perkins asking that they talk together before he signed any contract. Because of his "warm personal feeling for [Max], as man and friend," he next wrote Young, he would agree to such a talk but would keep him informed as to its outcome. "The whole matter," he confessed, "has got me a bit feverish." Anxious to keep Anderson and the book with Scribner's, the busy Max arrived in Marion on the early morning train on September 7 for two straight days of talk with him at Ripshin. By the time Max left he had persuaded Sherwood to talk with Mr. Scribner in New York before making a final decision. Explaining the outcome as well as he could to Young, Anderson admitted that "I'm afraid Stanley that I am more confused than ever," but assured him he would talk with him first in New York.[24]

Meanwhile, the book kept "pouring out." In the morning of September 12 he "Wrote a long piece I did not like so destroyed it and wrote another." During the next two mornings, working in the house by the fire rather than in his cabin, chilly because of the approach of fall, he seems to have written all of "Mary, the Dogs, and Theda Bara," memories of living in Palos Park. Then it took him two more mornings to do the short piece on "*The American Spectator,*" a good part of it a defense of Dreiser, one of the magazine's many editors, and one of its major weaknesses, he argued. On the sixteenth, his first *Spectator* morning, he wrote a confident letter to Young stating that he was putting off his choice between Harcourt and Scribner's until after he arrived in New York late in October. Perkins had reported Edward Weeks's interest in serializing the *Memoirs* in the *Atlantic Monthly*, and what, he cannily asked Stanley, was Harcourt's feeling about serials? And had Stanley found anyone interested in turning some of his stories into movies? It was a flash of foxiness out of his advertising days where he had learned how to use one company and client against another. Two days later he dropped into a four-day depression and inability to write brought on, he felt, by his weeks of "intense writing"; though he was probably also realizing that he had only deferred, not made as he must, a vexing decision.[25]

His depression broke on September 22 with the activity of packing up. Since Eleanor had to leave for New York and her job that evening, they moved into Marion where, at Rosemont, they kept a small apartment arranged for them and where he now wrote and slept for a month. The fall was extraordinarily beautiful that year, as he repeatedly noted in his diary, and he was "terribly lonely" for Eleanor to share it with him. So glorious were the hills in their changing colors that he could not resist going back to Ripshin many afternoons to help ready the farm for winter or driving alone or with Laura Lu or even B. E. over Walker Mountain into the Rich Valley or along backroads among the hills. By early October, wherever he went by car or on foot "the whole mountain country [was] a sea of color." It was "the most beautiful fall [he had] ever known here." He could not have known, of course, that it was a kind of climax to his life at Ripshin, that he would not see another autumn, anywhere. Yet although he missed Eleanor to live with him in it, the surrounding sea of color buoyed him into writing. Day after day, with occasional exceptions, he would record a "good morning's work" on some unnamed piece for the *Memoirs*, and on the morning of October 2 he wrote a short story for the book based on a neighbor mountain man, Trealy Walls, whose first name he spelled Treely (changed in the 1969 *Memoirs* to Truly). Originally he was to be "a little Jesus Christly kind of man" in the aborted "fantasy" mountain childhood book he had described to John for illustration; in "Truly's Little House," however, he is realistically "a rather small athletic looking man with a red beard," one who had not helped build Anderson's house but a good farmer with a knack for making and keeping money, who had built a little house (a privy) on stilts over the creek just upstream from Ripshin. Anderson embeds his instructive tale in the mind-set of mountain people he had come to know so well. Legally the house should have been built some distance from the stream, "but we did not think too much of the law in the hills."

What had the law done for us? It interfered when we wanted to make a little moon from our corn, raised on our own land. It collected taxes, wanted to regulate our trout fishing in mountain streams, at that time paid no attention to our roads. The law was a given, rather determined thing, far off, that occasionally lit down on us. It even wanted to decide, if you shot another man, whether you were in the right or in the wrong.

When "I," wishing to keep the creek clean for bathing, goes to ask Truly to move his house away from it, "I" makes the mistake of starting by citing the law, recognizes his mistake, and offers to pay the cost of moving. Truly is unpersuaded. Realizing that "I" would be in trouble if he has "the law on [Truly]," he waits for a time and one day meets Truly in the road, tells him that he hears from the neighbors that Truly won't move his house, but he himself has told them that they're wrong, "that Truly is as good a neighbor as they are." Truly grins, says "You're damned right I am," and moves his house that afternoon. Three years later Truly lets "I" dig a wagon load of wild azaleas from his land. When "I" offers to pay him for them, Truly scoffs, "What kind of neighbor would that make of me?" He starts to walk away, turns, grins, says, "I guess you might pay me for moving that little house." When "I" pays him, he walks away satisfied. Reading this tale, one understands why Anderson always insisted on a basic rule for country newspaper editors, or anyone: "Always leave a man with his self-respect."[26]

News from Chambrun about other pieces was mixed. When he wrote that the "For What?" story, which had been refused by several mass-market, well-paying magazines, could be accepted by the *Yale Review* for only thirty-five dollars, Anderson reluctantly agreed, but in less than a week the delighted agent reported that *This Week* would take "Big Fish" for five hundred. Other news was mostly good. Having already a lecture engagement in Detroit for the end of October, he was invited by Allan Seager, short story writer and professor of English at the University of Michigan, to speak at Ann Arbor near the Detroit date, and he could also get in a short visit to Olivet to see his friends there. *Home Town* was to be published in mid-October, and he thought an early copy, which Edwin Rosskam had sent him, was a good-looking volume with its many skillfully shot and selected photographs of small town scenes and people. Since this was to be his first book to appear in three years, he especially wanted it to be reviewed well and to sell well. Agreeing with Anderson that books are not bought but sold, Rosskam came to Marion on October 6 and spent much of the next day with him at Ripshin shooting publicity photos, to his annoyance since he disliked picture sessions, making, he complained, "a regular movie actor out of me." Nevertheless, Rosskam knew his business; he had Anderson inscribe a personal copy of *Home Town* to Eleanor Roosevelt, which he planned to present to her himself, persuaded him to send a copy to Henry Wallace, who came through obligingly with a fine letter of praise just right "for publicity," and in a day or two after the photo session had arranged for Anderson to speak at The Book Store in Washington early in November. Impressed and pleased by Rosskam's campaign, Anderson summarized it from long and not always happy experience: "Everything helps in getting a book launched." His own further contribution to the launching was a letter to Rosskam urging an investigation of the current South American interest in the United States, specifically seen in the publication of some of his books and stories in translation. Rosskam should send copies of *Home Town* to Juan Adolfo Vasquez, a young translator in La Plata, Argentina, interested in his works, and of course to María Luisa Bombal. A trip to South America was much on his mind.[27]

Heading northwest by train on October 21, he met his two lecture engagements—on the short story in Seager's literature class at the University of Michigan in the late afternoon of October 23, and on "The Life of the Writer," at a luncheon meeting of the Detroit English Club on the twenty-fifth, both, he wrote Laura Lu, going "off O.K." Then his Olivet friends Robert Ramsay and Glenn Gosling, who had heard the Detroit lecture, drove him to the college where he talked happily with all his faculty friends until after midnight, the next day spoke to the students about writing stories, and that evening was taken to a train that arrived in New York in the morning of the twenty-seventh. Eleanor, who had already engaged "a nice large room" for them at the Royalton, was deep into the campaign to elect Roosevelt for an unprecedented third term. In his diary entry for October 28, however, Sherwood showed his own priorities. "The whole town full of politics, women with buttons for voters on every corner. E[leanor wearing a 'button as big as your hat,' he wrote Laura Lu] going out to speak for Roosevelt, the newspapers against him, the President here. Nevertheless [during the day] I stayed at my own work . . . I did letters and then went back to work on my book. The bookstores filled with the new Home Town book."[28]

4.

Home Town, a set of essays on the American small town, is a compound of nostalgia and wide-traveled observation put together by the townsman who in *Winesburg* showed the dark side of a community more than its light, and now, as though balancing his masterpiece, genially shows the light side more than the dark. Opening with two of his essays published in *This Week,* "From Little Things" and "We Are All Small-Towners," he repeats his preference for "thinking small" since, as he puts it in a brief new essay completing his introductory group, in the daily intimacy of a town "the problem of living with others [is] a little closer, more persistently present." The following group of four essays takes the life of American towns impressionistically through the four seasons beginning with spring, which brings the "feel of earth invading the towns" from the blooming of the fruit trees and the planting of fields and gardens. Already, however, Anderson is making the reader aware of how modern industrialism has changed the old agriculture-centered towns, for the "almost universal owning of cars" and the "new big paved highways" have brought automobiles glowing through them in "endless rivers, [a sign of] American restlessness." With the essay on summer Anderson begins sketching economies characteristic of different sections of America—cotton in the Deep South, corn in the Midwest—then, in the autumn essay, the harvesting of cotton, of corn, of tobacco in the upper South, potatoes in northern New England and apples in the northern Pacific states. Winter "is the waiting time . . . the test time . . . of men's and women's ability to live together." Noticeably in the seasons group of essays and elsewhere in *Home Town,* Anderson emphasizes the two sections of American he knew best—the Midwest and the South.

The turn of the seasons concluded, he gives the remainder of his book, somewhat less than half the text, to essays on special aspects and institutions of the towns. There is the "small town individualist"—"character" would seem more accurate—such as the bachelor or the woman school teacher who lives alone; the kindly philosopher-mystic (much like Herman Hurd's father as described in the *Memoirs,* 1969, pp. 64–65); the censorious Carrie Nation–type who "hates all kinds of expressions of gaiety or joy"; the admired, capable professional man who at midlife goes to pieces and becomes the town drunkard. "Life in the towns," Anderson suddenly declares, "can be at times terrible or it can be infinitely amusing and absorbing"; it tests one's "skill in living with others." For legal systems in the towns he relies almost entirely on lengthy adaptations of his earlier piece on Virginia justice, concluding, as he had written before, that courtrooms are stages on which are played out "living drama of the everyday lives of everyday Americans." His discussion of small town weekly newspapers is the one he had made familiar in articles, speeches, and *Hello Towns!*— that they should be "intensely local," that their editors must not "rob people of their self-respect," that with the coming of standardization the weeklies began to rely too much on swatches of irrelevant boilerplate material, that since the Depression began younger people are leaving city journalism for the country weeklies and reinvigorating them. More perfunctory is his treatment of the churches, but he points out that membership in any particular church "fixes your social standing in the town life" and that the church is "the center of innumerable activities reaching into many phases of American small town life." He reports briefly but happily that local schools are now much improved, are more focused on training the individual student, have brought education "closer to everyday life." The final essay concentrates on changes in the small towns brought about by technology in modes of travel, especially the automobile, and in communication, especially movies and the radio, changes that helped break down the old isolation of towns. Social attitudes have slowly changed as well; the attitude toward sex is now more lenient, the problems of youth are given more consideration, perhaps most importantly—here the one flash of the early-thirties Anderson—the long oppression of labor by the owners of mines and factories has been met in these towns as elsewhere by a "new consciousness" in labor now that the New Deal has affirmed labor's right to organize. Whatever the effects of "modern machine-driven life," however, most towns will remain close to the land, "out of which," Anderson ends expansively, "has come the vast wealth that has made our America the land of rich possibilities it still remains."

Told, not in the brooding, probing voice of an observer of Winesburg, but in the relaxed, mostly cheerful one of a capable country editor, the text of *Home Town* is pleasant and informative, well suited to the "celebrate America" strain in American writing of the late 1930s and early 1940s. Very likely for this reason, although it is at best a minor work, it received probably more favorable reviews than any other of Anderson's books. By rough estimate 85 percent of some forty-four reviews were very or largely favorable; the praise of the Farm Security Administration photographs as straightforward, objective, revealing was practically unanimous. As the *Herald Tribune* reviewer put it, "The pictures and the text go together like peaches and cream." To be sure, one of the first reviewers, in the October 22 issue of the *New York Times*, considered the photographs "the real matter of the book"; whereas "Mr. Anderson rambles on about life in American small towns without saying much of anything new or getting anywhere in particular, but he says it amiably and characteristically." By

contrast, for example, R. L. Duffus covered the front page of the following Sunday *New York Times Book Review* with an enthusiastic summary
of the book, concluding that the photographers "who took the pictures
did jobs worthy of Mr. Anderson's prose." Again, the brief comment in the
December *Atlantic Monthly* praised text and pictures: "The result is that
Home Town is a book to own and be proud of owning, to give to the most
varied sorts of people, and be proud of giving." Anderson may have been
especially, if wryly, pleased with the recommendation in *Book-of-the-Month
Club* by William Allen White, who two decades earlier had dismissed
Winesburg, Ohio as "the picture of a maggoty mind; a snapshot from a
wapperjawed camera." Fine though the pictures are, "the Sherwood Anderson text is as genuine and as real a story of our rural towns as anyone
has written. Indeed, it is much more beautiful and true than the photographs." That old score was at least partly settled, and the reception of
Home Town in general should, Anderson hoped, bring in good sales during the Christmas season.[29]

5.

The problem of which publisher, Scribner's or Harcourt Brace, should have
the *Memoirs* had now to be faced and solved. As promised, he first talked
with Max Perkins, over lunch on November 2 at the Ritz, and they agreed
that Charles Scribner as head of the firm must be brought into the final discussion. Two days later, Sherwood took Eleanor with him to a lunch with
Harcourt people, and subsequently he talked with two other interested
publishers until the problem "got [him] down." On the eighteenth, he went
to the Scribner's offices for an hour-long meeting with Perkins and Scribner at which he "fought out" with the publisher his old conviction that
books are not bought but sold by the publishing firm, complaining "in a
pretty strong way" that Scribner's had not pushed *Puzzled America, Plays:
Winesburg and Others,* and *Kit Brandon* energetically. Scribner countered
that sales of the three books "had totaled no more than 6,500 copies"—
only *Kit* went into but by no means through three printings—and Max
later maintained that no amount of pushing would have produced much
better sales. Nevertheless, Anderson noted, "Mr. Scribner came across with
a fine offer on the new book." Still convinced, however, that Scribner's
"bad work" caused the poor sales of his three books, he had another lunch
with the persuasive Stanley Young and on November 22, weary of indecision, chose Harcourt Brace as publisher because he felt "more at home
with the fellows there." As usual, stress laid him up with a bad cold for
four days, in the midst of which he and Young agreed on a contract both
for the *Memoirs* and the mountain child book he still wanted to do. Later

he wrote Max an apologetic letter explaining his change and urging that their personal friendship continue.[30]

While all this harrowing indecision and decision was going on, the Andersons were immersed in their usual "strenuous" social life from lunch time onward, but he was able to spend two days in Washington to help advertise *Home Town* with a talk at The Book Store on November 8 and a reception the next day. During his stay there he spoke with Herbert Feis, his friend in the State Department, about his determination to take some kind of trip to South America and the possibility of his being sent there "on a kind of cultural mission, to contact South American writers etc"; but as with his inquiries about a Guggenheim Fellowship he could learn nothing definite. He discussed South America travel routes with Carlos Davila, and for funding he now turned to Robert Littell, associate editor of the *Reader's Digest*. Beginning with a talk at the Century Club on November 21 and another on December 3, the two, with DeWitt Wallace's approval, worked out a financial agreement in a series of letters. In general terms Anderson outlined his proposal for the trip.

What I would like to do is to get up into some South American town, say of five or ten thousand people, settle there for a time and try to get to know the people of such a town; that is to say, not public figures but the people such as a man might get to know in any one of our own towns, as far as possible getting to understand a little their way of thinking and feeling, and trying to pick up the little comedies and tragedies of their lives, much as I have always tried to do in relation to life in our own North American towns.

I do think it may well be quite possible to find for the *Reader's Digest* stories of everyday life in such a town which would be well worth while for your North American readers and that might possibly also strengthen your South American edition.

Perhaps, he suggested, the *Digest* would be willing to "gamble . . . $2,000 or even $2,500" on him. He did not mention that in such a town he also planned to finish and organize the *Memoirs* or that he was longing for a warm place to escape another New York winter and his usual flu attacks. Littell refused a gamble but made a cautiously phrased return offer "which is many yards higher than our usual ante": "If, as I hope, you settle in some rewarding spot and find a piece that you want to write, and if that piece is one we want to print, which I very much hope will be the case, we will pay you $2,000 for it." Anderson accepted his "fine offer" gratefully.[31]

Although his plans for the trip were far from definite, he was determined that sometime after Christmas he and Eleanor would definitely go. On November 11 he purchased a Linguaphone and a set of instructional records for "1 Spanish Conversational Course," and thereafter, for more days on than off, he worked an hour or more to learn the rudiments of the spoken language. Three weeks later he wrote María Luisa Bombal in Buenos Aires that presently they were planning to go through the Panama Canal to Chile and then perhaps to Peru and Argentina, and also to tell her of the Linguaphone and his hope "that by the time we arrive in South America I will at least be able to ask for something to eat, something to drink, and a place to sleep." Wanting more than Linguaphone instruction, he hired a tutor for himself and Eleanor to come to their hotel room beginning December 7 for an hour and a half three times a week. Margarita Madrigal was a "delightful" person, a skilled, lively teacher. Once while she was giving them a lesson, Ferdinand Schevill arrived unexpectedly for a three-day visit, and she at once sat him down with the Andersons to sing Spanish songs, she accompanying on her guitar. At the end of the year, however, Sherwood admitted ruefully that he had made little progress in speaking Spanish and could only hope that "persistence will somewhat make up for my stupidity."[32]

There remained the worrisome financial problem, not only for the expense of the trip but for future income generally. Like the businessman he had been, he had several schemes afloat for making money. Near the end of October, a Hollywood agent named Ned Brown had offered to facilitate getting some of his stories accepted for filming. Anderson was interested in Brown's proposal, but emphasized that he would not himself work in Hollywood or write movie scripts. By December 1, they had agreed that Brown would be his "only representative on the west coast"; though he wanted Brown to work closely with Anita Loos. Still, any income from having stories filmed would be all in the future. Working through Chambrun, he at first expressed interest in preparing a script in another medium, for a radio series, *Big Town*, but soon decided he had no time to do it. He was much put off at being interviewed about small towns on NBC radio the evening of November 19 by Edward Weeks, editor of the *Atlantic*; he did not like Weeks, and he intensely disliked the "artificial claptrap" of an audience directed when to applaud. Nevertheless, he remained interested in the possibilities of radio for experimentation, and by the twenty-eighth he was outlining to Chambrun his own proposal for "A very absorbing weekly program of the every day life in an imaginary American small town," a program that, he was sure, would appeal to the present "hunger in people to get back nearer to the soil"; but after discussing the proposal with several receptive people, he decided in mid-December that Laura Lu was right to advise against it lest it put him into the unhealthy "position of being some kind of public figure."[33]

So, his schemes evaporating, he continued to work on the *Memoirs*, pieces from which were, after all, proving his best sources of income. In mid-November he had arranged to have a stenographer, Justina ("Tina")

Van Deusen, "a very quick and intelligent" Smith College woman, come in to take dictation of his letters, and at least by the beginning of December he went back to his earlier practice of writing a first draft of a *Memoirs* episode in long hand, "a much faster method" for him, and then dictating a more finished draft to Tina. Among the first such pieces was "Crushed Artist," later, with an added section, titled "My Mother Said No," probably written and dictated in one session on December 6, perhaps given a final revision two days later, and sent to Chambrun on the ninth. It is an amusing reminiscence and doubtless true enough. Back when he "might have been twelve or thirteen," he devised a money-making "theatrical venture." He and Toughy McClary, "our local Huckleberry Finn," began staging a brief melodrama on a grass strip by the railroad station before passengers waiting between trains. Advancing with drawn (wooden) knives toward each other emitting dire threats, they would grapple to settle a long-standing blood feud. On their first encounter Sherwood as hero would seize Toughy's knife, but in a noble gesture would hold out both knives in open hand. Toughy as villain would seize both knives and stab Sherwood "to the heart." As he expired in appropriate agony, Toughy would run among the passengers successfully collecting nickels and dimes in his cap. Eventually, however, Sherwood's mother heard about this "smash hit," insisted that he stop the show—as being "too much like begging," and so ended his "first effort in the field of art." For "My Mother Said No," Anderson most conveniently received the usual $450 just before he sailed for South America.[34]

Perhaps already weary from days of pushing at the *Memoirs*, he was "suddenly knocked over" on December 9 by a flu attack, this one lasting for nearly a week. Schevill's visit brought back his energy, and he had put in two good days of writing. An early morning phone call from Marion on the eighteenth brought the devastating word Laura Lu had died. Although Eleanor was terribly shocked by the death of her mother, Sherwood noted admiringly that she was "standing up to it." He himself, after they had busily packed most of the day, felt "half crazed by this sudden disaster to all of us." They took the night train for home and the next morning found the "house at Marion stunned, the center of all life here gone." For three days while Rosemont was flooded with people come to pay their respects to the family, Sherwood tactfully but also because his "nerves [were] on edge" stayed mostly in the upstairs apartment, grieving also over "Mother Copenhaver" who had been, he wrote Karl and Helen, "certainly a second mother to me—that and a kind of sister too. The woman had a lot the spirit and the feeling of an artist and a wonderfully keen critical mind. It's a terrific blow." The funeral service was on Sunday the twenty-second, the day and the countryside, he noted, "beautiful, as though nature were welcoming Mother." His short memorial to her was read, and he liked the minister, but the rest of the services at the church and the cemetery struck him as so Christianly "vulgar" that throughout "the whole performance [he] played an imaginary game of croquet with Mother."[35]

The next morning he went back to work on the *Memoirs,* finishing the foreword, and he continued writing on the book for several mornings including Christmas day, for which this year there were none of the usual preparations. At frequent conferences of the whole gathered family it was decided that Eleanor should be the executor of her mother's estate, and Sherwood usefully drove her and other family members around on errands. The house seemed strange to him now, as though the dead woman, who had been "so filled with life," had left no "sense of death" there, he wrote son John, "Just a kind of queer disappointment that she doesn't suddenly walk through the door." On December 27, he and Eleanor, she still in "a great mess as executor," still bearing up admirably despite her grief, took a train to Knoxville for a two-day YWCA meeting, leaving, being there, and returning in rain, both of them feeling, as Sherwood wrote Lankes, that the death of this "great woman . . . has left a great hole in our lives." Only with his last diary entry for 1940 did the sadness lift. He had a good morning's work, the whole family drove to Ripshin where John Sullivan was keeping everything in good condition, and where, Sherwood noted touchingly, "My little dog very happy to see me which made me glad."[36]

14

The Storyteller's Ending

T HE LATE fall and early winter of 1940 had been a hard time for Anderson physically and emotionally. He had had a serious cold and a bad case of the flu, had agonized for days over leaving Scribner's for Harcourt, and had been devastated by the death of Laura Lu, his long-cherished friend. On January 3, Eleanor left Marion for Chicago for three weeks of YWCA work, and he took the evening train for New York, where, settled in again at the Royalton, he shortly had a brief but intense recurrence of the flu and in less than a week after recovery from that was "slaughtered by the worst head and chest cold yet" for ten days, half the time in bed. Missing Eleanor intensely, war news in the papers on his nerves, he was often depressed, "blue." He was "hating New York," he noted in his diary for January 13, "Want a warm place."[1]

Some days went better. Occasionally, not frequently, he had a good morning of writing or an afternoon of dictation with Tina on the *Memoirs,* and on the fourteenth, with his usual enthusiasm for a new project, he did a rough draft of a half-hour radio play, "Above Suspicion," one of a series of plays celebrating American freedoms by ten writers comprising The Free Company to be presented on CBS from February 23 through May 4. Anderson's theme was freedom from persecution by police, but he never did finish off the draft. In the afternoons, Margarita Madrigal often came to give him Spanish lessons; and when he felt well enough, he spent considerable time trying to find a date for passage to Chile on a Grace Line ship not already fully booked, a task in which he was being assisted by a new friend in the Editors' Press Service, one Roberto Rendueles, whom he regarded as a "very sweet real person, a Spanish gentleman." Evenings he dined alone in his room, when ill, or with friends, four times with his oldest friend of all, John Emerson, who seemed to have recovered completely from "the manic depressant thing . . . at least for the time."[2]

His own depression continued. Even after Eleanor returned on the twentieth in the midst of his slaughtering cold, he felt "so low and n.g. [no good]—so blue, so worthless." He feared that out of a sense of family obligation she might want to return to Rosemont to care for her father, who constantly irritated him; he was discouraged and ashamed that, as he put it, he "could not be a better lover," possibly a reference to some depression-related sexual inadequacy; he wondered dismally how she could love him given "these times, when I do not live." Near the end of January, when it was assured that he and Eleanor would be sailing on February 28, he decided to leave wintry New York and head for the warm South to recover from his series of illnesses, to get back to mornings of good writing, and to escape, physically if possible, from his depression, his overwhelming fear of being to Eleanor "excess baggage." On January 28 he took the evening train for Marion, spent the next day there, already "feeling a bit less blue and worthless," and on the thirtieth began driving south toward Tampa, where he hoped to find a Spanish family with whom to live and so "sharpen up" his uncertain command of the spoken language. After three wearying days of driving he reached Tampa on February 1, took a room at the Hotel Thomas Jefferson, and spent the following three days in bed with a recurrence of the flu.[3]

The results of the Tampa trip were mixed. Despite more cold and rain than sunshine and warmth, he was able to recover fairly quickly from the last onslaught of the flu, and he got in five good mornings of work, at least two on the *Memoirs,* the others on an article designed for the *Reader's Digest* on Spanish Americans, "God Bless the Americas." This last was prompted by conversations, in English, with a pleasant couple named Cortina, Mary a teacher of Spanish at the University of Tampa and Joseph a workman. As often happened, writing steadily and well brought him out of his depression; but though the Cortinas were informative, they were not a substitute for a family he had hoped to live among like the Troutdale Greears. The "few older Spanish families," he wrote Eleanor, "either haven't heard of me or are shy, thinking they aren't intellectual enough." His plan a failure, he left Tampa on February 12, days earlier than he had intended, and at noon on the fourteenth reached Marion, where Eleanor was already waiting for him. They had exactly two weeks left to prepare for their voyage through the Panama Canal to Valparaiso, where their long stay in Chile would begin and from which they presumably planned to depart for home sometime in June after a visit to Buenos Aires to see Bombal, Vazquez, and others. Apparently at the urging of Rendueles, the Grace Line had agreed to pay their round-trip fares for, as Sherwood wrote to Mary Emmett, "'Good Neighbor' purposes," his version of President Roosevelt's "Good Neighbor" policy toward South America countries. As for a town in Chile suitable for their extended stay, Carlos Davila was now in Santiago and would advise.[4]

During his last week in Marion he spent much time answering letters, unabashedly, for example, telling Robert Littell, to whom he was sending the article for *Reader's Digest,* that he had been living with a Spanish family in Tampa "for the last few weeks," and perhaps more truthfully telling Rendueles that, "I think now, that if I can get over my embarrassment in speaking I can begin to get along rapidly as soon as I am where I hear Spanish spoken constantly." Four mornings straight he "really got to work again" on the *Memoirs.* He spent one afternoon at his beloved Ripshin, where as usual John Sullivan had everything in shape, and another afternoon he drove to Abingdon, where he could arrange for his passport through a federal court. For three evenings he talked contentedly with Andy Funk, still his best male friend in town. Then on February 23 he and Eleanor took the overnight train for New York, both by now excited over the prospect of the voyage and the new foreign countries, new people, new experiences.[5]

In New York for the few days left before their ship sailed, Anderson "ran about town seeing people." While A. Caprile, New York representative of the Buenos Aires *La Nación,* helpfully gave him letters to some South Americans, Edward Cardenas, editor of the Spanish American edition of *Reader's Digest,* had to tell him that "God Bless the Americas" had been refused; but Chambrun presented him with a check for $450 from *This Week* for "My Mother Said No" (published as "I Was a Bad Boy"), a useful going-away present. His most satisfying meeting was at the offices of the Viking Press on his last day before sailing. Back in November he had written a long, tactful letter to Ben Huebsch requesting that in accordance with current publishing contracts he be allowed to purchase from Viking the copyrights, plates, and unsold copies of his collections of short stories *The Triumph of the Egg* and *Horses and Men* and possibly his other out-of-print books. Huebsch agreed to sell rights to all of Anderson's books published by John Lane and himself except for *Winesburg, Ohio* and *A Story Teller's Story,* and on February 17 Anderson acquired all rights to six of his first eight books at a cost to him of "$1993.00 borrowed money."[6]

At the end of their few crowded days in New York came, of course, the farewell parties and dinners. The first of these, cocktails at Mary Emmett's home, dinner at a fine restaurant, was on February 26. At the final celebration on the evening of the twenty-seventh brother Karl, James Boyd, and Paul Rosenfeld were also guests for cocktails at the Galantières' apartment, followed by dinner at the Rendueles home. What happened at the Galantières' could later have reminded Sherwood of his opening sentence to an editorial he had recently "dashed off" for the Marion College student publication, the *Squib:* "All our lives are controlled by some trifling incident." He was in the best of spirits at soon being in motion toward a new promising land, and to celebrate he began drinking his favorite, martini with an olive, one after the other, Eleanor trying unsuccessfully to restrain him, until he had drunk five or six of them. The conversation was a lively one on modern writers, including, Karl recalled, Sherwood's nonfavorites, Hemingway and Sinclair Lewis. "Well do I [Karl] remember Sherwood, as a final emphasis of his opinion on some contemporary writer, holding a toothpick spiked with sausage and snapping his teeth on it and swallowing part of the toothpick. That act, it is said, was the means of his death." Karl's recollection of the act was probably accurate, though not his conclusion, for it suggests Sherwood's carelessness about toothpicks as he became progressively more drunk on an unusual number of martinis. What would eventually kill him was a three-inch toothpick in the olive of one of his last martinis, a toothpick he swallowed, not a part, but whole.[7]

At 11 AM on February 28, the Andersons boarded the Grace Line's *Santa Lucia* docked at Pier 58 on West Sixteenth Street. On deck before they went to their stateroom (No. 41) they were photographed, Eleanor smiling happily, Sherwood unsmiling, as was fellow passenger Thornton Wilder, also caught in this photograph. Later, when Sherwood became ill, Wilder assured Eleanor of any assistance he could give. The liner sailed at noon. It was a cold, snowy day, and when the ship got into the Atlantic, the wind was very strong, the ocean very rough. The second day out the weather was so stormy that when fellow passenger Freda Kirchwey, editor of the *Nation,* found the Andersons in the lounge before lunch, it was half empty. Sherwood told her that

he was on his way to South America to meet writers in several countries and to get closer to what was going on in various cultural fields. He was not on an official errand. Although he carried letters of introduction from people in the State Department, he was on his own, a writer going to meet his fellow craftsmen on terms of friendship and common interests.

Because of "cramps across his lower abdomen," as the ship's hospital report stated, he did not eat lunch that March 1, and by the following day he was having painful cramps and was seriously ill. Kirchwey saw him only briefly thereafter, but each time, as she described it, "he was uncompromisingly optimistic . . . viewed his ailment with amiable contempt . . . and came through spasms of pain without relinquishing his certainty that the attack would be defeated in the end by his determination to do what he had set out to do." Eleanor, however, remained worried about him. On the morning of March 5 he felt well enough to have a breakfast of eggs and tea, but by noon he was having such violent abdominal pains that he was given morphine, which had little effect on him, and Eleanor persuaded the ship's doctor to have the Colón Hospital radioed for an ambulance to meet the ship when it would dock at nearby Cristobal at the Atlantic end of the Panama Canal. While she was packing their bags, Kirchwey came in to say goodbye since she too was disembarking at Cristobal.

He was still in pain and still stubbornly cheerful. In a dismal attempt at lightness I said, "Well, I see you couldn't bear to go on down the coast without me." "You expect pretty costly tribute from your admirers, don't you, my girl?" he answered. "I'll let them examine me here at the Canal and do what they have to do and then I'll catch the next boat. They aren't going to spoil my trip."

That evening the *Santa Lucia* came into dock, and Sherwood was transferred by ambulance to the Colón Hospital. "It was then," writes Dr. B. H. Kean, who later performed the autopsy, "that Anderson's condition took a sharp turn for the worse. On March 8 his pulse began to race, accelerating until he lapsed into a state of delirium, delirium became coma, and he died," at 5:40 PM that day of peritonitis, exact cause for which was unknown to the hospital doctors. That night his body was taken by train to Gorgas Hospital at the top of Ancon Hill in Panama City at the Pacific end of the Canal, and on the morning of the ninth Dr. Kean discovered during his autopsy in the Gorgas morgue that exact cause. A three-inch "well preserved" wooden toothpick had projected through the lower part of the colon into the abdominal cavity. That afternoon Kean called on Eleanor, who had moved to the Tivoli Hotel at the bottom of the Ancon Hill, to assure her that "all arrangements for shipping the body back to the States had been made" and to confirm from her the hypothesis that the toothpick had come from the olive of one of Sherwood's martinis.[8]

After delays Eleanor was able to leave Cristobal on March 18 on the Grace Line *Santa Clara,* the ship carrying the embalmed body of her husband. The liner docked at New York on the twenty-fourth, and on the next day she brought him home to Marion. At 11 AM on the twenty-sixth the funeral service was held at Rosemont, a brief and "unpretentious ceremony . . . just as Sherwood Anderson would have wished it," as it was described by Davis T. Ratcliffe, an admirer of his writings who was driving through Marion that day and stopped "to pay tribute to a great writer and to catch a glimpse of the spirit of a great man." Dr. J. J. Scherer, Eleanor's uncle, a Lutheran minister in Richmond whom Sherwood had liked, read the Lord's Prayer, and the Reverend John Brokhoff, pastor of the Marion Lutheran Church, read the Twenty-third Psalm. The Marion College choir sang "sweetly." Although Paul Rosenfeld was present, Pastor Brokhoff read his tribute, "The Man of Good Will," "during which," Ratcliffe wrote, "by coincidence, the municipal siren of Marion wailed long and loud, as if to express the sorrow of all the people." Stanley Young read a tribute from Theodore Dreiser to his "wise, kind, affectionate, forgiving" friend. So the service ended.[9]

The *Smyth County News* would report that the casket was covered by an American flag sent by the War Department to recognize Anderson's military service. Among the pallbearers were such old friends as Andy Funk, Dave Greear, Burt Dickinson, and John Sullivan. Present also, in addition to his many Smyth and Grayson county friends, were family—brothers Karl and Ray, Bob, John, and Mimi—and friends from away—Mary Emmett, Paul Green, Roberto Rendueles, the Galantières, Wharton Esherick, Roger Sergel, and Ferdinand Schevill. Ratcliffe recounted that he "drove behind a car with an Oklahoma license plate as the procession of some 30 cars wound its way" up steep Round Hill to Round Hill Cemetery at the top. "There, on the green slope overlooking the town, Dr. Scherer read the Beatitudes as a warm March sun gave a final blessing from a cloudless and a smokeless sky. Sherwood Anderson, lover of the simplicity and real beauty of life, was buried." The stone marking his grave was designed by Wharton Esherick. On a rough-cut slab a smooth half-circle of stone, concave in back, swoops upward to a lower and an upper point. On its front, near its base, under his name is carved in block letters the epitaph he himself had long since chosen: "Life not death is the great adventure." It was the personal truth by which, to the extent possible, he had lived his life.[10]

After all the public ceremonies were completed, Andy Funk led a small group of men friends to the workshop behind his house where he made fine wood cabinets and had often talked with Sherwood. Here he set a block of hard wood into his lathe and had each man take a turn at the chisel until the block was cut into the shape of a goblet. Filling the goblet with wine that he and Sherwood had made, he drank from it, then handed it to the next man to drink and so on among them until all had drunk. It was a secular communion celebrating the lost friend of whom Andy had already written in tribute.

Over the entire world, wherever good literature is loved and known, people will mourn the passing of Sherwood Anderson.

Yet his tribute had been to something more:

The people of Marion and Smyth and Grayson counties have lost, in his passing, more than Sherwood Anderson the great writer. They have lost Sherwood Anderson their good friend and good neighbor. We did not look at him through his books or magnify him through his fame. We found and loved the man for what he was.[11]

Notes

In the interest of readability, many typographical errors in quotations were silently corrected. In a few places, *sic* or details such as names, places, or dates were added to clarify a point.

CHAPTER 1. BREAK-UP

1. "About Obituary Notices," *Smyth County News,* Mar. 22, 1928, p. 2.
2. "To Our Readers!" *Smyth County News,* Jan. 26, 1928, p. 6. SA to John Anderson, ?Feb. 1928. "The Young Writer," *Periwig* 1 (Feb. 1928): 4–5. "In Washington," *Smyth County News,* Feb. 9, 1928, pp. 1, 3; reprinted in SA, *Hello Towns!* pp. 118–26.
3. SA to John Anderson, ?Feb. 1928. Interviews, WBR with Dickinson, June 18 and June 19, 1953. Sutton, ed., *Letters to Bab,* p. 307, n. 4.
4. "Buck Fever Says," *Smyth County News,* Mar. 1, 1928, p. 1, Aug. 30, 1928, p. 2; "A Town Eyesore," *Smyth County News,* Apr. 26, 1928, p. 1; "Two Town Eyesores to Go," *Smyth County News,* June 7, 1928, p. 1; "Will You Help Buella," *Smyth County News,* May 10, 1928, p. 1; "Kiwanis Meeting Devoted to Roads," *Smyth County News,* May 31, 1928, p. 1. SA to Alexander, ca. Jan. 3, 1931.
5. SA to Alexander, ca. Jan. 3, 1931.
6. "Two Town Eyesores to Go," *Smyth County News,* June 7, 1928, p. 1; "Mamie Palmer, Bootleg Queen, in Dying Condition," *Smyth County News,* Sept. 13, 1928, p. 3; "County Housekeeping," *Smyth County News,* Sept. 20, 1928, p. 1. SA to Alexander, ca. Jan. 3, 1931.
7. SA to Alexander, ca. Jan. 3, 1931; to Lankes, Apr. 12, 1928; to Bab, ?late Apr. 1928. "Book Notes," *Smyth County News,* Apr. 5, 1928, p. 4; "Some More New Books," June 28, 1928, p. 6; "What Say!" Oct. 25, 1928, p. 8; "Buck Fever Says," Feb. 9, 1928, p. 1. Interview, WBR with Joe Stephenson, Sept. 6, 1955.
8. Raymond W. Weaver, deviser, "A Complete Handbook of Opinion," *Vanity Fair* 30 (Apr. 1928): 68–69, 114, 116. SA to Dimand, Jan. 31, 1928.
9. SA to Finley, ?early Apr. 1928, Apr. 8, 1928. Interview, WBR with William Wright, June 17, 1953.

10. SA to Finley, ?mid-Apr. 1928 (two letters); to Roger Sergel, Mar. 26, 1928; to Otto Liveright, May 1, 1928.
11. SA to Finley, ?mid-Apr. 1928 (two letters), ?late Apr. 1928.
12. SA to Otto Liveright, May 1, 1928, ca. May 16, 1928, ca. June 3, 1928; Robert Bridges to Otto Liveright, May 24, 1928. "Small Town Notes," *Vanity Fair* 30 (June 1928): 58, 120, p. 58. "Buck Fever Says," *Smyth County News,* June 7, 1928, p. 1.
13. "To Think About," *Smyth County News,* May 17, 1928, p. 1. "Exultation," *Hello Towns!* pp. 197–204. "In New York," *Smyth County News,* June 21, 1928, p. 8, reprinted in *Hello Towns!* pp. 232–34. SA to Burton Emmett, June 26, 1928.
14. SA to Burton Emmett, June 26, 1928.
15. "Troutdale Burned Out," *Smyth County News,* June 21, 1928, p. 1; "Editorial Statement," *Smyth County News,* July 19, 1928, p. 1; "After Election," *Smyth County News,* July 12, 1928, p. 3; "The Smyth County Newspaper Office," *Smyth County News,* July 12, 1928, p. 8.
16. SA to Finley, ?early June 1928, ?Aug. 1928; to Stein, July 31, 1928; to Alfred Dashiell, July 22, 1928. "Behind the Scenes," *Scribner's* 84 (Sept. 1928): 41–43, p. 41.
17. SA to Church, Aug. 15, 1928. "What Say!" *Smyth County News,* Aug. 16, 1928, p. 10. Interview, WBR with Burt L. Dickinson, June 19, 1953.
18. Elizabeth Anderson and Gerald R. Kelly, *Miss Elizabeth: A Memoir* (Boston: Little, Brown, 1969), pp. 174–75. "First Time Up," *Smyth County News,* Aug. 30, 1928, p. 1.
19. *Miss Elizabeth,* pp. 185–87. Interview, WBR with William Wright, June 18, 1953.
20. Interviews, WBR with Elizabeth Prall Anderson, Dec. 17, 1959; with Dickinson, June 18, 1953. Elizabeth Prall Anderson to Hans W. Poppe, Sept. 15, 1947 (copy of letter).
21. William Spratling, *File on Spratling: An Autobiography* (Boston: Little, Brown, 1967), p. 123. Interviews, WBR with Wright, June 18, 1953; with Burt L. Dickinson, June 19, 1953. SA to Eleanor Copenhaver Anderson, May 7, 1930, May 22, 1930.
22. SA to Finley, ?Aug. 1928; to Church, Aug. 15, 1928; to Isidor Schneider, Sept. 25, 1928; to Otto Liveright, Sept. 19, 1928. "Civic Clubs," *Smyth County News,* Sept. 20, 1928, p. 1.
23. Otto Liveright could not market "Among the Drifters," and it was published in *Hello Towns!* pp. 216–23.
24. SA to Burton Emmett, June 26, 1928; to Stewart, June 18, 1934.
25. *Miss Elizabeth,* pp. 139–41. *Today* 2 (July 21, 1934): 6–7, 24.
26. "In the Town," *Smyth County News,* Sept. 20, 1928, p. 2; "Thank You Ladies and Gentlemen," *Smyth County News,* Oct. 18, 1928, p. 1; "Will You Sell Your Newspapers?" *Smyth County News,* Nov. 8, 1928, p. 2, and *Outlook and Independent* 150 (Dec. 5, 1928): 1286–87; "Editor Away," *Smyth County News,* Nov. 22, 1928, p. 3. Leigh to SA, Oct. 30, 1928; Leonard B. Hurley to SA, Nov. 14, 1928. *Miss Elizabeth,* p. 185.

27. SA to Otto Liveright, ca. Dec. 6, 1928; to Burton Emmett, ca. Dec. 1, 1928, Dec. 6, 1928; to Bockler, ?Jan. 1929; to Donald Freeman, Jan. 14, 1929; Mary Vernon Greer to Stanley Pargellis, Sept. 17, 1958. "What Say!" *Smyth County News,* Dec. 6, 1928, p. 8. Interview, WBR with Bockler, June 12, 1953.

28. SA to Burton Emmett, Dec. 6, 1928; to Finley, Dec. 1928.

29. SA to Burton Emmett, Dec. 21, 1928; to Eleanor Copenhaver Anderson, Apr. 4, 1930. *Miss Elizabeth,* p. 187; Interview, Modlin and Campbell, "Interview with Mrs. Sherwood Anderson," pp. 67–68, 70, in Hilbert H. Campbell and Charles E. Modlin, eds., *Sherwood Anderson: Centennial Studies.* "Personals," *Smyth County News,* May 17, 1928, p. 3.

30. SA to Eleanor Copenhaver Anderson, Apr. 4, 1930; to Finley, Dec. 17, 1928. "Buck Fever Says," *Smyth County News,* Dec. 13, 1928, p. 1. Original Bill [for divorce] (File No. 138), filed Feb. 1, 1932, at Smyth County Courthouse, Marion. "Transcription of Burt Dickinson's profile of Sherwood Anderson (written to his daughter, Frances Dickinson Ackerly, in 1951)," May 16, 1951, kindly sent me by Welford D. Taylor. *Miss Elizabeth,* pp. 188–89. Interview, WBR with William Dennes, May 29, 1959.

CHAPTER 2. THE YEAR OF THE CRASH

1. "Personal Notes," *Smyth County News,* Jan. 10, 1929, p. 1.

2. W. Colston Leigh to SA, Sept. 11, 1928; SA to Daugherty, Jan. 14, 1929; to the Schevills, Jan. 16, 1929; to Finley, Jan. 15, 1929; to Bockler, ?Jan. 1929; to Leigh, Jan. 14, 1929.

3. SA to Finley, Jan. 15, 1929, ?after Jan. 15, 1929; to Horace Liveright, Jan. 15, 1929.

4. SA to Jane Heap, ca. Jan. 15, 1929; to Parkhurst Whitney, Jan. 15, 1929; to Henry F. Pringle, Jan. 23, 1919; to Eleanor Copenhaver Anderson, Feb. 2, 1929; to Finley, ca. Feb. 1, 1929; to Cornelia Lane Anderson, Feb. 21, 1929; to Donald Freeman, Feb. 1, 1929; to Kahn, Jan. 26, 1929. "Let's Go Somewhere," *Outlook and Independent* 151 (Feb. 13, 1929): 247, 278, 280. Interview, WBR with Dickinson, June 18, 1953.

5. "A Traveler's Notes," *Smyth County News,* Feb. 7, 1929, p. 1; Feb. 14, 1929, p. 5.

6. SA to Horace Liveright, ca. Feb. 13, 1929; to Hélène Boussinesq, Feb. 1, 1929; Boussinesq to SA, Jan. 13, 1929. SA to Bockler, ca. Feb. 21, 1929. "Leon Bazalgette," *Smyth County News,* Feb. 7, 1929, p. 8 (reprinted as "Death on a Winter Day," pp. 9–12 in *No Swank* [Philadelphia: Centaur Press, 1934]). Interview, WBR with Dickinson, June 18, 1953.

7. SA to Cornelia Lane Anderson, Feb. 21, 1929; to Burton Emmett, Feb. 21, 1929; to Eleanor Copenhaver Anderson, ca. Feb. 21, 1929, ca. Feb. 4, 1929; to Horace Liveright, Feb. 21, 1929, ca. Feb. 23, 1929.

8. SA to Burton Emmett, Mar. 10, 1929. Calverton to SA, ?Feb. 1929. SA to Horace Liveright, Mar. 9, 1929; to Koskull, ca. Mar. 11, 1929. Dickinson to Elizabeth Prall Anderson, Mar. 7, 1929; Koskull to SA, Jan. 29, 1929, Oct. 16, 1935. Record Conveyance Office Book 451 Folio 230/Apr. 29, 1929, Register

of Conveyances, New Orleans. "Impressions of an Inauguration," *Smyth County News,* Mar. 7, 1929, pp. 1, 4; "New Subscribers," *Smyth County News,* Sept. 6, 1928, p. 4; "Fear," *Smyth County News,* June 24, 1929, pp. 4–5.

9. Horace Liveright to SA, Mar. 2, 1929, Mar. 7, 1929. SA to Horace Liveright, Mar. 5, 1929, Mar. 9, 1929. Burton Emmett to SA, Mar. 7, 1929. SA to Burton Emmett, Mar. 10, 1929.

10. "Sherwood Anderson," *Yale Review Magazine* 93 (July 1928): 209–43. SA to Macdonald, Mar. 8, 1929; to Finley, Mar. 9, 1929.

11. SA to Koskull, ca. Mar. 11, 1929; to Finley, Apr. 2, 1929; to John Anderson, Apr. 2, 1929. "A Traveler's Notes," *Smyth County News,* Mar. 28, 1929, p. 1; Apr. 4, 1929, p. 8.

12. SA to Burton Emmett, Apr. 2, 1929; to Lankes, Jan. 15, 1929.

13. SA to Eleanor Copenhaver Anderson, ?Apr. 1929. "A Traveler's Notes," *Smyth County News,* May 2, 1929, p. 10.

14. SA to Lewis, Apr. 16, 1929, May 6, 1929; to Doris Ulmann, Apr. 2, 1929; to Horace Liveright, Apr. 3, 1929.

15. SA to Eleanor Copenhaver Anderson, Apr. 21, 1929; to Young, ca. May 13, 1929. Hansen, "The First Reader," *New York World,* Apr. 18, 1929, p. 15. Hutchison, "The Village Oracle Speaks," *New York Times Book Review,* Apr. 28, 1929, p. 1. Interview, WBR with B. L. Dickinson, June 18, 1953.

16. "Sherwood Anderson and the Small Towns," *Minneapolis Journal,* Apr. 28, 1929, p. 4.

17. SA to Eleanor Copenhaver Anderson, Apr. 29, 1929, Apr. 21, 1929; to Koskull, Apr. 29, 1929, ca. Apr. 25, 1929; Koskull to SA, Apr. 3, 1929, Feb. 4, 1930, Nov. 3, 1931. "What Say!" *Smyth County News,* May 2, 1929, p. 10. Charles E. Modlin, ed., *Sherwood Anderson's Love Letters to Eleanor Copenhaver Anderson,* p. 10, n. 2. "Two Irishmen," pp. 31–34, in *No Swank,* p. 31.

18. SA to Koskull, Apr. 29, 1929; Robert Lane Anderson to Barr, Apr. 22, 1929. "Virginia," *Vanity Fair* 32 (Aug. 1929): 66, 74.

19. SA to Freeman, May 10, 1929.

20. O'Brien to SA, May 15, 1929. Otto Liveright to SA, May 29, 1929. SA to Freeman, May 22, 1929; to the Schevills, June 2, 1929.

21. SA to Eleanor Copenhaver Anderson, ca. June 7, 1929, June 12, 1929, ca. June 15, 1929, June 15, 1929, ca. June 26, 1929. See Modlin's very helpful notes to these letters in his edition of *Anderson's Love Letters.*

22. SA to Horace Liveright, ca. June 25, 1929; to Eleanor Copenhaver Anderson, July 17, 1929, July 31, 1929, late July 1929. Bockler to SA, May 23, 1929. "Anderson Is Expelled on Rumanian Trip," *New York Times,* Mar. 9, 1929, p. 6. "What Say!" *Smyth County News,* July 11, 1929, p. 8. Interviews, WBR with Bockler, June 12, 1953; with Charles H. Funk, June 23, 1953.

23. SA to Karl Anderson, Nov. 30 [1929?]; to Horace Liveright, ca. July 6, 1929; to Lambert Davis, ca. July 3, 1929; to Robert Lane Anderson, ca. Nov. 3, 1929.

24. Koskull to SA, Oct. 22, 1929. SA to Koskull, late July 1929; to Burton Emmett, July 24, 1929.

25. Mary Vernon Greer to Stanley Pargellis, Sept. 17, 1958. SA to Koskull, late

July 1929; to Bockler, Feb. 10, 1931. Koskull to SA, Oct. 22, 1929. Interview, WBR with Charles H. Funk, June 23, 1953.

26. SA to Horace Liveright, ca. July 21, 1929; Aug. 9, 1929; to Lambert Davis, ca. July 25, 1929; to Burton Emmett, Aug. 22, 1929, Aug. 28, 1929. Bockler to SA, Sept. 30. "Newspapers/The Boss Makes a Speech," *Smyth County News,* Aug. 15, 1929, p. 1.

27. "Noted Writers Aid Textile Strikers . . . Group Headed by Dreiser, Anderson and Fannie Hurst," *New York Times,* Aug. 19, 1929, p. 39.

28. SA to Mimi Anderson, ca. Sept. 5, 1929; to Burton Emmett, Sept. 14, 1929; to Horace Liveright, ca. Sept. 30, 1929. Mildred Adams, "A Small-Town Editor Airs His Mind," *New York Times Magazine,* Sept. 22, 1929, pp. 3, 20.

29. SA to Eleanor Copenhaver Anderson, Sept. 28, 1929, Oct. 21, 1929; to Mimi Anderson, Sept. 24, 1929.

30. SA to Eleanor Copenhaver Anderson, Oct. 22, 1929; Otto Liveright to Robert Bridges, Oct. 4, 1929.

31. SA to Eleanor Copenhaver Anderson, Oct. 26, 1929, Oct. 22, 1929, ca. late Oct. 1929.

32. SA to Robert Lane Anderson, ca. Nov. 3, 1929; to Eleanor Copenhaver Anderson , Oct. 26, 1929, Oct. 27, 1929, ca. Oct. 31, 1929, Nov. 4, 1929; to Horace Liveright, Dec. 5, 1929, Dec. 10, 1929.

33. SA to Eleanor Copenhaver Anderson, Jan. 6, 1930, ca. Nov. 30, 1929, Nov. 29, 1929; to Horace Liveright, Nov. 9, 1929, Dec. 3, 1929, Dec. 16, 1929; to Burton Emmett, Nov. 18, 1929. "What Say!" *Smyth County News,* Nov. 28, 1929, p. 8. Interview, WBR with Charles H. Funk, June 23, 1953.

34. SA to Eleanor Copenhaver Anderson, Dec. 5, 1929, Dec. 6–7, 1929; Marion Anderson Spear to WBR, July 18, 1991.

35. SA to Rosenfeld, Jan. 11, 1930; to the Schevills, ca. Dec. 28, 1929, ca. May 7, 1930; to Horace Liveright, Dec. 16, 1929; to Eleanor Copenhaver Anderson, Dec. 25, 1929.

36. SA to the Schevills, ca. Dec. 31, 1929. "Divorced Wife of Novelist Is Found Dead," *Chicago Daily Tribune,* Dec. 27, 1929, p. 5. "Ex-Wife of Anderson, Novelist, Found Dead," *New York Times,* Dec. 27, 1929, p. 12.

37. Interview, WBR with Harriet Walker Welling, Feb. 21, 1970. SA to the Schevills, ca. Dec. 31, 1929. "Mrs. Anderson Is Buried with Poetry, Music," *Chicago Daily Tribune,* Jan. 1, 1930, p. 44.

38. SA to Eleanor Copenhaver Anderson, ca. Dec. 30, 1929.

39. SA to the Schevills, ca. Dec. 31, 1929.

CHAPTER 3. FACTORIES AND SPEECHES

1. SA to Horace Liveright, ca. Jan. 2, 1930; to the Schevills, ca. Jan. 8, 1930. "A Traveler's Notes," *Smyth County News,* Jan. 9, 1930, p. 1.

2. SA to Rosenfeld, Jan. 11, 1930; to Eleanor Copenhaver Anderson, Jan. 23, 1930, Apr. 1, 1930. "Traveler's Notes: Adrift in Georgia," *Smyth County News,* Feb. 6, 1930, p. 1.

3. "Novelist Comes Here for Visit" and "High Praise Is Accorded Julia and Julian

Harris," *Macon Telegraph,* Jan. 17, 1930, p. 1, and Jan. 19, 1930, pp. 1, 15. Susan Myrick, "sherwood anderson," unpublished, undated article, copies kindly sent me by Susan Myrick and by Stephen C. Enniss. Myrick to WBR, Nov. 13, 1964.

4. Myrick, "sherwood anderson," pp. 7–8. SA, "A Traveler's Notes," *Smyth County News,* Feb. 13, 1930, p. 8. SA to Bockler, ca. Mar. 5, 1930; to Eleanor Copenhaver Anderson, Jan. 17, 1930, Jan. 23, 1930.

5. SA to Julian Harris, ca. Jan. 25, 1930; to the Sergels, ?late Jan. 1930; to Church, Jan. 26, 1930; to Eleanor Copenhaver Anderson, Jan. 29, 1930. Chronology furnished by Charles E. Modlin.

6. SA to Burton Emmett, ca. Feb. 3, 1930; to Eleanor Copenhaver Anderson, Feb. 9, 1930. Modlin's Chronology. "Machine Song" was published as "Machine Song: Automobile" in *Household Magazine* 30 (Oct. 1930): 3, and became the opening piece in *Perhaps Women.*

7. SA to the Sergels, ?late Jan. 1930; to Nelson Antrim Crawford, Feb. 20, 1930.

8. Otto Liveright to SA, Feb. 13, 1930, Apr. 11, 1930; John Hall Wheelock to SA, Mar. 19, 1930, Mar. 27, 1930, Apr. 8, 1930; SA to Wheelock, Mar. 24, 1930, Apr. 3, 1930, ca. Apr. 15, 1930.

9. SA to Eleanor Copenhaver Anderson, Feb. 11, 1930, Feb. 14, 1930, Feb. 12, 1930; to Mimi Anderson, ca. Feb. 20, 1930.

10. SA to Crawford, Feb. 20, 1930; to Horace Liveright, ca. Feb. 26, 1930; to Eleanor Copenhaver Anderson, Feb. 26, 1930, May 7, 1930, Mar. 6, 1930, Mar. 2, 1930. Modlin, *Anderson's Love Letters,* p. 59, n. 1, to 26 February 1930 letter; p. 61, n. 1. Eleanor Copenhaver Anderson to Amy Nyholm to WBR.

11. Blanche Gregory to SA, Feb. 19, 1930; SA to Eleanor Copenhaver Anderson, ca. Mar. 5, 1930, Mar. 6, 1930, Mar. 14, 1930, Mar. 11, 1930.

12. SA to Koskull, Mar. 11, 1930; to Eleanor Copenhaver Anderson, Mar. 11, 1930.

13. SA to Eleanor Copenhaver Anderson, Mar. 20, 1930, Apr. 1, 1930. *Nation* 130 (May 28, 1930): 620–22. In a letter to Charles Wright Thomas, Jan. 15, 1931, SA cited Deuteronomy as his source for the quotation. A parallel passage is of course Genesis 3:14–15 where Abram is commanded to "Lift up now thine eyes" and behold his people's new dwelling place.

14. SA to Burton Emmett, Mar. 11, 1930; to Wheelock, Mar. 24, 1930; Wheelock to SA, Mar. 27, 1930.

15. SA to Eleanor Copenhaver Anderson, Mar. 30, 1930, Apr. 4, 1930, Apr. 1, 1930, Apr. 5, 1930; to Wheelock, Apr. 3, 1930; to Bockler, ca. Apr. 4, 1930; to Mimi Anderson, Apr. 6, 1930.

16. SA to Eleanor Copenhaver Anderson, Apr. 9, 1930, Apr. 12, 1930; to Kahn, June 28, 1930; Burton Emmett to SA, July 7, 1930. In her "Sherwood Anderson," *Winesburg Eagle,* 14 (Summer 1989), 11, Caroline Greear recalls that the checks from Kahn and Emmett helped with the expenses of both brothers at "Tech High" in Atlanta, where David studied sculpture and Josh mechanics and electricity.

17. Wilson to SA, Apr. 11, 1930; SA to Wilson, ca. Apr. 14, 1930; to Burton Emmett, June 26, 1930, June 7, 1930; to the editors of *Scribner's,* May 18, 1930. "A Man's Mind," *New Republic* 63 (May 21, 1930): 22–23. James Feibleman, *Philosophers Lead Sheltered Lives* (New York: AMS Press), p. 183.

18. SA to Eleanor Copenhaver Anderson, Apr. 23, 1930, Apr. 28, 1930. Modlin, *Anderson's Love Letters,* p. 97, n. 2.
19. SA to Eleanor Copenhaver Anderson, Apr. 28, 1930, May 7, 1930, May 15, 1930; to Mimi Anderson, ca. May 7, 1930; Burton Emmett to SA, Apr. 4, 1930.
20. SA to Burton Emmett, ca. May 22, 1930, May 7, 1930; to Eleanor Copenhaver Anderson, May 7, 1930, May 10, 1930, May 15, 1930, May 22, 1930; to Crawford, ?late May 1930; to Wilson, May 19, 1930; Wheelock to SA, May 7, 1930, May 28, 1930. SA, "Real—Unreal," *New Republic* 63 (June 11, 1930): 103–4.
21. SA to Burton Emmett, June 26, 1930, Apr. 17, 1930.
22. SA to Wheelock, ca. June 6, 1930; Dashiell to Otto Liveright, May 29, 1930; SA to Watkins, Aug. 5, 1930.
23. SA to Burton Emmett, July 14, 1930; to Eleanor Copenhaver Anderson, Oct. 15, 1930, Mar. 2, 1931.
24. SA to Mimi Anderson, ca. June 26, 1930; to Eleanor Copenhaver Anderson, Aug. 13, 1930, July 11, 1930, July 20, 1930, Aug. 13, 1930; to Lankes, Aug. 7, 1930; to Bockler, July 30, 1930; to Burton Emmett, June 7, 1930; to the Schevills, after July 13, 1930.
25. SA to Blanche Chappell, Sept. 13, 1930; to Mimi Anderson, ca. June 26, 1930; to Church, Aug. 5, 1930. "Watch It," *Smyth County News,* Aug. 21, 1930, p. 8; "First Teachers Meeting," *Smyth County News,* Sept. 11, 1930, p. 5.
26. SA to Bockler, before Aug. 13, 1930, Aug. 16, 1930, Aug. 31, 1930, Nov. 26, 1930.
27. SA to Lankes, Sept. 1, 1930, Sept. 22, 1930; to Bockler, Sept. 21, 1930; to Chappell, Sept. 13, 1930; to Eleanor Copenhaver Anderson, Sept. 27, 1930; to the Schevills, ca. Oct. 6, 1930.
28. SA to Mimi Anderson, probably Oct. 2, 1930; to Eleanor Copenhaver Anderson, Oct. 15, 1930, ?Aug. 16, 1930; to the Schevills, ca. Oct. 6, 1930.
29. Barr to SA, Oct. 7, 1930, Oct. 10, 1930; SA to Lankes, Nov. 1, 1930. Arthur F. Raper, *The Tragedy of Lynching* (Chapel Hill: University of North Carolina Press, 1933), appendices, pp. 469–71, 481.
30. SA to Eleanor Copenhaver Anderson, ?ca. Oct. 10, 1930, Oct. 18, 1930, Oct. 24, 1930, Oct. 25, 1930, Oct. 15–16, 1930, Oct. 21, 1930, Oct. 28, 1930, Oct. 29, 1930, Oct. 30, 1930; to Bockler, ca. Nov. 12, 1930.
31. SA to Mimi Anderson, Nov. 1, 1930; to Burton Emmett, Nov. 10, 1930.
32. SA to Eleanor Copenhaver Anderson, Oct. 18, 1930; to Bockler, ca. Nov. 12, 1930; to Barr, ca. Nov. 12, 1930. "Stringfellow Barr and John Crowe Ransom Will Debate Merits of Agrarianism Versus Industrialism in South at City Auditorium," *Richmond Times-Dispatch,* Nov. 14, 1930, pp. 1, 3.
33. "Dr. Ransom Charges," *Richmond Times-Dispatch,* Nov. 15, 1930, pp. 1, 2; "The Barr-Ransom Debate," *Richmond Times-Dispatch,* Nov. 16, 1930, II, p. 2. SA to Bockler, Nov. 26, 1930. SA, untitled introduction to debate, unpublished ms. at Newberry Library.
34. Ray Lewis White, "Sherwood Anderson, American Labor, and Danville, Virginia," *Winesburg Eagle* 20 (Summer 1990): 1–9. SA to Mimi Anderson, ca. Dec. 19, 1930. SA, "Danville, Virginia," *New Republic* 65 (Jan. 21, 1931):

266–68. Louis Stanley, "Danville: Labor's Southern Outpost," *Nation* 132 (Jan. 21, 1931): 68–70. Tom Tippett, *When Southern Labor Stirs* (New York: Jonathan Cape & Harrison Smith, 1931), p. 250. Julian R. Meade, *I Live in Virginia* (New York: Longmans, Green and Co., 1935), 44–46. "Champions Mill Strikers," *New York Times,* Nov. 17, 1930, p. 19.

35. "What Say!" *Smyth County News,* Dec. 18, 1930, p. 8. SA to Bockler, ca. Nov. 17, 1930, Nov. 26, 1930; to Karl Anderson, ca. Nov. 22, 1930.

36. SA to Alexander, Dec. 30; Alexander to SA, Dec. 31, 1930; to Brownell, Dec. 18, 1930.

37. SA to Bab, Dec. 30, 1930; to Mimi Anderson, ca. Dec. 19, 1930; to Koskull, ca. Dec. 22, 1930.

38. SA to Church, Dec. 19, 1930; to Mimi Anderson, ca. Dec. 19, 1930; to Bockler, Dec. 25, 1930; to Bab, Dec. 30, 1930; to Eleanor Copenhaver Anderson, ca. Dec. 30, 1930.

CHAPTER 4. A SEMIPUBLIC FIGURE

1. SA to Ferdinand Schevill, early Jan. 1931; to Bockler, Jan. 2, 1931, Dec. 25, 1930; to Eleanor Copenhaver Anderson, Jan. 8, 1931, Jan. 25, 1931; to Burton Emmett, Jan. 21, 1931.

2. SA to Bockler, Dec. 13, 1930; to Eleanor Copenhaver Anderson, Jan. 7, 1931.

3. SA to Eleanor Copenhaver Anderson, ?Oct. 24, 1930, ca. Jan. 22, 1931, early Jan. 1931, Jan. 8, 1931.

4. SA to Eleanor Copenhaver Anderson, ca. Jan. 20, 1931, Jan. 8, 1931, Jan. 7, 1931.

5. SA to Eleanor Copenhaver Anderson, Jan. 12, 1931; Ella Boese to SA, ?Oct. 23, 1931; Martha Hall to SA, Oct. 20, 1931. "Maurice G. Long Is Taken by Death," *Washington Post,* Oct. 19, 1931, p. 2. *No Swank,* p. 33.

6. Tippett, *When Southern Labor Stirs,* pp. 249–52. SA to Eleanor Copenhaver Anderson, Jan. 14, 1931, Jan. 15, 1931. "8 Men, Women Fined in Strike Area Disorder," *Richmond Times-Dispatch,* Jan. 14, 1931, p. 1. "Speech Delivered by Sherwood Anderson to Striking Cotton Mill Workers of Danville, Va., January 13, 1931" (Mimeograph form, kindly given me by Mimi Anderson).

7. SA to Eleanor Copenhaver Anderson, Jan. 14, 1931, ca. Jan. 20, 1931; to Bockler, Jan. 16, 1931, Feb. 10, 1931; to John Edelman, after Mar. 10, 1931. Ray Lewis White has reprinted the speech from the *Trades Union News* in his "Sherwood Anderson, American Labor, and Danville, Virginia," *Winesburg Eagle* 15 (Summer 1990): 1–9.

8. SA to Eleanor Copenhaver Anderson, Jan. 14, 1931, Jan. 16, 1931, Jan. 15, 1931, Jan. 24, 1931, ca. Jan. 20, 1931, ca. Jan. 22, 1931, mid-Jan. 1931, Jan. 24, 1931, ca. Jan. 30, 1931.

9. SA to Eleanor Copenhaver Anderson, Jan. 27, 1931, ca. Jan. 30, 1931, Feb. 3, 1931. Leigh to SA, Jan. 25, 1931. SA to Leigh, Jan. 19, 1931, Jan. 28, 1931, Jan. 15, 1931; to James Feibleman, Jan. 15, 1931. "Weeklies Offer Chance for Those with 'Hunch' to Write—Anderson," *Roanoke Times,* Jan. 27, 1931, p. 2; "The Country Weekly," *Roanoke Times,* Jan. 28, 1931, p. 6.

10. SA to Bockler, Feb. 2, 1931; to Eleanor Copenhaver Anderson, Feb. 2, 1931, Feb. 1, 1931, Feb. 9, 1931, Feb. 3, 1931; to Karl Anderson, ca. Feb. 5, 1931.
11. SA to Eleanor Copenhaver Anderson, Feb. 3, 1931, Jan. 16, 1931, early Feb. 1931; to Bockler, Feb. 10, 1931; to John Anderson, Feb. 2, 1931.
12. SA to Eleanor Copenhaver Anderson, Feb. 6, 1931, Feb. 14, 1931, Feb. 15, 1931; to Bockler, Feb. 17, 1931.
13. SA to Eleanor Copenhaver Anderson, Feb. 14, 1931, ?Feb. 17, 1931, Feb. 16, 1931.
14. SA to Eleanor Copenhaver Anderson, Feb. 20, 1931, Feb. 21, 1931, Feb. 22, 1931, Mar. 2, 1931.
15. SA to Eleanor Copenhaver Anderson, Feb. 22, 1931, ?Feb. 28, 1931, Mar. 9, 1931, Mar. 3, 1931, ?Mar. 2, 1931.
16. Myrick, "sherwood anderson," pp. 14, 8–11. "Sherwood Anderson Arrives in Macon for Week's Visit," *Macon Telegraph,* Mar. 3, 1931, p. 1. SA to Eleanor Copenhaver Anderson, Mar. 3, 1931, Mar. 4, 1931, Mar. 4–5, 1931, Mar. 9, 1931. Myrick quotation on recordings quoted in Stephen Enniss, "Sherwood Anderson and Paul Gauguin: A Forgotten Review," *Studies in American Fiction* 18 (Spring 1990): 118–21, pp. 120–21, n. 12.
17. SA to Eleanor Copenhaver Anderson, Mar. 4, 1931, Mar. 7, 1931, Mar. 8, 1931; SA to Lankes, Mar. 5, 1931. Leigh's contract, Apr. 8, 1931. Concerning Burchfield, Welford D. Taylor to WBR, July 30, 1995, based on Taylor's examination of unpublished material.
18. SA to Eleanor Copenhaver Anderson, Mar. 5–6, 1931, Mar. 8, 1931, Mar. 9, 1931. *Smyth County News,* Mar. 12, 1931, p. 8, dated from Macon, Mar. 10.
19. SA's review, *Macon Telegraph,* Apr. 5, 1931, p. 5. Myrick, "sherwood anderson," pp. 8–11. Enniss, "Sherwood Anderson and Paul Gauguin," p. 119. SA to Bockler, ca. Nov. 17, 1930; to Eleanor Copenhaver Anderson, Mar. 9, 1931.
20. SA to Eleanor Copenhaver Anderson, Mar. 10, 1931; to Bockler, Mar. 11, 1931. "Travel Notes: Piney Woods," *Smyth County News,* Apr. 9, 1931, p. 1. "More Travel Notes," *Smyth County News,* Mar. 19, 1931, p. 8.
21. SA to Eleanor Copenhaver Anderson, Mar. 12, 1931, Mar. 23, 1931, ?Mar. 24, 1931. "Sherwood Anderson Pays Visit to City," *Times-Picayune,* Mar. 13, 1931, p. 2.
22. SA to Eleanor Copenhaver Anderson, Mar. 24, 1931, Mar. 25, 1931, Mar. 26, 1931, Mar. 29, 1931. Interview, WBR with Mary Chryst Anderson (Mrs. Robert L.), June 20, 1953.
23. SA to Eleanor Copenhaver Anderson, Mar. 24, 1931, Mar. 29, 1931, Mar. 30, 1931, Mar. 28, 1931, Apr. 5, 1931, Mar. 27, 1931; to Bockler, Mar. 30, 1931; to Lankes, Mar. 26, 1931.
24. SA to Bockler, probably Apr. 10, 1931; to Eleanor Copenhaver Anderson, ca. Apr. 13, 1931, Apr. 13, 1931.
25. SA to Eleanor Copenhaver Anderson, Apr. 12, 1931, ca. Apr. 13, 1931, Apr. 13, 1931, Apr. 16, 1931.
26. SA to Mimi Anderson, Apr. 18, 1931; to Eleanor Copenhaver Anderson, Apr. 21, 1931, Apr. 22, 1931, Apr. 24, 1931, Apr. 23, 1931. Printed announcement, "Northwestern University Lectures in Contemporary Thought," pp. 1–2.

27. Arthur W. Shumway, "Anderson Is New Type of Rural Editor/Noted Author Lectures on Country Journalism at Fisk Hall," *[?Northwester]n New[?s]*, Apr. 22, 1931, pp. 1–3.
28. SA to Eleanor Copenhaver Anderson, Apr. 24, 1931, Apr. 25, 1931, Apr. 23, 1931; SA to Philip Richard Davis, ca. Dec. 25, 1931. Davis, *A Country Editor Comes to Town* (Chicago: Peacock Press, 1931), twelve-page brochure. John Drury, "Grub Street Shavings," *Economy Spectator* 3 (Jan. 3, 1932), clipping in *A Country Editor* file at Newberry Library.
29. SA to Eleanor Copenhaver Anderson, Apr. 27, 1931, Apr. 29, 1931, Apr. 30, 1931.
30. SA to Karl Anderson, May 16, 1931; to Eleanor Copenhaver Anderson, May 1, 1931, May 4, 1931, May 6, 1931, May 7, 1931, May 11, 1931; to Laura Lu Copenhaver, May 12, 1931. Telegram, Long to Robert Lane Anderson, May 3, 1931.
31. SA to Eleanor Copenhaver Anderson, May 12, 1931, May 14, 1931.
32. SA to Eleanor Copenhaver Anderson, May 16, 1931, Apr. 21, 1931, May 24, 1931, May 17, 1931; to Stieglitz, May 29, 1931; to Laura Lu Copenhaver, May 30, 1931; to Rosenfeld, Apr. 7, 1931; to Wilson, after Apr. 15, 1931.
33. SA to Eleanor Copenhaver Anderson, May 17, 1931, May 18, 1931, May 17, 1931.
34. SA to Laura Lu Copenhaver, May 23, 1931, May 30, 1931; to Bockler, May 24, 1931; to Eleanor Copenhaver Anderson, ?May 19, 1931, May 29, 1931; to Long, June 5, 1931.
35. SA to Wilson, June 5, 1931, early July 1931; to Long, June 17, 1931; to Eleanor Copenhaver Anderson, June 11, 1931, June 12, 1931, June 15, 1931, June 20, 1931; to Waldie Van Eck, June 17, 1921. Robert Lane Anderson to Lankes, June 16, 1931; Wilson to Dos Passos, June 24, 1931, in Edmund Wilson, *Letters on Literature and Politics, 1912–1972*, ed. Elena Wilson (New York: Farrar, Straus and Giroux, 1977), p. 218.
36. SA to Eleanor Copenhaver Anderson, June 20, 1931; to Lankes, June 20, 1931.
37. SA to Eleanor Copenhaver Anderson, June 20, 1931, June 22, 1931, June 25, 1931, June 26, 1931, June 28, 1931.
38. SA to Bockler, after July 11, 1931; to John Anderson, late June 1931; to Lankes, July 11, 1931; to Laura Lu Copenhaver, two letters, ?late July 1931.
39. Deposition by SA accompanying "Original Bill (File No. 138)" in Smyth County Courthouse, Marion, filed Feb. 1, 1932. Interview, WBR with Dickinson, June 19, 1953.
40. SA to Eleanor Copenhaver Anderson, Aug. 4, 1931, ?Aug. 3, 1931, Aug. 8, 1931, Aug. 9, 1931, ca. Aug. 10, 1931, Aug. 15, 1931, Aug. 6, 1931, Aug. 14, 1931, Aug. 10, 1931, Aug. 17, 1931, Aug. 18, 1931, Aug. 24, 1931, Aug. 26, 1931, Aug. 31, 1931.
41. Ross, "Men, Women, and Machines," *New York Herald Tribune*, Sept. 20, 1931, p. 5; Stallings, "The Book of the Day," *Milwaukee Sentinel*, Sept. 19, 1931, p. 10; Hansen, "The First Reader," *New York World-Telegram*, Sept. 15, 1931, p. 25; Canby, "Machine-Made Men," *Saturday Review of Literature* 8 (Oct. 10, 1931): 183; D. F. G., "Sherwood Anderson on the Woman's

Era," *Boston Transcript,* Oct. 17, 1931, p. 1; "Maybe Men," *Time* 18 (Sept. 21, 1931): 55. SA to Karl Anderson, ca. Sept. 18, 1931; to Eleanor Copenhaver Anderson, ca. Sept. 27, 1931, Sept. 29, 1931.

42. SA to Eleanor Copenhaver Anderson, Oct. 11, 1931, Sept. 23, 1931, Oct. 2, 1931, Oct. 12, 1931; to Dashiell, Sept. 23, 1931, Sept. 8, 1931, Sept. 23, 1931, ca. Oct. 2, 1931, ca. Oct. 18, 1931; Dashiell to SA, Sept. 2, 1931, Sept. 25, 1931, Oct. 10, 1931, Oct. 20, 1931.

43. Karl Anderson to SA, Sept. 16, 1931, Dec. 29, 1931; SA to Eleanor Copenhaver Anderson, Sept. 24, 1931, Sept. 27, 1931, Sept. 23, 1931; to Bockler, Sept. 17, 1931. Interview, WBR with Mary Chryst Anderson, June 20, 1953.

44. SA to Eleanor Copenhaver Anderson, Sept. 26, 1931, Oct. 12, 1931, Oct. 3, 1931, Oct. 2, 1931, Oct. 4, 1931, probably Oct. 4, 1931, Oct. 6, 1931. "Maybe Men," *Time* 18 (Sept. 21, 1931): 55.

45. SA to Eleanor Copenhaver Anderson, Oct. 18, 1931, Oct. 19, 1931, Oct. 20, 1931, Oct. 21, 1931; to Bockler, ca. Oct. 21, 1931. "Maurice G. Long Is Taken by Death," *Washington Post,* Oct. 19, 1931, p. 2.

46. SA to Eleanor Copenhaver Anderson, Oct. 21, 1931, ca. Oct. 14, 1931, ca. Oct. 10, 1931, Oct. 22, 1931, Oct. 23, 1931; to Laura Lu Copenhaver, Oct. 24, 1931.

47. Details in this and the following two paragraphs are drawn from SA to Laura Lu Copenhaver, Oct. 24, 1931; to John Lineaweaver, Dec. 28, 1931; to Barr, May 20, 1932. "Southern Authors Informally Swap Views at University" and "Authors Urge More and Better Book Pages in the Newspapers," *Richmond Times-Dispatch,* Oct. 24 and Oct. 25, 1931, pp. 11 and 14; Emily Clark, *New York Herald Tribune Books,* Nov. 8, 1931, pp. 1–2; Josephine Pinckney, "Southern Writers' Congress," *Saturday Review of Literature* 8 (Nov. 7, 1931): 266; Joseph Blotner, *Faulkner: A Biography* (New York: Random House, 1974), vol. 1, pp. 705–15.

48. SA to Eleanor Copenhaver Anderson, Oct. 17, 1931, Oct. 29, 1931, ca. Oct. 30, 1931; Leigh to SA, Oct. 8, 1931, Dec. 16, 1931; Marion Anderson Spear to WBR, July 18, 1991. "Sees American Men Subdued by Women," *New York Times,* Oct. 31, 1931, p. 19; "Pre-Industrialist Edens," *New York Times,* Nov. 2, 1931, p. 20.

49. "Abolition of Family Debated by Authors," *New York Times,* Nov. 2, 1931, p. 19. *Sherwood Anderson's Memoirs* (1942), p. 471; (1969), p. 533. Charles E. Modlin, "Sherwood Anderson's Debate with Bertrand Russell," *Winesburg Eagle* 12 (Nov. 1986): 4–11.

50. "Shall the Home Be Abolished?" *Literary Digest* 111 (Nov. 28, 1931): 25–26. SA, "Machine Child-Rearing," *New York Times,* Nov. 8, 1931, sec. 9, p. 2. Leigh to SA, Dec. 16, 1931.

51. SA to Eleanor Copenhaver Anderson, Nov. 2, 1931, Nov. 5, 1931, probably Nov. 6, 1931, Nov. 12, 1931, Nov. 13, 1931, Nov. 14, 1931; to Max Eastman, Nov. 3, 1931, ca. Nov. 4, 1931; to Leigh, Nov. 5, 1931; Leigh to SA, Oct. 20, 1931. "Travel Notes," *Smyth County News,* Nov. 19, 1931, pp. 1, 8. "Heading for Matriarchy," *New York Times,* Nov. 23, 1931, p. 18. Leigh's contracts, Aug. 6, 1931, Mar. 28, 1931, June 11, 1931.

52. SA to Eleanor Copenhaver Anderson, Nov. 14, 1931, Nov. 15, 1931; to Laura Lu Copenhaver, Nov. 15, 1931. Leigh's contract, May 29, 1931.
53. SA to Eleanor Copenhaver Anderson, Nov. 15, 1931, Dec. 11, 1931, Nov. 26, 1931; to Laura Lu Copenhaver, Nov. 15, 1931. Richard Lingeman, *Theodore Dreiser: An American Journey 1908–1945* (New York: G. P. Putnam's Sons, 1990), vol. 2, pp. 354–62. Leigh's contracts, May 29, 1931, Sept. 21, 1931.
54. SA to Eleanor Copenhaver Anderson, Nov. 26, 1931, Nov. 28, 1931, Nov. 29, 1931, Nov. 30, 1931, Dec. 2, 1931.
55. SA to Eleanor Copenhaver Anderson, ?Dec. 3, 1931, Dec. 6, 1931; to Burton Emmett, Nov. 29, 1931; to Dreiser, ?Dec. 22, 1931. Dreiser to SA, Dec. 10, 1931. "Anderson Decries Our 'Speakeasy' Era," *New York Times,* Dec. 7, 1931, p. 24. "I Want to Be Counted," in Theodore Dreiser et al., *Harlan Miners Speak: Report on Terrorism in the Kentucky Coal Fields* (New York: Harcourt Brace, 1932), pp. 298–312.

CHAPTER 5. RADICAL

1. SA to Eleanor Copenhaver Anderson, Dec. 7, 1931, Dec. 11, 1931, Dec. 8, 1931, Dec. 9, 1931.
2. SA to Eleanor Copenhaver Anderson, Dec. 11, 1931, Dec. 9, 1931, Dec. 12, 1931, Dec. 14, 1931, Dec. [16], 1931, Dec. 16, 1931; to Mimi Anderson, Dec. 17, 1931. Modlin, *Anderson's Love Letters,* p. 208, n. 1. Leigh's contract, Dec. 7, 1931. "Miss Belle" was the wife of Dr. O. C. Sprinkle, pharmacist at the City Drug in Marion.
3. SA to Eleanor Copenhaver Anderson, Dec. 16, 1931, Dec. 29, 1931, Dec. 30–31, 1931, Jan. 1, 1932; to Mimi Anderson, Dec. 17, 1931. Bill in chancery, Smyth County Courthouse, Marion. Ray Lewis White, ed., *Sherwood Anderson's Secret Love Letters: For Eleanor, a Letter a Day,* introduction, pp. 9–10; letters, Jan. 1, Jan. 8, Jan. 28, Nov. 16, Aug. 3.
4. White, *Anderson's Secret Love Letters,* Jan. 1, Jan. 2, Jan. 3, Jan. 4.
5. SA to Karl Anderson, ca. Jan. 8, 1932; White, *Anderson's Secret Love Letters,* Jan. 5, Jan. 7, Jan. 8, Jan. 9.
6. White, *Anderson's Secret Love Letters,* Jan. 9, Jan. 11; SA to Eleanor Copenhaver Anderson, Jan. 10, 1932.
7. White, *Anderson's Secret Love Letters,* Jan. 12, Jan. 13, Jan. 16, Jan. 17, Jan. 19; SA to Eleanor Copenhaver Anderson, Jan. 13, 1932. Six Leigh contracts.
8. White, *Anderson's Secret Love Letters,* Jan. 23, Jan. 20, Jan. 27, Jan. 26, Jan. 28, Jan. 29, Jan. 31. SA to Eleanor Copenhaver Anderson, Jan. 20, 1932, Jan. 27, 1932, Jan. 28, 1932, Jan. 30, 1932; to Burton Emmett, Feb. 2, 1932.
9. White, *Anderson's Secret Love Letters,* Feb. 2; SA to Eleanor Copenhaver Anderson, Feb. 17, 1932. Original Bill (File No. 138), Smyth County Courthouse, Marion. Interview, WBR with Burt L. Dickinson.
10. White, *Anderson's Secret Love Letters,* Feb. 3, Feb. 8, Feb. 7; SA to Eleanor Copenhaver Anderson, Feb. 4, 1932, Feb. 5, 1932, Feb. 6, 1932.
11. SA to Eleanor Copenhaver Anderson, Feb. 5, 1932, Feb. 8, 1932; to Charles and Adelaide Walker, Feb. 5, 1932 (sent only to Eleanor Copenhaver Ander-

son); White, *Anderson's Secret Love Letters,* Feb. 13. Malcolm Cowley, *The Dream of the Golden Mountains: Remembering the 1930s* (New York: Viking Press, 1980), pp. 67–74.

12. White, *Anderson's Secret Love Letters,* Feb. 19, Feb. 11, Feb. 12, Feb. 20, Feb. 23, Feb. 24, Feb. 25, Feb. 26.

13. White, *Anderson's Secret Love Letters,* Feb. 28, Feb. 29, Mar. 4, Mar. 5, Mar. 11; SA to Eleanor Copenhaver Anderson, Mar. 3, 1932, Mar. 9, 1932.

14. White, *Anderson's Secret Love Letters,* Mar. 12, Feb. 10, Feb. 16.

15. White, *Anderson's Secret Love Letters,* Mar. 13; SA to Eleanor Copenhaver Anderson, Mar. 12, 1932. Leigh contract.

16. White, *Anderson's Secret Love Letters,* Mar. 14, Mar. 15, Mar. 16, Mar. 18, Mar. 19, Mar. 20; SA to Eleanor Copenhaver Anderson, Mar. 12, 1932, Mar. 17, 1932, Mar. 18, 1932; to Burton Emmett, Mar. 19, 1932; to Russell Spear, Mar. 18, 1932. Mimi Anderson to WBR, July 18, 1991. Leigh contracts. "Travel Notes," *Smyth County News,* Mar. 24, 1932, p. 3; Mar. 31, 1932, p. 3.

17. White, *Anderson's Secret Love Letters,* Mar. 20; SA to Eleanor Copenhaver Anderson, Mar. 20, 1932.

18. White, *Anderson's Secret Love Letters,* Mar. 21, Mar. 25, Mar. 22, Mar. 23, Mar. 24; SA to Eleanor Copenhaver Anderson , Mar. 21, 1932, Mar. 22, 1932. "Travel Notes," *Smyth County News,* Mar. 31, 1932, p. 4.

19. Leigh contract. "Calls Modern Press Vulgar," *Arizona Daily Star,* Mar. 24, 1932, p. 4. White, *Anderson's Secret Love Letters,* Mar. 24; SA to Eleanor Copenhaver Anderson, Mar. 24, 1932.

20. White, *Anderson's Secret Love Letters,* Mar. 25, Mar. 26, Mar. 27, Mar. 29, Mar. 31. "Travel Notes," *Smyth County News,* April 7, 1932, p. 8. Leigh contract. SA to Eleanor Copenhaver Anderson, Mar. 25, 1932, Mar. 28, 1932, Mar. 29, 1932, Mar. 31, 1932; to F. W. Reynolds, Dec. 9, 1931; to Laura Lu Copenhaver, ca. Apr. 3, 1932.

21. White, *Anderson's Secret Love Letters,* Apr. 1, Apr. 3, Apr. 4, Apr. 5, Apr. 6; SA to Bockler , Apr. 1, 1932; to Eleanor Copenhaver Anderson, Apr. 2–3, 1932, Apr. 6, 1932. Leigh contracts.

22. Leigh contracts. White, *Anderson's Secret Love Letters,* Apr. 7, Apr. 8, Apr. 9. "Travel Notes: Talkies," *Smyth County News,* May 5, 1932, p. 6. SA to Eleanor Copenhaver Anderson, Apr. 7, 1932.

23. White, *Anderson's Secret Love Letters,* Apr. 10. SA to Eleanor Copenhaver Anderson, Apr. 2–3, 1932, Apr. 11, 1932.

24. White, *Anderson's Secret Love Letters,* Apr. 11, Apr. 13, Apr. 14, Apr. 16, Apr. 17; SA to Eleanor Copenhaver Anderson, Apr. 14, 1932. Leigh contracts. David W. Hazen, "Editor, Novelist and Poet in City on Lecture Tour," *Morning Oregonian,* April 16, 1932, p. 7.

25. White, *Anderson's Secret Love Letters,* Apr. 18, Apr. 22, Apr. 13, Apr. 19, Apr. 20, Apr. 24, Apr. 23; SA to Wilson, Apr. 22, 1932. "Travel Notes: People and Events," *Smyth County News,* May 12, 1932, p. 7. Copy of typed "Manifesto."

26. White, *Anderson's Secret Love Letters,* Apr. 25, May 6; SA to Angelo, ca. Apr. 25, 1932; to Eleanor Copenhaver Anderson, May 13, 1932, May 3, 1932; to Laura Lu Copenhaver, ca. May 7, 1932.

27. White, *Anderson's Secret Love Letters,* May 1, May 2, May 7, May 9, May 6, May 5, May 11, May 15; SA to Laura Lu Copenhaver, May 13, 1932, Apr. 29, 1932.

28. SA to Laura Lu Copenhaver, May 13, 1932, May 17, 1932; to John Anderson, late Apr. 1932. White, *Anderson's Secret Love Letters,* May 13, May 15. Charles E. Modlin, ed., "'Dive Keeper': A New Story by Sherwood Anderson," *Winesburg Eagle* 19 (Winter 1994): 1–5.

29. SA to Laura Lu Copenhaver, May 17, 1931; to Eleanor Copenhaver Anderson, May 23, 1932, May 24, 1932. White, *Anderson's Secret Love Letters,* May 15, May 16, May 17, May 19, May 20, May 21, May 22, May 23.

30. White, *Anderson's Secret Love Letters,* June 4, June 1, June 10, June 20, May 25, June 11, June 19. SA to Eleanor Copenhaver Anderson, June 20, 1932; to Louis I. Jaffee, June 18, 1932; to Brooks, ca. May 25, 1932; to Bockler, June 11, 1932.

31. SA to Eleanor Copenhaver Anderson, June 19, 1932, July 9, 1932. White, *Anderson's Secret Love Letters,* June 25, June 30, July 1, July 2, July 3, July 12.

32. SA to Bockler, May 28, 1932; to Roger Sergel, June 7, 1932; to Paul Scherer, June 7, 1932; to Eleanor Copenhaver Anderson, ca. May 25, 1932, June 6, 1932. White, *Anderson's Secret Love Letters,* June 9.

33. White, *Anderson's Secret Love Letters,* July 2, July 14, July 15, July 18, July 23. SA to Eleanor Copenhaver Anderson, July 12, 1932; to Mimi Anderson, July 14, 1932, July 23, 1932; to Laura Lu Copenhaver, Aug. 2, 1932.

34. White, *Anderson's Secret Love Letters,* Aug. 1, July 27, Aug. 2, Aug. 8. SA to Roger Sergel, ca. July 27, 1932; to Burton Emmett, July 28, 1932; to Laura Lu Copenhaver, Aug. 3, 1932, Aug. 2, 1932. "A Writer's Notes," *New Masses* 8 (Aug. 1932): 10. Stationery of the National Committee.

35. SA to Mimi Anderson, July 23, 1932; to Laura Lu Copenhaver, Aug. 2, 1932, Aug. 3, 1932. Robert Lane Anderson to Mimi Anderson, July 30, 1932. White, *Anderson's Secret Love Letters,* July 30, Aug. 5, Aug. 9, Aug. 6.

36. "Troops Drive Veterans from Capital," *New York Times,* July 29, 1932, pp. 1, 3.

37. "To 'Challenge' Hoover on Ejecting Veterans" and "Challenge to Hoover Planned by Writers," *New York Times,* Aug. 9, 1932, p. 4, and Aug. 10, 1932, p. 2. "President Too Busy For Bonus Protest," *New York Times,* Aug. 11, 1932, p. 2, an extended account printing part of the statement SA began reading. "When Are Authors Insulted?" *Bookman* 75 (Oct. 1932): 564. SA to Hoover, Aug. 10, 1932; to Eleanor Copenhaver Anderson, Aug. 10, 1932, Aug. 11, 1932. White, *Anderson's Secret Love Letters,* Aug. 11.

38. White, *Anderson's Secret Love Letters,* Aug. 12, Aug. 13. SA to Eleanor Copenhaver Anderson, Aug. 12, 1932.

39. SA to Eleanor Copenhaver Anderson, Aug. 14, 1932; to Ferdinand Schevill, Sept. 22, 1932; to Mimi Anderson, Aug. 16, 1932; to the Emmetts, Aug. 18, 1932. White, *Anderson's Secret Love Letters,* Aug. 15, Aug. 16, Aug. 18.

40. SA to Eleanor Copenhaver Anderson, Aug. 18, 1932, Aug. 19, 1932, Aug. 22, 1932, Aug. 21, 1932, Aug. 23, 1932, Aug. 25, 1932, Aug. 26, 1932; to the Emmetts, Aug. 18, 1932. White, *Anderson's Secret Love Letters,* Aug. 19–Aug. 25.

41. White, *Anderson's Secret Love Letters,* Aug. 26, Aug. 27. SA to Eleanor Copenhaver Anderson, Aug. 26, 1932, Aug. 27, 1932. Herbert R. Lottman, *The Left Bank: Writers, Artists, and Politics from the Popular Front to the Cold War* (Boston: Houghton Mifflin, 1982), pp. 50–52. "2,000 Pacifists Open Parley in Amsterdam," *New York Times,* Aug. 28, 1932, p. 2.

42. "At Amsterdam," *New Masses* 8 (Nov. 1932): 11. White, *Anderson's Secret Love Letters,* Aug. 29.

43. SA to Eleanor Copenhaver Anderson, Aug. 29, 1932, Aug. 31, 1932. Manifesto, reprinted in *Smyth County News,* Sept. 15, 1932, p. 2. Lottman, *The Left Bank,* p. 52.

44. SA to Eleanor Copenhaver Anderson, Aug. 30, 1932, Aug. 25, 1932, Aug. 27, 1932; to Ida Dailes, Nov. 18, 1932. *Modern Quarterly* 6 (Summer 1932): 11–19, p. 12. *New Masses* 8 (Sept. 1932): 6–10, pp. 8–9.

45. White, *Anderson's Secret Love Letters,* Aug. 31, Sept. 2, Sept. 11, Sept. 8, Sept. 6, Sept. 5, Sept. 7. SA to Eleanor Copenhaver Anderson, Aug. 31, 1932, Sept. 3, 1932.

46. White, *Anderson's Secret Love Letters,* Sept. 9, Sept. 12, Sept. 13, Sept. 10, Sept. 14, Sept. 15, Sept. 16. SA to Eleanor Copenhaver Anderson, Sept. 12, 1932. "Form Group to Back Foster," *New York Times,* Sept. 12, 1932, p. 3. "Men Useless to Women, Sherwood Anderson Says," *New York World-Telegram,* Sept. 16, 1932, p. 28.

47. Hansen, "The First Reader," *New York World-Telegram,* Sept. 19, 1932, p. 23; Gannett, "Books and Things," *New York Herald Tribune,* Sept. 19, 1932, p. 11; Stallings, "The Book of the Day," *Sun,* Sept. 20, 1932, p. 28; William Soskin, "Reading and Writing," *Evening Post,* Sept. 20, 1932. SA to Eleanor Copenhaver Anderson, Sept. 29, 1932; to Karl Anderson, Sept. 24, 1932. White, *Anderson's Secret Love Letters,* Sept. 26, Sept. 21.

48. Hicks, "Red Pilgrimage," *New Republic* 73 (Dec. 21, 1932): 168–69; Chamberlain, "Mr. Anderson's 'Labor' Novel," *New York Times Book Review,* Sept. 25, 1932, p. 6; Geoffrey Stone, "*Beyond Desire,*" *Bookman* 75 (Oct. 1932): 642–43; Ted Robinson, "Bully Book by Hemingway," *Cleveland Plain Dealer,* Sept. 25, 1932, Amusement section, p. 11; "Beyond Control," *Time* 20 (Oct. 17, 1932): 52. White, *Anderson's Secret Love Letters,* Oct. 15.

CHAPTER 6. UNSETTLED

1. SA to Eleanor Copenhaver Anderson, Sept. 29, 1932, Sept. 25, 1932, Sept. 26, 1932, Sept. 23, 1932, Sept. 30, 1932. White, *Anderson's Secret Love Letters,* Sept. 18, Sept. 28, Sept. 29.

2. Barr to SA, Sept. 29, 1932, Oct. 3, 1932. SA to Barr, ca. Oct. 1, 1932, Oct. 5, 1932, Oct. 13, 1932; to Eleanor Copenhaver Anderson, Oct. 6, 1932, Oct. 7, 1932, Oct. 11, 1932, Oct. 12, 1932. *Virginia Quarterly Review* 9 (Jan. 1933): 108–14. White, *Anderson's Secret Love Letters,* Oct. 12.

3. SA to Eleanor Copenhaver Anderson, Oct. 1, 1932, Oct. 1–2, 1932, Oct. 17, 1932, Oct. 11, 1932. White, *Anderson's Secret Love Letters,* Oct. 8, Oct. 13.

4. White, *Anderson's Secret Love Letters,* Oct. 15, Oct. 20, Oct. 21, Oct. 22,

Oct. 25, Oct. 26. SA to Laura Lu Copenhaver and Bascom E. Copenhaver, Oct. 23, 1932, Oct. 24, 1932, Oct. 26, 1932; to Mimi Anderson, Oct. 31, 1932; to Roger Sergel, Oct. 26, 1932; to Eleanor Copenhaver Anderson, Oct. 29, 1932; to the Emmetts, Nov. 14, 1932.

5. SA to Mimi Anderson, Oct. 31, 1932; to Karl Anderson, Oct. 28, 1932; to Eleanor Copenhaver Anderson, Oct. 28, 1932, Oct. 31, 1932, Sept. 20, 1932, Oct. [31], 1932, Nov. 1, 1932. League of Professional Groups, *Culture and the Crisis* (New York: Workers Library Publishers, 1932).

6. SA to Mimi Anderson, Oct. 31, 1932; to Roger Sergel, Nov. 9, 1932; to Eleanor Copenhaver Anderson, Oct. 30, 1932, Nov. 5, 1932, Nov. 9, 1932. White, *Anderson's Secret Love Letters,* Oct. 31.

7. White, *Anderson's Secret Love Letters,* Nov. 10, Nov. 11, Nov. 17. SA to Eleanor Copenhaver Anderson, Nov. 10.

8. White, *Anderson's Secret Love Letters,* Nov. 17, Nov. 18, Nov. 15, Nov. 20, Nov. 19, Nov. 13, Nov. 14, Nov. 24, Dec. 11. Interview, WBR with Charles H. Funk, June 22, 1953.

9. SA to Karl Anderson, Jan. 19, 1933; to Thomas Smith, Dec. 2, 1932; to Barton, Nov. 26, 1932, Dec. 7, 1932; to Eleanor Copenhaver Anderson, mid-Nov. 1932. "The Wonder Boys in 52d Street," *New York Times,* Nov. 1, 1931, sec. 8, p. 3. J. Brooks Atkinson, "The Play: A Lampooning of the Screen," *New York Times,* Oct. 24, 1931, p. 20.

10. SA to Ruth Sergel, Dec. 2, 1932; to Barton, Dec. 3, 1932, Dec. 7, 1932.

11. SA to Eleanor Copenhaver Anderson, Dec. 14, 1932, Dec. 16, 1932; to Mimi Anderson, Dec. 19, 1932; to Mary Emmett, Dec. 27, 1932; to Roger Sergel, ?mid-Dec. 1932.

12. SA to Mary Emmett, Dec. 27, 1932; to the Emmetts, Jan. 19, 1933; to Mimi Anderson, Jan. 9, 1933; to Mabel Connick, Jan. 19, 1933; to Karl Anderson, Jan. 19, 1933; to the Sergels, ca. Jan. 14, 1933.

13. SA to Bockler, Jan. 20, 1933; to Laura Lu Copenhaver, ca. Jan. 19, 1933; to Eleanor Copenhaver Anderson, Jan. 18, 1933, Jan. 22, 1933; to Smith, Dec. 2, 1932.

14. SA to Laura Lu Copenhaver, Jan. 20, 1933, ?late Jan. 1933, Jan. 1933; to Rosenfeld, Jan. 20, 1933; to Karl Anderson, Jan. 19, 1933; to Marco Morrow, ca. Jan. 25, 1933; to Eleanor Copenhaver Anderson, ?Jan 1933; to Dreiser, Jan. 25, 1933.

15. SA to the Emmetts, Jan. 19, 1933; to Laura Lu Copenhaver, Feb. 12–13, 1933; to Dreiser, Feb. 7, 1933; to Ferdinand Schevill, Mar. 2, 1933.

16. SA to Dreiser, Feb. 7, 1933, Feb. 27, 1933; to Eleanor Copenhaver Anderson, Feb. 10, 1933; to Mabel Connick, Jan. 19, 1933; to Mimi Anderson, Feb. 12, 1933; to Bockler and Katharine B., Feb. 12, 1933; to Finley, ca. Feb. 23, 1933; to Marco Morrow, ?mid-Feb. 1933, ca. Mar. 18, 1933.

17. SA to Marco Morrow, ca. mid-Mar. 1933; to Roger Sergel, ca. Mar. 20, 1933; to Kraft, late Feb. 1933; to Adelaide Walker, before Mar. 22, 1933; Kraft to SA, Apr. 5, 1932, June 23, 1932, Feb. 28, 1933. *American Spectator* 1 (May 1933): 1. Olin Downes, "Gruenberg's 'Jones' In Premiere," *New York Times,* Jan. 1, 1933, sec. 9, p. 6; "Felicitate Gruenberg," *New York Times,* Jan. 11, 1933, p. 23.

18. Kraft to SA, Mar. 14, 1933; SA to Kraft, Mar. 18, 1933, ca. Mar. 20, 1933; to Dreiser, ca. Mar. 20, 1933.
19. SA to Eleanor Copenhaver Anderson, ca. July 26, 1933; to Roger Sergel, late Feb. 1933; to Marco Morrow, ca. Mar. 18, 1933; to Kraft and Gruenberg, Mar. 26 or 27, 1933; to Kraft, Mar. 18, 1933; to Mimi Anderson, Mar. 21, 1933, early Mar. 1933.
20. SA to Mimi Anderson, Mar. 24, 1933, Apr. 4, 1933; to Karl Anderson, Apr. 4, 1933; to Kraft, ca. Apr. 3, 1933; to Roger Sergel, ca. Apr. 15, 1933.
21. SA to Mimi Anderson, Apr. 27, 1933. "Liveright, Inc. Put into Bankruptcy," *New York Times,* May 5, 1933, p. 16; "A Writer Should Be Poor," *New York Times,* Apr. 20, 1933, p. 15; "Novelist Calls Film Trail Real Path to Fame," *New York Herald Tribune,* Apr. 20, 1933, p. 13.
22. SA to Roger Sergel, ca. Apr. 27, 1933; to Laura Lu Copenhaver, ca. Apr. 22, 1933, Apr. 27, 1933; to Burton Emmett, ?July 5, 1933. Gannett, "Books and Things," *New York Herald Tribune,* April 13, 1933, p. 15; Hansen, "The First Reader," *New York World-Telegram,* Apr. 15, 1933, p. 13; Marsh, "The Story Teller's Return," *New York Herald Tribune Books,* Apr. 16, 1933, p. 4; H. M. W., *Boston Transcript,* Apr. 29, 1933, p. 1.
23. SA to Roger Sergel, ca. Apr. 27, 1933, ca. May 1, 1933; ca. May 4, 1933; to Laura Lu Copenhaver, ca. May 1, 1933; to Frieda Fishbein, May 6, 1933. "Liveright, Inc. Put into Bankruptcy," *New York Times,* May 5, 1933, p. 16. "Liveright in Difficulties," *Publishers' Weekly* 123 (May 13, 1933): 1546.
24. SA to Tom Brandon, May 6, 1933; to Frieda Fishbein, May 6, 1933; to Laura Lu Copenhaver, ca. May 1, 1933; to Blum, May 6, 1933; to H. L. Mencken, ca. May 1, 1933.
25. SA to Mrs. Friend (mother of Julius), May 10, 1933; to Sillcox, May 6, 1933; to Mimi Anderson, May 8, 1933; to Laura Lu Copenhaver, ca. May 1, 1933; to Roger Sergel, ca. May 4, 1933. Lardner to Richard Lardner Tobin, pp. 292–93 in Clifford M. Carruthers, ed., *Letters from Ring* (Flint, MI: Walden Press, 1979). "Paul Muni in 'Counselor-at Law,' at the Majestic, Brooklyn," *New York Herald Tribune,* April 30, 1933, sec. 7, p. 6. "American Authors Protest," *New York Times,* May 10, 1933, p. 11.
26. SA to Sillcox, May 6, 1933; to Barton, May 10, 1933; to Eleanor Copenhaver Anderson, May 18, 1933, May 21, 1933, May 22, 1933, May 23, 1933, ca. June 10, 1933, May 27, 1933.
27. SA to Eleanor Copenhaver Anderson, May 23, 1933, May 21, 1933, ca. June 7, 1933.
28. SA to Barton, May 10, 1933; to Eleanor Copenhaver Anderson, ca. June 8, 1933, ?June 9, 1933, ca. June 10, 1933, June 20, 1933, June 21, 1933, June 22, 1933; to Mimi Anderson, June 12, 1933; to Roger Sergel, ca. June 15, 1933. Kraft to SA, June 13, 1933. Letter, Dean Roger S. Bagnall, Graduate School of Arts and Sciences, Columbia University, to WBR, Mar. 10, 1993.
29. SA to Eleanor Copenhaver Anderson, June 22, 1933, June 23–24, 1933, June 26, 1933, June 25, 1933, June 23, 1933, June 27, 1933; to Roger Sergel, July 5, 1933.
30. Eleanor Copenhaver Anderson diary, Aug. 9, 1933, Aug. 31, 1933. Eleanor

Copenhaver Anderson to Mary Emmett, July 19, 1933. SA to Eleanor Copenhaver Anderson, July 24, 1933, July 18, 1933; to the Emmetts, July 24, 1933.

31. SA to the Emmetts, July 24; to Eleanor Copenhaver Anderson, July 27, 1933, July 26, 1933, ?July 26, 1933; to Roger Sergel, ca. July 22, 1933, July 5, 1933; to Ferdinand Schevill, July 26, 1933.

32. SA to Roger Sergel, July 29, 1933. *Publishers' Weekly* 123 (May 20, 1933): 1603; (June 3, 1933): 1817; (June 17, 1933): 1956; 124 (July 29, 1933): 298; (Aug. 19, 1933): 496. Walker Gilmer, *Horace Liveright: Publisher of the Twenties* (New York: D. Lewis), pp. 233–34, 268–69. Saxe Commins to SA, Aug. 24, 1933. Eleanor Copenhaver Anderson diary, July 31, 1933.

33. SA to Roger Sergel, ca. Aug. 3, 1933, late Aug. 1933, ca. Sept. 5, 1933; to Perkins, ca. Aug. 12, 1933; to Mary Emmett, Aug. 12, 1933.

34. Eleanor Copenhaver Anderson diary, Aug. 1, 2, 3, 4, 7, 10, 30, 31, 1933. Eleanor Copenhaver Anderson to Mary Emmett, Aug. 4, 1933, Aug. 11, 1933. SA to Perkins, ca. Aug. 12, 1933; to Harold Guinzburg, Aug. 14, 1933; to Eleanor Copenhaver Anderson, Oct. 2, 1933.

35. SA to Eleanor Copenhaver Anderson, ?Sept. 8, 1933, Sept. 5, 1933, Sept. 6, 1933; to the Emmetts, Sept. 22, 1933.

36. SA to Eleanor Copenhaver Anderson , Sept. 4, 1933; to the Emmetts, Sept. 15, 1933. "The Finding," *Memoirs* (1942), pp. 277–80; (1969), pp. 350–53.

37. SA to Laura Lu Copenhaver, Sept. 15, 1933; to the Emmetts, Sept. 19, 1933, Sept. 26, 29, 1933, Oct. 14, 1933; to Roger Sergel, ca. Sept. 30, 1933; to Laura Lu Copenhaver, Sept. 26, 1933. Eleanor Copenhaver Anderson diary, Sept. 23. Eleanor Copenhaver Anderson to the Emmetts, Nov. 5, 1933.

38. SA to the Emmetts, Oct. 8, 1933, Oct. 5, 1933; to Laura Lu Copenhaver, probably Oct. 5, 1933. Eleanor Copenhaver Anderson diary, Oct. 6.

39. SA to Dreiser, Oct. 3, 1933; Dreiser to SA, Oct. 17, 1933; Mencken to SA, May 5, 1933.

40. Dreiser to SA, Oct. 17, 1933; SA to the Emmetts, Oct. 14, 1933; to Eleanor Copenhaver Anderson, Oct. 16, 1933. Eleanor Copenhaver Anderson diary, Nov. 16.

41. Moley to SA, Sept. 28, 1933; SA to Roger Sergel, ca. Oct. 10, 1933; to the Emmetts, Oct. 14, 1933; to Eleanor Copenhaver Anderson, Oct. 16, 1933; to Dreiser, ca. Oct. 18, 1933.

42. Eleanor Copenhaver Anderson diary, Oct. 12, Nov. 16. SA to Eleanor Copenhaver Anderson, Oct. 16, 1933, Oct. 21, 1933; to Roger Sergel, late Oct. 1933, Nov. 24, 1933, Nov. 18, 1933; to Barton, Nov. 21, 1933; Eleanor Copenhaver Anderson to the Emmetts, Nov. 12.

43. Eleanor Copenhaver Anderson diary, Nov. 16, Oct. 16–20. Eleanor Copenhaver Anderson to the Emmetts, Nov. 12, 1933; SA to editors of *Today*, Nov. 13, 1933; to Roger Sergel, Nov. 18, 1933, ?late Oct. 1933.

44. SA to Barton, Nov. 21, 1933; to Roger Sergel, Nov. 24, 1933, ca. Nov. 30, 1933; to Thayer, Dec. 2, 1933; to Bockler, Dec. 4, 1933. Barton to SA, Nov. 29, 1933.

45. Eleanor Copenhaver Anderson diary, Nov. 16. SA to Laura Lu Copenhaver, ca. Nov. 24, 1933; to the Emmetts, Dec. 20, 1933. Eleanor Copenhaver An-

derson to the Emmetts, Nov. 25, 1933; to Mary Emmett, Dec. 11, 1933. "Dysentery in Chicago," *Time* 22 (Nov. 20, 1933): 29–30.

46. SA to Roger Sergel, ca. Dec. 8, 1933; to Eleanor Copenhaver Anderson, Dec. 13, 1933. "At the Mine Mouth," *Today* 1 (Dec. 30, 1933): 5, 19–21.

47. SA to Laura Lu Copenhaver, Dec. 13, 1933, before Dec. 25, 1933; to Ferdinand Schevill, Jan. 13, 1934; to Roger Sergel, Dec. 18, 1933; to the Emmetts, Dec. 20, 1933. "The Herald Angel Sings," *New York Times*, Dec. 10, 1933, sec. 10, pt. 2, p. 4.

48. Eleanor Copenhaver Anderson to the Emmetts, Dec. 29, 1933. SA to Laura Lu Copenhaver, Bascom E. Copenhaver, and May Scherer, Jan. 2, 1934; to the Emmetts, mid-Feb. 1934.

CHAPTER 7. ON, AND OFF, THE ROAD

1. SA to Moley, Jan. 5, 1934; Moley to SA, Jan. 11, 1934.
2. SA to the Emmetts, Jan. 14, 1934; to Maltz, Jan. 14, 1934; to Braver-Mann, Jan. 14, 1934; to Robert Lane Anderson, Jan. 13, 1934; to Fishbein, Jan. 25, 1934; to Stewart, Jan. 12, 1934, Jan. 21, 1934. Braver-Mann to SA, Dec. 22, 1933. Sillcox to Perkins, Jan. 16, 1934. Perkins to Sillcox, Jan. 17, 1934.
3. SA to Stewart, Jan. 12, 1934, Jan. 21, 1934, Jan. 24, 1934. Eleanor Copenhaver Anderson diary, Jan. 29. "Tough Babes in the Woods," *Today* 1 (Feb. 10, 1934): 6–7, 22.
4. SA to Stewart, Jan. 24, 1934; to Fishbein, Jan. 25, 1934; to Sillcox, Jan. 25, 1934; to T. G. McCall, Jan. 25, 1934; to Roger Sergel, Jan. 30, 1934. Document of agreement.
5. "Blue Smoke," *Today* 1 (Feb. 24, 1934): 6–7, 23.
6. Eleanor Copenhaver Anderson diary, Jan. 29, Feb. 28. "Gertrude Stein," *American Spectator* 2 (April 1934): 3. SA to Nathan and Boyd, Jan. 25, 1934; to Stewart, Jan. 31, 1934; to Roger Sergel, Jan. 30, 1934. Dreiser to SA, Jan. 4, 19[34].
7. Eleanor Copenhaver Anderson diary, Feb. 28. SA to Stewart, ca. Feb. 5, 1934, Feb. 13, 1934. "Price of Aristocracy," *Today* 1 (Mar. 10, 1934): 10–11, 23. "Tom Grey Could So Easily Lead Them," *Today* 1 (Mar. 24, 1934): 8–9, 23; published in *Puzzled America* (1935) as "A Union Meeting," pp. 113–23, with the seven-paragraph introduction deleted, probably because by early 1935 the NRA was under attack. On May 27 the Supreme Court ruled major provisions of it unconstitutional.
8. SA to Stewart, Feb. 21. "Personalities," renamed "New Paths for Old," *Today* 1 (Apr. 17, 1934): 12–13, 32, would be included in *Puzzled America* under the title "People," pp. 39–53.
9. Eleanor Copenhaver Anderson diary, Feb. 28. SA to Stewart, Feb. 28, 1934, Mar. 8, 1934. "I Want to Work," *Today* 1 (Apr. 28, 1934): 10–11, 22.
10. SA to Roger Sergel, Feb. 20, 1934, Mar. 5, 1934; to Stewart, Mar. 8, 1934; to Julius Friend, Apr. 5, 1934; to Marc and Lucile Antony, Apr. 5, 1934. "A New Chance for the Men of the Hills," *Today* 1 (May 12, 1934): 10–11, 22–23.
11. SA to Moley, Mar. 23, 1934; to Stewart, after Mar. 23, 1934, Apr. 5, 1934. "New Tyrants of the Land," *Today* 1 (May 26, 1934): 10–11, 20.

12. Moley to SA, Mar. 21, 1934; SA to Stewart, late Mar. 1934; to Roger Sergel, late Mar. 1934; to the Emmetts, Mar. 23. Eleanor Copenhaver Anderson diary, Jan. 29. Sillcox to SA, Mar. 16, 1934.

13. SA to Roger Sergel, Apr. 5, 1934; to Laura Lu Copenhaver, probably Apr. 7, 1934; to Blossom, Apr. 7, 1934. Eleanor Copenhaver Anderson to the Emmetts, Apr. 22, 1934.

14. Eleanor Copenhaver Anderson to the Emmetts, Apr. 13, 1934, May 8, 1934. SA to Laura Lu Copenhaver, after Apr. 15, 1934, May 6, 1934, ?May 18, 1934; to Stewart, May 4, 1934; to Mimi Anderson, May 11, 1934; to Roger Sergel, May 11, 1934; to the Emmetts, ca. May 18, 1934. John C. Wentz, "Anderson's *Winesburg* and the Hedgerow Theatre," *Modern Drama* 3 (May 1960): 42–51, the best account of this relationship.

15. SA to Mimi Anderson, May 11, 1934; to Roger Sergel, ca. May 5, 1934; to Editors, *Scribner's*, ca. May 18, 1934. Dashiell to SA, May 28, 1934.

16. SA to Mimi Anderson, May 11, 1934; to Laura Lu Copenhaver, May 18, 1934; to Stewart, June 18, 1934; to K. S. White, May 11, 1934. Eleanor Copenhaver Anderson diary, June 5, July 4. *American Magazine* 118 (Aug. 1934): 81–82. *New Yorker* 10 (June 9, 1934): 77–80.

17. Eleanor Copenhaver Anderson to the Emmetts, Apr. 22, 1934, ?Mar. 25, 1934. SA to James Creelman, Apr. 5, 1934; to Stein, Mar. 24, 1934, Apr. 6, 1934; to Laura Lu Copenhaver, ?Apr. 7, 1934; to Mimi Anderson, May 11, 1934. Mimi Anderson to WBR, July 18, 1991.

18. SA to the Emmetts, ca. May 15, 1934. Eleanor Copenhaver Anderson to the Emmetts, Apr. 22, 1934. Eleanor Copenhaver Anderson diary, June 5.

19. Wentz, "Anderson's *Winesburg*," passim. SA, "The Good Life at Hedgerow," *Esquire* 6 (October 1936): 51, 198A, 198B, 199; reprinted as "Jasper Deeter," the dedication in SA, *Plays: Winesburg and Others*, pp. xi–xxii.

20. Eleanor Copenhaver Anderson diary, June 5.

21. Eleanor Copenhaver Anderson diary, June 5. SA to Deeter, May 6, 1934; to Nathan and Boyd, June 12; to Stewart, June 18, 1934; to Burton Emmett, ca. June 12, 1934. Deeter to SA, June 11, 1934. Stewart to SA, June 22, 1934. "Paying for Old Sins," *Nation* 139 (July 11, 1934): 49–50.

22. SA to Dreiser, June 22, 1934; to Roger Sergel, July 2, 1934. Eleanor Copenhaver Anderson diary, July 4. Wentz, "Anderson's *Winesburg*," pp. 48–50. "'Winesburg' Debut Quiet," *New York World Telegram*, July 2, 1934, p. 12. Nearly thirty years later (Oct. 30, 1962) Eleanor told W. A. Swanberg in an interview for his *Dreiser* (pp. 419, 571) that her mother *had* seen Dreiser's genitals, had murmured "Disgusting," and had fled; however, the diary entry, made three days after the event, contradicts her later memory. It also supports Swanberg's suggestion that SA the story teller invented his account (see *Memoirs* [1942], pp. 337–38; [1969], pp. 457–58) of a naked Dreiser being given a shower bath by a boy with a garden hose in front of the group of breakfasters.

23. SA to Deeter, July 9, 1934. Wentz, "Anderson's *Winesburg*," p. 46.

24. SA to Stallings, June 14, 1934. Robert Garland, "Small Town Realism Marks 'Winesburg, O.,'" *New York World Telegram*, Aug. 20, 1934, p. 10.

25. SA to Deeter, July 9, 1934.

26. Eleanor Copenhaver Anderson diary, July 5, July 31, July 13, July 22. SA to Deeter, July 9, 1934.

27. SA to Sumner Blossom, Aug. 7, 1934. Stewart to SA, Aug. 9, 1934, Aug. 14, 1934. "Jug of Moon," *Today* 2 (Sept. 15, 1934): 6–7, 23. The story is reprinted in the 1942 edition of the *Memoirs,* pp. 389–94, as the unnamed opening episode of a section titled "Why I Live Where I Live," but is properly not included in White's 1969 edition. Anderson's title for the story was "The Death of Bill Graves"; apparently the not-very-appropriate "Jug of Moon" was assigned by some editor at *Today.* (See Stewart to SA, Aug. 9, 1934, SA's notation, Aug. 14, 1934.)

28. Stewart to SA, Aug. 14, 1934; Mason to SA, July 12, 1934, Sept. 24, 1934; SA to Mason, July 17, 1934, ca. Sept. 26, 1934.

29. Eleanor Copenhaver Anderson diary, Aug. 10, Aug. 14, Aug. 29, Sept. 11. SA to Roger Sergel, early Aug. 1934; to Perkins, Aug. 27, 1934, early Sept. 1934.

30. Eleanor Copenhaver Anderson diary, Sept. 11, Sept. 20. SA to Eleanor Copenhaver Anderson, Sept. 18 or 19, 1934; to Mimi Anderson and Russell, ca. Sept. 20, 1934; to Mason, Sept. 26, 1934, ca. Sept. 26, 1934. Perkins to SA, Sept. 10, 1934. Mason to SA, Sept. 24, 1934, Sept. 29, 1934.

31. SA to Mason, ca. Oct. 6, 1934, ca. Oct. 11, 1934, ca. Oct. 22, 1934; to Perkins, ca. Oct. 3, 1934, Oct. 6, 1934, ca. Oct. 19, 1934. Mason to SA, Oct. 9, 1934. Perkins to SA, Oct. 5, 1934, Oct. 18, 1934. "Please Let Me Explain" first published as "A Plan," *Modern Monthly* 7 (Feb. 1933): 13–16.

32. SA to Roger Sergel, ca. Oct. 21, 1934; to Mason, ca. Oct. 22, 1934, Nov. 6, 1934; to Laura Lu Copenhaver, Oct. 11, 1934; to Stewart, Oct. 29, 1934, Nov. 4, 1934, Nov. 5, 1934; to Eleanor Copenhaver Anderson, Oct. 29, 1934. "Young Man from West Virginia," *Today* 3 (Dec. 1, 1934): 5, 23–24; reprinted as "They Elected Him" in *Puzzled America.*

33. SA to Stewart, Nov. 4; to Koskull, ?early Nov. 1934. Stewart to SA, Nov. 5, 1934. Eleanor Copenhaver Anderson diary, Nov. 11.

34. SA to Mason, Nov. 6, 1934; to Coombs, Oct. 29, 1934. Eleanor Copenhaver Anderson diary, Nov. 11, 12, 13.

35. Eleanor Copenhaver Anderson diary, Nov. 16, 18, 19, 22. SA to Stewart, Nov. 11, 1934.

36. SA to Stewart, Nov. 12, 1934; to Perkins, ca. Nov. 22, 1934, ca. Nov. 28, 1934. Perkins to SA, Nov. 13, 1934. "Sherwood Anderson Goes Home," *Today* 3 (Dec. 8, 1934): 6–7, 23; reprinted in *Puzzled America* as "Night in a Corn Town."

37. Eleanor Copenhaver Anderson diary, Nov. 25, Dec. 3, Dec. 6. "Village Wassail," *Today* 3 (Jan. 26, 1935): 8–9, 20. *Saint Paul Pioneer Press,* Dec. 1, 4, 1934, p. 1. "Northwest Unafraid," *Today* 3 (Jan. 12, 1935): 8–9, 22–23, reprinted slightly revised as "Olsonville" in *Puzzled America.*

38. SA to Stein, Oct. 25, 1934. Eleanor Copenhaver Anderson diary, Dec. 6. "Who's Fannie? Local Girl? Gertrude Asks," *Saint Paul Pioneer Press,* Dec. 8, 1934, pp. 1, 4.

39. Eleanor Copenhaver Anderson diary, Dec. 6, Dec. 11. SA to Church, Dec. 11, 1934.

40. Toklas to "Elizabeth" [Eleanor], June 6, 1961, in Hilbert H. Campbell, "Three Unpublished Letters of Alice B. Toklas," *English Language Notes* 20 (March/June 1983): 47–51; p. 49. Since Toklas had come to know SA's third wife fairly well in 1927, the confusion of names is understandable. Eleanor Copenhaver Anderson diary, Dec. 11, 13. SA to Stein, Dec. 20, 1934.

41. SA to Church, Dec. 11, 1934; to Roger Sergel, Dec. 14, 1934; to Perkins, Jan. 2, 1935. Eleanor Copenhaver Anderson diary, Dec. 13, Jan. 17, 1935, Jan. 3, 1935.

42. SA to Church, Dec. 30, 1934.

CHAPTER 8. LOOKING FOR AN ART FORM

1. Mason to SA, Jan. 8, 1935. "Books and Things," *New York Herald Tribune*, Dec. 24, 1934, p. 7; "From Sherwood Anderson," *Today* 3 (Jan. 26, 1935): 18; *New Yorker* 10 (Dec. 29, 1934): 57–58; *Time* 24 (Dec. 31, 1934): 39. Eleanor Copenhaver Anderson diary, Jan. 17, 1935. *New York Times Book Review* (Nov. 25, 1934, p. 14) had briefly noted under "Books and Authors" that *No Swank* would be published "on Dec. 3," a date corrected to Dec. 8 by Lewis Gannett in a four-line notice, "Out Today," at the bottom of his "Books and Things" column in the *New York Herald Tribune*, Dec. 8, 1934, p. 13.

2. SA to Stewart, Jan. 2, 1935; to Perkins, Jan. 5, 1935. "Revolt in South Dakota" published under the title "War of the Winds," *Today* 3 (Feb. 23, 1935): 8–9, 20; published under original title in *Puzzled America*. "Feud," *American Magazine* 119 (Feb. 1935): 71, 112–14.

3. SA to Roger Sergel, Jan. 8, 1935, ca. Jan. 14, 1935. Eleanor Copenhaver Anderson diary, Jan. 17.

4. "Anderson Talks on 'Experiments' at Group Theater," *Times-Picayune,* Jan. 16, 1935, p. 4. Eleanor Copenhaver Anderson diary, Jan. 17.

5. Eleanor Copenhaver Anderson diary, Jan. 17, Jan. 31, Jan. 22, Jan. 27. SA to Frank [Copenhaver], Feb. 16, 1935; to Perkins, ca. Jan. 23, 1935, (telegram) Jan. 24, 1935; to Bockler, Jan. 29, 1935; to Scribner's, Jan. 27, 1935. Maxwell Perkins's secretary to SA, Jan. 25, 1935.

6. Eleanor Copenhaver Anderson diary, Feb. 10, Feb. 20. SA to Frank Copenhaver, Feb. 16, 1935; to Roger Sergel, Feb. 16, 1935. Myrick, "sherwood anderson," p. 11.

7. Eleanor Copenhaver Anderson diary, Jan. 27. SA to Roger Sergel, Feb. 16, 1935. "Such a Rotten and Stupid Way," p. 22 in "Public Enemy No. 1," *The Crisis* 42 (Jan. 1935): 6–7, 22–23. "Nobody's Home," *Today* 3 (March 30, 1935): 6–7, 20–21.

8. *Today* 3 (April 20, 1935): 6–7, 22–23.

9. SA to Scribner's, Jan. 27, 1935; to Roger Sergel, Feb. 16, 1935; to Perkins, Mar. 2, 1935.

10. Eleanor Copenhaver Anderson diary, Feb. 10, Feb. 20.

11. Stein to SA, ?Jan. 12, 1935. Eleanor Copenhaver Anderson to Frank Graham, Feb. 22, 1935. SA to Stein, Feb. 23, 1935. Toklas to Carl Van Vechten, Feb. 21, 1935, in Edward Burns, ed., *The Letters of Gertrude Stein and Carl Van Vechten 1913–1946* (New York: Columbia University Press, 1935), vol. 1,

pp. 392–94. "Gertrude Stein Does Not Repeat . . . ," *Times-Picayune*, Feb. 19, 1935, pp. 1, 2. Eleanor Copenhaver Anderson diary, Feb. 20, 21. Toklas, *What Is Remembered* (New York: Holt, Rinehart and Winston, 1963), p. 151. Preston, "A Conversation," *Atlantic* 156 (Aug. 1935): 187–94, p. 190.

12. Eleanor Copenhaver Anderson diary, Feb. 21, Feb. 24. SA to Stein, Feb. 23, 1935. "Author Returns to Favorite City after Vacation," *Times-Picayune*, Feb. 24, 1935, p. 4.

13. SA to Roger Sergel, ?Mar. 6, 1935.

14. "Jewish Women to Aid Refugees from Reich," *New York Times*, Mar. 15, 1935, p. 6. SA to Laura Lu Copenhaver, Mar. 1935; to Eleanor Copenhaver Anderson, Mar. 11, 1935, Mar. 21, 1935; to Stein, Mar. 22, 1935.

15. SA to Eleanor Copenhaver Anderson, Mar. 21, 1935, Mar. 23, 1935; to Laura Lu Copenhaver, Mar. 27, 1935, Mar. 31, 1935, Apr. 2, 1935.

16. Gannett, "Books and Things," New York Herald Tribune, Mar. 30, 1935, p. 9; North, "Sherwood Anderson Stages a Comeback," *Chicago Daily News,* April 3, 1935, p. 9; Adamie, "A Puzzled American," *Saturday Review of Literature,* April 13, 1935, p. 621; Bates, "The American Countryman," *New York Herald Tribune Books,* April 7, 1935, p. 5; Stein, "Gertrude Stein Reviews New Anderson Book/Praises 'Puzzled America' in Her Own Way," *Chicago Daily Tribune,* May 4, 1935, p. 14.

17. SA to Scribner's, Jan. 27, 1935; to Perkins, Feb. 24, 1935.

18. Perkins to SA, Feb. 20, 1935; SA to Perkins, Feb. 24, 1935.

19. SA to Laura Lu Copenhaver, Mar. 31, 1935, Apr. 2, 1935; to Feibleman, Apr. 8, 1935; to the Sergels, Apr. 13, 1935; to Roger Sergel, Apr. 16, 1935, Apr. 24, 1935; to Perkins, Apr. 20, 1935. "Miss Copenhaver to Make Speech before Macon 'Y,'" *Macon Telegraph*, Apr. 17, 1935; "Famous Author Visits in City," *Macon Telegraph*, Apr. 18, 1935, p. 1; "'Y. W.' Is Called Industrial Index," *Macon Telegraph*, Apr. 19, 1935, p. 2. Myrick, "sherwood anderson," p. 11.

20. SA to Perkins, Apr. 4, 1935; to Burton Emmett, Apr. 20, 1935; to Esherick, Apr. 20, 1935. Perkins to SA, Mar. 29, 1935. Wolfe to SA, July 8, 1935.

21. SA to Roger Sergel, Apr. 24, 1935, June 3, 1935; to Dreiser, May 9, 1935; to Funk, ?late May 1935. "Burton Emmett, Art Patron, Dies," *New York Times,* May 7, 1935, p. 23. SA, "Burton Emmett," *Colophon* 1, New Series (Summer 1935): 7–9.

22. Eleanor Copenhaver Anderson diary, Feb. 10. Gaston to SA, Feb. 9, 1935. SA to Gaston, Feb. 12, 1935. James Schevill, *Sherwood Anderson: His Life and Work*, p. 318. "34 Indicted by U.S. Jury in Franklin Rum Ring; Bribery, Theft Charged," *Richmond Times-Dispatch*, Feb. 8, 1935, pp. 1, 11. SA, "Man and His Imagination," pp. 39–79 in Augusto Centeno, ed., *The Intent of the Artist* (Princeton, NJ: Princeton University Press, 1941), p. 56.

23. I am grateful to Welford Taylor for the loan of his microfilm of the scrapbook and for his "Kit Brandon: A Reidentification," *Newberry Library Bulletin* 6 (July 1971): 263–67. SA to Gaston, May 24, 1935; to Perkins, May 24, 1935. "Woman Pilot of 'Rum Cargoes' On Stand in Roanoke Trials," *Richmond Times-Dispatch*, May 23, 1935, pp. 1, 17. SA, "City Gangs Enslave Moonshine Mountaineers," *Liberty* 12 (Nov. 2, 1935): 12–13, p. 13.

24. "Woman Pilot of Whiskey Cars Is Placed on Stand," *Roanoke Times*, May 24, 1935, p. 1; "Woman Pilot of 'Rum Runners,'" *Richmond Times-Dispatch*, May 23, 1935, pp. 1, 17; "Roanoke's Union of Bootleggers Gets into Trial," May 9, 1935, p. 1; "Woman Pilot of Liquor Caravans Completes Story," *Roanoke Times*, May 25, 1935, p. 1. SA, "City Gangs," p. 13.

25. *Today* 4 (June 8, 1935): 5, 21. "Tugwell Pledges New Conservation," *New York Times*, May 16, 1935, pp. 1, 15. Stewart to SA, Mar. 29, 1935.

26. SA to Friedman, May 31, 1935; to Roger Sergel, June 3, 1935, ?after June 19, 1935; to Mary Emmett, June 16, 1935, (telegram) June 25, 1935; to Sillcox, June 19, 1935; to Karl Anderson, ca. June 20, 1935. "Final Testimony Being Given in Conspiracy Case," *Roanoke Times*, June 25, 1935, p. 1.

27. SA, "Man and His Imagination," pp. 56–57. SA, "City Gangs," p. 13. "Final Testimony."

28. "20 Convicted in Franklin Liquor Ring," *Richmond Times-Dispatch*, July 2, 1935, pp. 1, 9. Eleanor Copenhaver Anderson to Gaston, July 3, 1935; SA to Gaston, Aug. 3, 1935.

29. Eleanor Copenhaver Anderson to Sumner Blossom, June 22, 1935; to Gaston, July 3, 1935; to Sillcox, July 30, 1935; to Oursler, July 9, 1935; to Fishbein, July 10, 1935. William H. McReynolds to SA, July 20, 1935. SA to Gaston, Aug. 3, 1935.

30. SA to Sillcox, Aug. 8, 1935; to Perkins, Aug. 1, 1935, Aug. 16, 1935; to Karl Anderson, ca. June 20, 1935; to Ferdinand Schevill, ?late Nov. 1935. Eleanor Copenhaver Anderson to Ivan von Auw, July 25, 1935; to Sillcox, July 30, 1935; to Mary Emmett, Aug. 13, 1935; to Henry Goddard Leach, Aug. 27, 1935. J. Friend to SA, June 19, 1935. "Mother" is one of four plays by U.S. playwrights in Wilde, ed., *Contemporary One-Act Plays from Nine Countries* (Boston: Little, Brown, 1936). "Dinner in Thessaly," *Forum and Century* 95 (Jan. 1936): 40–41. SA would send "Playthings" to *Scribner's*, which turned it down, and subsequently to two different literary agents, who were unable to place it. It was first published in Rosenfeld's *The Sherwood Anderson Reader* under the title "Nobody Laughed" (pp. 2–11); and Charles Modlin included it in a re-edited text under that title in *Certain Things Last*, pp. 307–17.

31. Eleanor Copenhaver Anderson to Mary Emmett, Aug. 13, 1935. SA to Charles Bocker, late Oct. 1935; to Eleanor Copenhaver Anderson, Nov. 13, 1935, and n. 2 in Modlin, *Anderson's Love Letters*, p. 303; to Mary Emmett, ?ca. Sept. 13, 1935.

32. SA to Bockler, Nov. 20, 1935; to Perkins, ca. Oct. 15, 1935, Nov. 8, 1935; to Funk, late Oct. 1935; to Roger Sergel, ?Sept. 15, 1935; to John Anderson, late Oct. 1935.

33. Perkins to SA, Sept. 17, 1935. SA to Roger Sergel, ?Sept. 16, 1935; to Karl Anderson, before Oct. 30, 1935; to Laura Lu Copenhaver, ca. Oct. 6, 1935. Edward Alden Jewell, "Art Collection of Emmett Seen," *New York Times*, Oct. 2, 1935, p. 21, and "Machine Age in Decorative Rhythms," *New York Times*, Oct. 6, 1935, sec. 11, p. 9. SA, "Lindsay and Masters," *New Republic* 85 (Dec. 5, 1935): 194–95.

34. Scribner's to SA, Oct. 3, 1935. SA to Perkins, Oct. 25, 1935. A note on this

letter (not in SA's hand) together with Perkins to SA, Oct. 26, 1935, confirms the royalty amount as being $522.28, not the $636 SA mistakenly states to Laura Lu Copenhaver. SA to Laura Lu Copenhaver, ca. Oct. 6, 1935; to Mary Emmett, ?Sept. 13, 1935; to Moley, ca. Sept. 23, 1935, after Sept. 24, 1935. Moley to SA, Sept. 24, 1935. Schevill, *Sherwood Anderson,* p. 314. "Boardwalk Fireworks," *Today* (Nov. 9, 1935): 6–7, 19. SA gives the vote as 28,851 to 10,826, roughly three to one. In "Craft Unionists Win A. F. of L. Row," *New York Times,* Oct. 17, 1935, p. 12, Louis Stark gives it as 18,025 to 10,924, less than two to one.

35. SA to Laura Lu Copenhaver, Oct. 18, 1935, Oct. 21, 1935, Oct. 22, 1935, Oct. 25, 1935, early Oct. 1935; to "Hilda" (Baroness von Koskull), Nov. 1, 1935; to Funk, ?Nov. 14, 1935. Burnett to SA, Sept. 26, 1935, Oct. 22, 1935. "Why Men Write," *Story* 8 (Jan. 1936): 2, 4, 103, 105.

36. Houghton Mifflin published the first two volumes of the *Letters* in 1927, the third in 1929. SA to Dreiser, after Dec. 6, 1935; to John Anderson, late Oct. 1935, early Nov. 1935; to Laura Lu Copenhaver, ca. Nov. 18, 1935, Nov. 3, 1935; to Bockler, ?Nov. 7, 1935; to Church, ca. Nov. 23, 1935. Edward Alden Jewell, "Exhibition of Art by Van Gogh Opens," *New York Times,* Nov. 5, 1935, p. 23; "Crowds for Art," *New York Times,* Nov. 11, 1935, p. 22.

37. SA to Laura Lu Copenhaver, ca. Nov. 10, 1935, ca. Nov. 16, 1935; to Deeter, Nov. 16, 1935.

38. SA to Laura Lu Copenhaver, ca. Nov. 27, 1935; to Roger Sergel, ca. Dec. 6, 1935. The text of "Mrs. Wife" is that established by Charles E. Modlin for his edition *Certain Things Last.* The story was later revised by Laura Lu Copenhaver and published under SA's name as "A Moonlight Walk," *Redbook* 70 (Dec. 1937): 43–45, 100–104. See Karen Coats, "Reclaiming 'Mrs. Wife,'" *Winesburg Eagle* 16 (Summer 1991): 9–12.

39. SA to Laura Lu Copenhaver, Nov. 23, 1935, ca. Nov. 16, 1935; to Eleanor Copenhaver Anderson, Oct. 18, 1935, Nov. 13, 1935. Eleanor Copenhaver Anderson diary, Feb. 24, 1936.

CHAPTER 9. THE YEAR OF *KIT BRANDON*

1. SA to Roger Sergel, early Dec. 1935, ca. Dec. 10, 1935, ca. Dec. 18, 1935; to Laura Lu Copenhaver, Nov. 23, 1935, ca. Nov. 27, 1935, after Dec. 3, 1935; to Henry and Katharine Van Meier, Nov. 23, 1935; to Mary Emmett, late Nov. 1935; to Bockler, Dec. 7, 1935; to O'Keeffe, after Dec. 9, 1935; to Perkins, Dec. 22, 1935, Dec. 18, 1935; to Phillips, Dec. 12, 1935. Perkins to SA, Dec. 16, 1935.

2. SA to Phillips, Dec. 12, 1935, late Dec. 1935; to Mary Emmett, Dec. 16, 1935, ca. Dec. 20, 1935.

3. SA to Perkins, before Dec. 14, 1935. SA, "A Good One," *New Republic* 85 (Jan. 8, 1936): 259.

4. SA to Perkins, ca. Dec. 18, 1935; to Mary Emmett, Dec. 30, 1935; to Karl Anderson, ca. Jan. 2, 1936; to Eleanor Copenhaver Anderson, Dec. 31, 1935. Perkins to SA, Dec. 26, 1935. SA diary, Jan. 1, 1936, Jan. 9, 1936. Eleanor

Copenhaver Anderson diary, Jan. 1, 1936. SA kept diaries from Jan. 1, 1936, to Feb. 28, 1941, shortly before his death. These have been very capably edited by Hilbert H. Campbell, *The Sherwood Anderson Diaries, 1936–1941.*

5. SA to Dreiser, Dec. 22, 1935, Jan. 12, 1936. Dreiser to SA, Jan. 2, 1936.

6. SA diary, Jan. 4–8, 1936, Jan. 12, Jan. 14. SA to Roger Sergel, early Jan. 1936; to Barbour, Jan. 10, 193[6], misdated by typist as "1935"; to Church, Jan. 13, 1936; to Eleanor Copenhaver Anderson, Jan. 14, 1936.

7. SA to Mary Emmett, Jan. 15, 1936. SA diary, Jan. 17–21. "Anderson Hails Improved Press," *Richmond Times-Dispatch,* Jan. 17, 1936, p. 10. SA to N. Bryllion Fagin, Dec. 35, Jan. 20, 193[6]; to Deeter, Jan. 15, 1936. Eleanor Copenhaver Anderson diary, Jan. 18.

8. SA diary, Jan. 22–Feb. 4; Eleanor Copenhaver Anderson diary, Jan. 21–Feb. 3. "Novelist Speaks," *Herald and Examiner,* Jan. 24, 1936, p. [30]. SA to Karl Anderson, Feb. 16, 1936; to Roger Sergel, Feb. 4, 1936.

9. Eleanor Copenhaver Anderson diary, Feb. 3, Feb. 4, Feb. 7, Feb. 11. SA to Stewart, ?Feb. 23, 1936; to Witter Bynner, Feb. 10, 1936; to Perkins, ?Feb. 25, 1936.

10. SA diary, Feb. 6, Mar. 6, Mar. 11. Eleanor Copenhaver Anderson diary, Feb. 17, Feb. 10, Feb. 21, Feb. 24, Mar. 1, Mar. 2, Mar. 12. SA to Mary Emmett, late Oct. 1935; to Laura Lu Copenhaver, Feb. 12, 1936.

11. SA diary, Feb. 6–13; Eleanor Copenhaver Anderson diary, Feb. 5–14. SA, "What Say!" *Smyth County News,* Feb. 27, 1936, p. 2. SA to Phillips, Feb. 11, 1936; to Laura Lu Copenhaver, Feb. 23, 1936.

12. SA diary, Mar. 15–29; Eleanor Copenhaver Anderson diary, Mar. 15–21. SA to Laura Lu Copenhaver, Mar. 21, 1936, Mar. 28, 1936; to Roger Sergel, Apr. 1, 1936; to Mary Emmett, Mar. 28, 1936. Modlin, ed., *Sherwood Anderson: Selected Letters,* p. 202, nn. 1, 2. "Women Must Act for World Peace, Speaker Asserts," *Times-Picayune,* March 25, 1936, p. 4.

13. SA diary, Apr. 1–9. Eleanor Copenhaver Anderson diary, Apr. 1. SA to Roger Sergel, ca. Mar. 9, 1936; to Bernd, May 1, 1936. Myrick, "sherwood anderson," pp. 11–14.

14. SA diary, Apr. 12–13, May 18. SA to Roger Sergel, May 2, 1936; to Laura Lu Copenhaver, May 25, 1936; to Patricia Meredith, Apr. 2, 1937.

15. SA to Mary Emmett, Apr. 11, 1936; to Roger Sergel, Apr. 15, 1936; to Laura Lu Copenhaver, Apr. 18, 1936, May 4, 1936; to Perkins, Apr. 13, 1936, Apr. 22, 1936; to Myrick, May 1, 1936. Perkins to SA, May 4, 1936. SA diary, Apr. 15–17, Apr. 20–May 1, May 4–8.

16. SA diary, May 26, May 25, June 3. SA to Editors, *New Yorker,* June 11, 1936; to Deeter, July 3, 1936. Eleanor Copenhaver Anderson to Helene Richards, July 31, 1936.

17. *Man Has Hands* exists at the Newberry Library in a number of typescripts of various scenes, some stapled together, others separate. Act 1 clearly ends with scene 3 since the last page of that typescript concludes with the direction, "(Curtain)/Intermission." Stapled in sequence with scene 3 are scene 4 (canceled, see next paragraph of text) and scene 5, the conclusion of the play, these two scenes constituting at some point in composition or rearrangement a good part of act 2.

18. SA to Laura Lu Copenhaver, May 17, 1936, May 25, 1936; to Roger Sergel, May 26, 1931. Eleanor Copenhaver Anderson diary, May 10. SA diary, May 24.

19. SA to Mary Emmett, May 19, 1936, July 1, 1936. SA diary, May 31, June 8, June 14, June 18–19.

20. SA diary, June 16, June 12, June 17.

21. SA diary, June 22–23, June 25, June 27, July 1–5. SA to JA, June 26, 1936; to Roger Sergel, June 21, 1936. Deeter to SA, June 19, 1936. Eleanor Copenhaver Anderson diary, June 4–5.

22. SA diary, July 9–12, July 25. SA to Mary Emmett, July 15, 1936, ca. July 31, 1936; to Roger Sergel, June 21, 1936; to Perkins, June 18, 1936; to Rosenfeld, Aug. 14, 1936. Perkins to SA, June 25, 1936. Eleanor Copenhaver Anderson diary, July 25, 1936.

23. SA to Perkins, June 29, 1936, July 3, 1936, July 6, 1936, ca. July 13, 1936, July 25, 1936; to Mary Emmett, July 21, 1936. Perkins to SA, June 25, 1936, July 8, 1936. Eleanor Copenhaver Anderson diary, July 23–24.

24. SA to Perkins, June 29, 1936, ca. Aug. 14, 1936, Aug. 7, 1936; to Phillips, Sept. 17, 1936. Perkins to SA, Aug. 27, 1936. SA diary, July 16, Aug. 2, July 29, Aug. 1, Aug. 4, Aug. 9. Eleanor Copenhaver Anderson diary, Aug. 2, Aug. 13. Sergel, "Of Sherwood Anderson and 'Kit Brandon,'" *Book Buyer* 2 (Nov. 1936): 2–4. Later Sergel recalled that SA was too tired to read the proofs of *Kit*, refused his offer to read them, and returned them "uncorrected." (Schevill, *Sherwood Anderson,* p. 318.) The article, SA's diary entries, and his correspondence with Perkins show that Sergel's recollection was unaccountably inaccurate.

25. SA diary, Aug. 13–29, Sept. 3–22. SA to Phillips, Sept. 17, 1936; to Ferdinand Schevill, Sept. 8, 1936, Sept. 24, 1936; to Mary Emmett, July 1, 1936, Aug. 20, 1936; to Eleanor Copenhaver Anderson, Sept. 21, 1936, Sept. 22, 1936. Eleanor Copenhaver Anderson diary, Sept. 3.

26. SA diary, Sept. 28–Oct. 2, Oct. 9, Oct. 15. SA to Laura Lu Copenhaver, Oct. 2, 1936, Oct. 11, 1936, Oct. 13, 1936. Campbell, *Anderson Diaries,* p. 357, n. 191. SA to Huebsch, July 16, 1936.

27. SA diary, Oct. 5, Oct. 13, Oct. 21, Oct. 7, Oct. 29, Oct. 30–31.

28. SA diary, Oct. 13–15. In his "Sherwood Anderson and Boxing" (*Winesburg Eagle* 11 [Nov. 1985]: 1–3) Charles Modlin makes a good case that since "Boomer," instead of the correct "Bomber" in Louis's nickname, was SA's error in the surviving typescript and since he misspelled "bomb" as "boom" in other contexts, the word should hereafter be spelled correctly in title and text. I have maintained SA's odd spelling on the grounds that (a) as a fan of Louis SA must have often seen the name spelled correctly many times, and (b) by analogy with SA's insistence on spelling "Eleanor" as "Elenore," it is possible that he preferred his idiosyncratic spelling. After slight revision by Laura Lu Copenhaver the piece was published in *Signatures* 3 (Winter 1937–38): 302–8.

29. SA to Perkins, Sept. 25, 1936, Oct. 9, 1936. SA diary, Oct. 7, Oct. 11, Oct. 21. Rorty, "Heaven Won't Protect the Working Girl," *Advance* 22 (Nov. 1936): 25–26. Van Doren, *Nation* 143 (Oct. 17, 1936): 452–53.

30. SA to Perkins, Aug. 7, 1936.
31. "Roanoke's Union of Bootleggers Gets into Trial," *Roanoke Times,* May 9, 1935. "A Mountain Marriage," *Fight Against War and Fascism* 3 (October 1936): 16–17, 25.
32. Roger Sergel, "Of Sherwood Anderson and 'Kit Brandon,'" p. 2.

CHAPTER 10. SLIPPAGE

1. SA to Perkins, ca. Sept. 20, 1936; to Moley, Sept. 25, 1936; to Laura Lu Copenhaver, Dec. 7, 1936, Nov. 4, 1936, Nov. 5, 1936, Oct. 16, 1936. Perkins to SA, Oct. 15, 1936, Oct. 19, 1936. A. Scott Berg, *Max Perkins: Editor of Genius* (New York: E. P. Dutton, 1978), p. 381. On February 9, 1995, Kiley L. Thompson of Simon & Schuster, of which Scribner's is now an imprint, answered my query as to whether sales records of the individual books were available by reporting that after diligent but unsuccessful search, he had concluded that the original "ledgers were either destroyed or are no longer in the possession of the company."
2. SA to Laura Lu Copenhaver, Oct. 22, 1936; to Mary Emmett, Nov. 2, 1936, Nov. 26, 1936; to Roger Sergel, ca. Nov. 25, 1936, Nov. 27, 1936; to Karl Anderson, ca. Dec. 20, 1936. SA diary, Oct. 24 and p. 357, n. 182, Nov. 2–3, Nov. 7, Nov. 21–26. Eleanor Copenhaver Anderson diary, Nov. 20. "7,000 in Day View Times Book Fair," *New York Times,* Nov. 8, 1936, sec. 2, p. 10.
3. SA to Roger Sergel, Nov. 27, 1936. SA diary, Nov. 24. Eleanor Copenhaver Anderson diary, Nov. 24–25. Lovett's "Sherwood Anderson" would be reprinted in Malcolm Cowley, ed. *After the Genteel Tradition: American Writers Since 1910* (New York: Norton, 1937), pp. 88–99.
4. SA to Mary Emmett, Nov. 26, 1936, Dec. 6, 1936; to RS, Dec. 1, 1936; to Laura Lu Copenhaver, Dec. 7, 1936. Roger Sergel to SA, Dec. 1, 1936. SA diary, Nov. 28, Dec. 1, Dec. 5–7.
5. SA diary, Dec. 8–31, passim. SA to Roger Sergel, Dec. 23, 1936; to Van Eck, Dec. 30, 1936. "Straws in the Wind," *Scribner's* 101 (Jan. 1937): 14, 16.
6. SA diary, Jan. 1–7. Eleanor Copenhaver Anderson diary, Jan. 9. Grace Vanamee to SA, Jan. 6, 1937, Jan. 12, 1937.
7. SA diary, Jan. 12–14. Eleanor Copenhaver Anderson diary, Jan. 12–14. SA to Perkins, Feb. 3, 1937.
8. SA diary, Jan. 15–21. Eleanor Copenhaver Anderson diary, Jan. 15–21. SA to Roger Sergel, Feb. 4, 1937; to Mary Emmett, Jan. 22, 1937, Jan. 24, 1937. "Sit-Downers Stick," *Digest,* 123 (Feb. 13, 1937): 8. See also SA to E. L. Greever, Feb. 18, 1937 (Jones and Rideout, eds., *Letters of Sherwood Anderson,* p. 374), where he argues that limited violence by the strikers against company violence might be acceptable.
9. SA diary, Jan. 22–Feb. 10. Eleanor Copenhaver Anderson diary, Jan. 26–Feb. 11. SA to Mary Emmett, Feb. 24, 1937; to Perkins, Feb. 3, 1937. Eleanor Copenhaver Anderson to Karl Anderson, Feb. 28, 1937. Perkins to SA, Feb. 6, 1937.
10. Eleanor Copenhaver Anderson diary, Jan. 25, Feb. 2–28. SA diary, Feb. 10–Mar. 8.

11. SA diary, Mar. 8–20, Mar. 23. SA to Mary Emmett, Mar. 18, 1937.

12. SA diary, Mar. 21–29. SA to Davison, Mar. 23, 1937; to Perkins, Mar. 26, 1937, ca. Mar. 27, 1937; to Mary Emmett, Mar. 23, 1937. Davison to SA, Mar. 10, 1937. Perkins to SA, Mar. 10, 1937.

13. "Friend," *PM* [later continued as *A-D*]: *An Intimate Journal for Art Directors, Production Managers and Their Associates* 3 (1937): 2–4. Lucile Charles to SA, Oct. 7, 1936, Oct. 20, 1936, Feb. 15, 1937, Jan. 25, 1937, Feb. 4, 1937. Merrill Denison to Frederick Willis, memo on Radio Plays Series, Nov. 26, 1936. "Where the Play's the Thing," *New York Times*, Aug. 15, 1937, sec. 10, p. 10.

14. SA to Deeter, Apr. 15, 1937. Eleanor Copenhaver Anderson diary, Mar. 22. *Textiles,* pp. 3–22 in William Kozlenko, ed., *Contemporary One-Act Plays: Radio Plays Folk Plays Social Plays* (New York: Charles Scribner's Sons, 1938).

15. SA diary, Mar. 30–Apr. 8. SA to John Anderson, Apr. 2, 1937; to Charles, Apr. 9, 1937; to Laura Lu Copenhaver, Apr. 3, 1937. Wolfe to Hamilton Basso, Apr. 28, 1937, in Elizabeth Nowell, ed., *The Letters of Thomas Wolfe* (New York: Charles Scribner's Sons, 1956), p. 616. Charles to SA, Apr. 8, 1937.

16. SA diary, Apr. 9–10, Apr. 13–14, Apr. 17, Apr. 22–25. Eleanor Copenhaver Anderson diary, Apr. 9. SA to Charles, Apr. 13, 1937.

17. SA diary, Apr. 26–May 6. SA to Lankes, Mar. 23, 1937, May 4, 1937; to Roger Sergel, May 4, 1937, May 19, 1937; to Laura Lu Copenhaver, May 6, 1937. Campbell, *Anderson Diaries,* p. 363, n. 51. Anon, *"Kit Brandon," Times Literary Supplement,* Apr. 3, 1937, p. 256.

18. SA to Laura Lu Copenhaver, May 6, 1937; to Lankes, May 28, 1937; to Roger Sergel, May 4, 1937. SA diary, May 5, May 27. Eleanor Copenhaver Anderson diary, May 27. Farrell, "A Memoir on Sherwood Anderson," *Perspective* 7 (Summer 1954): 83–88.

19. SA diary, May 29–June 9, June 14, June 23–July 19 passim. SA to Roger Sergel, June 2; to Mary Emmett, June 2; to Earle Birney, June 9, 1937. "Personal Protest," *Forum* 17 (Aug. 1937): 168–69. Birney, "Proletarian Literature: Theory and Practice," *Forum* 17 (May 1937): 58–60.

20. SA diary, May 13, June 2, June 22, July 6. Chambrun to SA, May 17, 1937, June 1, 1937, June 9, 1937, June 24, 1937, July 2, 1937, Aug. 7, 1937, July 15, 1937. SA to Chambrun, July 6, 1937; to Huebsch, June 12, 1937; to Marshall A. Best, June 21, 1937. Campbell, "Sherwood Anderson and His 'Editor,'" *Papers of the Bibliographical Society of America* 79 (1985): 229–32. Jacques Chambrun could not place "Two Lovers" for months since, as he wrote SA on July 10, 1937, "the big circulation magazines shy away from" stories with much drinking in them. On Nov. 12, 1938, he wrote that he finally sold it to *Story* for their "usual" price of twenty-five dollars. It was published in *Story* 14 (Jan.–Feb. 1939): 16–25.

21. SA diary, June 9–July 18 passim. Eleanor Copenhaver Anderson diary, June 16, July 6, July 9. Ray Lewis White, "Anderson's Will and Testament," *Winesburg Eagle* 21 (Summer 1996): 3–5, p. 3.

22. SA diary, July 19–26. Eleanor Copenhaver Anderson diary, July 22, July 25–26. SA to Roger Sergel, July 9, 1937. Ruth Sergel's secretary to SA, July 12, 1937. Davison to SA, June 12, 1927.

23. SA to Karl Anderson, Aug. 26, 1937. SA diary, July 27–Aug. 9. Eleanor Copenhaver Anderson diary, July 30, July 29. Martha Monigle, "Sherwood Anderson," *Michigan Quarterly Review* 9 (Winter 1970): 55–56.

24. Eleanor Copenhaver Anderson diary, July 29, Aug. 5, July 28, Aug. 10. SA diary, July 31–Aug. 10. Whit Burnett, "Writing on Thin Air," *Story* 11 (Oct. 1937): 7–8, 94–97. SA to Perkins, ca. Aug. 20, 1937. Natalie Davison to SA, Oct. 27, 1937. Idell Durrett, "Silent Author Discovered; Sherwood Anderson's Here," *Rocky Mountain News,* Aug. 9, 1937, p. 5. SA's undated letter to Shaw, printed as the "Foreword" to Lloyd Shaw, *Cowboy Dances: A Collection of Western Square Dances* (Caldwell, ID: The Caxton Printers, 1939). Shaw to SA, Jan. 3, 1939, requesting such a "brief introduction."

25. SA diary, Aug. 11–28. Eleanor Copenhaver Anderson diary, Aug. 14, Aug. 22, Aug. 27. "Listen, Hollywood!" *Photoplay Magazine* 52 (Mar. 1938): 29, 93. SA to Perkins, ca. Aug. 20, 1937; to Mary Emmett, Aug. 23, 1937. Perkins to SA, Aug. 18, 1937.

26. Eleanor Copenhaver Anderson diary, Aug. 24. SA to Pearson, Aug. 26, 1937. "Author's Note," p. 1453 in Benét and Pearson, eds., *The Oxford Anthology of American Literature* (New York: Oxford University Press, 1938).

27. Pearson to SA, Sept. 13, 1937. SA to Pearson, after Sept. 13, 1937.

28. SA diary, Aug. 26–29, Aug. 31. "We Little Children of the Arts" was first published under that title in White's 1969 *Memoirs,* pp. 317–28. The "Ben" section of the piece was revised ("Ben" changed to "Jerry") and under the title "For What?" first published in the *Yale Review* 30 (Summer 1941): 750–58. Paul Rosenfeld used the "For What?" version in his 1942 edition of the *Memoirs,* pp. 227–33.

29. SA diary, Aug. 29, Sept. 1, Sept. 5, Sept. 8–9, Sept. 13–14. SA to Mary Emmett, Sept. 9, 1937; to Perkins, Sept. 9, 1937, after Sept. 14, 1937. Eleanor Copenhaver Anderson diary, Sept. 9, Sept. 13.

30. Eleanor Copenhaver Anderson diary, Sept. 1, Sept. 18, Sept. 21–22. SA diary, Sept. 16. Perkins to SA, Sept. 14, 1937. SA to Perkins, after Sept. 14, 1937. Eleanor Copenhaver Anderson to Meriweather Smith, Sept. 24, 1937.

31. W. J. Simons, "Anderson's Plays Issued in Book Form," *San Francisco Chronicle,* Sept. 5, 1937, p. D3. Eaton, "Our Country! Right or———," *New York Herald Tribune Books,* Oct. 31, 1937, sec. 10, p. 22. Jack, "Sherwood Anderson Turns to the Stage," *New York Times Book Review,* Nov. 14, 1937, p. 9. Anon, "*Plays: Winesburg and Others,*" *Theatre Arts Monthly* 21 (Oct. 1937): 824–25.

32. William Kozlenko to SA, Sept. 21, 1937, Oct. 2, 1937.

33. SA diary, Sept. 19–20. SA to Robert Lane Anderson, Sept. 20, 1937; to Wolfe, Sept. 19, 1937 [Eleanor Copenhaver Anderson diary, Sept. 19; letter itself is in Thomas Wolfe collection at University of North Carolina, Chapel Hill]. Wolfe to SA, Sept. 22, 1937, printed in Nowell, ed., *The Letters of Thomas Wolfe,* pp. 654–66.

34. Eleanor Copenhaver Anderson diary, Sept. 15, Oct. 20. SA to Cullen, Sept. 16, 1937; to Mary Emmett, Sept. 9, 1937. SA diary, Sept. 24, Sept. 26, Sept. 21–22, Oct. 6–11, Oct. 18–21.

35. SA diary, Oct. 22, Oct. 25, Nov. 4, Nov. 27. SA to Laura Lu Copenhaver, Nov. 9, 1937. Chambrun to SA, Dec. 8, 1937. The text of the story used here is that in Modlin, *Certain Things Last,* pp. 297–306. See Modlin's Editorial Note, pp. 353–57, for Laura Lu Copenhaver's moralizing suggestions for revision, which like those in "Mrs. Wife" altered Anderson's point in the ending. "Not Sixteen" would not be published until it appeared, somewhat revised by Rosenfeld, in *Tomorrow* 5 (March 1946): 28–32.

36. Eleanor Copenhaver Anderson diary, Oct. 26. SA diary, Oct. 26, Dec. 20, Nov. 5–7. J. Benjamin Townsend, ed., *Charles Burchfield's Journals: The Poetry of Place* (Albany: State University of New York Press, 1993), p. 23. Interview, WBR with Dahlberg, Dec. 6, 1960. Blotner, *Faulkner,* vol. 2, 974–75.

37. SA diary, Feb. 25, 1938. *Memoirs* (1942), pp. 473–77; (1969), 462–66. SA to Laura Lu Copenhaver, Oct. 24–31. "Sherwood Anderson: An Appreciation," *Atlantic* 191 (June 1953): 27–29. In his *Faulkner* (vol. 2, p. 974), Blotner, a careful scholar, makes the understandable mistake of suggesting that "It seems likely" that the supposed New York cocktail party occurred at some time just prior to Anderson's visit, but at the time of writing he did not have the evidence in *The Sherwood Anderson Diaries.*

38. Cullen to SA, Nov. 8, 1937. SA to Laura Lu Copenhaver, Nov. 11, 1937, Nov. 14, 1937; to Cullen, Nov. 17, 1937. SA diary, Nov. 11–23.

39. SA to Roger Sergel, ?Nov. 27, 1937; to Phillips, Dec. 8, 1937. SA diary, Nov. 7, Nov. 24–Dec. 19 passim.

40. SA diary, Nov. 24–Dec. 22 passim. Chambrun to SA, Dec. 24, 1937. SA to DeVries, Nov. 28, 1937; to Laura Lu Copenhaver, Nov. 26, 1937, Dec. 7, 1937.

41. SA to Laura Lu Copenhaver, Dec. 6, 1937, Dec. 16, 1937; to Cullen, Dec. 20, 1937; to Wolfe, Dec. 17, 1937. SA diary, Dec. 1; Eleanor Copenhaver Anderson diary, Dec. 2. For a number of details concerning the end of the Anderson-Wolfe relationship I have drawn on Elizabeth Nowell, *Thomas Wolfe: A Biography* (Garden City, NY: Doubleday & Co., 1960), pp. 408–12; Nowell, ed., *The Letters of Thomas Wolfe,* pp. 687–91; David Herbert Donald, *Look Homeward: A Life of Thomas Wolfe* (Boston: Little, Brown & Co., 1987), pp. 430–31. On p. 430 of Donald's book he notes of Eleanor's explanation: "Mrs. Sherwood Anderson to William A. Jackson, Jan. 11, 1949, copy, Nowell MSS. . . ." The explanation is quoted in full in Campbell, *Anderson Diaries,* pp. 367–68, n. 157. See also Hilbert Campbell, "Sherwood Anderson and Thomas Wolfe," *Resources for American Literary Study* 21, no. 1 (1995): 58–67.

42. SA diary, Dec. 17. Claudine Chonez, "Du Middle-West á Greenwich Village: Avec Sherwood Anderson, Européen d'Amerique," *Les Nouvelles Littéraires* 806 (Mar. 26, 1938): 6. Quotations from her article are in my translation.

43. SA diary, Dec. 21, Dec. 3. SA to Roger Sergel, Dec. 22, 1935.

44. SA diary, Dec. 23–31.

CHAPTER 11. GOING TOWARD PIECES

1. SA diary, Jan. 1–31, 1938, passim. SA to Mary Emmett, Jan. 10, 1938; to Laura Lu Copenhaver, Jan. 15, 1938, Jan. 24, 1938 (added note by Eleanor

Copenhaver Anderson). Chambrun to SA, Jan. 8, 1938. Eleanor Copenhaver Anderson diary, Feb. 8, 1938. "Virginia Country Squires" was published in *Coronet* 3 (Mar. 1938): 6–10.

2. SA diary, Feb. 1–6. The Mooney piece, "You Be the American Zola," would be published under the title "Backstage with a Martyr" in *Coronet* 8 (July 1940): 39–41, and in *Memoirs* (1942), pp. 421–22. Under Anderson's title it appeared in *Memoirs* (1969), pp. 542–45.

3. SA diary, Feb. 7–15. SA to the Sergels, Feb. 13, 1938; to Laura Lu Copenhaver, Feb. 15, 1938. Eleanor Copenhaver Anderson diary, Feb. 9, Feb. 13. Perkins to SA, Feb. 8, 1938. Since the Scribner's payments did not include any royalties from *Plays,* the total must represent, for the most part, the small sales of *Kit Brandon.*

4. SA to Laura Lu Copenhaver, Feb. 19, 1938; to Karl Anderson, Feb. 27, 1938; to Mary Emmett, ca. Feb. 28, 1938. SA diary, Feb. 16–18, Feb. 20, Feb. 25, Feb. 28, Mar. 1, Mar. 3–5. Eleanor Copenhaver Anderson diary, Feb. 21, Mar. 1, Mar. 4.

5. SA diary, Mar. 7–8, Mar. 11–12, Mar. 14–15. SA to Laura Lu Copenhaver, Mar. 18, 1938; to Mary Emmett, Mar. 15, 1938; to John Emerson, Apr. 16, 1938. Eleanor Copenhaver Anderson to parents, Mar. 9, 1938. Eleanor Copenhaver Anderson diary, Mar. 3, Mar. 13, Mar. 15–16.

6. Eleanor Copenhaver Anderson diary, Feb. 21, Mar. 13, Feb. 23, Feb. 25, Mar. 3.

7. Spratling, *File on Spratling,* pp. 120–23. Eleanor Copenhaver Anderson diary, Mar. 16, covering the meeting with Spratling on May 15. SA diary, Mar. 16. The tone of *Miss Elizabeth,* published only two years after *File on Spratling,* does not suggest that she still "cared" for Sherwood; but I should record that in my two interviews with her on December 16–17, 1959, she received me very hospitably and answered all my questions openly and without sign of resentment toward her former husband.

8. Eleanor Copenhaver Anderson diary, Mar. 17, Mar. 20, Mar. 23. SA diary, Mar. 19–24. SA to Mary Emmett, Mar. 25, 1938.

9. SA diary, Mar. 25–Apr. 14 passim. Eleanor Copenhaver Anderson diary, Mar. 25.

10. SA diary, Apr. 15–20, Apr. 25. To Roger Sergel, ca. Apr. 21, 1938; to Mary Emmett, Mar. 25, 1938, Apr. 23, 1938; to Perkins, Apr. 15, 1938.

11. SA to Mannados Book Shop, undated draft of response to a letter to SA, Apr. 18, 1938; to Mary Emmett, Apr. 23, 1938, May 1, 1938, June 1, 1938, June 3, 1938; to Roger Sergel, May 5, 1938. Subsequently the manuscript was held by the Dartmouth College Library for several years and was later purchased by the Newberry Library Associates and presented to the Library's SA Collection in 1969, the fiftieth anniversary of the publication of the book. See Hilbert H. Campbell, "Winesburg at Dartmouth," *Winesburg Eagle* 17 (1992): 11.

12. SA diary, May 24, May 26, June 1, June 5, June 7, June 9. SA to Mary Emmett, June 9, 1938; to Karl Anderson, ?June 23, 1938; to Chambrun, July 2, 1938; to Funk, June 29, 1938; to Perkins, July 25, 1938. Eleanor Copenhaver Anderson diary, June 6. Chambrun to Eleanor Copenhaver Anderson, June 16, 1938.

13. SA diary, July 3–19. SA to Mary Emmett, July 10, 1938; to Perkins, July 25, 1938.
14. SA to Perkins, July 25, 1938; to the Galantières, ca. Aug. 29, 1938. SA diary, July 20, Aug. 5, July 24, July 29, Aug. 7, Aug. 9, Aug. 21.
15. SA diary, Aug. 18–22, Aug. 29. SA to Perkins, Sept. 7, 1938; to Roger Sergel, ca. Sept. 7, 1938. In his replies to SA, Sept. 16, 1938, and Sept. 23, 1938, Perkins encouraged his textbook proposal.
16. SA diary, Sept. 1, Sept. 4, Sept. 10, Sept. 13–18. Eleanor Copenhaver Anderson diary, Sept. 1.
17. Eleanor Copenhaver Anderson diary, Sept. 1, Sept. 26, Sept. 16. SA to Perkins, Sept. 20, 1938, July 25, 1938. SA diary, Oct. 29.
18. SA to Arnold F. Gates, ?Oct. 27, 1938; to Eleanor Copenhaver Anderson, Oct. 26, 1938. SA diary, Sept. 29–Oct. 18. Chambrun to SA, Oct. 22, 1938, Oct. 26, 1938.
19. SA diary, Oct. 29, Nov. 1–22. SA to Mary Emmett, Nov. 3, 1938; to Roger Sergel, ca. Nov. 18, 1938.
20. SA diary, Oct. 17–Dec. 9 passim, Sept. 14–15, 1939.
21. Chambrun to SA, Nov. 12, 1938, Dec. 23, 1938. SA to the League of American Writers, Nov. 25, 1938; to Rifka Angel, ca. Nov. 17, 1938; to Roger Sergel, ca. Nov. 17, 1938.
22. SA diary, Nov. 30–Dec. 31, passim. Brewer to SA, Dec. 7, 1938, Dec. 17, 1938. SA to Mary Emmett, Dec. 20, 1938.

CHAPTER 12. A SORT OF RESCUE

1. SA diary, Jan. 1–8, 1939. SA to Funk, Jan. 7, 1939; to Mary Emmett, Jan. [5], 1939; to Eleanor Copenhaver Anderson, Jan. 7, 1939, Jan. 9, 1939; to Laura Lu Copenhaver, Jan. 7, 1939. "Noted Author to Come Here," [?*Olivet College Echo*], Jan. 5, 1939, pp. 1, 4. Interview, WBR with Glenn and Laura Gosling, May 11, 1959.
2. Gosling interview. Brewer to SA, Dec. 7, 1938. SA diary, Jan. 9–22. SA to Cullen, Nov. 16, 1939; to Roger Sergel, Jan. 13; to Phillips, Nov. 14; to Mary Emmett, Jan. 24.
3. SA to Roger Sergel, Jan. 17. Gosling interview. "Legacies of Ford Madox Ford," *Coronet* 8 (August 1940): 135–36.
4. SA to Laura Lu Copenhaver, Jan. 21, 1939. SA diary, Jan. 20. The lecture was printed and published "By Olivet College" in 1939.
5. SA diary, Jan. 21–27. Brewer to SA, Feb. 10, 1939. Robie Macauley, "The Dean in Exile: Notes on Ford Madox Ford as Teacher," *Shenandoah* 4 (Spring 1953): 43–48, p. 47. SA to Edward Davison, Jan. 29, 1939; to Cullen, Feb. 7, 1939.
6. SA diary, Jan. 28–Feb. 1. SA to Funk, Jan. 31, 1939; to Gilbert Wilson, ?Feb. 17, 1939; to Cullen, Feb. 7, 1939; to Eleanor Copenhaver Anderson, Jan. 26, 1939. Jessie C. Treichler to Howard Mumford Jones, Apr. 14, 1952.
7. SA diary, Feb. 2–6. SA to Eleanor Copenhaver Anderson, Jan. 26, 1939, Mar. 7, 1939.
8. Unpublished typescript in the Newberry Library. See following note 11.

9. SA diary, Feb. 15–Mar. 7. Perkins to SA, Feb. 25, 1939, and undated Scribner's accounting department notes; Chambrun to SA, Feb. 23, 1939; Gosling to SA, ?Feb. 25, 1939. SA to Gosling, Mar. 2, 1939, Mar. 6, 1939.

10. SA diary, Mar. 8–18. SA to Mary Emmett, Mar. 27, 1939; to Eleanor Copenhaver Anderson, Mar. 15, 1939; to Chambrun, Mar. 27, 1939. Chambrun to SA, Mar. 29, 1939. Goslings interview. "I Live a Dozen Lives," *American Magazine* 128 (Oct. 1939): 58.

11. SA diary, Mar. 19–Apr. 1. SA to Feibleman, Mar. 30, 1939; to Mary Emmett, Mar. 27, 1939, Apr. 1, 1939. Chambrun to SA, Mar. 29, 1939. As the Chambrun-Anderson correspondence makes clear, Anderson's reference in his March 25 diary entry to the sale of the "editorial" was his error for "article." For some unknown reason, the *American Magazine,* after sending the $400 check to Chambrun for "How I Ran a Small-Town Newspaper," did not publish the article.

12. SA diary, Apr. 3–8. SA to young man, Apr. 9, 1939, Apr. 17, 1939.

13. SA diary, Apr. 11–22. Chambrun to SA, Apr. 15, 1939, Apr. 14, 1939. SA to Mary Emmett, Apr. 19, 1939.

14. The text used is that in Modlin, *Certain Things Last,* pp. 288–96.

15. SA diary, July 6, 1938, Aug. 5, 1938, Apr. 15, 1939. SA to Steele, Aug. 29, 1938. The oblique evidence is in a letter of April 18, 1939, from Chambrun in part responding to a query by Anderson, now lost, about this story he was writing: "Of course it will be quite all right to change the names in the case." This suggests that Anderson was writing about actual persons, including the "unforgettable character," whose names he knew but hesitated to use.

16. SA to Roger Sergel, ca. Feb. 14, 1939; to Feis, Apr. 17, 1939; to Rolland, May 1, 1939. SA diary, Apr. 23–24. On the letterhead of a release of Aug. 10, 1936, by the recently formed Comité Mondial, SA and Dos Passos are listed as members of the Conseil de Présidence. In a letter of June 6 the secretary general of the Comité informed him that his name had been removed (SA to Francis Jourdain, June 30, 1939).

17. SA diary, Apr. 25–June 2. Chambrun to SA, July 8, 1939. SA to Lankes, Apr. 29, 1939; to Roger Sergel, May 13, 1939.

18. SA to Roger Sergel, May 13, 1939; to Van Meier, Apr. 21, 1939; to Perkins, May 29, 1939; to Davila, Sept. 19, 1939. SA diary, Apr. 27, May 7, May 30, May 13, May 24, May 29, June 1, June 8. Bombal, "En Nueva York con Sherwood Anderson," *La Nacion,* Oct. 8, 1939, 2, p. 3.

19. SA diary, June 11–July 2. Eleanor Copenhaver Anderson to Chambrun, July 3. Chambrun to SA, July 1, 1939; to Eleanor Copenhaver Anderson, July 8, 1939. SA's own text is reprinted as "Unforgotten" in *Memoirs* (1969), pp. 76–85; the 1942 *Memoirs* prints "Discovery of a Father," pp. 45–49.

20. SA finished "a short story—Tim and General Grant" on Nov. 11, 1940 (diary), but it would first be published in Rosenfeld, *Sherwood Anderson Reader,* pp. 846–50.

21. SA diary, July 1–17. "Homage to Ford Madox Ford 1875–1939," pp. 441–94 in *New Directions* 7 (1942): 459. Brewer to SA, July 1, 1939.

22. SA diary, July 18–27. SA to Roger Sergel, May 13, 1939; to Mary Emmett,

Aug. 3, 1939; to Eleanor Copenhaver Anderson, July 21, 1939. Porter to George Platt Lynes, July 28, 1939. "U.S. Authors Gather on Olivet Campus," *Lansing News,* ?July 20, 1939, pp. 1, 6. The photograph, dated 1940 in Campbell, *Anderson Diaries,* p. 309, and July 28, 1937, in Isabel Bayley, ed., *Letters of Katherine Anne Porter* (New York: Atlantic Monthly Press, 1990), n.p., with quotation, must be dated *1939* since it appears in the Olivet College Bulletin of "March, 1940," along with other photographs of "Who's Who" at the 1939 conference, announcing the 1940 conference.

23. SA diary, July 19–27. "Olivet Writers' and Readers' Conference," *Olivet College Bulletin* 38 (May 1939). SA to De Vries, Aug. 9, 1939. Interview, WBR with Glenn Gosling, May 11, 1959. Brewer to SA, Aug. 3, 1939.

24. SA to Gosling, Apr. 26, 1939, May 19, 1939. Gosling to SA, May 16, 1939.

25. SA diary, July 28–Aug. 8. SA to Mary Emmett, Aug. 3, 1939; to Getts, July 31, 1939; to Wallace, Aug. 2, 1939. Getts to SA, July 24, 1939.

26. SA to Laura Lu Copenhaver, ?Aug. 4, 1939; to Chambrun, Sept. 2, 1939; to Rose Schulman, Aug. 27, 1939; to Gosling, Sept. 6, 1939. Chambrun to SA, Sept. 5, 1939. SA diary, Aug. 7, Aug. 23–26, Aug. 29, Sept. 13. Interview, WBR with Gosling, May 11, 1959.

27. Curry, ed., *The "Writer's Book" by Sherwood Anderson.* Considerably edited by Rosenfeld, "Prelude" would be included in the 1942 *Memoirs* as "The Sound of the Stream," pp. 429–45.

28. SA to Mary Emmett, Aug. 29, 1939; to Perkins, Aug. 9, 1939; to Centeno, Aug. 23, 1939. Perkins to SA, Aug. 3, 1939.

29. SA to Gingrich, Aug. 29, 1939; to Chambrun, Sept. 19, 1939. SA diary, Sept. 14–15. "Here They Come," *Esquire* 13 (Mar. 1940): 80–81.

30. SA diary, Sept. 18–20. Hogan, "The Big White Portico of Sherwood Anderson," *Winesburg Eagle* 5 (Apr. 1980): 1–4, and 6 (Nov. 1980): 1–5.

31. SA diary, Sept. 21, Sept. 24–29. SA to Laura Lu Copenhaver, Sept. 24, 1939, Sept. 26, 1939; to Minnie Stevenson, Sept. 16, 1939; to Eleanor Copenhaver Anderson, Sept. 26, 1939, Sept. 27, 1939. "Peter Astra Wins $9,000 Futurity . . . ," *New York Times,* Sept. 26, 1939, p. 31. "Davis's 2-Year-Old Victor," *New York Times,* Sept. 27, 1939, p. 36.

32. SA diary, Oct. 2–6. SA to Chambrun, Oct. 2, 1939, Oct. 6, 1939; to Roger Sergel, Oct. 17, 1939. Chambrun to SA, Oct. 10, 1939, Nov. 21, 1939, Sept. 18, 1939, Dec. 1, 1939, Jan. 3, 1940. "So You Want to Be a Writer?" *Saturday Review of Literature* 21 (Dec. 9, 1939): 13–14; *Reader's Digest* 36 (Jan. 1940): 109–11. Published in the issue of *This Week* for Feb. 11, 1940, under the title "From Little Things," "Why Not Oak Hill?" would become the first section of SA's next book, *Home Town.*

33. SA diary, Oct. 8–19. SA to Allen Tate, Oct. 14, 1939. "Man and His Imagination," pp. 39–79 in Augusto Centeno, ed., *The Intent of the Artist* (Princeton: Princeton University Press, 1941), a slightly expanded version of the original lecture.

34. SA diary, Oct. 20–25.

35. SA diary, Oct. 26–Nov. 5. SA to Wilson, Oct. 26, 1939; to Laura Lu Copenhaver, Oct. 25, 1939; to Roger Sergel, Nov. 6, 1939.

36. SA diary, Nov. 6–15. SA to the Galantières, Nov. 20, 1939; to Laura Lu Copenhaver, Nov. 14, 1939. Stanton Delaplane, "Sherwood Anderson—Interviewed: From Him, Many Laughs, But Little Information," *San Francisco Chronicle*, Nov. 12, 1939, p. 6.

37. SA diary, Nov. 15–19. Chambrun to SA, Dec. 1, 1939. "San Francisco at Christmas," *San Francisco Chronicle*, Dec. 24, 1939, p. 19. SA to the Galantières, Nov. 20, 1939.

38. SA diary, Nov. 20–29, Dec. 4. SA to Laura Lu Copenhaver, Nov. 28, 1939. Chambrun to SA, Dec. 4, 1939. "For What?" would be accepted by the *Yale Review* on Sept. 19, 1940, for "an honorarium of thirty-five dollars" (Helen McAfee to Chambrun), but it would be published posthumously in the *Review*'s Summer 1941 issue and payment then made (Chambrun to Eleanor Copenhaver Anderson, June 12, 1941).

39. SA to Roger Sergel, Dec. 16, 1939; to Laura Lu Copenhaver, Nov. 28, 1939. "Why Not?" appears under the title "We Little Children of the Arts" in *Memoirs* (1942), pp. 227–33. A much expanded and revised version of "We Little Children of the Arts" is in White's Critical Edition of the *Memoirs*, pp. 317–28.

40. SA diary, Nov. 29–Dec. 3, Dec. 28. SA to Monte Bartlett, Nov. 12, 1939; to Roger Sergel, Dec. 16, 1939, Jan. 27, 1940; to Ted and Natalie Davison, Dec. 15, 1939; to August Derleth, Jan. 30, 1940; to Laura Lu Copenhaver, Nov. 14, 1939. SA had read the first two installments of Huxley's novel in *Harper's Magazine* for November and December 1939.

41. SA diary, Dec. 4–18. SA to the Galantières, Dec. 7, 1939; to Centeno, Oct. 26, 1939; to Cullen, Dec. 15, 1939; to Roger Sergel, Dec. 16, 1939. Brewer to SA, Nov. 4, 1939, Nov. 20, 1939. "Maury Maverick in San Antonio," *New Republic* 102 (Mar. 25, 1940): 398–400.

42. SA diary, Dec. 19–31. SA to Feibleman, ca. Dec. 14, 1939.

43. "The Finding," *Memoirs* (1942), pp. 278–80; (1969), pp. 350–53. A newly edited text is available in Modlin and White, eds., *Winesburg, Ohio*, pp. 155–59. SA to the Emmetts, Sept. 15, 1933.

44. "Foreword," *Memoirs* (1969), p. 21; "This Book," *Memoirs* (1942), p. 7.

CHAPTER 13. HOME TOWN, MEMOIRS, AND OTHERS

1. Eleanor Copenhaver Anderson diary, Jan. 1, 1940. SA diary, Jan. 1–7. Chambrun to SA, Jan. 3, 1940. Wallace to SA, Jan. 3, 1940. Under the title "From Little Things" SA's piece was published in *This Week*, Feb. 11, 1940, p. 2.

2. SA to Mary Emmett, Jan. 3, 1940; to Roger Sergel, Jan. 3, 1940; to Joseph Henry Jackson, Jan. 29, 1940. SA diary, Jan. 5–11, Nov. 15, 1939.

3. SA diary, Jan. 11–30. Although SA sent "In a Field" (pp. 336–40 in *A Story Teller's Story*) to Chambrun on Jan. 17, 1940, it was first published with SA's later changes by Charles E. Modlin in *Winesburg Eagle* 8 (Apr. 1983): 1–6. Benét, "The Dark Field," *Saturday Review of Literature* 1 (Oct. 18, 1924): 200. SA to Laura Lu Copenhaver, Jan. 25, 1940, Jan. 31, 1940; to Cornelia Lane Anderson, Jan. 27, 1940. Chambrun to SA, Jan. 16, 1940, Jan. 17, 1940,

Feb. 3, 1940, Apr. 5, 1940. "Oh, the Big Words!" *This Week,* March 31, 1940, p. 2. Although Jacques Chambrun had received this last piece by Feb. 3, SA's letter to him of February 13 indicates that either SA was considering revisions or was supplying an outline for Chambrun to use in approaching Mrs. Meloney at *This Week.*

4. SA diary, Jan. 15, 29. SA to Laura Lu Copenhaver, Jan. 31, 1940.

5. SA to Gosling, Jan. 17, 1940; to Laura Lu Copenhaver, Jan. 31, 1940, Feb. 1, 1940. SA diary, Jan. 14, Jan. 21, Feb. 9, Mar. 17, Mar. 25, Mar. 30, Mar. 27, Apr. 1, Jan. 31.

6. SA diary, Jan. 16–17, Mar. 27–30, May 21. SA to Laura Lu Copenhaver, Jan. 29, 1940, Mar. 30, 1940. Robert E. Spiller, ed., *The Van Wyck Brooks–Lewis Mumford Letters* (New York: E. P. Dutton, 1970), pp. 175, 126.

7. SA diary, Feb. 5–10. SA to Laura Lu Copenhaver, Feb. 8, 1940, Feb. 12, 1940. Note 23, p. 381 in Campbell, *Anderson Diaries,* corrects the obvious error in the subject of Eleanor's conference in Jones and Rideout, *Letters of Sherwood Anderson,* p. 458, n. 6.

8. SA diary, Feb. 13–Mar. 4. Getts to SA, July 24, 1939, Jan. 15, 1940. Since the fee was for $300 but SA received from Getts a check for $217.50, it is clear that certain of his travel expenses as well as Getts's commission of 25 percent were to be deducted from any fee. SA to Rosskam, Mar. 15, 1940.

9. SA to Stryker, Mar. 28, 1940; to A. S. Burack, Apr. 5, 1940; to Laura Lu Copenhaver, Mar. 30, 1940. D. W. Hall (of Jacques Chambrun, Inc.) to SA, Apr. 8, 1940, Apr. 12, 1940. SA diary, Apr. 6–20. The shortened "A Writer's Conception of Realism" was published in the *Writer* 54 (January 1941): 3–6. "American Small Town" was published as "We Are All Small-Towners," *This Week Magazine,* June 16, 1940, p. 2.

10. SA diary, Apr. 26–May 15, May 20. SA to Laura Lu Copenhaver, Mar. 30, 1940; to Mary Emmett, Apr. 29, 1940; to John Anderson, ?Apr. 3, 1940; to Roger Sergel, Sept. 3, 1940. Peter Kihss, "Sherwood Anderson Fooled in One of His Protests," *New York World-Telegram,* May 22, 1940, p. 19. SA's letter to John describes as leads for his proposed illustrations the mountain characters with whom SA intends to "play," including a lumberman-hunter father, a half-Indian mother, one son of seventeen, a tomboy daughter of twelve, and "a young boy—7," and such neighbors as a crazy old woman who follows turkey hens in order to sit on the eggs they may lay.

11. SA diary, May 16–29. SA to Van Meier, May 21, 1940; to White, May 22, 1940; to Koppell, May 21, 1940; to Chambrun, May 23, 1940; to Cullen, May 22, 1940. Chambrun to SA, May 6, 1940, June 11, 1940. Wallace to SA, May 23, 1940, May 29, 1940. "The Dance Is On" finally appeared, in very slightly revised form in the *Rotarian* 58 (June 1941): 7. It appears in its original form in the *Memoirs* (1942), pp. 494–95; (1969), pp. 552–53. The anecdote is printed in Jones and Rideout, *Letters of Sherwood Anderson,* pp. 461–62.

12. SA diary, May 31–June 20. SA to Lankes, June 4, 1940. Chambrun to SA, June 17, 1940.

13. SA diary, June 21–28. SA to Roger Sergel, June 25, 1940.

14. SA diary, July 1–4. The *Memoirs* text used here is that of 1969, pp. 85–89. The relevant section in the 1942 text is on pp. 61–66.
15. Interview, WBR with Karl Anderson, June 30, 1953.
16. *Memoirs* (1969); pp. 89–100; (1942), pp. 66–74.
17. *Memoirs* (1969), pp. 86, 431–35.
18. SA to Young, July 9, 1940. SA diary, July 4–14. Conference Program.
19. SA diary, July 15–25. SA to Judd, Aug. 1, 1940, Aug. 16, 1940; to Eleanor Copenhaver Anderson, July 19, 1940; to Laura Lu Copenhaver, July 22, 1940. Eleanor Copenhaver Anderson diary, July 23, 27. Brewer to SA, Sept. 7, 1940.
20. SA diary, July 26–30. Eleanor Copenhaver Anderson diary, July 27.
21. SA diary, July 31–Aug. 2. Eleanor Copenhaver Anderson diary, July 31. SA to Young, Aug. 16, 1940. Apparently another version of "One by One" would eventually be revised by a "collaborator" after SA's death and published as "Little People and Big Words," in *Reader's Digest* 39 (Sept. 1941): 118–20. (See Chambrun letters to Eleanor Copenhaver Anderson, June 9, 1941, through Aug. 16, 1941.) Although Eleanor Copenhaver Anderson did not like the revision by the collaborator, and presumably the 25 percent fee he charged, the *Digest* paid its top fee of $1,500 for the piece, she receiving $975.
22. SA to Young, Aug. 16, 1940. SA diary, Aug. 6–7, 11. Eleanor Copenhaver Anderson diary, Aug. 6–7. Chambrun to SA, Aug. 26, 1940, Sept. 27, 1940. "Stolen Day" ["Big Fish"], *This Week* (April 27, 1941): 8, 15, reprinted in *Memoirs* (1969), pp. 33–57, but not in *Memoirs* (1942).
23. SA diary, July 8. "The Persistent Liar" would eventually be published in *Tomorrow* 6 (Sept. 1946): 10–12.
24. SA diary, Aug. 14–24, Sept. 7–8. Young to SA, Aug. 7, 1940. "I See Grace Again," *Memoirs* (1969), pp. 294–304. SA to Perkins, ?Aug. 10, 1940, Aug. 23, 1940, Aug. 29, 1940; to Young, Aug. 25, 1940, Aug. 31, 1940, Sept. 9, 1940.
25. SA to Young, Sept. 9, 1940. SA diary, Sept. 12–21. "Mary, the Dogs, and Theda Bara," *Memoirs* (1969), pp. 420–31; (1942), pp. 306–31. "Spectator," *Memoirs* (1969), pp. 534–37.
26. SA diary, Sept. 22, Oct. 18, Oct. 9–10, Oct. 2. SA to Mary Emmett, Oct. 8, 1940; to John Anderson, ?Apr. 3, 1940. *Memoirs* (1969), 504–7. Campbell, *Anderson Diaries,* p. 383, n. 101.
27. Chambrun to SA, Sept. 20, 1940, Sept. 25, 1940. Getts to SA, Aug. 1, 1940. SA to Seager, Sept. 24, 1940. Brewer to SA, Oct. 14, 1940. SA to Stryker, Oct. 12, 1940; to Wallace, Oct. 18, 1940; to Rosskam, Sept. 25, 1940, Oct. 18, 1940, Oct. 11, 1940, Oct. 16, 1940. SA diary, Oct. 6–7.
28. SA diary, Oct. 21–28. SA to Brewer, Sept. 24, 1940; to Rosskam, Oct. 8, 1940; to Laura Lu Copenhaver, Oct. 27, 1940, Nov. 1, 1940.
29. Richard F. Crandall, "Cheerful Chekov of America's Whistle Stops," *New York Herald Tribune Books,* Oct. 27, 1940, p. 5. Ralph Thompson, "Books of the Times," *New York Times,* Oct. 22, 1940, p. 21. Duffus, "The Small Towns of America," *New York Times Book Review,* Oct. 27, 1940, pp. 1, 30, p. 30. Anon, "Bookshelf," *Atlantic Monthly* 166 (Dec. 1940): n.p. White,

"Home Town," Book-of-the-Month Club News (Jan. 1941): 5–6, p. 6. White, "The Other Side of Main Street," *Collier's* 68 (July 30, 1921): 7–8, 18–19, p. 7. I have found no records of sales numbers of *Home Town,* but Eleanor and John Anderson as "Executrix and Executor of the Estate of Sherwood Anderson" reported 1941 royalty income from the publisher of only $208.84 and 1942 royalty income of $65.40, figures indicating that sales were weak. (White, "Anderson's Will and Estate," p. 4.)

30. SA diary, Nov. 2, 4, 18–20, 22–26. SA to Laura Lu Copenhaver, Nov. 3, 1940. A. Scott Berg, *Max Perkins: Editor of Genius* (New York: Dutton, 1978), pp. 381–82. Scribner manufacturing records graciously sent WBR by Margaret M. Sherry, Special Collections Archivist, Princeton University Libraries, Mar. 28, 1995. SA to Perkins, Nov. 30, 1940.
31. SA to Laura Lu Copenhaver, Nov. 3, 1940; to Roger Sergel, ?Nov. 12, 1940. SA diary, Nov. 8–9, 6, 13, Dec. 3. SA to Littell, Dec. 5, 1940, Dec. 26, 1940. Littell to SA, Dec. 12, 1940, Dec. 18, 1940.
32. Linguaphone Institute receipt, Nov. 11, 1940. SA to Bombal, Nov. 30, 1940; to Madrigal, Dec. 3, 1940; to Augusto Centeno, Dec. 31, 1940. SA diary, Nov. 11, Dec. 7, Dec. 15.
33. SA to Brown, Oct. 30, 1940, Dec. 1, 1940; to Monte Bartlett, Nov. 15, 1940, Nov. 21, 1940; to Lankes, Dec. 5, 1940; to Chambrun, Nov. 28, 1940; to Laura Lu Copenhaver, Dec. 15, 1940. SA diary, Nov. 19.
34. SA to Stryker, Nov. 21, 1940; to Laura Lu Copenhaver, Dec. 12, 1940. SA diary, Dec. 6–9, Jan. 1, 1941. Campbell, *Anderson Diaries,* p. 385, note 134. Chambrun to SA, Feb. 25, 1941, Jan. 25, 1941. Richard L. Field to Chambrun, Jan. 24, 1941. "My Mother Said No" was published under the title "I Was a Bad Boy," *This Week,* May 18, 1941, pp. 12, 17. First part partially reprinted in *Memoirs* (1942), pp. 36–39; both parts partially reprinted in *Memoirs* (1969), pp. 69–73.
35. SA diary, Dec. 9–22, Jan. 1, 1941. SA to Karl and Helen Anderson, Dec. 21, 1940; to Marie Mattingly Meloney, Dec. 21, 1940.
36. SA diary, Dec. 23–31. SA to John Anderson, Dec. 24, 1940; to Lankes, Dec. 31, 1940.

CHAPTER 14. THE STORYTELLER'S ENDING

1. SA diary, Jan. 3–25.
2. SA diary, Jan. 4–26, Dec. 16, 1940. Late in January SA sent his draft of "Above Suspicion" to the chairman of the Free Company, James Boyd, who later completed it. The play was aired on May 4, the last of the series, as "a tribute to [Anderson's] memory." David E. Whisnant, *James Boyd* (New York: Twayne, 1972), pp. 135, 159, n. 30. James Boyd et al., *The Free Company Presents . . .* (New York: Dodd, Mead, 1941), pp. 270–71.
3. SA to Eleanor Copenhaver Anderson, Jan. 29, 1941, Jan. 3, 1941, Jan. 14, 1941, undated letter cited in Modlin, *Anderson's Love Letters,* p. 329, n. 1; to John Anderson, Jan. 26, 1941. SA diary, Jan. 28–Feb. 4, 1941.
4. SA to Eleanor Copenhaver Anderson, Feb. 8, 1941; to Juan Adolfo Vazquez,

Dec. 15, 1941; to Roger Sergel, Jan. 26, 1941; to Mary Emmett, Feb. 16, 1941; to Davila, Jan. 26, 1941. SA diary, Feb. 5–14.

5. SA to Littell, Feb. 17, 1941; to Rendueles, Feb. 17, 1941; to Feis, Feb. 17, 1941, Feb. 19, 1941. SA diary, Feb. 15–23. February 21, 1941, fourth of the "Four mornings straight," is the last date in SA's diary recording work on the *Memoirs,* which remained unfinished at the time of his death. Ray Lewis White in the introduction to his 1969 Critical Edition explains (pp. xxviii–xxxiii) how Paul Rosenfeld, with some assistance from Eleanor and Roger Sergel, edited the first version of *Sherwood Anderson's Memoirs.* Published April 9, 1942, it would be well received by a majority of reviewers, a number of them observing its mixture of accurate memory and fiction. Probably as a result of the decline in his literary reputation the book sold only 2,550 copies between publication date and October 15, 1942 (Young to Eleanor Copenhaver Anderson, Oct. 19, 1942). More recently his significant contributions to American literature are being recognized.

6. SA diary, Feb. 24–27. Chambrun to SA, Feb. 25, 1941. SA to Huebsch, Nov. 30, 1940, Jan. 18, 1941, Feb. 21, 1941.

7. SA diary, Feb. 26–27. WBR, ed., "Memories of Sherwood Anderson," *Winesburg Eagle* 16 (Winter 1991): 14. SA, "Chance Rules Us All," with "Afterword" by Helen Caudill Barranger, *Winesburg Eagle* 20 (Summer 1995): 1–3. B. H. Kean, M.D., with Tracy Dahlby, *M.D.: One Doctor's Adventures Among the Famous and Infamous from the Jungles of Panama to a Park Avenue Practice* (New York: Ballantine Books, 1990), pp. 92–96.

8. SA diary, Feb. 28, final entry. Campbell, *Anderson Diaries,* p. 386, n. 13. Wilder to Eleanor Copenhaver Anderson, n.d. Kirchwey, "Sherwood Anderson," *Nation* 152 (Mar. 22, 1941): 313–14. Kean, *M.D.,* pp. 92–96, 36. In a telegram to Mimi dated Mar. 8, 1941, Robert gives the time of their father's death as "5:40" PM; Kean gives the time as "five." Karl would remain convinced that "Sherwood's death was not necessary, had the ship's doctor not so objected to having a famous Chilean doctor meet the boat at Colon. [Randolph] had cabled to her that she should get immediate contact with this doctor" ("Memories of Sherwood Anderson," p. 14).

9. "To Bury Anderson in Virginia," *New York Times,* Mar. 19, 1941, p. 21. Robert L. Anderson, "As His Home Town Knew Him," *Smyth County News,* Mar. 13, 1941, pp. 1, 6. Davis T. Ratcliffe, "A Blessing on the Hilltop," *Winesburg Eagle* 9 (Apr. 1984): 5. Rosenfeld and Dreiser tributes, *Smyth County News,* Apr. 3, 1941, p. 6.

10. "Sherwood Anderson Is Buried in Round Hill," *Smyth County News,* Mar. 27, 1941, p. 1.

11. "Both Barrels" [Charles Funk], "Sherwood Anderson, Our Friend and Neighbor," *Smyth County News,* Mar. 23, 1941, p. 2.

Selected Bibliography

PRIMARY SOURCES

Beyond Desire. New York: Liveright, 1932.
Dark Laughter. New York: Boni and Liveright, 1925.
Death in the Woods and Other Stories. New York: Liveright, 1933.
Hello Towns! New York: Liveright, 1929.
Home Town. New York: Alliance Book Corp., 1940.
Horses and Men. New York: B. W. Huebsch, 1923.
Kit Brandon. New York: Charles Scribner's Sons, 1936.
Many Marriages. New York: B. W. Huebsch, 1923.
Marching Men. New York: John Lane Company, 1917.
Mid-American Chants. New York: John Lane, 1918.
A New Testament. New York: Boni and Liveright, 1927.
No Swank. Philadelphia: Centaur Press, 1934.
Perhaps Women. New York: Liveright, 1931.
Plays: Winesburg and Others. New York: Charles Scribner's, 1937.
Poor White. New York: B. W. Huebsch, 1920.
Puzzled America. New York: Charles Scribner's Sons, 1935.
Sherwood Anderson's Notebook. New York: Boni and Liveright, 1926.
A Story Teller's Story. New York: B. W. Huebsch, 1924.
Tar: A Midwest Childhood. New York: Boni and Liveright, 1926.
The Triumph of the Egg. New York: B. W. Huebsch, 1921.
Windy McPherson's Son. New York: John Lane, 1916; rev. ed., New York, B. W. Huebsch, 1922.
Winesburg, Ohio. New York: B. W. Huebsch, 1919.

EDITED AND CRITICAL WORKS

Anderson, David. *Critical Essays on Sherwood Anderson.* Boston: G. K. Hall, 1981.
———, ed. *Sherwood Anderson: An Introduction and Interpretation.* New York: Holt, 1967.
Anderson, Elizabeth, and Gerald R. Kelly. *Miss Elizabeth: A Memoir.* Boston: Little, Brown, 1969.

Bruyère, Claire. *Sherwood Anderson: l'impuissance créatrice*. Paris: Klincksieck, 1985.

Burbank, Rex. *Sherwood Anderson*. New York: Twayne, 1964.

Campbell, Hilbert H., ed. *The Sherwood Anderson Diaries, 1936–1941*. Athens: University of Georgia Press, 1987.

Campbell, Hilbert H., and Charles E. Modlin, eds. *Sherwood Anderson: Centennial Studies*. Troy, NY: Whitston Publishing Co., 1976.

Crowley, John W., ed. *New Essays on Winesburg, Ohio*. Cambridge: Cambridge University Press, 1990.

Curry, Sister Martha Mulroy, ed. *The "Writer's Book" by Sherwood Anderson*. Metuchen, NJ: Scarecrow Press, 1975.

Dunne, Robert. *A New Book of the Grotesque*. Kent, OH: Kent State University Press, 2005.

Fanning, Michael. *France and Sherwood Anderson: Paris Notebook, 1921*. Baton Rouge: Louisiana State University Press, 1976.

Howe, Irving. *Sherwood Anderson*. New York: William Sloane Associates, 1951.

Jones, Howard Mumford, and Walter B. Rideout, eds. *Letters of Sherwood Anderson*. Boston: Little, Brown, 1953.

Modlin, Charles E., ed. *Certain Things Last: The Selected Short Stories of Sherwood Anderson*. New York: Four Walls and Eight Windows, 1992.

———, ed. *The Egg and Other Stories*. New York: Penguin, 1998.

———, ed. *Sherwood Anderson: Selected Letters*. Knoxville: University of Tennessee Press, 1984.

———, ed. *Sherwood Anderson's Love Letters to Eleanor Copenhaver Anderson*. Athens: University of Georgia Press, 1989.

Modlin, Charles E., and Ray Lewis White, eds. *Winesburg, Ohio*. New York: Norton, 1996.

Ohashi, Kichinosuke, ed. *The Complete Works of Sherwood Anderson*. 20 vols. Kyoto: Rinsen Book Co., 1982.

Papinchak, Robert Allen. *Sherwood Anderson: A Study of the Short Fiction*. New York: Twayne, 1992.

Rideout, Walter B., ed. *Sherwood Anderson: A Collection of Critical Essays*. Englewood Cliffs, NJ: Prentice-Hall, 1974.

Rosenfeld, Paul, ed. *The Sherwood Anderson Reader*. Boston: Houghton Mifflin, 1947.

———, ed. *Sherwood Anderson's Memoirs*. New York: Harcourt, Brace, 1942.

Salzman, Jack, David D. Anderson, and Kichinosuke Ohashi, eds. *Sherwood Anderson: The Writer at His Craft*. Mamaroneck, NY: Appel, 1979.

Schevill, James. *Sherwood Anderson: His Life and Work*. Denver: University of Denver Press, 1951.

Sheehy, Eugene P., and Kenneth A. Lohf. *Sherwood Anderson: A Bibliography*. Los Gatos, CA: Talisman Press, 1960.

Small, Judy Jo. *A Reader's Guide to the Short Stories of Sherwood Anderson*. New York: G. K. Hall, 1994.

Sutton, William A., ed. *Letters to Bab: Sherwood Anderson to Marietta D. Finley, 1916–1933*. Urbana: University of Illinois Press, 1985.

————, ed. *The Road to Winesburg: A Mosaic of the Imaginative Life of Sherwood Anderson.* Metuchen, NJ: Scarecrow Press,1972.

Taylor, Welford Dunaway, ed. *The Buck Fever Papers.* Charlottesville: University Press of Virginia, 1971.

Taylor, Welford Dunaway, and Charles E. Modlin, eds. *Southern Odyssey: Selected Writings by Sherwood Anderson.* Athens: University of Georgia Press, 1997.

Townsend, Kim. *Sherwood Anderson.* Boston: Houghton Mifflin, 1987.

White, Ray Lewis, ed. *Sherwood Anderson: Early Writings.* Kent, OH: Kent State University Press, 1989.

————, ed. *Sherwood Anderson/Gertrude Stein.* Chapel Hill: University of North Carolina Press, 1972.

————. *Sherwood Anderson: A Reference Guide.* Boston: G. K. Hall, 1977.

————, ed. *Sherwood Anderson's Memoirs: A Critical Edition.* Chapel Hill: University of North Carolina Press, 1969.

————, ed. *Sherwood Anderson's Secret Love Letters: For Eleanor, a Letter a Day.* Baton Rouge: Louisiana State University Press, 1991.

————, ed. *Sherwood Anderson's Winesburg, Ohio.* Athens: Ohio University Press, 1997.

Williams, Kenny J. *A Storyteller and a City.* DeKalb: Northern Illinois Press, 1988.

Index